Introduction to Operations and Technology Management

2nd edition

| PEARSON COLLECTIONS |

PEARSON

Cover Art: Courtesy of Photodisc/Getty Images

Pearson Learning Solutions, 501 Boylston Street, Suite 900, Boston, MA 02116

A Pearson Education Company
www.pearsoned.com

ISBN 10: 132367943X

ISBN 13: 9781323679432

Printed in the USA

Table of Contents

Rob Walls/Alamy

McDonald's continually seeks ways to re-design and improve its processes so as to provide better quality and menu choices to its customers at a lower cost, with more sustainable resources.

PROCESS STRATEGY AND ANALYSIS

McDonald's Corporation

As a global food service retailer, McDonald's has more than 35,000 restaurants around the world, and 70 million customers visit them each day. It employs 1.9 million people who work for McDonald's and its franchisees across more than 100 countries. Even though the company is a leader in its industry, things were not so good in 2002, when customer complaints were growing more frequent and bitter. McDonald's began listening to the customers again and changed its processes to reflect it. The board brought on a new CEO who had spent 20 years on the operational side of the business. With a zeal for measuring customer satisfaction and sharing the data freely with operators, he pulled off a turnaround that stunned everyone in the business with its speed and scope. Initiatives were launched to collect performance measures and revamp McDonald's processes to meet customer expectations. Data on speed of service; food temperature; presentation and taste; cleanliness of the counter, tables and condiment islands; even whether the counter crewperson smiles at diners, was collected using mystery shoppers. Operators could pinpoint lingering problems, and performance measures focused operators' attention on needed process changes. Customers were encouraged to report their experience at a particular U.S. restaurant by e-mail, regular mail, or toll-free telephone call.

Another initiative was to send 900 operations missionaries into the field, each visiting stores multiple times to fine-tune processes while also conducting day-long seminars where store managers could share tips from corporate kitchen gurus—such as where to place staff—that would shave precious

From Chapter 2 of *Operations Management: Processes and Supply Chains*, Eleventh Edition. Lee J. Krajewski, Manoj K. Malhotra, and Larry P. Ritzman.

seconds off average service times. The process was changed back to toasting buns rather than microwaving them, giving them an even sweeter caramelized flavor. Other initiatives were taken on McDonald's fast lane. Outdoor menu boards were placed with more pictures and fewer words. An LED display confirmed what customers ordered, reducing confusion later on. Premium sandwiches were put in boxes rather than paper wrappers, saving a few seconds, and boxes were color coded by sandwich to improve speed and accuracy. Processes were also changed to become environment friendly, all the way from the counters of McDonald's restaurants into its supply chain. All these changes resulted in greater profitability and share price over ten years, as performance measurement and process analysis increased customer value and the bottom line.

Lately, however, the growth has stagnated. Same-store sales slipped 0.1 percent, which marked a second quarterly decline in 2013. The menu got overly complicated as more items were added to suit a wider range of tastes. This created bottlenecks in the kitchen, which slowed service and turned off customers. Some items, like chicken wings, were too pricey for customers' taste and resulted in 10 million pounds of unsold wings. To regain focus, McDonalds is now redesigning its kitchens to include prep tables that would give employees more space for assembling food. In addition, $3 billion in capital expenditures is being budgeted in 2014 for opening new restaurants and refurbishing existing ones. Apart from making the menu more relevant to closely reflect customer preferences, more employees would also be hired at peak hours and weekends to increase speed of service.

Even at successful firms like McDonald's, it is easy to lose touch over time. Careful design and execution of processes that appropriately reflect product designs and market trends ultimately drive business outcomes and financial success.

Source: Julie Jargon, "McDonald's Says Its Restaurants Got Too Complicated," *Wall Street Journal*, January 24, 2014; Daniel Kruger, "You Want Data with That?" *Forbes*, vol. 173, no. 6 (March 2004), pp. 58–60; **http://www.mcdonalds.com**, June 26, 2014.

LEARNING GOALS *After reading this chapter, you should be able to:*

1. Understand the process structure in services and how to position a service process on the customer-contact matrix.
2. Understand the process structure in manufacturing and how to position a manufacturing process on the product-process matrix.
3. Explain the major process strategy decisions and their implications for operations.
4. Discuss how process decisions should strategically fit together.
5. Compare and contrast the two commonly used strategies for change, and understand a systematic way to analyze and improve processes.
6. Discuss how to document and evaluate processes.
7. Identify the commonly used approaches for effectively redesigning and managing processes.

Processes involve the use of an organization's resources to provide something of value and are perhaps the least understood and managed aspect of a business. No service can be provided and no product can be made without a process, and no process can exist without at least one service or product. Even with talented and motivated people, a firm cannot gain competitive advantage with faulty processes. Process decisions as such are strategic in nature. They should further a company's long-term competitive goals. In making process decisions, managers focus on controlling such competitive priorities as quality, flexibility, time, and cost. As exemplified by McDonald's, process management is an ongoing activity, with the same principles applying to both first-time and redesign choices. Many different choices are available in selecting human resources, equipment, outsourced services, materials, work flows, and methods that transform inputs into outputs. Another choice is which processes are to be done in-house and which processes are to be outsourced—that is, done outside the firm and purchased as materials and services. This decision helps to define the supply chain.

In this chapter, we focus on **process strategy**, which specifies the pattern of decisions made in managing processes so that the processes will achieve their competitive priorities, as well as **process analysis**, which is the documentation and detailed understanding of how work is performed and how it can be redesigned. Process decisions directly affect the process itself and indirectly the services and the products that it provides. All parts of an organization, as well as external suppliers and customers across the supply chain, need to be involved to ensure that processes are providing the most value to their internal and external customers.

Process strategy guides a variety of process decisions, and in turn is guided by operations strategy and the organization's ability to obtain the resources necessary to support them. We begin by defining four basic process decisions: (1) process structure, (2) customer involvement, (3) resource flexibility, and (4) capital intensity. We discuss these decisions for both service and manufacturing processes. We pay particular attention to ways in which these decisions fit together, depending on factors such as competitive priorities, customer contact, and volume, which in turn lead to two basic change strategies for analyzing and modifying processes: (1) process reengineering and (2) process improvement. Both these approaches need process analysis to identify and implement changes.

Three principles concerning process strategy are particularly important:

1. The key to successful process decisions is to make choices that fit the situation and that make sense together. They should not work at cross-purposes, with one process optimized at the expense of other processes. A more effective process is one that matches key process characteristics and has a close *strategic fit.*
2. Although this section of the text focuses on individual processes, they are the building blocks that eventually create the firm's whole supply chain. The cumulative effect on customer satisfaction and competitive advantage is huge.
3. Whether processes in the supply chain are performed internally or by outside suppliers and customers, management must pay particular attention to the interfaces between processes. Dealing with these interfaces underscores the need for cross-functional coordination.

Whether dealing with processes for offices, service providers, or manufacturers, operations managers must consider four common process decisions. Figure 1 shows that they are all important steps toward an effective process design. These four decisions are best understood at the process or subprocess level rather than at the firm level.

- **Process structure** determines the process type relative to the kinds of resources needed, how resources are partitioned between them, and their key characteristics. A **layout** is the physical arrangement of operations (or departments) relative to each other.
- **Customer involvement** reflects the ways in which customers become part of the process and the extent of their participation.
- **Resource flexibility** is the ease with which employees and equipment can handle a wide variety of products, output levels, duties, and functions.
- **Capital intensity** is the mix of equipment and human skills in a process. The greater the cost of equipment relative to the cost of labor, the greater is the capital intensity.

The concepts that we develop around these four decisions establish a framework within which we can address the appropriate process design in every situation. We establish the patterns of choices

process strategy
The pattern of decisions made in managing processes so that they will achieve their competitive priorities.

process analysis
The documentation and detailed understanding of how work is performed and how it can be redesigned.

process structure
The process type relative to the kinds of resources needed, how resources are partitioned between them, and their key characteristics.

layout
The physical arrangement of operations (or departments) relative to each other.

customer involvement
The ways in which customers become part of the process and the extent of their participation.

resource flexibility
The ease with which employees and equipment can handle a wide variety of products, output levels, duties, and functions.

▼ **FIGURE 1**
Major Decisions for Effective Processes

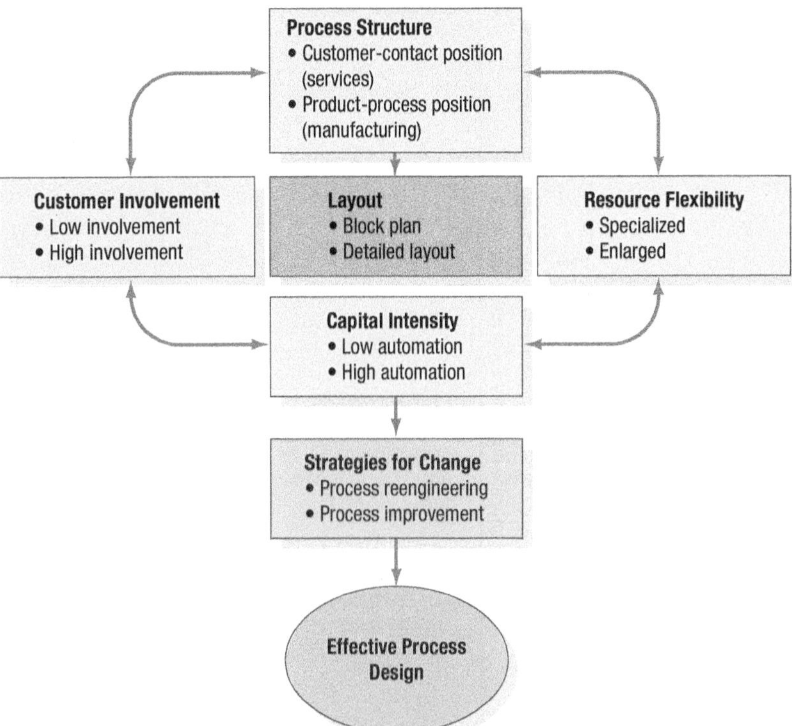

capital intensity

The mix of equipment and human skills in a process.

that create a good fit between the four decisions. For example, if you walk through a manufacturing facility where materials flow smoothly from one work station to the next (which we will define later to be a *line* process), you would be tempted to conclude that all processes should be line processes. They seem so efficient and organized. However, converting to a line process would be a big mistake if volumes are low and the products made are customized. Resources must be more flexible to handle a variety of products in such a situation. The result is a more disorganized appearance with jobs crisscrossing in many different directions depending on the product being made. Despite appearances, this process is the best choice.

Process Structure in Services

One of the first decisions a manager makes in designing a well-functioning process is to choose a process type that best achieves the competitive priorities for that process. Strategies for designing processes can be quite different, depending on whether a service is being provided or a product is being manufactured. We begin with service processes, given their huge implication for workforce resources in industrialized countries.

customer contact

The extent to which the customer is present, is actively involved, and receives personal attention during the service process.

A process strategy that gets customers in and out of a fast-food restaurant quickly would not be the right process strategy for a five-star restaurant, where customers seek a leisurely dining experience. To gain insights, we must start at the process level and recognize key contextual variables associated with the process. A good process strategy for a service process depends first and foremost on the type and amount of customer contact. **Customer contact** is the extent to which the customer is present, is actively involved, and receives personal attention during the service process. Face-to-face interaction, sometimes called a *moment of truth* or *service encounter*, brings the customer and service providers together. At that time, customer attitudes about the quality of the service provided are shaped. Table 1 shows several dimensions of customer contact. Many levels are possible on each of the five dimensions. Also, some parts of a process can have low contact and other parts of a process can have high contact.

TABLE 1 DIMENSIONS OF CUSTOMER CONTACT IN SERVICE PROCESSES

Dimension	High Contact	Low Contact
Physical presence	Present	Absent
What is processed	People	Possessions or information
Contact intensity	Active, visible	Passive, out of sight
Personal attention	Personal	Impersonal
Method of delivery	Face-to-face	Regular mail or e-mail

Customer-Contact Matrix

The customer-contact matrix, shown in Figure 2, brings together three elements: (1) the degree of customer contact, (2) customization, and (3) process characteristics. The matrix is the starting point for evaluating and improving a process.

FIGURE 2 ▶ Customer-Contact Matrix for Service Processes

MyOMLab Animation

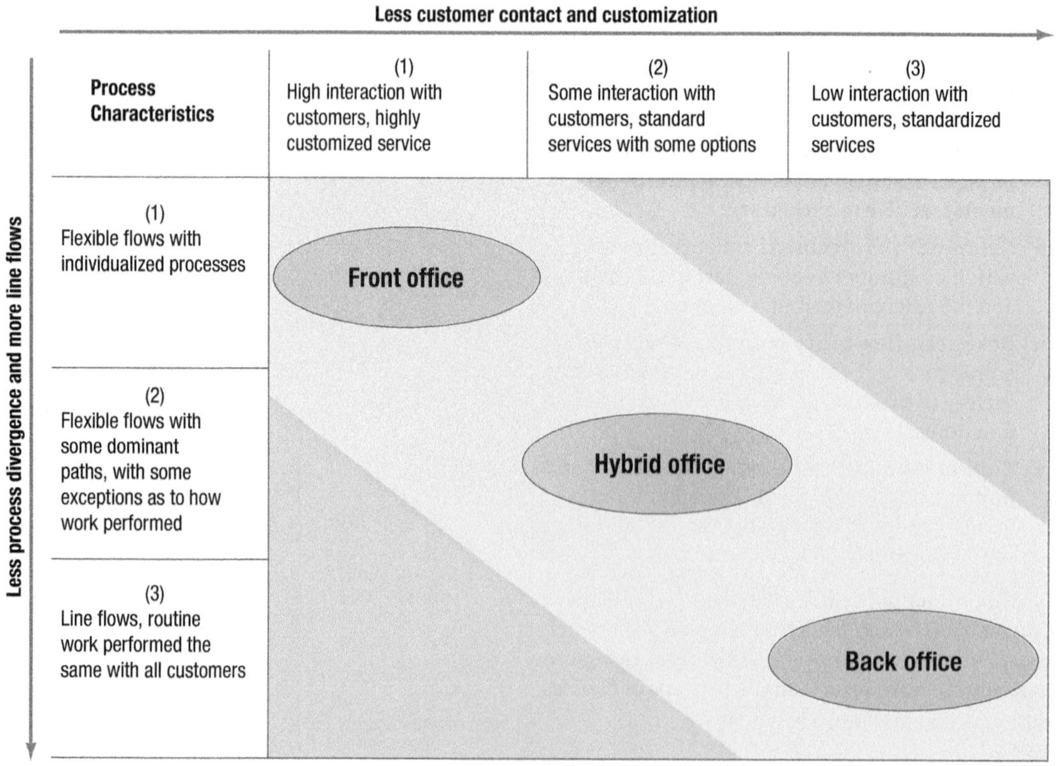

Customer Contact and Customization The horizontal dimension of the matrix represents the service provided to the customer in terms of customer contact and competitive priorities. A key competitive priority is how much customization is needed. Positions on the left side of the matrix represent high customer contact and highly customized services. The customer is more likely to be present and active. The process is more likely to be visible to the customer, who receives more personal attention. The right side of the matrix represents low customer contact, passive involvement, less personalized attention, and a process out of the customer's sight.

process divergence
The extent to which the process is highly customized with considerable latitude as to how its tasks are performed.

flexible flow
The customers, materials, or information move in diverse ways, with the path of one customer or job often crisscrossing the path that the next one takes.

line flow
The customers, materials, or information move linearly from one operation to the next, according to a fixed sequence.

front office
A process with high customer contact where the service provider interacts directly with the internal or external customer.

hybrid office
A process with moderate levels of customer contact and standard services with some options available.

Process Divergence and Flow The vertical dimension of the customer-contact matrix deals with two characteristics of the process itself: (1) process divergence and (2) flow. Each process can be analyzed on these two dimensions.

Process divergence is the extent to which the process is highly customized with considerable latitude as to how its tasks are performed. If the process changes with each customer, virtually every performance of the service is unique. Examples of highly divergent service processes where many steps in them change with each customer are found in consulting, law, and architecture. A service with low divergence, on the other hand, is repetitive and standardized. The work is performed exactly the same with all customers and tends to be less complex. Certain hotel services and telephone services are highly standardized to ensure uniformity.

Closely related to divergence is how the customer, object, or information being processed flows through the service facility. Work progresses through the sequence of steps in a process, which could range from highly diverse to linear. When divergence is considerable, the work flow tends to be more flexible. A **flexible flow** means that the customers, materials, or information move in diverse ways, with the path of one customer or job often crisscrossing the path that the next one takes. Each one can follow a carefully preplanned path, even though the first impression is one of disorganized, jumbled flows. Such an appearance goes naturally with high process divergence. A **line flow** means that the customers, materials, or information move linearly from one operation to the next, according to a fixed sequence. When diversity is low and the process standardized, line flows are a natural consequence.

Service Process Structuring

Figure 2 shows several desirable positions in the matrix that effectively connect the service product with the process. The manager has three process structures, which form a continuum, to choose from: (1) front office, (2) hybrid office, and (3) back office. It is unlikely that a process can be a top performer if a process lies too far from one of these diagonal positions, occupying instead one of the extreme positions represented by the light blue triangles in the matrix (refer to Figure 2). Such positions represent too much of a disconnect between the service provided and process characteristics.

Front Office A **front-office** process has high customer contact where the service provider interacts directly with the internal or external customer. Because of the customization of the service and variety of service options, many of the steps in it have considerable divergence. Work flows are flexible, and they vary from one customer to the next. The high-contact service process tends to be adapted or tailored to each customer.

Hybrid Office A hybrid office tends to be in the middle of the five dimensions in Table 1, or perhaps high on some contact measures and low on others. A **hybrid-office** process has moderate levels of customer contact and standard services, with some options available from which the customer chooses. The work flow progresses from one workstation to the next, with some dominant paths apparent.

Monkey Business/Fotolia

A financial consultant discusses options with a couple at their home. This process scores high on customer contact, because the customers are present, take an active part in creating the service, receive personal attention, and have a face-to-face meeting.

back office
A process with low customer contact and little service customization.

Back Office A **back-office** process has low customer contact and little service customization. The work is standardized and routine, with line flows from one service provider to the next until the service is completed. Preparing the monthly client fund balance reports in the financial services industry is a good example. It has low customer contact, low divergence, and a line flow.

Serge Kozak/Corbis

Employees discuss work with one another and their supervisor. Employees in these work stations are in a back office, because they have low customer contact and little service customization.

Process Structure in Manufacturing

Many processes at a manufacturing firm are actually services to internal or external customers, and so the previous discussion on services applies to them. Similarly, manufacturing processes can be found in service firms. Clarity comes when viewing work at the process level, rather than the organizational level. Here we focus instead on the manufacturing processes. Because of the differences between service and manufacturing processes, we need a different view on process structure.

Product–Process Matrix

The product-process matrix, shown in Figure 3, brings together three elements: (1) volume, (2) product customization, and (3) process characteristics. It synchronizes the product to be manufactured with the manufacturing process itself.

A good strategy for a manufacturing process depends first and foremost on volume. Customer contact, a primary feature of the customer-contact matrix for services, normally is not a consideration for manufacturing processes (although it *is* a factor for the many service processes throughout manufacturing firms). For many manufacturing processes, high product customization means lower volumes for many of the steps in the process. The vertical dimension of the product–process matrix deals with the same two characteristics in the customer-contact matrix: process divergence and flow. Each manufacturing process should be analyzed on these two dimensions, just as was done for a service process.

FIGURE 3 ▶
Product-Process Matrix for Manufacturing Processes
MyOMLab Animation

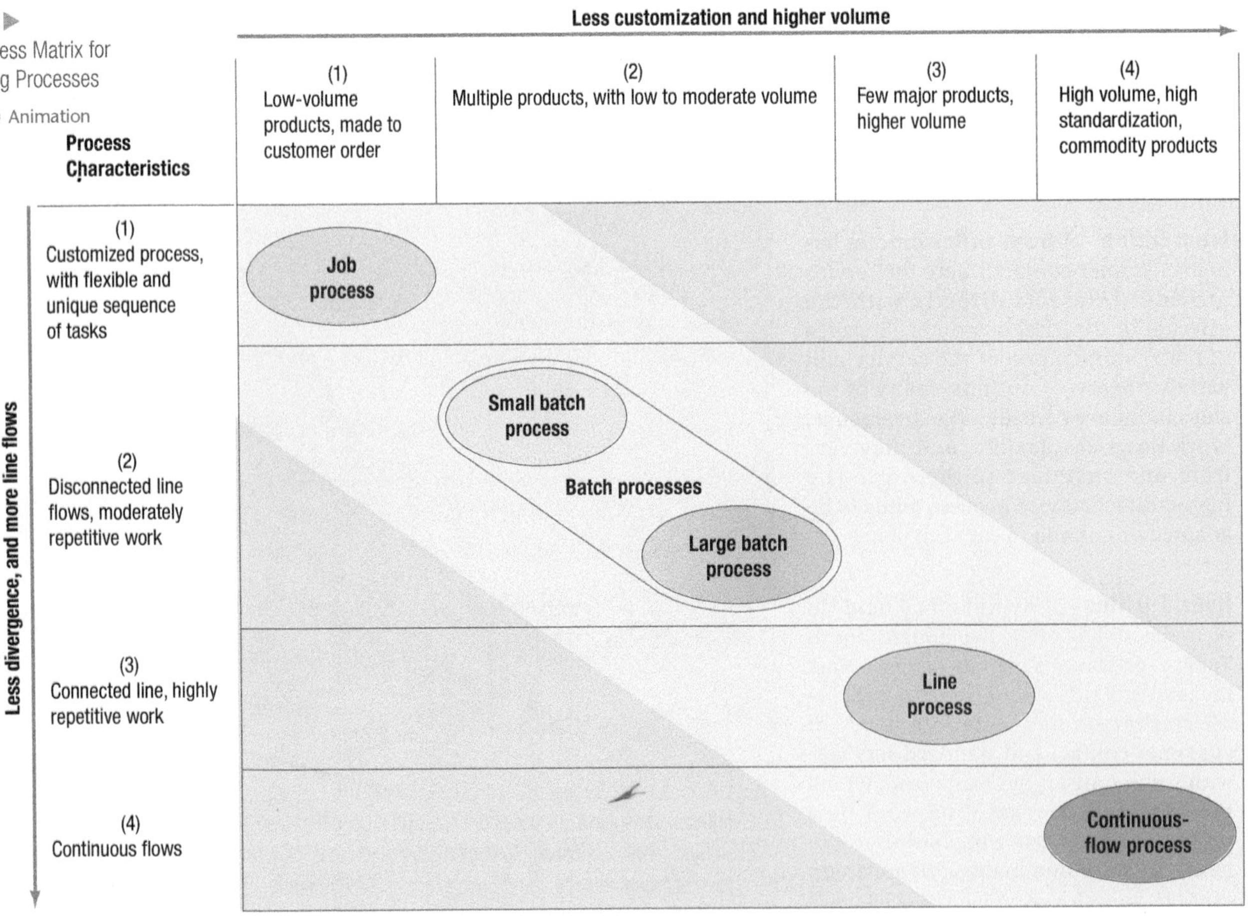

Less customization and higher volume

Less divergence, and more line flows

Process Characteristics	(1) Low-volume products, made to customer order	(2) Multiple products, with low to moderate volume	(3) Few major products, higher volume	(4) High volume, high standardization, commodity products
(1) Customized process, with flexible and unique sequence of tasks	Job process			
(2) Disconnected line flows, moderately repetitive work		Small batch process Batch processes Large batch process		
(3) Connected line, highly repetitive work			Line process	
(4) Continuous flows				Continuous-flow process

Manufacturing Process Structuring

Figure 3 shows several desirable positions (often called *process choices*) in the product-process matrix that effectively connect the manufactured product with the process. **Process choice** is the way of structuring the process by organizing resources around the process or organizing them around the products. Organizing around the process means, for example, that all milling machines are grouped together and process all products or parts needing that kind of transformation. Organizing around the product means bringing together all the different human resources and equipment needed for a specific product and dedicating them to producing just that product. The manager has four process choices, which form a continuum, to choose from: (1) job process, (2) batch process, (3) line process, and (4) continuous-flow process. As with the customer-contact matrix, it is unlikely that a manufacturing process can be a top performer if its position is too far from the diagonal. The fundamental message in Figure 3 is that the best choice for a manufacturing process depends on the volume and degree of customization required of the process. The process choice might apply to an entire manufacturing process or just one subprocess nested within it.

process choice

A way of structuring the process by organizing resources around the process or organizing them around the products.

Job Process A **job process** creates the flexibility needed to produce a wide variety of products in significant quantities, with considerable divergence in the steps performed. Customization is high and volume for any one product is low. The workforce and equipment are flexible to handle considerable task divergence. Companies choosing job processes often bid for work. Typically, they make products to order and do not produce them ahead of time. Each new order is handled as a single unit—as a job. Examples are machining a metal casting for a customized order or producing customized cabinets.

With a job process, all equipment and workers capable of certain types of work are positioned together. Because customization is high and most jobs have a different sequence of steps, this process choice creates flexible flows through the operations rather than a line flow.

job process

A process with the flexibility needed to produce a wide variety of products in significant quantities, with considerable divergence in the steps performed.

Batch Process The batch process is by far the most common process choice found in practice, leading to terms such as *small batch* or *large batch* to further distinguish one process choice from another. A **batch process** differs from the job process with respect to volume, variety, and quantity. The primary difference is that volumes are higher because the same or similar products or parts going into them are produced repeatedly. Some of the components going into the final product may be processed in advance. Production lots are handled in larger quantities (or *batches*) than they are with job processes. A batch of one product (or component part going into it or perhaps other products) is processed, and then production is switched to the next one. Eventually, the first product is produced again. A batch process has average or moderate volumes, but process divergence is still too great to warrant dedicating a separate process for each product. The process flow is flexible, but more dominant paths emerge than at a job process, and some segments of the process have a line flow. Examples of a batch process are making standard components that feed an assembly line or some processes that manufacture capital equipment.

batch process

A process that differs from the job process with respect to volume, variety, and quantity.

Line Process A **line process** lies between the batch and continuous processes on the continuum; volumes are high and products are standardized, which allows resources to be organized around particular products. Divergence is minimal in the process or line flows, and little inventory is held between the processing steps. Each step performs the same process over and over, with little variability in the products manufactured. Production and material handling equipment is specialized. Products created by a line process include the assembly of computers, automobiles, appliances, and toys.

Standard products are produced in advance of their need and held in inventory so that they are ready when a customer places an order. Product variety is possible by careful control of the addition of standard options to the main product.

line process

A process that lies between the batch and continuous processes on the continuum; volumes are high and products are standardized, which allows resources to be organized around particular products.

Continuous-Flow Process A **continuous-flow process** is the extreme end of high-volume standardized production, with rigid line flows. Process divergence is negligible. Its name derives from the way materials move through the process. Usually, one primary material (such as a liquid, a gas, or a powder) moves without stopping through the process. A continuous-flow process differs from a line process in one important respect: Materials (be they undifferentiated or discrete) flow through the process without stopping until the whole batch is finished. The time span can be several shifts or even several months. Examples of a continuous-flow process are petroleum refining; chemical processes; paper manufacturing; and processes making steel, soft drinks, and food.

continuous-flow process

The extreme end of high-volume standardized production and rigid line flows, with production not starting and stopping for long time intervals.

Production and Inventory Strategies

Strategies for manufacturing processes differ from those in services not only because of low customer contact and involvement but also because of the ability to use inventories not only as purchased materials but also in the form of subassemblies or finished products. There are clearly exceptions to this rule as Avis has an inventory of autos to rent, and FedEx has an inventory of in-process parcels. Design-to-order, make-to-order, assemble-to-order, and make-to-stock strategies are four approaches to inventory that should be coordinated with process choice.

Design-to-Order Strategy A firm uses a **design-to-order strategy** when it can design new products that do not currently exist, and then manufacture them to meet unique customer specifications. Typically a job process is employed to create a highly customized product, such as a designer pair of shoes for a particular client.

design-to-order strategy

A strategy that involves designing new products that do not currently exist, and then manufacturing them to meet unique customer specifications.

Make-to-Order Strategy Manufacturers that make products to customer specifications in low volumes tend to use the **make-to-order strategy**, coupling it with job or small batch processes. Even though the product is based on a standard design, it is a more complex process than assembling a final product from standard components. This strategy provides a high degree of customization and typically uses job or small batch processes. The processes have high divergence. Specialized medical equipment, castings, and expensive homes are suited to the make-to-order strategy.

make-to-order strategy

A strategy used by manufacturers that make products to customer specifications in low volumes.

Assemble-to-Order Strategy The **assemble-to-order strategy** is an approach to producing a wide variety of products from relatively few subassemblies and components after the customer orders are received. Typical competitive priorities are variety and fast delivery times. The assemble-to-order strategy often involves a line process for assembly and a batch process for fabrication. Because they are devoted to manufacturing standardized components and subassemblies in high volumes, the fabrication processes focus on creating appropriate amounts of component inventories for the assembly processes. Once the specific order from the customer is received, the assembly processes create the product from standardized components and subassemblies produced by the fabrication processes.

assemble-to-order strategy

A strategy for producing a wide variety of products from relatively few subassemblies and components after the customer orders are received.

Stocking finished products would be economically prohibitive because the numerous possible options make forecasting relatively inaccurate. Thus, the principle of **postponement** is applied, whereby the final activities in the provision of a product are delayed until the orders are received. The assemble-to-order strategy is also linked to **mass customization**, where highly divergent processes generate a wide variety of customized products at reasonably low costs.

postponement

The strategy of delaying final activities in the provision of a product until the orders are received.

mass customization

The strategy that uses highly divergent processes to generate a wide variety of customized products at reasonably low costs.

Make-to-Stock Strategy Manufacturing firms that hold items in stock for immediate delivery, thereby minimizing customer delivery times, use a **make-to-stock strategy**. This strategy is feasible for standardized products with high volumes and reasonably accurate forecasts. It is the inventory strategy of choice for line or continuous-flow processes. Examples of products produced with a make-to-stock strategy include garden tools, electronic components, soft drinks, and chemicals.

make-to-stock strategy

A strategy that involves holding items in stock for immediate delivery, thereby minimizing customer delivery times.

Combining a line process with the make-to-stock strategy is sometimes called **mass production**. It is what the popular press commonly envisions as the classical manufacturing process, because the environment is stable and predictable, with workers repeating narrowly defined tasks with low divergence.

mass production

A term sometimes used in the popular press for a line process that uses the make-to-stock strategy.

Layout

Selecting process structures for the various processes housed in a facility is a strategic decision, but must be followed by a more tactical decision—creating a layout. A *layout* is the physical arrangement of operations (or departments) created from the various processes and puts them in tangible form. For organizational purposes, processes tend to be clustered together into operations or departments. An *operation* is a group of human and capital resources performing all or part of one or more processes. For example, an operation could be several customer service representatives in a customer reception area; a group of machines and workers producing cell phones; or a marketing department. Regardless of how processes are grouped together organizationally, many of them cut across departmental boundaries. The flows across departmental lines could be informational, services, or products. Process structures that create more flows across departmental lines, as with job or batch processes, are the most challenging layout problems.

Process Strategy Decisions

Having covered process structure decisions in both service and manufacturing organizations, we turn our attention now to the other three major process strategy decisions shown in Figure 1—customer involvement, resource flexibility, and capital intensity.

Customer Involvement

Customer involvement reflects the ways in which customers become part of the process and the extent of their participation. As illustrated in Managerial Practice 1, it is especially important for many service processes such as eBay, particularly if customer contact is (or should be) high.

Possible Advantages The advantages of a more customer-focused process might increase the net value to the customer. Some customers seek active participation in and control over the service process, particularly if they will enjoy savings in both price and time. The manager must assess whether advantages outweigh disadvantages, judging them in terms of the competitive priorities and customer satisfaction. More customer

MANAGERIAL PRACTICE 1 Customer Involvement at eBay

Most manufacturers do not have to contend with customers waltzing around their shop floors, showing up intermittently and unannounced. Such customer contact can introduce considerable variability, disrupting carefully designed production processes. Costs and quality can be adversely affected. While customer contact is an issue even with manufacturers (each process does have at least one customer), extensive customer contact and involvement are business as usual for many processes of service providers. Customers at restaurants or rental car agencies are directly involved in performing the processes. The area where the sales person interacts with the customer *is* the shop floor.

How much should customers be involved in a process, so as to provide timely delivery and consistent quality, and at sustainable cost? Various ways are available—some accommodate customer-introduced variability and some reduce it. eBay provides two services: It provides sellers a platform for selling their goods or services, and it provides buyers a platform to find the goods and services they want. From a business perspective, providing these two services generates a high degree of variability in the demands for the company's resources. eBay illustrates one way to accommodate that kind of variability—provide an online auction house. As an online auction house, eBay accommodates high volumes as well as service order variability from customers seeking to buy and sell an endless number of items. eBay customers also have variability in technological capability, some with considerable Internet experience and some needing more handholding. Such variability would greatly complicate workforce scheduling if eBay's customers were not involved in many of its processes. eBay's process strategy utilizing customer involvement has been successful. Founded in 1995 in California, it now has 145 million active buyers globally buying and selling more than 650 million listed items with revenue of about $16.5 billion per year. It connects hundreds of millions of people around the world every day with only 31,800 employees. This relatively small workforce is possible in the face of customer-induced variability because its customers perform virtually all of the selling and buying processes through the e-commerce platform eBay.com and other vertical shopping sites. When the customer is responsible for much of the work, the right labor is provided at the right moment.

Kristoffer Tripplaar/Alamy

At any given time eBay has approximately 650 million listings worldwide, and yet its workforce consists of just 31,800 employees. The explanation? Customers do most of the work in eBay's buying and selling processes.

Source: Frances X. Frei, "Breaking the Trade-Off between Efficiency and Service," *Harvard Business Review* (November 2006), pp. 93–101; **http://en.wikipedia.org/wiki/Ebay** (May 31, 2014); **https://finance.yahoo.com/q/pr?s=EBAY+Profile** (May 31, 2014); **http://www.ebayinc.com/who_we_are/one_company** (May 31, 2014).

involvement can mean better quality, faster delivery, greater flexibility, and even lower cost. Self-service is the choice of many retailers, such as gasoline stations, supermarkets, and bank services. Manufacturers of products (such as toys, bicycles, and furniture) may also prefer to let the customer perform the final assembly because product, shipping, and inventory costs frequently are lower. In fact, IKEA Furniture Company's business model is based on customers being actively involved in its processes.

Customer involvement can also help coordinate across the supply chain. Emerging technologies allow companies to engage in an active dialogue with customers and make them partners in creating value and forecasting future demand. Suppliers to automobile companies can be close collaborators in the process of developing new vehicles and are no longer passive providers of materials and services. The same is true for distributors. Walmart does more than just distribute Procter & Gamble's products: It shares daily sales information and works with Procter & Gamble in managing inventories and warehousing operations.

Ramin Talaie/Corbis

A customer at Starbucks, a large coffee shop chain, places his order in the correct way. By structuring the ordering process for counter clerks and customers, Starbucks can deal efficiently with the variety in products offered, and with no hit on the service experience.

Jetta Productions/Getty Images

A car mechanic must be flexibly cross-trained at many different tasks in order to repair a wide variety of cars from different manufacturers.

Possible Disadvantages Customer involvement is not always a good idea. In some cases, giving the customer more active contact in a service process will just be disruptive, making the process less efficient. Managing the timing and volume of customer demands becomes more challenging if the customer is physically present and expects prompt delivery. Exposing the facilities and employees to the customer can have important quality implications (favorable or unfavorable). Such changes make interpersonal skills a prerequisite to the service provider's job, but higher skill levels come at a cost. It also might mean having many smaller decentralized facilities closer to the various customer concentration areas if the customer comes to the service providers.

Resource Flexibility

Just as managers must account for customer contact when making customer involvement decisions, so must they account for process divergence and diverse process flows when making resource flexibility decisions in Figure 1. For example, high task divergence and flexible process flows require more flexibility of the process's resources—its employees, facilities, and equipment. Employees need to perform a broad range of duties, and equipment must be general purpose. Otherwise, resource utilization will be too low for economical operations.

flexible workforce

A workforce whose members are capable of doing many tasks, either at their own workstations or as they move from one workstation to another.

Workforce Operations managers must decide whether to have a **flexible workforce**. Members of a flexible workforce are capable of doing many tasks, either at their own workstations or as they move from one workstation to another. However, such flexibility often comes at a cost, requiring greater skills and thus more training and education. Nevertheless, benefits can be large: Worker flexibility can be one of the best ways to achieve reliable customer service and alleviate capacity bottlenecks. Resource flexibility helps to absorb the feast-or-famine workloads in individual operations that are caused by low-volume production, divergent tasks, flexible flows, and fluid scheduling.

The type of workforce required also depends on the need for volume flexibility. When conditions allow for a smooth, steady rate of output, the likely choice is a permanent workforce that expects regular full-time employment. If the process is subject to hourly, daily, or seasonal peaks and valleys in demand, the use of part-time or temporary employees to supplement a smaller core of full-time employees may be the best solution. However, this approach may not be practical if knowledge and skill requirements are too high for a temporary worker to grasp quickly.

MyOMLab

Tutor 1 in MyOMLab demonstrates how to do break-even analysis for equipment selection.

Equipment Low volumes mean that process designers should select flexible, general-purpose equipment. Figure 4 illustrates this relationship by showing the total cost lines for two different types of equipment that can be chosen for a process. Each line represents the total annual cost of the process at different volume levels. It is the sum of fixed costs and variable costs. When volumes are low (because customization is high), process 1 is the better choice. It calls for inexpensive general-purpose equipment, which keeps investment in equipment low and makes fixed costs (F_1) small. Its variable unit cost is high, which gives its total cost line a relatively steep slope. Process 1 does the job, but not at peak efficiency.

Conversely, process 2 is the better choice when volumes are high and customization is low. Its advantage is low variable unit cost, as reflected in the flatter total cost line. This efficiency is possible when customization is low because the equipment can be designed for a narrow range of products or tasks. Its disadvantage is high equipment investment and, thus, high fixed costs (F_2). When annual volume produced is high enough, spreading these fixed costs over more units produced, the advantage of low variable costs more than compensates for the high fixed costs.

▼ **FIGURE 4**
Relationship between Process Costs and Product Volume

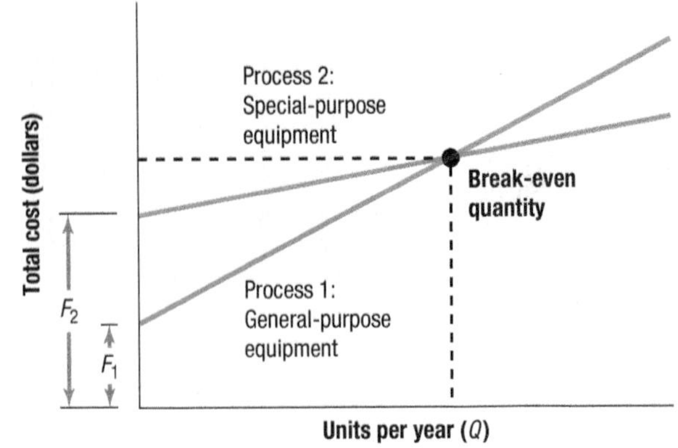

The break-even quantity in Figure 4 is the quantity at which the total costs for the two alternatives are equal. At quantities beyond this point, the cost of process 1 exceeds that of process 2. Unless the firm expects to sell more than the break-even amount, which is unlikely with high customization and low volume, the capital investment of process 2 is not warranted.

Capital Intensity

Capital intensity is the mix of equipment and human skills in the process; the greater the cost of equipment relative to the cost of labor, the greater is the capital intensity. As the capabilities of technology increase and its costs decrease, managers face an ever-widening range of choices, from operations utilizing very little automation to those requiring task-specific equipment and little human intervention. **Automation** is a system, process, or piece of equipment that is self-acting and self-regulating. Although automation is often thought to be necessary to gain competitive advantage, it has both advantages and disadvantages. Thus, the automation decision requires careful examination.

automation
A system, process, or piece of equipment that is self-acting and self-regulating.

fixed automation
A manufacturing process that produces one type of part or product in a fixed sequence of simple operations.

flexible (or programmable) automation
A manufacturing process that can be changed easily to handle various products.

industrial robot
Versatile, computer-controlled machine programmed to perform various tasks.

Automating Manufacturing Processes Substituting labor-saving capital equipment and technology for labor has been a classic way of improving productivity and quality consistency in manufacturing processes. If investment costs are large, automation works best when volume is high, because more customization typically means reduced volume. Gillette, for example, spent $750 million on the production lines and robotics that gave it a capacity to make 1.2 billion razor cartridges a year. The equipment is complicated and expensive. Only with such high volumes could this line process produce the product at a price low enough that consumers could afford to buy it.

One big disadvantage of capital intensity can be the prohibitive investment cost for low-volume operations (see Figure 4). Generally, capital-intensive operations must have high utilization to be justifiable. Also, automation does not always align with a company's competitive priorities. If a firm offers a unique product or high-quality service, competitive priorities may indicate the need for hand labor and individual attention rather than new technology. A case in point is the downstream processes in Gillette's supply chain that package and store the razor cartridges. It customizes the packaging for different regions of the world, so that volumes for any one type of package are much lower. As a result of the low volumes, Gillette does not use expensive automation for these processes. In fact, it outsources them. It produces razor cartridges to stock using highly automated processes and then packages them in customized fashion at remote locations on demand.

Manufacturers use two types of automation: (1) fixed and (2) flexible (or programmable). Particularly appropriate for line and continuous-flow process choices, **fixed automation** produces one type of part or product in a fixed sequence of simple operations. Operations managers favor fixed automation when demand volumes are high, product designs are stable, and product life cycles are long. These conditions compensate for the process's two primary drawbacks: (1) large initial investment cost and (2) relative inflexibility. However, fixed automation maximizes efficiency and yields the lowest variable cost per unit if volumes are high.

Flexible (or programmable) automation can be changed easily to handle various products. The ability to reprogram machines is useful for both low-customization and high-customization processes. In the case of high customization, a machine that makes a variety of products in small batches can be programmed to alternate between products. When a machine has been dedicated to a particular product or family of products, as in the case of low customization and a line flow, and the product is at the end of its life cycle, the machine can simply be reprogrammed with a new sequence of tasks for a new product. An **industrial robot**, which is a versatile, computer-controlled machine programmed to perform various tasks, is a classic example of flexible automation. These "steel-collar" workers operate independently of human control. A robot's arm has up to six standard movements. The robot's "hand" can be changed to perform different tasks, such as materials handling, assembly, and testing.

James Hardy/PhotoAlto/Alamy

R.R. Donnelly has been able to achieve flexible automation by receiving books digitally and preparing them to go to press electronically. This allows the company to put books on press more quickly and print smaller more manageable quantities in a single print run.

Automating Service Processes Using capital inputs as a labor-saving device is also possible for service processes. In educational services, for example, long-distance learning technology now can supplement or even replace the traditional classroom experience by using books, computers, Web sites, and videos as facilitating goods that go with the service. Justifying technology need not be limited to cost reduction. Sometimes, it can actually allow more task divergence by making available a wide menu of choices to the customer. It can also improve quality by being more consistent.

David R. Frazier/Newscom

Regional automated mail sorting facility in Boise, Idaho. Automating service processes in high volume environments such as these save labor and justify expensive capital investments.

The need for volume to justify expensive automation is just as valid for service processes as for manufacturing processes. Increasing the volume lowers the cost per dollar of sales. Volume is essential for many capital-intensive processes in the transportation, communications, and utilities industries.

Economies of Scope If capital intensity is high, resource flexibility usually is low. In certain types of manufacturing operations, such as machining and assembly, programmable automation breaks this inverse relationship between resource flexibility and capital intensity. It makes possible both high capital intensity and high resource flexibility, creating economies of scope. **Economies of scope** reflect the ability to produce multiple products more cheaply in combination than separately. In such situations, two conflicting competitive priorities—customization and low price—become more compatible. However, taking advantage of economies of scope requires that a family of parts or products have enough collective volume to utilize equipment fully.

economies of scope

Economies that reflect the ability to produce multiple products more cheaply in combination than separately.

Economies of scope also apply to service processes. Consider, for example, Disney whose managers used the Internet to reap the benefits of economies of scope. They aggressively linked their Internet processes with one another and with other parts of Disney. A flexible technology that handles many services together can be less expensive than handling each one separately, particularly when the markets are not too volatile.

Strategic Fit

The manager should understand how the four major process decisions tie together, so as to spot ways of improving poorly designed processes. The choices should fit the situation and each other. When the fit is more *strategic*, the process will be more effective. We examine services and manufacturing processes, looking for ways to test for strategic fit.

Decision Patterns for Service Processes

After analyzing a process and determining its position on the customer-contact matrix in Figure 2, it may be apparent that it is improperly positioned, either too far to the left or right, or too far to the top or bottom. Opportunities for improvement become apparent. Perhaps, more customization and customer contact is needed than the process currently provides. Perhaps, instead, the process is too divergent, with unnecessarily flexible flows. Reducing divergence might reduce costs and improve productivity.

The process should reflect its desired competitive priorities. Front offices generally emphasize top quality and customization, whereas back offices are more likely to emphasize low-cost operation, consistent quality, and on-time delivery. The process structure selected then points the way to appropriate choices on customer involvement, resource flexibility, and capital intensity. High customer contact at a front-office service process means:

1. *Process Structure.* The customer (internal or external) is present, actively involved, and receives personal attention. These conditions create processes with high divergence and flexible process flows.
2. *Customer Involvement.* When customer contact is high, customers are more likely to become part of the process. The service created for each customer is unique.
3. *Resource Flexibility.* High process divergence and flexible process flows fit with more flexibility from the process's resources—its workforce, facilities, and equipment.
4. *Capital Intensity.* When volume is higher, automation and capital intensity are more likely. Even though higher volume is usually assumed in the back office, it is just as likely to be in the front office for financial services. Information technology is a major type of automation at many service processes, which brings together both resource flexibility and automation.

Of course, this list provides general tendencies rather than rigid prescriptions. Exceptions can be found, but these relationships provide a way of understanding how service process decisions can be linked coherently.

Decision Patterns for Manufacturing Processes

Just as a service process can be repositioned in the customer-contact matrix, a manufacturing process can also be moved in the product-process matrix. Changes can be made either in the horizontal direction of Figure 3 by changing the degree of customization and volume, or they can be moved in the vertical direction by changing process divergence. Competitive priorities must be considered when translating strategy into specific manufacturing processes. Figure 5 shows some usual tendencies found in practice. Job and small batch processes are usual choices if top quality, on-time delivery, and flexibility (customization, variety, and volume flexibility) are given primary emphasis. Large batch, line, and continuous-flow processes match up with an emphasis on low-cost operations, consistent quality, and delivery speed.

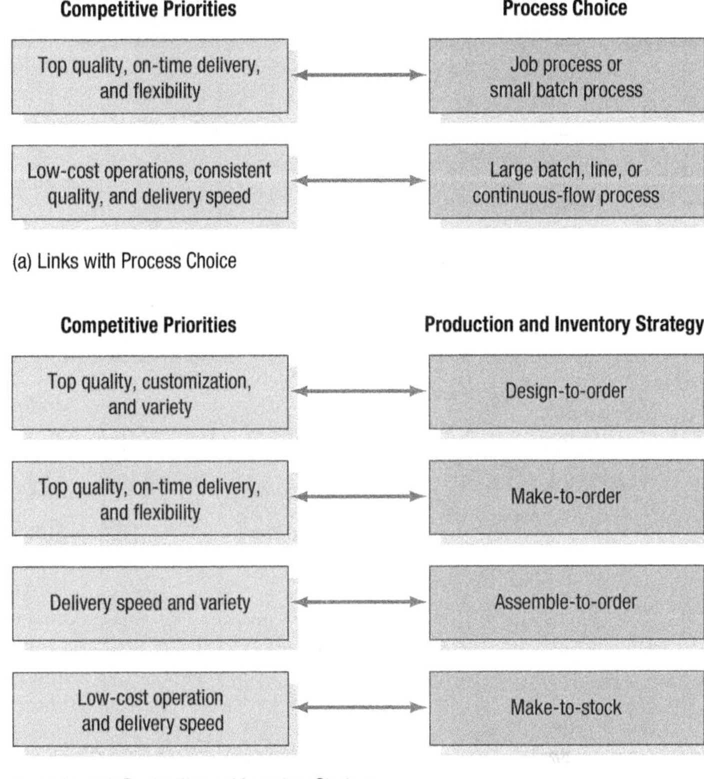

▲ **FIGURE 5**
Links of Competitive Priorities with Manufacturing Strategy

The production and inventory strategy should also be chosen to be consistent with the competitive priorities emphasized. As shown in Figure 5, the design-to-order strategy is consistent with top quality, customization, and variety. The focus is on meeting the unique needs of the customers by specifically designing a variety of products according to the customer specifications. The make-to-order strategy matches up with flexibility (particularly customization) and top quality. Because delivery speed is more difficult, meeting due dates and on-time delivery get the emphasis on the time dimension. The assemble-to-order strategy allows delivery speed and flexibility (particularly variety) to be achieved, whereas the make-to-stock strategy is the usual choice if delivery speed and low-cost operations are emphasized. Keeping an item in stock ensures quick delivery because it is generally available when needed, without delays in producing it. High volumes open up opportunities to reduce costs.

The process structure selected once again points the way to appropriate choices on customer involvement, resource flexibility, and capital intensity. High volumes per part type at a manufacturing process typically mean:

1. *Process Structure.* High volumes, combined with a standard product, make a line flow possible. It is just the opposite where a job process produces to specific customer orders.
2. *Customer Involvement.* Customer involvement is not a factor in most manufacturing processes, except for choices made on product variety and customization. Less discretion is allowed with line or continuous-flow processes to avoid the unpredictable demands required by customized orders.
3. *Resource Flexibility.* When volumes are high and process divergence is low, flexibility is not needed to utilize resources effectively, and specialization can lead to more efficient processes.
4. *Capital Intensity.* High volumes justify the large fixed costs of an efficient operation.

Gaining Focus

In the past, new services or products often were added to a facility in the name of better utilizing fixed costs and keeping everything under the same roof. The result was a jumble of competitive priorities, process structures, and technologies. In the effort to do everything, nothing was done well.

Focus by Process Segments A facility's operations often can neither be characterized nor actually designed for one set of competitive priorities and one process choice. At a services facility, some parts of the process might seem like a front office and other parts like a back office. Such arrangements can be effective, provided that sufficient focus is given to each process by the management segmenting them into separate operations that are relatively autonomous.

Plants within plants (PWPs) are different operations within a facility with individualized competitive priorities, processes, and workforces under the same roof. Boundaries for PWPs may be established by physically separating subunits or simply by revising organizational relationships. At each PWP, customization, capital intensity volume, and other relationships are crucial and must be complementary. The advantages of PWPs are fewer layers of management, greater ability to rely on team problem solving, and shorter lines of communication between departments.

plants within plants (PWPs)
Different operations within a facility with individualized competitive priorities, processes, and workforces under the same roof.

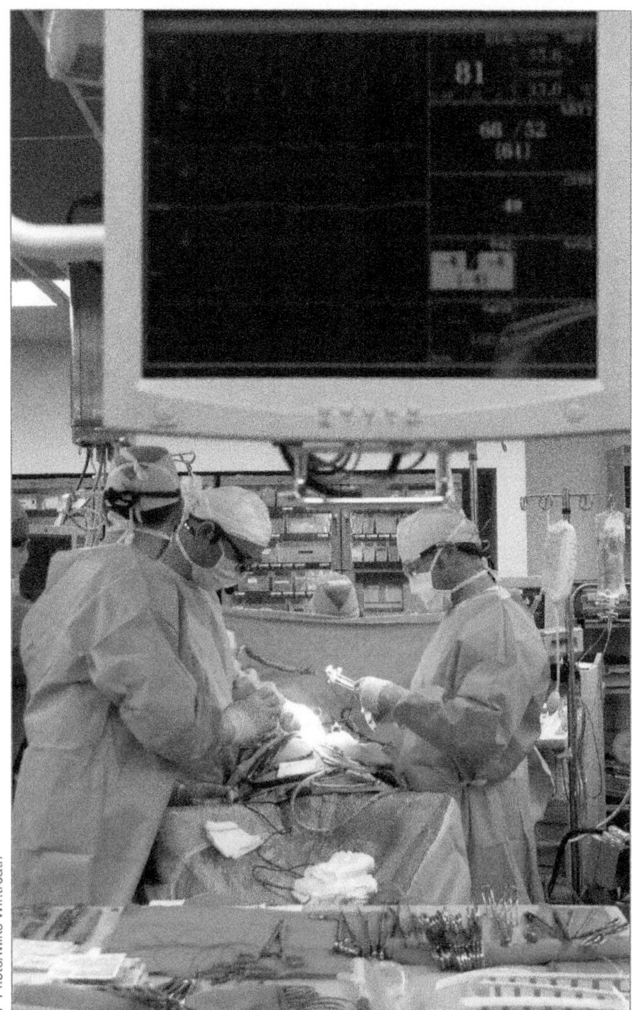
AP Photo/Mike Wintroath

Focused factories are not just found in manufacturing. This single-specialty facility focuses just on heart surgery and has all the advanced resources need that cannot be provided by a general hospital. Another example is the Toronto-based Shouldice Clinic, which focuses just on hernias.

Focused Service Operations Service industries also implement the concepts of focus and PWPs. Specialty retailers opened stores with smaller, more accessible spaces. These focused facilities generally chipped away at the business of large department stores. Using the same philosophy, some department stores now focus on specific customers or products. Remodeled stores create the effect of many small boutiques under one roof.

Focused Factories Hewlett-Packard, Rolls-Royce, Japan's Ricoh and Mitsubishi, and Britain's Imperial Chemical Industries PLC are some of the firms that created **focused factories**, splitting large plants that produced all the company's products into several specialized smaller plants. The theory is that narrowing the range of demands on a facility will lead to better performance because management can concentrate on fewer tasks and lead a workforce toward a single goal.

Strategies for Change

The four major process decisions represent broad, strategic issues and define the nature of the processes a firm needs to compete effectively. However, decisions that are made must be translated into actual process designs or redesigns. There are two different but complementary philosophies for process design and change: (1) process reengineering and (2) process improvement. Process analysis, supported by the tools described later, is needed regardless of whether reengineering or process improvement is attempted. An individual or a whole team examines the process and looks for ways to streamline tasks, eliminate whole processes entirely, cut expensive materials or services, improve the environment, or make jobs safer. By comprehensively analyzing the process, one must find the ways to trim costs and delays and to improve customer satisfaction.

Process Reengineering

Reengineering is the fundamental rethinking and radical redesign of processes to improve performance dramatically in terms of cost, quality, service, and speed. Process reengineering is about reinvention rather than incremental improvement. It is strong medicine and not always needed or successful. Pain, in the form of layoffs and large cash outflows for investments in information technology, almost always accompanies massive change. However, reengineering processes can have big payoffs. Table 2 lists the key elements of the overall approach.

focused factories

The result of a firm's splitting large plants that produced all the company's products into several specialized smaller plants.

reengineering

The fundamental rethinking and radical redesign of processes to improve performance dramatically in terms of cost, quality, service, and speed.

TABLE 2 | KEY ELEMENTS OF REENGINEERING

Element	Description
Critical processes	The emphasis of reengineering should be on core business processes. Normal process-improvement activities can be continued with the other processes.
Strong leadership	Senior executives must provide strong leadership for reengineering to be successful. Otherwise, cynicism, resistance ("we tried that before"), and boundaries between departments can block radical changes.
Cross-functional teams	A team, consisting of members from each functional area affected by the process change, is charged with carrying out a reengineering project. Self-managing teams and employee empowerment are the rule rather than the exception.
Information technology	Information technology is a primary enabler of process engineering. Most reengineering projects design processes around information flows, such as customer order fulfillment.
Clean-slate philosophy	Reengineering requires a "clean-slate" philosophy—that is, starting with the way the customer wants to deal with the company. To ensure a customer orientation, teams begin with internal and external customer objectives for the process.
Process analysis	Despite the clean-slate philosophy, a reengineering team must understand things about the current process: what it does, how well it performs, and what factors affect it. The team must look at every procedure involved in the process throughout the organization.

Reengineering has led to many successes and will continue to do so. However, it is not simple or easily done, nor is it appropriate for all processes or all organizations. The best understanding of a process, and how to improve it, often lies with the people who perform the work each day, not with cross-functional teams or top management.

Process Improvement

Process improvement is the systematic study of the activities and flows of each process to improve it. Its purpose is to "learn the numbers," understand the process, and dig out the details. Once a process is really understood, it can be improved. The relentless pressure to provide better quality at a lower price means that companies must continually review all aspects of their operations. Process improvement goes on, whether or not a process is reengineered. There is always a better way. Most processes can be improved if someone thinks of a way and implements it effectively. Indeed, companies will either adapt processes to the changing needs of customers or cease to exist. Long-term success comes from managers and employees who really understand their businesses. But all too often, highly publicized efforts that seem to offer quick-fix solutions fail to live up to expectations over the long haul, be they programs for conceptualizing a business vision, conducting culture transformation campaigns, or providing leadership training.

process improvement
The systematic study of the activities and flows of each process to improve it.

Process Analysis

Process analysis is the documentation and detailed understanding of how work is performed and how it can be redesigned. Looking at the strategic issues can help identify opportunities for improvement. Do gaps exist between a process's competitive priorities and its current competitive capabilities. Do multiple measures of cost, top quality, quality consistency, delivery speed, and on-time delivery meet or exceed expectations? Is there a good *strategic fit* in the process? If the process provides a service, does its position on the customer-contact matrix (see Figure 2) seem appropriate? How does the degree of customer contact match up with process structure, customer involvement, resource flexibility, and capital intensity? Similar questions should be asked about manufacturing processes regarding the strategic fit between process choice, volume, and product customization.

Process analysis begins with identifying and defining a new opportunity for improvement and ends with implementing and controlling a revised process, and which we capture through the Six Sigma Process Improvement Model. Other approaches to process improvement are statistical process control and process capability analysis and value stream mapping.

Six Sigma Process Improvement Model Figure 6 shows the Six Sigma Process Improvement Model, a five-step procedure that leads to improvements in-process performance. This model can be applied to projects involving incremental improvements to processes or to projects requiring major changes, including a redesign of an existing process or the development of a new process.

The following steps comprise the model:

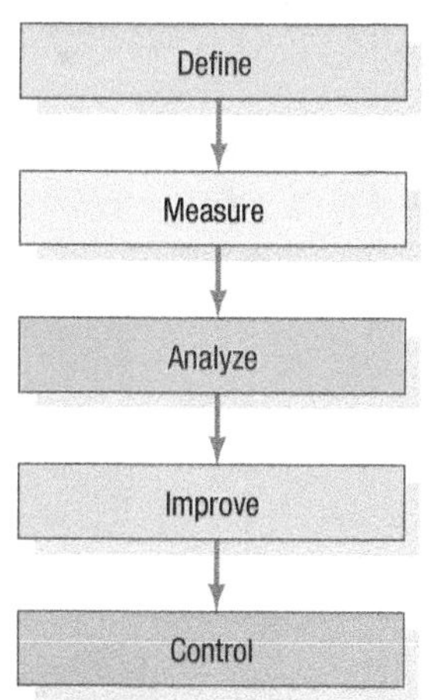

▲ **FIGURE 6**
Six Sigma Process Improvement Model

- *Define.* The scope and boundaries of the process to be analyzed are first established. Is it a broad process that stretches across the whole organization, involving many steps and many employees, or is it a more narrowly bracketed nested subprocess that is just part of one person's job? A process's scope can be too narrow or too broad. For example, a broadly defined process that outstrips the resources available, sometimes called "trying to boil the ocean," is doomed because it will increase employee frustration without producing any results. The resources that management assigns to improving or reengineering a process should match the scope of the process. Once scope is established, determine the characteristics of the process's output that are critical to customer satisfaction and identify any gaps between these characteristics and the process's capabilities. Get a picture of the current process by documenting it using techniques outlined in this chapter.
- *Measure.* It is important to have good performance measures to evaluate a process for clues on how to improve it. **Metrics** are performance measures for the process and the steps within it. A good place to start is with competitive priorities, but they need to be specific. The analyst creates multiple measures of quality, customer satisfaction, time to perform each step or the whole process, cost, errors, safety, environmental measures, on-time delivery, flexibility, and the like. Once the metrics are identified, it is time to collect information on how the process is currently performing on each one. Measurement can be rough-cut estimates or quite extensive. It is important to quantify the work the process does that affects the gap. Select what to measure, identify data sources, and prepare a data collection plan.
- *Analyze.* Use the data on measures to perform process analysis to determine where improvements are necessary. A careful analysis of the process and its performance on the selected metrics should

metrics
Performance measures that are established for a process and the steps within it.

uncover *disconnects*, or gaps, between actual and desired performance. Illogical, missing, or extraneous steps can cause performance gaps. They can also be caused by metrics that reinforce the silo mentality of individual departments when the process spans across several departments. The analyst or design team should dig deep to find the root causes of performance gaps. For instance, techniques for analyzing wait times and delays can provide important information. Whether or not major redesign is necessary, establish procedures to make the desired outcome routine.

- *Improve.* Using analytical and creative thinking, the design team generates a long list of ideas for improvements. These ideas are then sifted and analyzed. Ideas that are justifiable, where benefits outweigh costs, are reflected in a new process design that can meet the new performance objectives. The new design should be documented "as proposed." Combining the new process design with the documentation of the current process gives the analysts clear before and after pictures. The new documentation should make clear how the revised process will work and the performance expected for the various metrics used. Implement the changes.
- *Control.* After the implementation, monitor the process to make sure that high performance levels are maintained. Once again, data analysis tools can be used to control the process. Implementation is more than developing a plan and carrying it out. Many processes have been redesigned effectively, but never get implemented. People resist change: "We have always done it that way" or "we tried that before." Widespread participation in process analysis is essential, not only because of the work involved but also because it builds commitment. It is much easier to implement something that is partly your own idea. In addition, special expertise may be needed, such as for developing software. New jobs and skills may be needed, involving training and investments in new technology. Implementation and control brings to life the steps needed to bring the redesigned process online. Management or the steering committee must make sure that the implementation project goes according to schedule.

Green Belt

An employee who achieved the first level of training in a Six Sigma program and spends part of his or her time teaching and helping teams with their projects.

Black Belt

An employee who reached the highest level of training in a Six Sigma program and spends all of his or her time teaching and leading teams involved in Six Sigma projects.

Master Black Belt

Full-time teachers and mentors to several Black Belts.

Successful users have found that it is essential to rigorously follow the steps in the Six Sigma Improvement Model, which is sometimes referred to as the *DMAIC process* (whose name comes from using the first letter of each step in the model). To accomplish the goals of Six Sigma, employees must be trained in the "whys" and the "how-tos" of process performance and what it means to customers, both internal and external. Successful firms using Six Sigma develop a cadre of internal teachers who then are responsible for teaching and assisting teams involved in a process-improvement project. These teachers have different titles depending on their experience and level of achievement. "**Green Belts**" devote part of their time to teaching and helping teams with their projects and the rest of their time to their normally assigned duties. "**Black Belts**" are full-time teachers and leaders of teams involved in Six Sigma projects. Finally, "**Master Black Belts**" are full-time teachers who review and mentor "Black Belts."

flowchart

A diagram that traces the flow of information, customers, equipment, or materials through the various steps of a process.

Documenting and Evaluating the Process

Three major techniques for effectively documenting and evaluating processes are (1) flowcharts, (2) work measurement techniques, and (3) process charts. They allow you to "lift the lid and peer inside" to see how an organization does its work. You can see how a process operates, at any level of detail, and how well it is performing. Trying to create one of these charts might even reveal a lack of any established process. It may not be a pretty picture, but it is how work actually gets done. Techniques for documenting the process lend themselves to finding performance gaps, generating ideas for process improvements, and documenting the look of a redesigned process.

Wavebreak Media Ltd./Alamy

Young designer presenting a flow chat during a meeting. The use of flowcharts can help in documenting and evaluating processes.

Flowcharts

A **flowchart** traces the flow of information, customers, equipment, or materials through the various steps of a process. Flowcharts are also known as flow diagrams, process maps, relationship maps, or blueprints. Flowcharts have no precise format and typically are drawn with boxes (with a brief description of the step inside), and with lines and arrows to show sequencing. The rectangle (□) shape is the usual choice for a box, although other shapes (O, ⬭, ⬡, ▽, or ▭) can differentiate between different types of steps (e.g., operation, delay, storage, and inspection). Colors and shading can also call attention to different types of steps, such as those particularly high on process divergence. Divergence is also communicated when an outgoing arrow from a step splits into two or more arrows that lead to different boxes. Although many representations are acceptable, there must be agreement on the conventions used. They can be given as a key somewhere in the flowchart, and/or described in accompanying text. It is also important to communicate *what* (e.g., information, customer order, customer, and materials) is being tracked.

You can create flowcharts with several programs. Microsoft PowerPoint offers many different formatting choices for flowcharts (see the Flowchart submenu under AutoShapes). The tutorials "Flowcharting in Excel" and "Flowcharting in PowerPoint" in MyOMLab offer other options. Other powerful software packages for flowcharting and drawing diagrams (such as organization charts and decision trees) are SmartDraw (**http://www.smartdraw.com**), Microsoft Visio (**http://www.microsoft.com/office/visio**), and Micrografx (**http://www.micrografx.com**). Often, free downloads are available at such sites on a trial basis.

MyOMLab

Flowcharts can be created for several levels in the organization. For example, at the strategic level, they could show the core processes and their linkages. At this level, the flowcharts do not have much detail; however, they give a bird's eye view of the overall business. Just identifying a core process is often helpful. However, in this chapter, we focus at the process level, where we get into the details of the process being analyzed. Many steps may have subprocesses nested within them. Rather than representing everything in one flowchart, an overview of the whole process can first be created. Subsequently flowcharts can be developed to flesh out nested processes. This nesting approach often becomes a practical necessity because only so much detail can be shown in any single flowchart.

Swim Lane Flowchart One of the most commonly used forms of a flowchart is the **swim lane flowchart**. It is a visual representation that groups functional areas responsible for different subprocesses into lanes. It is most appropriate when the business process spans several department boundaries, and where parallel lines similar to lanes in a swimming pool separate each department or a functional area. Swim lanes are labeled according to the functional groups they represent and can be arranged either horizontally or vertically.

swim lane flowchart

A visual representation that groups functional areas responsible for different subprocesses into lanes. It is most appropriate when the business process spans several department boundaries.

The swim lane flowchart in Figure 7 illustrates the order placement and acceptance process at a manufacturing company. The process starts when an order is generated by a customer and ends when

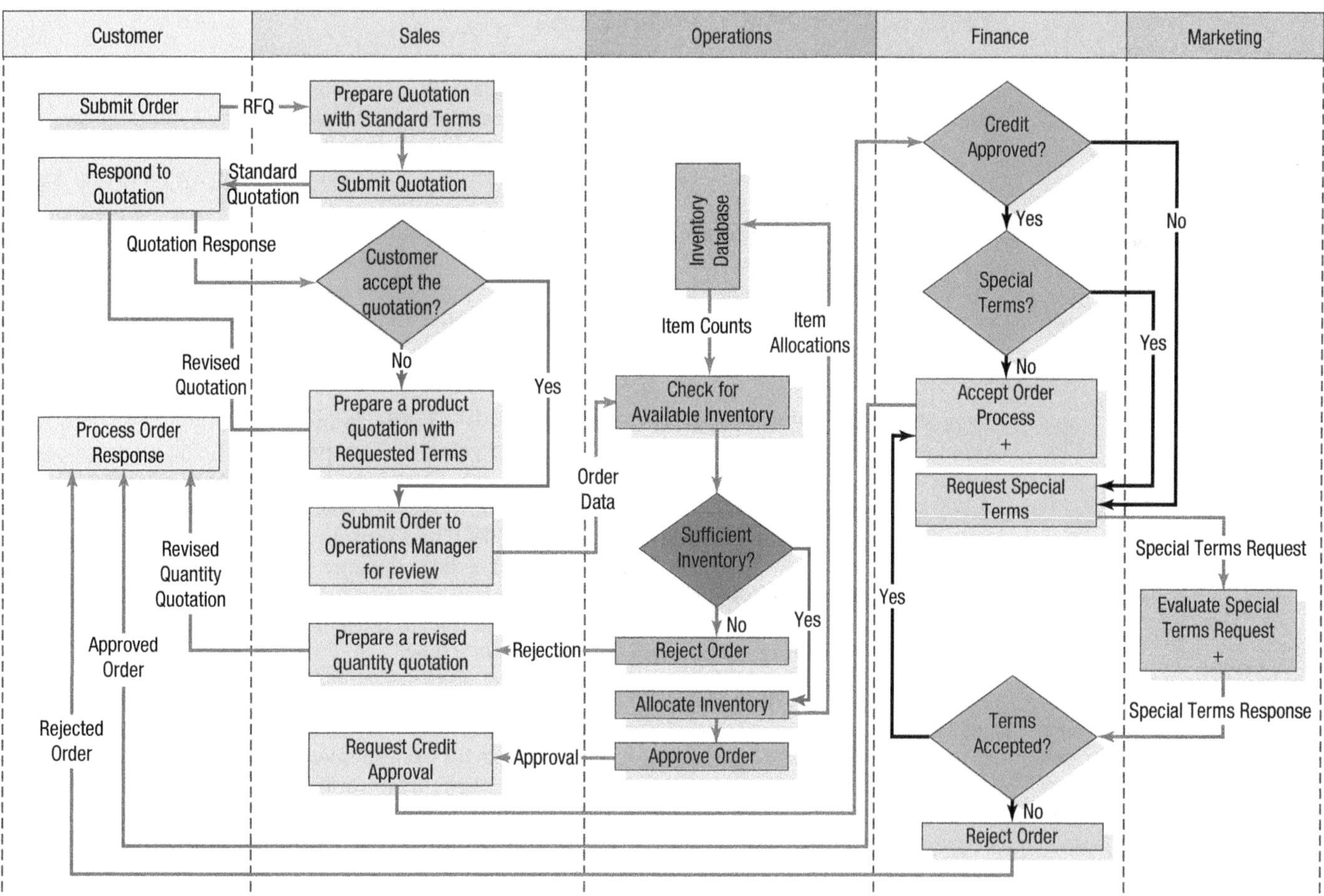

▲ FIGURE 7
Swim Lane Flowchart of the Order-Filling Process Showing Handoffs between Departments

Source: D. Kroenke, *Using MIS*, 4th ed., © 2012. Reprinted and electronically reproduced by permission of Pearson Education, Inc., Upper Saddle River, New Jersey.

the order is actually rejected, modified, or approved by the company in consultation with the customer. All functions contributing to this process are included in the flowchart. The columns represent different departments or functional areas, and the steps appear in the department column where they are performed. The customer is also shown as one of the column headings. This approach shows the *handoffs* from one department to another when the outgoing arrow from a step goes to another column. Special dotted-line arrows are one way to show handoffs. Handoffs are points where cross-functional coordination is at particular risk due to the silo mentality. Misunderstandings, backlogs, and errors are more likely at these points.

Figure 7 illustrates one other feature. The diamond shape (◊) represents a yes/no decision or outcome, such as the results of an inspection or recognition of different kinds of customer requirements. In Figure 7, the diamond represents three yes/no decision points within finance, and one each within sales and operations. These yes/no decision points are more likely to appear when a process is high in divergence.

Swim lane flowcharts allow the process analyst and managers to look at the horizontal organization rather than the vertical organization and departmental boundaries implied by a typical organizational chart. Swim lane flowcharts show how organizations produce their outputs through cross-functional work processes and allow the design team to see all the critical interfaces between functions and departments.

service blueprint

A special flowchart of a service process that shows which steps have high customer contact.

Service Blueprint A **service blueprint** is a special flowchart of a service process that shows which steps have high customer contact. It uses a dotted line of visibility to identify which steps are visible to the customer (and thus are more of a front-office process) and those that are not (back-office process). Of course, visibility is just one aspect of customer contact, and it may not adequately capture how actively the customer is involved or how much personal attention is required. A service blueprint can use colors, shading, or box shapes, instead of the lines of visibility, to show the extent and type of customer contact. Another approach to service blueprinting is to tag each step with a number, and then have an accompanying table that describes in detail the customer contact for each numbered step. There is no one "right way" to create a flow chart or service blueprint.

Work Measurement Techniques

time study

A work measurement method using a trained analyst to perform four basic steps in setting a time standard for a job or process: selecting the work elements (or nested processes) within the process to be studied, timing the elements, determining the sample size, and setting the final standard.

MyOMLab

Process documentation would not be complete without estimates of the average time each step in the process would take. Time estimates are needed not just for process-improvement efforts but for capacity planning, constraint management, performance appraisal, and scheduling. Estimating task times can be as simple as making a reasoned guess, asking a knowledgeable person, or taking notes while observing the process. More extensive studies involve collecting data for several weeks, consulting cost accounting data, or checking data recorded in information systems.

Formal techniques are also available that rely on the judgment of skilled observers: (1) the time study method, (2) the elemental standard data method, (3) the predetermined data method, and (4) work sampling. A fifth method, (5) learning curve analysis, is particularly appropriate when a new product or process is introduced and the time per unit produced has not yet stabilized. The method chosen depends on the purpose of the data, process type (job, batch, or line), and degree of product customization.

Time Study Method **Time study** uses a trained analyst to perform four basic steps in setting a time standard for a job or process: (1) selecting the work elements (steps in a flowchart or process chart) within the process to be studied, (2) timing the elements, (3) determining the sample size, and (4) setting the final standard. It is essentially the average time observed, adjusted for normal effort and making an allowance for breaks, unavoidable delays, and the like. The analyst records time spent on each element of the process being studied using a stopwatch, and records the time spent on each element for several repetitions. The analyst assigns a performance rating for each element to adjust for normal effort. Some elements may be performed faster or slower than normal, in the analyst's judgment. The allowance is expressed as a proportion or percent of the total *normal* time.

elemental standard data

A database of standards compiled by a firm's analysts for basic elements that they can draw on later to estimate the time required for a particular job, which is most appropriate when products or services are highly customized, job processes prevail, and process divergence is great.

Elemental Standard Data Method Another method is needed when products or services are highly customized, job processes prevail, and process divergence is great. **Elemental standard data** is a database of standards compiled by a firm's analysts for basic elements that they can draw on later to estimate the time required for a particular job. This approach works well when work elements within certain jobs are similar to those in other jobs. Sometimes, the time required for a work element depends on variable characteristics of the jobs, such as the amount of metal to be deposited for a welding process. In such cases, an equation that relates these characteristics to the time required is also stored in the database. Another method, such as time study or past records, still must be used to compile the normal times (before the allowance is added) stored in the database.

EXAMPLE 1 **Time Study of Watch Assembly Process**

A process at a watch assembly plant has been changed. The process is divided into three work elements. A time study has been performed with the following results. The time standard for the process previously was 14.5 minutes. Based on the new time study, should the time standard be revised?

Christopher Bosset/Bloomberg/Getty Images

Workers seen on a watch assembly line at the Jaeger-LeCoultre factory in Le Sentier, Switzerland.

SOLUTION

The new time study had an initial sample of four observations, with the results shown in the following table. The performance rating factor (RF) is shown for each element (to adjust for normal effort), and the allowance for the whole process is 18 percent of the total *normal* time.

	Obs 1	Obs 2	Obs 3	Obs 4	Average (min)	RF	Normal Time
Element 1	2.60	2.34	3.12	2.86	2.730	1.0	2.730
Element 2	4.94	4.78	5.10	4.68	4.875	1.1	5.363
Element 3	2.18	1.98	2.13	2.25	2.135	0.9	1.922
					Total Normal Time = **10.015 minutes**		

The normal time for an element in the table is its average time, multiplied by the RF. The total normal time for the whole process is the sum of the normal times for the three elements, or 10.015 minutes. To get the standard time (ST) for the process, just add in the allowance, or

$$ST = 10.015(1 + 0.18) = \mathbf{11.82} \text{ minutes/watch}$$

DECISION POINT

The time to assemble a watch appears to have decreased considerably. However, based on the precision that management wants, the analyst decided to increase the sample size before setting a new standard. MyOMLab Supplement H, "Measuring Output Rates," gives more information on determining the number of additional observations needed.

MyOMLab

Predetermined Data Method The **predetermined data method** divides each work element even more, into a series of micromotions that make up the element. The analyst then consults a published database that contains the normal times for the full array of possible micromotions. A process's normal time can then be calculated as the sum of the times given in the database for the elements performed in the process. This approach makes most sense for highly repetitive processes with little process divergence and line flows. The micromotions (such as reach, move, or apply pressure) are very detailed.

predetermined data method
A database approach that divides each work element into a series of micromotions that make up the element. The analyst then consults a published database that contains the normal times for the full array of possible micromotions.

Work Sampling Method **Work sampling** estimates the proportion of time spent by people or machines on different activities, based on observations randomized over time. Examples of these activities include working on a service or product, doing paperwork, waiting for instructions, waiting for maintenance, or being idle. Such data can then be used to assess a process's productivity, estimate the allowances needed to set standards for other work measurement methods, and spot areas for process improvement. It is best used when the processes are highly divergent with flexible flows. Figure 8 shows the input data and numerical results for one week of observations. It shows an idle time of 23.81 percent for the week and also reports that 237 more observations are needed to achieve the confidence and precision levels required with the input data.

work sampling
A process that estimates the proportion of time spent by people or machines on different activities, based on observations randomized over time.

MyOMLab

Learning Curve Analysis The time estimation techniques just covered assume that the process is stable. If the process is revised, then just repeat the method for the revised process after it stabilizes. Learning curve analysis, on the other hand, takes into account that learning takes place on an ongoing basis, such as when new products or services are introduced frequently. With instruction and repetition,

(a) Input Data and Numerical Results

Increase Observations | Remove An Observation

Confidence z	1.96	**Precision p**	0.05

Observation Period	**Times Busy**	**Times Idle**	**Observations**
Monday	6	1	7
Tuesday	5	2	7
Wednesday	7	0	7
Thursday	9	2	11
Friday	5	5	10
Total	32	10	42

(b) Idle Time and Observations Required

Portion of idle times	0.2381
Total observations required	279
Additional observations required	237

▲ **FIGURE 8**
Work Sampling Study of Admission Clerk at Health Clinic Using OM Explorer's *Time Study* Solver.

learning curve

A line that displays the relationship between processing time and the cumulative quantity of a product or service produced.

MyOMLab

workers learn to perform jobs more efficiently, process improvements are identified, and better administration methods are created. These learning effects can be anticipated with a **learning curve**, a line that displays the relationship between processing time and the cumulative quantity of a product or service produced. The time required to produce a unit or create a service decreases as more units or customers are processed. The learning curve for a process depends on the rate of learning and the actual or estimated time for the first unit processed. Figure 9 demonstrates the learning curve assuming an 80 percent learning rate, with the first unit taking 120,000 hours and the cumulative average time for the first 10 units produced. The learning rate deals with each *doubling* of the output total. The time for the second unit is 80 percent of the first (or 120,000 × .80 = 96,000 hours), the time for the fourth unit is 80 percent of the second unit (or 96,000 × .80 = 76,800 hours), and so on.

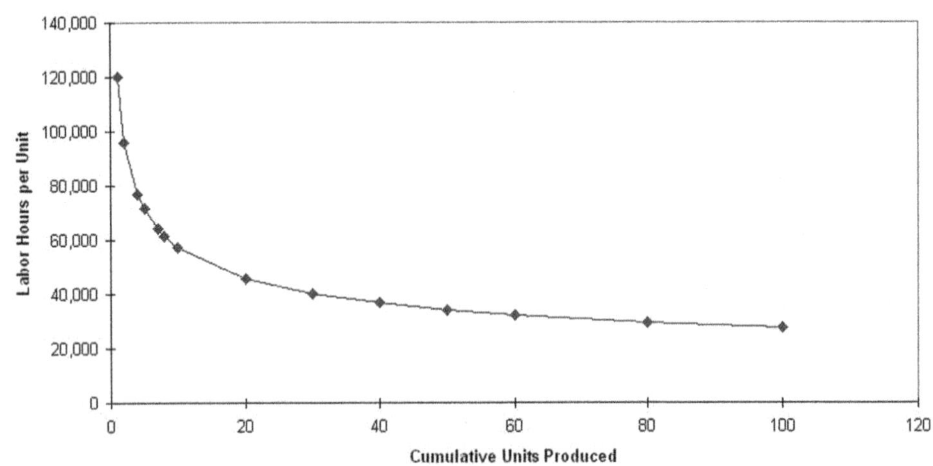

Time for first unit	120,000
Unit number	10
Time for unit 10	57,172
Cumulative average time per unit	75,784

▲ **FIGURE 9**
Learning Curve with 80% Learning Rate Using OM Explorer's *Learning Curves* Solver.

process chart

An organized way of documenting all the activities performed by a person or group of people, at a workstation, with a customer, or on materials.

Process Charts

A **process chart** is an organized way of documenting all the activities performed by a person or group of people at a workstation, with a customer, or working with certain materials. It analyzes a process using a table, and provides information about each step in the process. In contrast to flowcharts, swim lane flowcharts, and service blueprints, it requires the time estimates (see work measurement techniques covered in the last section). Often it is used to drill down to the job level for an individual person, a team, or a focused nested process. It can have many formats. Here, we group the type of activities for a typical process into five categories:

- *Operation.* Changes, creates, or adds something. Drilling a hole or serving a customer are examples of operations.
- *Transportation.* Moves the study's subject from one place to another (sometimes called *materials handling*). The subject can be a person, a material, a tool, or a piece of equipment. A customer walking from one end of a counter to the other, a crane hoisting a steel beam to a location, and a conveyor carrying a partially completed product from one workstation to the next are examples of transportation. It could also be the shipment of a finished product to the customer or a warehouse.

- *Inspection.* Checks or verifies something but does not change it. Getting customer feedback, checking for blemishes on a surface, weighing a product, and taking a temperature reading are examples of inspections.
- *Delay.* Occurs when the subject is held up awaiting further action. Time spent waiting for a server; time spent waiting for materials or equipment; cleanup time; and time that workers, machines, or workstations are idle because they have no work to complete are examples of delays.
- *Storage.* Occurs when something is put away until a later time. Supplies unloaded and placed in a storeroom as inventory, equipment put away after use, and papers put in a file cabinet are examples of storage.

Depending on the situation, other categories can be used. For example, subcontracting for outside services might be a category, temporary storage and permanent storage, or environmental waste might be three separate categories. Choosing the right category for each activity requires taking the perspective of the subject charted. A delay for the equipment could be inspection or transportation for the operator.

To complete a chart for a new process, the analyst must identify each step performed. If the process is an existing one, the analyst can actually observe the steps and categorize each step according to the subject being studied. The analyst then records the distance traveled and the time taken to perform each step. After recording all the activities and steps, the analyst summarizes the steps, times, and distances data. Figure 10 shows a process chart prepared using OM Explorer's *Process Chart* Solver. It is for a patient with a twisted ankle being treated at a hospital. The process begins at the entrance and ends with the patient exiting after picking up the prescription.

After a process is charted, the analyst sometimes estimates the annual cost of the entire process. It becomes a benchmark against which other methods for performing the process can be evaluated. Annual labor cost can be estimated by finding the product of (1) time in hours to perform the process each time, (2) variable costs per hour, and (3) number of times the process is performed each year, or

$$\begin{matrix}\text{Annual}\\ \text{labor cost}\end{matrix} = \begin{pmatrix}\text{Time to perform}\\ \text{the process in hours}\end{pmatrix}\begin{pmatrix}\text{Variable costs}\\ \text{per hour}\end{pmatrix}\begin{pmatrix}\text{Number of times process}\\ \text{is performed per year}\end{pmatrix}$$

MyOMLab

Tutor 2 in MyOMLab provides a new example to practice creating process charts.

Process:	Emergency room admission
Subject:	Ankle injury patient
Beginning:	Enter emergency room
Ending:	Leave hospital

Insert Step

Append Step

Remove Step

Summary

Activity	Number of Steps	Time (min)	Distance (ft)
Operation ●	5	23.00	
Transport ➡	9	11.00	815
Inspect ■	2	8.00	
Delay ◗	3	8.00	
Store ▼	—	—	

Step No.	Time (min)	Distance (ft)	●	➡	■	◗	▼	Step Description
1	0.50	15.0		X				Enter emergency room, approach patient window
2	10.00		X					Sit down and fill out patient history
3	0.75	40.0		X				Nurse escorts patient to ER triage room
4	3.00				X			Nurse inspects injury
5	0.75	40.0		X				Return to waiting room
6	1.00					X		Wait for available bed
7	1.00	60.0		X				Go to ER bed
8	4.00					X		Wait for doctor
9	5.00				X			Doctor inspects injury and questions patient
10	2.00	200.0		X				Nurse takes patient to radiology
11	3.00		X					Technician x-rays patient
12	2.00	200.0		X				Return to bed in ER
13	3.00					X		Wait for doctor to return
14	2.00		X					Doctor provides diagnosis and advice
15	1.00	60.0		X				Return to emergency entrance area
16	4.00		X					Check out
17	2.00	180.0		X				Walk to pharmacy
18	4.00		X					Pick up prescription
19	1.00	20.0		X				Leave the building

◀ **FIGURE 10**
Process Chart for Emergency Room Admission

MyOMLab Animation

For example, if the average time to serve a customer is 4 hours, the variable cost is \$25 per hour, and 40 customers are served per year, then the labor cost is \$4,000 per year (or 4 hrs/customer × \$25/hr × 40 customers/yr).

In the case of the patient in Figure 10, this conversion would not be necessary, with total patient time being sufficient. What is being tracked is the patient's time, not the time and costs of the service providers.

You can design your own process chart spreadsheets to bring out issues that are particularly important for the process you are analyzing, such as categories for customer contact, process divergence, and the like. You can also track performance measures other than time and distance traveled, such as error rates. In addition, you can also create a different version of the process chart spreadsheet that examines processes much as done with flowcharts, except now in the form of a table. The columns that categorize the activity type could be replaced by one or more columns reporting different metrics of interest, rather than trying to fit them into a flowchart. Although it might not look as elegant, it could be just as informative—and easier to create.

The leader of a design team presents several charts that document a process in their office that they are analyzing. He is identifying several areas of substandard performance across a range of different metrics. The next step will be to redesign the process. The flipchart on the right will be quite useful in generating rapid fire ideas from the team on how the process might be improved.

Data Analysis Tools

Metrics and performance information complete the documentation of a process. The specific metrics analysts choose depends on the process being analyzed and on the competitive priorities. Good starting points are the per-unit processing time and cost at each step, and the time elapsed from beginning to end of the process. Capacity utilization, environmental issues, and customer (or job) waiting times reveal where in the process delays are most likely to occur. Customer satisfaction measures, error rates, and scrap rates identify possible quality problems.

Metrics can be displayed in various ways. Sometimes, they can be added directly on the flowchart or process chart. When the number of metrics gets unwieldy, another approach is to create a supporting table for the chart. Its rows are the steps in the flowchart, swim lane flowchart, service blueprint, or process chart. The columns are the current performance, goals, and performance gaps for various metrics. Various tools are available to help you understand the causes of these performance gaps and problems. Here we present six tools: (1) checklists, (2) histograms and bar charts, (3) Pareto charts, (4) scatter diagrams, (5) cause-and-effect diagrams, and (6) graphs. Many of them were developed initially to analyze quality issues, but they apply equally well to process analysis in general.

checklist

A form used to record the frequency of occurrence of certain process failures.

process failure

Any performance shortfall, such as error, delay, environmental waste, rework, and the like.

histogram

A summarization of data measured on a continuous scale, showing the frequency distribution of some process failure (in statistical terms, the central tendency and dispersion of the data).

bar chart

A series of bars representing the frequency of occurrence of data characteristics measured on a yes-or-no basis.

Checklists Data collection through the use of a checklist is often the first step in the analysis of a metric. A **checklist** is a form used to record the frequency of occurrence of certain process failures. A **process failure** is any performance shortfall, such as error, delay, environmental waste, rework, and the like. The characteristics may be measurable on a continuous scale (e.g., weight, customer satisfaction on a 1 to 7 scale, unit cost, scrap loss percentage, time, or length) or on a yes-or-no basis (e.g., customer complaint, posting error, paint discoloration, or inattentive servers).

Histograms and Bar Charts Data from a checklist often can be presented succinctly and clearly with histograms or bar charts. A **histogram** summarizes data measured on a continuous scale, showing the frequency distribution of some process failure (in statistical terms, the central tendency and dispersion of the data). Often the mean of the data is indicated on the histogram. A **bar chart** (see Figure 11) is a series of bars representing the frequency of occurrence of data characteristics measured on a yes-or-no basis. The bar height indicates the number of times a particular process failure was observed.

Pareto Charts When managers discover several process problems that need to be addressed, they have to decide which should be attacked first. Vilfredo Pareto, a nineteenth-century Italian scientist whose statistical work focused on inequalities in data, proposed that most of an "activity" is caused by relatively few of its factors. In a restaurant quality problem, the activity could be customer complaints and the factor could be "discourteous server." For a manufacturer, the activity could be product defects and the factor could be "missing part." Pareto's concept, called the 80–20 rule, is that 80 percent of the activity is caused by 20 percent of the factors. By concentrating on the 20 percent of the factors (the "vital few"), managers can attack 80 percent of the process failure problems. Of course, the exact percentages vary with each situation, but inevitably relatively few factors cause most of the performance shortfalls.

The few vital factors can be identified with a **Pareto chart**, a bar chart on which the factors are plotted along the horizontal axis in decreasing order of frequency (see Figure 12). The chart has two vertical axes, the one on the left showing frequency (as in a histogram) and the one on the right showing the cumulative percentage of frequency. The cumulative frequency curve identifies the few vital factors that warrant immediate managerial attention.

Pareto chart
A bar chart on which factors are plotted along the horizontal axis in decreasing order of frequency.

EXAMPLE 2 Pareto Chart for a Restaurant

The manager of a neighborhood restaurant is concerned about the lower numbers of customers patronizing his eatery. Complaints have been rising, and he would like to find out what issues to address and present the findings in a way his employees can understand.

MyOMLab
Active Model 1 in MyOMLab provides additional insights on this Pareto chart example and its extensions.

MyOMLab
Tutor 3 in MyOMLab provides a new example on creating Pareto charts.

SOLUTION

The manager surveyed his customers over several weeks and collected the following data:

Complaint	Frequency
Discourteous server	12
Slow service	42
Cold dinner	5
Cramped tables	20
Atmosphere	10

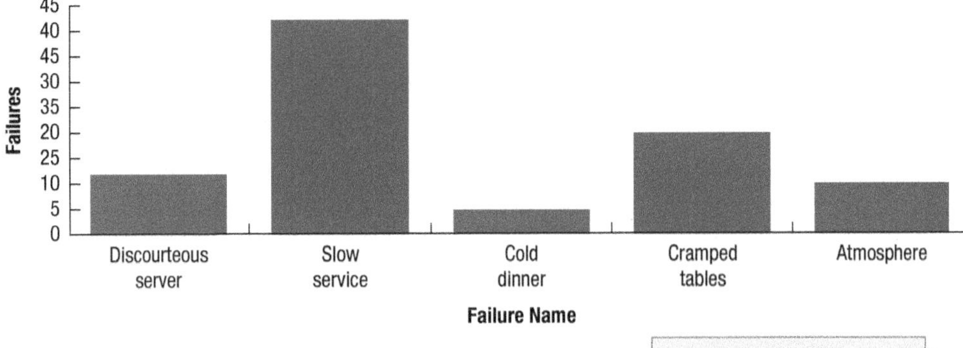

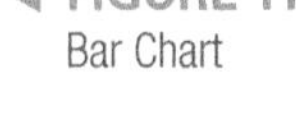
◀ FIGURE 11
Bar Chart

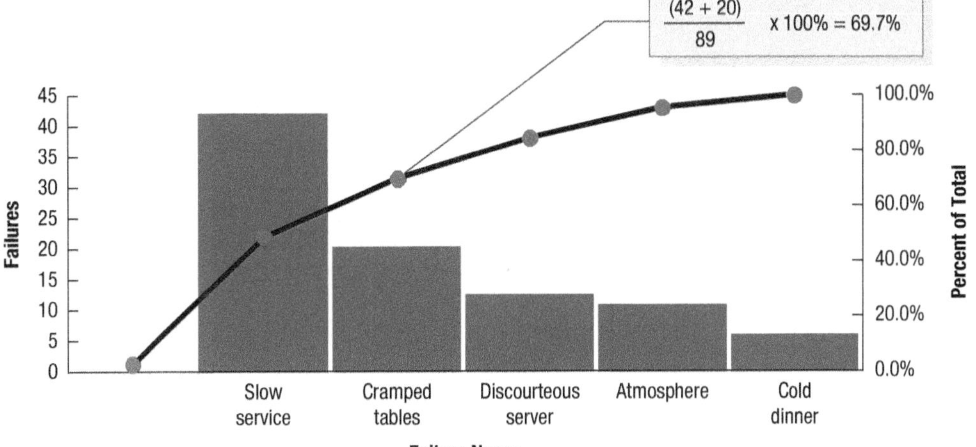

◀ FIGURE 12
Pareto Chart

Figure 11 is a bar chart and Figure 12 is a Pareto chart, both created with OM Explorer's *Bar, Pareto, and Line Charts* Solver. They present the data in a way that shows which complaints are more prevalent (the vital few). You can reformat these charts for any yes-or-no metrics by unprotecting the spreadsheet and then making your revisions. Another approach is to create your own spreadsheets from scratch. More advanced software with point-and-click interfaces include Minitab (**http://www.minitab.com/index.htm**), SAS (**http://www.sas.com/rnd/app/qc.html**), and Microsoft Visio (**http://www.microsoft.com/office/visio**).

DECISION POINT

It was clear to the manager (and all employees) which complaints, if rectified, would cover most of the process failure problems in the restaurant. First, slow service will be addressed by training the existing staff, adding another server, and improving the food preparation process. Removing some decorative furniture from the dining area and spacing the tables better will solve the problem with cramped tables. The Pareto chart shows that these two problems, if rectified, will account for almost 70 percent of the complaints.

scatter diagram

A plot of two variables showing whether they are related.

Scatter Diagrams Sometimes managers suspect that a certain factor is causing a particular process failure. A **scatter diagram**, which is a plot of two variables showing whether they are related, can be used to verify or negate the suspicion. Each point on the scatter diagram represents one data observation. For example, the manager of a castings shop may suspect that casting defects are a function of the diameter of the casting. A scatter diagram could be constructed by plotting the number of defective castings found for each diameter of casting produced. After the diagram is completed, any relationship between diameter and number of process failures will be clear.

cause-and-effect diagram

A diagram that relates a key performance problem to its potential causes.

Cause-and-Effect Diagrams An important aspect of process analysis is linking each metric to the inputs, methods, and process steps that build a particular attribute into the service or product. One way to identify a design problem is to develop a **cause-and-effect diagram** that relates a key performance problem to its potential causes. First developed by Kaoru Ishikawa, the diagram helps management trace disconnects directly to the operations involved. Processes that have no bearing on a particular problem are not shown on the diagram.

The cause-and-effect diagram sometimes is called a *fishbone diagram*. The main performance gap is labeled as the fish's "head," the major categories of potential causes as structural "bones," and the likely specific causes as "ribs." When constructing and using a cause-and-effect diagram, an analyst identifies all the major categories of potential causes for the problem. These might be personnel, machines, materials, and processes. For each major category, the analyst lists all the likely causes of the performance gap. Under personnel might be listed "lack of training," "poor communication," and "absenteeism." Creative thinking helps the analyst identify and properly classify all suspected causes. The analyst then systematically investigates the causes listed on the diagram for each major category, updating the chart as new causes become apparent. The process of constructing a cause-and-effect diagram calls management and worker attention to the primary factors affecting process failures. Example 3 demonstrates the use of a cause-and-effect diagram by a firm manufacturing air conditioners.

EXAMPLE 3 Analysis of Inadequate Production of Headers

A process improvement team is working to improve the production output at the Johnson Manufacturing plant's Header Cell that manufactures a key component, headers, used in commercial air conditioners. A header is part of the circulatory system of a commercial air conditioner that moves coolant between various components such as the evaporator coil and the condenser coil. Currently, the header production cell is scheduled separately from the main work in the plant. Often, individual headers are not sequenced to match the product they go into on the final assembly line in a timely fashion, and so the product can sit in queue waiting for a header.

SOLUTION

As a first step, the team conducted extensive on-site observations across the six processing steps within the cell, followed by the transport of the finished header to the air conditioner assembly area for installation into an air conditioner unit. The six processing steps included:

1. Cut copper pipes to the appropriate length.
2. Punch vent and stub holes into the copper log.
3. Weld a steel supply valve onto the top of the copper log.

4. Braze end caps and vent plugs to the copper log.
5. Braze stub tubes into each stub hole in the copper log.
6. Add plastic end caps to protect the newly created header.

To analyze all the possible causes of the problem, the team constructed a cause-and-effect diagram, shown in Figure 13. The main problem, inadequate header production, is the head of the diagram. The team brainstormed all possible causes, and together they identified several major categories: management, manpower, method, measurement, machine, and materials, or the 6 M's. Several suspected causes were identified for each major category.

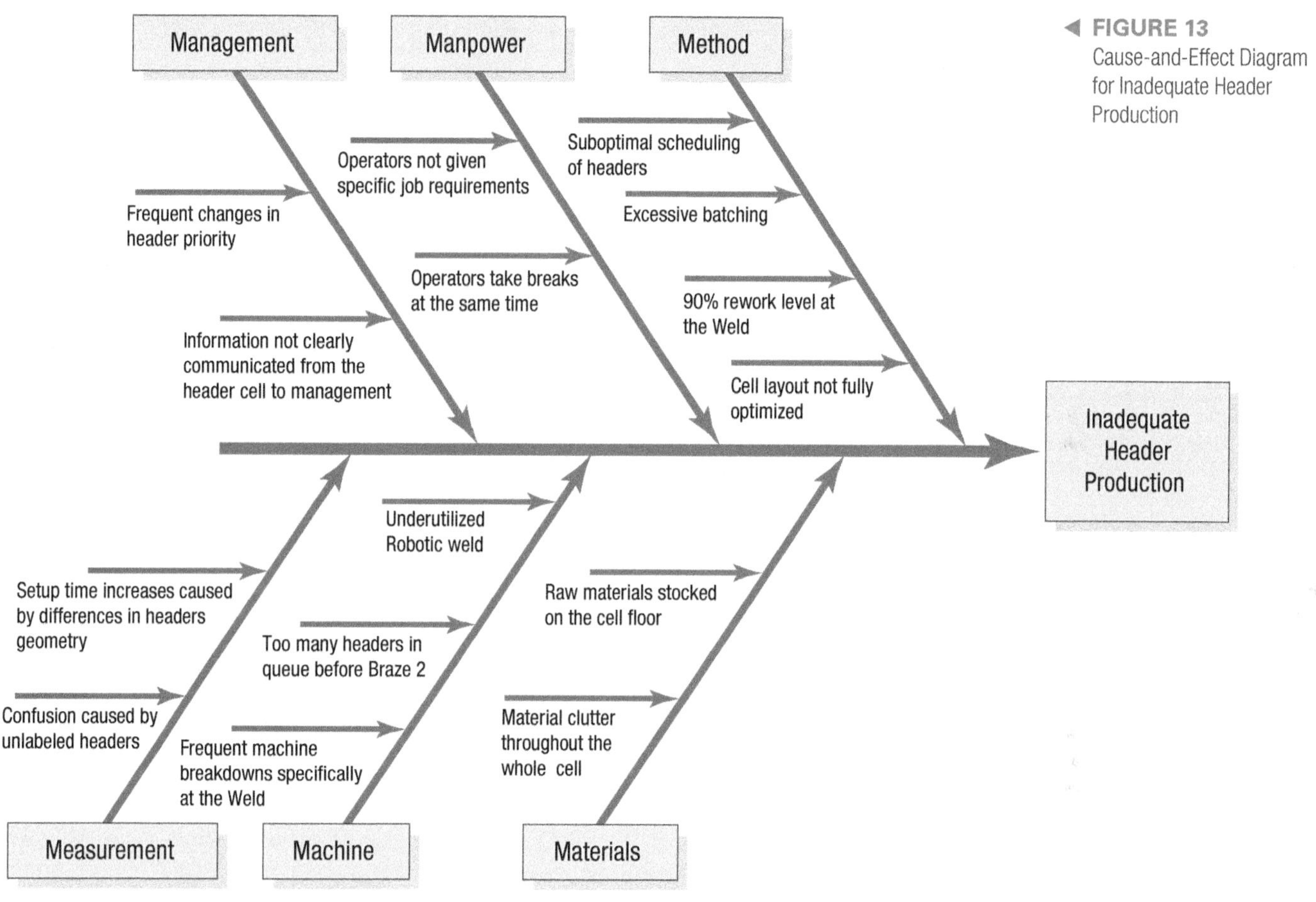

FIGURE 13 Cause-and-Effect Diagram for Inadequate Header Production

DECISION POINT

The improvement team noted several immediate issues that were slowing down production of headers. These issues included operators batching individual jobs (method branch) into groups to save walking time, which was further exasperated by the availability of raw materials stocked on the shop floor (materials branch) and the lack of specific job requirement (management branch). Further, there were many instances of individual tasks not being done correctly, and thus having to be redone; such as the 90 percent rework rate at weld (method branch). The next step in this process improvement was to eliminate the raw material on the floor, improve quality at the weld machine, and move each header individually using a header-specific cart.

Graphs Visualizing data in user-friendly ways can greatly enhance process analysis. **Graphs** represent data in a variety of pictorial formats, such as line charts and pie charts. *Line charts* represent data sequentially with data points connected by line segments to highlight trends in the data. Line charts are used in control charts. Pie charts represent process factors as slices of a pie; the size of each slice is in proportion to the number of occurrences of the factor. Pie charts are useful for showing data from *a group of factors* that can be represented as percentages totaling 100 percent.

graphs
Representations of data in a variety of pictorial forms, such as line charts and pie charts.

Each of the tools for improving quality may be used independently, but their power is greatest when they are used together. In solving a process-related problem, managers often must act as detectives, sifting data to clarify the issues involved and deducing the causes. We call this process *data snooping.* Example 4 demonstrates how the tools for improving quality can be used for data snooping.

EXAMPLE 4 Identifying Causes of Poor Headliner Process Failures

The Wellington Fiber Board Company produces headliners, the fiberglass components that form the inner roof of passenger cars. Management wanted to identify which process failures were most prevalent and to find the cause.

SOLUTION

Figure 14 shows the sequential application of several tools for improving quality.

FIGURE 14 Application of the Tools for Improving Quality

Step 1. Checklist

Headliner failures

Process failure	Tally	Total
A. Tears in fabric	IIII	4
B. Discolored fabric	III	3
C. Broken fiber board	𝍸𝍸𝍸𝍸𝍸𝍸𝍸I	36
D. Ragged edges	𝍸II	7
		Total 50

Step 2. Pareto Chart

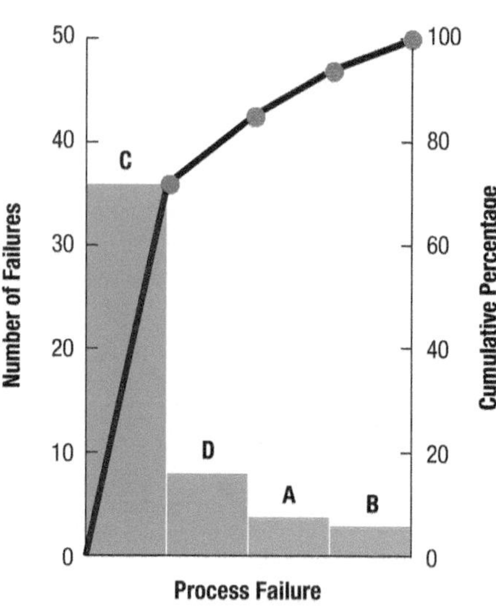

Step 3. Cause-and-Effect Diagram

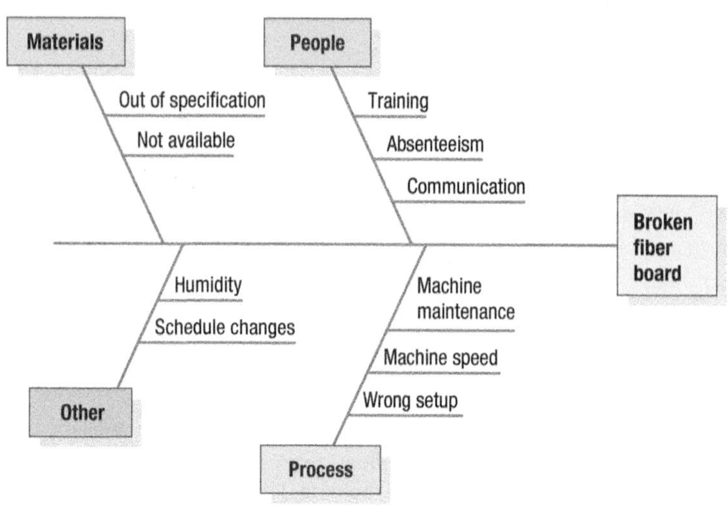

Step 4. Bar Chart

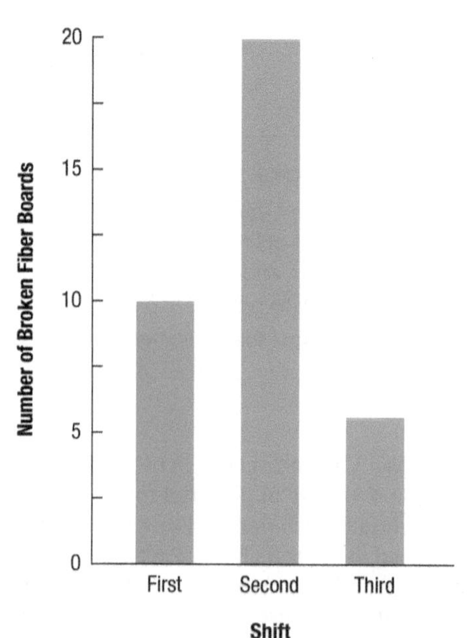

Step 1. A checklist of different types of process failures was constructed from last month's production records.

Step 2. A Pareto chart prepared from the checklist data indicated that broken fiber board accounted for 72 percent of the process failures.

Step 3. A cause-and-effect diagram for broken fiber board identified several potential causes for the problem. The one strongly suspected by the manager was employee training.

Step 4. The manager reorganized the production reports into a bar chart according to shift because the personnel on the three shifts had varied amounts of experience.

DECISION POINT

The bar chart indicated that the second shift, with the least experienced workforce, had most of the process failures. Further investigation revealed that workers were not using proper procedures for stacking the fiber boards after the press operation, which caused cracking and chipping. The manager set up additional training sessions focused on board handling. Although the second shift was not responsible for all the process failures, finding the source of many of the failures enabled the manager to improve the performance of her operations.

A simulation model goes one step further than static data analysis tools, because it can show how the process dynamically changes over time. **Process simulation** is the act of reproducing the behavior of a process, using a model that describes each step. Once the process is modeled, the analyst can make changes in the model to measure the impact on certain metrics, such as response time, waiting lines, resource utilization, and the like.

process simulation

The act of reproducing the behavior of a process, using a model that describes each step.

MyOMLab

Redesigning and Managing Process Improvements

A doctor pinpoints an illness after a thorough examination of the patient, and then the doctor recommends treatments based on the diagnosis; so it is with processes. After a process is documented, metrics data are collected, and disconnects are identified, the process analyst or design team puts together a set of changes that will make the process better. At this step, people directly involved in the process are brought in to get their ideas and inputs.

brainstorming

Letting a group of people, knowledgeable about the process, propose ideas for change by saying whatever comes to mind.

Questioning and Brainstorming

Sometimes, ideas for reengineering or improving a process become apparent after documenting the process and carefully examining the areas of substandard performance, handoffs between departments, and steps where customer contact is high. Example 4 illustrated how such documentation pointed to a better way of handling the fiber boards through better training. In other cases, the better solution is less evident. Ideas can be uncovered (because there is always a better way) by asking six questions about each step in the process, and a final series of questions about the process as a whole:

1. *What* is being done?
2. *When* is it being done?
3. *Who* is doing it?
4. *Where* is it being done?
5. *How* is it being done?
6. *How* well does it do on the various metrics of importance?

Answers to these questions are challenged by asking still another series of questions. *Why* is the process even being done? *Why* is it being done where it is being done? *Why* is it being done when it is being done?

Creativity can also be stimulated by **brainstorming**, letting a group of people knowledgeable about the process propose ideas for change by saying whatever comes to mind. A facilitator records the ideas on a flipchart, so that all can see. Participants are discouraged from evaluating any of the ideas generated during the session. The purpose is

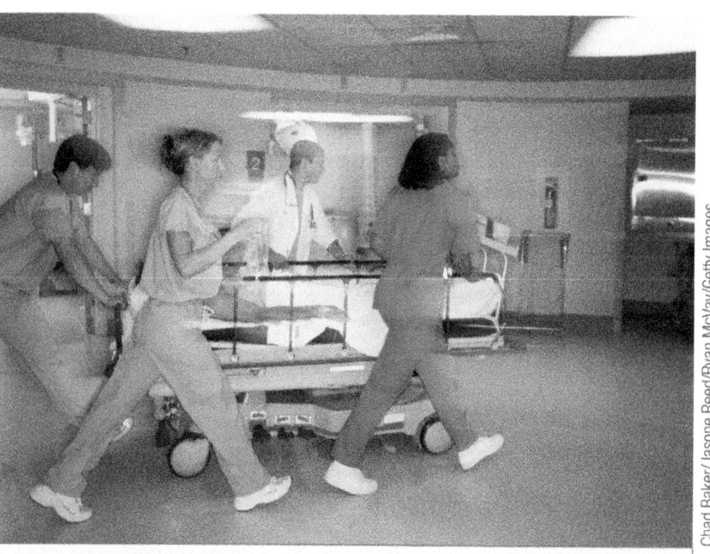

Baptist Memorial Hospital in Memphis, Tennessee, holds "huddle meetings" at least three times a day seeking out process improvements. The meetings bring together the hospital's house supervisor, housekeeping supervisor, and key nurses. Improvements have been dramatic. In 2011, the hospital was ranked in the top 5 percent nationally for emergency medicine.

to encourage creativity and to get as many ideas as possible, no matter how far-fetched the ideas may seem. The participants of a brainstorming session need not be limited to the design team as long as they have seen or heard the process documentation. A growing number of big companies are taking advantage of the Internet and specially designed software to run brainstorming sessions that allow people at far-flung locations to "meet" online and hash out solutions to particular problems. The technology lets employees see, and build on, one another's ideas, so that one person's seed of a notion can grow into a practical plan.

After the brainstorming session is over, the design team moves into the "get real" phase: They evaluate the different ideas. The team identifies the changes that give the best payoffs for process redesign. The redesign could involve issues of capacity, technology, or even location.

The redesigned process is documented once again, this time as the "after" view of the process. Expected payoffs are carefully estimated, along with risks. For changes involving investments, the time value of money must be considered. The impact on people (skills, degree of change, training requirements, and resistance to change) must also be factored into the evaluation of the new design.

MyOMLab

Benchmarking

Benchmarking can be another valuable source for process redesign. **Benchmarking** is a systematic procedure that measures a firm's processes, services, and products against those of industry leaders. Companies use benchmarking to better understand how outstanding companies do things so that they can improve their own processes.

benchmarking

A systematic procedure that measures a firm's processes, services, and products against those of industry leaders.

Benchmarking focuses on setting quantitative goals for improvement. *Competitive* benchmarking is based on comparisons with a direct industry competitor. *Functional* benchmarking compares areas such as administration, customer service, and sales operations with those of outstanding firms in any industry. For instance, Xerox benchmarked its distribution function against L.L. Bean's because L.L. Bean is renowned as a leading retailer in distribution efficiency and customer service. *Internal* benchmarking involves using an organizational unit with superior performance as the benchmark for other units. This form of benchmarking can be advantageous for firms that have several business units or divisions. All forms of benchmarking are best applied in situations where you are looking for a long-term program of continuous improvement.

Typical measures used in benchmarking include cost per unit, service upsets (breakdowns) per customer, processing time per unit, customer retention rates, revenue per unit, return on investment, and customer satisfaction levels.

Collecting benchmarking data can sometimes be a challenge. Internal benchmarking data is surely the most accessible. One way of benchmarking is always available—tracking the performance of a process over time. Functional benchmarking data are often collected by professional associations or consulting firms. Several corporations and government organizations have agreed to share and standardize performance benchmarks. The American Productivity and Quality Center, a nonprofit organization, created thousands of measures, as Figure 15 illustrates. A full range of metrics can be explored at **http://www.apqc.org**. Another source is the Supply Chain Council, which has defined key metrics in its Supply Chain Operations Reference (SCOR) model.

Implementing

Implementing a beautifully redesigned process is only the beginning to continually monitoring and improving processes. Metrics goals must be continually evaluated and reset to fit changing requirements. Avoid the following seven mistakes when managing processes:[2]

1. *Not Connecting with Strategic Issues.* Is particular attention being paid to core processes, competitive priorities, impact of customer contact and volume, and strategic fit during process analysis?
2. *Not Involving the Right People in the Right Way.* Does process analysis closely involve the people performing the process, or those closely connected to it as internal customers and suppliers?
3. *Not Giving the Design Teams and Process Analysts a Clear Charter, and then Holding Them Accountable.* Does management set expectations for change and maintain pressure for results? Does it allow paralysis in process-improvement efforts by requiring excessive analysis?
4. *Not Being Satisfied Unless Fundamental "Reengineering" Changes Are Made.* Is the radical change from process reengineering the expectation? If so, the cumulative effect of many small improvements that could be made incrementally could be lost. Process management efforts should not be limited to downsizing or to reorganization only, even though jobs may be eliminated or the

[2]Geary A. Rummler and Alan P. Brache, *Improving Performance*, 2nd ed. (San Francisco: Jossey-Bass, 1995), pp. 126–133.

FIGURE 15
Illustrative Benchmarking Metrics by Type of Process

Customer Relationship Process

- Total cost of "enter, process, and track orders" per $1,000 revenue
- System costs of process per $100,000 revenue
- Value of sales order line item not fulfilled due to stockouts, as percentage of revenue
- Percentage of finished goods sales value that is returned
- Average time from sales order receipt until manufacturing or logistics is notified
- Average time in direct contact with customer per sales order line item
- Energy consumed in transporting product
- Total distance traveled for products
- Green house gas emissions

Order Fulfillment Process

- Value of plant shipments per employee
- Finished goods inventory turnover
- Reject rate as percentage of total orders processed
- Percentage of orders returned by customers due to quality problems
- Standard customer lead time from order entry to shipment
- Percentage of orders shipped on time
- Use of non-renewable energy sources
- Use of toxic ingredients
- Safe and healthy work environment

New Service/Product Development Process

- Percentage of sales due to services/products launched last year
- Cost of "generate new services/products" process per $1,000 revenue
- Ratio of projects entering the process to projects completing the process
- Time to market for existing service/product improvement project
- Time to market for new service/product project
- Time to profitability for existing service/product improvement project

Supplier Relationship Process

- Cost of "select suppliers and develop/maintain contracts" process per $1,000 revenue
- Number of employees per $1,000 of purchases
- Percentage of purchase orders approved electronically
- Average time to place a purchase order
- Total number of active vendors per $1,000 of purchases
- Percentage of value of purchased material that is supplier certified
- Amount of toxic chemicals used in supplies production process
- Energy consumed in transporting raw materials and parts
- Total distance traveled for raw materials and parts
- Green house gas emissions
- Supplier's use of toxic chemicals in production process
- Percentage of child labor used by supplier

Support Process

- Systems cost of finance function per $1,000 revenue
- Percentage of finance staff devoted to internal audit
- Total cost of payroll processes per $1,000 revenue
- Number of accepted jobs as percentage of job offers
- Total cost of "source, recruit, and select" process per $1,000 revenue
- Average employee turnover rate

structure changed. It should not be limited to big technological innovation projects, even though technological change occurs often.

5. *Not Considering the Impact on People.* Are the changes aligned with the attitudes and skills of the people who must implement the redesigned process? It is crucial to understand and deal with the *people side* of process changes.
6. *Not Giving Attention to Implementation.* Are processes redesigned but never implemented? A great job of flowcharting and benchmarking is of only academic interest if the proposed changes are not implemented. Sound project management practices are required.
7. *Not Creating an Infrastructure for Continuous Process Improvement.* Is a measurement system in place to monitor key metrics over time? Is anyone checking to see whether anticipated benefits of a redesigned process are actually being realized?

Failure to manage processes is failure to manage the business. Managers must make sure that their organization spots new performance gaps in the continual search for process improvements. Process redesign efforts need to be part of periodic reviews and even annual plans.

LEARNING GOALS IN REVIEW

Learning Goal	Guidelines for Review	MyOMLab Resources
1 Understand the process structure in services and how to position a service process on the customer-contact matrix	The section "Process Structure in Services" shows at the process level the key contextual variables associated with service processes and how they relate to each other. There is a key figure in this section: Figure 2 brings together three key elements: (1) the degree of customer contact, (2) customization, and (3) process characteristics. It shows how the degree of customer contact and customization are linked with process divergence and line flows.	
2 Understand the process structure in manufacturing and how to position a manufacturing process on the product-process matrix.	See the section "Process Structure in Manufacturing" which focuses on the manufacturing processes. Figure 3 brings together three key elements: (1) volume, (2) product customization, and (3) process characteristics. The key drivers are customization and volume, which are linked with line flows and the extent of repetitive work. See the video "Manufacturing Process Structure Choices" to understand how SOME BURROS Mexican Restaurant, WT Graphix Custom Embroidery and Silk Screening, and Crayola make trade-offs between customization and volume in designing their processes.	**Video:** Manufacturing Process Structure Choices
3 Explain the major process strategy decisions and their implications for operations.	"Process Strategy Decisions" explains three major process strategy decisions shown in Figure 1. Apart from process structure, these include customer involvement, resource flexibility, and capital intensity. Note that customer involvement has advantages and disadvantages, resource flexibility applies to both workforce and equipment, and economies of scope in certain situations can break the inverse relationship between resource flexibility and capital intensity.	**OM Explorer Tutor:** Break-Even for Equipment Selection **POM for Windows:** Break-Even Analysis
4 Discuss how process decisions should strategically fit together.	See "Strategic Fit" for a detailed discussion of how managers should understand how the four major process decisions tie together in service and manufacturing firms, so as to spot ways of improving poorly designed processes.	
5 Compare and contrast the two commonly used strategies for change, and understand a systematic way to analyze and improve processes.	The section "Strategies for Change" explains two different but complementary philosophies for process design and change: (1) process reengineering and (2) process improvement. The Six Sigma DMAIC model for process improvement then shows a systematic way in which processes can be defined, measured, analyzed, improved, and controlled.	
6 Discuss how to document and evaluate processes.	The section "Documenting and Evaluating the Process" discusses three major techniques for effectively documenting and evaluating processes including (1) flowcharts, (2) work measurement techniques, and (3) process charts. Review the Solved Problems for examples of flowchart, process chart, and Pareto chart construction. The time study method, elemental standard data method, predetermined data method, work sampling method, and learning curve analysis are briefly described in the "Work Measurement Techniques" section. Pareto charts and cause-and-effect diagrams help you to understand the causes of performance gaps.	**Video:** Process Analysis at Starwood **Cases:** Custom Molds, Inc.; José's Authentic Mexican Restaurant **OM Explorer Solvers:** Learning Curve Analysis; Measuring Output Rates; Process Charts; Pareto Charts **OM Explorer Tutors:** Process Charts; Pareto Charts **POM for Windows:** Learning Curve Analysis; Measuring Output Rates **Supplement I:** Learning Curve Analysis
7 Identify the commonly used approaches for effectively redesigning and managing processes.	The section "Redesigning and Managing Process Improvements" discusses how the process analyst puts together a set of changes that will make the process better. Then seven mistakes to avoid when managing processes are discussed at the end. There must be a continual search for process improvements.	

Key Terms

assemble-to-order strategy
automation
back office
bar chart
batch process
benchmarking
Black Belt
brainstorming
capital intensity
cause-and-effect diagram
checklist
continuous-flow process
customer contact
customer involvement
design-to-order strategy
economies of scope
elemental standard data
fixed automation
flexible (or programmable) automation
flexible flow
flexible workforce
flowchart
focused factories
front office
graphs
Green Belt
histogram
hybrid office
industrial robot
job process
layout
learning curve
line flow
line process
make-to-order strategy
make-to-stock strategy
mass customization
mass production
Master Black Belt
metrics
Pareto chart
plants within plants (PWPs)
postponement
predetermined data method
process analysis
process chart
process choice
process divergence
process failure
process improvement
process simulation
process strategy
process structure
reengineering
resource flexibility
scatter diagram
service blueprint
swim lane flowchart
time study
work sampling

Solved Problem 1

MyOMLab Video

Create a flowchart for the following telephone-ordering process at a retail chain that specializes in selling books and music CDs. It provides an ordering system via the telephone to its time-sensitive customers besides its regular store sales.

First, the automated system greets customers and identifies whether they have a tone or pulse phone. Customers choose 1 if they have a tone phone; otherwise, they wait for the first available service representative to process their request. If customers have a tone phone, they complete their request by choosing options on the phone. First, the system checks to see whether customers have an existing account. Customers choose 1 if they have an existing account or choose 2 if they want to open a new account. Customers wait for the service representative to open a new account if they choose 2.

Next, customers choose between the options of making an order, canceling an order, or talking to a customer representative for questions and/or complaints. If customers choose to make an order, then they specify the order type as a book or a music CD, and a specialized customer representative for books or music CDs picks up the phone to get the order details. If customers choose to cancel an order, then they wait for the automated response. By entering the order code via phone, customers can cancel the order. The automated system says the name of the ordered item and asks for the confirmation of the customer. If the customer validates the cancellation of the order, then the system cancels the order; otherwise, the system asks the customer to input the order code again. After responding to the request, the system asks whether the customer has additional requests; if not, the process terminates.

SOLUTION

Figure 16 shows the flowchart.

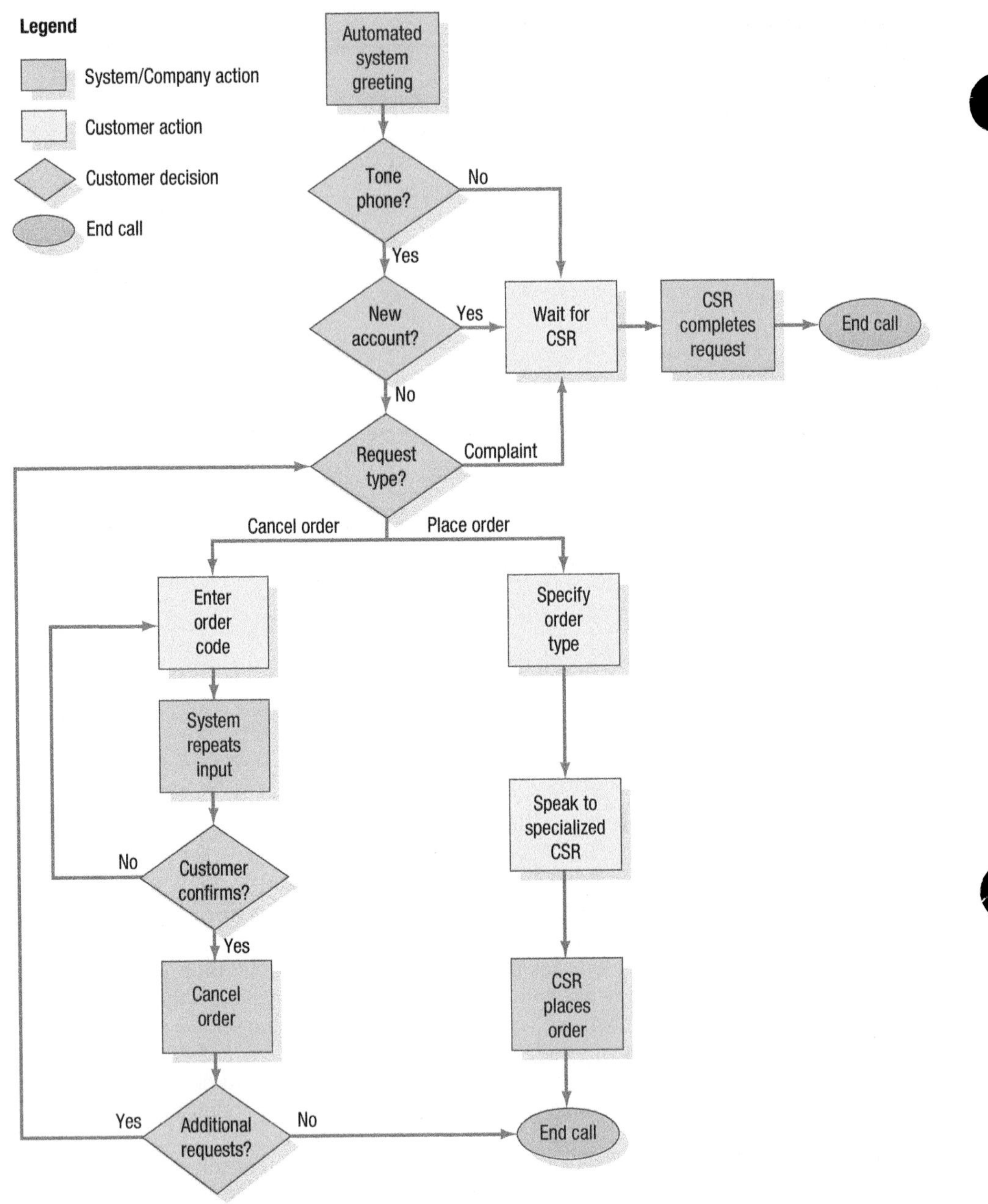

FIGURE 16 ▶ Flowchart of Telephone Ordering Process

Solved Problem 2

An automobile service is having difficulty providing oil changes in the 29 minutes or less mentioned in its advertising. You are to analyze the process of changing automobile engine oil. The subject of the study is the service mechanic. The process begins when the mechanic directs the customer's arrival and ends when the customer pays for the services.

SOLUTION

Figure 17 shows the completed process chart. The process is broken into 21 steps. A summary of the times and distances traveled is shown in the upper right-hand corner of the process chart.

The times add up to 28 minutes, which does not allow much room for error if the 29-minute guarantee is to be met and the mechanic travels a total of 420 feet.

Process:	Changing engine oil
Subject:	Mechanic
Beginning:	Direct customer arrival
Ending:	Total charges, receive payment

Insert Step

Append Step

Remove Step

Summary				
Activity		Number of Steps	Time (min)	Distance (ft)
Operation	●	7	16.50	
Transport	➡	8	5.50	420
Inspect	■	4	5.00	
Delay	◗	1	0.70	
Store	▼	1	0.30	

Step No.	Time (min)	Distance (ft)	●	➡	■	◗	▼	Step Description
1	0.80	50.0		X				Direct customer into service bay
2	1.80		X					Record name and desired service
3	2.30				X			Open hood, verify engine type, inspect hoses, check fluids
4	0.80	30.0		X				Walk to customer in waiting area
5	0.60		X					Recommend additional services
6	0.70					X		Wait for customer decision
7	0.90	70.0		X				Walk to storeroom
8	1.90		X					Look up filter number(s), find filter(s)
9	0.40				X			Check filter number(s)
10	0.60	50.0		X				Carry filter(s) to service pit
11	4.20		X					Perform under-car services
12	0.70	40.0		X				Climb from pit, walk to automobile
13	2.70		X					Fill engine with oil, start engine
14	1.30				X			Inspect for leaks
15	0.50	40.0		X				Walk to pit
16	1.00				X			Inspect for leaks
17	3.00		X					Clean and organize work area
18	0.70	80.0		X				Return to auto, drive from bay
19	0.30						X	Park the car
20	0.50	60.0		X				Walk to customer waiting area
21	2.30		X					Total charges, receive payment

◀ **FIGURE 17**
Process Chart for Changing Engine Oil

Solved Problem 3

What improvement can you make in the process shown in Figure 17?

SOLUTION

Your analysis should verify the following three ideas for improvement. You may also be able to come up with others.

a. **Move Step 17 to Step 21.** Customers should not have to wait while the mechanic cleans the work area.

b. **Store Small Inventories of Frequently Used Filters in the Pit.** Steps 7 and 10 involve travel to and from the storeroom. If the filters are moved to the pit, a copy of the reference material must also be placed in the pit. The pit will have to be organized and well lighted.

c. **Use Two Mechanics.** Steps 10, 12, 15, and 17 involve running up and down the steps to the pit. Much of this travel could be eliminated. The service time could be shortened by having one mechanic in the pit working simultaneously with another working under the hood.

Solved Problem 4

Vera Johnson and Merris Williams manufacture vanishing cream. Their packaging process has four steps: (1) mix, (2) fill, (3) cap, and (4) label. They have had the reported process failures analyzed, which shows the following:

Process failure		Frequency
Lumps of unmixed product		7
Over- or underfilled jars		18
Jar lids did not seal		6
Labels rumpled or missing		29
	Total	60

Draw a Pareto chart to identify the vital failures.

SOLUTION

Defective labels account for 48.33 percent of the total number of failures:

$$\frac{29}{60} \times 100\% = 48.33\%$$

Improperly filled jars account for 30 percent of the total number of failures:

$$\frac{18}{60} \times 100\% = 30.00\%$$

The cumulative percent for the two most frequent failures is

$$48.33\% + 30.00\% = 78.33\%$$

Lumps represent $\frac{7}{60} \times 100\% = 11.67\%$ of failures; the cumulative percentage is

$$78.33\% + 11.67\% = 90.00\%$$

Defective seals represent $\frac{6}{60} \times 100\% = 10\%$ of failures; the cumulative percentage is

$$10\% + 90\% = 100.00\%$$

The Pareto chart is shown in Figure 18.

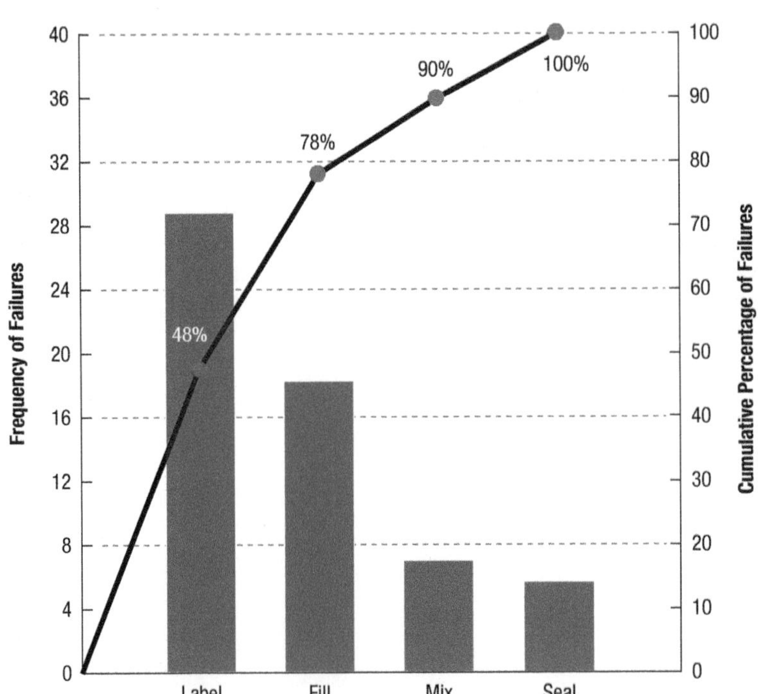

FIGURE 18 ▶ Pareto Chart

Discussion Questions

1. What processes at manufacturing firms are really service processes that involve considerable customer contact? Can customer contact be high, even if the process only has internal customers?
2. Consider this sign seen in a local restaurant: "To-go orders do NOT include complimentary chips and salsa. If you have any questions, see our management, NOT our employees." What impact does this message have on its employees, their service processes, and customer satisfaction? Contrast this approach with the one taken by a five-star restaurant. Are the differences primarily due to different competitive priorities?
3. How do the process strategies of eBay and McDonald's differ, and how do their choices relate to customer-introduced variability?
4. Medical technology can outfit a patient with an artificial heart or cure vision defects with the touch of a laser. However, hospitals still struggle with their back-office processes, such as getting X-ray files from radiology on the fourth floor to the first-floor view boxes in the emergency room without having to send a runner. More than 90 percent of the estimated 30 billion health transactions each year are conducted by telephone, fax, or mail. To what extent, and how, can information technology improve productivity and quality for such processes? Remember that some doctors are not ready to give up their pads and pencils, and many hospitals have strong lines drawn around its departments, such as pharmacy, cardiology, radiology, and pediatrics.
5. Consider the range of processes in the financial services industry. What position on the customer-contact matrix would the process of selling financial services to municipalities occupy? The process of preparing monthly fund balance reports? Explain why they would differ.
6. Rate operators at a call center, who respond to queries from customers who call in about the company's product, on each of the five dimensions of customer contact in Table 1. Use a seven-point scale, where 1 = very low and 7 = very high. For example, the operators newer are physically present with the customer, and so they would get a score of 1 for physical presence. Explain your ratings, and then calculate a combined score for the overall customer contact. Did you use equal weights in calculating the combined score? Why or why not? Where is your process positioned on the customer-contact matrix? Is it properly aligned? Why or why not?
7. Continuous improvement recognizes that many small improvements add up to sizable benefits. Will continuous improvement take a company at the bottom of an industry to the top? Explain.
8. The Hydro-Electric Company (HEC) has three sources of power. A small amount of hydroelectric power is generated by damming wild and scenic rivers; a second source of power comes from burning coal, with emissions that create acid rain and contribute to global warming; the third source of power comes from nuclear fission. HEC's coal-fired plants use obsolete pollution-control technology, and an investment of several hundred million dollars would be required to update it. Environmentalists urge HEC to promote conservation and purchase power from suppliers that use the cleanest fuels and technology.

   However, HEC is already suffering from declining sales, which have resulted in billions of dollars invested in idle equipment. Its large customers are taking advantage of laws that permit them to buy power from low-cost suppliers. HEC must cover the fixed costs of idle capacity by raising rates charged to its remaining customers or face defaulting on bonds (bankruptcy). The increased rates motivate even more customers to seek low-cost suppliers, the start of a death spiral for HEC. To prevent additional rate increases, HEC implements a cost-cutting program and puts its plans to update pollution controls on hold.

   Form sides and discuss the ethical, environmental, and political issues and trade-offs associated with HEC's strategy.
9. Paul O'Neill, former U.S. Treasury Secretary, estimated that arguably half of the $2 trillion a year that Americans spend on health care is needlessly wasted. Brainstorm up to 10 blue-sky ideas to solve the following problems:
   a. A typical retail pharmacy spends 20 percent of its time playing telephone tag with doctors trying to find out what the intent was for a given prescription.
   b. After the person responsible for filling the prescription determines what they think they are supposed to do, errors can be made even in filling the prescription. For example, administering an adult dose (rather than the dose for a premature baby) of Heparin in a preemie ICU is fatal.
   c. Drugs get distributed at a hospital on a batch basis. For example, carts can be filled on Monday, Wednesday, and Friday. A huge volume of drugs can come back on Monday because they are not consumed on the wards between Friday and Monday, patient conditions changed, or the doctor decided on a different intervention. A technician spends the rest of the day restocking the shelves with the returns and 40 percent of the intravenous materials prepared on Friday morning are poured down the drain.
   d. Sometimes the administration of the drug was not done on the agreed schedule, because the nurses were busy doing something else.
   e. For every bed in an acute care hospital system, someone falls during the year. Most falls occur after 11 P.M. and before 6 A.M. Sometimes a bone is fractured, leading to immobilization and then pneumonia.
   f. One in every 14 people who goes to a U.S. hospital gets an infection they did not bring with them.

Problems

The OM Explorer and POM for Windows software is available to all students using this text. Go to **http://www.pearsonhighered.com/krajewski** to download these computer packages. If you purchased MyOMLab, you also have access to Active Models software and significant help in doing the following problems. Check with your instructor on how best to use these resources. In many cases, the instructor wants you to understand how to do the calculations by hand. At the least, the software provides a check on your calculations. When calculations are particularly complex and the goal is interpreting the results in making decisions, the software replaces entirely the manual calculations.

Process Strategy Decisions

Problems 1, 2, and 3 apply break-even analysis to process decisions.

1. Dr. Gulakowicz is an orthodontist. She estimates that adding two new chairs will increase fixed costs by $150,000, including the annual equivalent cost of the capital investment and the salary of one more technician. Each new patient is expected to bring in $3,000 per year in additional revenue, with variable costs estimated at $1,000 per patient. The two new chairs will allow Dr. Gulakowicz to expand her practice by as many as 200 patients annually. How many patients would have to be added for the new process to break even?

2. Two different manufacturing processes are being considered for making a new product. The first process is less capital-intensive, with fixed costs of only $50,000 per year and variable costs of $700 per unit. The second process has fixed costs of $400,000 but has variable costs of only $200 per unit.

a. What is the break-even quantity beyond which the second process becomes more attractive than the first?

b. If the expected annual sales for the product is 800 units, which process would you choose?

3. The operations manager at Sebago Manufacturing is considering three proposals for supplying a critical component for its new line of electric watercraft. Proposal one is to purchase the component, proposal two is make the component in-house using rebuilt equipment, and proposal three is to purchase new, highly automated equipment. The costs associated with each proposal are provided in the table below.

Proposal	Annual cost of capital required	Variable cost of each component
One: purchase	$0.00	$22.00
Two: make with rebuilt equipment	$150,000.00	$14.00
Three: make with new equipment	$450,000.00	$12.50

At what quantity range will each option be preferred?

Documenting and Evaluating the Process

4. Consider the Custom Molds, Inc., case at the end of this chapter. Prepare a flowchart of the mold fabrication process and the parts manufacturing process, showing how they are linked. For a good tutorial on how to create flowcharts, see **http://www.hci.com.au/hcisite5/library/materials/Flowcharting.htm**. Also check out the Flowcharting Tutor in Excel in MyOMLab.

5. Do Problem 4 using a process chart spreadsheet of your own design, one that differs from the *Process Chart* Solver in OM Explorer. It should have one or more columns to record information or metrics that you think are relevant, be they external customer contacts, time delays, completion times, percent rework, costs, capacity, or demand rates. Your entries should show what information you would collect, even though only part of it is available in the case.

6. Founded in 1970, ABC is one of the world's largest insurance companies with locations in 28 countries. Given the following description, flowchart the new policy setup process as it existed in 1970:

Individual customers who wanted to set up a new policy would visit one of ABC's 70 branch offices or make contact with an agent. They would then fill out an application and sometimes attach a check. The branch office then sent the application package through company mail to the XYZ division in London. In addition, a customer might also fill out the application at home and send it directly to any number of ABC locations, which would then transfer it to the London operation. Once received, XYZ separated the various parts of the application, then scanned and digitized it. The electronic image was then retrieved from a server and delivered to an associate's desktop client computer. The associate was responsible for entering the information on the form into the appropriate database. If the information supplied on the application was complete, a confirmation notice was automatically printed and sent to the customer. If the information was incomplete, then another associate, trained to deal with customers on the telephone, would call the customer to obtain the additional information. If the customer noticed something wrong on the confirmation notice received, she or he would either call a toll-free number or send in a letter describing the problem. The Customer Problem Resolution division dealt with problems arising at this point. An updated confirmation notice was sent to the customer. If the information was correct, the application transaction was complete.

7. Do Problem 6 using a process chart spreadsheet of your own design, one that differs from the *Process Chart* Solver in OM Explorer. It should have one or more columns to record information or metrics that you think should be collected to analyze the process (see Problem 5).

8. Prepare a flowchart of the field service division process at DEF, as described here. Start from the point where a call is received and end when a technician finishes the job.

DEF was a multibillion dollar company that manufactured and distributed a wide variety of electronic, photographic, and reprographic equipment used in many engineering and medical system applications. The Field Service Division employed 475 field service technicians, who performed maintenance and warranty repairs on the equipment sold by DEF. Customers would call DEF's National Service Center (NSC), which received about 3,000 calls per day. The NSC staffed its call center with about 40 call-takers. A typical incoming service call was received at the NSC and routed to one of the call-takers, who entered information about the machine, the caller's name, and the type of problem into DEF's mainframe computer. In some cases, the call-taker attempted to help the customer fix the problem. However, call-takers were currently only able to avoid about 10 percent of the incoming emergency maintenance service calls. If the service call could not be avoided, the call-taker usually stated the following script: "Depending upon the availability of our technicians, you should expect to see a technician sometime between now and (now +X)." ("X" was the target response time based on the model number and the zone.) This information was given to the customer because many customers wanted to know when a tech would arrive on site.

Call-takers entered service call information on DEF's computer system, which then sent the information electronically to the regional dispatch center assigned to that customer location. (DEF had four regional dispatch centers with a total of about 20 dispatchers.) Service call information was printed on a small card at the dispatch center. About every hour, cards were ripped off the printer and given to the dispatcher assigned to that customer location. The dispatcher placed each card on a magnetic board under the name of a tech that the dispatcher believed would be the most likely candidate for the service call, given the location of the machine, the current location of the tech, and the tech's training profile. After completing a service call, techs called the dispatcher in the regional dispatch center, cleared the call, and received a new call assigned by the dispatcher. After getting the service call from a dispatcher, a tech called the customer to give an expected time of arrival, drove to the customer site, diagnosed the problem, repaired the machine if parts were available in the van, and then telephoned the dispatcher for the next call. If the tech did not have the right parts for a repair, the tech informed the NSC, and the part was express mailed to the customer; the repair was done the next morning.

9. Big Bob's Burger Barn would like to graphically depict the interaction among its lunch-ordering customers and its three employees. Customers come into the restaurant and eat there rather than drive through and eat in the car. Using the brief process descriptions below, develop a service blueprint.

Fry Employee: receive customer order from counter employee, retrieve uncooked food, drop food into fry vat, wrap cooked food into special packaging, place wrapped items on service counter.

Grill Employee: receive customer order from counter employee, retrieve uncooked food, place food onto grill, build sandwich with requested condiments, deliver sandwich to Counter Employee.

Counter Employee: take order from customer, transmit appropriate orders to Fry and Grill Employee, transact payment, retrieve drinks, wrap sandwich, package order, and deliver order to customer.

10. Your class has volunteered to work for Referendum 13 on the November ballot, which calls for free tuition and books for all college courses except Operations Management. Support for the referendum includes assembling 10,000 yard signs (preprinted water-resistant paper signs to be glued and stapled to a wooden stake) on a fall Saturday. Construct a flowchart and a process chart for yard sign assembly. What inputs in terms of materials, human effort, and equipment are involved? Estimate the amount of volunteers, staples, glue, equipment, lawn and garage space, and pizza required.

11. Suppose you are in charge of a large mailing to the alumni of your college inviting them to contribute to a scholarship fund. The letters and envelopes have been individually addressed (mailing labels were not used). The letters are to be processed (matched with correct envelope, time estimated to be 0.2 minutes each), folded (0.12 minutes each), and stuffed into the correct envelope (0.10 minutes each). The envelopes are to be sealed (0.05 minutes each), and a large commemorative stamp is to be placed in the upper right-hand corner of each envelope (0.10 minutes each).

a. Make a process chart for this activity, assuming that it is a one-person operation.

b. Estimate how long it will take to stuff, seal, and stamp 2,000 envelopes. Assume that the person doing this work is paid $8 per hour. How much will it cost to process 2,000 letters?

c. Consider each of the following process changes. Which changes would reduce the time and cost of the current process?

- Each letter has the same greeting, "Dear Alumnus or Alumna," instead of the person's name.
- Mailing labels are used and have to be put on the envelopes (0.10 minutes each).
- Prestamped envelopes are used.
- Envelopes are stamped by a postage meter which can stamp 200 letters per minute.
- Window envelopes are used.
- A preaddressed envelope is included with each letter for contributions (adds 0.05 minutes to stuffing step).

d. Would any of these changes be likely to reduce the effectiveness of the mailing? If so, which ones? Why?

e. Would the changes that increase time and cost be likely to increase the effectiveness of the mailing? Why or why not?

12. Diagrams of two self-service gasoline stations, both located on corners, are shown in Figure 19(a) and (b). Both have two rows of four pumps and a booth at which an attendant receives payment for the gasoline. At neither station is it necessary for the customer to pay in advance. The exits and entrances are marked on the diagrams. Analyze the flows of cars and people through each station.

a. Which station has the more efficient flows from the standpoint of the customer?

b. Which station is likely to lose more potential customers who cannot gain access to the pumps because another car is headed in the other direction?

c. At which station can a customer pay without getting out of the car?

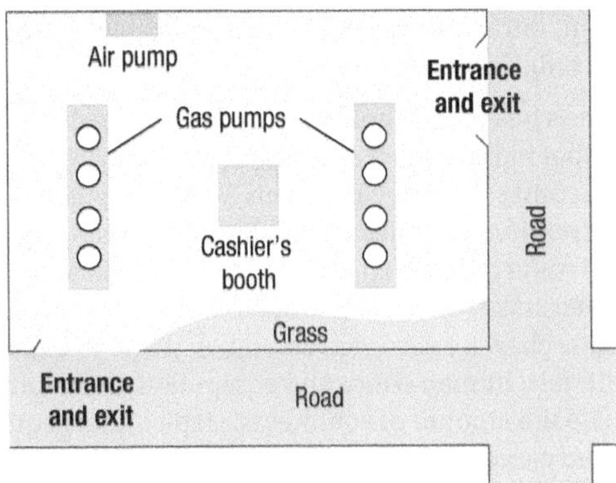

(a)

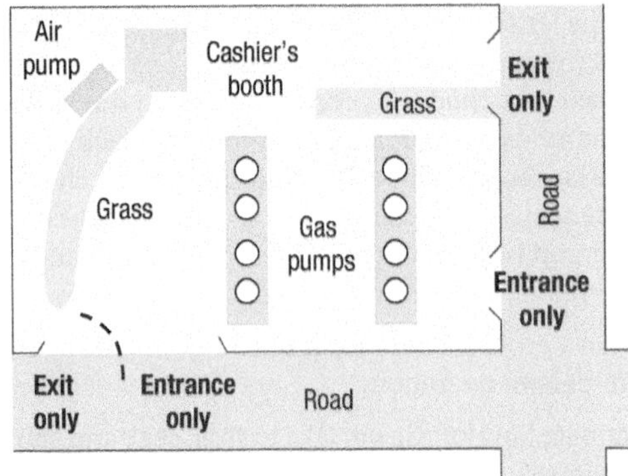

(b)

▲ **FIGURE 19**
Two Self-Service Gasoline Stations

13. The management of the Just Like Home Restaurant has asked you to analyze some of its processes. One of these processes is making a single-scoop ice cream cone. Cones can be ordered by a server (for table service) or by a customer (for takeout).

Figure 20 illustrates the process chart for this operation.

- The ice cream counter server earns $10 per hour (including variable fringe benefits).
- The process is performed 10 times per hour (on average).
- The restaurant is open 363 days a year, 10 hours a day.

a. Complete the Summary (top-right) portion of the chart.

b. What is the total labor cost associated with the process?

c. How can this operation be made more efficient? Make a process chart using OM Explorer's *Process Charts* Solver of the improved process. What are the annual labor savings if this new process is implemented?

14. As a graduate assistant, your duties include grading and keeping records for Operations Management course homework assignments. Five sections for 40 students each are offered each semester. A few graduate students attend sections 3 and 4. Graduate students must complete some extra work to higher standards for each assignment. Every student delivers (or is supposed to deliver) directly to (under) the door of your office one homework assignment every Tuesday. Your job is to correct the homework, record grades, sort the papers by class section, sort by student last name in

FIGURE 20 ▶
Process Chart for Making Ice Cream Cones

Process:	Making one ice cream cone
Subject:	Server at counter
Beginning:	Walk to cone storage area
Ending:	Give it to server or customer

Insert Step

Append Step

Remove Step

Summary			
Activity	Number of Steps	Time (min)	Distance (ft)
Operation ●			
Transport ➡			
Inspect ■			
Delay ◗			
Store ▼			

Step No.	Time (min)	Distance (ft)	●	➡	■	◗	▼	Step Description
1	0.20	5.0		X				Walk to cone storage area
2	0.05		X					Remove empty cone
3	0.10	5.0		X				Walk to counter
4	0.05		X					Place cone in holder
5	0.20	8.0		X				Walk to sink area
6	0.50					X		Ask dishwasher to wash scoop
7	0.15	8.0		X				Walk to counter with clean scoop
8	0.05		X					Pick up empty cone
9	0.10	2.5		X				Walk to flavor ordered
10	0.75		X					Scoop ice cream from container
11	0.75		X					Place ice cream in cone
12	0.25				X			Check for stability
13	0.05	2.5		X				Walk to order placement area
14	0.05		X					Give server or customer the cone

alphabetical order, and return the homework papers to the appropriate instructors (not necessarily in that order). There are some complications. A fair majority of the students sign their names legibly, others identify work with their correct ID number, and a few do neither. Rarely do students identify their section number or graduate status. Prepare a list of process chart steps and place them in an efficient sequence.

15. At the Department of Motor Vehicles (DMV), the process of getting license plates for your car begins when you enter the facility and take a number. You walk 50 feet to the waiting area. During your wait, you count about 30 customers waiting for service. You notice that many customers become discouraged and leave. When a number is called, if a customer stands, the ticket is checked by a uniformed person, and the customer is directed to the available clerk. If no one stands, several minutes are lost while the same number is called repeatedly. Eventually, the next number is called, and more often than not, that customer has left too. The DMV clerk has now been idle for several minutes but does not seem to mind.

After 4 hours, your number is called and checked by the uniformed person. You walk 60 feet to the clerk, and the process of paying city sales taxes is completed in four minutes. The clerk then directs you to the waiting area for paying state personal property tax, 80 feet away. You take a different number and sit down with some different customers who are just renewing licenses. There is a 1-hour, 40-minute wait this time, and after a walk of 25 feet you pay property taxes in a process that takes two minutes. Now that you have paid taxes, you are eligible to pay registration and license fees. That department is 50 feet away, beyond the employees' cafeteria.

The registration and license customers are called in the same order in which personal property taxes were paid. There is only a 10-minute wait and a 3-minute process. You receive your license plates, take a minute to abuse the license clerk, and leave exactly 6 hours after arriving.

Make a process chart using OM Explorer's *Process Charts* Solver to depict this process, and suggest improvements.

16. Refer to the process chart for the automobile oil change in Solved Problem 2. Calculate the annual labor cost if:

- The mechanic earns $40 per hour (including variable fringe benefits).
- The process is performed twice per hour (on average).
- The shop is open 300 days a year, 10 hours a day.

a. What is the total labor cost associated with the process?

b. If steps 7, 10, 12, and 15 were eliminated, estimate the annual labor savings associated with implementing this new process.

17. A time study of an employee assembling peanut valves resulted in the following set of observations. What is the standard time, given a performance rating of 95 percent and an allowance of 20 percent of the total normal time?

Average Time (seconds)	Observations
15	14
20	12
25	15

18. An initial time study was done on a process with the following results (in minutes). Based on the data obtained so far, assuming an allowance of 20 percent of the normal time, what do you estimate for the time per customer served, based on this preliminary sample?

Element	Performance Rating	Obs 1	Obs 2	Obs 3	Obs 4	Obs 5
Element 1	70	4	3	5	4	3
Element 2	110	8	10	9	11	10
Element 3	90	6	8	7	7	6

19. A work sampling study was conducted to determine the proportion of the time a worker is idle. The following information was gathered on a random basis:

Day	Number of Times Worker Idle	Total Number of Observations
Monday	17	44
Tuesday	18	56
Wednesday	14	48
Thursday	16	60

a. Based on these preliminary results, what percent of the time is the worker working?

b. If idle time is judged to be excessive, what additional categories might you add to a follow-up work sampling study to identify the root causes?

20. A contractor is preparing a bid to install swimming pools at a new housing addition. The estimated time to build the first pool is 35 hours. The contractor estimates an 85 percent learning rate. Without using the computer:

a. How long do you estimate the time required to install the second pool?

b. How long do you estimate the time required to install the fourth pool?

21. Return to Problem 20. Using OM Explorer's Learning Curves Solver, how long do you estimate the time required to install the fifth pool? What is your estimate of the total time for all five pools?

22. On RainTite Window's manual assembly line, a new employee can usually assemble their first window unit in 30 minutes. Management assumes a 90 percent learning rate.

a. How long should a new employee take to assemble their second window if management is correct in their assumption? How long should the 16th window take?

b. On RainTite's semi-automated line, a new employee takes 45 minutes to assemble their first window; however, the learning rate is 75 percent. At how many windows produced will the semi-automated line's employee take less time to produce a window than an employee on the manual line?

23. The manager of Perrotti's Pizza collects data concerning customer complaints about pizza delivery. Either the pizza arrives late, or the wrong pizza is delivered.

Problem	Frequency
Topping is stuck to box lid	17
Pizza arrives late	35
Wrong topping or combination	9
Wrong style of crust	6
Wrong size	4
Pizza is partially eaten	3
Pizza never arrives	6

a. Use a Pareto chart to identify the "vital few" delivery problems. Comment on potential root causes of these problems and identify any especially egregious quality failures.

b. The manager of Perrotti's Pizza is attempting to understand the root causes of late pizza delivery and has asked each driver to keep a log of specific difficulties that create late deliveries. After one week, the logs included the following entries:

delivery vehicle broke down, couldn't make it across town to deliver second pizza in time, couldn't deliver four pizzas to four different customers in time, kitchen was late in producing order, got lost, order ticket was lost in production, couldn't read address on ticket and went to wrong house.

Organize these causes into a cause-and-effect diagram.

24. Smith, Schroeder, and Torn (SST) is a short-haul household furniture moving company. SST's labor force, selected from the local community college football team, is temporary and part-time. SST is concerned with recent complaints, as tabulated on the following tally sheet:

Complaint	Tally
Broken glass	卌 卌 |||
Delivered to wrong address	卌 ||||
Furniture rubbed together while on truck	卌 卌 卌 卌
Late delivery	卌
Late arrival for pickup	卌 卌 卌 |||
Missing items	卌 卌 卌 卌 卌 |
Nicks and scratches from rough handling	卌 卌
Soiled upholstery	卌 |||

a. Draw a bar chart and a Pareto chart using OM Explorer to identify the most serious moving problems.

b. The manager of Smith, Schroeder, and Torn is attempting to understand the root causes of complaints. He has compiled the following list of issues that occurred during problem deliveries:

truck broke down, ran out of packing boxes, multiple deliveries in one day caused truck to be late, no furniture pads, employee dropped several items, drive got lost on route to address, ramp into truck was bent, no packing tape, new employee doesn't know how to pack, moving dolly has broken wheel, employee late to work

Organize these causes into a cause-and-effect diagram.

25. Rick DeNeefe, manager of the Golden Valley Bank credit authorization department, recently noticed that a major competitor was advertising that applications for equity loans could be approved within two working days. Because fast credit approval was a competitive priority, DeNeefe wanted to see how well his department was doing relative to the competitor's. Golden Valley stamps each application with the date and time it is received and again when a decision is made. A total of 104 applications were received in March. The time required for each decision, rounded to the nearest hour, is shown in the following table. Golden Valley's employees work 8 hours per day.

Decision Process Time (hours)	Frequency
8	8
11	19
14	28
17	10
20	25
23	4
26	10
Total	104

a. Draw a bar chart for these data.

b. Analyze the data. How is Golden Valley Bank doing with regard to this competitive priority?

26. Last year, the manager of the service department at East Woods Ford instituted a customer opinion program to find out how to improve service. One week after service on a vehicle was performed, an assistant would call the customer to find out whether the work had been done satisfactorily and how service could be improved. After one year of gathering data, the assistant discovered that the complaints could be grouped into the following five categories:

Complaint	Frequency
Unfriendly atmosphere	5
Long wait for service	17
Price too high	20
Incorrect bill	8
Needed to return to correct problem	50
Total	100

a. Use OM Explorer to draw a bar chart and a Pareto chart to identify the significant service problems.

b. Categorize the following causes of complaints into a cause-and-effect diagram: tools, scheduling, defective parts, training, billing system, performance measures, diagnostic equipment, and communications.

27. Oregon Fiber Board makes roof liners for the automotive industry. The manufacturing manager is concerned about product quality. She suspects that one particular failure, tears in the fabric, is related to production-run size. An assistant gathers the following data from production records:

Run	Size	Failures (%)	Run	Size	Failures (%)
1	1,000	3.5	11	6,500	1.5
2	4,100	3.8	12	1,000	5.5
3	2,000	5.5	13	7,000	1.0
4	6,000	1.9	14	3,000	4.5
5	6,800	2.0	15	2,200	4.2
6	3,000	3.2	16	1,800	6.0
7	2,000	3.8	17	5,400	2.0
8	1,200	4.2	18	5,800	2.0
9	5,000	3.8	19	1,000	6.2
10	3,800	3.0	20	1,500	7.0

a. Draw a scatter diagram for these data.

b. Does there appear to be a relationship between run size and percent failures? What implications does this data have for Oregon Fiber Board's business?

28. Grindwell, Inc., a manufacturer of grinding tools, is concerned about the durability of its products, which depends on the permeability of the sinter mixtures used in production. Suspecting that the carbon content might be the source of the problem, the plant manager collected the following data:

Carbon Content (%)	Permeability Index
5.5	16
3.0	31
4.5	21
4.8	19
4.2	16
4.7	23
5.1	20
4.4	11
3.6	20

a. Draw a scatter diagram for these data.

b. Is there a relationship between permeability and carbon content?

c. If low permeability is desirable, what does the scatter diagram suggest with regard to the carbon content?

29. The operations manager for Superfast Airlines at Chicago's O'Hare Airport noticed an increase in the number of delayed flight departures. She brainstormed possible causes with her staff:

- Aircraft late to gate
- Acceptance of late passengers
- Passengers arriving late at gate
- Passenger processing delays at gate
- Late baggage to aircraft
- Other late personnel or unavailable items
- Mechanical failures

Draw a cause-and-effect diagram to organize the possible causes of delayed flight departures into the following major categories: equipment, personnel, material, procedures, and other factors beyond managerial control. Provide a detailed set of causes for each major cause identified by the operations manager, and incorporate them in your cause-and-effect diagram.

30. Plastomer, Inc., specializes in the manufacture of high-grade plastic film used to wrap food products. Film is rejected and scrapped for a variety of reasons (e.g., opacity, high carbon content, incorrect thickness or gauge, scratches, etc.). During the past month, management collected data on the types of rejects and the amount of scrap generated by each type. The following table presents the results:

Type of Failure	Amount of Scrap (lbs.)
Air bubbles	500
Bubble breaks	19,650
Carbon content	150
Unevenness	3,810
Thickness or gauge	27,600
Opacity	450
Scratches	3,840
Trim	500
Wrinkles	10,650

Draw a Pareto chart to identify which type of failure management should attempt to eliminate first.

31. Management of a shampoo bottling company introduced a new 13.5-ounce pack and used an existing machine, with some modifications, to fill it. To measure filling consistency by the modified machine (set to fill 13.85 ounces), an analyst collected the following data (volume in ounces) for a random sample of 100 bottles:

a. Draw a histogram for these data.

b. Bottles with less than 12.85 ounces or more than 14.85 ounces are considered to be out of specification. Based on the sample data, what percentage of the bottles filled by the machine will be out of specification?

Bottle Volume (ounces)									
13.0	13.3	13.6	13.2	14.0	12.9	14.2	12.9	14.5	13.5
14.1	14.0	13.7	13.4	14.4	14.3	14.8	13.9	13.5	14.3
14.2	14.1	14.0	13.9	13.9	14.0	14.5	13.6	13.3	12.9
12.8	13.1	13.6	14.5	14.6	12.9	13.1	14.4	14.0	14.4
13.1	14.1	14.2	12.9	13.3	14.0	14.1	13.1	13.6	13.7
14.0	13.6	13.2	13.4	13.9	14.5	14.0	14.4	13.9	14.6
12.9	14.3	14.0	12.9	14.2	14.8	14.5	13.1	12.7	13.9
13.6	14.4	13.1	14.5	13.5	13.3	14.0	13.6	13.5	14.3
13.2	13.8	13.7	12.8	13.4	13.8	13.3	13.7	14.1	13.7
13.7	13.8	13.4	13.7	14.1	12.8	13.7	13.8	14.1	14.3

32. This problem should be solved as a team exercise:

Shaving is a process that most men perform each morning. Assume that the process begins at the bathroom sink with the shaver walking (say, 5 feet) to the cabinet (where his shaving supplies are stored) to pick up bowl, soap, brush, and razor. He walks back to the sink, runs the water until it gets warm, lathers his face, shaves, and inspects the results. Then he rinses the razor; dries his face; walks over to the cabinet to return the bowl, soap, brush, and razor; and comes back to the sink to clean it up and complete the process.

a. Develop a process chart for shaving. (Assume suitable values for the time required for the various activities involved in the process.)

b. Brainstorm to generate ideas for improving the shaving process. Having fewer than 20 ideas is unacceptable. (Do not try to evaluate the ideas until the group has compiled as complete a list as possible. Otherwise, judgment will block creativity.)

33. At Conner Company, a custom manufacturer of printed circuit boards, the finished boards are subjected to a final inspection prior to shipment to its customers. As Conner's quality assurance manager, you are responsible for making a presentation to management on quality problems at the beginning of each month. Your assistant has analyzed the reject memos for all the circuit boards that were rejected during the past month. He has given you a summary statement listing the reference number of the circuit board and the reason for rejection from one of the following categories:

A = Poor electrolyte coverage

B = Improper lamination

C = Low copper plating

D = Plating separation

E = Improper etching

For 50 circuit boards that had been rejected last month, the summary statement showed the following:

C B C C D E C C B A D A C C C B C A C D C A C C B
A C A C B C C A C A A C C D A C C C E C C A B A C

a. Prepare a tally sheet (or checklist) of the different reasons for rejection.

b. Develop a Pareto chart to identify the more significant types of rejection.

c. Examine the causes of the most significant type of defect, using a cause-and-effect diagram.

Active Model Exercise

This Active Model appears in MyOMLab. Continuing on with Example 2, it allows you to evaluate the structure of a Pareto chart.

QUESTIONS

1. What percentage of overall complaints does discourteous service account for?
2. What percentage of overall complaints do the three most common complaints account for?
3. How does it affect the chart if we eliminate discourteous service?

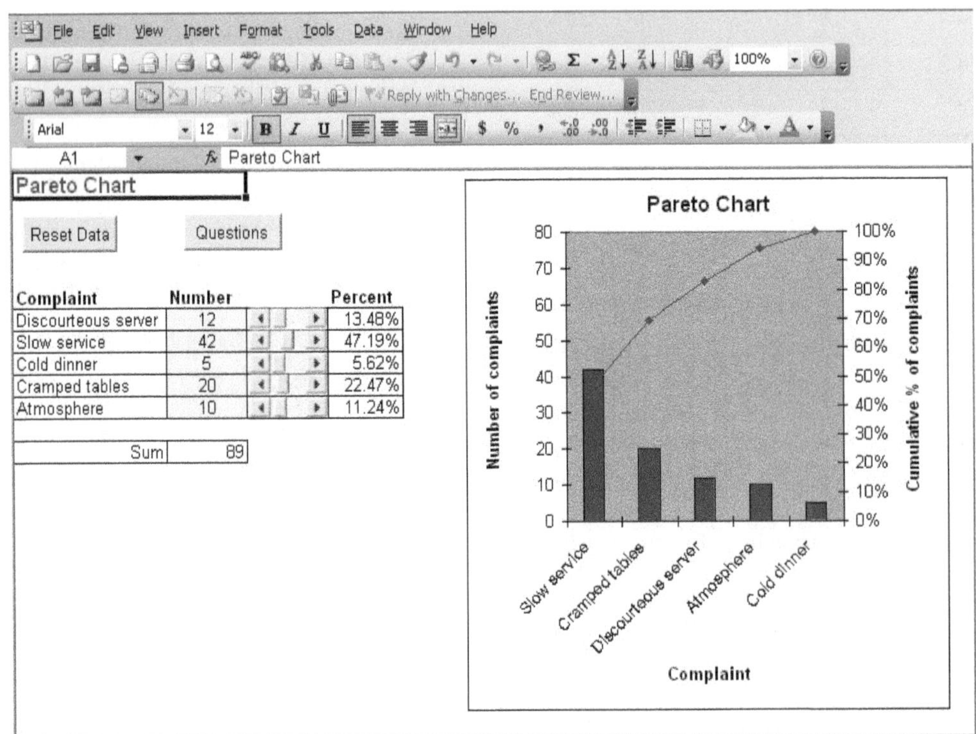

VIDEO CASE Manufacturing Process Structure Choices

The features and layout of The Phoenician property of Starwood Hotels and Resorts at Scottsdale, Arizona, are shown in the following figure. Starwood Hotels and Resorts is no stranger to process improvement. In fact, the president's letter in a recent annual report stated that through ". . .benchmarking, Six Sigma, and recognition of excellence, [Starwood is] driving results in a virtual cycle of self-improvement at all levels of the Company." Recognizing that improved processes in one department of a single hotel, if rolled out across the organization, could lead to significant improvements, the company recently created a program called Power of Innovation, or POI.

The Power of Innovation program in Starwood seeks to capture best practices that exist throughout hotels across all brands in North America. An internal team with expertise in kitchen preparation and production, laundry, stewarding, front office, and housekeeping works with individual properties to build upon and maximize the existing knowledge of local property management teams. The team usually spends about a week on property entrenched in operations to really see day-to-day activity over an extended period. Of particular interest is scheduling the workforce to meet the demand of each hotel's individual operations while streamlining operations processes.

At the Westin Galleria-Oaks in Houston, Texas, for example, the POI team helped management achieve a 6 percent productivity improvement in the kitchen preparation and production job, with a reduction of 2,404 hours used and $23,320 in annual payroll savings alone. At the same time, other POI projects at the hotel generated an additional $14,400 in annual payroll savings.

The Phoenician in Scottsdale also had a visit from the POI team. One area the team focused on was stewarding. The typical stewarding process includes the following duties: dishwashing, kitchen trash removal, polishing silver, and assisting with banquet meal food prep lines. Stewards support eight kitchens and two bakeries and work with housekeeping in keeping public areas, such as restrooms and pool cabanas, clean.

A flowchart that diagrams the existing stewarding process that the team documented is shown in the figure. In any given day, a particular steward may provide support to more than one kitchen and be called upon to do a variety of tasks.

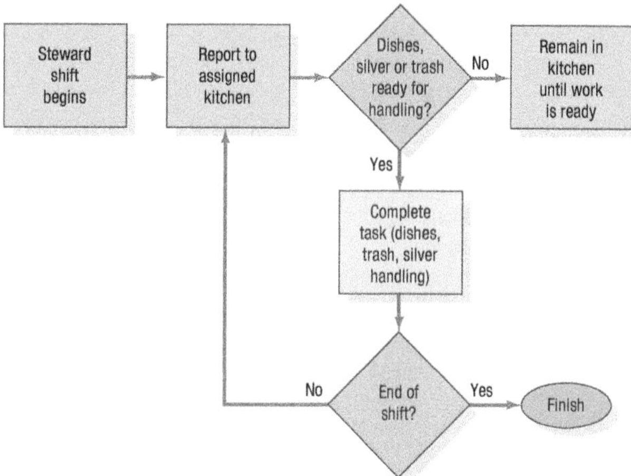

Before the POI team arrived, stewards were dedicated to a particular kitchen or area during their shift. Each kitchen required stewarding coverage as outlined by the executive chef, so more than one steward may be assigned to an area. A certain amount of stewarding work could be forecast by the food and beverage manager, based on scheduled banquets, afternoon teas, conference buffets, and restaurant reservations. Considerable uncertainty also arose from traffic generated by leisure travelers and local clientele, meaning that stewards assigned to designated areas periodically did not have a steady flow of work.

On a weekly basis, activity levels for the dedicated stewarding staff were determined, based on executive chef input. Other factors considered in the weekly planning included prior year activity, special events and holidays, and

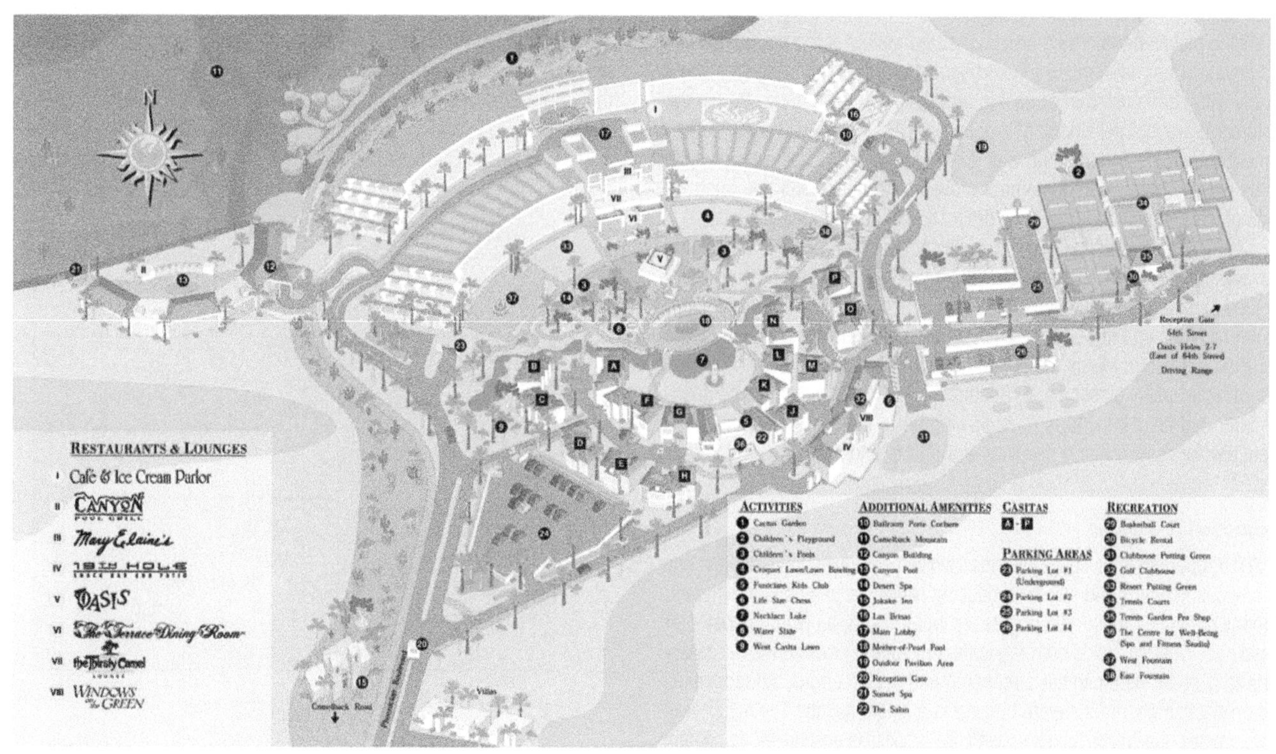

number of children. With this information, the executive steward created a summary of all meals, called covers, by location, date, and time of day. Then an Excel spreadsheet template was used to create the schedule for deployment of stewarding staff throughout the resort's kitchens and restaurants.

In performing its analysis, the POI team examined staff availability, banquet events, restaurants, occupied room counts, and other drivers of business to areas supported by stewards. Time studies were done to determine how far stewards were traveling throughout the property, and how long it took to perform each stewarding task. Some restaurants and kitchens did not require full-time coverage by a steward, so the steward would be assigned multiple kitchens to fill a work shift. In the case of coverage between the 19th Hole restaurant on one side of the resort and the Canyon Building on the other side, that steward would walk one-half mile, one way, to take care of duties in both locations because they lacked enough work for a dedicated steward in each location.

Often, stewards had downtime as they waited for banquet dishes to be cleared, or kitchen pots and utensils to be brought in for cleaning. Some restaurants had china with special cleaning requirements, meaning those dishes had to be handwashed instead of being placed in an automated sanitizing dishwasher. This situation required a dedicated steward to perform that task.

Time studies revealed how long it took stewards to move from one kitchen to the next. The studies also helped the POI team understand how long it took to wash dishes in the five-star restaurant versus the casual poolside dining area's kitchen. Additionally, the studies uncovered building design and landscaping limitations that prevented staff from moving between kitchens quickly. In some cases, a maze of corridors added miles to the distances covered each day, and thick privacy hedges barred entry to sidewalk shortcuts.

QUESTIONS

1. How can the management specifically improve the stewarding process at The Phoenician? Using the information provided, create a flowchart illustrating the new process.
2. What are the benefits that the POI program can bring to Starwood? Can these benefits be extended to other processes and properties within the Starwood system?
3. Of the seven mistakes organizations can make when managing processes (see last section of this chapter), which ones might Starwood be most at risk of making? Why?

CASE Custom Molds, Inc.

Custom Molds, Inc., manufactures custom-designed molds for plastic parts and produces custom-made plastic connectors for the electronics industry. Located in Tucson, Arizona, Custom Molds was founded by the father-and-son team of Tom and Mason Miller in 1997. Tom Miller, a mechanical engineer, had more than 20 years of experience in the connector industry with AMP, Inc., a large multinational producer of electronic connectors. Mason Miller graduated from the Arizona State University in 1996 with joint degrees in chemistry and chemical engineering.

The company was originally formed to provide manufacturers of electronic connectors with a source of high-quality, custom-designed molds for producing plastic parts. The market consisted mainly of the product design and development divisions of those manufacturers. Custom Molds worked closely with each customer to design and develop molds to be used in the customer's product development processes. Thus, virtually every mold had to meet exacting standards and was somewhat unique. Orders for multiple molds would arrive when customers moved from the design and pilot-run stage of development to large-scale production of newly designed parts.

As the years went by, Custom Molds's reputation grew as a designer and fabricator of precision molds. Building on this reputation, the Millers decided to expand into the limited manufacture of plastic parts. Ingredient-mixing facilities and injection-molding equipment were added, and by the mid-2000s, Custom Molds developed its reputation to include being a supplier of high-quality plastic parts. Because of limited capacity, the company concentrated its sales efforts on supplying parts that were used in limited quantities for research and development efforts and in preproduction pilot runs.

Production Processes

By 2010, operations at Custom Molds involved two distinct processes: one for fabricating molds and one for producing plastic parts. Although different, in many instances these two processes were linked, as when a customer would have Custom Molds both fabricate a mold and produce the necessary parts to support the customer's research and design efforts. All fabrication and production operations were housed in a single facility. The layout was characteristic of a typical job shop, with like processes and similar equipment grouped in various places in the plant. Figure 21 shows a layout of the plant floor. Multiple pieces of various types of high-precision machinery, including milling, turning, cutting, and drilling equipment, were located in the mold-fabrication area.

Fabricating molds is a skill-oriented, craftsman-driven process. When an order is received, a design team, comprising a design engineer and one of 13 master machinists, reviews the design specifications. Working closely with the customer, the team establishes the final specifications for the mold and gives them to the master machinist for fabrication. It is always the same machinist who was assigned to the design team. At the same time, the purchasing department is given a copy of the design specifications, from which it orders the appropriate raw materials and special tooling. The time needed to receive the ordered materials is usually three to four weeks. When the materials are received for a particular mold, the plant master scheduler reviews the workload of the assigned master machinist and schedules the mold for fabrication.

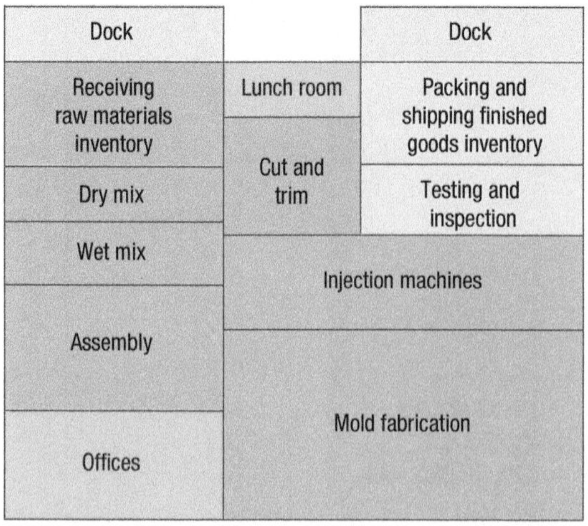

▲ **FIGURE 21**
Plant Layout

Fabricating a mold takes from two to four weeks, depending on the amount of work the machinist already has scheduled. The fabrication process itself takes only three to five days. Upon completion, the mold is sent to the testing and inspection area, where it is used to produce a small number of parts on one of the injection-molding machines. If the parts meet the design specifications established by the design team, the mold is passed on to be cleaned and polished. It is then packed and shipped to the customer. One day is spent inspecting and testing the mold and a second day cleaning, polishing, packing, and shipping it to the customer. If the parts made by the mold do not meet design specifications, the mold is returned to the master machinist for retooling and the process starts over. Currently, Custom Molds has a published lead time of nine weeks for delivery of custom-fabricated molds.

The manufacturing process for plastic parts is somewhat different from that for mold fabrication. An order for parts may be received in conjunction with an order for a mold to be fabricated. In instances where Custom Molds has previously fabricated the mold and maintains it in inventory, an order may be just for parts. If the mold is already available, the order is reviewed by a design engineer, who verifies the part and raw material specifications. If the design engineer has any questions concerning the specifications, the customer is contacted and any revisions to specifications are mutually worked out and agreed upon.

Upon acceptance of the part and raw material specifications, raw material orders are placed and production is scheduled for the order. Chemicals and compounds that support plastic-parts manufacturing are typically ordered and received within one week. Upon receipt, the compounds are first dry-mixed and blended to achieve the correct composition. Then the mixture is wet-mixed to the desired consistency (called *slurry*) for injection into molding machines. When ready, the slurry is transferred to the injection-molding area by an overhead pipeline and deposited in holding tanks adjacent to the injection machines. The entire mixing process takes only one day.

When the slurry is staged and ready, the proper molds are secured—from inventory or from the clean and polish operation if new molds were fabricated for the order—and the parts are manufactured. Although different parts require different temperature and pressure settings, the time to produce a part is relatively constant. Custom Molds has the capacity to produce 5,000 parts per day in the injection-molding department; historically, however, the lead time for handling orders in this department has averaged one week. Upon completion of molding, the parts are taken to the cut and trim operation, where they are disconnected and leftover flashing is removed. After being inspected, the parts may be taken to assembly or transferred to the packing and shipping area for shipment to the customer. If assembly of the final parts is not required, the parts can be on their way to the customer two days after being molded.

Sometimes, the final product requires some assembly. Typically, this entails attaching metal leads to plastic connectors. If assembly is necessary, an additional three days are needed before the order can be shipped. Custom Molds is currently quoting a three-week lead time for parts not requiring fabricated molds.

The Changing Environment

In early 2015, Tom and Mason Miller began to realize that the electronics industry they supplied, along with their own business, was changing. Electronics manufacturers had traditionally manufactured their own component parts to reduce costs and ensure a timely supply of parts. By the mid-1990s, this trend had changed. Manufacturers were developing strategic partnerships with parts suppliers to ensure the timely delivery of high-quality, cost-effective parts. This approach allowed funds to be diverted to other uses that could provide a larger return on investment.

The impact on Custom Molds could be seen in sales figures over the past three years. The sales mix was changing. Although the number of orders per year for mold fabrication remained virtually constant, orders for multiple molds were declining, as shown in the following table:

	NUMBER OF ORDERS		
Order Size	**Molds 2012**	**Molds 2013**	**Molds 2014**
1	80	74	72
2	60	70	75
3	40	51	55
4	5	6	5
5	3	5	4
6	4	8	5
7	2	0	1
8	10	6	4
9	11	8	5
10	15	10	5
Total orders	230	238	231

The reverse was true for plastic parts, for which the number of orders per year had declined, but for which the order sizes were becoming larger, as illustrated in the following table:

	NUMBER OF ORDERS		
Order Size	**Parts 2012**	**Parts 2013**	**Parts 2014**
50	100	93	70
100	70	72	65
150	40	30	35
200	36	34	38
250	25	27	25
500	10	12	14
750	1	3	5
1,000	2	2	8
3,000	1	4	9
5,000	1	3	8
Total orders	286	280	277

During this same period, Custom Molds began having delivery problems. Customers were complaining that parts orders were taking four to five weeks instead of the stated three weeks and that the delays were disrupting production schedules. When asked about the situation, the master scheduler said that determining when a particular order could be promised for delivery was difficult. Bottlenecks were occurring during the production process, but where or when they would occur could not be predicted. The bottlenecks always seemed to be moving from one operation to another.

Tom Miller thought that he had excess labor capacity in the mold-fabrication area. So, to help push through those orders that were behind schedule, he assigned one of the master machinists the job of identifying and expediting those late orders. However, that tactic did not seem to help much. Complaints about late deliveries were still being received. To add to the problems, two orders had been returned recently because of the number of defective parts. The Millers knew that something had to be done. The question was, "What?"

QUESTIONS

1. What are the major issues facing Tom and Mason Miller?
2. What are the competitive priorities for Custom Molds's processes and the changing nature of the industry?
3. What alternatives might the Millers pursue? What key factors should they consider as they evaluate these alternatives?

Source: This case was prepared by Dr. Brooke Saladin, Wake Forest University, as a basis for classroom discussion.

CASE José's Authentic Mexican Restaurant

"Two bean tacos, a chicken burrito grande, and a side order of Spanish rice, please." Ivan Karetski called his table's order into the kitchen as he prepared the beverage orders. Business was brisk. Karetski liked it that way. Lots of customers meant lots of tips and, as a struggling graduate student, the extra income was greatly appreciated. Lately, however, his tips had been declining.

José's is a small, 58-seat restaurant that offers a reasonably broad range of Mexican food prepared and presented in a traditional Mexican style. It is located in New England in a mature business district on the edge of a large metropolitan area. The site is adjacent to a central artery and offers limited free off-street parking. The restaurant's interior decoration promotes the Mexican theme: The walls appear to be made of adobe and are draped with serapes, the furniture is Spanish–Mexican style, and flamenco guitar and mariachi alternate as background music.

Patrons enter the restaurant through a small vestibule that opens directly into the dining area; there is no separate waiting area. Upon arrival, patrons are greeted by a hostess and either seated directly or apprised of the expected wait. Seating at José's is usually immediate except for Friday and Saturday nights when waits of as long as 45 minutes can be encountered. Because space inside for waiting is very limited, patrons must remain outside until their party is called. José's does not take reservations.

After seating patrons, the hostess distributes menus and fills glasses with water. If standards are being met, the waiter assigned to the table greets the patrons within one minute of their being seated. (Being a traditional Mexican restaurant, its entire wait staff is male.) The waiter introduces himself, announces the daily specials, and takes the beverage orders. After delivering the beverages, the waiter takes the meal orders.

The menu consists of 23 main entrees assembled from eight basic stocks (chicken, beef, beans, rice, corn tortillas, flour tortillas, tomatoes, and lettuce) and a variety of other ingredients (fruits, vegetables, sauces, herbs, and spices). Before the dining hours begin, the cook prepares the basic stocks so that they can be quickly combined and finished off to complete the requested meals. The typical amount of time needed to complete a meal once it has been ordered is 12 minutes. A good portion of this time is for final cooking, so several meals may be in preparation at the same time. As can be imagined, one of the skills a good cook needs is to be able to schedule production of the various meals ordered at a table so that they are ready at approximately the same time. Once all the meals and any side dishes have been completed by the cook, the waiter checks to see that all meals are correct and pleasing to the eye, corrects any mistakes, and adds any finishing touches. When everything is in order, he assembles them on a tray and delivers them to the table. From this point on, the waiter keeps an eye on the table to detect when any additional service or assistance is needed.

When the diners at the table appear to be substantially finished with their main meal, the waiter approaches, asks if he can clear away any dishes, and takes any requests for dessert or coffee. When the entire meal has been completed, the waiter presents the bill and shortly thereafter collects payment. José's accepts cash or major credit card but no checks.

Karetski feels that his relationship with the cook is important. As the cook largely controls the quality of the food, Karetski wants to stay on good terms with him. He treats the cook with respect, tries to place the items on his order slip in the sequence of longest preparation time, and makes sure to write clearly so that the orders are easy to read. Although it is not his job, he helps out by fetching food stocks from the refrigerator or the storage area when the cook is busy and by doing some of the food preparation himself. The cook has been irritable lately, complaining of the poor quality of some of the ingredients that have been delivered. Last week, for example, he received lettuce that appeared wilted and chicken that was tough and more bone than meat. During peak times, it can take more than 20 minutes to get good meals delivered to the table.

Karetski had been shown the results of a customer survey that management conducted last Friday and Saturday during the evening mealtime. The following table shows a summary of the responses:

Customer Survey Results		
Were you seated promptly?	Yes: 70	No: 13
Was your waiter satisfactory?	Yes: 73	No: 10
Were you served in a reasonable time?	Yes: 58	No: 25
Was your food enjoyable?	Yes: 72	No: 11
Was your dining experience worth the cost?	Yes: 67	No: 16

As Karetski carried the tray of drinks to the table, he wondered whether the recent falloff in tips was due to anything that he could control.

QUESTIONS

1. How should process outcomes and quality be defined at this restaurant?
2. What are the restaurant's costs of process failures?
3. Use some of the tools for process analysis to assess the situation at José's.

Source: This case was prepared by Larry Meile, Boston College, as a basis for classroom discussion.

Selected References

Andersen, Bjørn. *Business Process Improvement Toolbox,* 2nd ed. Milwaukee, Wisconsin: American Society for Quality, 2007.

Ahire, Sanjay L., and Manoj K. Malhotra. "Scripting a Holistic Rx for Process Improvement at Palmetto Health Imaging Centers." *Journal of Global Business and Organizational Excellence*, vol. 30, no. 2 (January/February 2011), pp. 23–35.

Baghai, Ramin, Edward H. Levine, and Saumya S. Sutaria. "Service-Line Strategies for U.S. Hospitals." *The McKinsey Quarterly* (July 2008), pp. 1–9.

Bhuiyan, Nadjia, Amit Baghel, and Jim Wilson. "A Sustainable Continuous Improvement Methodology at an Aerospace Company," *International Journal of Productivity and Performance Management,* vol. 55, no. 8 (2006), pp. 671–687.

Booth, Alan. "The Management of Technical Change: Automation in the UK and USA since 1950." *The Economic History Review*, vol. 62, no. 2 (May 2009), pp. 493–494.

Brink, Harold, Senthil Muthiah, and Rajan Naik. "A Better Way to Automate Service Operations." *McKinsey on Business Technology*, vol. 20 (Summer, 2010), pp. 1–10.

Carey, Susan. "Case of the Vanishing Airport Lines." *Wall Street Journal*, vol. 250, no. 33 (August 9, 2007), pp. B1-B4.

Chase, Richard B., and Uday M. Apte. "A History of Research in Service Operations: What's the Big Idea?" *Journal of Operations Management,* vol. 25 (2007), pp. 375–386.

Davenport, Thomas H. "The Coming Commoditization of Processes." *Harvard Business Review*, (June 2005), pp. 101–108.

Edmondson, Amy C. "The Competitive Imperative of Learning." *Harvard Business Review*, vol. 86 (July/August, 2008), pp. 1–13.

Fisher, Anne. "Get Employees to Brainstorm Online." *Fortune*, vol. 150, no. 11 (November 2004), p. 72.

Fisher, Marshall L. "Bob Hayes: Forty Years of Leading Operations Management into Uncharted Waters." *Production and Operations Management,* vol. 16, no. 2, (March/April 2007), pp. 159–168.

Fleming, John H., Curt Coffman, and James K. Harter. "Manage Your Human Sigma." *Harvard Business Review* (July/August 2005), pp. 101–108.

Greasley, A. "Using Process Mapping and Business Process Simulation to Support a Process-Based Approach to Change in a Public Sector Organisation." *Technovation*, vol. 26 (2006), pp. 95–103.

Grosskopf, Alexander, Gero Decker, and Mathias Weske. *The Process: Business Process Modelling Using BPMN.* Tampa, Florida: Meghan-Kiffer Press, 2009.

Grover, Varun, and Manoj K. Malhotra. "Business Process Reengineering: A Tutorial on the Concept, Evolution, Method, Technology, and Application." *Journal of Operations Management*, vol. 15, no. 3 (1997), pp. 194–213.

Hall, J. M., and M. E. Johnson. "When Should a Process Be Art, Not Science?" *Harvard Business Review*, vol. 87, no. 3 (2009), pp. 58–66.

Hammer, Michael. "Deep Change: How Operational Innovation Can Transform Your Company." *Harvard Business Review*, vol. 82, no. 4 (April 2004), pp. 85–93.

Hammer, Michael. "The Process Audit." *Harvard Business Review*, vol. 82, no. 4 (April 2007), pp. 111–123.

Hammer, Michael. "What Is Business Process Management?" *Handbook on Business Process Management,* vol. 1 (2010), pp. 3–16.

Hartvigsen, David. *SimQuick: Process Simulation with Excel,* 2nd ed. Upper Saddle River, NJ: Prentice Hall, 2004.

Hayes, Robert. *Operations, Strategy, and Technology: Pursuing the Competitive Edge,* Hoboken, NJ: Wiley, 2005.

Hill, Terry. *Manufacturing Strategy: Text and Cases,* 3rd ed. Homewood, IL: Irwin/McGraw-Hill, 2000.

Jack, Eric, and John Collis. "Strengthen and Tone: A Flexible Approach to Operations Can Build Some Serious Muscle." *APICS Magazine* (June 2006), pp. 35–38.

Jain, Rashmi, Angappa Gunasekaran, and Anithashree Chandrasekaran. "Evolving Role of Process Reengineering: A Perspective of Employers." *Industrial and Commercial Training*, vol. 41, no. 7 (2009), pp. 382–390.

Jensen, John B., Sanjay L. Ahire, and Manoj K. Malhotra. "Trane/Ingersoll Rand Combines Lean and Operations Research Tools to Redesign Feeder Manufacturing Operations." *Interfaces*, vol. 43, no. 4 (2013), pp. 325–340.

Jeston, John, and Johan Nelis. *Management by Process: A Roadmap to Sustainable Business Process Management.* Oxford, UK: Elsevier, 2008.

Johansson, Pontus, and Jan Olhager. "Linking Product-Process Matrices for Manufacturing and Industrial Service Operations." *International Journal of Production Economics*, vol. 104, (2006), pp. 615–624.

Karmarkar, Uday. "Will You Survive the Services Revolution?" *Harvard Business Review*, vol. 82, no. 6 (June 2004), pp. 100–107.

Kulpa, Margaret K., and Kent A. Johnson. *Interpeting the CMMI: A Process Improvement Approach*, 2nd ed. Boca Raton, FL: Auerbach Publications, 2008.

Kung, Peter, and Claus Hagen. "The Fruits of Business Process Management: An Experience Report from a Swiss Bank." *Business Process Management Journal*, vol. 13, no. 4 (2007), pp. 477–487.

La Ferla, Beverly. "Mapping the Way to Process Improvement." *IEE Engineering Management* (December 2004/January 2005), pp. 16–17.

Lee, Hau L. "The Triple-A Supply Chain." *Harvard Business Review* (October 2004), pp. 102–112.

Malhotra, Manoj K., and Larry P. Ritzman. "Resource Flexibility Issues in Multistage Manufacturing." *Decision Sciences*, vol. 21, no. 4 (1990), pp. 673–690.

Metters, Richard, Kathryn King-Metters, and Madeleine Pullman. *Successful Service Operations Management.* Mason, OH: South-Western, 2003.

Prajogo, Daniel. "The Implementation of Operations Management Techniques in Service Organisations." *International Journal of Operations & Production Management*, vol. 26, no. 12 (2006), pp. 1374–1390.

Rayport, Jeffrey F., and Bernard J. Jaworski. "Best Face Forward." *Harvard Business Review*, vol. 82, no. 12 (2003), pp. 47–58.

Rummler, Geary A., and Alan P. Brache. *Improving Performance*, 2nd ed. San Francisco: Jossey-Bass Inc., 1995.

Safizadeh, M. Hossein, Joy M. Field, and Larry P. Ritzman. "An Empirical Analysis of Financial Services Processes with a Front-Office or Back-Office Orientation." *Journal of Operations Management*, vol. 21, no. 5 (2003), pp. 557–576.

Safizadeh, M. Hossein, Larry P. Ritzman, and Debasish Mallick. "Revisiting Alternative Theoretical Paradigms in Manufacturing." *Production and Operations Management*, vol. 9, no. 2 (2000), pp. 111–127.

Scott, Bradley, S., Anne E. Wilcock, and Vinay Kanetkar. "A Survey of Structured Continuous Improvement Programs in the Canadian Food Sector." *Food Control*, vol. 20 (2009), 209–217.

Sehgal, Sanjay, B. S. Sahay, and S. K. Goyal. "Reengineering the Supply Chain in a Paint Company." *International Journal of Productivity and Performance Management*, vol. 55, no. 8 (2006), pp. 655–670.

Skinner, Wickham. "Operations Technology: Blind Spot in Strategic Management." *Interfaces*, vol. 14 (January/February 1984), pp. 116–125.

Swink, Morgan, and Anand Nair. "Capturing the Competitive Advantages of AMT: Design-Manufacturing Integration as a Complementary Asset." *Journal of Operations Management*, vol. 25 (2007), pp. 736–754.

Zomerdijk, Leonieke G., and Jan de Vries. "Structuring Front Office and Back Office Work in Service Delivery Systems." *International Journal of Operations & Production Management*, vol. 27, no. 1 (2007), pp. 108–131.

Annette M. Drowlette/Agusta Chronicle/ZUMAPRESS.com/Newscom

Accurate forecasting is crucial to maintaining the proper amount of product in the supply chain. Kimberly-Clark recently incorporated demand-signal data—information on actual consumer sales—into its forecasting system and greatly increased the accuracy of the forecasts. Here a worker moves pallets of paper products at a Kimberly-Clark warehouse in Beech Island, South Carolina.

FORECASTING

Kimberly-Clark

What do Kleenex tissues, Huggies diapers, and Scott paper towels all have in common? They are all produced by Kimberly-Clark, a $21 billion multi-national company based in Irving, Texas. With 106 production and warehouse facilities worldwide one can only imagine the complexity of ensuring that retail customers located in 175 countries receive their orders on time. Any time the retailer's inventories are out of sync with production forecasts, it can have a dramatic effect on Kimberly-Clark's bottom line: empty shelves at the retail level force consumers to seek out competitors' products while too much inventory at Kimberly-Clark is very costly. For example, during the high-volume flu season a one-day reduction in safety stock inventories translates into a $10 million savings across the supply chain network. It is no wonder that forecast accuracy is a top priority at Kimberly-Clark. Forecast errors drive the need for safety stocks (greater forecast errors equate to greater uncertainty in demands) and result in inefficient operations and higher costs. Consequently, Kimberly-Clark undertook a major project to improve its forecasting performance.

Prior to the onset of the project, forecasts were based on historical shipment data. The shipments were geared to satisfy actual customer orders. Intuitively, those data should be good for making forecasts of future orders. However, actual shipments may be subject to all sorts of anomalies such as supply disruptions, factory or transportation capacity limits, or severe weather, all of which could delay the shipments and miss the dates the customer actually wanted the

From Chapter 8 of *Operations Management: Processes and Supply Chains*, Eleventh Edition. Lee J. Krajewski, Manoj K. Malhotra, and Larry P. Ritzman.

product. Perhaps the biggest problem with using past shipment data for making forecasts is that it is backward-looking; forecasts assume that what happened in the past will happen in the future. Such an approach will miss spikes in consumer demand. For example, Hurricane Sandy pummeled the east coast in 2012 and caused a drop in the sales of paper products in the northeast region. Estimating weekly sales on the basis of historical shipment data when there was no storm will be fraught with errors; even managerial judgment to temper the forecasts will not provide much relief. When would consumers in the northeast turn their attention from buying generators and portable lighting products to paper towels and diapers again?

The project to improve forecasting performance was a major part of a larger project to create a demand-driven supply chain. Kimberly-Clark reduced the number of production facilities and warehouses, opened new larger facilities, and repurposed others to handle a smaller set of customers or to ship only promotional items. All told, this design not only improved logistical efficiency but also simplified the forecasting effort. The key, however, to creating a demand-driven supply chain was to incorporate demand-signal data—information about actual consumer purchases—into its plans to resupply retailers with product. In close collaboration with Terra Technology, whose Multi-Enterprise Demand Sensing (MDS) system was chosen for the forecasting tool, Kimberly-Clark incorporated the point-of-sale data (POS) from three of its largest retail customers in North America. The software uses that data along with inventory in the distribution channel, shipments from warehouses, and the retailer's own forecasts to create a daily operational forecast. These inputs are re-evaluated weekly for their influence on the forecast. For example, POS might be the best predictor of a shipment forecast on a three-week horizon, but actual orders could be the best predictor for the current week. A new metric for evaluating forecast performance was created; it was defined as the absolute difference between shipments and forecast and reported as a percentage of shipments. Using that metric and the new forecasting system, Kimberly-Clark observed forecast error reductions as high as 35 percent in the first week of the horizon and 20 percent on a two-week horizon. These forecast error reductions can translate into one to three weeks reduction in safety stocks.

Sources: James A. Cooke, "Kimberly-Clark Connects Its Supply Chain to the Store Shelf," *DC Velocity*, April 10, 2013; Paul Taylor, "Demand Forecasting Pays Off for Kimberly-Clark," *Financial Times*, September 10, 2011; Heather Clancy, "Kimberly-Clark Makes Sense of Demand," *CGT*, **http://consumergoods.edgl.com**; Kimberly-Clark Annual Report, 2013, **http://www.Kimberly-Clark.com.**

LEARNING GOALS *After reading this chapter, you should be able to:*

1. Explain how managers can change demand patterns.
2. Describe the two key decisions on making forecasts.
3. Calculate the five basic measures of forecast errors.
4. Compare and contrast the four approaches to judgmental forecasting.
5. Use regression to make forecasts with one or more independent variables.
6. Make forecasts using the five most common statistical approaches for time-series analysis.
7. Describe the six steps in a typical forecasting process.

Balancing supply and demand begins with making accurate forecasts, and then reconciling them across the supply chain as shown by Kimberly-Clark. A **forecast** is a prediction of future events used for planning purposes. Planning, on the other hand, is the process of making management decisions on how to deploy resources to best respond to the demand forecasts. Forecasting methods may be based on mathematical models that use available historical data, or on qualitative methods that draw on managerial experience and judgments, or on a combination of both.

forecast

A prediction of future events used for planning purposes.

In this chapter our focus is on demand forecasts. We begin with different types of demand patterns. We examine forecasting methods in three basic categories: (1) judgment, (2) causal, and (3) time-series methods. Forecast errors are defined, providing important clues for making better forecasts. We next consider the forecasting techniques themselves, and then how they can be combined to bring together insights from several sources. We conclude with overall processes for making forecasts and designing the forecasting system.

Forecasts are useful for both managing processes and managing supply chains. At the supply chain level, a firm needs forecasts to coordinate with its customers and suppliers. At the process level, output forecasts are needed to design the various processes throughout the organization, including identifying and dealing with in-house bottlenecks.

As you might imagine, the organization-wide forecasting process cuts across functional areas. Forecasting overall demand typically originates with marketing, but internal customers throughout the organization depend on forecasts to formulate and execute their plans as well. Forecasts are critical inputs to business plans, annual plans, and budgets. Finance needs forecasts to project cash flows and capital requirements. Human resources uses forecasts to anticipate hiring and training needs. Marketing is an important source for sales forecast information because it is closest to external customers. Operations and supply chain managers need forecasts to plan output levels, purchases of services and materials, workforce and output schedules, inventories, and long-term capacities. Managers at all levels need estimates of future demands, so that they can plan activities that are consistent with the firm's competitive priorities.

Using Operations to Create Value

MANAGING PROCESSES

Process Strategy and Analysis
Quality and Performance
Capacity Planning
Constraint Management
Lean Systems
Project Management

MANAGING CUSTOMER DEMAND

→ **Forecasting**
Inventory Management
Operations Planning and Scheduling
Resource Planning

MANAGING SUPPLY CHAINS

Supply Chain Design
Supply Chain Logistic Networks
Supply Chain Integration
Supply Chain Sustainability

Managing Demand

Before we get into the tools and techniques for forecasting demands, it is important to understand that the timing and sizing of customer demand can often be manipulated. Accurately forecasting customer demand is a difficult task because the demand for services and goods can vary greatly. For example, demand for lawn fertilizer predictably increases in the spring and summer months; however, the particular weekends when demand is heaviest may depend on uncontrollable factors such as the weather. These demand swings are costly to satisfy for any process, even if they are predictable. However, managers can often do two things to alleviate the pains of demand swings. First, understand the demand pattern they are facing; second, employ one or more options to alleviate any avoidable swings.

Demand Patterns

Forecasting demand requires uncovering the underlying patterns from available information. The repeated observations of demand for a service or product in their order of occurrence form a pattern known as a **time series**. There are five basic patterns of most demand time series:

time series

The repeated observations of demand for a service or product in their order of occurrence.

1. *Horizontal.* The fluctuation of data around a constant mean.
2. *Trend.* The systematic increase or decrease in the mean of the series over time.
3. *Seasonal.* A repeatable pattern of increases or decreases in demand, depending on the time of day, week, month, or season.
4. *Cyclical.* The less predictable gradual increases or decreases in demand over longer periods of time (years or decades).
5. *Random.* The unforecastable variation in demand.

Cyclical patterns arise from two influences. The first is the business cycle, which includes factors that cause the economy to go from recession to expansion over a number of years. The other influence is the service or product life cycle, which reflects the stages of demand from development through decline. Business cycle demand is difficult to predict because it is affected by national or international events.

The four patterns of demand—horizontal, trend, seasonal, and cyclical—combine in varying degrees to define the underlying time pattern of demand for a service or product. The fifth pattern,

FIGURE 1 ▶
Patterns of Demand

MyOMLab Animation

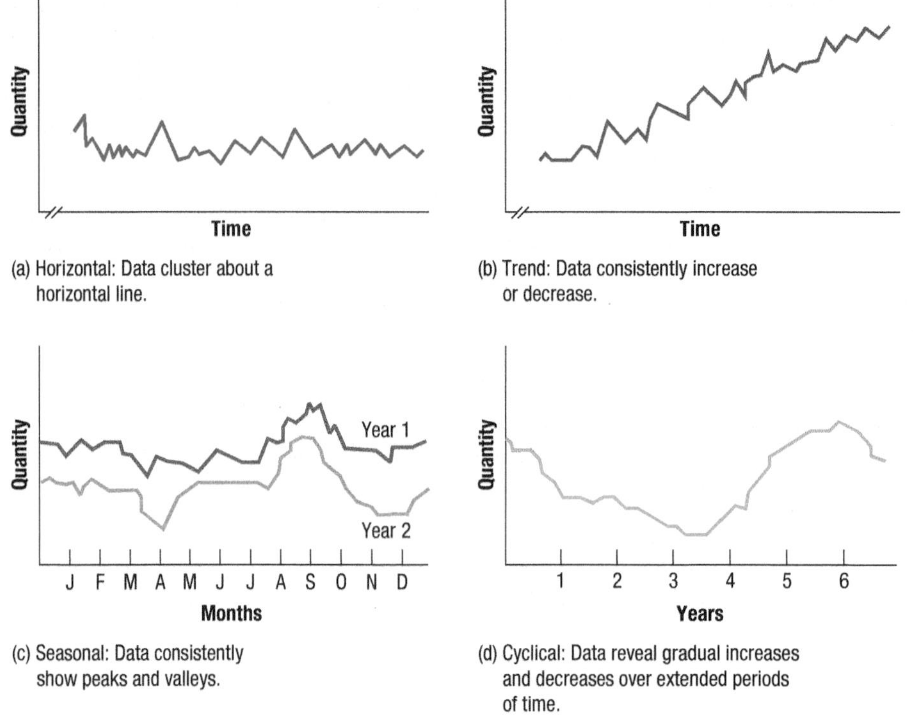

(a) Horizontal: Data cluster about a horizontal line.

(b) Trend: Data consistently increase or decrease.

(c) Seasonal: Data consistently show peaks and valleys.

(d) Cyclical: Data reveal gradual increases and decreases over extended periods of time.

random variation, results from chance causes and thus, cannot be predicted. Random variation is an aspect of demand that makes every forecast ultimately inaccurate. Figure 1 shows the first four patterns of a demand time series, all of which contain random variations.

Demand Management Options

Matching supply with demand becomes a challenge when forecasts call for uneven demand patterns—and uneven demand is more the rule than the exception. Demand swings can be from one month to the next, one week to the next, or even one hour to the next. Peaks and valleys in demand are costly or can cause poor customer service. Air New Zealand can lose sales because capacity is exceeded for one of its flights, while another of its flights to the same destination at about the same time has many empty seats. If nothing is done to even out demand, sales are lost or greater capacity cushions might be needed. All come at an extra cost. Here we deal with **demand management**, the process of changing demand patterns using one or more demand options.

demand management
The process of changing demand patterns using one or more demand options.

Various options are available in managing demand, including complementary products, promotional pricing, prescheduled appointments, reservations, revenue management, backlogs, backorders, and stockouts. The manager may select one or more of them, as we illustrate below.

Complementary Products One demand option for a company to even out the load on resources is to produce **complementary products**, or services that have similar resource requirements but different demand cycles. For example, manufacturers of matzoh balls for the Jewish Passover holiday are in a seasonal business. The B. Manischewitz Company, a kosher foods manufacturer in Jersey City, New Jersey, previously experienced 40 percent of its annual sales for the 8-day Passover holiday alone. It expanded toward markets with year-round appeal such as low-carb, low-fat foods, including canned soups and crackers, borscht, cake mixes, dressing and spreads, juices, and condiments.

complementary products
Services or products that have similar resource requirements but different demand cycles.

For service providers, a city parks and recreation department can counterbalance seasonal staffing requirements for summer activities by offering ice skating, tobogganing, or indoor activities during the winter months. The key is to find services and products that can be produced with the existing resources and can level off the need for resources over the year.

Promotional Pricing Promotional campaigns are designed to increase sales with creative pricing. Examples include automobile rebate programs, price reductions for winter clothing in the late summer months, reduced prices for hotel rooms during off-peak periods, and "two-for-the-price-of-one" automobile tire sales. Lower prices can increase demand for the product or service from new and existing customers during traditional slack periods or encourage customers to move up future buying.

Prescheduled Appointments Service providers often can schedule customers for definite periods of order fulfillment. With this approach, demand is leveled to not exceed supply capacity. An appointment system assigns specific times for service to customers. The advantages of this method are timely customer service and the high utilization of service personnel.

Doctors, dentists, lawyers, and automobile repair shops are examples of service providers that use appointment systems. Doctors can use the system to schedule parts of their day to visit hospital patients, and lawyers can set aside time to prepare cases. Care must be taken to tailor the length of appointments to individual customer needs rather than merely scheduling customers at equal time intervals.

Reservations Reservation systems, although quite similar to appointment systems, are used when the customer actually occupies or uses facilities associated with the service. For example, customers reserve hotel rooms, automobiles, airline seats, and concert seats. The major advantage of reservation systems is the lead time they give service managers and the ability to level demand. Managers can deal with no-shows with a blend of overbooking, deposits, and cancellation penalties. Sometimes overbooking means that a customer with reservations cannot be served as promised. In such cases, bonuses can be offered for compensation. For example, an airline passenger might not only get on the next available flight, but also may be given a free ticket for a second flight sometime in the future.

Revenue Management A specialized combination of the pricing and reservation options for service providers is revenue management. **Revenue management** (sometimes called *yield management*) is the process of varying price at the right time for different customer segments to maximize revenues generated from existing supply capacity. It works best if customers can be segmented, prices can be varied by segment, fixed costs are high, variable costs are low, service duration is predictable, and capacity is lost if not used (sometimes called *perishable capacity*). Airlines, hotels, cruise lines, restaurants (early-bird specials), and rental cars are good examples. Computerized reservation systems can make hour-by-hour updates, using decision rules for opening or closing price classes depending on the difference between supply and continually updated demand forecasts. In the airlines industry, prices are lowered if a particular airline flight is not selling as fast as expected, until more seats are booked. Alternately, if larger than expected demand is developing, prices for the remaining seats may be increased. Last-minute business travelers pay the higher prices, whereas leisure travelers making reservations well in advance and staying over the weekend get the bargain prices. Southwest Airlines now segments its customers by creating a "Business Select" ticket class that rewards more perks to frequent fliers willing to pay higher prices.

revenue management
Varying price at the right time for different customer segments to maximize revenues yielded by existing supply capacity.

Backlogs Much like the appointments or reservations of service providers, a **backlog** is an accumulation of customer orders that a manufacturer has promised for delivery at some future date. Manufacturers in the supply chain that maintain a backlog of orders as a normal business practice can allow the backlog to grow during periods of high demand and then reduce it during periods of low demand. Airplane manufacturers do not promise instantaneous delivery, as do wholesalers or retailers farther forward in the supply chain. Instead, they impose a lead time between when the order is placed and when it is delivered. For example, an automotive parts manufacturer may agree to deliver to the repair department of a car dealership a batch of 100 door latches for a particular car model next Tuesday. The parts manufacturer uses that due date to plan its production of door latches within its capacity limits. Firms that are most likely to use backlogs—and increase the size of them during periods of heavy demand—make customized products and tend to have a make-to-order strategy. Backlogs reduce the uncertainty of future production requirements and also can be used to level demand. However, they become a competitive disadvantage if they get too big.

backlog
An accumulation of customer orders that a manufacturer has promised for delivery at some future date.

Backorders and Stockouts A last resort in demand management is to set lower standards for customer service, either in the form of backorders or stockouts. Not to be confused with a backlog, a **backorder** is a customer order that cannot be filled when promised or demanded but is filled later. Demand may be too unpredictable or the item may be too costly to hold it in inventory. Although the customer is not pleased with the delay, the customer order is not lost and it is filled at a later date. In contrast, a **stockout** is an order that cannot be satisfied, resulting in a loss of the sale. A backorder adds to the next period's demand requirement, whereas a stockout does not. Backorders and stockouts can lead dissatisfied customers to do their future business with another firm. Generally, backorders and stockouts are to be avoided.

backorder
A customer order that cannot be filled when promised or demanded but is filled later.

stockout
An order that cannot be satisfied, resulting in a loss of the sale.

aggregation

The act of clustering several similar services or products so that forecasts and plans can be made for whole families.

judgment methods

A forecasting method that translates the opinions of managers, expert opinions, consumer surveys, and salesforce estimates into quantitative estimates.

causal methods

A quantitative forecasting method that uses historical data on independent variables, such as promotional campaigns, economic conditions, and competitors' actions, to predict demand.

time-series analysis

A statistical approach that relies heavily on historical demand data to project the future size of demand and recognizes trends and seasonal patterns.

Combinations of demand options can also be used. For example, a manufacturer of lighting equipment had several products characterized as "slow movers with spikes," where only 2 or 3 units were sold for several weeks, and then suddenly there was a huge order for 10,000 units the next week. The reason is that their product was purchased by commercial property managers who might be upgrading the lighting in a large office building. The result was a forecasting nightmare and having to resort to high cost supply options to meet the demand spikes. The breakthrough in solving this problem was to combine the pricing and backlog options. Contractors are now offered a 3 percent discount (the pricing option) on any order in excess of 10,000 units that are placed five or more weeks before they are needed (the backlog option). The advanced warning allows the manufacturer to smooth out its production processes, saving millions of dollars annually.

Key Decisions on Making Forecasts

Before using forecasting techniques, a manager must make two decisions: (1) what to forecast, and (2) what type of forecasting technique to select for different items.

Deciding What to Forecast

Although some sort of demand estimate is needed for the individual services or goods produced by a company, forecasting total demand for groups or clusters and then deriving individual service or product forecasts may be easiest. Also, selecting the correct unit of measurement (e.g., units, customers, or machine-hours) for forecasting may be as important as choosing the best method.

Level of Aggregation Few companies err by more than 5 percent when forecasting the annual total demand for all their services or products. However, errors in forecasts for individual items and shorter time periods may be much higher. Recognizing this reality, many companies use a two-tier forecasting system. They first cluster (or "roll up") several similar services or products in a process called **aggregation**, making forecasts for families of services or goods that have similar demand requirements and common processing, labor, and materials requirements. Next, they derive forecasts for individual items, which are sometimes called stock-keeping units. A *stock-keeping unit (SKU)* is an individual item or product that has an identifying code and is held in inventory somewhere along the supply chain, such as in a distribution center.

Mark Lennihan/Associated Press

A Moto X phone manufactured by Motorola Mobility. Motorola considerably improved its demand forecasting process by closely collaborating with its major retailers, obtaining point-of-sale data from them.

Units of Measurement Rather than using dollars as the initial unit of measurement, forecasts often begin with service or product units, such as individual products, express packages to deliver, or customers needing maintenance service or repairs for their cars. Forecasted units can then be translated to dollars by multiplying them by the unit price. If accurately forecasting demand for a service or product is not possible in terms of number of units, forecast the standard labor or machine-hours required of each of the critical resources.

Choosing the Type of Forecasting Technique

Forecasting systems offer a variety of techniques, and no one of them is best for all items and situations. The forecaster's objective is to develop a useful forecast from the information at hand with the technique that is appropriate for the different patterns of demand. Two general types of forecasting techniques are used: judgment methods and quantitative methods. **Judgment methods** translate the opinions of managers, expert opinions, consumer surveys, and salesforce estimates into quantitative estimates. Quantitative methods include causal methods, time-series analysis, and trend projection with regression. **Causal methods** use historical data on independent variables, such as promotional campaigns, economic conditions, and competitors' actions, to predict demand. **Time-series analysis** is a statistical approach that relies heavily on historical demand data to project the future size of demand and recognizes trends and seasonal patterns. **Trend projection with regression** is a hybrid between a time-series technique and the causal method.

Forecast Error

For any forecasting technique, it is important to measure the accuracy of its forecasts. Forecasts almost always contain errors. Random error results from unpredictable factors that cause the forecast to deviate from the actual demand. Forecasting analysts try to minimize forecast errors by selecting appropriate forecasting models, but eliminating all forms of errors is impossible.

Forecast error for a given period t is simply the difference found by subtracting the forecast from actual demand, or

$$E_t = D_t - F_t$$

where

$$E_t = \text{forecast error for period } t$$

$$D_t = \text{actual demand for period } t$$

$$F_t = \text{forecast for period } t$$

This equation (notice the alphabetical order with D_t coming before F_t) is the starting point for creating several measures of forecast error that cover longer periods of time.

There are five basic measures of forecast error: CFE, MSE, (σ), MAD, and MAPE. Figure 2 shows the output from the *Error Analysis* routine in Forecasting's dropdown menu of POM for Windows. Part (a) gives a big picture view of how well the forecast has been tracking the actual demand. Part (b) shows the detailed calculations needed to obtain the summary error terms. Finally, Part (c) gives the summary error measures summarized across all 10 time periods, as derived from Part (b).

trend projection with regression

A forecasting model that is a hybrid between a time-series technique and the causal method.

forecast error

The difference found by subtracting the forecast from actual demand for a given period.

Cumulative Sum of Forecast Errors

The **cumulative sum of forecast errors (CFE)** measures the total forecast error:

$$\text{CFE} = \Sigma E_t$$

CFE is a cumulative sum. Figure 2(b) shows that it is the sum of the errors for all 10 periods. For any given period, it would be the sum of errors up through that period. For example, it would be −8 (or −2 −6) for period 2. CFE is also called the *bias error* and results from consistent mistakes—the forecast is always too high or too low. This type of error typically causes the greatest disruption to planning efforts. For example, if a forecast is consistently lower than actual demand, the value of CFE will gradually get larger and larger. This increasingly large error indicates some systematic deficiency in the forecasting approach. The average forecast error, sometimes called the *mean bias*, is simply

$$\bar{E} = \frac{\text{CFE}}{n}$$

cumulative sum of forecast errors (CFE)

A measurement of the total forecast error that assesses the bias in a forecast.

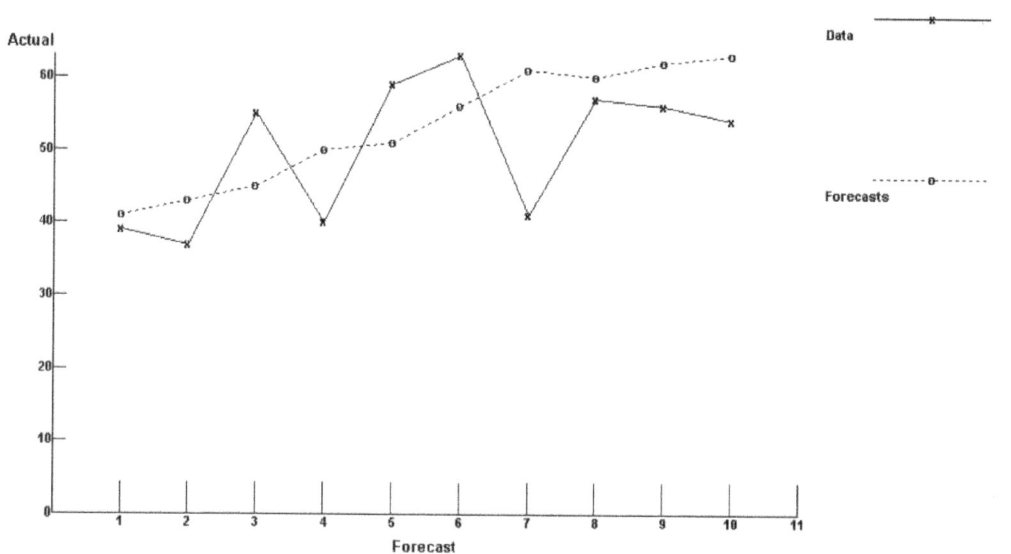

◄ FIGURE 2(a) Graph of Actual and Forecast Demand Using *Error Analysis* of Forecasting in POM for Windows

FIGURE 2(b) ▶ Detailed Calculations of Forecast Errors

		Forecast	Error	|Error|	Error^2	|Pct Error|
Past period 1	39	41	-2	2	4	5.128%
Past period 2	37	43	-6	6	36	16.216%
Past period 3	55	45	10	10	100	18.182%
Past period 4	40	50	-10	10	100	25%
Past period 5	59	51	8	8	64	13.559%
Past period 6	63	56	7	7	49	11.111%
Past period 7	41	61	-20	20	400	48.78%
Past period 8	57	60	-3	3	9	5.263%
Past period 9	56	62	-6	6	36	10.714%
Past period 10	54	63	-9	9	81	16.667%
TOTALS	501		-31	81	879	170.621%
AVERAGE	50.1		-3.1	8.1	87.9	17.062%
			(Bias)	(MAD)	(MSE)	(MAPE)
				Std dev	29.648	

Dispersion of Forecast Errors

mean squared error (MSE)
A measurement of the dispersion of forecast errors.

standard deviation of the errors (σ)
A measurement of the dispersion of forecast errors.

mean absolute deviation (MAD)
A measurement of the dispersion of forecast errors.

The **mean squared error (MSE)**, **standard deviation of the errors** (σ), and **mean absolute deviation (MAD)** measure the dispersion of forecast errors attributed to trend, seasonal, cyclical, or random effects:

$$\text{MSE} = \frac{\sum E_t^2}{n}$$

$$\sigma = \sqrt{\frac{\sum (E_t - \overline{E})^2}{n - 1}}$$

$$\text{MAD} = \frac{\sum |E_t|}{n}$$

Figure 2(b) shows the squared error in period 1 is 4, and MSE is 87.9 for the whole sample. The standard deviation of the errors, shown as 29.648 in Figure 2(b), is calculated using a separate function available in Excel. The absolute value of the error in period 2 is 6, and MAD is 1 across the whole sample.

The mathematical symbol $| \; |$ is used to indicate the absolute value—that is, it tells you to disregard positive or negative signs. If MSE, σ, or MAD is small, the forecast is typically close to actual demand; by contrast, a large value indicates the possibility of large forecast errors. The measures do differ in the way they emphasize errors. Large errors get far more weight in MSE and σ because the errors are squared. MAD is a widely used measure of forecast error and is easily understood; it is merely the mean of the absolute forecast errors over a series of time periods, without regard to whether the error was an overestimate or an underestimate.

mean absolute percent error (MAPE)
A measurement that relates the forecast error to the level of demand and is useful for putting forecast performance in the proper perspective.

Mean Absolute Percent Error

The **mean absolute percent error (MAPE)** relates the forecast error to the level of demand and is useful for putting forecast performance in the proper perspective:

$$\text{MAPE} = \frac{(\sum |E_t| / D_t)(100)}{n} \text{ (expressed as a percentage)}$$

For example, an absolute forecast error of 100 results in a larger percentage error when the demand is 200 units than when the demand is 10,000 units. MAPE is the best error measure to use when making comparisons between time series for different SKUs. Looking again at Figure 2(b), the percent error in period 2 is 16.22 percent, and MAPE, the average over all 10 periods, is 17.062 percent.

Finally, Figure 2(c) summarizes the key error terms across all 10 time periods. They are actually found in selected portions of Figure 2(b). For example, CFE is −31, which is in the error column of Figure 2(b) in the TOTALS row. MAD is 1, found in the $|$Error$|$ column and AVERAGE row. Finally, MAPE is 17.062%, which is in the $|$Pct Error$|$ column and AVERAGE row.

▼ **FIGURE 2(c)** Error Measures

Measure	Value
Error Measures	
CFE (Cumulative Forecast Error)	-31
MAD (Mean Absolute Deviation)	8.1
MSE (Mean Squared Error)	87.9
Standard Deviation of Errors	29.648
MAPE (Mean Absolute Percent	17.062%

EXAMPLE 1

Calculating Forecast Error Measures

The following table shows the actual sales of upholstered chairs for a furniture manufacturer and the forecasts made for each of the last 8 months. Calculate CFE, MSE, σ, MAD, and MAPE for this product.

Month, t	Demand, D_t	Forecast, F_t	Error, E_t	Error, Squared, E_t^2	Absolute Error, $\lvert E_t \rvert$	Absolute Percent Error, $(\lvert E_t \rvert / D_t)(100)$
1	200	225	−25	625	25	12.5%
2	240	220	20	400	20	8.3
3	300	285	15	225	15	5.0
4	270	290	−20	400	20	7.4
5	230	250	−20	400	20	8.7
6	260	240	20	400	20	7.7
7	210	250	−40	1,600	40	19.0
8	275	240	35	1,225	35	12.7
		Total	−15	5,275	195	81.3%

SOLUTION

Using the formulas for the measures, we get

Cumulative forecast error (bias):

CFE = −15 (the bias, or the sum of the errors for all time periods in the time series)

Average forecast error (mean bias):

$$\bar{E} = \frac{\text{CFE}}{n} = \frac{-15}{8} = -1.875$$

Mean squared error:

$$\text{MSE} = \frac{\Sigma E_t^2}{n} = \frac{5{,}275}{8} = 659.4$$

Standard deviation of the errors:

$$\sigma = \sqrt{\frac{\Sigma[E_t - (-1.875)]^2}{7}} = 27.4$$

Mean absolute deviation:

$$\text{MAD} = \frac{\Sigma|E_t|}{n} = \frac{195}{8} = 24.4$$

Mean absolute percent error:

$$\text{MAPE} = \frac{[\Sigma|E_t|/D_t]100}{n} = \frac{81.3\%}{8} = 10.2\%$$

A CFE of −15 indicates that the forecast has a slight bias to overestimate demand. The MSE, σ, and MAD statistics provide measures of forecast error variability. A MAD of 24.4 means that the average forecast error was 24.4 units in absolute value. The value of σ, 27.4, indicates that the sample distribution of forecast errors has a standard deviation of 27.4 units. A MAPE of 10.2 percent implies that, on average, the forecast error was within about 10 percent of actual demand. These measures become more reliable as the number of periods of data increases.

DECISION POINT

Although reasonably satisfied with these forecast performance results, the analyst decided to test out a few more forecasting methods before reaching a final forecasting method to use for the future.

Computer Support

Computer support, such as from OM Explorer or POM for Windows, makes error calculations easy when evaluating how well forecasting models fit with past data. Errors are measured across past data, often called the *history file* in practice. They show the various error measures across the entire history file for each forecasting method evaluated. They also make forecasts into the future, based on the method selected.

Judgment Methods

Forecasts from quantitative methods are possible only when there is adequate historical data, (i.e., the *history file*). However, the history file may be nonexistent when a new product is introduced or when technology is expected to change. The history file might exist but be less useful when certain events (such as rollouts or special packages) are reflected in the past data, or when certain events are expected to occur in the future. In some cases, judgment methods are the only practical way to make a forecast. In other cases, judgment methods can also be used to modify forecasts that are generated by quantitative methods. They may recognize that one or two quantitative models have been performing particularly well in recent periods. Adjustments certainly would be called for if the forecaster has important contextual knowledge. *Contextual knowledge* is knowledge that practitioners gain through experience, such as cause-and-effect relationships, environmental cues, and organizational information that may have an effect on the variable being forecast. Adjustments also could account for unusual circumstances, such as a new sales promotion or unexpected international events. They could also have been used to remove the effect of special one-time events in the history file before quantitative methods are applied. Four of the more successful judgment methods are as follows: (1) salesforce estimates, (2) executive opinion, (3) market research, and (4) the Delphi method.

salesforce estimates

The forecasts that are compiled from estimates of future demands made periodically by members of a company's salesforce.

executive opinion

A forecasting method in which the opinions, experience, and technical knowledge of one or more managers are summarized to arrive at a single forecast.

technological forecasting

An application of executive opinion to keep abreast of the latest advances in technology.

market research

A systematic approach to determine external consumer interest in a service or product by creating and testing hypotheses through data-gathering surveys.

Delphi method

A process of gaining consensus from a group of experts while maintaining their anonymity.

linear regression

A causal method in which one variable (the dependent variable) is related to one or more independent variables by a linear equation.

dependent variable

The variable that one wants to forecast.

Salesforce estimates are forecasts compiled from estimates made periodically by members of a company's salesforce. The salesforce is the group most likely to know which services or products customers will be buying in the near future and in what quantities. Forecasts of individual salesforce members can be combined easily to get regional or national sales estimates. However, individual biases of the salespeople may taint the forecast. For example, some people are naturally optimistic, whereas others are more cautious. Adjustments in forecasts may need to be made to account for these individual biases.

Executive opinion is a forecasting method in which the opinions, experience, and technical knowledge of one or more managers or customers are summarized to arrive at a single forecast. All of the factors going into judgmental forecasts would fall into the category of executive opinion. Executive opinion can also be used for **technological forecasting**. The quick pace of technological change makes keeping abreast of the latest advances difficult.

Market research is a systematic approach to determine external consumer interest in a service or product by creating and testing hypotheses through data-gathering surveys. Conducting a market research study includes designing a questionnaire, deciding how to administer it, selecting a representative sample, and analyzing the information using judgment and statistical tools to interpret the responses. Although market research yields important information, it typically includes numerous qualifications and hedges in the findings.

The **Delphi method** is a process of gaining consensus from a group of experts while maintaining their anonymity. This form of forecasting is useful when no historical data are available from which to develop statistical models and when managers inside the firm have no experience on which to base informed projections. A coordinator sends questions to each member of the group of outside experts, who may not even know who else is participating. The coordinator prepares a statistical summary of the responses along with a summary of arguments for particular responses. The report is sent to the same group for another round, and the participants may choose to modify their previous responses. These rounds continue until consensus is obtained.

In the remainder of this chapter, we turn to the commonly used quantitative forecasting approaches.

Causal Methods: Linear Regression

Causal methods are used when historical data are available and the relationship between the factor to be forecasted and other external or internal factors (e.g., government actions or advertising promotions) can be identified. These relationships are expressed in mathematical terms and can be complex. Causal methods are good for predicting turning points in demand and for preparing long-range forecasts. We focus on linear regression, one of the best known and most commonly used causal methods.

In **linear regression**, one variable, called a dependent variable, is related to one or more independent variables by a linear equation. The **dependent variable** (such as demand for door hinges) is the one the manager wants to forecast. The **independent variables** (such as advertising expenditures and new housing starts) are assumed to affect the dependent variable and thereby "cause" the results observed in the past. Figure 3 shows how a linear regression line relates to the data. In technical terms, the regression line minimizes the squared deviations from the actual data.

independent variables
Variables that are assumed to affect the dependent variable and thereby "cause" the results observed in the past.

In the simplest linear regression models, the dependent variable is a function of only one independent variable and, therefore, the theoretical relationship is a straight line:

$$Y = a + bX$$

where

$Y =$ dependent variable

$X =$ independent variable

$a =$ Y-intercept of the line

$b =$ slope of the line

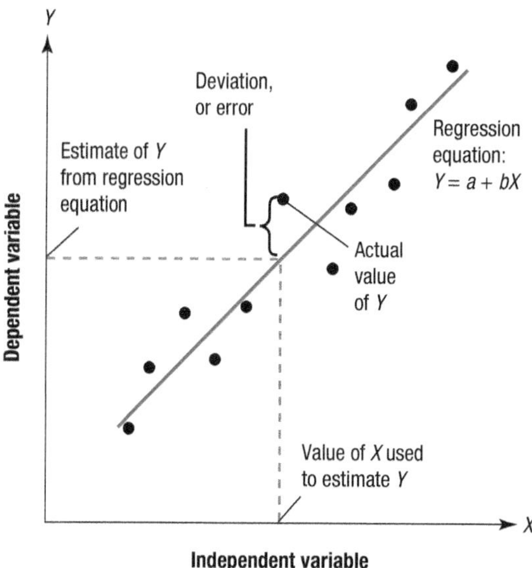

▲ FIGURE 3
Linear Regression Line Relative to Actual Demand

The objective of linear regression analysis is to find values of a and b that minimize the sum of the squared deviations of the actual data points from the graphed line. Computer programs are used for this purpose. For any set of matched observations for Y and X, the program computes the values of a and b and provides measures of forecast accuracy. Three measures commonly reported are (1) the sample correlation coefficient, (2) the sample coefficient of determination, and (3) the standard error of the estimate.

The *sample correlation coefficient*, r, measures the direction and strength of the relationship between the independent variable and the dependent variable. The value of r can range from -1.00 to $+1.00$. A correlation coefficient of $+1.00$ implies that period-by-period changes in direction (increases or decreases) of the independent variable are always accompanied by changes in the same direction by the dependent variable. An r of -1.00 means that decreases in the independent variable are always accompanied by increases in the dependent variable, and vice versa. A zero value of r means no linear relationship exists between the variables. The closer the value of r is to ± 1.00, the better the regression line fits the points.

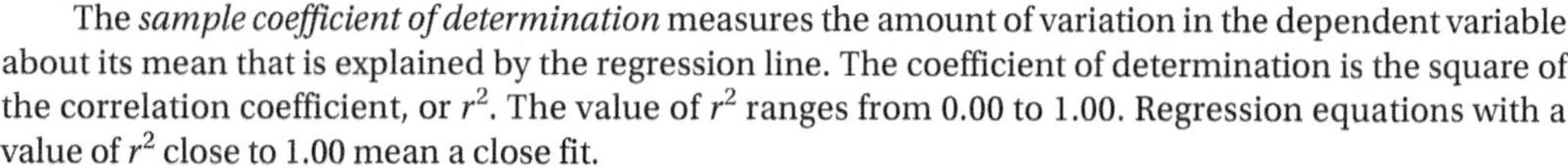

The *sample coefficient of determination* measures the amount of variation in the dependent variable about its mean that is explained by the regression line. The coefficient of determination is the square of the correlation coefficient, or r^2. The value of r^2 ranges from 0.00 to 1.00. Regression equations with a value of r^2 close to 1.00 mean a close fit.

The *standard error of the estimate*, s_{xy}, measures how closely the data on the dependent variable cluster around the regression line. Although it is similar to the sample standard deviation, it measures the error from the dependent variable, Y, to the regression line, rather than to the mean. Thus, it is the standard deviation of the difference between the actual demand and the estimate provided by the regression equation.

EXAMPLE 2 Using Linear Regression to Forecast Product Demand

The supply chain manager seeks a better way to forecast the demand for door hinges and believes that the demand is related to advertising expenditures. The following are sales and advertising data for the past 5 months:

MyOMLab
Active Model 1 in MyOMLab provides insight on varying the intercept and slope of the model.

Month	Sales (Thousands of Units)	Advertising (Thousands of $)
1	264	2.5
2	116	1.3
3	165	1.4
4	101	1.0
5	209	2.0

The company will spend $1,750 next month on advertising for the product. Use linear regression to develop an equation and a forecast for this product.

SOLUTION

We used POM for Windows to determine the best values of a, b, the correlation coefficient, the coefficient of determination, and the standard error of the estimate.

$$a = -8.135$$
$$b = 109.229X$$
$$r = 0.980$$
$$r^2 = 0.960$$
$$s_{yx} = 15.603$$

The regression equation is

$$Y = -8.135 + 109.229X$$

and the regression line is shown in Figure 4. The sample correlation coefficient, r, is 0.98, which is unusually close to 1.00 and suggests an unusually strong positive relationship exists between sales and advertising expenditures. The sample coefficient of determination, r^2, implies that 96 percent of the variation in sales is explained by advertising expenditures.

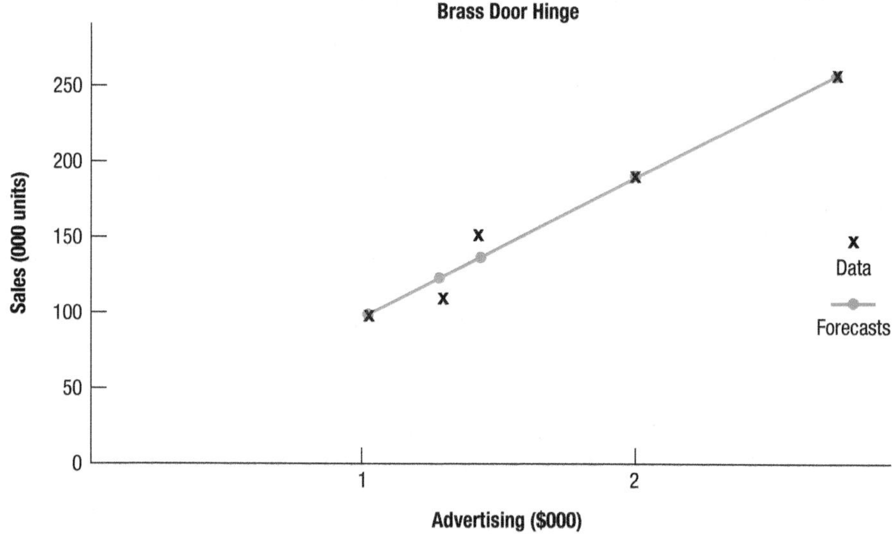

FIGURE 4 ▶ Linear Regression Line for the Sales and Advertising Data Using POM for Windows

DECISION POINT

The supply chain manager decided to use the regression model as input to planning production levels for month 6. As the advertising expenditure will be $1,750, the forecast for month 6 is $Y = -8.135 + 109.229(1.75) = 183.016$, or 183,016 units.

Often several independent variables may affect the dependent variable. For example, advertising expenditures, new corporation start-ups, and residential building contracts all may be important for estimating the demand for door hinges. In such cases, *multiple regression analysis* is helpful in determining a forecasting equation for the dependent variable as a function of several independent variables. Such models can be analyzed with POM for Windows or OM Explorer and can be quite useful for predicting turning points and solving many planning problems.

Time-Series Methods

Rather than using independent variables for the forecast as regression models do, time-series methods use historical information regarding only the dependent variable. These methods are based on the assumption that the dependent variable's past pattern will continue in the future. Time-series analysis identifies the underlying patterns of demand that combine to produce an observed historical pattern of the dependent variable and then develops a model to replicate it. In this section, we focus on five statistical time-series methods that address the horizontal, trend, and seasonal patterns of demand: simple moving averages, weighted moving averages, exponential smoothing, trend projection with regression, and multiplicative seasonal method. Before we discuss statistical methods, let us take a look at the simplest time-series method for addressing all patterns of demand—the naïve forecast.

Naïve Forecast

A method often used in practice is the **naïve forecast**, whereby the forecast for the next period (F_{t+1}) equals the demand for the current period (D_t). So if the actual demand for Wednesday is 35 customers, the forecasted demand for Thursday is 35 customers. Despite its name, the naïve forecast can perform well.

The naïve forecast method may be adapted to take into account a demand trend. The increase (or decrease) in demand observed between the last two periods is used to adjust the current demand to arrive at a forecast. Suppose that last week the demand was 120 units and the week before it was 108 units. Demand increased 12 units in 1 week, so the forecast for next week would be $120 + 12 = 132$ units. The naïve forecast method also may be used to account for seasonal patterns. If the demand last July was 50,000 units, and assuming no underlying trend from one year to the next, the forecast for this July would be 50,000 units. The method works best when the horizontal, trend, or seasonal patterns are stable and random variation is small.

naïve forecast

A time-series method whereby the forecast for the next period equals the demand for the current period, or Forecast $= D_t$.

Horizontal Patterns: Estimating the Average

We begin our discussion of statistical methods of time-series forecasting with demand that has no apparent trend, seasonal, or cyclical patterns. The horizontal pattern in a time series is based on the mean of the demands, so we focus on forecasting methods that estimate the average of a time series of data. The forecast of demand for *any* period in the future is the average of the time series computed in the current period. For example, if the average of past demand calculated on Tuesday is 65 customers, the forecasts for Wednesday, Thursday, and Friday are 65 customers each day.

Consider Figure 5, which shows patient arrivals at a medical clinic over the past 28 weeks. Assuming that the time series has only a horizontal and random pattern, one approach is simply to calculate the average of the data. However, this approach has no adaptive quality if there is a trend, seasonal, or cyclical pattern. The statistical techniques that do have an adaptive quality in estimating the average in a time series are (1) simple moving averages, (2) weighted moving averages, and (3) exponential smoothing. Another option is the simple average, but it has no adaptive capability.

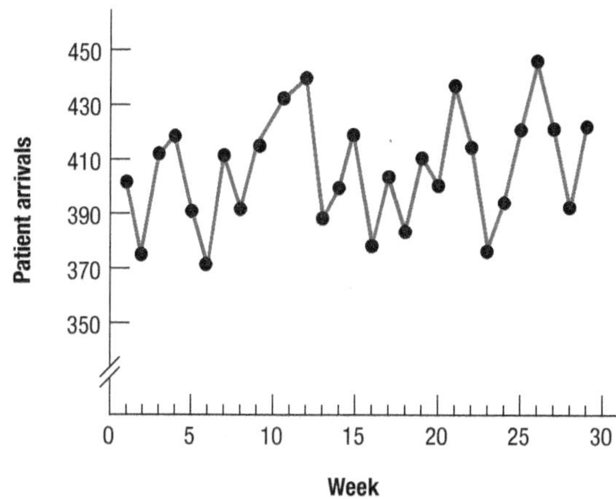

▲ **FIGURE 5**
Weekly Patient Arrivals at a Medical Clinic

Simple Moving Averages The **simple moving average method** simply involves calculating the average demand for the n most recent time periods and using it as the forecast for future time periods. For the next period, after the demand is known, the oldest demand from the previous average is replaced with the most recent demand and the average is recalculated. In this way, the n most recent demands are used, and the average "moves" from period to period.

Specifically, the forecast for period $t + 1$ can be calculated at the end of period t (after the actual demand for period t is known) as

simple moving average method

A time-series method used to estimate the average of a demand time series by averaging the demand for the n most recent time periods.

$$F_{t+1} = \frac{\text{Sum of last } n \text{ demands}}{n} = \frac{D_t + D_{t-1} + D_{t-2} + \cdots + D_{t-n+1}}{n}$$

where

D_t = actual demand in period t

n = total number of periods in the average

F_{t+1} = forecast for period $t + 1$

EXAMPLE 3 Using the Moving Average Method to Estimate Average Demand

a. Compute a *three-week* moving average forecast for the arrival of medical clinic patients in week 4. The numbers of arrivals for the past 3 weeks were as follows:

Week	Patient Arrivals
1	400
2	380
3	411

b. If the actual number of patient arrivals in week 4 is 415, what is the forecast error for week 4?

c. What is the forecast for week 5?

MyOMLab

Active Model 2 in MyOMLab provides insight on the impact of varying n using the example in Figure 5.

MyOMLab

Tutor 1 in MyOMLab provides another example to practice making forecasts with the moving average method.

SOLUTION

a. The moving average forecast at the end of week 3 is

$$F_4 = \frac{411 + 380 + 400}{3} = 397.0$$

b. The forecast error for week 4 is

$$E_4 = D_4 - F_4 = 415 - 397 = 18$$

c. The forecast for week 5 requires the actual arrivals from weeks 2 through 4, the 3 most recent weeks of data.

$$F_5 = \frac{415 + 411 + 380}{3} = 402.0$$

DECISION POINT

Thus, the forecast at the end of week 3 would have been 397 patients for week 4, which fell short of actual demand by 18 patients. The forecast for week 5, made at the end of week 4, would be 402 patients. If a forecast is needed now for week 6 and beyond, it would also be for 402 patients.

The moving average method may involve the use of as many periods of past demand as desired. Large values of n should be used for demand series that are stable, and small values of n should be used for those that are susceptible to changes in the underlying average. If n is set to its lowest level (i.e., 1), it becomes the naïve method.

weighted moving average method

A time-series method in which each historical demand in the average can have its own weight; the sum of the weights equals 1.0.

Weighted Moving Averages In the simple moving average method, each demand has the same weight in the average—namely, $1/n$. In the **weighted moving average method**, each historical demand in the average can have its own weight. The sum of the weights equals 1.0. For example, in a *three-period* weighted moving average model, the most recent period might be assigned a weight of 0.50, the second most recent might be weighted 0.30, and the third most recent might be weighted 0.20. The average is obtained by multiplying the weight of each period by the value for that period and adding the products together:

$$F_{t+1} = 0.50D_t + 0.30D_{t-1} + 0.20D_{t-2}$$

For a numerical example of using the weighted moving average method to estimate average demand, see Solved Problem 2 and Tutor 2 of OM Explorer in MyOMLab.

The advantage of a weighted moving average method is that it allows you to emphasize recent demand over earlier demand. (It can even handle seasonal effects by putting higher weights on prior years in the same season.) The forecast will be more responsive to changes in the underlying average of the demand series than the simple moving average forecast.

exponential smoothing method

A weighted moving average method that calculates the average of a time series by implicitly giving recent demands more weight than earlier demands.

Exponential Smoothing The **exponential smoothing method** is a sophisticated weighted moving average method that calculates the average of a time series by implicitly giving recent demands more weight than earlier demands, all the way back to the first period in the history file. It is the most frequently used formal forecasting method because of its simplicity and the small amount of data needed to support it. Unlike the weighted moving average method, which requires n periods of past demand and n weights, exponential smoothing requires only three items of data: (1) the last period's forecast; (2) the actual demand for this period; and (3) a smoothing parameter, alpha (α), which has a value between 0 and 1.0. The equation for the exponentially smoothed forecast for period $t + 1$ is calculated

$$F_{t+1} = \alpha D_t + (1 - \alpha)F_t$$

The emphasis given to the most recent demand levels can be adjusted by changing the smoothing parameter. Larger α values emphasize recent levels of demand and result in forecasts more responsive to changes in the underlying average. Smaller α values treat past demand more uniformly and result in more stable forecasts. Smaller α values are analogous to increasing the value of n in the moving average method and giving greater weight to past demand. In practice, various values of α are tried and the one producing the best forecasts is chosen.

Exponential smoothing requires an initial forecast to get started. There are several ways to get this initial forecast. OM Explorer and POM for Windows use as a default setting the actual demand in the first period, which becomes the forecast for the second period. Forecasts and forecast errors then are calculated beginning with period 2. If some historical data are available, the initial forecast can be found by calculating the average of several recent periods of demand. The effect of the initial estimate of the average on successive estimates of the average diminishes over time.

EXAMPLE 4 **Using Exponential Smoothing to Estimate Average Demand**

a. Reconsider the patient arrival data in Example 3. It is now the end of week 3, so the actual number of arrivals is known to be 411 patients. Using $\alpha = 0.10$, calculate the exponential smoothing forecast for week 4.

b. What was the forecast error for week 4 if the actual demand turned out to be 415?

c. What is the forecast for week 5?

MyOMLab

Active Model 3 in MyOMLab provides insight on the impact of varying α in Figure 5.

MyOMLab

Tutor 3 in MyOMLab provides a new practice example of how to make forecasts with the exponential smoothing method.

SOLUTION

a. The exponential smoothing method requires an initial forecast. Suppose that we take the demand data for the first 2 weeks and average them, obtaining $(400 + 380)/2 = 390$ as an initial forecast. (POM for Windows and OM Explorer simply use the actual demand for the first week as a default setting for the initial forecast for period 1, and do not begin tracking forecast errors until the second period). To obtain the forecast for week 4, using exponential smoothing with $D_3 = 411, \alpha = 0.10$, and $F_3 = 390$, we calculate the forecast for week 4 as

$$F_4 = 0.10(411) + 0.90(390) = 392.1$$

Thus, the forecast for week 4 would be 392 patients.

b. The forecast error for week 4 is

$$E_4 = 415 - 392 = 23$$

c. The new forecast for week 5 would be

$$F_5 = 0.10(415) + 0.90(392.1) = 394.4$$

or 394 patients. Note that we used F_4, not the integer-value forecast for week 4, in the computation for F_5. In general, we round off (when it is appropriate) only the final result to maintain as much accuracy as possible in the calculations.

DECISION POINT

Using this exponential smoothing model, the analyst's forecasts would have been 392 patients for week 4 and then 394 patients for week 5 and beyond. As soon as the actual demand for week 5 is known, then the forecast for week 6 will be updated.

Because exponential smoothing is simple and requires minimal data, it is inexpensive and attractive to firms that make thousands of forecasts for each time period. However, its simplicity also is a disadvantage when the underlying average is changing, as in the case of a demand series with a trend. Like any method geared solely to the assumption of a stable average, exponential smoothing results will lag behind changes in the underlying average of demand. Higher α values may help reduce forecast errors when there is a change in the average; however, the lags will still occur if the average is changing systematically. Typically, if large α values (e.g., > 0.50) are required for an exponential smoothing application, chances are good that another model is needed because of a significant trend or seasonal influence in the demand series.

Trend Patterns: Using Regression

Let us now consider a demand time series that has a trend. A *trend* in a time series is a systematic increase or decrease in the average of the series over time. Where a significant trend is present, forecasts from naïve, moving average, and exponential smoothing approaches are adaptive, but still lag behind actual demand and tend to be below or above the actual demand.

Trend projection with regression is a forecasting model that accounts for the trend with simple regression analysis. To develop a regression model for forecasting the trend, let the dependent variable, Y, be a period's demand and the independent variable, t, be the time period. For the first period, let $t = 1$; for the second period, let $t = 2$; and so on. The regression equation is

$$F_t = a + bt$$

One advantage of the trend projection with regression model is that it can forecast demand well into the future. The previous models project demand just one period ahead, and assume that demand beyond that will remain at that same level. Of course, all of the models (including the trend projection with regression model) can be updated each period to stay current. One *apparent* disadvantage of the trend with regression model is that it is not adaptive. The solution to this problem comes when you answer the following question. If you had the past sales of Ford automobiles since 1920, would you include each year in your regression analysis, giving equal weight to each year's sales, or include just the sales for more recent years? You most likely would decide to include just the more recent years, making your regression model more adaptive. The trend projection with regression model can thus be made more or less adaptive by the selection of historical data periods to include in the same way that moving average (changing n) or exponential smoothing (changing α) models do.

The trend projection with regression model can be solved with either the *Trend Projection with Regression* Solver or the *Time Series Forecasting* Solver in OM Explorer. Both solvers provide the regression coefficients, coefficient of determination r^2, error measures, and forecasts into the future. POM for Windows has an alternative model (we do not cover in the text, although a description is provided in MyOMLab) that includes the trend, called the *Trend-Adjusted Smoothing* model.

MyOMLab

The *Trend Projection with Regression* Solver focuses exclusively on trend analysis. Its graph gives a big-picture view of how well the model fits the actual demand. Its sliders allow you to control when the regression begins, how many periods are included in the regression analysis, and how many periods you want forecasted into the future. The *Time Series Forecasting* Solver, on the other hand, covers all time series models, including the trend projection with regression. It also computes a combination forecast, which we cover in a subsequent section on using multiple techniques.

EXAMPLE 5

Using Trend Projection with Regression to Forecast a Demand Series with a Trend

Medanalysis, Inc., provides medical laboratory services to patients of Health Providers, a group of 10 family-practice doctors associated with a new health maintenance program. Managers are interested in forecasting the number of blood analysis requests per week. Recent publicity about the damaging effects of cholesterol on the heart has caused a national increase in requests for standard blood tests. The arrivals over the last 16 weeks are given in Table 1. What is the forecasted demand for the next three periods?

TABLE 1 | ARRIVALS AT MEDANALYSIS FOR LAST 16 WEEKS

Week	Arrivals	Week	Arrivals
1	28	9	61
2	27	10	39
3	44	11	55
4	37	12	54
5	35	13	52
6	53	14	60
7	38	15	60
8	57	16	75

SOLUTION

Figure 6(a) shows the results using the *Trend Projection with Regression* Solver when all 16 weeks are included in the regression analysis, with Figure 6(b) showing the worksheet that goes with it.

Looking at the Results sheet of Figure 6(a), we see that the Y intercept of the trend line (a) is 28.50 and the slope of the line (b) is 2.35. Thus, the trend equation is $F_t = a + bt$, where t is the time period for which you are forecasting. The forecast for period 19 is $28.5 + 2.35(19) = 73$. The error terms are CFE $= 0$ (which is to be expected when the regression begins at the same time that error analysis begins), MAD $= 6.21$, MSE $= 52.96$, and MAPE $= 13.53$ percent. The coefficient of determination r^2 is decent at 0.69. The trend line is rising gently and reaches 73 for period 19. Each period the forecast predicts an increase of 2.35 arrivals per week.

FIGURE 6(a) ▶
Trend Projection with Regression Results

Solver - Trend Projection with Regression

Regression begins in period	1
Error analysis begins in period	1
Number of future forecasts	3

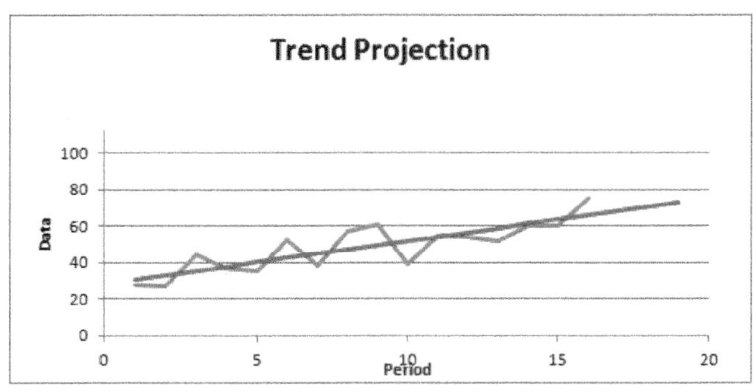

a (Y intercept)	28.50
b (slope or trend)	2.35
r2	0.69
CFE	0.00
MAD	6.21
MSE	52.96
MAPE	13.53%
Forecast for period 17	68.375
Forecast for period 18	70.72059
Forecast for period 19	73.06618

▼ **FIGURE 6(b)**
Detailed Calculations of Forecast Errors

				CFE	MSE	Averages MAD	MAPE
				0.000	**52.958**	**6.210**	**13.53%**
Period #	Actual Demand	Forecast	Error	Running CFE	Error Squared	Absolute Error	Abs % error
1	28	31	-2.846	-2.846	8.097	2.846	10.16%
2	27	33	-6.191	-9.037	38.331	6.191	22.93%
3	44	36	8.463	-0.574	71.626	8.463	19.23%
4	37	38	-0.882	-1.456	0.779	0.882	2.38%
5	35	40	-5.228	-6.684	27.331	5.228	14.94%
6	53	43	10.426	3.743	108.711	10.426	19.67%
7	38	45	-6.919	-3.176	47.874	6.919	18.21%
8	57	47	9.735	6.559	94.776	9.735	17.08%
9	61	50	11.390	17.949	129.725	11.390	18.67%
10	39	52	-12.956	4.993	167.855	12.956	33.22%
11	55	54	0.699	5.691	0.488	0.699	1.27%
12	54	57	-2.647	3.044	7.007	2.647	4.90%
13	52	59	-6.993	-3.949	48.897	6.993	13.45%
14	60	61	-1.338	-5.287	1.791	1.338	2.23%
15	60	64	-3.684	-8.971	13.571	3.684	6.14%
16	75	66	8.971	0.000	80.471	8.971	11.96%

Seasonal Patterns: Using Seasonal Factors

Seasonal patterns are regularly repeating upward or downward movements in demand measured in periods of less than one year (hours, days, weeks, months, or quarters). In this context, the time periods are called *seasons*. For example, customer arrivals at a fast-food shop on any day may peak between 11 A.M. and 1 P.M. and again from 5 P.M. to 7 P.M.

An easy way to account for seasonal effects is to use one of the techniques already described, but to limit the data in the time series to those time periods in the same season. For example, for a day-of-the-week seasonal effect, one time series would be for Mondays, one for Tuesdays, and so on. Such an approach accounts for seasonal effects, but has the disadvantage of discarding considerable information on past demand.

multiplicative seasonal method

A method whereby seasonal factors are multiplied by an estimate of average demand to arrive at a seasonal forecast.

Other methods are available that analyze all past data, using one model to forecast demand for all of the seasons. We describe only the **multiplicative seasonal method**, whereby an estimate of average demand is multiplied by seasonal factors to arrive at a seasonal forecast. The four-step procedure presented here involves the use of simple averages of past demand, although more sophisticated methods for calculating averages, such as a moving average or exponential smoothing approach, could be used. The following description is based on a seasonal pattern lasting one year and seasons of one month, although the procedure can be used for any seasonal pattern and season of any length.

1. For each year, calculate the average demand per season by dividing annual demand by the number of seasons per year.
2. For each year, divide the actual demand for a season by the average demand per season. The result is a *seasonal factor* for each season in the year, which indicates the level of demand relative to the average demand. For example, a seasonal factor of 1.14 calculated for April implies that April's demand is 14 percent greater than the average demand per month.
3. Calculate the average seasonal factor for each season, using the results from step 2. Add the seasonal factors for a season and divide by the number of years of data.
4. Calculate each season's forecast for next year. Begin by forecasting next year's annual demand using the naïve method, moving averages, exponential smoothing, or trend projection with regression. Then, divide annual demand by the number of seasons per year to get the average demand per season. Finally, make the seasonal forecast by multiplying the average demand per season by the appropriate seasonal factor found in step 3.

EXAMPLE 6 Using the Multiplicative Seasonal Method to Forecast the Number of Customers

The manager of the Stanley Steemer carpet cleaning company needs a quarterly forecast of the number of customers expected next year. The carpet cleaning business is seasonal, with a peak in the third quarter and a trough in the first quarter. The manager wants to forecast customer demand for each quarter of year 5, based on an estimate of total year 5 demand of 2,600 customers.

SOLUTION

The following table calculates the seasonal factor for each week.

It shows the quarterly demand data from the past 4 years, as well as the calculations performed to get the average seasonal factor for each quarter.

	YEAR 1		YEAR 2		YEAR 3		YEAR 4		
Quarter	Demand	Seasonal Factor (1)	Demand	Seasonal Factor (2)	Demand	Seasonal Factor (3)	Demand	Seasonal Factor (4)	Average Seasonal Factor [(1+2+3+4+)/4]
1	45	45/250 = 0.18	70	70/300 = 0.23333	100	100/450 = 0.22222	100	100/550 = 0.18182	0.2043
2	335	335/250 = 1.34	370	370/300 = 1.23333	585	585/450 = 1.30	725	725/550 = 1.31818	1.2979
3	520	520/250 = 2.08	590	590/300 = 1.96667	830	830/450 = 1.84444	1160	1160/550 = 2.10909	2.0001
4	100	100/250 = 0.40	170	170/300 = 0.56667	285	285/450 = 0.63333	215	215/550 = 0.39091	0.4977
Total	1,000		1,200		1,800		2,200		
Average	1,000/4 = 250		1,200/4 = 300		1,800/4 = 450		2,200/4 = 550		

For example, the seasonal factor for quarter 1 in year 1 is calculated by dividing the actual demand (45) by the average demand for the whole year $(1000/4 = 250)$. When this is done for all 4 years, we then can average the seasonal factors for quarter 1 over all 4 years. The result is a seasonal factor of 0.2043 for quarter 1.

Once seasonal factors are calculated for all four seasons (see last column in the table on the previous page), we then turn to making the forecasts for year 5. The manager suggests a forecast of 2,600 customers for the whole year, which seems reasonable given that the annual demand has been increasing by an average of 400 customers each year (from 1,000 in year 1 to 2,200 in year 4, or $1{,}200/3 = 400$). The computed forecast demand is found by extending that trend, and projecting an annual demand in year 5 of $2{,}200 + 400 = 2{,}600$ customers. (This same result is confirmed using the *Trend Projection with Regression* Solver of OM Explorer.) The quarterly forecasts are straight-forward. First, find the average demand forecast for year 5, which is $2{,}600/4 = 650$. Then multiple this average demand by the average seasonal index, giving us

Quarter	Forecast
1	$650 \times 0.2043 = 132.795$
2	$650 \times 1.2979 = 843.635$
3	$650 \times 2.0001 = 1{,}300.065$
4	$650 \times 0.4977 = 323.505$

Figure 7 shows the computer solution using the *Seasonal Forecasting* Solver in OM Explorer. Figure 7(b), the results, confirms all of the calculations made above. Notice in Figure 7(a), the inputs sheet that a computer demand forecast is provided as a default for year 5. However, there is an option for user-supplied demand forecast that overrides the computer-supplied forecast if the manager wishes to make a judgmental forecast based on additional information.

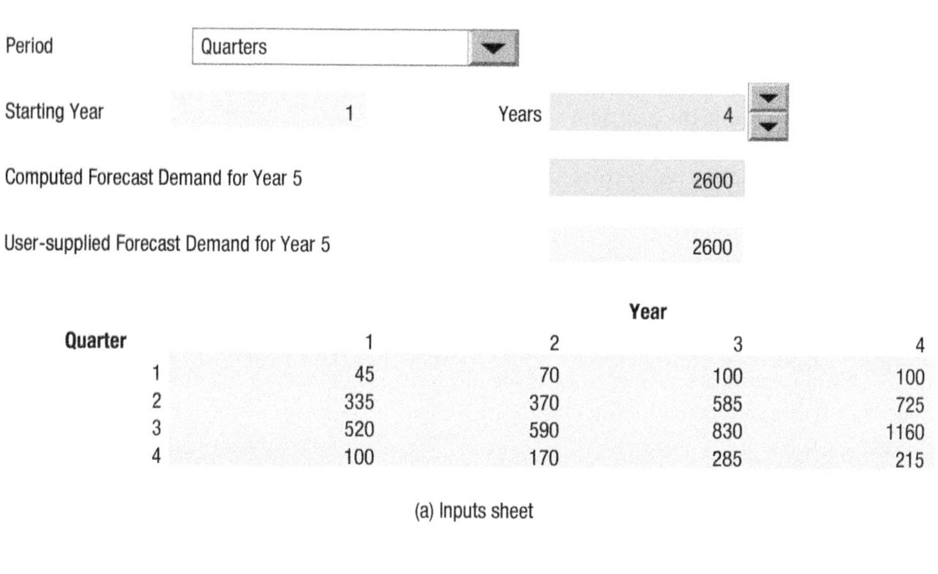

Quarter	Year 1	Year 2	Year 3	Year 4
1	45	70	100	100
2	335	370	585	725
3	520	590	830	1160
4	100	170	285	215

(a) Inputs sheet

Quarter	Seasonal Index	Forecast
1	0.2043	132.795
2	1.2979	843.635
3	2.0001	1300.065
4	0.4977	323.505

(b) Results

◀ **FIGURE 7**
Demand Forecasts Using the *Seasonal Forecasting* Solver of *OM Explorer*

DECISION POINT

Using this seasonal method, the analyst makes a demand forecast as low as 133 customers in the first quarter and as high as 1,300 customers in the third quarter. The season of the year clearly makes a difference.

additive seasonal method

A method in which seasonal forecasts are generated by adding a constant to the estimate of average demand per season.

An alternative to the multiplicative seasonal method is the **additive seasonal method**, whereby seasonal forecasts are generated by adding or subtracting a seasonal constant (say, 50 units) to the estimate of average demand per season. This approach is based on the assumption that the seasonal pattern is constant, regardless of average demand. The amplitude of the seasonal adjustment remains the same regardless of the level of demand.

Criteria for Selecting Time-Series Methods

Of all the time series forecasting methods available, which should be chosen? Forecast error measures provide important information for choosing the best forecasting method for a service or product. They also guide managers in selecting the best values for the parameters needed for the method: n for the moving average method, the weights for the weighted moving average method, α for the exponential smoothing method, and when regression data begins for the trend projection with regression method. The criteria to use in making forecast method and parameter choices include (1) minimizing bias (CFE); (2) minimizing MAPE, MAD, or MSE; (3) maximizing r^2 for trend projections using regression; (4) using a holdout sample analysis; (5) using a tracking signal; (6) meeting managerial expectations of changes in the components of demand; and (7) minimizing the forecast errors in recent periods. The first three criteria relate to statistical measures based on historical performance, the fourth is a test under realistic conditions, the fifth evaluates forecast performance and the potential need to change the method, the sixth reflects expectations of the future that may not be rooted in the past, and the seventh is a way to use whatever method seems to be working best at the time a forecast must be made.

Using Statistical Criteria Statistical performance measures can be used in the selection of which forecasting method to use. The following guidelines will help when searching for the best time-series models:

1. For projections of more stable demand patterns, use lower α values or larger n values to emphasize historical experience.
2. For projections of more dynamic demand patterns using the models covered in this chapter, try higher α values or smaller n values. When historical demand patterns are changing, recent history should be emphasized.

holdout sample

Actual demands from the more recent time periods in the time series that are set aside to test different models developed from the earlier time periods.

Using a Holdout Sample Often, the forecaster must make trade-offs between bias (CFE) and the measures of forecast error dispersion (MAPE, MAD, and MSE). Managers also must recognize that the best technique in explaining the past data is not necessarily the best technique to predict the future, and that "overfitting" past data can be deceptive. A forecasting method may have small errors relative to the history file, but may generate high errors for future time periods. For this reason, some analysts prefer to use a **holdout sample** as a final test (see Experiential Learning Exercise 1 at the end of this chapter). To do so, they set aside some of the more recent periods from the time series and use only the earlier time periods to develop and test different models. Once the final models have been selected in the first phase, they are tested again with the holdout sample. Performance measures, such as MAD and CFE, would still be used but they would be applied to the holdout sample. Whether this idea is used or not, managers should monitor future forecast errors, and modify their forecasting approaches as needed. Maintaining data on forecast performance is the ultimate test of forecasting power—rather than how well a model fits past data or holdout samples.

tracking signal

A measure that indicates whether a method of forecasting is accurately predicting actual changes in demand.

Using a Tracking Signal A **tracking signal** is a measure that indicates whether a method of forecasting is accurately predicting actual changes in demand. The tracking signal measures the number of MADs represented by the cumulative sum of forecast errors, the CFE. The CFE tends to be close to 0 when a correct forecasting system is being used. At any time, however, random errors can cause the CFE to be a nonzero number. The tracking signal formula is

$$\text{Tracking signal} = \frac{\text{CFE}}{\text{MAD}} \text{ or } \frac{\text{CFE}}{\text{MAD}_t}$$

Each period, the CFE and MAD are updated to reflect current error, and the tracking signal is compared to some predetermined limits. The MAD can be calculated in one of two ways: (1) as the simple average of all absolute errors (as demonstrated in Example 1) or (2) as a weighted average determined by the exponential smoothing method:

$$\text{MAD}_t = \alpha|E_t| + (1 - \alpha)\text{MAD}_{t-1}$$

If forecast errors are normally distributed with a mean of 0, the relationship between σ and MAD is simple:

$$\sigma = \left(\sqrt{\pi/2}\right)(\text{MAD}) \cong 1.25(\text{MAD})$$

$$\text{MAD} = 0.7978\sigma \cong 0.8\sigma$$

where

$$\pi = 3.1416$$

This relationship allows use of the normal probability tables to specify limits for the tracking signal. If the tracking signal falls outside those limits, the forecasting model no longer is tracking demand adequately. A tracking system is useful when forecasting systems are computerized because it alerts analysts when forecasts are getting far from desirable limits. Figure 8 shows tracking signal results for 23 periods plotted on a *control chart.* The control chart is useful for determining whether any action needs to be taken to improve the forecasting model. In the example, the first 20 points cluster around 0, as we would expect if the forecasts are not biased. The CFE will tend toward 0. When the underlying characteristics of demand change but the forecasting model does not, the tracking signal eventually goes out of control. The steady increase after the 20th point in Figure 8 indicates that the process is going out of control. The 21st and 22nd points are acceptable, but the 23rd point is not.

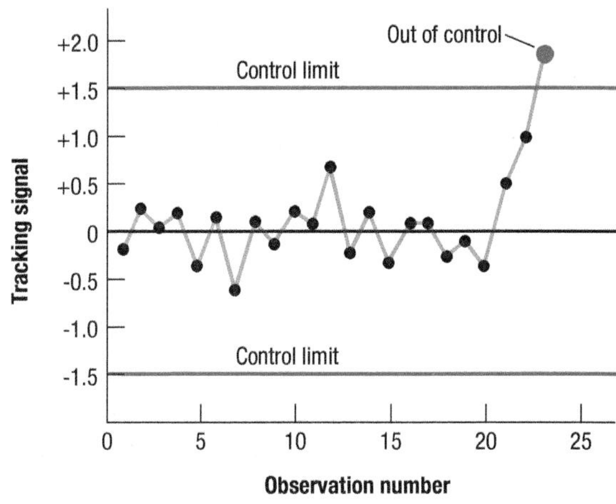

▲ FIGURE 8
Tracking Signal

Forecasting as a Process

Often companies must prepare forecasts for hundreds or even thousands of services or products repeatedly. For example, a large network of health care facilities must calculate demand forecasts for each of its services for every department. This undertaking involves voluminous data that must be manipulated frequently. However, software can ease the burden of making these forecasts and coordinating the forecasts between customers and suppliers. Many forecasting software packages are available, including Manugistics, Forecast Pro, and SAS. The forecasting routines in OM Explorer and POM for Windows give some hint of their capabilities. Forecasting is not just a set of techniques, but instead a process that must be designed and managed. While there is no one process that works for everyone, here we describe two comprehensive processes that can be quite effective in managing operations and the supply chain.

A Typical Forecasting Process

Many *inputs* to the forecasting process are informational, beginning with the *history file* on past demand. The history file is kept up-to-date with the actual demands. Clarifying notes and adjustments are made to the database to explain unusual demand behavior, such as the impact of special promotions and closeouts. Often the database is separated into two parts: *base* data and *nonbase* data. The second category reflects irregular demands. Final forecasts just made at the end of the prior cycle are entered in the history file so as to track forecast errors. Other information sources are from salesforce estimates, outstanding bids on new orders, booked orders, market research studies, competitor behavior, economic outlook, new product introductions, pricing, and promotions. If point-of-sale data are used, as is done by Kimberly-Clark in the opening vignette, then considerable information sharing will take place with customers. For new products, a history database is fabricated based on the firm's experience with prior products and the judgment of personnel.

Outputs of the process are forecasts for multiple time periods into the future. Typically, they are on a monthly basis and are projected out from six months to two years. Most software packages have the ability to "roll up" or "aggregate" forecasts for individual stock-keeping units (SKUs) into forecasts for whole product families. Forecasts can also be "blown down" or "disaggregated" into smaller pieces. In a make-to-stock environment, forecasts tend to be more detailed and can get down to specific individual products. In a make-to-order environment, the forecasts tend to be for groups of products. Similarly, if the lead times to buy raw materials and manufacture a product or provide a service are long, the forecasts go farther out into the future.

The forecast process itself, typically done on a monthly basis, consists of structured steps. These steps often are facilitated by someone who might be called a demand manager, forecast analyst, or demand/supply planner. However, many other people are typically involved before the plan for the month is authorized.

Step 1. The cycle begins mid-month just after the forecasts have been finalized and communicated to the stakeholders. Now is the time to update the history file and review forecast accuracy. At the end of the month, enter actual demand and review forecast accuracy.

Step 2. Prepare initial forecasts using some forecasting software package and judgment. Adjust the parameters of the software to find models that fit the past demand well and yet reflect the demand

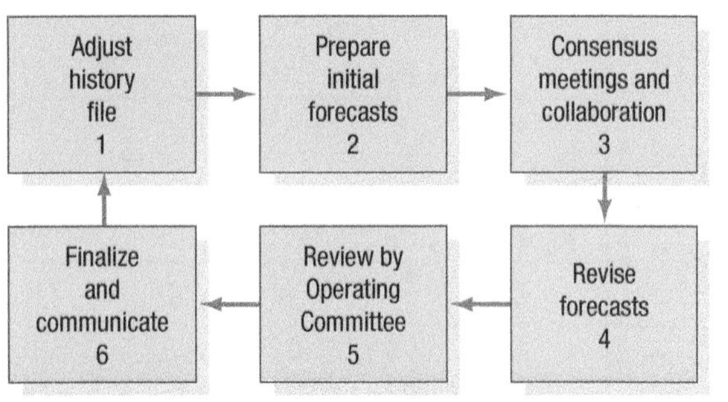

manager's judgment on irregular events and information about future sales pulled from various sources and business units.

Step 3. Hold consensus meetings with the stakeholders, such as marketing, sales, supply chain planners, and finance. Make it easy for business unit and field sales personnel to make inputs. Use the Internet to get collaborative information from key customers and suppliers. The goal is to arrive at consensus forecasts from all of the important players.

Step 4. Revise the forecasts using judgment, considering the inputs from the consensus meetings and collaborative sources.

Step 5. Present the forecasts to the operating committee for review and to reach a final set of forecasts. It is important to have a set of forecasts that everybody agrees upon and will work to support.

Step 6. Finalize the forecasts based on the decisions of the operating committee and communicate them to the important stakeholders. Supply chain planners are usually the biggest users.

As with all work activity, forecasting is a process and should be continually reviewed for improvements. A better process will foster better relationships between departments such as marketing, sales, and operations. It will also produce better forecasts. This principle is the first one in Table 2 to guide process improvements.

TABLE 2 | SOME PRINCIPLES FOR THE FORECASTING PROCESS

- Better processes yield better forecasts.
- Demand forecasting is being done in virtually every company, either formally or informally. The challenge is to do it well—better than the competition.
- Better forecasts result in better customer service and lower costs, as well as better relationships with suppliers and customers.
- The forecast can and must make sense based on the big picture, economic outlook, market share, and so on.
- The best way to improve forecast accuracy is to focus on reducing forecast error.
- Bias is the worst kind of forecast error; strive for zero bias.
- Whenever possible, forecast at more aggregate levels. Forecast in detail only where necessary.
- Far more can be gained by people collaborating and communicating well than by using the most advanced forecasting technique or model.

Source: From Thomas F. Wallace and Robert A. Stahl, *Sales Forecasting: A New Approach* (Cincinnati, OH: T. E. Wallace & Company, 2002), p. 112. Copyright © 2002 T.E. Wallace & Company. Used with permission.

Using Multiple Forecasting Methods

Step 2 of the forecasting process relates to preparing an initial forecast. However, we need not rely on a single forecasting method. Several different forecasts can be used to arrive at a forecast. Initial statistical forecasts using several time-series methods and regression are distributed to knowledgeable individuals, such as marketing directors and sales teams, (and sometimes even suppliers and customers) for their adjustments. They can account for current market and customer conditions that are not necessarily reflected in past data. Multiple forecasts may come from different sales teams, and some teams may have a better record on forecast errors than others.

combination forecasts

Forecasts that are produced by averaging independent forecasts based on different methods, different sources, or different data.

Research during the last two decades suggests that combining forecasts from multiple sources often produces more accurate forecasts. **Combination forecasts** are forecasts that are produced by averaging independent forecasts based on different methods, different sources, or different data. It is intriguing that combination forecasts often perform better over time than even the *best* single forecasting procedure. For example, suppose that the forecast for the next period is 100 units from technique 1 and 120 units from technique 2 and that technique 1 has provided more accurate forecasts to date. The combination forecast for next period, giving equal weight to each technique, is 110 units (or $0.5 \times 100 + 0.5 \times 120$). When this averaging technique is used consistently into the future, its combination forecasts often will be much more accurate than those of any single best forecasting technique (in this example, technique 1). Combining is most effective when the individual forecasts bring different kinds of information into the forecasting process. Forecasters have achieved excellent results by weighting forecasts equally, and this is a good starting point. However, unequal weights may provide better results under some conditions. Managerial Practice 1 shows how Fiskars Corporation successfully used combination forecasts.

MANAGERIAL PRACTICE 1 Combination Forecasts and the Forecasting Process

Fiskars Corporation, which generated more than $1.1 billion in sales in 2013, is the second oldest incorporated entity in the world and produces a variety of high-quality products such as garden shears, pruners, hand tools, scissors, ratchet tools, screwdrivers, and the like. Business is highly seasonal and prices quite variable. About 10 percent to 15 percent of the annual revenue comes from one-time promotions, and 25 percent to 35 percent of its products are new every year. Quality is very important at Fiskars; its scissors were selected as the Official Net-Cutting Scissors of the NCAA National Championship in 2014.

Given the highly volatile demand environment, Fiskars Brands, Inc., a subsidiary of Fiskars Corporation located in Madison, Wisconsin, needed to improve its forecasting process. It serves 2,000 customers ranging from large discounters to local craft stores providing about 2,300 products. Fiskars Brands introduced a statistical-based analysis in its forecasting process along with a Web-based business intelligence tool for reporting. It put much more emphasis on combination forecasts. Instead of asking members of the sales staff to provide their own forecasts, forecasts were sent to them, and they were asked for their validation and refinement. Their inputs are most useful relative to additions, deletions, and promotions. Converting multiple forecasts into one number (forecasts from time-series techniques, sales input, and customer input) creates more accurate forecasts by product. Fiskars's software has the ability to weigh each input. It gives more weight to a statistical forecast for in-line items, and inputs from the sales staff get much more weight for promoted products and new items.

It also segments products by value and forecastability so as to concentrate forecasting efforts on products that have the biggest impact on the business. High-value items that are easier to forecast (stable demand with low forecast errors to date) tend to do well with the time-series techniques, and **judgmental adjustments** are made with caution. High-value items that are difficult to forecast get top priority in the forecasting effort, and spark the need for collaboration with customers and suppliers. Much less attention is given to improving forecasts for low-value items for which there is some history and fairly steady demand.

Finally, Fiskars instituted a Web-based program that gives the entire company visibility to forecast information in whatever form it needs. For example, Finance wants monthly, quarterly, and yearly projections in dollars, whereas Operations wants projections in units as well as accuracy measures. Everybody can track updated forecast information by customer, brand, and product.

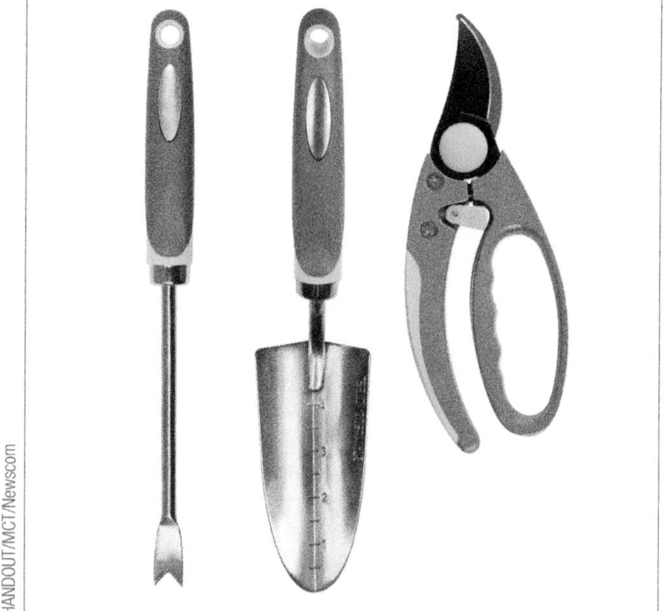

HANDOUT/MCT/Newscom

Fiskars Brands, Inc. totally overhauled its forecasting process for products such as those shown here. It introduced time-series methods, with much emphasis placed on combination forecasts. Sales staff added their judgmental modifications, which were combined with forecasts from several time-series techniques to produce more accurate forecasts down to the level of the product.

Source: David Montgomery, "Flashpoints for Changing Your Forecasting Process," *The Journal of Business Forecasting*, (Winter 2006–2007), pp. 35–37; **http://www.fiskars.com**, April 15, 2014.

OM Explorer and POM for Windows allow you to evaluate several forecasting models, and then you can create combination forecasts from them. In fact, the *Time-Series Forecasting* Solver of OM Explorer automatically computes a combination forecast as a weighted average, using the weights that you supply for the various models that it evaluates. The models include the naïve, moving average, exponential smoothing, and regression projector methods. Alternately, you can create a simple Excel spreadsheet that combines forecasts generated by POM for Windows to create combination forecasts. The *Time Series Forecasting* Solver also allows you evaluate your forecasting process with a holdout sample. The forecaster makes a forecast just one period ahead, and learns of given actual demand. Next the solver computes forecasts and forecast errors for the period. The process continues to the next period in the holdout sample with the forecaster committing to a forecast for the next period. To be informed, the forecaster should also be aware of how well the other forecasting methods have been performing, particularly in the recent past.

judgmental adjustment
An adjustment made to forecasts from one or more quantitative models that accounts for recognizing which models are performing particularly well in recent past, or take into account contextual information.

Another way to take advantage of multiple techniques is **focus forecasting**, which selects the best forecast (based on past error measures) from a group of forecasts generated by individual techniques. Every period, all techniques are used to make forecasts for each item. The forecasts are made with a computer because there can be 100,000 SKUs at a company, each needing to be forecast. Using the history file as the starting point for each method, the computer generates forecasts for the current period. The

focus forecasting
A method of forecasting that selects the best forecast from a group of forecasts generated by individual techniques.

Mark Peterson/CORBIS

Ever wonder how CPFR came into existence? Walmart has long been known for its careful analysis of cash register receipts and for working with suppliers to reduce inventories. To combat the ill effects of forecast errors on inventories, Benchmarking Partners, Inc. was funded in the mid-1990s by Walmart, IBM, SAP, and Manugistics to develop a software package. Walmart initiated the new system with Listerine, a primary product of Warner-Lambert (now produced by Johnson & Johnson). How did it work? Walmart and Warner-Lambert independently calculated the demand they expected for Listerine six months into the future, taking into consideration factors such as past sales trends and sales promotions. If the forecasts differed by more than a predetermined percentage, they exchanged written comments and supporting data. They went through as many cycles as needed to converge to an acceptable forecast. The program was successful; Walmart saw a reduction in stockouts from 15 percent to 2 percent, increased sales, and reduced inventory costs, while Warner-Lambert benefitted from a smoother production plan and lower average costs. The system was later generalized and called collaborative planning, forecasting, and replenishment, or CPFR.

forecasts are compared to actual demand, and the method that produces the forecast with the least error is used to make the forecast for the next period. The method used for each item may change from period to period.

Adding Collaboration to the Process

In step three of the forecasting process we try to achieve consensus of the forecast. One way to achieve that consensus in a formal way is to employ **collaborative planning, forecasting, and replenishment (CPFR)**, a process for supply chain integration that allows a supplier and its customers to collaborate on making the forecast by using the Internet. Traditionally, suppliers and buyers in most supply chains prepare independent demand forecasts. With CPFR, firms initiate customer-focused operations teams that share with retailers their real-time data and plans, including forecasts, inventories, sales to retailers' shelves, promotions, product plans, and exceptions. CPFR involves four interactive activities:

- **Strategy and Planning:** establish the ground rules for the collaborative relationship such as business goals, scope of collaboration, and assignment of roles and responsibilities.
- **Demand and Supply Management:** develop sales forecasts, procedures for order planning, and inventory positions.
- **Execution:** manage the generation of orders between supplier and customers and the production, shipment, and delivery of products for customer purchase.
- **Analysis:** monitor the planning process and operations for out of bound conditions and evaluate to achievement of business goals.

collaborative planning, forecasting, and replenishment (CPFR)

A process for supply chain integration that allows a supplier and its customers to collaborate on making the forecast by using the Internet.

Many firms have used CPFR to coordinate forecasts and plans up and down the supply chain. CPFR enables firms to collaborate with their retailers' distribution centers' customers and increase their ability to forecast effectively. The real key to a successful implementation of CPFR is the forging of a cultural alliance that involves peer-to peer relations and cross-functional teams.

Forecasting as a Nested Process

Forecasting is not a stand-alone activity. After all, demand is only half of the equation—the other half is supply. Future plans must be developed to supply the resources needed to meet the forecasted demand. Resources include the workforce, materials, inventories, dollars, and equipment capacity.

LEARNING GOALS IN REVIEW

Learning Goal	Guidelines for Review	MyOMLab Resources
1 Explain how managers can change demand patterns.	Review the section "Managing Demand," Focus on "Demand Management Options," and the eight ways managers can change demand patterns.	
2 Describe the two key decisions on making forecasts.	In the section "Key Decisions on Making Forecasts" focus on the considerations for deciding what to forecast and choosing the right forecasting technique.	
3 Calculate the five basic measures of forecast errors.	Review the section "Forecast Error" to understand CFE, MSE, σ, MAD, and MAPE. Study Figures 2 (a) and (b) for an example. Solved Problem 2 shows an example of MAD and Solved Problem 3 shows MAD and MAPE.	**POM for Windows:** Error Analysis
4 Compare and contrast the four approaches to judgmental forecasting.	The section "Judgment Methods" explains the differences between salesforce estimates, executive opinion, market research, and the Delphi method.	
5 Use regression to make forecasts with one or more independent variables.	The "Causal Methods: Linear Regression" section, and Example 2, describe how linear regression, when historical data is available, can express demand as a linear function of one or more independent variables. The computer is an essential tool for linear regression. In addition to Example 2, Solved Problem 1 provides the statistics on how well the regression equation fits the data.	**Active Model:** 1: Linear Regression **OM Explorer Solver:** Regression Analysis **POM for Windows:** Least Squares – Simple and Multiple Regression **POM for Windows:** Regression Projector
6 Make forecasts using the five most common statistical approaches for time-series analysis.	The "Time-Series Methods" explains the naïve method and the five statistical methods of simple moving average, weighted moving average, exponential smoothing, trend projection with regression, and multiplicative seasonal method that are used. Examples 3, 4, 5, and 6 demonstrate the methods, as do Solved Problems 2, 3 and 4. Also see Experiential Learning 1 for an in-class exercise requiring the use of time-series models to prepare a combination forecast.	**Active Models:** 2: Simple Moving Averages; 3: Exponential Smoothing **OM Explorer Tutors:** 1: Moving Average Method; 2: Weighted Moving Average Method; 3: Exponential Smoothing **OM Explorer Solvers:** Time Series Forecasting; Trend Projection with Regression; Seasonal Forecasting **POM for Windows:** Time Series Analysis **Student Data File:** Experiential Exercise 1 Data
7 Describe the six steps in a typical forecasting process.	See the section "Forecasting as a Process" and the six steps involved. There is much more complexity when you realize the number of SKUs involved and the need to update the history file. Be sure to understand how combination forecasts work into step 2 and how CPFR is integral to step 3.	**Video:** Forecasting and Supply Chain Management at Deckers Outdoor Corporation

Key Equations

Forecast Error

1. Forecast error measures:

$$E_t = D_t - F_t$$

$$\text{CFE} = \sum E_t$$

$$\bar{E} = \frac{\text{CFE}}{n}$$

$$\text{MSE} = \frac{\sum E_t^2}{n}$$

$$\sigma = \sqrt{\frac{\Sigma(E_t - \bar{E})^2}{n - 1}}$$

$$\text{MAD} = \frac{\Sigma|E_t|}{n}$$

$$\text{MAPE} = \frac{(\Sigma|E_t|/D_t)(100\%)}{n}$$

Causal Methods: Linear Regression

2. Linear regression:

$$Y = a + bX$$

Time-Series Methods

3. Naïve forecasting:

$$\text{Forecast} = D_t$$

4. Simple moving average:

$$F_{t+1} = \frac{D_t + D_{t-1} + D_{t-2} + \cdots + D_{t-n+1}}{n}$$

5. Weighted moving average:

$$F_{t+1} = \text{Weight}_1(D_t) + \text{Weight}_2(D_{t-1}) + \text{Weight}_3(D_{t-2}) + \cdots + \text{Weight}_n(D_{t-n+1})$$

6. Exponential smoothing:

$$F_{t+1} = \alpha D_t + (1 - \alpha)F_t$$

7. Trend Projection using Regression

$$F_t = a + bt$$

8. Tracking signal:

$$\frac{\text{CFE}}{\text{MAD}} \text{ or } \frac{\text{CFE}}{\text{MAD}_t}$$

9. Exponentially smoothed error:

$$\text{MAD}_t = \alpha|E_t| + (1 - \alpha)\text{MAD}_{t-1}$$

Key Terms

additive seasonal method
aggregation
backlog
backorder
causal methods
collaborative planning, forecasting, and replenishment (CPFR)
combination forecasts
complementary products
cumulative sum of forecast errors (CFE)
demand management
dependent variable
Delphi method
executive opinion
exponential smoothing method
focus forecasting
forecast
forecast error
holdout sample
independent variables
judgment methods
judgmental adjustment
linear regression
market research
mean absolute deviation (MAD)
mean absolute percent error (MAPE)
mean squared error (MSE)
multiplicative seasonal method
naïve forecast
revenue management
salesforce estimates
simple moving average method
standard deviation of the errors (σ)
stockout
technological forecasting
time series
time-series analysis
tracking signal
trend projection with regression
weighted moving average method

Solved Problem 1

Chicken Palace periodically offers carryout five-piece chicken dinners at special prices. Let Y be the number of dinners sold and X be the price. Based on the historical observations and calculations in the following table, determine the regression equation, correlation coefficient, and coefficient of determination. How many dinners can Chicken Palace expect to sell at \$3.00 each?

Observation	Price (X)	Dinners Sold (Y)
1	\$2.70	760
2	\$3.50	510
3	\$2.00	980
4	\$4.20	250
5	\$3.10	320
6	\$4.05	480
Total	\$19.55	3,300
Average	\$3.258	550

SOLUTION

We use the computer (*Regression Analysis* Solver of OM Explorer or *Regression Projector* module of POM for Windows) to calculate the best values of a, b, the correlation coefficient, and the coefficient of determination.

$$\begin{aligned} a &= 1{,}454.60 \\ b &= -277.63 \\ r &= -0.84 \\ r^2 &= 0.71 \end{aligned}$$

The regression line is

$$Y = a + bX = 1{,}454.60 - 277.63X$$

The correlation coefficient ($r = -0.84$) shows a negative correlation between the variables. The coefficient of determination ($r^2 = 0.71$) is not too large, which suggests that other variables (in addition to price) might appreciably affect sales.

If the regression equation is satisfactory to the manager, estimated sales at a price of \$3.00 per dinner may be calculated as follows:

$$\begin{aligned} Y &= a + bX = 1{,}454.60 - 277.63(3.00) \\ &= 621.71 \text{ or } 622 \text{ dinners} \end{aligned}$$

Solved Problem 2

The Polish General's Pizza Parlor is a small restaurant catering to patrons with a taste for European pizza. One of its specialties is Polish Prize pizza. The manager must forecast weekly demand for these special pizzas so that he can order pizza shells weekly. Recently, demand has been as follows:

Week	Pizzas	Week	Pizzas
June 2	50	June 23	56
June 9	65	June 30	55
June 16	52	July 7	60

a. Forecast the demand for pizza for June 23 to July 14 by using the simple moving average method with $n = 3$. Then, repeat the forecast by using the weighted moving average method with $n = 3$ and weights of 0.50, 0.30, and 0.20, with 0.50 applying to the most recent demand.

b. Calculate the MAD for each method.

SOLUTION

a. The simple moving average method and the weighted moving average method give the following results:

Current Week	Simple Moving Average Forecast for Next Week	Weighted Moving Average Forecast for Next Week
June 16	$\frac{52 + 65 + 50}{3} = 55.7$ or 56	$[(0.5 \times 52) + (0.3 \times 65) + (0.2 \times 50)] = 55.5$ or 56
June 23	$\frac{56 + 52 + 65}{3} = 55.7$ or 58	$[(0.5 \times 56) + (0.3 \times 52) + (0.2 \times 65)] = 56.6$ or 57
June 30	$\frac{55 + 56 + 52}{3} = 54.3$ or 54	$[(0.5 \times 55) + (0.3 \times 56) + (0.2 \times 52)] = 54.7$ or 55
July 7	$\frac{60 + 55 + 56}{3} = 57.0$ or 57	$[(0.5 \times 60) + (0.3 \times 55) + (0.2 \times 56)] = 57.7$ or 58

Forecasts in each row are for the next week's demand. For example, the simple moving average and weighted moving average forecasts (both are 56 units) calculated after learning the demand on June 16 apply to June 23's demand forecast.

b. The mean absolute deviation is calculated as follows:

		SIMPLE MOVING AVERAGE		WEIGHTED MOVING AVERAGE	
Week	**Actual Demand**	**Forecast for This Week**	**Absolute Errors $\|E_t\|$**	**Forecast for This Week**	**Absolute Errors $\|E_t\|$**
June 23	56	56	$\|56 - 56\| = 0$	56	$\|56 - 56\| = 0$
June 30	55	58	$\|55 - 58\| = 3$	57	$\|55 - 57\| = 2$
July 7	60	54	$\|60 - 54\| = 6$	55	$\|60 - 55\| = 5$
			$\text{MAD} = \frac{0 + 3 + 6}{3} = 3.0$		$\text{MAD} = \frac{0 + 2 + 5}{3} = 2.3$

For this limited set of data, the weighted moving average method resulted in a slightly lower mean absolute deviation. However, final conclusions can be made only after analyzing much more data.

Solved Problem 3

MyOMLab Video

The monthly demand for units manufactured by the Acme Rocket Company has been as follows:

Month	Units	Month	Units
May	100	September	105
June	80	October	110
July	110	November	125
August	115	December	120

a. Use the exponential smoothing method to forecast the number of units for June to January. The initial forecast for May was 105 units; $\alpha = 0.2$.

b. Calculate the absolute percentage error for each month from June through December and the MAD and MAPE of forecast error as of the end of December.

c. Calculate the tracking signal as of the end of December. What can you say about the performance of your forecasting method?

SOLUTION

a.

Current Month, t	Calculating Forecast for Next Month $F_{t+1} = \alpha D_t + (1 - \alpha)F_t$	Forecast for Month $t + 1$
May	0.2(100) + 0.8(105) = 104.0 or 104	June
June	0.2(80) + 0.8(104.0) = 99.2 or 99	July
July	0.2(110) + 0.8(99.2) = 101.4 or 101	August
August	0.2(115) + 0.8(101.4) = 104.1 or 104	September
September	0.2(105) + 0.8(104.1) = 104.3 or 104	October
October	0.2(110) + 0.8(104.3) = 105.4 or 105	November
November	0.2(125) + 0.8(105.4) = 109.3 or 109	December
December	0.2(120) + 0.8(109.3) = 111.4 or 111	January

b.

Month, t	Actual Demand, D_t	Forecast, F_t	Error, $E_t = D_t - F_t$	Absolute Error, $\lvert E_t \rvert$	Absolute Percentage Error, $(\lvert E_t \rvert / D_t)(100\%)$
June	80	104	−24	24	30.0%
July	110	99	11	11	10.0
August	115	101	14	14	12.0
September	105	104	1	1	1.0
October	110	104	6	6	5.5
November	125	105	20	0	16.0
December	120	109	11	11	9.2
Total	765		39	87	83.7%

$$\text{MAD} = \frac{\Sigma \lvert E_t \rvert}{n} = \frac{87}{7} = 12.4 \text{ and MAPE} = \frac{(\Sigma \lvert E_t \rvert / D_t)(100)}{n} = \frac{83.7\%}{7} = 11.96\%$$

c. As of the end of December, the cumulative sum of forecast errors (CFE) is 39. Using the mean absolute deviation calculated in part (b), we calculate the tracking signal:

$$\text{Tracking signal} = \frac{\text{CFE}}{\text{MAD}} = \frac{39}{12.4} = 3.14$$

The probability that a tracking signal value of 3.14 could be generated completely by chance is small. Consequently, we should revise our approach. The long string of forecasts lower than actual demand suggests use of a trend method.

Solved Problem 4

The Northville Post Office experiences a seasonal pattern of daily mail volume every week. The following data for two representative weeks are expressed in thousands of pieces of mail:

Day	Week 1	Week 2
Sunday	5	8
Monday	20	15
Tuesday	30	32
Wednesday	35	30
Thursday	49	45
Friday	70	70
Saturday	15	10
Total	224	210

a. Calculate a seasonal factor for each day of the week.

b. If the postmaster estimates 230,000 pieces of mail to be sorted next week, forecast the volume for each day of the week.

SOLUTION

a. Calculate the average daily mail volume for each week. Then, for each day of the week, divide the mail volume by the week's average to get the seasonal factor. Finally, for each day, add the two seasonal factors and divide by 2 to obtain the average seasonal factor to use in the forecast (see part [b]).

	WEEK 1		WEEK 2		
Day	**Mail Volume**	**Seasonal Factor (1)**	**Mail Volume**	**Seasonal Factor (2)**	**Average Seasonal Factor [(1) + (2)]/2**
Sunday	5	5/32 = 0.15625	8	8/30 = 0.26667	0.21146
Monday	20	20/32 = 0.62500	15	15/30 = 0.50000	0.56250
Tuesday	30	30/32 = 0.93750	32	32/30 = 1.06667	1.00209
Wednesday	35	35/32 = 1.09375	30	30/30 = 1.00000	1.04688
Thursday	49	49/32 = 1.53125	45	45/30 = 1.50000	1.51563
Friday	70	70/32 = 2.18750	70	70/30 = 2.33333	2.26042
Saturday	15	15/32 = 0.46875	10	10/30 = 0.33333	0.40104
Total	224		210		
Average	224/7 = 32		210/7 = 30		

b. The average daily mail volume is expected to be 230,000/7 = 32,857 pieces of mail. Using the average seasonal factors calculated in part (a), we obtain the following forecasts:

Day	**Calculation**		**Forecast**
Sunday	0.21146(32,857) =		6,948
Monday	0.56250(32,857) =		18,482
Tuesday	1.00209(32,857) =		32,926
Wednesday	1.04688(32,857) =		34,397
Thursday	1.51563(32,857) =		49,799
Friday	2.26042(32,857) =		74,271
Saturday	0.40104(32,857) =		13,177
		Total	230,000

Discussion Questions

1. Figure 9 shows summer air visibility measurements for Denver, Colorado. The acceptable visibility standard is 100, with readings above 100 indicating clean air and good visibility, and readings below 100 indicating temperature inversions caused by forest fires, volcanic eruptions, or collisions with comets.

   a. Is a trend evident in the data? Which time-series techniques might be appropriate for estimating the average of these data?

   b. A medical center for asthma and respiratory diseases located in Denver has great demand for its services when air quality is poor. If you were in charge of developing a short-term (say, 3-day) forecast of visibility, which causal factor(s) would you analyze? In other words, which external factors hold the potential to significantly affect visibility in the *short term*?

   c. Tourism, an important factor in Denver's economy, is affected by the city's image. Air quality, as measured by visibility, affects the city's image. If you were responsible for development of tourism, which causal factor(s) would you analyze to forecast visibility for the *medium term* (say, the next two summers)?

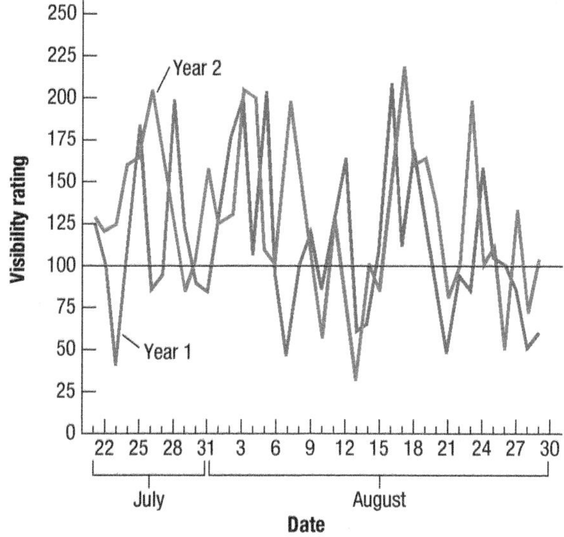

▲ FIGURE 9
Summer Air Visibility Measurements

d. The federal government threatens to withhold several hundred million dollars in Department of Transportation funds unless Denver meets visibility standards within 8 years. How would you proceed to generate a *long-term* judgment forecast of technologies that will be available to improve visibility in the next 10 years?

2. Kay and Michael Passe publish *What's Happening?*—a biweekly newspaper to publicize local events. *What's Happening?* has few subscribers; it typically is sold at checkout stands. Much of the revenue comes from advertisers of garage sales and supermarket specials. In an effort to reduce costs associated with printing too many papers or delivering them to the wrong location, Michael implemented a computerized system to collect sales data. Sales-counter scanners accurately record sales data for each location. Since the system was implemented, total sales volume has steadily declined. Selling advertising space and maintaining shelf space at supermarkets are getting more difficult.

Reduced revenue makes controlling costs all the more important. For each issue, Michael carefully makes a forecast based on sales data collected at each location. Then, he orders papers to be printed and distributed in quantities matching the forecast. Michael's forecast reflects a downward trend, which *is* present in the sales data. Now only a few papers are left over at only a few locations. Although the sales forecast accurately predicts the actual sales at most locations, *What's Happening?* is spiraling toward oblivion. Kay suspects that Michael is doing something wrong in preparing the forecast but can find no mathematical errors. Tell her what is happening.

Problems

The OM Explorer and POM for Windows software is available to all students using this text. Go to **http://www.pearsonhighered.com/krajewski** to download these computer packages. If you purchased MyOMLab, you also have access to Active Models software and significant help in doing the following problems. Check with your instructor on how best to use these resources. In many cases, the instructor wants you to understand how to do the calculations by hand. At the least, the software provides a check on your calculations. When calculations are particularly complex and the goal is interpreting the results in making decisions, the software entirely replaces the manual calculations.

Causal Methods: Linear Regression

1. Demand for oil changes at Garcia's Garage has been as follows:

Month	Number of Oil Changes
January	41
February	46
March	57
April	52
May	59
June	51
July	60
August	62

a. Use simple linear regression analysis to develop a forecasting model for monthly demand. In this application, the dependent variable, Y, is monthly demand and the independent variable, X, is the month. For January, let $X = 1$; for February, let $X = 2$; and so on.

b. Use the model to forecast demand for September, October, and November. Here, $X = 9, 10$, and 11, respectively.

2. At a hydrocarbon processing factory, process control involves periodic analysis of samples for a certain process quality parameter. The analytic procedure currently used is costly and time consuming. A faster and more economical alternative procedure has been proposed. However, the numbers for the quality parameter given by the alternative procedure are somewhat different from those given by the current procedure, not because of any inherent errors but because of changes in the nature of the chemical analysis.

Management believes that if the numbers from the new procedure can be used to forecast reliably the corresponding numbers from the current procedure, switching to the new procedure would be reasonable and cost effective. The following data were obtained for the quality parameter by analyzing samples using both procedures:

Current (Y)	Proposed (X)	Current (Y)	Proposed (X)
3.0	3.1	3.1	3.1
3.1	3.9	2.7	2.9
3.0	3.4	3.3	3.6
3.6	4.0	3.2	4.1
3.8	3.6	2.1	2.6
2.7	3.6	3.0	3.1
2.7	3.6	2.6	2.8

a. Use linear regression to find a relation to forecast Y, which is the quality parameter from the current procedure, using the values from the proposed procedure, X.

b. Is there a strong relationship between Y and X? Explain.

3. Ohio Swiss Milk Products manufactures and distributes ice cream in Ohio, Kentucky, and West Virginia. The company wants to expand operations by locating another plant in northern Ohio. The size of the new plant will be a function of the expected demand for ice cream within the area served by the plant. A market survey is currently under way to determine that demand.

Ohio Swiss wants to estimate the relationship between the manufacturing cost per gallon and the number of gallons sold in a year to determine the demand for ice cream and, thus, the size of the new plant. The following data have been collected:

a. Develop a regression equation to forecast the cost per gallon as a function of the number of gallons produced.

Plant	Cost per Thousand Gallons (Y)	Thousands of Gallons Sold (X)
1	$ 1,015	416.9
2	973	472.5
3	1,046	250.0
4	1,006	372.1
5	1,058	238.1
6	1,068	258.6
7	967	597.0
8	997	414.0
9	1,044	263.2
10	1,008	372.0
Total	$10,182	3,654.4

b. What are the correlation coefficient and the coefficient of determination? Comment on your regression equation in light of these measures.

c. Suppose that the market survey indicates a demand of 325,000 gallons in the Bucyrus, Ohio area. Estimate the manufacturing cost per gallon for a plant producing 325,000 gallons per year.

4. A manufacturing firm has developed a skills test, the scores from which can be used to predict workers' production rating factors. Data on the test scores of various workers and their subsequent production ratings are shown.

Worker	Test Score	Production Rating	Worker	Test Score	Production Rating
A	53	45	K	54	59
B	36	43	L	73	77
C	88	89	M	65	56
D	84	79	N	29	28
E	86	84	O	52	51
F	64	66	P	22	27
G	45	49	Q	76	76
H	48	48	R	32	34
I	39	43	S	51	60
J	67	76	T	37	32

a. Using POM for Windows' least squares-linear regression module, develop a relationship to forecast production ratings from test scores.

b. If a worker's test score was 80, what would be your forecast of the worker's production rating?

c. Comment on the strength of the relationship between the test scores and production ratings.

5. The materials handling manager of a manufacturing company is trying to forecast the cost of maintenance for the company's fleet of over-the-road tractors. The manager believes that the cost of maintaining the tractors increases with their age. The following data was collected:

Age (years)	Yearly Maintenance Cost ($)	Age (years)	Yearly Maintenance Cost ($)
4.5	619	5.0	1,194
4.5	1,049	0.5	163
4.5	1,033	0.5	182
4.0	495	6.0	764
4.0	723	6.0	1,373
4.0	681	1.0	978
5.0	890	1.0	466
5.0	1,522	1.0	549
5.5	987		

a. Use POM for Windows' least squares-linear regression module to develop a relationship to forecast the yearly maintenance cost based on the age of a tractor.

b. If a section has 20 three-year-old tractors, what is the forecast for the annual maintenance cost?

Time-Series Methods

6. Marianne Kramer, the owner of Handy Man Rentals, rents carpet cleaners to contractors and walk-in customers. She is interested in arriving at a forecast of rentals so that she can order the correct quantities of supplies that go with the cleaners. Data for the last 10 weeks are shown here.

Week	Rentals	Week	Rentals
1	15	6	20
2	16	7	24
3	24	8	27
4	18	9	18
5	23	10	16

a. Prepare a forecast for weeks 6 through 10 by using a 4-week moving average. What is the forecast for week 11?

b. Calculate the mean absolute deviation as of the end of week 10.

7. Sales for the past 12 months at Computer Success are given here.

Month	Sales ($)	Month	Sales ($)
January	3,000	July	6,300
February	3,400	August	7,200
March	3,700	September	6,400
April	4,100	October	4,600
May	4,700	November	4,200
June	5,700	December	3,900

a. Use a three-month moving average to forecast the sales for the months May through December.

b. Use a four-month moving average to forecast the sales for the months May through December.

c. Compare the performance of the two methods by using the mean absolute deviation as the performance criterion. Which method would you recommend?

d. Compare the performance of the two methods by using the mean absolute percent error as the performance criterion. Which method would you recommend?

e. Compare the performance of the two methods by using the mean squared error as the performance criterion. Which method would you recommend?

8. Bradley's Copiers sells and repairs photocopy machines. The manager needs weekly forecasts of service calls so that he can schedule service personnel. Use the actual demand in the first period for the forecast for the first week so error measurement begins in the second week. The manager uses exponential smoothing with $\alpha = 0.20$. Forecast the number of calls for week 6, which is next week.

Week	Actual Service Calls
1	29
2	27
3	41
4	18
5	33

9. Consider the sales data for Computer Success given in Problem 7.

a. Use a 3-month weighted moving average to forecast the sales for the months April through December. Use weights of (4/8), (3/8), and (1/8), giving more weight to more recent data.

b. Use exponential smoothing with $\alpha = 0.6$ to forecast the sales for the months April through December. Assume that the initial forecast for January was $3,200. Start error measurement in April.

c. Compare the performance of the two methods by using the mean absolute deviation as the performance criterion, with error measurement beginning in April. Which method would you recommend?

d. Compare the performance of the two methods by using the mean absolute percent error as the performance criterion, with error measurement beginning in April. Which method would you recommend?

e. Compare the performance of the two methods by using the mean squared error as the performance criterion, with error measurement beginning in April. Which method would you recommend?

10. A convenience store recently started to carry a new brand of soft drink. Management is interested in estimating future sales volume to determine whether it should continue to carry the new brand or replace it with another brand. The table below provides the number of cans sold per week. Use both the trend projection with regression and the exponential smoothing (let $\alpha = 0.4$ with an initial forecast for week 1 of 617) methods to forecast demand for week 13. Compare these methods by using the mean absolute deviation and mean absolute percent error performance criteria. Does your analysis suggest that sales are trending and if so, by how much?

Week	1	2	3	4	5	6	7	8	9	10	11	12
Sales	617	617	648	739	659	623	742	704	724	715	668	740

11. Community Federal Bank in Dothan, Alabama, recently increased its fees to customers who use employees as tellers. Management is interested in whether its new fee policy has increased the number of customers now using its automatic teller machines to that point that more machines are required. The following table provides the number of automatic teller transactions by week. Use trend projection with regression to forecast usage for weeks 13–16.

Week	1	2	3	4	5	6	7	8	9	10	11	12
Transactions	512	527	631	434	482	539	577	518	526	636	623	461

12. The number of heart surgeries performed at Heartville General Hospital has increased steadily over the past several years. The hospital's administration is seeking the best method to forecast the demand for such surgeries in year 6. The data for the past 5 years are shown.

Year	Demand
1	45
2	50
3	52
4	56
5	58

The hospital's administration is considering the following forecasting methods. Begin error measurement in year 3 so all methods are compared for the same years.

i. Exponential smoothing, with $\alpha = 0.6$. Let the initial forecast for year 1 be 45, the same as the actual demand.

ii. Exponential smoothing, with $\alpha = 0.9$. Let the initial forecast for year 1 be 45, the same as the actual demand.

iii. Trend projection with regression.

iv. Two-year moving average.

v. Two-year weighted moving average, using weights 0.6 and 0.4, with more recent data given more weight.

vi. If MAD is the performance criterion chosen by the administration, which forecasting method should it choose?

vii. If MSE is the performance criterion chosen by the administration, which forecasting method should it choose?

viii. If MAPE is the performance criterion chosen by the administration, which forecasting method should it choose?

13. The following data are for calculator sales in units at an electronics store over the past 9 weeks:

Week	Sales	Week	Sales
1	46	6	58
2	49	7	62
3	43	8	56
4	50	9	63
5	53		

Use trend projection with regression to forecast sales for weeks 10–13. What are the error measures (CFE, MSE, σ, MAD, and MAPE) for this forecasting procedure? How about r^2?

14. The demand for Krispee Crunchies, a favorite breakfast cereal of people born in the 1940s, is experiencing a decline. The company wants to monitor demand for this product closely as it nears the end of its life cycle. The following table shows the actual sales history for January–October. Generate forecasts for November–December, using the trend projection with regression method. Looking at the accuracy of its forecasts over the history file, as well as the other statistics provided, how confident are you in these forecasts for November–December?

Month	Sales	Month	Sales
January	890,000	July	710,000
February	800,000	August	730,000
March	825,000	September	680,000
April	840,000	October	670,000
May	730,000	November	
June	780,000	December	

15. Forrest and Dan make boxes of chocolates for which the demand is uncertain. Forrest says, "That's life." On the other hand, Dan believes that some demand patterns exist that could be useful for planning the purchase of sugar, chocolate, and shrimp. Forrest insists on placing a surprise chocolate-covered shrimp in some boxes so that "You never know what you'll get." Quarterly demand (in boxes of chocolates) for the last 3 years follows:

Quarter	Year 1	Year 2	Year 3
1	3,000	3,300	3,502
2	1,700	2,100	2,448
3	900	1,500	1,768
4	4,400	5,100	5,882
Total	10,000	12,000	13,600

a. Use intuition and judgment to estimate quarterly demand for the fourth year.

b. If the expected sales for chocolates are 14,800 cases for year 4, use the multiplicative seasonal method to prepare a forecast for each quarter of the year. Are any of the quarterly forecasts different from what you thought you would get in part (a)?

16. The manager of Alaina's Garden Center must make the annual purchasing plans for rakes, gloves, and other gardening items. One of the items the company stocks is Fast-Grow,

a liquid fertilizer. The sales of this item are seasonal, with peaks in the spring, summer, and fall months. Quarterly demand (in cases) for the past 2 years follows:

Quarter	Year 1	Year 2
1	45	67
2	339	444
3	299	329
4	222	283
Total	905	1,123

If the expected sales for Fast-Grow are 1,850 cases for year 3, use the multiplicative seasonal method to prepare a forecast for each quarter of the year.

17. The manager of a utility company in the Texas panhandle wants to develop quarterly forecasts of power loads for the next year. The power loads are seasonal, and the data on the quarterly loads in megawatts (MW) for the last 4 years are as follows:

Quarter	Year 1	Year 2	Year 3	Year 4
1	103.5	94.7	118.6	109.3
2	126.1	116.0	141.2	131.6
3	144.5	137.1	159.0	149.5
4	166.1	152.5	178.2	169.0

The manager estimates the total demand for the next year at 600 MW. Use the multiplicative seasonal method to develop the forecast for each quarter.

18. D Franklin Tooling, Inc., manufactures specialty tooling for firms in the paper-making industry. All of their products are engineer-to-order and so the company never knows exactly what components to purchase for a tool until a customer places an order. However, the company believes that weekly demand for a few components is fairly stable. Component 135.AG is one such item. The last 26 weeks of historical use of component 135.AG is recorded below.

Week	Demand	Week	Demand
1	137	14	131
2	136	15	132
3	143	16	124
4	136	17	121
5	141	18	127
6	128	19	118
7	149	20	120
8	136	21	115
9	134	22	106
10	142	23	120
11	125	24	113
12	134	25	121
13	118	26	119

Use OM Explorer's *Time Series Forecasting* Solver to evaluate the following forecasting methods. Start error measurement in the fifth week, so all methods are evaluated over the same time interval. Use the default settings for initial forecasts.

i. Naïve (1-Period Moving Average)

ii. 3-Period Moving Average

iii. Exponential Smoothing, with $\alpha = .28$

iv. Trend Projection with Regression

v. Which forecasting method should management use, if the performance criterion it chooses is:

- CFE?
- MSE?
- MAD?
- MAPE?

19. D Create an Excel spreadsheet on your own that can create combination forecasts for Problem 18. Create a combination forecast using all four techniques from Problem 18. Give each technique an equal weight. Create a second combination forecast by using the three techniques that seem best based on MAD. Give equal weight to each technique. Finally, create a third forecast by equally weighting the two best techniques. Calculate CFE, MAD, MSE, and MAPE for the combination forecast. Are these forecasts better or worse than the forecasting techniques identified in Problem 18?

20. D The director of a large public library must schedule employees to reshelf books and periodicals checked out of the library. The number of items checked out will determine the labor requirements. The following data reflect the number of items checked out of the library for the past 3 years:

Month	Year 1	Year 2	Year 3
January	1,847	2,045	1,986
February	2,669	2,321	2,564
March	2,467	2,419	2,635
April	2,432	2,088	2,150
May	2,464	2,667	2,201
June	2,378	2,122	2,663
July	2,217	2,206	2,055
August	2,445	1,869	1,678
September	1,894	2,441	1,845
October	1,922	2,291	2,065
November	2,431	2,364	2,147
December	2,274	2,189	2,451

The director needs a time-series method for forecasting the number of items to be checked out during the next month. Find the best simple moving average forecast you can. Decide what is meant by "best" and justify your decision.

D = Difficult Problem

21. Using the data in Problem 20 and the Time Series Solver of OM Explorer, find the best exponential smoothing parameter alpha that minimizes MAD. Let the forecast for period 1 be the actual data for period 1, and begin the error analysis in period 2.

22. Using the data in Problem 20, find the trend projection with regression model using the Time Series Forecasting Solver of OM Explorer. Compare the performance of this method with the exponential smoothing method from Problem 21. Let the error analysis begin in period 2 (so that both exponential smoothing and trend projection are analyzed over the same time horizon).Which of these two methods would you choose if MAD is the key error measure?

23. Cannister, Inc., specializes in the manufacture of plastic containers. The data on the monthly sales of 10-ounce shampoo bottles for the past 5 years are as follows:

Year	1	2	3	4	5
January	742	741	896	951	1,030
February	697	700	793	861	1,032
March	776	774	885	938	1,126
April	898	932	1,055	1,109	1,285
May	1,030	1,099	1,204	1,274	1,468
June	1,107	1,223	1,326	1,422	1,637
July	1,165	1,290	1,303	1,486	1,611
August	1,216	1,349	1,436	1,555	1,608
September	1,208	1,341	1,473	1,604	1,528
October	1,131	1,296	1,453	1,600	1,420
November	971	1,066	1,170	1,403	1,119
December	783	901	1,023	1,209	1,013

a. Using the multiplicative seasonal method, calculate the monthly seasonal indices.

b. Develop a simple linear regression equation to forecast annual sales. For this regression, the dependent variable, Y, is the demand in each year and the independent variable, X, is the index for the year (i.e., $X = 1$ for year 1, $X = 2$ for year 2, and so on until $X = 5$ for year 5).

c. Forecast the annual sales for year 6 by using the regression model you developed in part (b).

d. Prepare the seasonal forecast for each month by using the monthly seasonal indices calculated in part (a).

24. The Midwest Computer Company serves a large number of businesses in the Great Lakes region. The company sells supplies and replacements and performs service on all computers sold through seven sales offices. Many items are stocked, so close inventory control is necessary to assure customers of efficient service. Recently, business has been increasing, and management is concerned about stockouts. A forecasting method is needed to estimate requirements several months in advance so that adequate replenishment quantities can be purchased. An example of the sales growth experienced during the last 50 months is the growth in demand for item EP-37, a laser printer cartridge, shown in Table 3.

a. Develop a trend projection with regression solution using OM Explorer. Forecast demand for month 51.

b. A consultant to Midwest's management suggested that new office building leases would be a good leading indicator for company sales. The consultant quoted a recent university study finding that new office building leases precede office equipment and supply sales by 3 months. According to the study findings, leases in month 1 would affect sales in month 4, leases in month 2 would affect sales in month 5, and so on. Use POM for Windows' linear regression module to develop a forecasting model for sales, with leases as the independent variable. Forecast sales for month 51.

c. Which of the two models provides better forecasts? Explain.

TABLE 3 | EP-37 SALES AND LEASE DATA

Month	EP-37 Sales	Leases	Month	EP-37 Sales	Leases
1	80	32	26	1,296	281
2	132	29	27	1,199	298
3	143	32	28	1,267	314
4	180	54	29	1,300	323
5	200	53	30	1,370	309
6	168	89	31	1,489	343
7	212	74	32	1,499	357
8	254	93	33	1,669	353
9	397	120	34	1,716	360
10	385	113	35	1,603	370
11	472	147	36	1,812	386
12	397	126	37	1,817	389

D = Difficult Problem

Month	EP-37 Sales	Leases	Month	EP-37 Sales	Leases
13	476	138	38	1,798	399
14	699	145	39	1,873	409
15	545	160	40	1,923	410
16	837	196	41	2,028	413
17	743	180	42	2,049	439
18	722	197	43	2,084	454
19	735	203	44	2,083	441
20	838	223	45	2,121	470
21	1,057	247	46	2,072	469
22	930	242	47	2,262	490
23	1,085	234	48	2,371	496
24	1,090	254	49	2,309	509
25	1,218	271	50	2,422	522

25. A certain food item at P&Q Supermarkets has the demand pattern shown in the following 24-period table. **D**

Period	Demand	Period	Demand
1	33	13	37
2	37	14	43
3	31	15	56
4	39	16	41
5	54	17	36
6	38	18	39
7	42	19	41
8	40	20	58
9	41	21	42
10	54	22	45
11	43	23	41
12	39	24	38

a. Use the Combination forecasting method of the Time Series Forecasting Solver of OM Explorer. Let error analysis begin in month 6, and include (1) a 5-period moving average (with a combination weight of 0.33), (2) an exponential smoothing model with $\alpha = 0.20$ (with a combination weight of 0.33), and (3) trend projection (with a combination weight of 0.33). What is the MAD of this model? What is the forecast for month 25?

b. The need to account for seasonality is apparent if you look at a graph of the trend line. There is a spike in demand in the 5th period of each 5-period cycle. Unfortunately, OM Explorer's Seasonal Forecasting Solver does not cover the case where there are 5 periods in a cycle (or seasons in a year). You must do some manual calculations. Begin by calculating the seasonal factor for each period in each of the first 4 cycles, and then calculating the average seasonal factor for each period (see Example 6). Now estimate the total demand for cycle 5 using OM Explorer's Trend Projection routine in the Time Series Solver. The dependent variables are the total demands for the first 4 cycles. Now multiply the average demand estimate for the 5th cycle by the seasonal factor for the 5th period. This is your forecast for month 25. To calculate the errors (including MAD) for the multiplicative seasonal method for all cycles (except for the 5th month in the 5th cycle), calculate MAD manually. You might instead use the Error Analysis Module of POM for Windows.

c. How do the forecasts by the two methods compare? Which one is likely to give the better forecast, based on MAD?

26. The data for the visibility chart in Discussion Question 1 are shown in Table 4. The visibility standard is set at 100. Readings below 100 indicate that air pollution has reduced visibility, and readings above 100 indicate that the air is clearer. **D**

a. Use several methods to generate a visibility forecast for August 31 of the second year. Which method seems to produce the best forecast?

b. Use several methods to forecast the visibility index for the summer of the third year. Which method seems to produce the best forecast? Support your choice.

D = **Difficult Problem**

TABLE 4 | VISIBILITY DATA

Date	Year 1	Year 2	Date	Year 1	Year 2	Date	Year 1	Year 2
July 22	125	130	Aug 5	105	200	Aug 19	170	160
23	100	120	6	205	110	20	125	165
24	40	125	7	90	100	21	85	135
25	100	160	8	45	200	22	45	80
26	185	165	9	100	160	23	95	100
27	85	205	10	120	100	24	85	200
28	95	165	11	85	55	25	160	100
29	200	125	12	125	130	26	105	110
30	125	85	13	165	75	27	100	50
31	90	105	14	60	30	28	95	135
Aug 1	85	160	15	65	100	29	50	70
2	135	125	16	110	85	30	60	105
3	175	130	17	210	150			
4	200	205	18	110	220			

27. (D) Tom Glass forecasts electrical demand for the Flatlands Public Power District (FPPD). The FPPD wants to take its Comstock power plant out of service for maintenance when demand is expected to be low. After shutdown, performing maintenance and getting the plant back on line takes two weeks. The utility has enough other generating capacity to satisfy 1,550 megawatts (MW) of demand while Comstock is out of service. Table 5 shows weekly peak demands (in MW) for the past several autumns. When next in year 6 should the Comstock plant be scheduled for maintenance?

TABLE 5 | WEEKLY PEAK POWER DEMANDS

	AUGUST			SEPTEMBER				OCTOBER				NOVEMBER	
Year	**1**	**2**	**3**	**4**	**5**	**6**	**7**	**8**	**9**	**10**	**11**	**12**	**13**
1	2,050	1,925	1,825	1,525	1,050	1,300	1,200	1,175	1,350	1,525	1,725	1,575	1,925
2	2,000	2,075	2,225	1,800	1,175	1,050	1,250	1,025	1,300	1,425	1,625	1,950	1,950
3	1,950	1,800	2,150	1,725	1,575	1,275	1,325	1,100	1,500	1,550	1,375	1,825	2,000
4	2,100	2,400	1,975	1,675	1,350	1,525	1,500	1,150	1,350	1,225	1,225	1,475	1,850
5	2,275	2,300	2,150	1,525	1,350	1,475	1,475	1,175	1,375	1,400	1,425	1,550	1,900

28. (D) A manufacturing firm seeks to develop a better forecast for an important product, and believes that there is a trend to the data. OM Explorer's *Trend Projection with Regression* Solver has been set up with the 47 demands in the history file. Note the "Load Problem 28 Data" button in the *Trend Projection with Regression* Solver that when clicked will automatically input the demand data. Otherwise, you can enter the demand data directly into the Inputs sheet.

Yr	1	2	3	4
Jan	4507	4589	4084	4535
Feb	4400	4688	4158	4477
Mar	4099	4566	4174	4601
Apr	4064	4485	4225	4648
May	4002	4385	4324	4860
Jun	3963	4377	4220	4998
Jul	4037	4309	4267	5003
Aug	4162	4276	4187	4960
Sep	4312	4280	4239	4943
Oct	4395	4144	4352	5052
Nov	4540	4219	4331	5107
Dec	4471	4052	4371	

(D) = Difficult Problem

a. What is your forecast for December of Year 4, making period 1 as the starting period for the regression?

b. The actual demand for period 48 was just learned to be 5,100. Add this demand to the Inputs file and change the starting period for the regression to period 2 so that the number of periods in the regression remains unchanged. How much or little does the forecast for period 49 change from the one for period 48? The error measures? Are you surprised?

c. Now change the time when the regression starts to period 25 and repeat the process. What differences do you note now? What forecast will you make for period 49?

VIDEO CASE Forecasting and Supply Chain Management at Deckers Outdoor Corporation

Deckers Outdoor Corporation's footwear products are among some of the most well-known brands in the world. From UGG sheepskin boots and Teva sport sandals to Simple shoes, Deckers flip-flops, and Tsubo footwear, Deckers is committed to building niche footwear brands into global brands with market leadership positions. Net sales for fiscal year 2007 were close to $449 million. In addition to traditional retail store outlets for Deckers' footwear styles, the company maintains an active and growing "direct to consumer" e-commerce business. Since most retail stores cannot carry every style in every color and size, the company offers the full line for each of its brands directly to consumers through the brands' individual Web sites. Online sales at its virtual store are handled by its e-commerce group. Customers who want a pair of shoes not available at the retail store can always buy from the virtual store.

Pearson

Customer orders for Decker footwear are broken down by brand and sent to headquarters in Goletta, CA. where the order is entered into the system.

Founded in 1973, the company manufactured a single line of sandals in a small factory in Southern California. The challenges of managing the raw materials and finished goods inventories were small compared to today's global sourcing and sales challenges for the company's various brands. Today, each brand has its own development team and brand managers who generate, develop, and test-market the seasonal styles that appear on the shelves of retailers such as Nordstrom, Lord & Taylor, REI, the Walking Company, and the company's own UGG brand retail stores in the United States and Japan.

At Deckers, forecasting is the starting point for inventory management, sales and operations planning, resource planning, and scheduling—in short, managing its supply chain. It carries a considerable amount of seasonal stock. Shoes with seasonal demand that are left over at the end of their season must be sold at heavily discounted prices. Its products fall into three categories: (1) carry-over items that were sold in prior years, (2) new items that look similar to past models, and (3) completely new designs that are fashionable with no past history.

Twice a year, the brand development teams work on the fall and spring product lines. They come up with new designs about one year in advance of each season. Each brand (UGG, Teva, Simple, Tsubo, and Deckers) contains numerous products. The materials for new designs are selected and tested in prototypes. Approved designs are put into the seasonal line-up. Forecasts must be made at both the product and aggregate levels months before the season begins. "Bottoms-up" forecasts for each product begin by analyzing any available history files of past demand. Judgment forecasts are also important inputs, particularly for the second and third categories of shoes that are not carry-overs. For example, Char Nicanor-Kimball is an expert in spotting trends in shoe sales and makes forecasts for the virtual store. For new designs, historical sales on similar items are used to make a best guess on demand for those items. This process is facilitated by a forecasting and inventory system on the company's Intranet. At the same time, the sales teams for each brand call on their retail accounts and secure customer orders of approved designs for the coming season. Then, the virtual store forecasts are merged with orders from the retail store orders to get the total seasonal demand forecasted by product. Next, the product forecasts are "rolled up" by category and "top down" forecasts are also made.

These forecasts then go to top management where some adjustments may be made to account for financial market conditions, consumer credit, weather, demographic factors, and customer confidence. The impact of public relations and advertising must also be considered.

Actually, forecasting continues on throughout the year on a daily and weekly basis to "get a handle" on demand. Comparing actual demand with what was forecasted for different parts of the season also helps the forecasters make better forecasts for the future and better control inventories.

Based on initial demand forecasts, the company must begin sourcing the materials needed to produce the footwear. The company makes most of its products in China and sources many of the raw materials there as well. For UGG products sheepskin sourcing occurs in Australia with top grade producers, but the rawhide tanning still takes places in China. With potential suppliers identified and assurance from internal engineering that the footwear can be successfully made, the engineering and material data are handed over to the manufacturing department to determine how best to make the footwear in mass quantities. At this point, Deckers places a seasonal "buy" with its suppliers.

The orders for each product are fed into the manufacturing schedules at the Chinese factories. All the products for a given brand are manufactured at the same factory. While Deckers agents negotiate the raw materials contracts early in the development process, the factories only place the orders for the raw materials when the company sends in the actual orders for the finished goods. No footwear is made by the factories until orders are received.

At the factories, finished goods footwear is inspected and packaged for the month-long ocean voyage from Hong Kong to ports in the United States. Deckers ships fifty containers a week from its Chinese manufacturing sources, each holding approximately 5,000 pairs of shoes. Ownership of the finished goods transfers from the factories to Deckers in Hong Kong.

When the shipping containers arrive in the United States, the footwear is transferred to Deckers' distribution centers in Southern California. Teva products are warehoused in Ventura, California; all other products are handled by the company's state-of-the-art facility in Camarillo, California. Typically, Deckers brings product into the distribution centers two to three months in advance of expected needs so that the production at the suppliers' factories and the labor activities at the distribution centers are leveled. There are definitive spikes in the demand for footwear, with Teva spiking in Quarter 1 and UGG spiking in Quarter 4. The leveling approach works to keep costs low in the supply chain. However, it also means that Deckers must maintain sizeable inventories. Most shipments from suppliers come in to the distribution centers and are stored in inventory for one to two months awaiting a customer order. By the time the footwear is stocked in the distribution center, the company knows which retail customers will be getting the various products, based on the orders booked months earlier. Then, according to delivery schedules negotiated with the customers, the company begins filling orders and shipping products to retail locations. The warehouse tracks incoming shipments, goods placed on the shelves for customers, and outgoing orders. The inventory system helps manage the customer order filling process.

Because the booked orders are a relatively large proportion of the total orders from retailers, and the number of unanticipated orders is very small, only small safety stocks are needed to service the retailers. Occasionally, the purchase order from Deckers to one of its suppliers matches the sales order from the customer. In such a case, Deckers uses a "cross-dock" system. When the shipment is received at the distribution center, it is immediately checked in and loaded on another truck for delivery to customers. Cross docking reduces the need to store vast quantities of product for long periods of time and cuts down on warehousing expenses for Deckers. The company has been successful in turning its inventory over about four times a year, which is in line with footwear industry standards.

The online sales traffic is all managed centrally. In fact, for ordering and inventory management purposes, the online side of the business is treated just like another major retail store account. As forecasted seasonal orders are generated by each brand's sales team, a manufacturing order for the online business is placed by the e-commerce sales team at the same time. However, unlike the retail outlets that take delivery of products on a regular schedule, the inventory pledged to the online business is held in the distribution center until a Web site order is received. Only then is it shipped directly to the consumer who placed the online order. If actual demand exceeds expected demand, Char Nicanor-Kimball checks if more inventory can be secured from other customer orders that have scaled back.

The forecasting and supply chain management challenges now facing Deckers are two-fold. First, the company plans to grow the brands that have enjoyed seasonal sales activity into year-round footwear options for consumers by expanding the number of products for those brands. For example, most sales for UGG footwear occur in the fall/winter season. Sales for Teva historically have been in the spring and summer. Product managers are now working to develop styles that will allow the brands to cross over the seasons. Second, the company plans to expand internationally, and will have retail outlets in Europe, China, and other Asian locations in the very near future. Company managers are well aware of the challenges and opportunities such global growth will bring, and are taking steps now to assure that the entire supply chain is prepared to forecast and handle the demand when the time comes.

QUESTIONS

1. How much does the forecasting process at Deckers correspond with the "typical forecasting process" described at the end of this chapter?
2. Based on what you see in the video, what kinds of information technology are used to make forecasts, maintain accurate inventory records, and project future inventory levels?
3. What factors make forecasting at Deckers particularly challenging? How can forecasts be made for seasonal, fashionable products for which there is no history file? What are the costs of over-forecasting demand for such items? Under-forecasting?
4. What are the benefits of leveling aggregate demand by having a portfolio of products that create 365-day demand?
5. Deckers plans to expand internationally, thereby increasing the volume of shoes it must manage in the supply chain and the pattern of material flows. What implications does this strategy have on forecasting, order quantities, logistics, and relationships with its suppliers and customers?

CASE Yankee Fork and Hoe Company

The Yankee Fork and Hoe Company is a leading producer of garden tools ranging from wheelbarrows, mortar pans, and hand trucks to shovels, rakes, and trowels. The tools are sold in four different product lines ranging from the top-of-the-line Hercules products, which are rugged tools for the toughest jobs, to the Garden Helper products, which are economy tools for the occasional user. The market for garden tools is extremely competitive because of the simple design of the products and the large number of competing producers. In addition, more people are using power tools, such as lawn edgers, hedge trimmers, and thatchers, reducing demand for their manual counterparts. These factors compel Yankee to maintain low prices while retaining high quality and dependable delivery.

Garden tools represent a mature industry. Unless new manual products can be developed or a sudden resurgence occurs in home gardening, the prospects for large increases in sales are not bright. Keeping ahead of the competition is a constant battle. No one knows this better than Alan Roberts, president of Yankee.

The types of tools sold today are, by and large, the same ones sold 30 years ago. The only way to generate new sales and retain old customers is to provide superior customer service and produce a product with high customer value. This approach puts pressure on the manufacturing system, which has been having difficulties lately. Recently, Roberts has been receiving calls from long-time customers, such as Sears and True Value Hardware Stores, complaining about late shipments. These customers advertise promotions for garden tools and require on-time delivery.

Roberts knows that losing customers like Sears and True Value would be disastrous. He decides to ask consultant Sharon Place to look into the matter and report to him in one week. Roberts suggests that she focus on the bow rake as a case in point because it is a high-volume product and has been a major source of customer complaints of late.

Planning Bow Rake Production

A bow rake consists of a head with 12 teeth spaced 1 inch apart, a hardwood handle, a bow that attaches the head to the handle, and a metal ferrule that reinforces the area where the bow inserts into the handle. The bow is a metal strip that is welded to the ends of the rake head and bent in the middle to form a flat tab for insertion into the handle. The rake is about 64 inches long.

Place decides to find out how Yankee plans bow rake production. She goes straight to Phil Stanton, who gives the following account:

> Planning is informal around here. To begin, marketing determines the forecast for bow rakes by month for the next year. Then they pass it along to me. Quite frankly, the forecasts are usually inflated—must be their big egos over there. I have to be careful because we enter into long-term purchasing agreements for steel, and having it just sitting around is expensive. So I usually reduce the forecast by 10 percent or so. I use the modified forecast to generate a monthly final-assembly schedule, which determines what I need to have from the forging and woodworking areas. The system works well if the forecasts are good. But when marketing comes to me and says they are behind on customer orders, as they often do near the end of the year, it wreaks havoc with the schedules. Forging gets hit the hardest. For example, the presses that stamp the rake heads from blanks of steel can handle only 7,000 heads per day, and the bow rolling machine can do only 5,000 per day. Both operations are also required for many other products.

Because the marketing department provides crucial information to Stanton, Place decides to see the marketing manager, Ron Adams. Adams explains how he arrives at the bow rake forecasts.

> Things do not change much from year to year. Sure, sometimes we put on a sales promotion of some kind, but we try to give Phil enough warning before the demand kicks in—usually a month or so. I meet with several managers from the various sales regions to go over shipping data from last year and discuss anticipated promotions, changes in the economy, and shortages we experienced last year. Based on these meetings, I generate a monthly forecast for the next year. Even though we take a lot of time getting the forecast, it never seems to help us avoid customer problems.

The Problem

Place ponders the comments from Stanton and Adams. She understands Stanton's concerns about costs and keeping inventory low and Adams's concern about having enough rakes on hand to make timely shipments. Both are also somewhat concerned about capacity. Yet she decides to check actual customer demand for the bow rake over the past 4 years (in Table 6) before making her final report to Roberts.

QUESTIONS

1. Comment on the forecasting system being used by Yankee. Suggest changes or improvements that you believe are justified.
2. Develop your own forecast for bow rakes for each month of the next year (year 5). Justify your forecast and the method you used.

TABLE 6 | FOUR-YEAR DEMAND HISTORY FOR THE BOW RAKE

	DEMAND			
Month	**Year 1**	**Year 2**	**Year 3**	**Year 4**
1	55,220	39,875	32,180	62,377
2	57,350	64,128	38,600	66,501
3	15,445	47,653	25,020	31,404
4	27,776	43,050	51,300	36,504
5	21,408	39,359	31,790	16,888
6	17,118	10,317	32,100	18,909
7	18,028	45,194	59,832	35,500
8	19,883	46,530	30,740	51,250
9	15,796	22,105	47,800	34,443
10	53,665	41,350	73,890	68,088
11	83,269	46,024	60,202	68,175
12	72,991	41,856	55,200	61,100

EXPERIENTIAL LEARNING 1 Forecasting a Vital Energy Statistic

The following time-series data capture the weekly average of East Coast crude oil imports in thousands of barrels per day.

QUARTER 2 YEAR 1		QUARTER 3 YEAR 1		QUARTER 4 YEAR 1		QUARTER 1 YEAR 2	
Week	**Data**	**Week**	**Data**	**Week**	**Data**	**Week**	**Data**
1	1,160	14	1,116	27	1,073	40	994
2	779	15	1,328	28	857	41	1,307
3	1,134	16	1,183	29	1,197	42	997
4	1,275	17	1,219	30	718	43	1,082
5	1,355	18	1,132	31	817	44	887
6	1,513	19	1,094	32	946	45	1,067
7	1,394	20	1,040	33	725	46	890
8	1,097	21	1,053	34	748	47	865
9	1,206	22	1,232	35	1,031	48	858
10	1,264	23	1,073	36	1,061	49	814
11	1,153	24	1,329	37	1,074	50	871
12	1,424	25	1,096	38	941	51	1,255
13	1,274	26	1,125	39	994	52	980

Your instructor has a "holdout" sample representing the values for Week 53 and beyond. Your task is to use the POM for Windows *Time Series Forecasting* module and the history file to project this statistic into the future. If you have MyOMLab, the demand data is available in the *Experimental Exercise 1* Data file. It can be pasted into the Data Table of the *Time Series Forecasting* module. Otherwise, you can enter the demand data directly into the Data Table. Prior to your next class meeting:

a. Use the POM for Windows *Time Series Forecasting* module to locate the best naïve, moving average, weighted moving average, and trend projection with regression models that you think will most accurately forecast demand during the holdout sample. *Begin your error calculations with week 5.*

b. Create an Excel spreadsheet that begins with inputs of the four forecasts from the *Time Series Forecasting* module. Its purpose is to develop a combination forecast that will serve as your team's forecasts for each period. Assign a weight to each forecast model (the sum of all four forecast weights for one period should equal 1.0) and develop a "combination forecast" by multiplying each forecast by its weight. Keep the weights constant for the whole history file as you search for the best set of weights. If you do not like a particular model, give it a weight of 0. Calculate appropriate forecast error measures for your combination forecast in your Excel spreadsheet.

c. Create a management report that shows your period-by-period forecasts and their overall historical CFE and MAPE performance for each model and your combination forecast.

In-Class Exercise–Part 1

a. Input into your Excel spreadsheet the forecasts from the POM for Windows *Time Series Forecasting* module to get the combination forecast for the first period (week 53) in the holdout sample. The combination forecast is considered your team's forecast.

b. Enter the actual data announced by your instructor, and have Excel compute appropriate forecast error measures for your four models and the combination forecast. Decide on any revisions of weights for the combination forecast.

c. Update the POM for Windows *Time Series Forecasting* module with the actual demand for the new period and get the new forecasts.

In-Class Exercise–Part 2

a. Input the forecasts from the POM for Windows *Time Series Forecasting* module into your Excel spreadsheet to get the final combination forecast for the next period (week 54). At this point, you may change this period's weights on each forecasting technique going into the combination forecast. You have no contextual information, but may observe that one model has been performing particularly well in the last few periods. Your team might have different opinions, but you must reach a consensus.

b. Enter the actual data announced by your instructor, with Excel computing appropriate forecast error measures for your four models and the combination forecast.

c. Update the POM for Windows *Time Series Forecasting* module with the actual demand for the new period and get the new forecasts.

In-Class Exercise–Parts 3 and beyond

Continue in the fashion of Parts 1 and 2 to produce forecasts as directed by your instructor. At the end of the exercise, create a second management report that shows for the holdout sample your period-by-period forecasts, their individual forecast errors and percent deviations for each model and your combination forecast. Explain your logic regarding any changes made to your combination forecast weights over the holdout period.

Source: This experiential exercise was prepared as an in-class exercise prepared by Dr. John Jensen, University of South Carolina, as a basis for classroom discussion. By permission of John B. Jensen.

Selected References

Armstrong, J. Scott. "Findings from Evidence-based Forecasting: Methods for Reducing Forecast Error." *International Journal of Forecasting,* vol. 22, no. 3 (2006), pp. 583–598.

Armstrong, J. Scott. (ed.). *Principles of Forecasting: A Handbook for Researchers and Practitioners.* Norwell, MA: Kluwer Academic Publishers, 2001. Also visit http://www.forecastingprinciples.com for valuable information on forecasting, including frequently asked questions, a forecasting methodology tree, and a dictionary.

Attaran, Mohsen, and Sharmin Attaran. "Collaborative Supply Chain Management." *Business Process Management Journal,* vol. 13, no. 13 (June 2007), pp. 390–404.

Cederlund, Jerold P., Rajiv Kohli, Susan A. Sherer, and Yuliang Yao. "How Motorola Put CPFR into Action." *Supply Chain Management Review* (October 2007), pp. 28–35.

Daugherty, Patricia J., R. Glenn Richey, Anthony S. Roath, Soonhong Min, Haozhe Chen, Aaron D. Arndt, and Stefan E. Genchev. "Is Collaboration Paying Off for Firms?" *Business Horizons* (2006), pp. 61–70.

Fildes, Robert, Paul Goodwin, Michael Lawrence, and Konstantinos Nikolopoulos. "Effective Forecasting and Judgmental Adjustments: An Empirical Evaluation and Strategies for Improvement in Supply-Chain Planning." *International Journal of Forecasting,* vol. 25, no. 1 (2009), pp. 3–23.

Lawrence, Michael, Paul Goodwin, Marcus O'Connor, and Dilek Onkal. "Judgmental Forecasting: A Review of Progress over the Last 25 Years." *International Journal of Forecasting* (June 2006), pp. 493–518.

Makridakis, S., R. Hogarth, and A. Gaba. "Why Forecasts Fail? What to Do Instead?" *MIT Sloan Management Review,* vol. 51, no. 2 (2010), pp. 83–90.

McCarthy, Teresa, Donna F. Davis, Susan L. Golicic, and John T. Mentzer. "The Evolution of Sales Forecasting Management: A 20-Year Longitudinal Study of Forecasting Practices." *Journal of Forecasting,* vol. 25 (2006), pp. 303–324.

Min, Hokey, and Wen-Bin Vincent Yu. "Collaborative Planning, Forecasting and Replenishment: Demand Planning in Supply Chain Management." *International Journal of Information Technology and Management,* vol. 7, no. 1 (2008), pp. 4–20.

Montgomery, David. "Flashpoints for Changing Your Forecasting Process." *The Journal of Business Forecasting* (Winter 2006–2007), pp. 35–42.

Saffo, Paul. "Six Rules for Effective Forecasting." *Harvard Business Review* (July–August 2007), pp. 1–30.

Smaros, Johanna. "Forecasting Collaboration in the European Grocery Sector: Observations from a Case Study." *Journal of Operations Management,* vol. 25, no. 3 (April 2007), pp. 702–716.

Smith, Larry. "West Marine: A CPFR Success Story." *Supply Chain Management Review* (March 2006), pp. 29–36.

Syntetos, Aris, Konstantinos Nikolopoulos, John Boylan, Robert Fildes, and Paul Goodwin. "The Effects of Integrating Management Judgement into Intermittent Demand Forecasts." *International Journal of Production Economics,* vol. 118, no. 1 (March, 2009), pp. 72–81.

Wikipedia. "Collaborative Planning, Forecasting, and Replenishment," http:en.wikipedia.org/wiki/Collaborative Planning Forecasting and Replenishment (April, 2011).

Hardware, Software, and Mobile Systems

Cam Forset, the operations manager of Falcon Security, asked Mateo Thomas, CEO, Joni Campbell, CFO, and Alexis Moore, head of sales, to come down to the small hangar bay to see how the testing of the new 3D-printed drone is coming along. Mateo asked Cam to investigate the possibility of using 3D-printed parts to make drones in-house rather than buy them from vendors. This could be a tremendous cost-savings opportunity and give the company greater flexibility in updating its current fleet of drones.

Cam waves to Mateo and Joni to come over and look at the screen that she and Alexis are looking at. The screen is showing a live video feed from the new drone as it flies around the perimeter of the building.

"Well, it works—sort of," Cam says to Mateo and Joni with a forced smile. "It's *pretty* stable, and we can get streaming video. I just wish it hadn't taken 2 weeks to get it running." Cam's voice has an undeniably displeased tone.

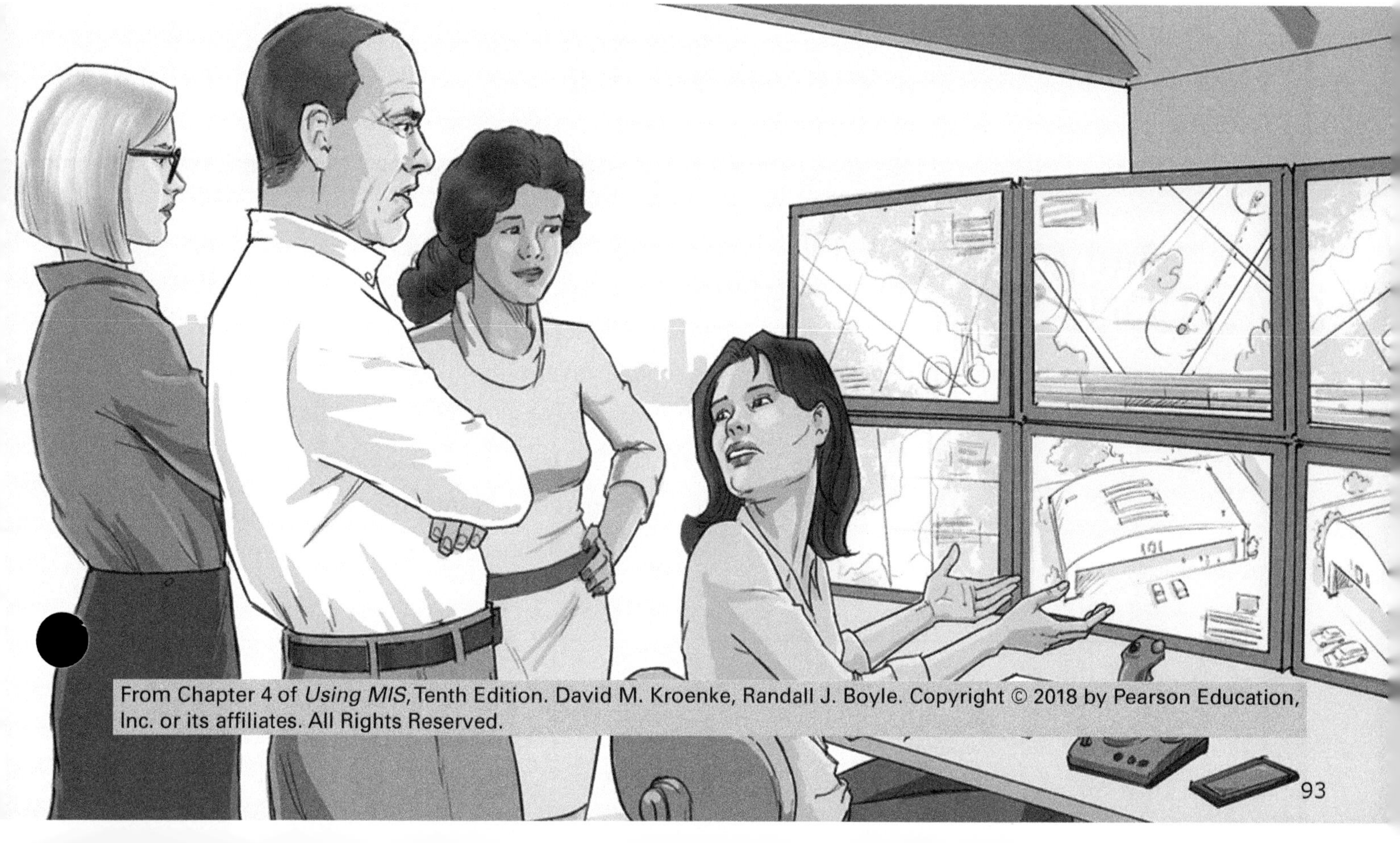

"That's OK. What was the total cost to make it?" Mateo asks.

"Well, this specific quad cost nearly nothing. We harvested all of the internals from a couple broken quads we had lying around. Everything else we printed." Cam points to a rack of dismantled quadcopters. "We found some free designs on the Web, but we had to make some changes so they would work with our internals."

"Well, that's good news, isn't it?" Mateo asks.

"Well, not really," Cam says with a skeptical tone. "If we wanted to build more drones, we'd need to harvest more parts from existing drones or buy generic parts and try to see if they'll work together."

Joni and Mateo both look confused. Mateo shakes his head and asks, "Well, why didn't you build it with generic parts in the first place?"

"Honestly, we weren't sure we could make it work even if we used existing internal components. I've never *made* a quadcopter before," Cam says flatly. "We ended up printing about 20 parts, but we still needed motors, a speed controller, a flight control board, a radio transmitter and receiver, propellers, batteries, and a charger."

"We also needed to make sure it could integrate with our internal systems. We didn't want to start experimenting with generic components until we knew we could actually make a quad that could fly," she adds.

"So your next step is to take out the existing internal components and replace them with generic parts to see if they will work, right?" Mateo asks.

"Well..." Cam starts to say.

Joni interrupts, "It probably won't matter if the generic components work or not. Essentially we've just replaced the frame, skids, and a few other parts to hold the camera. We still have to buy the other nonprintable component parts. Those won't be cheap. Add in the additional labor costs to assemble and test each quad..." she trails off.

"Plus the time and labor to integrate them with our internal systems," Alexis picks up her train of thought. "It won't be easy or cheap."

"Exactly," Cam says. "3D printing our own drones isn't going to save us enough money. There aren't enough parts that can be replaced. Yes, the passive recharging platform we developed using 3D-printed parts was a huge success. It has allowed us to automate the recharging process and extend the reach of our drones. But I just don't think 3D printing our own drones is going reduce our hardware costs enough to justify us becoming a drone manufacturer."

"3D printing our own drones isn't going to save us enough money."

Image source: rommma/Fotolia

Study QUESTIONS

- **Q1** What do business professionals need to know about computer hardware?
- **Q2** How can new hardware affect competitive strategies?
- **Q3** What do business professionals need to know about software?
- **Q4** Is open source software a viable alternative?
- **Q5** What are the differences between native and Web applications?
- **Q6** Why are mobile systems increasingly important?
- **Q7** What are the challenges of personal mobile devices at work?
- **Q8** 2027?

Mateo looks disappointed. "Well, maybe you're right. I really wish there was some way to make it work. It just seems like we keep burning through cash buying dozens of drones that become obsolete in a few years. It's really frustrating being on the cutting edge."

"You mean the bleeding edge...right?" Joni says with a smirk.

Chapter PREVIEW

What would you do if you were Mateo? Or Joni? Would you go ahead and build your own customized drones? It might give you a unique competitive advantage down the road. You might be able to hire someone who is an expert at building drones and save a lot of money. Is Cam being too conservative? If you're wondering why, as a future business professional, you need to know about hardware and software, think about those questions. Those and others of greater complexity—most likely ones involving technology that will be invented between now and the time you start working—will come your way.

You don't need to be an expert. You don't need to be a hardware engineer or a computer programmer. You do need to know enough, however, to be an effective consumer. You need the knowledge and skills to ask important, relevant questions and understand the answers.

We begin with basic hardware concepts and how innovations in hardware could affect businesses. Next, we will discuss software concepts, open source software development, and the differences between native and Web applications. Following that, we'll discuss the importance of mobile systems and the challenges created when employees bring their computers to work. Finally, we'll wrap up by forecasting trends in hardware and software in 2027.

Q1 What Do Business Professionals Need to Know About Computer Hardware?

Most people think of computer hardware as a laptop, a desktop, a server, or maybe even a tablet. As time passes, the way we think of computer hardware is changing. Take phones as an example. Twenty-five years ago, they were strictly used for voice communication. No one would have considered a phone a piece of computer hardware.

Fast-forward to today. Smartphones have substantial processing power, the ability to connect to networks, internal memory, and virtual keyboards and can interconnect with other devices. Now a "phone" is essentially a powerful piece of computing hardware. Computing hardware is also being integrated into other devices such as watches, glasses, TVs, cars, and even toothbrushes.

Computer hardware consists of electronic components and related gadgetry that input, process, output, and store data according to instructions encoded in computer programs or software. All hardware today has more or less the same components, at least to the level that is important to us. We'll begin with those components, and then we'll quickly survey basic types of computers.

Hardware Components

Every computer has a **central processing unit (CPU)**, which is sometimes called "the brain" of the computer. Although the design of the CPU has nothing in common with the anatomy of animal brains, this description is helpful because the CPU does have the "smarts" of the machine.

The CPU selects instructions, processes them, performs arithmetic and logical comparisons, and stores results of operations in memory. Some computers have two or more CPUs. A computer with two CPUs is called a **dual-processor** computer. **Quad-processor** computers have four CPUs. Some high-end computers have 16 or more CPUs.

CPUs vary in speed, function, and cost. Hardware vendors such as Intel, Advanced Micro Devices, and National Semiconductor continually improve CPU speed and capabilities while reducing CPU costs. Whether you or your department needs the latest, greatest CPU depends on the nature of your work.

The CPU works in conjunction with **main memory**. The CPU reads data and instructions from memory and then stores the results of computations in main memory. Main memory is sometimes called **RAM**, for random access memory.

All computers include **storage hardware**, which is used to save data and programs. Magnetic disks (also called hard disks) are the most common storage device. **Solid-state storage (SSD)** (or an SSD drive) is much faster than traditional magnetic storage because it stores information using nonvolatile electronic circuits. SSD drives are gaining in popularity but are several times more expensive than magnetic hard disks. USB flash drives are small, portable solid-state storage devices that can be used to back up data and transfer it from one computer to another. Optical disks such as CDs and DVDs are also popular portable storage media.

Types of Hardware

Figure 1 lists the basic types of hardware. **Personal computers** (PCs) are classic computing devices that are used by individuals. In the past, PCs were the primary computer used in business. Today, they are gradually being supplanted by tablets and other mobile devices. The Mac Pro is an example of a modern PC. Apple brought **tablets** to prominence with the iPad. In 2012, Microsoft announced Surface and Google announced the Nexus series, all tablets. Smartphones are cell phones with processing capability; the Samsung Galaxy S7 is a good example. Today, because it's hard to find a cell phone that isn't "smart," people often just call them phones.

A **server** is a computer that is designed to support processing requests from many remote computers and users. A server is essentially a PC on steroids. A server differs from a PC principally because of what it does. The relationship between PCs and servers is similar to the relationship between clients and servers at a typical restaurant. Servers take requests from clients and then bring them things. In restaurants this is food and silverware. In computing environments servers can send Web pages, email, files, or data to PCs. PCs, tablets, and smartphones that access servers are called **clients**. As of 2017, a good example of a server is the Dell PowerEdge server.

Finally, a **server farm** is a collection of, typically, thousands of servers. (See Figure 2.) Server farms are often placed in large truck trailers that hold 5,000 servers or more. Typically a trailer has two large cables coming out of it; one is for power, and the other is for data communications. The operator of the farm backs a trailer into a pre-prepared slab (in a warehouse or sometimes out in the open air), plugs in the power and communications cables, and, voilà, thousands of servers are up and running!

Hardware Type	Example (s)
Personal computer (PC) *Including desktops and laptops*	Apple Mac Pro
Tablet *Including e-book readers*	iPad, Microsoft Surface, Google Nexus, Kindle Fire
Smartphone	Samsung Galaxy, iPhone
Server	Dell PowerEdge Server
Server farm	Racks of servers (Figure 2)

FIGURE 1
Basic Types of Hardware

FIGURE 2
Server Farm
Source: © Andrew Twort/Alamy

Increasingly, server infrastructure is delivered as a service via the Internet that is often referred to as *the cloud.*

The capacities of computer hardware are specified according to data units, which we discuss next.

Computer Data

Computers represent data using **binary digits**, called **bits**. A bit is either a zero or a one. Bits are used for computer data because they are easy to represent physically, as illustrated in Figure 3. A switch can be either closed or open. A computer can be designed so that an open switch represents zero and a closed switch represents one. Or the orientation of a magnetic field can represent a bit: magnetism in one direction represents a zero; magnetism in the opposite direction represents a one. Or, for optical media, small pits are burned onto the surface of the disk so that they will reflect light. In a given spot, a reflection means a one; no reflection means a zero.

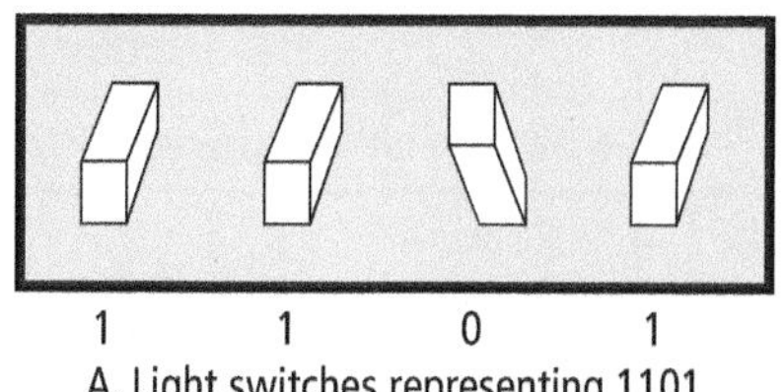

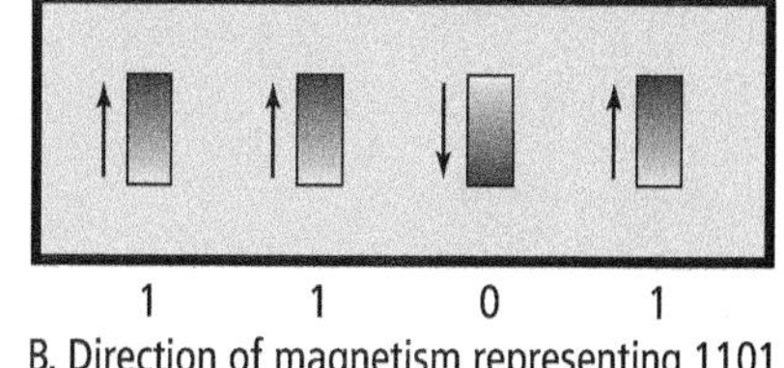

1 1 0 1
C. Reflection/no reflection representing 1101

FIGURE 3
Bits Are Easy to Represent Physically

Computer Data Sizes

All forms of computer data are represented by bits. The data can be numbers, characters, currency amounts, photos, recordings, or whatever. All are simply a string of bits. For reasons that interest many but are irrelevant for future managers, bits are grouped into 8-bit chunks called **bytes**. For character data, such as the letters in a person's name, one character will fit into one byte. Thus, when you read a specification that a computing device has 100 million bytes of memory, you know that the device can hold up to 100 million characters.

Bytes are used to measure sizes of noncharacter data as well. Someone might say, for example, that a given picture is 100,000 bytes in size. This statement means the length of the bit string that represents the picture is 100,000 bytes or 800,000 bits (because there are 8 bits per byte).

The specifications for the size of main memory, disk, and other computer devices are expressed in bytes. Figure 4 shows the set of abbreviations that are used to represent data storage capacity. A **kilobyte**, abbreviated **KB**, is a collection of 1,024 bytes. A **megabyte**, or **MB**, is 1,024 kilobytes. A **gigabyte**, or **GB**, is 1,024 megabytes; a **terabyte**, or **TB**, is 1,024 gigabytes; a **petabyte**, or **PB**, is 1,024 terabytes; an **exabyte**, or **EB**, is 1,024 petabytes; and a **zettabyte**, or **ZB**, is 1,024 exabytes. Sometimes you will see these definitions simplified as 1KB equals 1,000 bytes and 1MB equals 1,000K, and so on. Such simplifications are incorrect, but they do ease the math.

To put these sizes in perspective consider that Walmart processes about 40 PB worth of customer data per day.[1] Facebook processes about 600 TB each day, in a 300PB data warehouse.[2] The super-secret NSA data center in Utah is estimated to hold about 12 EB of data.[3] And Cisco estimates that annual global Internet traffic volume will exceed 2.0 ZB by the end of 2019.[4]

Specifying Hardware with Computer Data Sizes

Computer disk capacities are specified according to the amount of data they can contain. Thus, a 500GB disk can contain up to 500GB of data and programs. There is some overhead, so it is not quite 500GB, but it's close enough.

You can purchase computers with CPUs of different speeds. CPU speed is expressed in cycles called *hertz*. In 2016, a slow personal computer had a speed of 3.0 Gigahertz. A fast personal computer had a speed of 3.5+ Gigahertz, with multiple processors. An employee who does only simple tasks such as word processing does not need a fast CPU; a 2.0 Gigahertz CPU will be fine. However, an employee who processes large, complicated spreadsheets or who manipulates large database files or edits large picture, sound, or video files needs a fast computer like a dual processor with 3.5 Gigahertz or more. Employees whose work requires them to use many large applications at the same time need 12 GB or more of RAM. Others can do with less.

One last comment: The cache and main memory are **volatile**, meaning their contents are lost when power is off. Magnetic and optical disks are **nonvolatile**, meaning their contents survive when power is off. If you suddenly lose power, the contents of unsaved memory—say, documents

Term	Definition	Abbreviation
Byte	Number of bits to represent one character	
Kilobyte	1,024 bytes	KB
Megabyte	1,024 KB = 1,048,576 bytes	MB
Gigabyte	1,024 MB = 1,073,741,824 bytes	GB
Terabyte	1,024 GB = 1,099,511,627,776 bytes	TB
Petabyte	1,024 TB = 1,125,899,906,842,624 bytes	PB
Exabyte	1,024 PB = 1,152,921,504,606,846,976 bytes	EB
Zettabyte	1,024 EB = 1,180,591,620,717,411,303,424 bytes	ZB

FIGURE 4
Important Storage-Capacity Terminology

that have been altered—will be lost. Therefore, get into the habit of frequently (every few minutes or so) saving documents or files that you are changing. Save your documents before your roommate trips over the power cord.

Q2 How Can New Hardware Affect Competitive Strategies?

Organizations are interested in new hardware because they represent potential opportunities, or threats, to their ability to generate revenue. It's important to keep an eye on new tech hardware for the same reason you watch the weather forecast. You care about how the future will affect you.

Below we will look at four new hardware developments that have the potential to disrupt existing organizations.

Internet of Things

The first disruptive force that has the power to change business is the **Internet of Things (IoT)**. This is the idea that objects are becoming connected to the Internet so they can interact with other devices, applications, or services. Everyday objects are being embedded with hardware capable of sensing, processing, and transmitting data. Objects can then connect to a network and share data with any other application, service, or device.

Take your mobile phone, for example; it's probably a smartphone. But it wasn't always "smart." It started out as a simple device that just handled voice calls. Over time it became a **smart device** by adding more processing power, more memory, Internet access, Wi-Fi connectivity, and the ability to interconnect with other devices and applications (Figure 5). People began to use their mobile phones much differently than before. It also changed the way businesses operate. In 2015, *Amazon.com* reported that more than 70 percent of its customers shopped using a mobile device.[5]

FIGURE 5
Smartphone Development
Source: Grgroup/Fotolia

What happens when other devices become smart? How would your life change if you had access to a smart car, smart home appliances, or an entire smart building? Within a few short decades it's possible that you could interact with nearly every object around you from your smartphone. In fact, your devices will be able to talk to other devices, anticipate your actions, make changes, and configure themselves.

This shift away from "dumb" devices to interconnected smart devices is not lost on businesses. Consumers like smart devices and are willing to pay more for them. Businesses want to improve the existing devices they manufacture into a smart devices and then sell them for twice as much. If they don't, someone else will.

The iPhone, for example, was introduced by Apple Inc., a computing hardware and software company. The mobile phone market was already mature. Industry leaders could have created a smartphone, but they didn't. Apple's success with portable audio players (iPod) and mobile phones (iPhone) was a shot across the bow of other hardware manufacturers. A wave of smart devices is coming.

Impact of the Internet of Things

The impact of IoT will be felt by many different high-tech industries. Smart devices need microprocessors, memory, wireless network connections, a power source, and new software. These devices will also need new protocols, more bandwidth, and tighter security, and they will consume more energy.

A good example of this push toward smart devices is General Electric's (GE) Industrial Internet.[6] GE's Industrial Internet is a broad program focused on creating smart devices, analyzing the data from these devices, and then making changes that increase efficiencies, reduce waste, and improve decision making. GE sees the greatest potential for smart devices in hospitals, power grids, railroads, and manufacturing plants.

GE estimates that an average airline using smart devices in its jet aircraft could save an average of 2 percent in fuel consumption. The resulting fuel and carbon dioxide savings would be the equivalent of removing 10,000 cars from the road.[7]

Microsoft has also made tremendous gains using smart devices. Microsoft has created a network of 125 smart buildings spread over 500 acres in Redmond, Washington (Figure 6).[8]

FIGURE 6
Microsoft's Redmond, WA, Campus
Source: Ian Dagnall/Alamy

Its operations center processes 500 million data transactions every day from 30,000 devices, including heaters, air conditioners, lights, fans, and doors.

Microsoft engineers were able to reduce energy costs by 6 percent to 10 percent a year by identifying problems like wasteful lighting, competing heating and cooling systems, and rogue fans. For Microsoft, that's millions of dollars. What if every corporate building were a smart building? When you consider that 40 percent of the world's energy is consumed in corporate buildings, you can start to get an idea of the immense financial cost savings. Indirectly, this would also have a huge environmental and economic impact worldwide.

Digital Reality Devices

The second disruptive force that has the power to change business is digital reality devices. Digital reality devices are an emerging technology with tremendous potential to revolutionize our daily lives. Much like the emergence of the Internet in the mid-1990s, these devices will create entirely new types of companies and change the way people live, work, shop, and entertain themselves. It's estimated that the digital reality market will be $150 billion by 2020.[9]

There are different levels of digital reality on a continuum from completely *real* environments to completely **virtual** environments, or simulated nonphysical environments. Before you start to think about how digital reality devices will affect business, you need to understand how the levels of digital reality differ. First, **reality** is the state of things as they actually exist. If you're reading the paper version of this text with your eyes, contact lenses, or glasses, you're seeing the real world without any digital alteration. You are (hopefully) experiencing reality.

Next comes augmented reality. **Augmented reality (AR)** is the altering of reality by overlaying digital information on real-world objects. Examples of AR devices include Google Glass ($1,250), Epson's Moverio Smart Glasses ($700), and Daqri Smart Helmet (est. $5,000 to $15,000). Essentially, these devices work like heads-up displays, giving users information about the real world they're experiencing. For example, an AR device could provide users directions in the form of virtual arrows being displayed on the roadway. Users could also read virtual emails displayed in the air or see virtual health data projected in front of them as they exercise.

The next step on the digital reality continuum, as shown in Figure 7, is mixed reality. **Mixed reality (MR)** is the combination of the real physical world with interactive virtual images or objects. Microsoft (HoloLens, $3,000) and Meta (Meta 2, $949) released their MR devices in early 2016. Both companies are marketing these devices to developers interested in creating digital reality applications. MR devices are generally perceived as having greater potential than AR devices due to their ability to interact with virtual objects in real time.

For example, using AR you could view a 2D virtual weather forecast projected on your wall. But with MR you would see a real-time 3D virtual model of your city created on your coffee table (Figure 8). It would show a virtual tornado moving toward the city, and you could interact with the 3D weather application to see its projected path. And this is just one example. Imagine watching sporting events live in high-definition 3D in the middle of your room.

There's one problem when discussing AR and MR devices. Currently, the term *augmented reality* isn't applied consistently. It's common to hear AR used to describe both AR and MR devices.[10]

	Reality	Augmented Reality	Mixed Reality	Virtual Reality
Example	Glasses	Google Glass	Microsoft HoloLens	Facebook's Oculus Rift
Virtual Information	No	Yes	Yes	Yes
Virtual Objects	No	No	Yes	Yes
Virtual World	No	No	No	Yes

FIGURE 7
Levels of Digital Reality

But this is normal for emerging technologies. Terms are created, refined, and stored in common speech as the technology develops. So don't be surprised to hear AR used to describe both types of digital reality.

The last step on the digital reality continuum is **virtual reality (VR)**, or a completely computer-generated virtual world with interactive digital objects. Here you'll find devices like Facebook's Oculus Rift ($599), Sony's PlayStation VR ($399), and Samsung Gear VR ($99). These are completely immersive experiences that try to create a strong **sense of presence**, or the illusion that a virtual experience is real. In other words, if a device were able to create a strong sense of presence, you'd lean back and hold on tight if you were on a virtual roller coaster about to go off the track.

Impact of Digital Reality Devices

Digital reality devices are developing in much the same way cellular phones developed over the past 20 years. In fact, it's entirely possible that the AR market could disrupt the smartphone market. Imagine taking calls, browsing the Web, messaging friends, and watching a movie without ever taking your smartphone out of your pocket.

The application of digital reality devices extends beyond personal use as well. Organizations are currently building digital reality applications for education, training, collaboration, new product design, "holoportation," gaming, sports, advertising, tourism, and shopping. For example, Lowe's new Holoroom allows customers to design and visualize their ideal room before they commit to major changes. Case Western Reserve University has partnered with Microsoft to develop 3D mixed-reality applications to teach anatomy in an interactive environment.[11]

The full impact of digital reality devices won't be understood for years—we just don't know how they'll be used. Even experts in the field are just starting to understand the implications of how digital reality devices will change organizations. The shift from 2D flat screens to a 3D virtual world is like changing vocations from being a painter to being a sculptor. It requires new skills, processes, tools, and ways of thinking. Digital reality devices are truly one of the most transformative innovations in hardware to come along in the past 20 years.

Self-driving Cars

The third disruptive force that could change the way businesses operate is self-driving cars. A **self-driving car** (also known as a driverless car) uses a variety of sensors to navigate like a traditional car but without human intervention. It will be full of advanced hardware and integrated software

FIGURE 8
Digital Reality Applications

Source: © Peshkov/Fotolia

and is the epitome of a mobile system. In fact, it will be so mobile that it will be able to move without anyone being in the car (Figure 9). Yes, self-driving cars are in your very near future.

A recent report by KPMG indicates that self-driving cars will be a reality as soon as 2020, with full adoption by 2040.[12] Most auto manufacturers (Mercedes-Benz, Nissan, Audi, and BMW) say they will have self-driving cars by 2020.[13] Google recently announced that it is partnering with Fiat Chrysler to make 100 driverless minivans.[14] Google's existing two-seater cars have logged more than 1.5 million miles. The Mercedes-Benz F 015 was the hit of the CES 2015 show when it drove itself onstage and opened its saloon-style doors, revealing passenger seats facing each other. It looks like the race to develop self-driving cars is heating up. The competition will be fierce.

Self-driving cars will make things easier, cheaper, and safer. They'll also disrupt well-established industries.

Self-driving Cars Make Things Easier

Imagine how a self-driving car will change the lives of a typical family. A self-driving car could allow Dad to review sales reports while "driving" to work. He's much less stressed out—and more productive—during his commute than he was with his old car. The self-driving car could then drop off the kids at school—without Dad in the car—and return home to take Mom to work.

After work the family goes shopping and is dropped off curbside at the store. No need to park anymore. It's safer too. While shopping, Dad gets a message from his college-aged daughter that she needs the car sent to pick her up from the airport. Dad's glad he won't have to drive all the way out there.

Dad remembers when he had to drive himself. It was a long and painful process. Now the car plans the route for him, fills itself up with gas, communicates with intersections so he never gets a

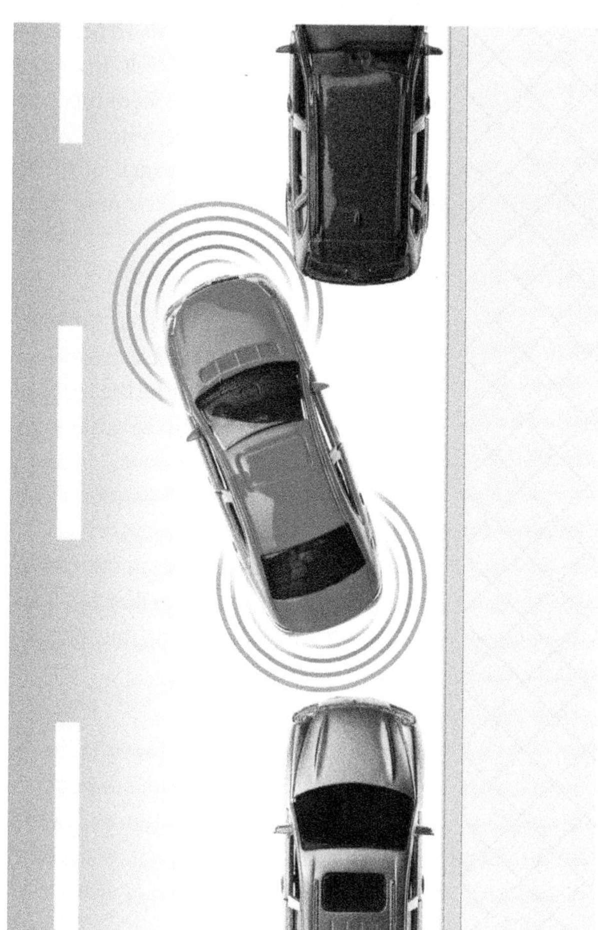

FIGURE 9
Future Cars Will Drive Themselves
Source: Dan Race/Fotolia

red light, and reroutes itself if there's an accident or traffic. Most importantly, he doesn't get mad at other drivers. Traveling is just easier now.

Later the family plans a vacation to a distant locale. Taking the self-driving car is the way to go. No airport security lines, family members don't have to get frisked by overzealous TSA agents, they get comfortable seats that face each other, they don't have to pay for their bags, and they don't have to rent a car when they get there. Plus, they can leave anytime they like.

Sometimes it's nice to leave for vacation at night and sleep while you're "driving." Driving isn't bad when you don't actually drive.

Self-driving Cars Make Things Cheaper

You've seen how a self-driving car can make your life easier. But what about cost? Will it be more expensive or less expensive than the car you have now?

Self-driving cars will probably be much less expensive over time than your current car. Early adopters will pay a premium when self-driving cars first hit the market, but that's true of most new products.

Cost savings will show up in several ways. In the above scenario, you may have noticed that the family had only one car. Self-driving cars will be used more effectively than cars are used now. Most cars sit dormant for 22 hours a day. Sharing a self-driving car could eliminate the need to have multiple cars. That's a big cost savings.

You'll see more cost savings because a self-driving car will drive better than you. You'll save on fuel because it will drive more efficiently (less braking, revving the engine, and street racing!). You will avoid costly traffic tickets, parking tickets, and DUI citations.

Your car insurance will drop dramatically. It may be so low that you won't even need it anymore. In a report about the effect of self-driving cars on the insurance industry KPMG estimated that accident frequency will drop by 80 percent by the year 2040. Subsequently, the personal automobile industry will shrink to 40 percent of its current size.[15]

They're probably right. Self-driving cars will probably take a big chunk out of the $150B, paid each year in car insurance premiums. And they should. Your future self-driving car will be safer because its crash avoidance systems will apply the brakes before you're even aware of a problem. It will be able to know the exact locations, velocities, and routes of all cars within the vicinity. Automobile accidents may become a thing of the past.

Self-driving Cars Will Make Things Safer

Yes, you read that right—safer. Currently, 90 percent of motor vehicle crashes are caused by human error.[16] Motor vehicle crashes are the leading cause of death for people ages 3 to 33. Spending time driving may be the most dangerous thing you do all day.

Your car will be able to see better than you, react more quickly than you, and have better information about your driving environment. It will be able to communicate with other cars around it, dynamically analyze traffic patterns, avoid construction sites, and contact emergency services if needed.

Self-driving cars will mean safer driving, fewer accidents, fewer drunk drivers, fewer road-rage incidents, and fewer auto–pedestrian accidents. Cars will be able to go faster with fewer accidents. In the future, manual driving may be a risky and expensive hobby.

Self-driving Cars Will Disrupt Businesses

Self-driving cars have the potential to disrupt well-established industries. Self-driving cars may mean fewer cars on the road. Fewer cars on the road may mean fewer cars sold (transportation), fewer auto loans written (finance), fewer automobile insurance policies underwritten (insurance), fewer auto parts sold due to fewer accidents (manufacturing), and fewer parking lots (real estate). If they didn't have to drive, consumers might take more trips by car than by plane or train (transportation).

The production of self-driving cars will mean more jobs for engineers, programmers, and systems designers. There will be more computer hardware, sensors, and cameras in the vehicle. Corporations may not completely see the far-reaching effects of self-driving cars on existing industries.

How will self-driving cars disrupt your personal life? Suppose you get married in a few years and have a child. Will your child ever drive a car? Will driving a "manual" car be too costly? Your potential offspring may never learn how to drive a car. But that may not be too strange. Do you know how to ride a horse? Your ancestors did.

3D Printing

The fourth disruptive force that has the power to change businesses is 3D printing. 3D printing will not only change the competitive landscape, but it may change the nature of businesses themselves. Think back to the Falcon Security case at the start of this chapter. The Falcon Security team chose not to make its own drones because doing so wasn't going to save the company enough money. It didn't want to use 3D printing to become a drone manufacturer.

While manufacturing wasn't right for Falcon, it is a viable option for some companies. Consider how Nike has used 3D printing to improve the way it designs and creates shoes. It recently used a 3D printer to create the world's first 3D-printed cleat plate for a shoe called the Nike Vapor Laser Talon.[17] Nike chose to use a 3D printer to produce the cleat because it could create the optimal geometric shapes for optimal traction. Using a 3D printer, it could design and produce a lighter and stronger cleat much more quickly than before. In fact, Nike did just that when it produced a pair of custom-designed sprinting shoes (the Nike Zoom Superfly Flyknit) for gold-medal Olympian Allyson Felix to be worn at the 2016 Olympic games in Rio.[18]

3D printers have the potential to affect a broad array of industries beyond sporting equipment. You can get an idea of the scope of change when you realize that 3D printers can print in more than just plastics (Figure 10). They can print in metals, ceramics, foods, and biological material too.

At CES 2015, industry leader MakerBot announced that it will begin selling composite filaments that can be used in its 3D printers. These new composite filaments combine traditional PLA (polylactic acid) thermoplastic with materials like wood, bronze, iron, and limestone. While each

FIGURE 10
3D Printer
Source: Seraficus/iStock/Getty Images

type of composite filament will require a new 3D print head, the printed objects will look and behave like their real-world counterparts.

Take the ability to 3D-print in a variety of materials and look for opportunities across the aerospace, defense, automotive, entertainment, and healthcare industries. What happens when it becomes feasible to 3D-print extra-large objects like cars,[19] planes, boats, houses, and drones?

Below are three examples of nontraditional 3D printing. Consider how disruptive each one would be to its respective industry:

- 3D Systems new ChefJet™ Pro can print complex sugary structures in flavors like chocolate, vanilla, mint, cherry, sour apple, and watermelon.[20] With a ChefJet, even a culinary novice could produce intricate, beautiful, and fully customized deserts.
- Researchers at the Harvard School of Engineering and Applied Sciences were able to print a 3D biological structure with blood vessels that could deliver nutrients and remove waste.[21] This development means doctors will be able to print fully functional replacements for damaged tissues by simply pressing print. Not only could this save lives, but it could also lower insurance premiums and the overall cost of health care.
- Professor Behrokh Khoshnevis of the University of Southern California has built a large-scale 3D printer that can print an entire house in 24 hours.[22] This 3D home printer would create more stable and better insulated structures, use less materials, reduce workplace injuries, automatically install heating and plumbing, and produce the home at a fraction of the cost.

Q3 What Do Business Professionals Need to Know About Software?

Innocuous-looking applications can be custom-made for malicious purposes.

As a future manager or business professional, you need to know the essential terminology and software concepts that will enable you to be an intelligent software consumer. To begin, consider the basic categories of software shown in Figure 11.

Every computer has an **operating system (OS)**, which is a program that controls that computer's resources. Some of the functions of an operating system are to read and write data, allocate main memory, perform memory swapping, start and stop programs, respond to error conditions, and facilitate backup and recovery. In addition, the operating system creates and manages the user interface, including the display, keyboard, mouse, and other devices.

Although the operating system makes the computer usable, it does little application-specific work. If you want to check the weather or access a database, you need application programs such as an iPad weather application or Oracle's customer relationship management (CRM) software.

Both client and server computers need an operating system, though they need not be the same. Further, both clients and servers can process application programs. The application's design determines whether the client, the server, or both process it.

You need to understand two important software constraints. First, a particular version of an operating system is written for a particular type of hardware. For example, Microsoft Windows

FIGURE 11
Categories of Computer Software

	Operating System	Application Programs
Client	Programs that control the client computer's resources	Applications that are processed on client computers
Server	Programs that control the server computer's resources	Applications that are processed on server computers

works only on processors from Intel and companies that make processors that conform to the Intel instruction set (the commands that a CPU can process). With other operating systems, such as Linux, many versions exist for many different instruction sets.

Second, two types of application programs exist. **Native applications** are programs that are written to use a particular operating system. Microsoft Access, for example, will run only on the Windows operating system. Some applications come in multiple versions. For example, there are Windows and Macintosh versions of Microsoft Word. But unless you are informed otherwise, assume that a native application runs on just one operating system. Native applications are sometimes called **thick-client applications**.

A **Web application** (also known as a **thin-client application**) is designed to run within a computer browser such as Firefox, Chrome, Opera, or Edge (formerly Internet Explorer). Web applications run within the browser and can run on any type of computer. Ideally, a Web application can also run within any browser, though this is not always true as you will learn.

Consider next the operating system and application program categories of software.

What Are the Major Operating Systems?

The major operating systems are listed in Figure 12. Consider each.

FIGURE 12
Major Operating Systems

Category	Operating System	Used for	Remarks
Nonmobile Clients	Windows	Personal computer clients	Most widely used operating system in business. Current version is Windows 10. Includes a touch interface.
	Mac OS	Macintosh clients	First used by graphic artists and others in arts community; now used more widely. First desktop OS to provide a touch interface. Current version is the macOS Sierra.
	Unix	Workstation clients	Popular on powerful client computers used in engineering, computer-assisted design, architecture. Difficult for the nontechnical user. Almost never used by business clients.
	Linux	Just about anything	Open source variant of Unix. Adapted to almost every type of computing device. On a PC, used with Libre Office application software. Rarely used by business clients.
Mobile Clients	Symbian	Nokia, Samsung, and other phones	Popular worldwide, but less so in North America.
	BlackBerry OS	Research in Motion BlackBerries	Device and OS developed for use by business. Very popular in beginning, but losing market share to iOS and Android.
	iOS	iPhone, iPod Touch, iPad	Rapidly increasing installed base with success of the iPhone and iPad. Based on Mac OS X.
	Android	Samsung, Google, HTC, and Sony smartphones; tablets	Linux-based phone/tablet operating system from Google. Rapidly increasing market share.
	Windows 10 (mobile)	Nokia and Microsoft Surface	Windows 10 tailored specifically for mobile devices. Full Windows 10 on Surface Pro.
Servers	Windows Server	Servers	Businesses with a strong commitment to Microsoft.
	Unix	Servers	Fading from use. Replaced by Linux.
	Linux	Servers	Very popular. Aggressively pushed by IBM.

Nonmobile Client Operating Systems

Nonmobile client operating systems are used on personal computers. The most popular is **Microsoft Windows**. Some version of Windows resides on more than 85 percent of the world's desktops, and, if we consider just business users, the figure is more than 95 percent. The most recent version of Windows is Windows 10. Net Applications estimates that overall market share of Windows as of 2016 is Windows 10 at 15.3 percent, Windows 8.1 at 9.9 percent, Windows 8 at 3.2 percent, Windows 7 at 47.8 percent, Windows Vista at 1.4 percent, and Windows XP at 10.6 percent.[23] It's interesting to note that Microsoft dropped support for Windows XP in 2014 despite the fact that it is still more popular than Windows Vista, Windows 8, and Windows 8.1.

Windows 8 was a major rewrite of prior versions. Windows 8 was distinguished by what Microsoft calls **modern-style applications**.[24] These applications, now carried over into Windows 10, are touch-screen oriented and provide context-sensitive, pop-up menus. They can also be used with a mouse and keyboard. Microsoft claims that modern-style applications work just as well on portable, mobile devices, such as tablet computers, as they do on desktop computers. One key feature of modern-style applications is the minimization of menu bars, status lines, and other visual overhead. Figure 13 shows an example of a modern-style version of searching for images in Windows Explorer.

Apple Computer, Inc., developed its own operating system for the Macintosh, **Mac OS**. The current version is macOS Sierra. Apple touts it as the world's most advanced desktop operating system, and, until Windows 8, it was without doubt. Windows 10 now gives it a run for the money in terms of that title.

Until recently, Mac OS was used primarily by graphic artists and workers in the arts community. But for many reasons, Mac OS has made headway into the traditional Windows market. According to Net Applications, as of 2016, desktop operating system market share was divided between versions of Windows (88.8 percent), Mac OS X (9.6 percent), and Linux (1.6 percent).[25]

Mac OS was designed originally to run the line of CPU processors from Motorola, but today a Macintosh with an Intel processor is able to run both Windows and the Mac OS.

Unix is an operating system that was developed at Bell Labs in the 1970s. It has been the workhorse of the scientific and engineering communities since then. Unix is seldom used in business.

Linux is a version of Unix that was developed by the open source community. This community is a loosely coupled group of programmers who mostly volunteer their time to contribute code to

FIGURE 13
Example of the Modern-Style Interface
Source: Windows 10, Microsoft Corporation.

develop and maintain Linux. The open source community owns Linux, and there is no fee to use it. Linux can run on client computers, but usually only when budget is of paramount concern. By far, Linux is most popular as a server OS. According to *DistroWatch.com*, the top five most popular versions of Linux as of 2016 were Linux Mint, Debian GNU/Linux, Ubuntu, openSUSE, and Fedora.[26]

Mobile Client Operating Systems

Figure 12 also lists the five principal mobile operating systems. **Symbian** is popular on phones in Europe and the Far East, but less so in North America. **BlackBerry OS** was one of the most successful early mobile operating systems and was used primarily by business users on BlackBerry devices. It has lost market share to iOS, Android, and Windows 10.

iOS is the operating system used on the iPhone, iPod Touch, and iPad. When first released, it broke new ground with its ease of use and compelling display, features that are now being copied by the BlackBerry OS and Android. With the popularity of the iPhone and iPad, Apple has been increasing its market share of iOS, and, according to Net Applications, it is used on 28 percent of mobile devices.[27] The current version of iOS is iOS 9.

Android is a mobile operating system licensed by Google. Android devices have a very loyal following, especially among technical users. Net Applications estimates Android's market share to be nearly 62 percent.

Most industry observers would agree that Apple has led the way, both with the Mac OS and the iOS, in creating easy-to-use interfaces. Certainly, many innovative ideas have first appeared in a Macintosh or iSomething and then later were added, in one form or another, to Android and Windows.

Users who want Windows 10 on mobile devices will get either **Windows 10 (mobile)** on smartphones or a full version of Windows 10 on Surface Pro devices. Windows garners about 4 percent of the mobile OS market share.

The smartphone market has always been huge, but recently, e-book readers and tablets have substantially increased the market for mobile client operating systems. As of 2015, 68 percent of Americans owned a smartphone, and 45 percent owned a tablet in addition to their smartphone.[28]

Server Operating Systems

The last three rows of Figure 12 show the three most popular server operating systems. **Windows Server** is a version of Windows that has been specially designed and configured for server use. It has much more stringent and restrictive security features than other versions of Windows and is popular on servers in organizations that have made a strong commitment to Microsoft.

Unix can also be used on servers, but it is gradually being replaced by Linux.

Linux is frequently used on servers by organizations that want, for whatever reason, to avoid a server commitment to Microsoft. IBM is the primary proponent of Linux and in the past has used it as a means to better compete against Microsoft. Although IBM does not own Linux, IBM has developed many business systems solutions that use Linux. By using Linux, neither IBM nor its customers have to pay a license fee to Microsoft.

Virtualization

Virtualization is the process by which one physical computer hosts many different virtual (not literal) computers within it. One operating system, called the **host operating system**, runs one or more operating systems as applications. Those hosted operating systems are called **virtual machines (vm)**. Each virtual machine has disk space and other resources allocated to it. The host operating system controls the activities of the virtual machines it hosts to prevent them from interfering with one another. With virtualization, each vm is able to operate exactly the same as it would if it were operating in a stand-alone, nonvirtual environment.

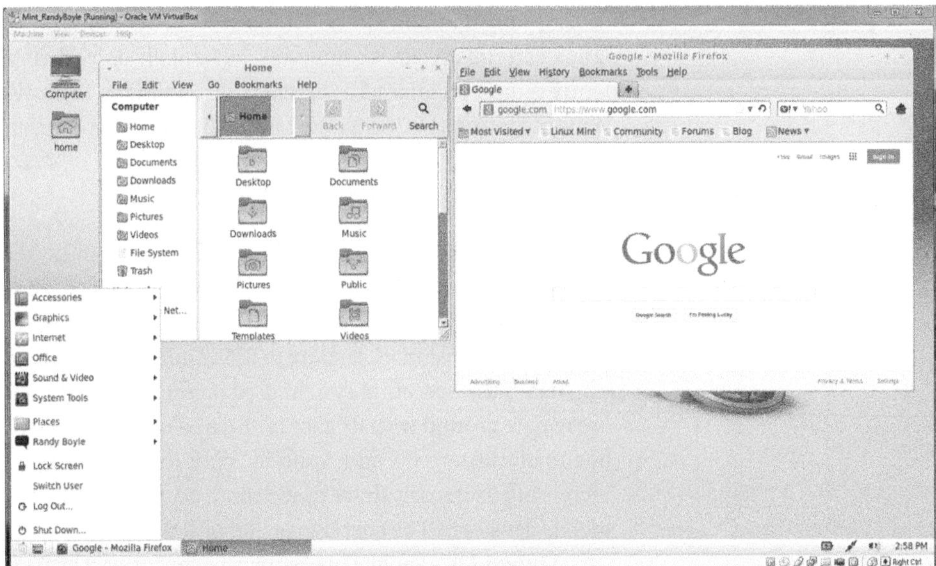

FIGURE 14
Linux Mint Virtual Machine Running in Microsoft Windows 7 Professional
Source: Windows 10, Microsoft Corporation.

Three types of virtualization exist:

- PC virtualization
- Server virtualization
- Desktop virtualization

With **PC virtualization**, a personal computer, such as a desktop or laptop, hosts several different operating systems. Say a user needs to have both Linux and Windows running on a computer for a training or development project. In that circumstance, the user can load software like Oracle VirtualBox or VMWare Workstation on the host operating system in order to create Linux and Windows virtual machines. The user can run both systems on the same hardware at the same time if the host operating system has sufficient resources (i.e., memory and CPU power) as shown in Figure 14.

With **server virtualization**, a server computer hosts one or more other server computers. In Figure 15, a Windows Server computer is hosting two virtual machines. Users can log on to either of those virtual machines, and they will appear as normal servers. Figure 16 shows how virtual machine VM3 appears to a user of that server. Notice that a user of VM3 is running a browser that is accessing SharePoint.

PC virtualization is interesting as well as quite useful. Desktop virtualization, on the other hand, has the potential to be revolutionary. With **desktop virtualization**, a server hosts many

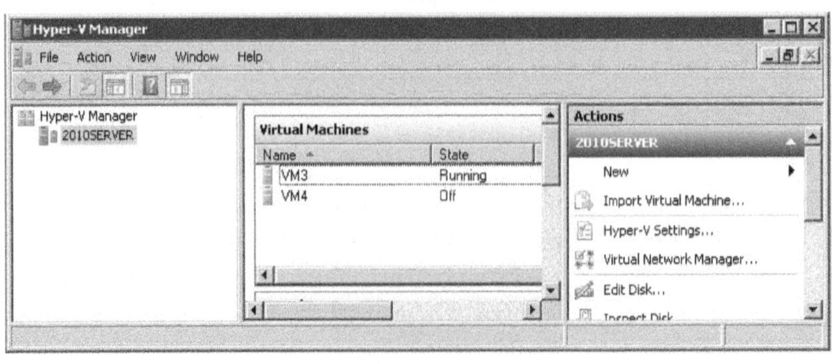

FIGURE 15
Windows Server Computer Hosting Two Virtual Machines
Source: Windows 10, Microsoft Corporation.

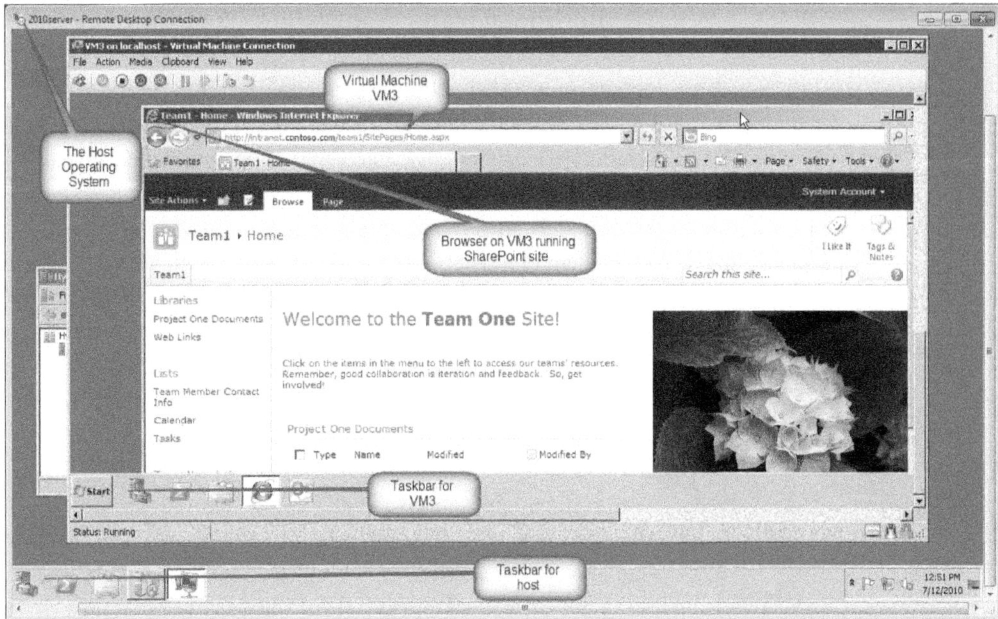

FIGURE 16
Virtual Machine Example
Source: Windows 10, Microsoft Corporation.

versions of desktop operating systems. Each of those desktops has a complete user environment and appears to the user to be just another PC. However, the desktop can be accessed from any computer to which the user has access. Thus, you could be at an airport and go to a terminal computer and access your virtualized desktop. To you, it appears as if that airport computer is your own personal computer. Using a virtual desktop also means that you wouldn't have to worry about losing a corporate laptop or confidential internal data. Meanwhile, many other users could have accessed the computer in the airport, and each thought he or she had his or her personal computer.

Desktop virtualization is in its infancy, but it might have major impact during the early years of your career.

Own Versus License

When you buy a computer program, you are not actually buying that program. Instead, you are buying a **license** to use that program. For example, when you buy a Mac OS license, Apple is selling you the right to use Mac OS. Apple continues to own the Mac OS program. Large organizations do not buy a license for each computer user. Instead, they negotiate a **site license**, which is a flat fee that authorizes the company to install the product (operating system or application) on all of that company's computers or on all of the computers at a specific site.

In the case of Linux, no company can sell you a license to use it. It is owned by the open source community, which states that Linux has no license fee (with certain reasonable restrictions). Large companies such as IBM and smaller companies such as RedHat can make money by *supporting* Linux, but no company makes money selling Linux licenses.

What Types of Applications Exist, and How Do Organizations Obtain Them?

Some applications are designed to be free but gather data about the people who use them.

Application software performs a service or function. Some application programs are general purpose, such as Microsoft Excel or Word. Other application programs provide specific functions. QuickBooks, for example, is an application program that provides general ledger and other accounting functions. We begin by describing categories of application programs and then describe sources for them.

Horizontal-market application software provides capabilities common across all organizations and industries. Word processors, graphics programs, spreadsheets, and presentation programs are all horizontal-market application software.

Examples of such software are Microsoft Word, Excel, and PowerPoint. Examples from other vendors are Adobe's Acrobat, Photoshop, and PageMaker and Jasc Corporation's Paint Shop Pro. These applications are used in a wide variety of businesses across all industries. They are purchased off the shelf, and little customization of features is necessary (or possible). They are the automobile equivalent of a sedan. Everybody buys them and then uses them for different purposes.

Vertical-market application software serves the needs of a specific industry. Examples of such programs are those used by dental offices to schedule appointments and bill patients, those used by auto mechanics to keep track of customer data and customers' automobile repairs, and those used by parts warehouses to track inventory, purchases, and sales. If horizontal-market applications are sedans, then vertical-market applications would be construction vehicles, like an excavator. They meet the needs of a specific industry.

Vertical applications usually can be altered or customized. Typically, the company that sold the application software will provide such services or offer referrals to qualified consultants who can provide this service.

One-of-a-kind application software is developed for a specific, unique need. The U.S. Department of Defense develops such software, for example, because it has needs that no other organization has.

You can think of one-of-a-kind application software as the automotive equivalent of a military tank. Tanks are developed for a very specific and unique need. Tanks cost more to manufacture than sedans, and cost overruns are common. They take longer to make and require unique hardware components. However, tanks are highly customizable and fit the requirements of a heavy-duty battle vehicle very well.

If you're headed into battle, you wouldn't want to be driving a four-door sedan. Sometimes paying for a custom vehicle, while expensive, is warranted. It all depends on what you're doing. Militaries, for example, purchase sedans, construction vehicles, and tanks. Each vehicle fills its own need. You can buy computer software in exactly the same ways: **off-the-shelf software**, **off-the-shelf with alterations software**, or **custom-developed software**.

Organizations develop custom application software themselves or hire a development vendor. Like buying a tank, such development is done in situations where the needs of the organization are so unique that no horizontal or vertical applications are available. By developing custom software, the organization can tailor its application to fit its requirements.

Custom development is difficult and risky. Staffing and managing teams of software developers is challenging. Managing software projects can be daunting. Many organizations have embarked on application development projects only to find that the projects take twice as long—or longer—to finish than planned. Cost overruns of 200 percent and 300 percent are not uncommon.

In addition, every application program needs to be adapted to changing needs and changing technologies. The adaptation costs of horizontal and vertical software are amortized over all the users of that software, perhaps thousands or millions of customers. For custom-developed software, however, the using organization must pay all of the adaptation costs itself. Over time, this cost burden is heavy.

Because of the risk and expense, custom development is the last-choice alternative, used only when there is no other option. Figure 17 summarizes software sources and types.

What Is Firmware?

Firmware is computer software that is installed into devices such as printers, print servers, and various types of communication devices. The software is coded just like other software, but it is installed into special, read-only memory of the printer or other device. In this way, the program becomes part of the device's memory; it is as if the program's logic is designed into the device's

FIGURE 17
Software Sources and Types

Software Type	Software Source: Off-the-shelf	Off-the-shelf and then customized	Custom-developed
Horizontal applications	(shaded)		
Vertical applications	(shaded)	(shaded)	
One-of-a-kind applications			(shaded)

circuitry. Therefore, users do not need to load firmware into the device's memory. Firmware can be changed or upgraded, but this is normally a task for IS professionals.

Q4 Is Open Source Software a Viable Alternative?

To answer this question, you first need to know something about the open source movement and process. Most computer historians would agree that Richard Matthew Stallman is the father of the movement. In 1983, he developed a set of tools called **GNU** (a self-referential acronym meaning *GNU Not Unix*) for creating a free Unix-like operating system. Stallman made many other contributions to open source, including the **GNU general public license (GPL) agreement,** one of the standard license agreements for open source software. Stallman was unable to attract enough developers to finish the free Unix system but continued making other contributions to the open source movement.

In 1991 Linus Torvalds, working in Helsinki, began work on another version of Unix, using some of Stallman's tools. That version eventually became Linux, the high-quality and very popular operating system discussed previously.

The Internet proved to be a great asset for open source, and many open source projects became successful, including:

- LibreOffice (default office suite in Linux distributions)
- Firefox (a browser)
- MySQL (a DBMS)
- Apache (a Web server)
- Ubuntu (a Windows-like desktop operating system)
- Android (a mobile device operating system)
- Cassandra (a NoSQL DBMS)
- Hadoop (a BigData processing system)

Why Do Programmers Volunteer Their Services?

To a person who has never enjoyed writing computer programs, it is difficult to understand why anyone would donate his or her time and skills to contribute to open source projects. Programming is, however, an intense combination of art and logic, and designing and writing a complicated computer program can be exceedingly pleasurable (and addictive). Many programmers joyfully write computer programs—day after day. If you have an artistic and logical mind, you ought to try it.

The first reason that people contribute to open source is that it is great fun! Additionally, some people contribute to open source because it gives them the freedom to choose the projects they work on. They may have a programming day job that is not terribly interesting—say, writing a program to manage a computer printer. Their job pays the bills, but it's not fulfilling.

In the 1950s, Hollywood studio musicians suffered as they recorded the same style of music over and over for a long string of uninteresting movies. To keep their sanity, those musicians would

SO WHAT? NEW FROM CES 2016

What's new in hardware? It's the Consumer Electronics Show (CES) held in Las Vegas every January: 3,600 exhibitors and 170,000 hardware-gawking attendees whipped to frenzy by loud music, screaming video, and hyperventilating media. It's a show that only Las Vegas can do!

What's hot this year? How about:

1. **Transparent and Flexible TVs:** New TV developments are a perennial CES favorite. Why? Because everyone watches TV, and hardware geeks are prime buyers, spending big money for the latest gee-whiz features. UHD (Ultra High Definition) TVs that display 4K (2160p) and 8K (4320p) were commonplace at CES this year. But Panasonic's prototype transparent display looks like a typical HD TV when it's showing a movie, then turns into a normal piece of tinted glass when you're done. LG's new 18-inch flexible display was also a hit. It rolls up just like a sheet of paper when you're done watching your favorite show.
2. **DietSensor:** The winner of the coveted CES 2016 Best of Innovation Award was DietSensor. This small, handheld device pairs with your smartphone and scans the food you're about to eat. It determines the amount of carbohydrates, fats, and proteins in the food using a "molecular sensor." Once the scan is complete, you set the amount of that food you plan to eat, and the DietSensor calculates the calories. If you're on a diet and counting calories, DietSensor makes it easy to stay on track.
3. **"it" Smart Bed:** You will spend about one-third of your life sleeping–that's roughly 26 years. Sleep Number intends to make your sleep more informative. The company's new "it" bed uses biometric sensors to track your heart rate, breathing, sleeping patterns, and movement. Based on the data collected, the bed suggests adjustments to the level of firmness, comfort, and support. It can also be linked with other cloud services to provide insights into factors that might affect your sleep. For example, data from the "it" bed can be combined with temperature data gathered in your bedroom. It can then analyze your sleep patterns over a range of temperatures to determine the optimal room temperature for your best night's sleep. Getting a better night's rest may not seem like a big deal now, but over 26 years it adds up.

Source: Dpa picture alliance/Alamy Stock Photo

4. **Family Hub Smart Refrigerator:** Samsung's new Wi-Fi–enabled smart fridge has cameras inside that display its contents to any linked mobile device. Suppose you're shopping at the grocery store and can't remember if you have enough lemons for your famous lemon meringue pie. Just tap the fridge app on your smartphone and you can immediately see the contents of your refrigerator. The smart fridge can also display shared calendars, photos, and notes from your mobile device; stream music directly from Internet using apps like Pandora; or even stream video from your smart TV.

Questions

1. What trends do you see pushing innovation in televisions? Why are these important to consumers?
2. What types of sensors like DietSensor might be useful for other IoT devices?
3. Why might doctors and nutritionists be interested in a device like DietSensor?
4. How could a smart bed benefit from being paired with a smartphone?
5. What other devices do you think could benefit from becoming "smart" devices? Why?
6. What security or privacy concerns might be associated with a smart fridge?

gather on Sundays to play jazz, and a number of high-quality jazz clubs resulted. That's what open source is to programmers: a place where they can exercise their creativity while working on projects they find interesting and fulfilling.

Another reason for contributing to open source is to exhibit one's skill, both for pride and to find a job or consulting employment. A final reason is to start a business selling services to support an open source product.

How Does Open Source Work?

The term **open source** means that the source code of the program is available to the public. **Source code** is computer code as written by humans and understandable by humans. Figure 18 shows a portion of the computer code written for the ARES project.

Source code is compiled into **machine code** that is processed by a computer. Machine code is, in general, not understandable by humans and cannot be modified. When a user accesses a Web site, the machine code version of the program runs on the user's computer. We do not show machine code in a figure because it would look like this:

1101001010010111111001110111100100011100000111111011101111100111...

In a **closed source** project, say, Microsoft Office, the source code is highly protected and only available to trusted employees and carefully vetted contractors. The source code is protected like gold in a vault. Only those trusted programmers can make changes to a closed source project.

With open source, anyone can obtain the source code from the open source project's Web site. Programmers alter or add to this code depending on their interests and goals. In most cases,

FIGURE 18
Source Code Sample

```
/// <summary>
/// Allows the page to draw itself.
/// </summary>
private void OnDraw(object sender, GameTimerEventArgs e)
{
    SharedGraphicsDeviceManager.Current.GraphicsDevice.Clear(Color.CornflowerBlue);

    SharedGraphicsDeviceManager.Current.GraphicsDevice.Clear(Color.Black);

    // Render the Silverlight controls using the UIElementRenderer.
    elementRenderer.Render();

    // Draw the sprite
    spriteBatch.Begin();

    // Draw the rectangle in its new position
    for (int i = 0; i < 3; i++)
    {
        spriteBatch.Draw(texture[i], bikeSpritePosition[i], Color.White);
    }

    // Using the texture from the UIElementRenderer,

    // draw the Silverlight controls to the screen.
    spriteBatch.Draw(elementRenderer.Texture, Vector2.Zero, Color.White);

    spriteBatch.End();
}
```

programmers can incorporate code they find into their own projects. They may be able to resell those projects depending on the type of license agreement the project uses.

Open source succeeds because of collaboration. A programmer examines the source code and identifies a need or project that seems interesting. He or she then creates a new feature, redesigns or reprograms an existing feature, or fixes a known problem. That code is then sent to others in the open source project who evaluate the quality and merits of the work and add it to the product, if appropriate.

Typically, there is a lot of give and take. Or, there are many cycles of iteration and feedback. Because of this iteration, a well-managed project with strong peer reviews can result in very high quality code, like that in Linux.

So, Is Open Source Viable?

The answer depends on to whom and for what. Open source has certainly become legitimate. According to *The Economist*, "It is now generally accepted that the future will involve a blend of both proprietary and open-source software."[29] During your career, open source will likely take a greater and greater role in software. However, whether open source works for a particular situation depends on the requirements and constraints of that situation.

In some cases, companies choose open source software because it is "free." It turns out that this advantage may be less important than you'd think because in many cases support and operational costs swamp the initial licensing fee.

Q5 What Are the Differences Between Native and Web Applications?

Applications can be categorized as native applications that run on just one operating system or Web applications that run in browsers. In the latter case, the browser provides a more or less consistent environment for the application; the peculiarities of operating systems and hardware are handled by the browser's code and hidden from the Web application.

Figure 19 contrasts native and Web applications on their important characteristics. Consider the Native Applications column first.

Developing Native Applications

Native applications are developed using serious, heavy-duty, professional programming languages. Mac OS and iOS applications are constructed using Objective-C or the **Swift** programming language. Linux (Android) applications are constructed using Java, and Windows applications are constructed using C#, VB.NET, C++, and others. All of these languages are **object-oriented**, which means they can be used to create difficult, complex applications and, if used properly, will result in high-performance code that is easy to alter when requirements change. The particular characteristics of object-oriented languages are beyond the scope of this text.

Object-oriented languages can be used only by professional programmers who have devoted years to learning object-oriented design and coding skills. Typically, such developers were computer science majors in college.

The benefit of such languages is that they give programmers close control over the assets of the computing device and enable the creation of sophisticated and complex user interfaces. If the programs are well written, they perform fast and use memory efficiently. The limits on native applications are usually budgetary, not technological. As a businessperson, you can get just about any application you can afford.

The downside of native applications is that they are, well, native. They only run on the operating system for which they are programmed. An iOS application must be completely recoded in

	Native Applications	Web Applications
Development Languages	Objective-C Java C#, C++, VB.NET, Swift (object-oriented languages)	html5 css3 JavaScript (scripting language)
Developed by	Professional programmers, only	Professional programmers and technically oriented Web developers and business professionals
Skill level required	High	Low to high
Difficulty	High	Easy to hard, depending on application requirements
Developer's Degree	Computer science	Computer science Information systems Graphics design
User Experience	Can be superb, depending on programming quality	Simple to sophisticated, depending on program quality
Possible applications	Whatever you can pay for...	Some limits prohibit very sophisticated applications
Dependency	iOS, Android, Windows	Browser differences, only
Cost	High. Difficult work by highly paid employees, multiple versions required.	Low to high ... easier work by lesser-paid employees, only multiple browser files necessary. Sophisticated applications may require high skill and pay.
Application distribution	Via application stores (e.g., Apple Store)	Via Web sites
Example	Vanguard iPad application (free in Apple's iTunes store)	Seafood Web site: *www.wildrhodyseafood.com* Picozu editor: *www.picozu.com/editor*

FIGURE 19
Characteristics of Native and Web Applications

order to run on Android and recoded again to run on Windows.[30] Thus, to reach all users, an organization will need to support and maintain three separate versions of the same application. It will also have to staff and manage three different development teams, with three different skill sets.

As a general rule, the cost of native applications is high. Many organizations reduce that cost by outsourcing development to India and other countries, but native applications are still expensive relative to Web applications. The standard way to distribute native applications is via a company store, such as iTunes, owned by Apple. An excellent example of a native application is Vanguard's iPad application. It is easy to use, has complex functionality, and is highly secure, as you would expect. Companies such as Vanguard must and can afford to pay for exceedingly high-quality applications.

Developing Web Applications

The third column in Figure 19 summarizes Web application characteristics. Such applications run inside a browser such as Firefox, Chrome, Opera, or Edge. The browser handles the idiosyncrasies of the operating system and underlying hardware. In theory, an organization should be able to develop a single application and have it run flawlessly on all browsers on all devices. Unfortunately, there are some differences in the way that browsers implement the Web code. This means that some applications won't run correctly in some browsers.

As shown in the first row of Figure 19, Web development languages are html5, css3, and Javascript. html5 is the latest version of html. The advantages of this version are support for graphics, animation, 2D animations, and other sophisticated user experiences. css3 is used with html5 to specify the appearance of content coded in html. JavaScript is a scripting programming language that is much easier to learn than native-client languages. It is used to provide the underlying logic of the application.

Web applications can be written by professional programmers, and, indeed, most are. However, it is possible for technically oriented Web developers and business professionals to develop them as well. The entry-level technical skill required is low, and simple applications are relatively easy to develop. But sophisticated user experiences are difficult. Web application developers may have degrees in computer science, information systems, or graphics design.

The user experience provided by a Web application varies considerably. Some are simply fancy Web-based brochures (*www.wildrhodyseafood.com*); others are quite sophisticated, such as SpiroCanvas in Figure 20 (*www.gethugames.in/*) or, even more impressive, *www.biodigital.com* in Figure 21.

Web applications are limited by the capabilities of the browser. While browsers are becoming increasingly sophisticated, they cannot offer the full capabilities of the underlying operating system and hardware. Thus, Web applications are unable to support very specialized and complex applications, though this becomes less true each year.

As stated, the major advantage of Web over native applications is that they will run on any operating system and device. There are some browser differences, but these differences are very minor when compared with the differences among iOS, Android, and Windows. In general, unlike native applications, you can assume that a Web application has one code base and one development team.

Because Web applications can be developed by less skilled, lesser-paid employees and because only one code base and one development team are necessary, they are considerably cheaper to develop than native applications. However, this statement assumes applications of equivalent complexity. A simple native application can be cheaper to develop than a complex Web application.

Users obtain Web applications via the Internet. For example, when you go to *www.picozu.com/editor* the required html5, css3, and JavaScript files are downloaded automatically over the Web. Updates to the application are automatic and seamless. You need not install (or reinstall) anything. This difference is an advantage to the user; it makes it more difficult, however, to earn money from your application. Amazon, for example, will sell your native application and pay you a royalty.

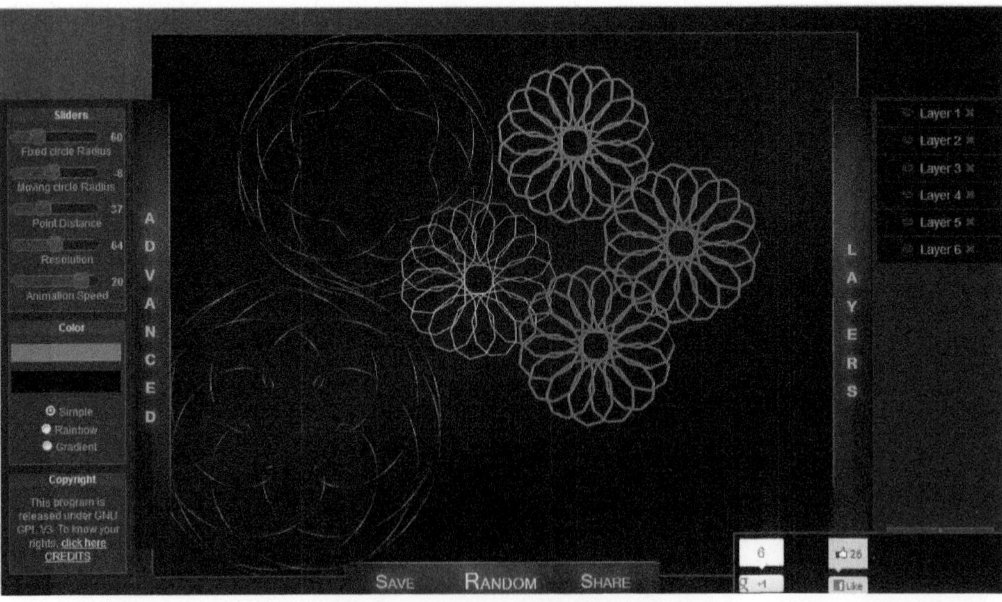

FIGURE 20
GethuGames' SpiroCanvas
Source: From www.gethugames.in/spirocanvas/.

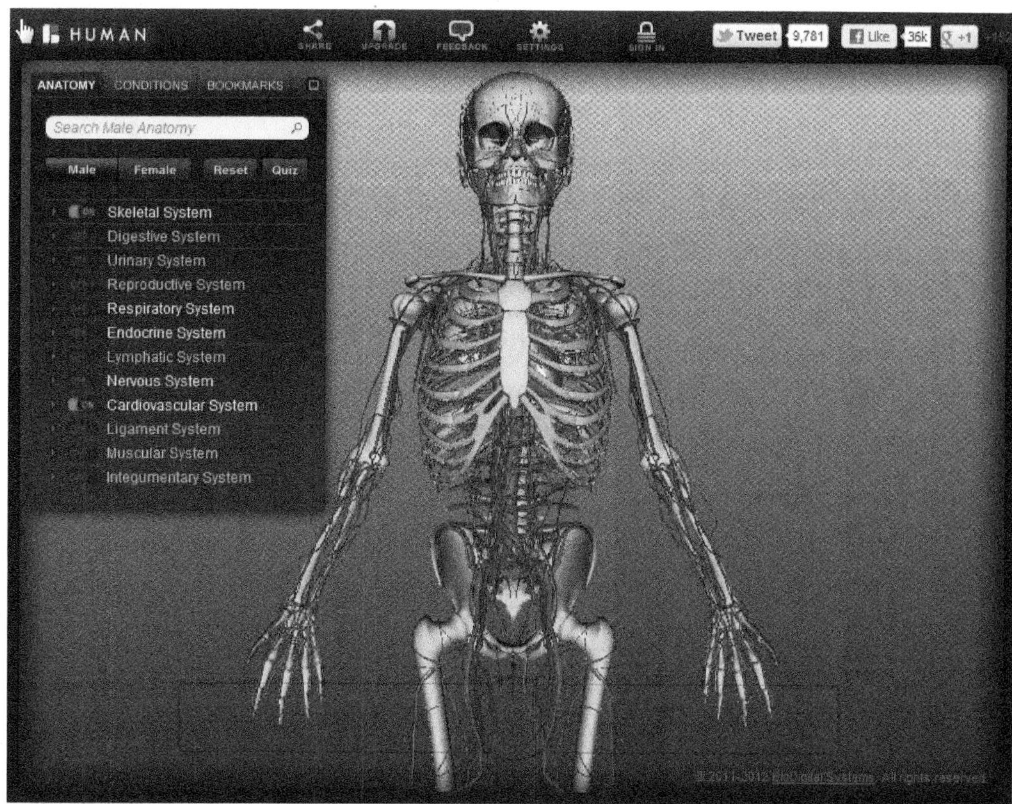

FIGURE 21
Sophisticated html5 Application
Source: Image created using the BioDigital Human (*www.biodigital.com*)

However, unless you require users to buy your Web application (which is possible but rare), you'll have to give it away.

Which Is Better?

You know the answer to that question. If it were clear-cut, we'd only be discussing one alternative. It's not. The choice depends on your strategy, your particular goals, the requirements for your application, your budget, your schedule, your tolerance for managing technical projects, your need for application revenue, and other factors. In general, Web applications are cheaper to develop and maintain, but they may lack the wow factor. You and your organization have to decide for yourselves!

Q6 Why Are Mobile Systems Increasingly Important?

Mobile systems are information systems that support users in motion. Mobile systems users access the system from *any place*—at home, at work, in the car, on the bus, or at the beach—using any smart device, such as a smartphone, tablet, or PC. The possibilities are endless.

Mobile systems users move not only geographically but also from device to device. The user who starts reading a book on an iPad on a bus, continues reading that book on a PC at work, and finishes it on a Kindle Fire at home is mobile both geographically and across devices.

As shown in Figure 22, the major elements in a mobile system are *users in motion, mobile devices, wireless connectivity*, and a *cloud-based resource.* A **mobile device** is a small, lightweight, power-conserving, computing device that is capable of wireless connectivity. Almost all mobile devices have a display and some means for data entry. Mobile devices include smartphones, tablets,

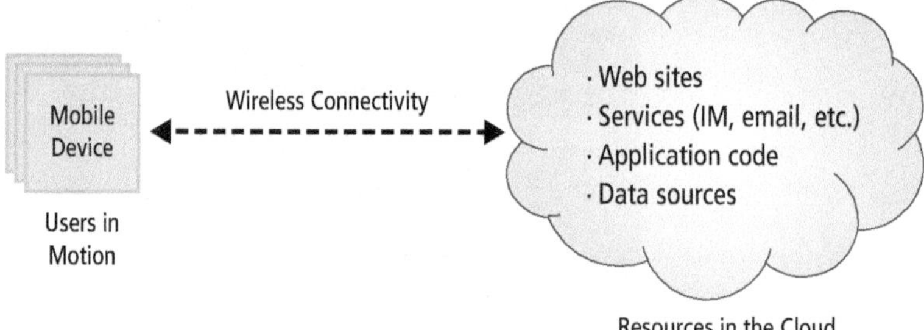

FIGURE 22
Elements of a Mobile Information System

smartwatches, and small, light laptops. Desktop computers, Xboxes, and large, heavy, power-hungry laptops are not mobile devices.

For now, just assume that the cloud is a group of servers on the other end of a connection with a mobile device. When downloading a book for a Kindle, for example, the cloud is one or more servers on the other end that store that book and download a copy of it to your device.

The major reason for the importance of mobile systems is the size of their market. According to Cisco, at the end of 2015 there were 7.9 billion mobile devices generating 3.7 exabytes of traffic per month.[31] By 2020, this will jump to 11.6 billion mobile devices generating more than 30.6 exabytes per month. That's 1.5 devices for every person on the planet. Smartphones will account for nearly 72 percent of global mobile traffic.[32]

It took seven years after the launch of the first iPhone (2007–2014) for smartphones to achieve mainstream use by 70 percent of the U.S. market.[33] That's faster than any other technology except television in the early 1950s, which tied the smartphone adoption rate. The February 2016 comScore Report shows 199 million people in the United States owned smartphones, which accounted for 79.3 percent of the mobile phone market.[34] The size of the mobile e-commerce, or **m-commerce**, market is expected to exceed $149B by 2019.[35]

Additionally, mobile use is favored by the young. According to Nielsen's measures of mobile device use, the younger the age group, the greater the percentage of people with mobile devices. Further, younger people have more devices per capita than older groups.[36] These young cohorts will further increase mobile systems use in the years to come.

Because of this vast and growing market, mobile systems are having a major impact on business and society today—impact that is forcing industry change while creating new career opportunities for mobile-IS-savvy professionals, as well as large numbers of new, interesting mobile- IS-related jobs.

Figure 23 summarizes the mobile-system impact for each of the five components of an information system. We will discuss each of the components in this figure, starting with hardware.

Hardware

Clearly, increasing demand for mobile systems means the sales of many more mobile devices, often at the expense of PC sales. Hewlett-Packard, a large PC manufacturer, learned this fact when it didn't respond quickly enough to the onslaught of mobile devices and was forced to eliminate 27,000 jobs in 2012. In the future, there will be high demand for innovative mobile devices as well as cheap copycats.

If you're reading this text, you're unlikely to be a hardware engineer, and if you're not living in Asia, you're also unlikely to be involved in hardware manufacturing. However, any market having 3.9 billion prospects is ripe with opportunities in marketing, sales, logistics, customer support, and related activities.

	Hardware	Software	Data	Procedures	People
Impact of mobile systems growth	Many, many more mobile devices will be sold.	Compact interfaces; new technology for active users; application scaling.	More data, but more information? Less device real estate means fewer ads possible.	Always on, always at work. Employee lifestyle becomes hybrid of personal and professional.	Ability to thrive in a dynamic environment more important.
Industry changes	PCs less important; high demand (and requirement) for innovative devices as well as cheap copycats.	html5, css3, and JavaScript increase capability of thin-clients.	Loss of control. Ad model in danger?	Personal mobile devices at work.	More part-time employees and independent contractors.
Career opportunities	Jobs for mobile device sales, marketing, support.	New technology levels the playing field for html5. Business expertise needed for mobile requirements. New companies!	Reporting and data mining even more important. Design of effective mobile reports.	Innovative use of just-in-time data. Need for adjusting business processes gives another premium to non-routine problem solvers.	Independent contractors (and some employees) work where and when they want. What is this new social organism?

FIGURE 23
Five Components of Mobile Change and Opportunity

Software

The reduced size of mobile devices requires the invention of new, innovative interfaces. The mobile user is an active user and expects an active screen experience. The premium will be for moving graphics, changing Web pages, and animation. Applications will need to scale from the very smallest to the very largest, while providing a user experience appropriate to the device's size.

Rapid technology change in mobile software continually levels the playing field. Today, for example, expert programmers in Objective-C better not relax. html5 and css3 are gaining popularity, and they will reduce the need for Objective-C expertise. Further, as you learned in 5, while languages like Objective-C are difficult and time-consuming to learn, html5, css3, and JavaScript are less so. With the reduced barrier to entry, hordes of less experienced and less educated new entrants will appear as competitors. You might be one of them.

Additionally, continually evolving software means new and exciting entrepreneurial opportunities. Are you sorry that you missed the early days working at Facebook? Right now, somewhere, there is another Mark Zuckerberg starting... well, what? Because of the continually changing software environment, new opportunities abound and will continue to do so for decades.

Data

Many more mobile systems mean an incredible amount of new data, data that professionals can use to create much more information. But more data doesn't necessarily mean more information. In fact, many business professionals believe they're drowning in data while starving for information. What can be done with all of this mobile-systems data to enable humans to conceive information of greater value to them? Data mining and better reporting are possibilities for you.

On the other hand, not all the news is good, at least not for many organizations. For one, smaller screens means less room for advertising, a factor that limited the success of the Facebook public offering in May 2012. Also, mobile systems increase the risk of organizations losing control over their data. In the past, employees used only computer equipment provided by the employer and connected only via employer-managed networks. In that situation, it is possible for the

ETHICS GUIDE

FREE APPS FOR DATA

You're sitting in your Introduction to MIS class, and the professor starts talking about how profitable software development can be. He points out that billionaires like Bill Gates (Microsoft), Larry Ellison (Oracle), Larry Page (Google), and Mark Zuckerberg (Facebook) all made their fortunes by developing useful software. But a vocal classmate jumps in and points out that he's never paid any of those people a penny. He uses Google Search, Gmail, and Facebook all for free. Yes, he uses Microsoft Office, but it's the free online version through OneDrive. Even the apps on his smartphone are free.

Then comes the perennial question, which also happens to be a major point of frustration for the tech industry: How do you make money from free apps? The professor says something about capturing market share, potential income, and future innovation. You're not buying it. You're interested in *real* income, not *potential* income.

Nick the Data Broker

The person sitting next to you, Nick, starts smiling broadly and nods his head. He's in your group for your big class project. He leans over and whispers, "If you're not paying for it, *you* are the product. Data is where you make money, not software. Give them the software, take the data, and make the money. It's simple."

You're a little confused at first. But then you think back to last Wednesday when you first met Nick. He said he was coming back to school to get a degree in MIS because he needed the technical knowledge for his new job with his brother's company. He explained that his brother was a data broker (sometimes called an information broker). He buys data about individuals from companies and then sells it to other companies for a profit. It sounded like they were doing really well. Before you could even ask if it was legal or ethical, Nick quipped, "Yes, of course it's legal. Everyone does it." He had obviously gotten this question before.

But was Nick right? He isn't a billionaire like Bill Gates. Nick was only concerned with buying and selling data. He wasn't interested in application development. But he did make a good point, and it got you thinking. What if you started a business that made applications that were designed to collect individual data? You could make dozens of useful apps, collect individual data, and then sell it to Nick.

But what data would Nick pay for? How much of it could you get? He wouldn't care about gaming data. But he would pay for data about user behavior like which Web sites they visit, where they're located, who their friends are, and what they purchase.

Flashlight Apps

At lunch, you do a few searches about how mobile applications can access data on smartphones. It turns out that users just have to grant the application permission(s), and it can access *any* data on the phone. Could that be right? *Any* data? This could be a gold mine. You get excited at the prospect of harvesting thousands of terabytes of data and selling them to Nick. You could retire in a month.

But then a sinking feeling comes over you. What if you're not the first person to think of this idea? What if someone else is already giving away apps and harvesting users' data. You decide to check the permissions for one of the most useful free applications you have on your phone—your flashlight app. You search for "flashlight app permissions" and you see dozens of news articles referencing a threat report by SnoopWall.[37]

The SnoopWall report looked at the permissions required by the top 10 flashlight apps for Android smartphones. The results were shocking. All of these apps did more than just turn a light on and off. They required permission to access data about your location, network connectivity, and USB storage. They also required permissions to install shortcuts, receive data to/from the Internet, modify your system settings, and disable your screen lock.

The app you use was third on the list. Not good. You decide to check to see whether the report was accurate. Were these apps harvesting all this data? You look at the first six flashlight apps that show up in Google Play. The results are shown in the table below. The bottom three rows show the changes in the number of permissions from 2013, 2014, and 2016.

Seeing all of the permissions required by these simple flashlight apps is distressing. Why would your flashlight need your GPS coordinates? Who was getting this data? What were they using it for? It looks like someone had already thought of your data-harvesting idea. It may be too late to make any money off the free-app-for-individual-data scheme. All of a sudden, these free apps don't look as attractive to you—as a consumer.

Permissions	Super-Bright LED Flashlight	Brightest Flashlight Free	Brightest LED Flashlight	Flashlight	High-Powered Flashlight	Tiny Flashlight + LED
Take pictures and videos	X	X	X	X	X	X
Receive data from Internet	X		X		X	
Control flashlight	X	X	X	X**	X	X
Change system display settings	X*		X*		X*	
Modify system settings	X*		X*		X*	
Prevent device from sleeping	X	X	X	X	X	X
View network connections	X	X	X	X	X	X
Full network access	X	X	X	X	X	X
Run at startup						X
Control vibration						X
Retrieve running apps			X*		X*	
Modify or delete the contents of your storage		X	X*		X*	
Read the contents of your storage		X	X*		X*	
View Wi-Fi connections		X	X*		X*	
Read phone status and identity		X	X		X*	
Read Home settings and shortcuts		X		X*		
Write Home settings and shortcuts				X*		
Disable your screen lock				X*		
Install shortcuts		X		X*		
Uninstall shortcuts		X		X*		
Approximate location		X			X*	
Precise location		X			X*	
Disable or modify status bar		X*				
Draw over other apps			X**			
Count 2013	20	15	13	9	15	6
Count 2014	8	15	13	9	15	7
Count 2016	6	14	8	5	6	7
* Dropped for 2016 ** Added for 2016						

DISCUSSION QUESTIONS

1. Consider the decision to create a free application designed to harvest individual data.
   a. Is this decision ethical according to the categorical imperative (pages 23–24)?
   b. Is this decision ethical according to the utilitarian perspective (pages 60–61)?
   c. How would users react if they knew their data was being harvested in exchange for a free app?
2. Suppose Google becomes aware that apps in the Google Play store are harvesting user data unrelated to the function of the application.
   a. Does it have a *legal* obligation to find out which apps are harvesting data inappropriately?
   b. Does it have an *ethical* obligation to find out which apps are harvesting data inappropriately?
   c. Does Google provide free apps in exchange for individual data? Why?
3. How hard should Google work at curating apps in Google Play to ensure that appropriate permissions are set?
4. In 2014, Symantec found that 17 percent of all Android apps were malware in disguise.[38] But a report by Google found that less than 1 percent of all Android devices had a potentially harmful application installed.[39]
   a. Is it ethical for Google to remove applications it considers inappropriate? Consider both the categorical imperative and utilitarian perspectives.
   b. Is it ethical for Google to limit permissions for certain applications? Consider both the categorical imperative and utilitarian perspectives.

organization to control who does what with which data and where. No longer. Employees come to work with their own mobile devices. Data leakage is inevitable.

With more people switching to mobile devices and with less room for ads, online advertising revenue may be sharply reduced, possibly endangering the revenue model that supports most of the Web's free content. If this happens, dramatic change is just around the corner!

Procedures

Mobile systems are always on. They have no business hours. And people who use mobile systems are equally always on. In the mobile world, we're always open for business. It is impossible to be out of the office. One consequence of always-on is the blending of our personal and professional lives. Such blending means, in part, that business will intrude on your personal life, and your personal life will intrude on your business. This intrusion can be distracting and stressful; on the other hand, it can lead to richer, more complex relationships.

Employees will expect to use their mobile devices at work, but should they? In truth, who can keep them from it? If the organization blocks them from connecting to the work-related networks, they can connect over the wireless networks that they pay for themselves. In this case, the organization is entirely out of the loop. Could employees send confidential corporate information through their personal mobile devices? We will discuss these issues in more detail in Q7.

Mobile systems offer the potential of **just-in-time data**, which is data delivered to the user at the precise time it is needed. A pharmaceutical salesperson uses just-in-time data when she accesses a mobile system to obtain the latest literature on a new drug while waiting for the doctor to whom she will pitch it. She needn't remember the drug's characteristics any longer than it takes her to walk down the hallway and make the sale.

Furthermore, some organizations will passively wait for change to happen, while others will proactively reengineer their processes to incorporate mobile systems for higher process quality. Either way, the need for business process change creates opportunity for creative, nonroutine business problem solvers.

People

Mobile systems change the value of our thinking. For example, just-in-time data removes the premium on the ability to memorize vast quantities of product data, but creates a premium for the ability to access, query, and present that data. Mobile systems increase the speed of business, giving an advantage to those who can nimbly respond to changing conditions and succeed with the unexpected.

With the ability to be connected and always on, organizations may find they can be just as effective with part-time employees and independent contractors. The increasing regulatory complexity and cost of full-time employees will create an incentive for organizations to do just that.

As that occurs, professionals who can thrive in a dynamic environment with little need for direct supervision will find that they can work both where and when they want, at least a good part of the time. Once you're always on and remote, it doesn't matter if you're always on in New Jersey or at a ski area in Vermont. New lifestyle choices become possible for such workers.

These mobile workers can work where they want and for whom they want. There won't be a boss looking over their shoulder. They can work multiple jobs with different companies at the same time! Companies may have to change the way they pay workers. Instead of paying employees by the hour, they would need to focus more on paying for productivity. This shift toward focusing on performance will empower great employees and make it harder for slackers to hide out in an organization. Companies will benefit from mobile workers too. They won't need as much expensive commercial office space. What an incredible time to be starting a business career!

Q7 What Are the Challenges of Personal Mobile Devices at Work?

So far, we've focused on mobile applications that organizations create for their customers and others to use. In this question we will address the use of mobile systems *within* organizations.

In truth, organizations today have a love/hate relationship with their employees' use of their own mobile devices at work. They love the cost-saving possibility of having employees buy their own hardware, but they hate the increased vulnerability and loss of control. The result, at least today, is a wide array of organizational attitudes.

Consider a recent report by Tech Pro Research that estimates 74 percent of companies have adopted BYOD or are planing to do so.[40] If you aren't already bringing your own device to work, you'll soon have to. Yet only 43 percent of all organizations have created an official mobile-use policy.[41]

Advantages and Disadvantages of Employee Use of Mobile Systems at Work

Figure 24 summarizes the advantages and disadvantages of employee use of mobile systems at work. Advantages include the cost savings just mentioned as well as greater employee satisfaction of using devices that they chose according to their own preferences rather than organization-supplied PCs. Because employees are already using these devices for their own purposes, they need less training and can be more productive. All of this means reduced support costs.

On the other hand, employee use of mobile devices has significant disadvantages. First, there is the real danger of lost or damaged data. When data is brought into employee-owned computing devices, the organization loses control over where it goes or what happens to it. IBM, for example, disallowed the use of Apple's voice searching application, Siri, on employees' mobile devices for just that reason.[42] Also, if an employee loses his or her device, the data goes with it, and when employees leave the organization, the data on their personal devices needs to be deleted somehow.

Organizations also lose control over the updating of software and the applications that users employ. This control loss leads to compatibility problems; users can process data, for example edit documents, with software that is incompatible with the organization's standard software. The result to the organization is a mess of inconsistent documents.

Possibly the greatest disadvantage of employee use of their own devices is the risk of infection. The organization cannot know where the users have been with their devices or what they've done when they've been there. The possibility of severe viruses infecting the organization's networks is real. Finally, all of these disadvantages can also lead, ironically, to greater support costs.

Given all that, organizations cannot avoid the issue. Whatever the costs and risks, employees are bringing their own devices to work. Ignoring the issue will simply make matters worse.

Advantages	Disadvantages
Cost savings	Data loss or damage
Greater employee satisfaction	Loss of control
Reduced need for training	Compatibility problems
Higher productivity	Risk of infection
Reduced support costs	Greater support costs

FIGURE 24
Advantages and Disadvantages of Employee Use of Mobile Systems at Work

Survey of Organizational BYOD Policy

A **bring your own device (BYOD) policy** is a statement concerning employees' permissions and responsibilities when they use their own device for organizational business. Figure 25 arranges BYOD policies according to functionality and control. Starting in the lower left-hand corner, the most primitive policy is to ignore mobile use. That posture, which provides neither functionality to the employee nor control to the organization, has no advantages and, as just stated, cannot last.

The next step up in functionality is for the organization to offer its wireless network to mobile devices, as if it were a coffee shop. The advantage to the organization of this policy is that the organization can sniff employees' mobile traffic, thus learning how employees are using their devices (and time) during work.

The next policy provides more functionality and somewhat more control. Here the organization creates secure application services using https that require employee sign-on and can be accessed from any device, mobile or not. Such applications can be used when employees are at work or elsewhere. These services provide controlled access to some organizations' assets.

A fourth policy is more of a strategic maneuver than a policy. The organization tells employees that they can sign on to the organization's network with their mobile devices, but the employee is financially responsible for any damage he or she does. The hope is that few employees know what their exposure is and hence decide not to do so.

A more enlightened policy is to manage the users' devices as if they were owned by the organization. With this policy, employees turn over their mobile devices to the IS department, which cleanses and reloads software and installs programs that enable the IS department to manage the device remotely. Numerous vendors license products called **mobile device management (MDM) software** that assist this process. These products install and update software, back up and restore mobile devices, wipe employer software and data from devices in the event the device is lost or the employee leaves the company, report usage, and provide other mobile device management data.

This policy benefits the organization, but some employees resist turning over the management of their own hardware to the organization. This resistance can be softened if the organization pays at least a portion of the hardware expense.

The most controlling policy is for the organization to declare that it owns any mobile device that employees connect to its network. To be enforceable, this policy must be part of the employee's contract. It is taken by organizations that manage very secure operations and environments.

Control

Functionality		Low ⟵				⟶ High
High	Full VPN Access to Organizational Systems			You're responsible for damage	We'll check it out, reload software and data, and manage it remotely	If you connect it, we own it
	Organizational Services on Public Internet		We'll offer limited systems you can access from any device			
	Access to Internet	We'll be a coffee shop				
Low	None	They don't exist				

FIGURE 25
Six Common BYOD Policies

BYOD Policy	Description	Advantage to Organization
They don't exist	Organization looks the other way when employees bring mobile devices to work.	None
We'll be a coffee shop	You'll be able to sign in to our wireless network using your mobile device.	Packet sniffing of employee mobile device use at work.
We'll offer limited systems you can access from any device	Organization creates https applications with sign-in and offers access to noncritical business systems.	Employees gain public access from any device, not just mobile devices, without having to use VPN accounts.
You're responsible for damage	Threatening posture to discourage employee use of mobile devices at work.	Appear to be permissive without actually being so.
We'll check it out, reload software, then manage remotely	Employees can use their mobile devices just as if they were computers provided by the corporate IS department.	Employee buys the hardware (perhaps with an employer's contribution).
If you connect it, we own it	Employees are not to use mobile devices at work. If they do, they lose them. Part of employment agreement.	Ultimate in control for highly secure work situations (intelligence, military).

FIGURE 26
Advantages of Example BYOD Policies

In some military/intelligence organizations, the policy is that any smart device that ever enters the workplace may never leave it. The advantages of these six policies are summarized in Figure 26.

BYOD policies are rapidly evolving, and many organizations have not yet determined what is best for them. If your employer has a committee to develop such policies, join it if you can. Doing so will provide a great way to gain exposure to the leading technology thinkers at your organization.

Q8 2027? 

There's a really old movie called *You've Got Mail* (1998) starring Tom Hanks and Meg Ryan. In it, the characters get really excited when they get "mail." The term *email* was so new at the time that it hadn't even caught on yet. You can see people in the movie reading newspapers and paper books. Oh, how times have changed.

Fast-forward to today. Email now comes in seconds after it's sent. You check your email during commercial breaks while you're watching TV, while you're driving in traffic, and while you're sitting on the toilet. Instead of checking your email with bated breath, you're dreading seeing more work pile up in your inbox. Or worse—bills, spam, and viruses.

New hardware and software have changed everyday life. People are always on, always connected, always communicating, always working and playing. This trend will continue. The Internet of Things will allow us to be continually connected to more and more devices. You'll be able to control your home, and everything in it, from your smartphone. Your home will be so smart that it will analyze you. It will see what, how, and when you do things and then anticipate your needs.

SECURITY GUIDE

POISONED APP-LES

Have you ever stopped to look up at the stars on a clear night and seen a faint white light tracking slowly across the sky? If so, you've seen a satellite orbiting the earth at speeds exceeding thousands of miles per hour. What may surprise you is that early spacecraft launched by NASA had less computing power than your smartphone. That's right—the small handheld device you use for checking social media and email and for playing games is more powerful than the first spacecraft. But why do you need all of that computing power? Phone calls and text messages don't seem to require massive processing power. Welcome to the era of the "app"!

Apps are the drivers of faster and more powerful smartphones. Apple and other smartphone manufacturers release new versions of their phones on an annual basis. Keeping up with the flashiest and most powerful apps drives the demand for faster processing chips and more memory. Advancements in both of these areas often happen without increasing the form factor of the phone or reducing battery life.

Smartphone users have a seemingly insatiable appetite for apps. In 2014, the Apple App Store contained more than 1.2 million apps, reported 75 billion app downloads, and listed 9 million registered app developers.[43] These apps allow you to do everything from making stock trades on the go to checking the latest weather conditions anywhere in the world. While most apps cost only a few dollars, many of them are free. You may be wondering, "How is this possible?" and "Are there any hidden costs?" You may be surprised to learn that free apps may not be such a great deal after all.

XcodeGhost Haunts iOS

The App Store is generally a well-regulated marketplace. Apps are screened for security vulnerabilities and vulgar content in order to create a safe experience for users. However, with more than a million applications available to consumers, it is inevitable that some malicious apps clear the screening process.

Apple recently reported that dozens of apps available on the App Store contained a malware application named XcodeGhost. Apps containing this malware reportedly accessed user credentials, hijacked URLs, were able to read and write data on devices, and compromised other iOS apps. WeChat, an app used extensively in China, was affected by XcodeGhost and contributed heavily to the tally of more than 500 million iOS users who could have been exposed to this dangerous malware.[44]

The malware was embedded in apps available on the App Store because developers chose to install a compromised version of the Xcode developers kit despite warnings that the software had been altered. Developers were downloading the compromised software because it had been posted on a server offering faster-than-standard download speeds.

Once this vulnerability had been identified, Apple notified users that the dangerous apps had been removed from the App Store and that they were collaborating with developers to ensure that this type of incident does not happen again. However, even with these apps identified and removed,

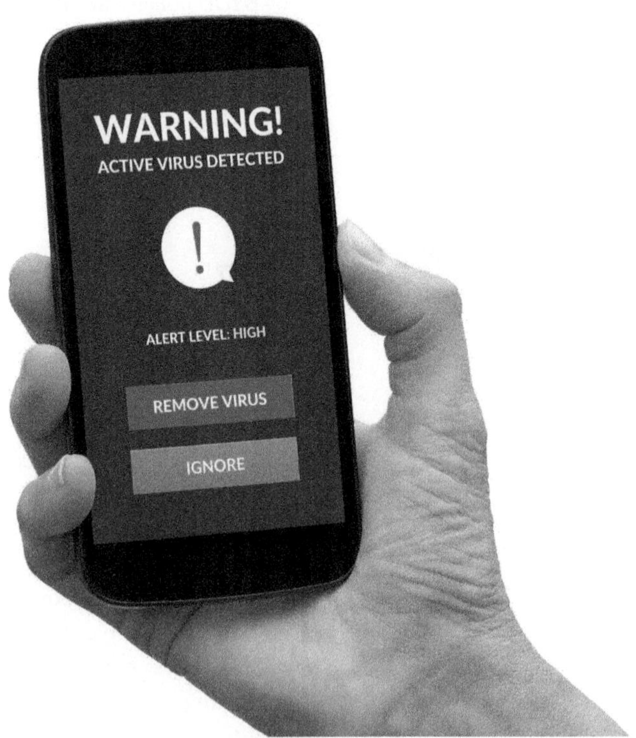

Source: © CarmenMurillo/iStock/Getty Images Plus

this security breach begs the question "What other vulnerabilities are lurking in the App Store, and have you already downloaded any of these potential threats?"

Installation App-rehension

Have you ever been using your phone and seen an alert message indicating that one of the apps on your phone was accessing your location information in the background? If so, were you worried? Did you allow the app to continue monitoring your location, or did you shut it off? A key point to consider is that an app does not have to be considered malware to be dangerous or invasive. In fact, many of the apps on your phone are likely accessing data that are unrelated to the app's specific purpose. For example, a survey of apps with built-in networking tools revealed that 13 out of 15 of these apps uploaded all user contacts on the phone to remote servers managed by the app developers.[45] Contact information can then be sold to advertisers and other third parties for a profit.

This type of indirect information gathering is why many of the apps downloaded from the App Store are free. End users end up paying for them with their privacy. But why do users tolerate an invasion of their privacy? Users often fail to review the usage agreement for each app.[46] Even more striking is that developers can change the terms of privacy agreements after a user has agreed to a prior version of the terms.

Despite the tremendous convenience, productivity, and entertainment afforded by our phones and apps, there are hidden costs. These hidden costs may include the risk of downloading dangerous software or inadvertently allowing apps access to private data. A little app-rehension may help users prevent a serious privacy invasion or data theft.

DISCUSSION QUESTIONS

1. Think about your use of various phone and computer apps and your interactions on social media. Have you ever experienced a breach of your privacy or personal data? What was the impact of this breach? Were you able to resolve it, or were you forced to live with the consequences?
2. Try to identify three different strategies that any smartphone user could follow in an attempt to minimize the risk of installing and using dangerous/risky apps.
3. Reflect on the trade-off between free apps and the potential privacy risks that these apps may introduce. Has this article changed your perception of free apps? If so, how?
4. Conduct an Internet search to identify if there have been any recent security vulnerabilities introduced through an app store (e.g., the App Store, Google Play, or Windows Phone Store). If so, conduct a brief investigation to see which apps are involved, how many people have been affected, and whether the vulnerability has been resolved.

Imagine your TV turning on every morning at just the right time so you can watch the markets open (see Figure 27). You smell fresh-baked bread, your shower turns on by itself, and your car knows exactly when to self-start so it's warm when you get in. Your self-driving car will let you work on your way to work. You'll see these anticipatory systems at your job too.

How will advances in hardware and software affect the types of jobs you'll go to? Ten years from now, the best-paying jobs will be ones that don't currently exist. The following are hot jobs today: IoT architect, marketing technologist, BigData architect, and DevOps manager. These job titles didn't exist 10 years ago. Ten years from now, there will be an entirely new set of jobs that you haven't heard of before.

How do you prepare for future jobs? What types of jobs will pay well? Regardless of your current college major, your future job will probably require a high level of tech skill. The best way to prepare for these types of jobs is to cultivate creativity, novel problem solving, and good judgment and have a sincere desire to learn new things.

Source: Alfredo Zorrilla

CAREER GUIDE

Name: Alfredo Zorrilla
Company: Microsoft Corp.
Job Title: Technical Account Manager
Education: University of Utah

1 How did you get this type of job?

When I interviewed for the role, I presented myself as a well-rounded candidate by highlighting a combination of soft and technical skills acquired as part of professional and academic experiences. The soft skills came as a result of several years serving in various customer service and relationship management roles at a major financial institution. Those skills include the ability to establish excellent interpersonal relationships, lead and work well with teams, and communicate in an effective and concise manner. The technical skills were acquired academically and include a broad understanding of a variety of IS topics like programming, networking, statistics, and system and database architecture and modeling.

2 What attracted you to this field?

Working as a technical account manager is a great way to combine relationship management with technical planning and troubleshooting. I realize that there's a certain romanticism around the stereotypical geek who can bang out 10,000 lines of code a day while chugging their favorite citrus-flavored soda and indulging in their preferred brand of crunchy cheesy-puffs, but I didn't want to just sit at a desk all day and "crush code." I also wanted to be involved in high-level strategy discussions with BDMs (business decision makers) and TDMs (technical decision makers). This field allows me to do a little of both.

3 What does a typical workday look like for you (duties, decisions, problems)?

There isn't a typical workday for me because there is always a different challenge or opportunity to tackle. I work directly with a very large Microsoft client, so some days I will be interacting with a VP of Infrastructure to learn more about the long-term IT goals of the organization and how they tie to its business priorities, while on others, I will be sitting side by side with a group of engineers trying to resolve a complex technical incident. I also have to work with several groups internally like Sales, Support, and the Product Group to ensure we are all achieving our mission of One Microsoft. The best way to describe what I do is this: work across every level of the client organization and leverage several different groups of my internal organization to ensure the customer is realizing maximum value from their software investments.

4 What do you like most about your job?

The best part about my job is the flexibility. Flexibility doesn't just mean that I can work whenever I want (which is true but does require a high level of self-motivation) but also that I can work toward my goals in whatever way I deem most efficient. We are encouraged to behave as "our own business," so even though there is an established set of best practices we can follow, how or if we implement them is ultimately up to us. Priority number one is for the clients to be happy with their Microsoft investment, and the best way to accomplish this is for their infrastructure to be stable.

5 What skills would someone need to do well at your job?

A successful technical account manager needs to wear many hats. One minute you may be discussing really technical problems with a systems engineer and the Microsoft Support team, and the next you may be presenting a solution to a VP or CIO alongside the Sales team. Therefore, the most important skill is to be able to interface successfully with anyone in the client and internal organizations. This requires the ability to communicate well, demonstrate a sense of empathy and ownership, solve problems quickly, work well under pressure, speak the languages of business and technology, and, above all, accomplish everything with high a level of integrity and accountability.

6 Are education or certifications important in your field? Why?

Absolutely. Continuing education and certifications are a great way to remain relevant and not become stale. Technology is changing at such a rapid pace that it is essential for organizations to become nimble so they can keep up with others in their industry. This makes it more important than ever to embrace and become acquainted with the latest trends so we can speak knowledgeably when the client expresses interest in pursuing a new direction. If we can't do that, a competitor surely will.

7 What advice would you give to someone who is considering working in your field?

Work toward achieving 300- to 400-level understanding in an area you are passionate about and 100- to 200-level understanding in everything else. The competition in the job market is fierce. If you can demonstrate you are an expert in one or two things but can also speak reasonably well to many others, you become a coveted candidate because many platforms are becoming increasingly interdependent. Also, build up a strong network, become part of a community, and leverage social media to broadcast yourself as a subject matter expert (SME) in a given topic. Blogging or contributing to sites like GitHub or Stack Overflow is a great way to achieve this.

8 What do you think will be hot tech jobs in 10 years?

Anything having to do with cloud, mobile, IoT, and BigData/analytics. The latter, in particular, will probably continue to experience tremendous growth as machine learning becomes more ubiquitous in industry.

FIGURE 27
Smart Home
Source: Si-Gal/iStock Vectors/Getty Images

ACTIVE REVIEW

Use this Active Review to verify that you understand the ideas and concepts that answer the chapter's study questions.

Q1 What do business professionals need to know about computer hardware?

List types of hardware and give an example of each. Define *bit* and *byte*. Explain why bits are used to represent computer data. Define the units of bytes used to size memory.

Q2 How can new hardware affect competitive strategies?

Define *IoT* and describe a smart device. Explain why smart devices are desirable. Give two examples of how businesses could benefit from smart devices. Describe the difference between AR, MR, and VR. Explain why sense of presence is important in virtual environments. Describe how self-driving cars could be safer and cheaper and make life easier. Explain how 3D printing works and how it could affect new product design, manufacturing, distribution, and consumer purchasing.

Q3 What do business professionals need to know about software?

Review Figure 12 and explain the meaning of each cell in this table. Describe three kinds of virtualization and explain the use of each. Explain the difference between software ownership and software licenses. Explain the differences among horizontal-market, vertical-market, and one-of-a-kind applications. Describe the three ways that organizations can acquire software.

Q4 Is open source software a viable alternative?

Define *GNU* and *GPL*. Name three successful open source projects. Describe four reasons programmers contribute to open source projects. Define *open source, closed source, source code*, and *machine code*. In your own words, explain why open source is a legitimate alternative but may or may not be appropriate for a given application.

Q5 What are the differences between native and Web applications?

In your own words, summarize the differences between native applications and Web applications. In high-level terms, explain the difference between object-oriented languages and scripting languages. Explain each cell of Figure 19. State which is better: native or Web applications. Justify your answer.

Q6 Why are mobile systems increasingly important?

Define *mobile systems*. Name and describe the four elements of a mobile system. Describe the size of the mobile market and explain why there are 3.9 billion mobile prospects. Explain why the mobile market will become stronger in the future. Explain why a problem for one organization is an opportunity for another. Using the five-component model, describe particular opportunities for each component. Define *just-in-time data* and explain how it changes the value of human thinking.

Q7 What are the challenges of personal mobile devices at work?

Summarize the advantages and disadvantages of employees' using mobile systems at work. Define *BYOD* and *BYOD policy*. Name six possible policies and compare them in terms of functionality and organizational control. Summarize the advantage of each to employers.

Q8 2027?

Explain how email usage has changed over the past 15 years. Describe how an anticipatory system might work. Explain how advances in hardware and software might change the types of jobs you take in the future.

Using Your Knowledge with Falcon Security

Suppose you are part of this Falcon Security team. Briefly summarize how the knowledge in this chapter would help you contribute. Explain why Falcon Security decided not make its own drones using 3D printing. Summarize the challenges it would face if it did decide to make its own drones.

KEY TERMS AND CONCEPTS

Android
Application software
Augmented reality (AR)
Binary digits
Bits
BlackBerry OS
Bring your own device (BYOD) policy
Bytes
Central processing unit (CPU)
Client
Closed source
Computer hardware
Custom-developed software
Desktop virtualization
Dual processor
Exabyte (EB)
Firmware
Gigabyte (GB)
GNU
GNU general public license (GPL) agreement
HoloLens
Horizontal-market application
Host operating system
Internet of Things (IoT)
iOS
Just-in-time data
Kilobyte (KB)
License
Linux
Mac OS
Machine code
Main memory
M-commerce
Megabyte (MB)
Microsoft Windows
Mixed reality (MR)
Mobile device
Mobile device management (MDM) software
Mobile systems
Modern-style application
Native application
Nonvolatile
Object-oriented
Off-the-shelf software
Off-the-shelf with alterations software
One-of-a-kind application
Open source
Operating system (OS)
PC virtualization
Personal computers
Petabyte (PB)
Quad processor
RAM
Reality
Self-driving car
Sense of presence
Server
Server farm
Server virtualization
Site license
Smart device
Solid-state storage (SSD)
Source code
Storage hardware
Swift
Symbian
Tablets
Terabyte (TB)
Thick-client application
Thin-client application
Unix
Vertical-market application
Virtual
Virtualization
Virtual machines (vm)
Virtual reality
Volatile
Web application
Windows 10 (mobile)
Windows Server
Zettabyte (ZB)

To complete the problems with the MyMISLab, go to EOC Discussion Questions in the MyLab.

USING YOUR KNOWLEDGE

1. MyMISLab Microsoft offers free licenses of certain software products to students at colleges and universities that participate in its DreamSpark program (formerly known as the Microsoft Developer Network [MSDN] Academic Alliance [AA]). If your college or university participates in this program, you have the opportunity to obtain hundreds of dollars of software for free. Here is a partial list of the software you can obtain:

- Microsoft Access 2016
- Microsoft OneNote 2016
- Microsoft Windows Server 2016
- Microsoft Project 2016
- Microsoft Visual Studio 2015
- Microsoft SQL Server 2016
- Microsoft Visio 2016

a. Search *www.microsoft.com*, *www.google.com*, or *www.bing.com* and determine the function of each of these software products.

b. Which of these software products are operating systems, and which are application programs?

c. Which of these programs are DBMS products?
d. Which of these programs should you download and install tonight?
e. Either (1) download and install the programs in your answer to part d or (2) explain why you would choose not to do so.
f. Does DreamSpark provide an unfair advantage to Microsoft? Why or why not?

2. Visit the Open Source Initiative's Web site at *www.opensource.org*. Summarize the mission of this foundation. Find the definition of open source on this site, and summarize that definition in your own words. Explain this foundation's role with regard to open source licenses. Summarize the process for having a license approved by the foundation. Describe the advantage of having the foundation's approval.

MyMISLab

3. Suppose that you are Cam at Falcon Security. List five criteria you would use in helping Falcon Security decide whether it should make its own drones. Justify your criteria.

MyMISLab

4. Describe how the class enrollment application at your university could benefit from a mobile application that uses the cloud.

5. Judging from your personal experience, describe the BYOD policy that appears to be in place at your university. Explain the advantages and disadvantages of the policy to you as a student and to the organization as a whole. How do you think that BYOD policy will change in the next five years? Explain your answer.

6. Read Q2 if you have not already done so. Critically evaluate the opinions of the author. Do you agree that advances in the IoT and self-driving cars will make life easier? Better? If so, say why. If not, explain what you think will happen when more smart devices and self-driving cars are adopted. Explain how you could prepare for a future high-tech job market.

COLLABORATION EXERCISE

Collaborate with a group of students to answer the following questions.

In March 2016, Microsoft released the development edition of its new mixed-reality head-mounted device named Microsoft **HoloLens**. HoloLens differs from digital reality devices like Meta 2 or Oculus Rift because it is a stand-alone, untethered computing device. In other words, it doesn't have to be plugged into a computer. It's a complete Windows 10 computer.[47]

HoloLens has a custom-built holographic CPU, an Intel 32-bit processor, 2 GB of RAM, and 64 GB of storage. It can be used for 2 to 3 hours without being recharged, and it comes with Bluetooth/Wi-Fi connectivity. It also comes with a 2-megapixel HD video camera, four microphones, motion sensors, light sensors, environmental cameras, and a depth-sensing camera.

As a result, HoloLens can do some pretty amazing things. It accepts voice commands and gesture commands (e.g., air tapping), it maps spaces in a room, and, most importantly, it creates holograms (virtual objects) in thin air. You can watch videos of how HoloLens works on its YouTube channel.

In a recent demonstration, Microsoft showed how HoloLens could be used collaboratively by having two people in different locations fix a plumbing problem together. A person with a broken pipe was wearing HoloLens, and a person who knew how to fix the pipe was in separate location. The person wearing the HoloLens could see 3D holographic arrows appear on the pipes indicating what needed to be done to fix the problem. The arrows were being hand-drawn on a tablet showing a live video feed from the HoloLens.

In another example, designers and engineers at Autodesk use HoloLens to collaboratively create new products.[48] Mechanical engineers, industrial designers, and marketing managers can all see the product as it's being designed. They don't have to iterate through numerous physical prototypes. They can make immediate changes to a virtual prototype before it's even built.

Volvo is using HoloLens in a similar way. The company has been able to reduce design times and potentially improve its manufacturing processes with the device. HoloLens also helps with sales. Using the device, customers can change the color of the car they're looking at with one click. Salespeople can also show customers interactive demonstrations of a car's built-in safety features (like automatic breaking sensors) in 3D holographic environments.

The potential uses for HoloLens are staggering. Gamers won't be stuck on the couch playing video games anymore; they will be able to play multiplayer holographic games anywhere with anyone—for 2 hours. HoloLens will also change the way people communicate. Microsoft engineers recently gave a demonstration of "holoportation" in which a real-time interactive 3D hologram of a person was holoported into another room. Users wearing HoloLens could interact with the person as if they were in the same room.

Many other applications in education, entertainment, tourism, design, engineering, and movies are being developed. And, because HoloLens is one of the first mixed-reality devices to become commercially available, it's likely that the best applications for this technology are still unknown. We simply don't know what people will use it for. What is clear, however, is that big names like Google, Microsoft, and Apple are making large investments into mixed-reality devices like HoloLens. They see the potential and are voting with their wallets.

RAND study states that there will be increased worldwide demand for workers who can apply new technology and products to solve business problems in innovative ways. Microsoft HoloLens is an excellent example of a new technology that will be applied innovatively.

7. Consider uses for HoloLens at your university. How might HoloLens be used in architecture, chemistry, law, medicine, business, geography, political science, art, music, or any other discipline in which your team has interest? Describe one potential application for HoloLens for five different disciplines.
8. List specific features and benefits for each of the five applications you selected in question 7.
9. Describe, in general terms, the work that needs to be accomplished to create the applications you identified in question 7.
10. Some people buy gaming consoles like Sony PlayStation and Microsoft Xbox because of exclusive games. Not all video games are available on all consoles. How important might applications be in the success of digital reality devices like HoloLens, Meta 2, and Oculus Rift?
11. You will sometimes hear the expression "Emerging technology is constantly leveling the playing field." In other words, technology eliminates competitive advantages of existing companies and enables opportunities for new companies. How does this statement pertain to HoloLens, iPad, Windows 10, Apple, and Google?

CASE STUDY

The Apple of Your i

A quick glance at Apple's stock history in Figure 28 will tell you that Apple is an incredibly successful and dramatic company, having peaks around the turn of the century, in 2007–2008, 2012 and again in 2015. At its high, it had the highest market value of any public company worldwide. Apple has been so successful that the NASDAQ stock exchange concluded Apple's price was skewing the price of the NASDAQ 100 Index and reduced Apple's weight in that index from 20 percent to 12 percent. As of this writing, Apple stock is trading at $95 after hitting a recent low of $56 in 2013.

But since Steve Jobs's death (October 5, 2011), there haven't been any groundbreaking products like the iPod, iPhone, and iPad. iWatch was released in 2015, but many initial reviews were tepid at best.[49] There were already several smartwatches

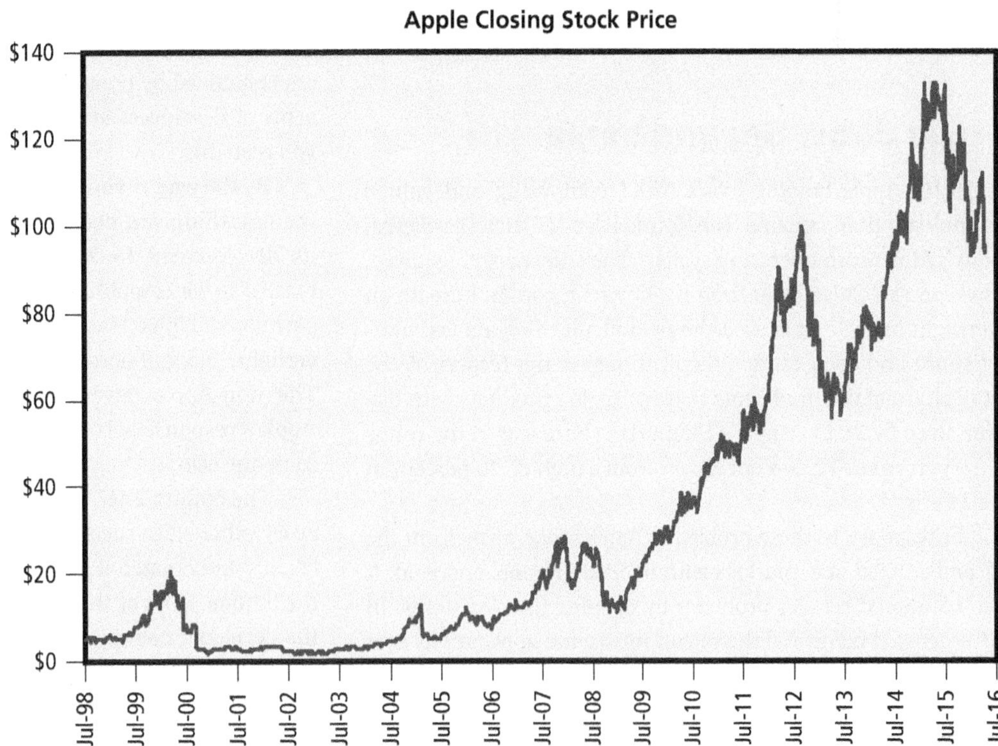

FIGURE 28
Growth in Apple Stock Price
Source: Financial data from *finance.yahoo.com*

on the market that had similar functionality, and it had performance issues. Most importantly, it wasn't clear if the iWatch provided enough value over the iPhone that was already in users' pockets. In short, it wasn't an immediate hit. So, what does the future look like for Apple and its shareholders? Uncertain, especially if you consider its past history without Jobs.

Early Success and Downfall

At the dawn of the personal computer age, in the early 1980s, Apple pioneered well-engineered home computers and innovative interfaces with its Apple II PC for the home and its Macintosh computer for students and knowledge workers. At one point, Apple owned more than 20 percent of the PC market, competing against many other PC vendors, most of which are no longer relevant (or in business).

However, Apple lost its way. In 1985, Steve Jobs, Apple's chief innovator, lost a fight with the Apple board and was forced out. He founded another PC company, NeXT, which developed and sold a groundbreaking PC product that was too innovative to sell well in that era. Meanwhile, Apple employed a succession of CEOs, starting with John Sculley, who was hired away from Pepsi-Cola where he'd enjoyed considerable success. Sculley's knowledge and experience did not transfer well to the PC business, however, and the company went downhill so fast that CNBC named him the 14th worst American CEO of all time.[50] Two other CEOs followed in Sculley's footsteps.

During this period, Apple made numerous mistakes, among them not rewarding innovative engineering, creating too many products for too many market segments, and losing the respect of the retail computer stores. Apple's PC market share plummeted.

Steve Jobs, Second Verse

In 1996, Apple bought Jobs's NeXT computing and gained technology that became the foundation of macOS Sierra, today's Macintosh operating system. The true asset it acquired, however, was Steve Jobs. Even he, however, couldn't create an overnight miracle. It is exceedingly difficult to regain lost market share and even more difficult to regain the respect of the retail channel that had come to view Apple's products with disdain. Even by 2011, Apple's PC market share was in the range of 10 percent to 12 percent, down from a high of 20 percent in the 1980s.

In response to these problems, Apple broke away from the PC and created new markets with its iPod, iPhone, and iPad. It also countered retailer problems by opening its own stores. In the process, it pioneered the sale of music and applications over the Internet.

iPod, iPhone, and iPad devices are a marvel of creativity and engineering. They exude not only ease of use, but also now/wow/fun coolness. By selling hot music for the iPod, Apple established a connection with a dynamic segment of the market that was willing to spend lots of money on bright, shiny objects. The ability to turn the iPhone on its side to rotate images probably sold more iPhones than anything else. With the iPad, portable devices became readable, and the market responded by awarding Apple a 44 percent share of the mobile market.[51] And Apple's success continues with the iPhone 7, which, as of this writing, is selling well.

All of this success propelled Apple's stores not only beyond vanilla retailers like Best Buy but also beyond the lofty heights of Tiffany & Co. In 2011, Apple stores were grossing more than $4,000 per square foot, compared with $3,000 for Tiffany and a mere $880 for Best Buy. Apple currently operates more than 447 such retail outlets and has welcomed more than a billion customer visits.[52]

Apple encourages customer visits and loyalty with its open and inviting sales floor, its Genius Bar help desk, and its incredibly well-trained and disciplined sales force. Salespeople, who are not commissioned, are taught to be consultants who help customers solve problems. Even some vocabulary is standardized. When an employee cannot solve a customer's problem, the word *unfortunately* is to be avoided; employees are taught to use the phrase *as it turns out* instead.[53] Try that on your next exam!

Apple has sold more than 25 billion songs through its iTunes online store, 130 million books through its iBookstore, and a mere 75 billion applications downloaded through its App Store. Apple is now the number-one PC software channel.[54]

To encourage the development of iPhone and iPad apps, Apple shares its revenue with application developers. That would be more than $25B paid to developers over the years![55] Developers responded by creating 1,000,000 iOS applications, and an army of developers are at work building thousands more while you read this.

By the way, if you want to build an iOS application, what's the first thing you need to do? Buy a Macintosh. Apple closed its development to any other development method. Adobe Flash? No way. Apple claims that Flash has too many bugs, and perhaps so. Thus, Flash developers are excluded. Microsoft Silverlight? Nope. Microsoft developers are out in the cold too. The non-Apple development community was furious, and Apple's response was, in essence, "Fine, we'll pay our $25B to someone else."

The bottom line? Until Jobs's death, every sales success fed every other sales success. Hot music fed the iPod. The iPod fed iTunes and created a growing customer base that was ripe for the iPhone. Sales of the iPhone fed the stores, whose success fed the developer community, which fed more applications, which fed the iPhone and set the stage for the iPad, which fed the App Store, which led to more loyal customers and, of course, to more developers.

Apple Without Steve Jobs

Apple's future is uncertain. It floundered when Jobs was fired in the 1990s, and it could flounder again. Sure, it'll be around for a long time, but the days of its incredible innovative leadership could be, alas, over.

QUESTIONS

12. Which of Porter's four competitive strategies does Apple engage in? Explain.

13. What do you think are the three most important factors in Apple's past success? Justify your answer.

14. Steve Jobs passed away in October 2011. Until his death, he had been the heart and soul of Apple's innovation. Today, 115,000 Apple employees continue onward in his absence. A huge question for many investors is whether the company can be successful without him. What do you think? What role did Jobs play? How can Apple respond to his loss? Would you be willing to invest in Apple without his leadership? Why or why not?

15. Microsoft took an early lead in the development of tablet devices (like the iPad), and it had the world's leading operating system and applications for more than 20 years. Provide five reasons why Microsoft has not been able to achieve the same success that Apple has. Most industry analysts would agree that the skills and abilities of Microsoft's 118,584 employees are as good, on average, as Apple's.

16. Considering your answers to the four questions above, if you had a spare $5,000 in your portfolio and wanted to buy an equity stock with it, would you buy AAPL (Apple)? Why or why not?

MyMISLab™

Go to the Assignments section of your MyLab to complete these writing exercises.

17. Suppose your first job after graduating from college is working at a large insurance company. Your boss asks you to analyze the impact self-driving cars will have on revenues from car insurance policies. List four ways self-driving cars could impact the insurance industry. Justify your answers.

18. Visit *www.distrowatch.com*. Click on one of the top five listed Linux distributions (like Mint, Ubuntu, Debian, Fedora, or OpenSUSE). Click on the Screenshots link for that distribution. List some similarities between this operating system and your current operating system. Summarize the advantages and disadvantages of switching from your current operating system to a Linux distribution.

ENDNOTES

1. Mark van Rijmenam, "Big Data at Walmart Is All About Big Numbers; 40 Petabytes a Day!," *Datafloq*, June 10, 2015, accessed April 29, 2016, *https://datafloq.com/read/big-data-walmart-big-numbers-40-petabytes/1175.*
2. Pamela Vagata and Kevin Wilfong, "Scaling the Facebook Data Warehouse to 300 PB," *Facebook.com*, accessed April 29, 2016, *https://code.facebook.com/posts/229861827208629/scaling-the-facebook-data-warehouse-to-300-pb.*
3. Kashmir Hill, "Blueprints of NSA's Ridiculously Expensive Data Center in Utah Suggest It Holds Less Info than Thought," *Forbes.com*, accessed April 29, 2016, *www.forbes.com/sites/kashmirhill/2013/07/24/blueprints-of-nsa-data-center-in-utah-suggest-its-storage-capacity-is-less-impressive-than-thought.*
4. Cisco Systems, Inc., "VNI Forecast Highlights," *Cisco.com*, accessed April 30, 2016, *www.cisco.com/c/en/us/solutions/service-provider/visual-networking-index-vni/vni-forecast.html.*
5. Todd Bishop, "Amazon Prime Adds More Than 3M New Members in 1 Week at Peak of Holiday Shopping Season," *GeekWire*, December 27, 2015, accessed April 29, 2016, *www.geekwire.com/2015/amazon-adds-3m-new-prime-members-in-one-week-in-december.*
6. General Electric, "Industrial Internet Insights Report for 2015," accessed April 29, 2016, *www.ge.com/digital/sites/default/files/industrial-internet-insights-report.pdf.*
7. Ibid.
8. Jennifer Warnick, "88 Acres: How Microsoft Quietly Built the City of the Future," Microsoft Corp., accessed April 29, 2016, *www.microsoft.com/en-us/news/stories/88acres/88-acres-how-microsoft-quietly-built-the-city-of-the-future-chapter-1.aspx.*
9. Jeffrey O'Brien, "The Race to Make Virtual Reality an Actual (Business) Reality," *Fortune*, May 1, 2016, accessed May 3, 2016, *http://fortune.com/virtual-reality-business.*
10. Eric Johnson, "Choose Your Reality: Virtual, Augmented or Mixed," *Re/code*, July 27, 2015, accessed May 3, 2016, *http://recode.net/2015/07/27/whats-the-difference-between-virtual-augmented-and-mixed-reality.*
11. See Microsoft's site for the latest MR applications being developed for HoloLens: *www.microsoft.com/microsoft-hololens/en-us.*
12. KPMG, "Automobile Insurance in the Era of Autonomous Vehicles," June 2015, accessed May 4, 2016, *www.kpmg.com/US/en/IssuesAndInsights/ArticlesPublications/Documents/automobile-insurance-in-the-era-of-autonomous-vehicles-survey-results-june-2015.pdf.*

13. Glenn Garvin, "Automakers Say Self-Driving Cars Are on the Horizon," *Miami Herald*, March 21, 2014, accessed May 22, 2016, *www.tampabay.com/news/business/autos/automakers-say-self-driving-cars-are-on-the-horizon/2171386*.
14. Bill Vlasic and Neal Boudette, "Google to Get Fiat Chrysler Minivans for Self-Driving Tests," *The New York Times*, May 3, 2016, accessed May 4, 2016, *www.nytimes.com/2016/05/04/technology/google-fiat-chrysler-minivans-self-driving.html*.
15. KPMG, "Automobile insurance in the era of autonomous vehicles," June 2015, accessed May 4, 2016, *www.kpmg.com/US/en/IssuesAndInsights/ArticlesPublications/Documents/automobile-insurance-in-the-era-of-autonomous-vehicles-survey-results-june-2015.pdf*.
16. Network of Employers for Traffic Safety, "10 Facts Employers Must Know," accessed May 4, 2016, *http://trafficsafety.org/safety/fleet-safety/10-facts-employers-must-know*.
17. Liz Stinson, "For Super Bowl, Nike Uses 3-D Printing to Create a Faster Football Cleat," *Wired*, January 10, 2014, accessed May 4, 2016, *www.wired.com/2014/01/nike-designed-fastest-cleat-history*.
18. Scott Grunewald, "Nike's 3D Printed Sprinting Shoe the Zoom Superfly Flyknit Will Be Worn at the 2016 Olympic Games in Rio," *3DPrint.com*, April 27, 2016, accessed May 4, 2016, *https://3dprint.com/131549/nike-zoom-superfly-flyknit*.
19. See EDAG's GENESIS prototype car at *www.EDAG.de*.
20. Jonathan Schwartz, "Will Food 3D Printing Really Become a 'Thing'?" VentureBeat, April 17, 2016, accessed May 4, 2016, *http://venturebeat.com/2016/04/17/will-food-3d-printing-really-become-a-thing*.
21. Dan Ferber, "An Essential Step Toward Printing Living Tissues," Harvard School of Engineering and Applied Sciences, February 19, 2014, accessed May 4, 2016, *www.seas.harvard.edu/news/2014/02/essential-step-toward-printing-living-tissues*.
22. Brian Krassenstein, "Contour Crafting Inventor Dr. Khoshnevis: Widespread 3D Printed Homes in 5 Years, High-Rises in 10 Years," *3DPrint.com*, March 31, 2015, accessed May 4, 2016, *https://3dprint.com/53437/contour-crafting-dr-khoshnevis*.
23. "Net Applications," accessed May 4, 2016, *www.netapplications.com*.
24. Previously called metro-style. Name change by Microsoft, reputedly because of a trademark lawsuit from Europe.
25. "Net Applications," accessed May 4, 2016, *www.netapplications.com*.
26. *DistroWatch.com*, accessed May 4, 2016, *www.distrowatch.com*.
27. "Net Applications," accessed May 4, 2016, *www.netapplications.com*.
28. Pew Research Center, "Device Ownership," July 1, 2015, accessed May 4, 2016, *www.pewresearch.org/data-trend/media-and-technology/device-ownership*.
29. "Unlocking the Cloud," *The Economist*, May 28, 2009.
30. Not quite true. Much of the design and possibly some of the code can be reused between native applications. But, for your planning, assume that it all must be redone. Not enough will carry over to make it worth considering.
31. Cisco Systems Inc., "Cisco Visual Networking Index: Global Mobile Data Traffic Forecast Update, 2015–2020," *Cisco.com*, February 3, 2016, accessed May 4, 2016, *www.cisco.com/c/en/us/solutions/collateral/service-provider/visual-networking-index-vni/white_paper_c11-520862.html*.
32. Ibid.
33. Horace Dediu, "Late Late Majority," *Asymco.com*, May 4, 2016, accessed May 4, 2016, *www.asymco.com/2014/07/08/late-late-majority*.
34. comScore, "comScore Reports February 2016 U.S. Smartphone Subscriber Market Share," April 6, 2016, accessed May 4, 2016, *www.comscore.com/Insights/Rankings/comScore-Reports-February-2016-US-Smartphone-Subscriber-Market-Share*.
35. Statista, "Mobile Retail E-commerce Sales in the United States from 2013 to 2019 (in Billion U.S. Dollars)," *Statista.com*, accessed May 4, 2016, *www.statista.com/statistics/249855/mobile-retail-commerce-revenue-in-the-united-states*.
36. The Nielsen Company, "Survey New U.S. Smartphone Growth By Age and Income," accessed May 2016, *www.nielsen.com/us/en/insights/news/2012/survey-new-u-s-smartphone-growth-by-age-and-income.html*.
37. SnoopWall, "SnoopWall Flashlight Apps Threat Assessment Report," October 1, 2014, *SnoopWall.com*, accessed May 4, 2016, *www.snoopwall.com/threat-reports-10-01-2014*.
38. Symantec Corporation, "Internet Security Report," *Symantec.com*, Volume 20, April 2015, accessed May 4, 2016, *www4.symantec.com/mktginfo/whitepaper/ISTR/21347932_GA-internet-security-threat-report-volume-20-2015-social_v2.pdf*.
39. Google, "Android Security 2014 Year in Review," *GoogleUserContent.com*, accessed May 4, 2016, *http://static.googleusercontent.com/media/source.android.com/en/us/devices/tech/security/reports/Google_Android_Security_2014_Report_Final.pdf*.
40. Teena Maddox, "Research: 74 Percent Using or Adopting BYOD," *ZDNet*, January 5, 2015, accessed May 4, 2016, *www.zdnet.com/article/research-74-percent-using-or-adopting-byod*.
41. "CDH," accessed May 4, 2016, *www.cdh.com*.
42. Robert McMillan, "IBM Worries iPhone's Siri Has Loose Lips," last modified May 24, 2012, *www.cnn.com/2012/05/23/tech/mobile/ibm-siri-ban/index.html?iphoneemail*.
43. Sarah Perez, "iTunes App Store Now Has 1.2 Million Apps, Has Seen 75 Billion Downloads to Date," *Tech Crunch, March 4, 2016, http://techcrunch.com/2014/06/02/itunes-app-store-now-has-1-2-million-apps-has-seen-75-billion-downloads-to-date*.
44. Joe Rossignol, "What You Need to Know About iOS Malware XcodeGhost," *MacRumors*, March 4, 2016, *www.macrumors.com/2015/09/20/xcodeghost-chinese-malware-faq*.
45. Larry Magid, "App Privacy Issues Deeply Troubling," *The Huffington Post*, March 4, 2016, *www.huffingtonpost.com/larry-magid/iphone-app-privacy_b_1290529.html*.
46. Terrie Morgan-Besecker, "Cellphone Apps Can Invade Your Privacy," *Government Technology*, March 4, 2016, *www.govtech.com/applications/Cellphone-Apps-Can-Invade-Your-Privacy.html*.
47. Horia Ungureanu, "TAG Microsoft, HoloLens, Augmented Reality Microsoft HoloLens Full Processor, RAM and Storage Specs Revealed: All You Need To Know," *Tech Times*, May 4, 2016, accessed May 5, 2016, *www.techtimes.com/articles/155683/20160504/microsoft-hololens-full-processor-ram-and-storage-specs-revealed-all-you-need-to-know.htm*.
48. Ken Yeung, "Microsoft Partners with Autodesk to bring 3D Product Design to HoloLens," *VentureBeat*, November 30, 2015, accessed May 5, 2016, *http://venturebeat.com/2015/11/30/microsoft-partners-with-autodesk-to-bring-3d-product-design-to-hololens*.
49. Will Shanklin, "Apple Watch Review: Elegant, Delightful ... and Completely Optional," April 29, 2015, *Gizmag.com*, accessed May 4, 2016, *www.gizmag.com/apple-watch-review-iwatch-review/37244*.
50. "Portfolio's Worst American CEOs of All Time," *CNBC.com*, accessed May 4, 2016, *www.cnbc.com/id/30502091?slide=8*.
51. Apple presentation at the Apple Worldwide Developers Conference, June 6, 2011.
52. TheStreet Transcripts, "Apple (AAPL) Earnings Report: Q1 2015 Conference Call Transcript," *TheStreet.com*, January 28, 2015, accessed May 4, 2016, *www.thestreet.com/story/13025362/4/apple-aapl-earnings-report-q1-2015-conference-call-transcript.html*.
53. Yukari Iwatani Kane and Ian Sherr, "Secrets from Apple's Genius Bar: Full Loyalty, No Negativity," *Wall Street Journal*, last modified June 15, 2011, *http://online.wsj.com/article/SB10001424052702304563104576364071955678908.html*.
54. Apple presentation at the Apple Worldwide Developers Conference, June 6, 2011.
55. Apple Inc., "App Store Rings in 2015 with New Records," *Apple.com*, January 8, 2015, accessed May 4, 2016, *www.apple.com/pr/library/2015/01/08App-Store-Rings-in-2015-with-New-Records.html*

APPLICATION EXERCISES

All exercise files can be found on the following Web site: *www.pearsonhighered.com/kroenke.*

AE1. Sometimes you will have data in one Office application and want to move it to another Office application without rekeying it. Often this occurs when data was created for one purpose but then is used for a second purpose. For example, Figure AE presents a portion of an Excel spreadsheet that shows the assignment of computers to employees.

Suppose you want to use this data to help you assess how to upgrade computers. Let's say, for example, that you want to upgrade all of the computers' operating systems to Windows 10. Furthermore, you want to first upgrade the computers that most need upgrading, but suppose you have a limited budget. To address this situation, you would like to query the data in Figure AE, find all computers that do not have Windows 10, and then select those with slower CPUs or smaller memory as candidates for upgrading. To do this, you need to move the data from Excel into Access.

Once you have analyzed the data and determined the computers to upgrade, you want to produce a report. In that case, you may want to move the data from Access back to Excel, or perhaps into Word. In this exercise, you will learn how to perform these tasks.

a. To begin, download the Excel file **Ch04Ex01_U10e.xlsx** into one of your directories. We will import the data in this file into Access, but before we do so, familiarize yourself with the data by opening it in Excel. Notice that there are three worksheets in this workbook. Close the Excel file.

b. Create a blank Access database. Name the database Ch04Ex01_Answer. Place it in some directory; it may be the same directory into which you have placed the Excel file, but it need not be. Close the default table that Access creates and delete it.

c. Now, we will import the data from the three worksheets in the Excel file **Ch04Ex01_U10e.xlsx** into a single table in your Access database. On the ribbon, select *External Data* and in the Import & Link section, click *Excel.* Start the import. For the first worksheet (Denver), you should select *Import the source data into a new table in the current database.* Ignore the warning about the first row by clicking OK. Be sure to click

	A	B	C	D	E	F	G	H
1	EmpLastName	EmpFirstName	Plant	Computer Brand	CPU (GHz)	Memory (GB)	Disk (TB)	OS
2	Ashley	Linda	Denver	Dell	3	16	2	Windows 10
3	Davidson	Victor	Denver	Dell	3	12	2	Windows 10
4	Ching	Diem Thi	Denver	HP	3	8	2.5	Windows 8
5	Collins	James	Denver	Dell	2.5	6	1	Windows 7
6	Corning	Haley	Denver	HP	3	8	2	Windows 8
7	Scott	Richard	Denver	HP	2.5	8	2.5	Windows 8
8	Corovic	Anna	Denver	Dell	4	12	3	Windows 10
9	Lane	Kathy	Denver	Lenovo	2.5	6	1	Windows 7
10	Wei	James	Denver	IBM	3	16	2	Windows 10
11	Dixon	Mary	Denver	IBM	2	6	1	Windows 7
12	Lee	Matthew	Denver	Dell	2.5	6	1	Windows 7
13	Duong	Steven	Denver	Dell	2	2	0.75	Vista
14	Bosa	William	Denver	HP	3	8	2.5	Windows 8
15	Drew	Tony	Denver	HP	3	8	2	Windows 8
16	Adams	Mark	Denver	HP	2.5	4	1	Windows 7
17	Lunden	Nicole	Denver	Lenovo	4	12	3	Windows 10
18	Utran	Bryan	Denver	Dell	3	8	2	Windows 8
19								
20		Primary Contact:	Kaye Davidson					

FIGURE AE
Sample Excel Data for Import
Source: Microsoft Corporation

First Row Contains Column Headings when Access presents your data. You can use the default Field types and let Access add the primary key. Name your table *Employees* and click *Finish*. There is no need to save your import script.

For the Miami and Boston worksheets, again click *External Data, Import Excel*, but this time select *Append a copy of the records to the table Employees*. Select the Miami worksheet and click *Finish*. Repeat to import the Boston office employees.

d. Open the *Employee* table and examine the data. Notice that Access has erroneously imported a blank line and the *Primary Contact* data into rows at the end of each data set. This data is not part of the employee records, and you should delete it (in three places—once for each worksheet). The *Employee* table should have a total of 40 records.

e. Create a parameterized query on this data. Place all of the columns except *ID* into the query. In the *OS* column, set the criteria to select rows for which the value is not *Windows 10*. In the *CPU* (GHz) column, enter the criterion: <=*[Enter cutoff value for CPU]* and in the *Memory* (GB) column, enter the criterion: <=*[Enter cutoff value for Memory]*. Test your query. For example, run your query and enter a value of 4 for CPU and 10 for memory. Verify that the correct rows are produced.

f. Use your query to find values of CPU and memory that give you as close to a maximum of 10 computers to upgrade as possible.

g. When you have found values of CPU and memory that give you 10, or nearly 10, computers to upgrade, leave your query open. Now, click *External data, Word*, and create a Word document that contains the results of your query. Adjust the column widths of the created table so that it fits on the page. Write a memo around this table explaining that these are the computers that you believe should be upgraded.

AE2. Assume you have been asked to create a spreadsheet to help make a buy-versus-lease decision about the servers for your organization. Assume that you are considering the servers for a 5-year period, but you do not know exactly how many servers you will need. Initially, you know you will need five servers, but you might need as many as 50, depending on the success of your organization's e-commerce activity. (By the way, many organizations are still making these calculations. However, those that have moved to the cloud no longer need to do so!)

a. For the buy-alternative calculations, set up your spreadsheet so that you can enter the base price of the server hardware, the price of all software, and a maintenance expense that is some percentage of the hardware price. Assume that the percent you enter covers both hardware and software maintenance. Also assume that each server has a 3-year life, after which it has no value. Assume straight-line depreciation for computers used less than 3 years, and that at the end of the 5 years you can sell the computers you have used for less than 3 years for their depreciated value. Also assume that your organization pays 2 percent interest on capital expenses. Assume the servers cost $2,500 each, and the needed software costs $1250. Assume that the maintenance expense varies from 2 to 7 percent.

b. For the lease-alternative calculations, assume that the leasing vendor will lease the same computer hardware you can purchase. The lease includes all the software you need as well as all maintenance. Set up your spreadsheet so that you can enter various lease costs, which vary according to the number of years of the lease (1, 2, or 3). Assume the cost of a 3-year lease is $285 per machine per month, a 2-year lease is $335 per machine per month, and a 1-year lease is $415 per machine per month. Also, the lessor offers a 5 percent discount if you lease from 20 to 30 computers and a 10 percent discount if you lease from 31 to 50 computers.

c. Using your spreadsheet, compare the costs of buy versus lease under the following situations. (Assume you either buy or lease. You cannot lease some and buy some.) Make assumptions as necessary and state those assumptions.

(1) Your organization requires 20 servers for 5 years.

(2) Your organization requires 20 servers for the first 2 years and 40 servers for the next 3 years.

(3) Your organization requires 20 servers for the first 2 years, 40 servers for the next 2 years, and 50 servers for the last year.

(4) Your organization requires 10 servers the first year, 20 servers the second year, 30 servers the third year, 40 servers the fourth year, and 50 servers the last year.

(5) For the previous case, does the cheaper alternative change if the cost of the servers is $4,000? If it is $8,000?

AE3. As you read in this chapter, open source software is popular because it's stable, customizable, and free. But you may not have used open source software before. In this project, you will download an alternate to the Microsoft Office suite called LibreOffice. It has applications for making documents (Writer), spreadsheets (Calc), presentations (Impress), databases (Base), and graphics (Draw) similar to those in Microsoft Office.

If you're used to Microsoft Office, it will take some time to become familiar with the LibreOffice interface. LibreOffice can do just about everything Microsoft Office can do, but it does it in a slightly different way. The main benefit of using LibreOffice is that it's totally free. You can install it as many times as you'd like on as many computers as you'd like.

a. Browse to *www.libreoffice.org*.

b. Click on the Download menu and select LibreOffice Fresh.

c. Download and install the latest version of LibreOffice. (There are LibreOffice versions for Windows, Mac OS X, and Linux.)

d. Open LibreOffice Calc. (There will be a shortcut on your desktop.)

e. Enter your name, date, and time into the new spreadsheet in cells A1, A2, and A3, respectively.

f. Click Tools and Options.

g. Expand the Load/Save menu and click on General.

h. Change the "Always save as" dropdown from ODF Spreadsheet to Microsoft Excel 2007-2013 XML and click OK. (You can do the same thing for documents and presentations.)

i. Click File, Save, and Save.

j. Take a screenshot with your name showing and paste it into your document. (You can take a screenshot by pressing Alt + Print Screen.)

k. Explain why more people don't use LibreOffice if it's free.

l. Explain why a systems administrator, who manages hundreds of servers (with Linux and Windows operating systems), might like using LibreOffice.

m. Explain why LibreOffice might be an important application for users or organizations in developing countries.

GLOSSARY

Android A mobile operating system that is a version of Linux. Android runs on the Google Nexus 7 and the Amazon Kindle Fire as well as many other mobile devices.

Application software Programs that perform a business function. Some application programs are general purpose, such as Excel or Word. Other application programs are specific to a business function, such as accounts payable.

Augmented reality (AR) The altering of reality by overlaying digital information on real world objects.

Binary digits See *bits.*

Bits The means by which computers represent data; also called binary digits. A bit is either a zero or a one.

BlackBerry OS One of the most successful early mobile operating systems; was primarily used by business users on BlackBerry devices.

Bring your own device (BYOD) policy An official organizational policy that states employees' permissions and responsibilities when using personal mobile devices for organizational business.

Bytes (1) 8-bit chunks of data. (2) Characters of data.

Central processing unit (CPU) The portion of a computer that selects instructions, processes them, performs arithmetic and logical comparisons, and stores results of operations in memory.

Client PCs, tablets, and smartphones that access servers via the cloud.

Closed source Source code that is highly protected and only available to trusted employees and carefully vetted contractors.

Computer hardware Electronic components and related gadgetry that input, process, output, store, and communicate data according to the instructions encoded in computer programs or software. One of the five fundamental components of an information system.

Custom-developed software Software tailor-made for a particular organization's requirements.

Database administration A person or department that develops procedures and practices to ensure efficient and orderly multiuser processing of the database, to control changes to database structure, and to protect the database.

Desktop virtualization Also called client virtualization and PC virtualization. The process of storing a user's desktop on a remote server. It enables users to run their desktop from many different client computers.

Dual processor A computer with two CPUs.

Exabyte (EB) 1,024 PB.

Firmware Computer software installed into devices such as printers, print servers, and various types of communication devices. The software is coded just like other software, but it is installed into special, programmable memory of the printer or other device.

Gigabyte (GB) 1,024 MB.

GNU A set of tools for creating and managing open source software. Originally created to develop an open source Unix-like operating system.

GNU general public license (GPL) agreement One of the standard license agreements for open source software.

Horizontal-market application Software that provides capabilities common across all organizations and industries; examples include word processors, graphics programs, spreadsheets, and presentation programs.

Host operating system In virtualization, the operating system that hosts the virtual operating systems.

Internet of Things (IoT) The idea that objects are becoming connected to the Internet so they can interact with other devices, applications, or services.

iOS The operating system used on the iPhone, iPod Touch, and iPad.

Just-in-time data Data delivered to the user at the time it is needed.

Kilobyte (KB) 1,024 bytes.

License A contract that stipulates how a program can be used. Most specify the number of computers on which the program can be installed; some specify the number of users who can connect to and use the program remotely. Such agreements also stipulate limitations on the liability of the software vendor for the consequences of errors in the software.

Linux A version of Unix developed by the open source community. The open source community owns Linux, and there is no fee to use it. Linux is a popular operating system for Web servers.

M-commerce E-commerce transacted using mobile devices.

Machine code Code compiled from source code and ready to be processed by a computer. Cannot be understood by humans.

Mac OS An operating system developed by Apple Computer, Inc., for the Macintosh. The current version is macOS Sierra.

Initially, Macintosh computers were used primarily by graphic artists and workers in the arts community, but today Macs are used more widely.

Main memory Memory that works in conjunction with the CPU. Stores data and instructions read by the CPU and stores the results of the CPU's computations.

Megabyte (MB) 1,024 KB.

Microsoft Windows The most popular nonmobile client operating system. Also refers to Windows Server, a popular server operating system that competes with Linux.

Mixed reality (MR) The combination of the real physical world with interactive virtual images or objects.

Mobile device A small, lightweight, power-conserving, computing device that is capable of wireless access.

Mobile device management (MDM) software Products that install and update mobile device software, back up and restore mobile devices, and wipe software and data from devices in the event the device is lost or the employee leaves the company. Such products also report usage and provide other mobile device management data.

Mobile systems Information systems that support users in motion.

Modern-style applications Windows applications that are touch-screen oriented and provide context-sensitive, popup menus.

Native application A thick-client application designed to work with a particular operating system and sometimes further limited to work only with a particular mobile device that runs that operating system.

Nonvolatile Memory that preserves data contents even when not powered (e.g., magnetic and optical disks). With such devices, you can turn the computer off and back on, and the contents will be unchanged.

Object-oriented When referring to languages, ones that can be used to create difficult, complex applications and, if used properly, will result in high-performance code that is easy to alter when requirements change.

Off-the-shelf software Software used without making any changes.

Off-the-shelf with alterations software Software bought off the shelf but altered to fit an organization's specific needs.

One-of-a-kind application Software developed for a specific, unique need, usually for a single company's requirements.

Open source (1) Source code available for a community to access. (2) A collaborative effort by which software developers create a product such as Linux; the developers often volunteer their time. In most cases, the jointly developed product can be used without paying a license fee.

Operating system (OS) A computer program that controls the computer's resources: It manages the contents of main memory, processes keystrokes and mouse movements, sends signals to the display monitor, reads and writes disk files, and controls the processing of other programs.

PC virtualization Synonym for desktop virtualization.

Personal computers Classic computing devices used by individuals. Examples of PCs include laptop or desktop computers.

Petabyte (PB) 1,024 TB.

Quad processor A computer with four CPUs.

RAM Random access memory. Another name for a computer's main memory.

Reality The state of things as they actually exist.

Self-driving car A driverless car that uses a variety of sensors to navigate like a traditional car but without human intervention.

Sense of presence The illusion that a virtual experience is real.

Server A computer that provides some type of service, such as hosting a database, running a blog, publishing a Web site, or selling goods. Server computers are faster, larger, and more powerful than client computers.

Server farm A large collection of server computers organized to share work and compensate for one another's failures.

Server virtualization The process of running two or more operating system instances on the same server. The host operating system runs virtual operating system instances as applications.

Site license A license purchased by an organization to equip all the computers on a site with certain software.

Smart device A device that has processing power, memory, network connectivity, and the ability to interconnect with other devices and applications.

Solid-state storage (SSD) Stores information using nonvolatile electronic circuits.

Source code Computer code written by humans and understandable by humans. Source code must be translated into machine code before it can be processed.

Storage hardware Hardware that saves data and programs. Magnetic disks are by far the most common storage device, although optical disks, such as CDs and DVDs, also are popular.

Swift Apple's programming language for OS X and iOS applications.

Symbian A mobile client operating system popular on phones in Europe and the Far East but less so in North America.

Tablets Computing devices that allow interaction through a flat touch screen.

Terabyte (TB) 1,024 GB.

Thick-client application A software application that requires programs other than just the browser on a user's computer; that is, requires code on both client and server computers. See also *native application*.

Thin-client application A software application that requires nothing more than a browser. Also called a Web application.

Unix An operating system developed at Bell Labs in the 1970s. It has been the workhorse of the scientific and engineering communities since then.

Vertical-market application Software that serves the needs of a specific industry. Examples of such programs are those used by dental offices to schedule appointments and bill patients, those used by auto mechanics to keep track of customer data and customers' automobile repairs, and those used by parts warehouses to track inventory, purchases, and sales.

Virtual A computer-generated world with interactive digital objects.

Virtualization The process whereby multiple operating systems run as clients on a single host operating system. Gives the appearance of many computers running on a single computer.

Virtual machines (vm) Computer programs that present the appearance of an independent operating system within a second host operating system. The host can support multiple virtual machines, possibly running different operating system programs (Windows, Linux), each of which is assigned assets such as disk space, devices, and network connections over which it has control.

Virtual reality A completely computer-generated virtual world with interactive digital objects.

Volatile Data that will be lost when the computer or device is not powered.

Web application A software application that requires nothing more than a browser. Also called a thin-client application.

Windows 10 (mobile) A Windows operating system designed for mobile devices.

Windows Server A version of Windows specifically designed and configured for server use. It has much more stringent and restrictive security procedures than other versions of Windows and is popular on servers in organizations that have made a strong commitment to Microsoft.

Zettabyte (ZB) 1,024 EB.

HoloLens Microsoft's head-mounted mixed-reality computing device capable of producing holographic objects that appear in the real world.

Database Processing

It's Friday night, and Cam Forset is on her way to an art show opening. She gets an urgent call from Jess Denkar, the head of security at PetroTex. PetroTex is a large oil refinery based in Texas and one of Falcon Security's biggest industrial clients. Jess is looking for information that could help him find out who stole almost $75,000 worth of custom piping and copper wiring.

Cam made sure Jess had her personal cell phone number and told him to call her anytime—day or night. She knows it's important to show Jess that the money PetroTex spends on Falcon's services is worth it. She immediately calls Toshio Sato, director of IT Services, and tells him to come back into the office. She also sends a text message to CEO Mateo Thomas and CFO Joni Campbell.

"Have you found anything yet?" Joni asks. She quickly sets down her purse at a nearby workstation and begins hovering behind Toshio.

"Not yet—we're working as fast as we can," Cam replies tersely. Cam wants to focus on helping Toshio find the correct security footage, not discuss the importance of the PetroTex account to Falcon Security.

"Is there anything I can do to help?" Joni wonders.

"No, we're just trying to find the right footage. There's a lot of it to review," Cam sighs.

"What's the problem? Why do we have to look through so much footage?"

Toshio is tempted to tell Joni that "we" aren't looking through anything. He's the one doing the searching. But he holds his tongue. "Well, the problem is we have footage of dozens of different buildings at PetroTex, from several different drones, over about a 2-week period. Tracking down the footage of exactly when the equipment was stolen means we have to search through hundreds of different video files. This could take all night," he answers matter-of-factly.

"There's got to be a faster way to do this. Can't we just search for the footage somehow?" Joni says.

"No," Toshio says calmly. "We don't have a way to track the data about the videos. The video files are sequentially numbered and stored in directories for a specific company. We can also see the date and time the video file was created, but there are several different drones. It's just..."

Cam interrupts Toshio to try to keep him from getting distracted. "Toshio and I have talked about creating a database to track all of our video files. We've just been busy trying to automate the data collection and storage process."

"Well, how long would it take to make it? How much would it cost?" Joni asks.

"We're not sure. We don't even know which database management system we'd use. Toshio and I have both used Microsoft Access, but Toshio mentioned something called MongoDB that might be better for tracking video files."

"We don't have a way to track the data about the videos."

Image source: rommma/Fotolia

Toshio pauses the video he's reviewing and starts pointing at a listing of video files in a directory. "Instead of searching through all of these manually, I could just specify characteristics about each video like company name, building name, date, time, and elevation. It would return the URLs for videos matching those characteristics. We'd know right where they are on our file server."

"Sounds good to me. Anything to keep us from spending our Friday nights looking through video footage. Let's do it," Joni quips.

Cam tries to get things back on track. "OK, great, we'll put it on our list. There's no doubt that a database will keep us from having to search through all this footage. For now, though, we should probably focus on finding the footage for Jess. We've got a lot to go through tonight."

Study QUESTIONS

Q1 What is the purpose of a database?

Q2 What is a database?

Q3 What is a database management system (DBMS)?

Q4 How do database applications make databases more useful?

Q5 How are data models used for database development?

Q6 How is a data model transformed into a database design?

Q7 How can Falcon Security benefit from a database system?

Q8 2027?

Chapter PREVIEW

Although you may not realize it, you access dozens, if not hundreds, of databases every day. Every time you make a cell phone call, log on to the Internet, or buy something online using a credit card, applications behind the scenes are processing numerous databases. Use Snapchat, Facebook, Twitter, or LinkedIn, and again applications are processing databases on your behalf. Google something, and yet again dozens of databases are processed to obtain the search results.

As a user, you need know nothing about the underlying technology. From your perspective, "it just works," to quote the late Steve Jobs. However, as a business professional in the 21st century, it's a different story. You need the knowledge of this chapter for four principal reasons:

1. When you participate in the development of any new business initiative, you need to know if database technology can facilitate your project goals. If so, you need sufficient knowledge to assess whether building that database is akin to building a small shed or is closer to building a skyscraper. Joni, in the opening vignette of this chapter, needs to have some knowledge to assess how hard (and thus how expensive) building that new database will be.
2. Because databases are ubiquitous in commerce, billions upon billions of bytes of data are stored every day. You need to know how to turn that data into a format from which you can construct useful information. To that end, you might use one of many different graphical tools to query that data. Or, to become truly proficient, you might learn SQL, an international standard language for querying databases. Many business professionals have done just that.
3. Business is dynamic, and information systems must adapt. Often such adaptation means that the structure of the database needs to be changed. Sometimes it means that entirely new databases must be created. As you will learn in this chapter, only the users, such as yourself, know what and how details should be stored. You may be asked to evaluate a data model like those described in Q4 to facilitate database change and creation.
4. Finally, you might someday find yourself or your department in a material mess. Maybe you don't know who has which equipment, or where certain tools are located, or what's really in your supply closet. In that case, you might choose to build your own database. Unless you're an IS professional, that database will be small and relatively simple, but it can still be very useful to you and your colleagues. Case Study illustrates one such example.

This chapter addresses the why, what, and how of database processing. We begin by describing the purpose of a database and then explain the important components of database systems. Next, we discuss data modeling and show how IS professionals use data models to design database structure. We then discuss how a database system could be used to solve the tracking problem at Falcon Security. We'll wrap up with pondering where database technology might be in 2027.

Q1 What Is the Purpose of a Database?

The purpose of a database is to keep track of things. When most students learn that, they wonder why we need a special technology for such a simple task. Why not just use a list? If the list is long, put it into a spreadsheet.

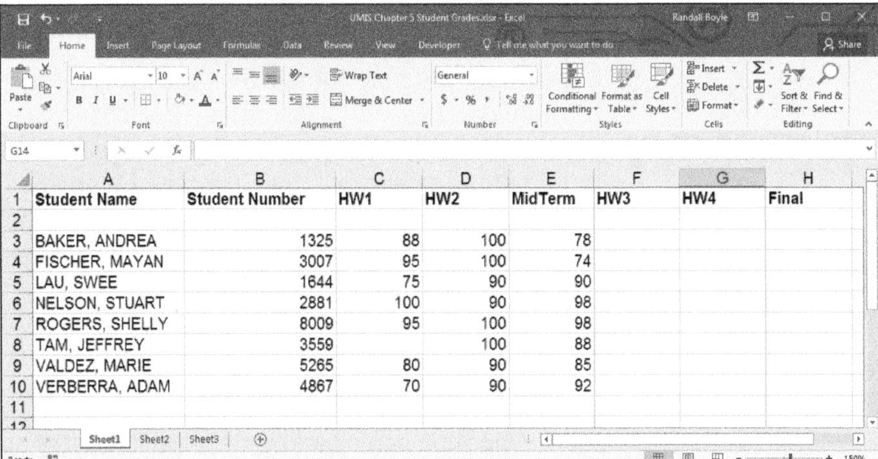

Student Name	Student Number	HW1	HW2	MidTerm	HW3	HW4	Final
BAKER, ANDREA	1325	88	100	78			
FISCHER, MAYAN	3007	95	100	74			
LAU, SWEE	1644	75	90	90			
NELSON, STUART	2881	100	90	98			
ROGERS, SHELLY	8009	95	100	98			
TAM, JEFFREY	3559		100	88			
VALDEZ, MARIE	5265	80	90	85			
VERBERRA, ADAM	4867	70	90	92			

FIGURE 1
A List of Student Grades Presented in a Spreadsheet
Source: Excel 2016, Windows 10, Microsoft Corporation.

In fact, many professionals do keep track of things using spreadsheets. If the structure of the list is simple enough, there is no need to use database technology. The list of student grades in Figure 1, for example, works perfectly well in a spreadsheet.

Suppose, however, that the professor wants to track more than just grades. Say that the professor wants to record email messages as well. Or perhaps the professor wants to record both email messages and office visits. There is no place in Figure 1 to record that additional data. Of course, the professor could set up a separate spreadsheet for email messages and another one for office visits, but that awkward solution would be difficult to use because it does not provide all of the data in one place.

Instead, the professor wants a form like that in Figure 2. With it, the professor can record student grades, emails, and office visits all in one place. A form like the one in Figure 2 is difficult, if not impossible, to produce from a spreadsheet. Such a form is easily produced, however, from a database.

The key distinction between Figures 1 and 2 is that the data in Figure 1 is about a single theme or concept. It is about student grades only. The data in Figure 2 has multiple themes; it shows student grades, student emails, and student office visits. We can make a general rule from these examples: Lists of data involving a single theme can be stored in a spreadsheet; lists that involve data with multiple themes require a database. We will say more about this general rule as this chapter proceeds.

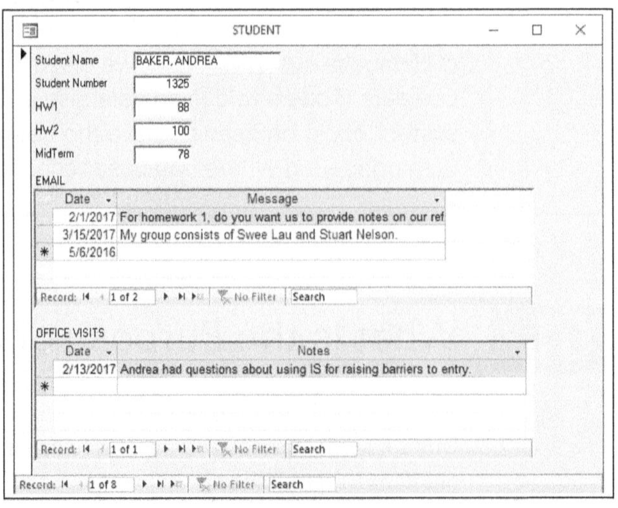

STUDENT

Student Name: BAKER, ANDREA
Student Number: 1325
HW1: 88
HW2: 100
MidTerm: 78

EMAIL

Date	Message
2/1/2017	For homework 1, do you want us to provide notes on our ref
3/15/2017	My group consists of Swee Lau and Stuart Nelson.
5/6/2016	

Record: 1 of 2 No Filter Search

OFFICE VISITS

Date	Notes
2/13/2017	Andrea had questions about using IS for raising barriers to entry.

Record: 1 of 1 No Filter Search

Record: 1 of 8 No Filter Search

FIGURE 2
Student Data Shown in a Form from a Database
Source: Access 2016, Windows 10, Microsoft Corporation.

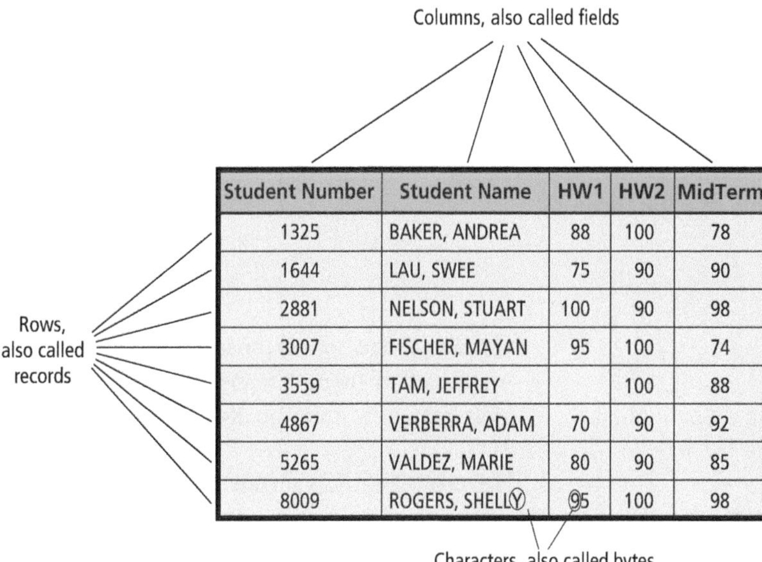

Student Number	Student Name	HW1	HW2	MidTerm
1325	BAKER, ANDREA	88	100	78
1644	LAU, SWEE	75	90	90
2881	NELSON, STUART	100	90	98
3007	FISCHER, MAYAN	95	100	74
3559	TAM, JEFFREY		100	88
4867	VERBERRA, ADAM	70	90	92
5265	VALDEZ, MARIE	80	90	85
8009	ROGERS, SHELLY	95	100	98

FIGURE 3
Student Table (also called a file)

Q2 What Is a Database?

A **database** is a self-describing collection of integrated records. To understand the terms in this definition, you first need to understand the terms illustrated in Figure 3. A **byte** is a character of data. In databases, bytes are grouped into **columns**, such as *Student Number* and *Student Name*. Columns are also called **fields**. Columns or fields, in turn, are grouped into **rows**, which are also called **records**. In Figure 3, the collection of data for all columns (*Student Number, Student Name, HW1, HW2,* and *MidTerm*) is called a *row* or a *record*. Finally, a group of similar rows or records is called a **table** or a **file**. From these definitions, you can see a hierarchy of data elements, as shown in Figure 4.

It is tempting to continue this grouping process by saying that a database is a group of tables or files. This statement, although true, does not go far enough. As shown in Figure 5, a database is a collection of tables *plus* relationships among the rows in those tables, *plus* special data, called

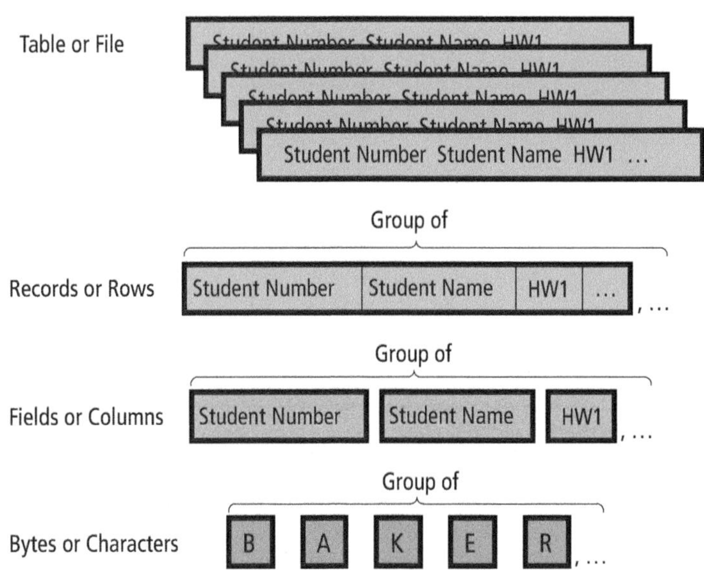

FIGURE 4
Hierarchy of Data Elements

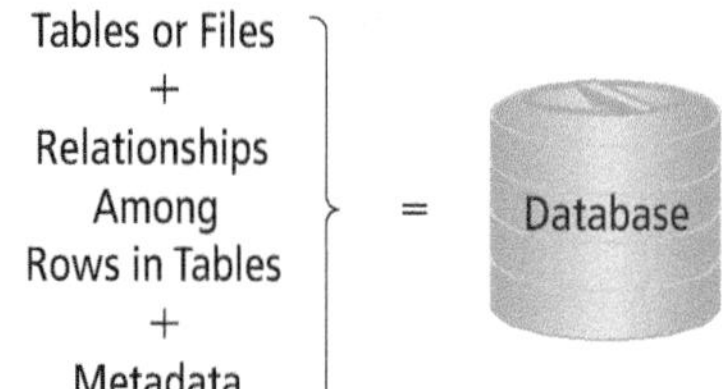

FIGURE 5
Components of a Database

metadata, that describes the structure of the database. By the way, the cylindrical symbol labeled "database" in Figure 5 represents a computer disk drive. It is used like this because databases are most frequently stored on disks.

Relationships Among Rows

Consider the terms on the left-hand side of Figure 5. You know what tables are. To understand what is meant by *relationships among rows in tables*, examine Figure 6. It shows sample data from the three tables *Email*, *Student*, and *Office_Visit*. Notice the column named *Student Number* in the *Email* table. That column indicates the row in *Student* to which a row of *Email* is connected. In the first row of *Email*, the *Student Number* value is 1325. This indicates that this particular email was received from the student whose *Student Number* is 1325. If you examine the *Student* table, you will see that the row for Andrea Baker has this value. Thus, the first row of the *Email* table is related to Andrea Baker.

FIGURE 6
Example of Relationships Among Rows

Email Table

EmailNum	Date	Message	Student Number
1	2/1/2018	For homework 1, do you want us to provide notes on our references?	1325
2	3/15/2018	My group consists of Swee Lau and Stuart Nelson.	1325
3	3/15/2018	Could you please assign me to a group?	1644

Student Table

Student Number	Student Name	HW1	HW2	MidTerm
1325	BAKER, ANDREA	88	100	78
1644	LAU, SWEE	75	90	90
2881	NELSON, STUART	100	90	98
3007	FISCHER, MAYAN	95	100	74
3559	TAM, JEFFREY		100	88
4867	VERBERRA, ADAM	70	90	92
5265	VALDEZ, MARIE	80	90	85
8009	ROGERS, SHELLY	95	100	98

Office_Visit Table

VisitID	Date	Notes	Student Number
2	2/13/2016	Andrea had questions about using IS for raising barriers to entry.	1325
3	2/17/2016	Jeffrey is considering an IS major. Wanted to talk about career opportunities.	3559
4	2/17/2016	Will miss class Friday due to job conflict.	4867

Now consider the last row of the *Office_Visit* table at the bottom of the figure. The value of *Student Number* in that row is 4867. This value indicates that the last row in *Office_Visit* belongs to Adam Verberra.

From these examples, you can see that values in one table relate rows of that table to rows in a second table. Several special terms are used to express these ideas. A **key** (also called a **primary key**) is a column or group of columns that identifies a unique row in a table. *Student Number* is the key of the *Student* table. Given a value of *Student Number*, you can determine one and only one row in *Student*. Only one student has the number 1325, for example.

Every table must have a key. The key of the *Email* table is *EmailNum*, and the key of the *Office_Visit* table is *VisitID*. Sometimes more than one column is needed to form a unique identifier. In a table called *City*, for example, the key would consist of the combination of columns (*City, State*) because a given city name can appear in more than one state.

Student Number is not the key of the *Email* or the *Office_Visit* tables. We know that about *Email* because there are two rows in *Email* that have the *Student Number* value 1325. The value 1325 does not identify a unique row; therefore, *Student Number* cannot be the key of *Email*.

Nor is *Student Number* a key of *Office_Visit*, although you cannot tell that from the data in Figure 6. If you think about it, however, there is nothing to prevent a student from visiting a professor more than once. If that were to happen, there would be two rows in *Office_Visit* with the same value of *Student Number*. It just happens that no student has visited twice in the limited data in Figure 6.

In both *Email* and *Office_Visit*, *Student Number* is a key, but it is a key of a different table, namely *Student*. Hence, the columns that fulfill a role like that of *Student Number* in the *Email* and *Office_Visit* tables are called **foreign keys**. This term is used because such columns are keys, but they are keys of a different (foreign) table than the one in which they reside.

Before we go on, databases that carry their data in the form of tables and that represent relationships using foreign keys are called **relational databases**. (The term *relational* is used because another, more formal name for a table like those we're discussing is **relation**.) You'll learn about another kind of database, or data store, in Q8 and in Case Study.

Metadata

Recall the definition of database: A database is a self-describing collection of integrated records. The records are integrated because, as you just learned, rows can be linked together by their key/foreign key relationship. Relationships among rows are represented in the database. But what does *self-describing* mean?

Database technology puts unprecedented ability to conceive information into the hands of users. But what do you do with that information when you find something objectionable? See the Ethics Guide given later in the chapter for an example case.

It means that a database contains, within itself, a description of its contents. Think of a library. A library is a self-describing collection of books and other materials. It is self-describing because the library contains a catalog that describes the library's contents. The same idea also pertains to a database. Databases are self-describing because they contain not only data, but also data about the data in the database.

Metadata is data that describes data. Figure 7 shows metadata for the *Email* table. The format of metadata depends on the software product that is processing the database. Figure 7 shows the metadata as it appears in Microsoft Access. Each row of the top part of this form describes a column of the *Email* table. The columns of these descriptions are *Field Name*, *Data Type*, and *Description*. *Field Name* contains the name of the column, *Data Type* shows the type of data the column may hold, and *Description* contains notes that explain the source or use of the column. As you can see, there is one row of metadata for each of the four columns of the *Email* table: *EmailNum*, *Date*, *Message*, and *Student Number*.

The bottom part of this form provides more metadata, which Access calls *Field Properties*, for each column. In Figure 7, the focus is on the *Date* column (note the light rectangle drawn around the *Date* row). Because the focus is on *Date* in the top pane, the details in the bottom pane pertain to the *Date* column. The Field Properties describe formats, a default value for Access to supply when a new row is created, and the constraint that a value is required for this column. It is not important

ETHICS GUIDE

QUERYING INEQUALITY?

MaryAnn Baker works as a data analyst in human relations at a large, multinational corporation. As part of its compensation program, her company defines job categories and assigns salary ranges to each category. For example, the category M1 is used for first-line managers and is assigned the salary range of $75,000 to $95,000. Every job description is assigned to one of these categories, depending on the knowledge and skills required to do that job. Thus, the job titles Manager of Customer Support, Manager of Technical Writing, and Manager of Product Quality Assurance are all judged to involve about the same level of management expertise and are all assigned to category M1.

One of MaryAnn's tasks is to analyze company salary data and determine how well actual salaries conform to established ranges. When discrepancies are noted, human relations managers meet to determine whether the discrepancy indicates a need to:

- Adjust the category's salary range;
- Move the job title to a different category;
- Define a new category; or Train the manager of the employee with the discrepancy on the use of salary ranges in setting employee compensation.

MaryAnn is an expert in creating database queries. Initially, she used Microsoft Access to produce reports, but much of the salary data she needs resides in the organization's Oracle database. At first she would ask the IS Department to extract certain data and move it into Access, but over time she learned that it was faster to ask IS to move all employee data from the operational Oracle database into another Oracle database created just for HR data analysis. Although Oracle provides a graphical query interface like that in Access, she found it easier to compose complex queries directly in SQL, so she learned it and, within a few months, became a SQL expert.

"I never thought I'd be doing this," she said. "But it turns out to be quite fun, like solving a puzzle, and apparently I'm good at it."

One day, after a break, MaryAnn signed into her computer and happened to glance at the results of a query that she'd left running while she was gone. "That's odd," she thought, "all the people with Hispanic surnames have lower salaries than the others." She wasn't looking for that pattern; it just happened to jump out at her as she glanced at the screen.

As she examined the data, she began to wonder if she was seeing a coincidence or if there was a discriminatory

pattern within the organization. Unfortunately for MaryAnn's purposes, the organization did not track employee race in its database, so she had no easy way of identifying employees of Hispanic heritage other than reading through the list of surnames. But, as a skilled problem solver, that didn't stop MaryAnn. She realized that many employees having Hispanic origins were born in certain cities in Texas, New Mexico, Arizona, and California. Of course, this wasn't true for all employees; many non-Hispanic employees were born in those cities, too, and many Hispanic employees were born in other cities. This data was still useful, however, because MaryAnn's sample queries revealed that the proportion of employees with Hispanic surnames who were also born in those cities was very high. "OK," she thought, "I'll use those cities as a rough surrogate."

Using birth city as a query criterion, MaryAnn created queries that determined employees who were born in the selected cities earned, on average, 23 percent less than those who were not. "Well, that could be because they work in lower-pay-grade jobs." After giving it a bit of thought, MaryAnn realized that she needed to examine wages and salaries within job categories. "Where," she wondered, "do people born in those cities fall in the ranges of their job categories?" So, she constructed SQL to determine where within a job category the compensation for people born in the selected cities fell. "Wow!" she said to herself, "almost 80 percent of the employees born in those cities fall into the bottom half of their salary range."

MaryAnn scheduled an appointment with her manager for the next day.

DISCUSSION QUESTIONS

When answering the following questions, suppose that you are MaryAnn:

1. Given these query results, do you have an ethical responsibility to do something? Consider both the categorical imperative and the utilitarian perspective.
2. Given these query results, do you have a personal or social responsibility to do something?
3. What is your response if your manager says, "You don't know anything; it could be that starting salaries are lower in those cities. Forget about it."
4. What is your response if your manager says, "Don't be a troublemaker; pushing this issue will hurt your career."
5. What is your response if your manager says, "Right. We already know that. Get back to the tasks that I've assigned you."
6. Suppose your manager gives you funding to follow up with a more accurate analysis, and, indeed, there is a pattern of underpayment to people with Hispanic surnames. What should the organization do? For each choice below, indicate likely outcomes:
   - **a.** Correct the imbalances immediately.
   - **b.** Gradually correct the imbalances at future pay raises.
   - **c.** Do nothing about the imbalances, but train managers not to discriminate in the future.
   - **d.** Do nothing.
7. Suppose you hire a part-time person to help with the more accurate analysis, and that person is so outraged at the outcome that he quits and notifies newspapers in all the affected cities of the organization's discrimination.
   - **a.** How should the organization respond?
   - **b.** How should you respond?
8. Consider the adage "Never ask a question for which you do not want the answer."
   - **a.** Is following that adage ethical? Consider both the categorical imperative and utilitarian perspectives.
   - **b.** Is following that adage socially responsible?
   - **c.** How does that adage relate to you, as MaryAnn?
   - **d.** How does that adage relate to you, as a future business professional?
   - **e.** With regard to employee compensation, how does that adage relate to organizations?

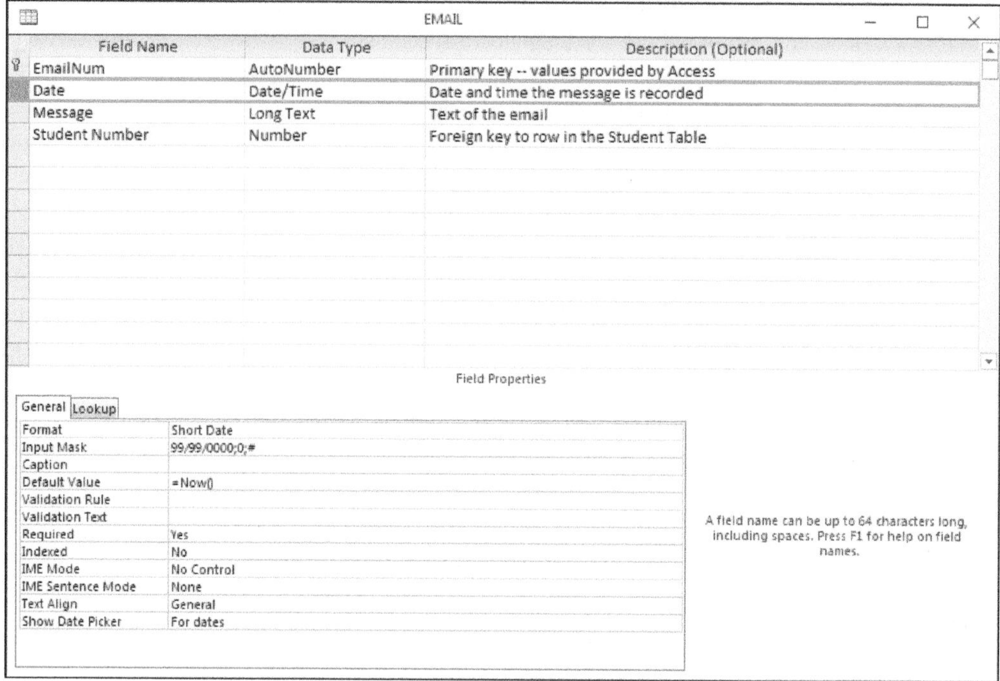

FIGURE 7
Sample Metadata (in Access)
Source: Access 2016, Windows 10, Microsoft Corporation.

for you to remember these details. Instead, just understand that metadata is data about data and that such metadata is always a part of a database.

The presence of metadata makes databases much more useful. Because of metadata, no one needs to guess, remember, or even record what is in the database. To find out what a database contains, we just look at the metadata inside the database.

Q3 What Is a Database Management System (DBMS)?

A **database management system (DBMS)** is a program used to create, process, and administer a database. As with operating systems, almost no organization develops its own DBMS. Instead, companies license DBMS products from vendors such as IBM, Microsoft, Oracle, and others. Popular DBMS products are **DB2** from IBM, **Access** and **SQL Server** from Microsoft, and **Oracle Database** from the Oracle Corporation. Another popular DBMS is **MySQL**, an open source DBMS product that is license-free for most applications.[1] Other DBMS products are available, but these five process the great bulk of databases today.

Note that a DBMS and a database are two different things. For some reason, the trade press and even some books confuse the two. A DBMS is a software program; a database is a collection of tables, relationships, and metadata. The two are very different concepts.

Creating the Database and Its Structures

Database developers use the DBMS to create tables, relationships, and other structures in the database. The form in Figure 7 can be used to define a new table or to modify an existing one. To create a new table, the developer just fills the new table's metadata into the form.

To modify an existing table—say, to add a new column—the developer opens the metadata form for that table and adds a new row of metadata. For example, in Figure 8 the developer has added a new column called *Response?*. This new column has the data type *Yes/No*, which means that the column can contain only one value—*Yes* or *No*. The professor will use this column to indicate whether he has responded to the student's email. A column can be removed by deleting its row in this table, though doing so will lose any existing data.

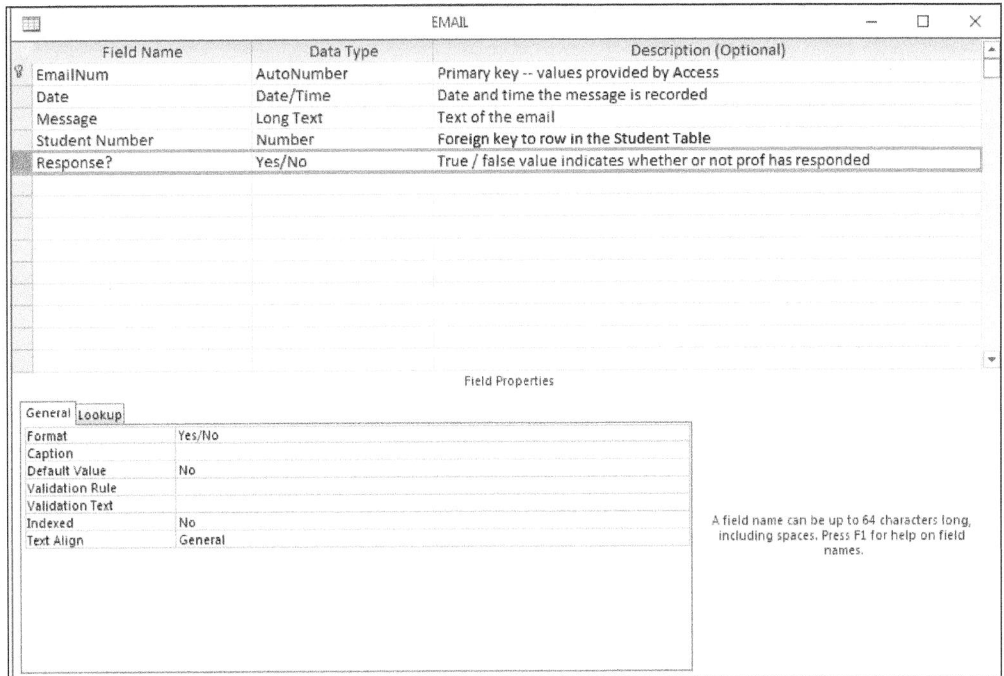

FIGURE 8

Adding a New Column to a Table (in Access)

Source: Access 2016, Windows 10, Microsoft Corporation.

Processing the Database

Organizations are collecting large amounts of data. Big data becomes a big target for hackers as described in the Security Guide given later in the chapter.

The second function of the DBMS is to process the database. Such processing can be quite complex, but, fundamentally, the DBMS provides applications for four processing operations: to read, insert, modify, or delete data. These operations are requested in application calls upon the DBMS. From a form, when the user enters new or changed data, a computer program behind the form calls the DBMS to make the necessary database changes. From a Web application, a program on the client or on the server calls the DBMS to make the change.

Structured Query Language (SQL) is an international standard language for processing a database. All five of the DBMS products mentioned earlier accept and process SQL (pronounced "see-quell") statements. As an example, the following SQL statement inserts a new row into the *Student* table:

```
INSERT INTO Student
([Student Number], [Student Name], HW1, HW2, MidTerm)
VALUES
(1000, 'Franklin, Benjamin', 90, 95, 100);
```

As stated, statements like this one are issued "behind the scenes" by programs that process forms and reports. Alternatively, they can be issued directly to the DBMS by an application program.

You do not need to understand or remember SQL language syntax. Instead, just realize that SQL is an international standard for processing a database. SQL can also be used to create databases and database structures. You will learn more about SQL if you take a database management class.

Administering the Database

A third DBMS function is to provide tools to assist in the administration of the database. **Database administration** involves a wide variety of activities. For example, the DBMS can be used to set up a security system involving user accounts, passwords, permissions, and limits for processing the database. To provide database security, a user must sign on using a valid user account before she can process the database.

Permissions can be limited in very specific ways. In the Student database example, it is possible to limit a particular user to reading only *Student Name* from the *Student* table. A different user could be given permission to read the entire *Student* table, but limited to update only the *HW1*, *HW2*, and *MidTerm* columns. Other users can be given still other permissions.

SO WHAT?

SLICK ANALYTICS

Spreadsheet software designed for small businesses is often misused. For example, if you use spreadsheet software to manage a dataset with several hundreds of thousands of rows of data, you will find that simple operations like sorting and saving updates to the data take several minutes. It is difficult to work effectively and efficiently when minutes are wasted on rudimentary operations. As companies continue to collect larger and larger datasets, there is demand for more robust and scalable data management solutions. These solutions must facilitate rather than hinder the rapid collection and analysis of important data.

Nowadays, a great deal of data collection, storage, and analysis has moved to the cloud. You may not realize it, but you are probably taking advantage of some sort of cloud-based storage solution right now. If you use applications like Dropbox, OneDrive, or Google Drive, you're using the cloud. You no longer need to transfer files from one device to the next using a flash drive or other physical storage medium. You can access your files on any device with Internet connectivity.

As a student, you've probably found cloud storage tremendously convenient (e.g., when sharing large files for a group project with peers). Businesses are harnessing the same power and convenience offered by the cloud, but on a much larger scale. Companies aren't just looking for the convenient file access, though; chief information officers (CIOs) are looking to merge the *storage* and *analysis* of data into one synergistic operation.

Drilling for Answers

Laredo Petroleum is an example of a company that has recognized the benefits offered by cloud analytics.[2] In a recent interview, the CIO described the cumbersome data analysis process the company had been using to improve its drilling operations. The company's old approach entailed the use of numerous spreadsheets and manual calculations that took a long time to perform. By the time actionable insights had been extracted from the data, the value of the information had already been diminished due to old age.

One important question Laredo Petroleum must answer is when it should clean chemical deposits in its wells. Cleaning these deposits boosts the efficiency of wells, but sending maintenance teams to clean the wells is costly. Laredo Petroleum transitioned from the antiquated spreadsheet-based approach of analyzing this problem to using a cloud-based analytics platform. This new approach made data management more scalable, data analysis more robust, and data accessibility better. Data could now be accessed on both traditional PCs and mobile devices at any time and in any location.[3]

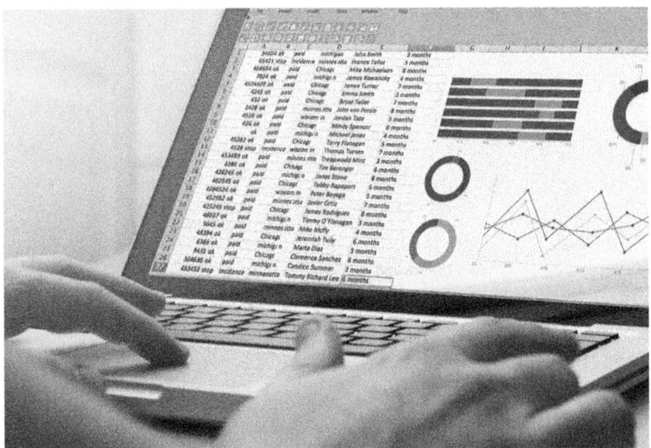

Source: © Georgejmclittle/Fotolia

Cloud analytics provide a much nimbler information systems architecture. It can respond to changes in market conditions more easily (e.g., the glut in the world oil supply and subsequent bottoming out of oil prices that began in 2015 has affected how Laredo Petroleum does business). Laredo Petroleum isn't the only company that has identified cloud analytics as a viable solution for surviving and thriving in a world driven by Big Data. A recent study reported that global cloud analytics would grow by 46 percent through 2020.[4] The widespread interest in cloud analytics is likely driven by improvements in data storage and analysis functionality like enhanced scalability, parallelism across devices, resource pooling, and agile virtualization[5].

Cloudburst?

It's easy to tout the benefits of cloud services, but you may be wondering if there are downsides. Think about your own use of cloud services. Are there any aspects of storing your files in the cloud that concern you? Some people are apprehensive about storing their photos and financial data (e.g., tax returns) in the cloud. Are their data being stored securely? Is it safe to allow your personal data out in the "wild" where it is out of your control?

There are other risks too. Could your data be permanently lost due to a system failure or a malicious insider at your cloud service provider?[6] Could a denial-of-service attack against your cloud service provider render your data inaccessible for an extended period of time?[7] As with any system, security often comes at the expense of convenience. As a business leader, you must consider if the *benefits* of cloud-based services outweigh the potential *risks*, which in some cases may turn into real losses.

Questions

1. Have you chosen to store any of your personal data in the cloud? If so, do you store all of your data or only certain types of data? If not, what factors have inhibited you from putting your data in the hands of a cloud provider? If you don't use cloud-based storage, how do you back up your data?
2. This article discussed the specific example of a petroleum company using cloud-based data analytics to improve decision making. What other industries can you identify that would benefit from the ability to capture large quantities of data in real time, analyze the data, and then use the results of those analyses to make better decisions?
3. This article mentions that some users may decide to manage their data "in house" rather than use cloud-based services and risk losing access to their data in the event of a denial-of-service (DoS) attack. Take a few minutes to research what a DoS attack is and how it could prevent users from accessing their data. Be prepared to explain this concept to another classmate or the class.
4. In a business setting, what types of organizations would place greater value on security rather than convenience? What types of organizations would prioritize convenience over security?

Source: Clint Boulton, "Oil company hopes to strike efficiency with cloud analytics," CIO.com, November 10, 2015, accessed March 27, 2016, http://www.cio.com/article/3003498/cloud-computing/oil-company-hopes-to-strike-efficiency-with-cloud-analytics.html; James Kobielus, "The all-consuming future of cloud analytics," InfoWorld.com, March 20, 2015, accessed March 27, 2016, http://www.infoworld.com/article/2899662/big-data/the-all-consuming-future-of-cloud-analytics.html; Fahmida Y. Rashid, "The dirty dozen: 12 cloud security threats," InfoWorld.com, March 11, 2016, accessed March 27, 2016, http://www.infoworld.com/article/3041078/security/the-dirty-dozen-12-cloud-security-threats.html;

In addition to security, DBMS administrative functions include backing up database data, adding structures to improve the performance of database applications, removing data that are no longer wanted or needed, and similar tasks.

For important databases, most organizations dedicate one or more employees to the role of database administration. Figure 9 summarizes the major responsibilities for this function. You will learn more about this topic if you take a database management course.

Category	Database Administration Task	Description
Development	Create and staff DBA function	Size of DBA group depends on size and complexity of database. Groups range from one part-time person to small group.
	Form steering committee	Consists of representatives of all user groups. Forum for community-wide discussions and decisions.
	Specify requirements	Ensure that all appropriate user input is considered.
	Validate data model	Check data model for accuracy and completeness.
	Evaluate application design	Verify that all necessary forms, reports, queries, and applications are developed. Validate design and usability of application components.
Operation	Manage processing rights and responsibilities	Determine processing rights/restrictions on each table and column.
	Manage security	Add and delete users and user groups as necessary; ensure that security system works.
	Track problems and manage resolution	Develop system to record and manage resolution of problems.
	Monitor database performance	Provide expertise/solutions for performance improvements.
	Manage DBMS	Evaluate new features and functions.
Backup and Recovery	Monitor backup procedures	Verify that database backup procedures are followed.
	Conduct training	Ensure that users and operations personnel know and understand recovery procedures.
	Manage recovery	Manage recovery process.
Adaptation	Set up request tracking system	Develop system to record and prioritize requests for change.
	Manage configuration change	Manage impact of database structure changes on applications and users.

FIGURE 9
Summary of Database Administration (DBA) Tasks

Q4 How Do Database Applications Make Databases More Useful?

A set of database tables, by itself, is not very useful; the tables in Figure 6 contain the data the professor wants, but the format is awkward at best. The data in database tables can be made more useful, or more available for the conception of information, when it is placed into forms like that in Figure 2 or other formats.

A **database application** is a collection of forms, reports, queries, and application programs[8] that serves as an intermediary between users and database data. Database applications reformat database table data to make it more informative and more easily updated. Application programs also have features that provide security, maintain data consistency, and handle special cases.

The specific purposes of the four elements of a database application are:

Forms	View data; insert new, update existing, and delete existing data
Reports	Structured presentation of data using sorting, grouping, filtering, and other operations
Queries	Search based on data values provided by the user
Application programs	Provide security, data consistency, and special purpose processing, (e.g., handle out-of-stock situations)

Database applications came into prominence in the 1990s and were based on the technology available at that time. Many existing systems today are long-lived extensions to those applications; the ERP system SAP is a good example of this concept. You should expect to see these kinds of applications during the early years of your career.

Today, however, many database applications are based on newer technology that employs browsers, the Web, and related standards. These browser-based applications can do everything the older ones do, but they are more dynamic and better suited to today's world. To see why, consider each type.

Traditional Forms, Queries, Reports, and Applications

In most cases, a traditional database is shared among many users. In that case, the application shown in Figure 10 resides on the users' computers and the DBMS and database reside on a server computer. A network, in most cases *not* the Internet, is used to transmit traffic back and forth between the users' computers and the DBMS server computer.

FIGURE 10
Components of a Database Application System

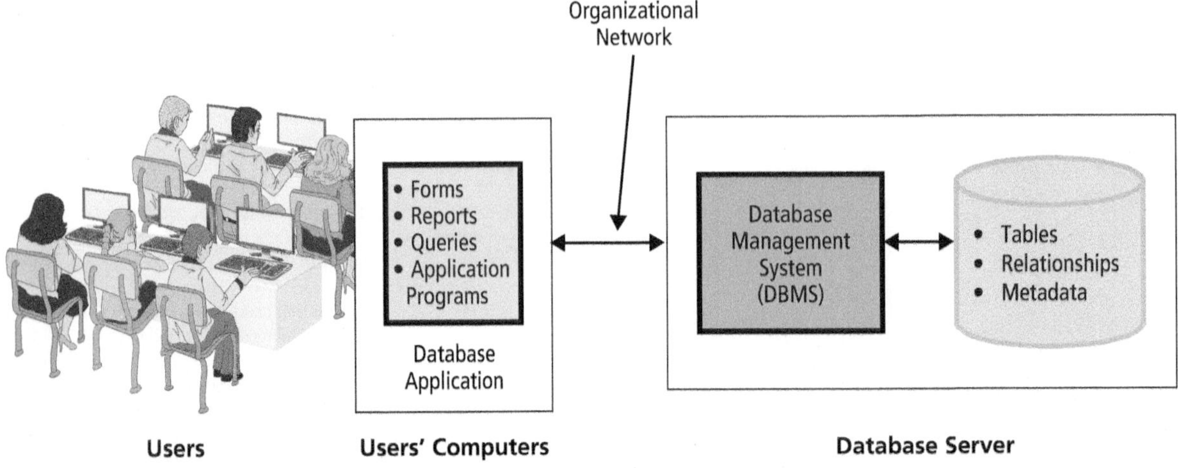

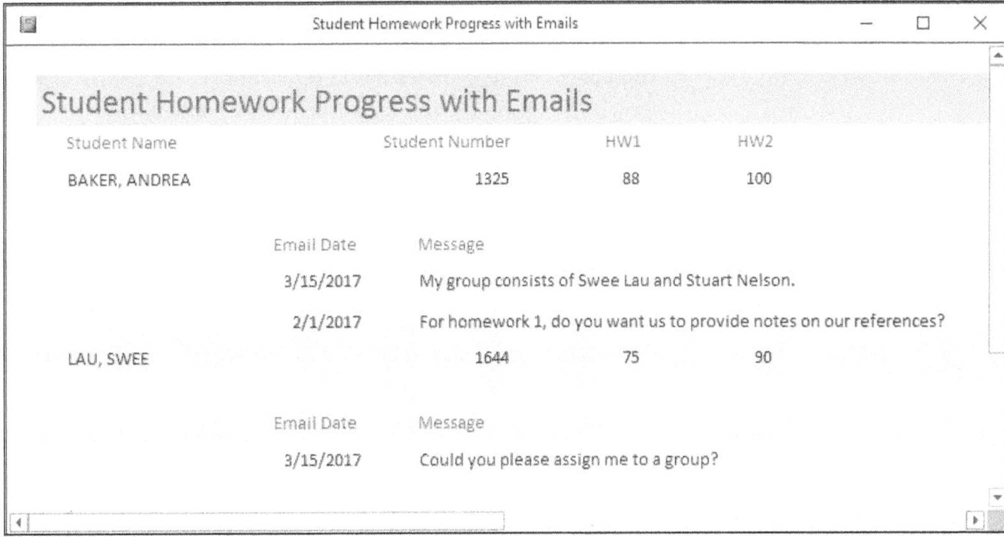

FIGURE 11
Example of a Student Report

Single-user databases like those in Microsoft Access are an exception. With such databases, the application, the DBMS, and the database all reside on the user's computer.

Traditional forms appeared in window-like displays like that in Figure 2. They serve their purpose; users can view, insert, modify, and delete data with them, but by today's standards, they look clunky.

Figure 11 shows a traditional report, which is a static display of data, placed into a format that is meaningful to the user. In this report, each of the emails for a particular student is shown after the student's name and grade data. Figure 12 shows a traditional query. The user specifies query criteria in a window-like box (Figure 12a), and the application responds with data that fit those criteria (Figure 12b).

Traditional database application programs are written in object-oriented languages such as C++ and VisualBasic (and even in earlier languages like COBOL). They are thick applications that need to be installed on users' computers. In some cases, all of the application logic is contained in a program on users' computers and the server does nothing except run the DBMS and serve up data. In other cases, some application code is placed on both the users' computers and the database server computer.

As stated, in the early years of your career, you will still see traditional applications, especially for enterprise-wide applications like ERP and CRM. Most likely, you will also be concerned, as a user if not in a more involved way, with the transition from such traditional applications into browser-based applications.

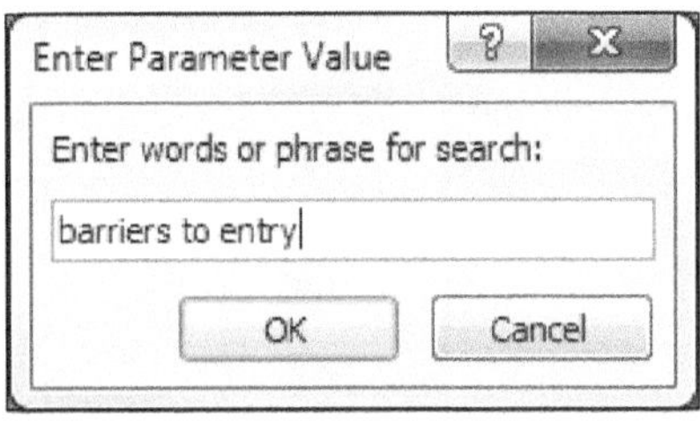

FIGURE 12A
Sample Query Form Used to Enter Phrase for Search
Source: Access 2016, Windows 10, Microsoft Corporation.

FIGURE 12B
Sample Query Results of Query Operation
Source: Access 2016, Windows 10, Microsoft Corporation.

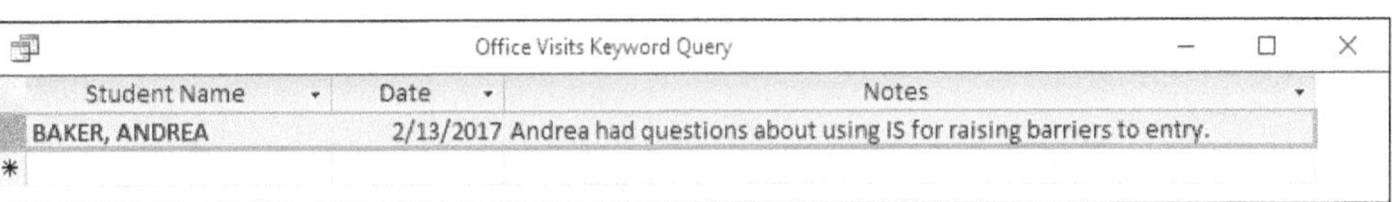

Browser Forms, Reports, Queries, and Applications

The databases in browser-based applications are nearly always shared among many users. As shown in Figure 13, the users' browsers connect over the Internet to a Web server computer, which in turn connects to a database server computer (often many computers are involved on the server side of the Internet).

Browser applications are thin-client applications that need not be preinstalled on the users' computers. In most cases, all of the code for generating and processing the application elements is shared between the users' computers and the servers. JavaScript is the standard language for user-side processing. Languages like C# and Java are used for server-side code, though JavaScript is starting to be used on the server with an open source product named Node.js.

Browser database application forms, reports, and queries are displayed and processed using html and, most recently, using html5, css3, and JavaScript. Figure 14 shows a browser form that is used to create a new user account in Office 365. The form's content is dynamic; the user can click on the blue arrow next to *Additional Details* to see more data. Also, notice the steps on the left-hand side that outline the process that the administrator will follow when creating the new account. The current step is shown in color. Compare and contrast this form with that in Figure 2; it is cleaner, with much less chrome.

Figure 15 illustrates a browser report that shows the content of a SharePoint site. The content is dynamic; almost all of the items can be clicked to produce other reports or take other actions. The user can search the report in the box in the upper-right-hand corner to find specific items.

Browser-based applications can support traditional queries, but more exciting are **graphical queries**, in which query criteria are created when the user clicks on a graphic. Figure 16 shows a map of one of the facilities protected by Falcon Security. The user can click on any one of the video icons on the map, and the click will initiate a query to return a list of all the videos available from that location.

Security requirements are more stringent for browser-based Internet applications than for traditional ones. Most traditional applications run within a corporate network protected from threats common on the Internet. Browser-based applications that are open to the public, over the Internet, are far more vulnerable. Thus, protecting security is a major function for browser-based Internet application programs. Like traditional database application programs, they need to

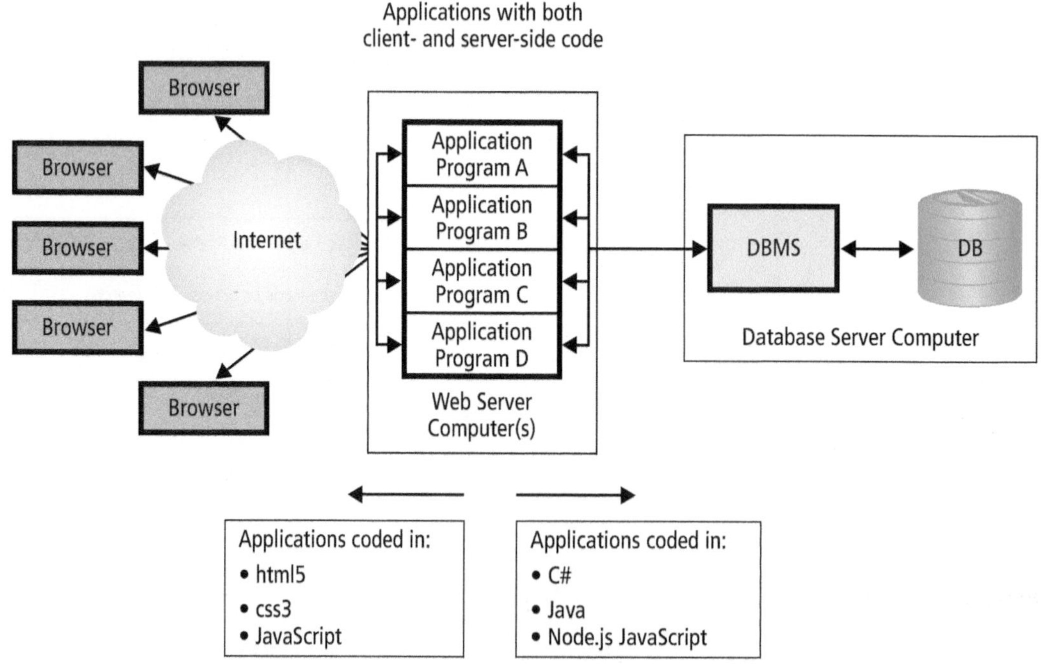

FIGURE 13
Four Application Programs on a Web Server Computer

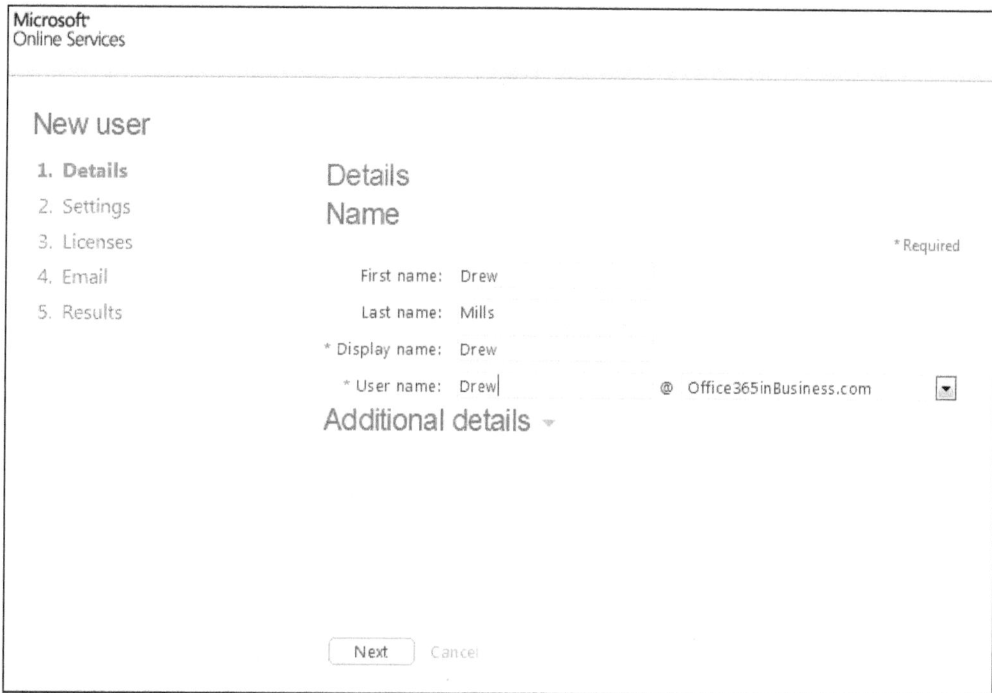

FIGURE 14
Account Creation Browser Form
Source: Windows 10, Microsoft Corporation.

provide for data consistency and to handle special conditions as well. As an example of the need for data consistency, consider the problems introduced by multi-user processing.

Multi-user Processing

Most traditional and browser-based applications involve multiple users processing the same database. While such **multi-user processing** is common, it does pose unique problems that you, as a future manager, should know about. To understand the nature of those problems, consider the following scenario, which could occur on either a traditional or browser-based application.

At a ticket vendor's Web site, two customers, Andrea and Jeffrey, are both attempting to buy tickets to a popular event. Andrea uses her browser to access the site and finds that two tickets are available. She places both of them in her shopping cart. She doesn't know it, but when she opened the order form, she invoked an application program on the vendor's servers that read a database to

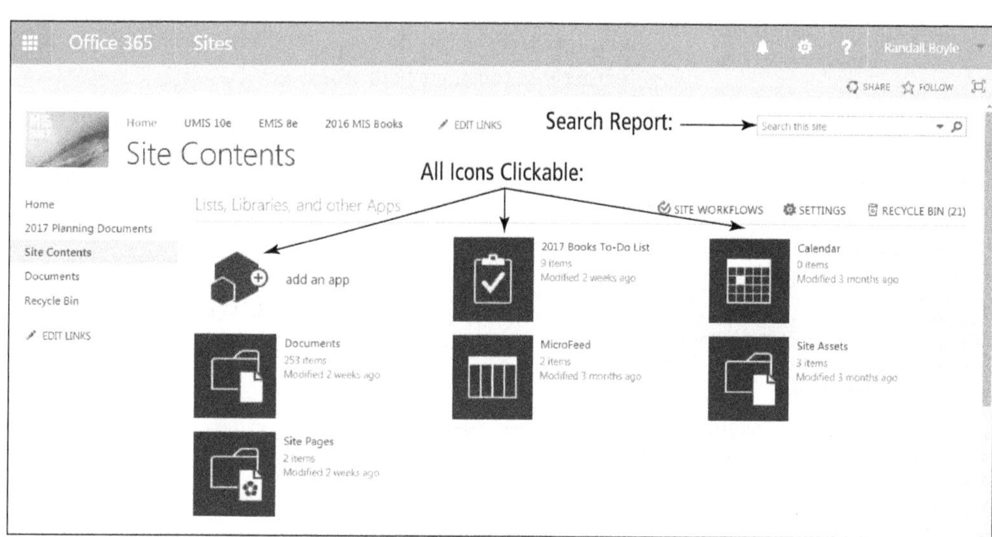

FIGURE 15
Browser Report
Source: Windows 10, Microsoft Corporation.

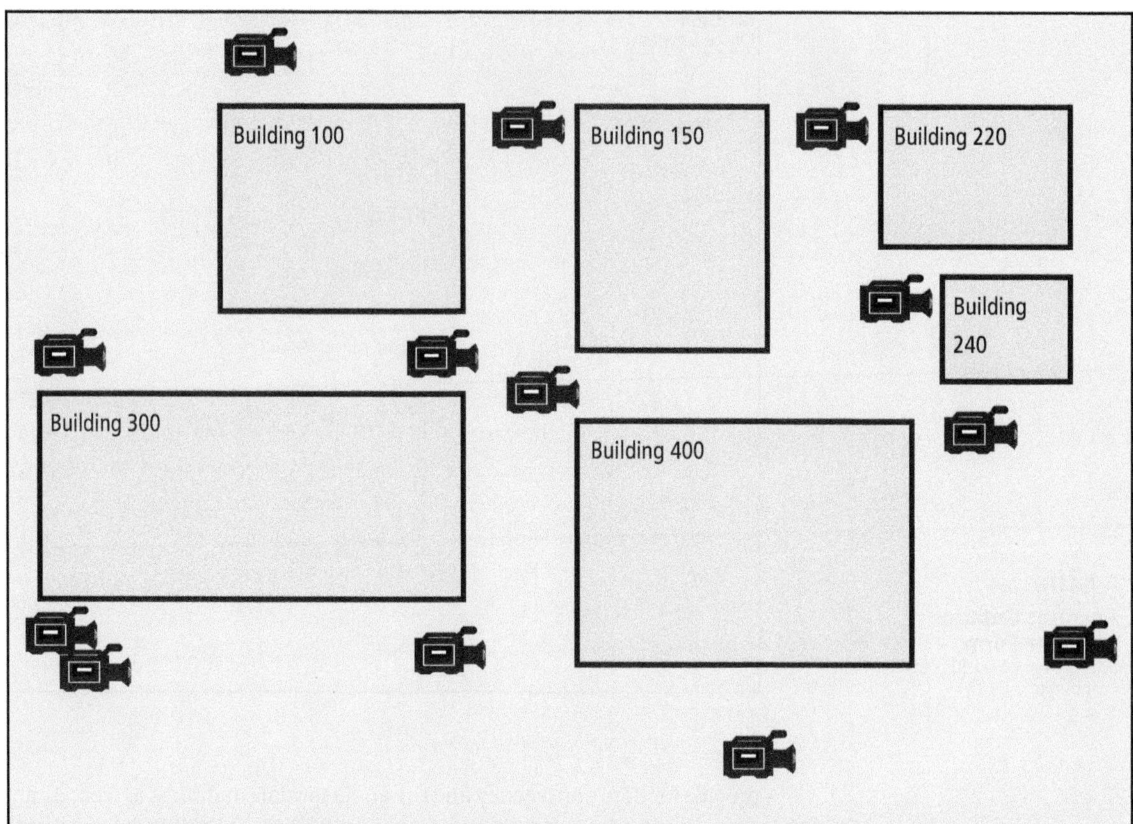

FIGURE 16
Graphical Query: User Clicks on Video Icon to Find All Videos from That Location

find that two tickets are available. Before she checks out, she takes a moment to verify with her friend that they still want to go.

Meanwhile, Jeffrey uses his browser and also finds that two tickets are available because his browser activates that same application that reads the database and finds (because Andrea has not yet checked out) that two are available. He places both in his cart and checks out.

Meanwhile, Andrea and her friend decide to go, so she checks out. Clearly, we have a problem. Both Andrea and Jeffrey have purchased the same two tickets. One of them is going to be disappointed.

This problem, known as the **lost-update problem**, exemplifies one of the special characteristics of multi-user database processing. To prevent this problem, some type of locking must be used to coordinate the activities of users who know nothing about one another. Locking brings its own set of problems, however, and those problems must be addressed as well. We will not delve further into this topic here, however.

Be aware of possible data conflicts when you manage business activities that involve multi-user processing. If you find inaccurate results that seem not to have a cause, you may be experiencing multi-user data conflicts. Contact your IS department for assistance.

Q5 How Are Data Models Used for Database Development?

You may learn about the process for developing information systems in detail in other courses. However, business professionals have such a critical role in the development of database applications that we need to anticipate part of that discussion here by introducing two topics—data modeling and database design.

Because the design of the database depends entirely on how users view their business environment, user involvement is critical for database development. Think about the Student database. What data should it contain? Possibilities are: *Students, Classes, Grades, Emails, Office_Visits, Majors, Advisers, Student_Organizations*—the list could go on and on. Further, how much detail should be included in each? Should the database include campus addresses? Home addresses? Billing addresses?

In fact, there are unlimited possibilities, and the database developers do not and cannot know what to include. They do know, however, that a database must include all the data necessary for the users to perform their jobs. Ideally, it contains that amount of data and no more. So, during database development, the developers must rely on the users to tell them what to include in the database.

Database structures can be complex, in some cases very complex. So, before building the database the developers construct a logical representation of database data called a **data model**. It describes the data and relationships that will be stored in the database. It is akin to a blueprint. Just as building architects create a blueprint before they start building, so, too, database developers create a data model before they start designing the database.

To learn more about a career as a database engineer, see the Career Guide given later in the chapter.

Figure 17 summarizes the database development process. Interviews with users lead to database requirements, which are summarized in a data model. Once the users have approved (validated) the data model, it is transformed into a database design. That design is then implemented into database structures. We will consider data modeling and database design briefly in the next two sections. Again, your goal should be to learn the process so that you can be an effective user representative for a development effort.

What Is the Entity-Relationship Data Model?

The **entity-relationship (E-R) data model** is a tool for constructing data models. Developers use it to describe the content of a data model by defining the things (*entities*) that will be stored in the database and the *relationships* among those entities. A second, less popular tool for data modeling is the **Unified Modeling Language (UML)**. We will not describe that tool here. However, if you learn how to interpret E-R models, with a bit of study you will be able to understand UML models as well.

Entities

An **entity** is some thing that the users want to track. Examples of entities are *Order, Customer, Salesperson,* and *Item*. Some entities represent a physical object, such as *Item* or *Salesperson*; others represent a logical construct or transaction, such as *Order* or *Contract*. For reasons beyond this discussion, entity names are always singular. We use *Order*, not *Orders*; *Salesperson*, not *Salespersons*.

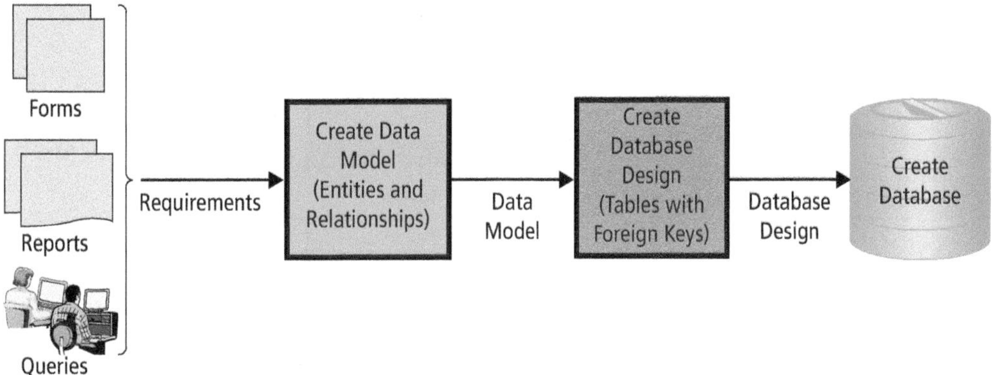

FIGURE 17
Database Development Process

Entities have **attributes** that describe characteristics of the entity. Example attributes of *Order* are *OrderNumber, OrderDate, SubTotal, Tax, Total,* and so forth. Example attributes of *Salesperson* are *SalespersonName, Email, Phone,* and so forth.

Entities have an **identifier**, which is an attribute (or group of attributes) whose value is associated with one and only one entity instance. For example, *OrderNumber* is an identifier of *Order* because only one *Order* instance has a given value of *OrderNumber*. For the same reason, *CustomerNumber* is an identifier of *Customer*. If each member of the sales staff has a unique name, then *SalespersonName* is an identifier of *Salesperson*.

Before we continue, consider that last sentence. Is the salesperson's name unique among the sales staff? Both now and in the future? Who decides the answer to such a question? Only the users know whether this is true; the database developers cannot know. This example underlines why it is important for you to be able to interpret data models because only users like you will know for sure.

Figure 18 shows examples of entities for the Student database. Each entity is shown in a rectangle. The name of the entity is just above the rectangle, and the identifier is shown in a section at the top of the entity. Entity attributes are shown in the remainder of the rectangle. In Figure 18, the *Adviser* entity has an identifier called *AdviserName* and the attributes *Phone, CampusAddress,* and *EmailAddress*.

Observe that the entities *Email* and *Office_Visit* do not have an identifier. Unlike *Student* or *Adviser*, the users do not have an attribute that identifies a particular email. We *could* make one up. For example, we could say that the identifier of *Email* is *EmailNumber*, but if we do so we are not modeling how the users view their world. Instead, we are forcing something onto the users. Be aware of this possibility when you review data models about your business. Do not allow the database developers to create something in the data model that is not part of your business world.

Relationships

Entities have **relationships** to each other. An *Order*, for example, has a relationship to a *Customer* entity and also to a *Salesperson* entity. In the Student database, a *Student* has a relationship to an *Adviser*, and an *Adviser* has a relationship to a *Department*.

Figure 19 shows sample *Department, Adviser,* and *Student* entities and their relationships. For simplicity, this figure shows just the identifier of the entities and not the other attributes. For this sample data, *Accounting* has three professors—Jones, Wu, and Lopez—and *Finance* has two professors—Smith and Greene.

The relationship between *Advisers* and *Students* is a bit more complicated because in this example, an adviser is allowed to advise many students and a student is allowed to have many advisers. Perhaps this happens because students can have multiple majors. In any case, note that Professor Jones advises students 100 and 400 and that student 100 is advised by both Professors Jones and Smith.

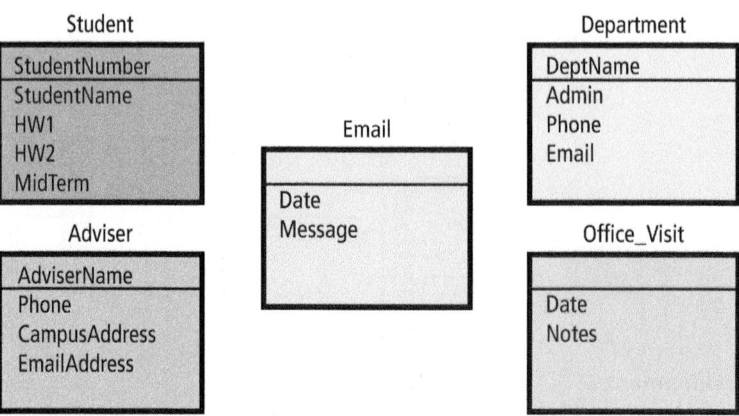

FIGURE 18
Student Data Model Entities

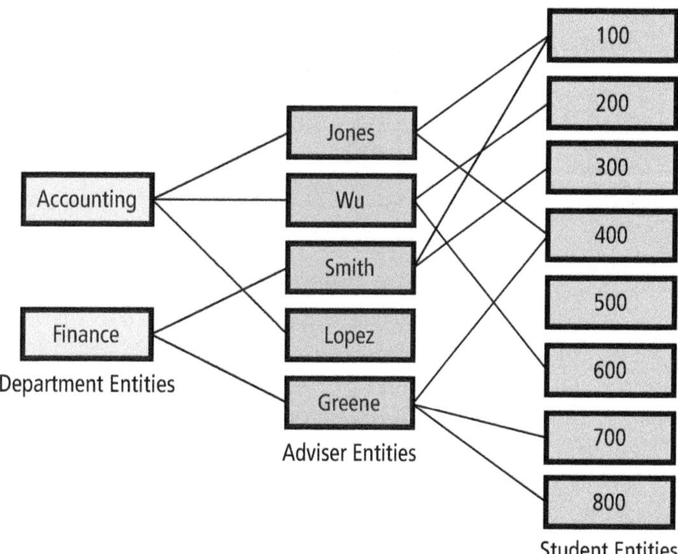

FIGURE 19
Example of Department, Adviser, and Student Entities and Relationships

Diagrams like the one in Figure 19 are too cumbersome for use in database design discussions. Instead, database designers use diagrams called **entity-relationship (E-R) diagrams**. Figure 20 shows an E-R diagram for the data in Figure 19. In this figure, all of the entities of one type are represented by a single rectangle. Thus, there are rectangles for the *Department*, *Adviser*, and *Student* entities. Attributes are shown as before in Figure 18.

Additionally, a line is used to represent a relationship between two entities. Notice the line between *Department* and *Adviser*, for example. The vertical bar on the left side of the relationship means that an adviser works in just one department. The forked lines on the right side of that line signify that a department may have more than one adviser. The angled lines, which are referred to as **crow's feet**, are shorthand for the multiple lines between *Department* and *Adviser* in Figure 19. Relationships like this one are called **1:N**, or **one-to-many relationships**, because one department can have many advisers, but an adviser has at most one department.

Now examine the line between *Adviser* and *Student*. Notice the crow's feet that appear at each end of the line. This notation signifies that an adviser can be related to many students and that a student can be related to many advisers, which is the situation in Figure 19. Relationships like this one are called **N:M**, or **many-to-many relationships**, because one adviser can have many students and one student can have many advisers.

Students sometimes find the notation N:M confusing. Interpret the *N* and *M* to mean that a variable number, greater than one, is allowed on each side of the relationship. Such a relationship is not written *N:N* because that notation would imply that there are the same number of entities on each side of the relationship, which is not necessarily true. *N:M* means that more than one entity is allowed on each side of the relationship and that the number of entities on each side can be different.

Figure 21 shows the same entities with different assumptions. Here, advisers may advise in more than one department, but a student may have only one adviser, representing a policy that students may not have multiple majors.

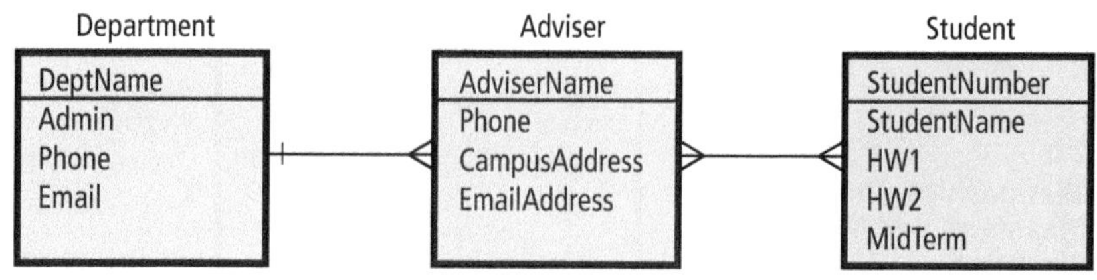

FIGURE 20
Sample Relationships Version 1

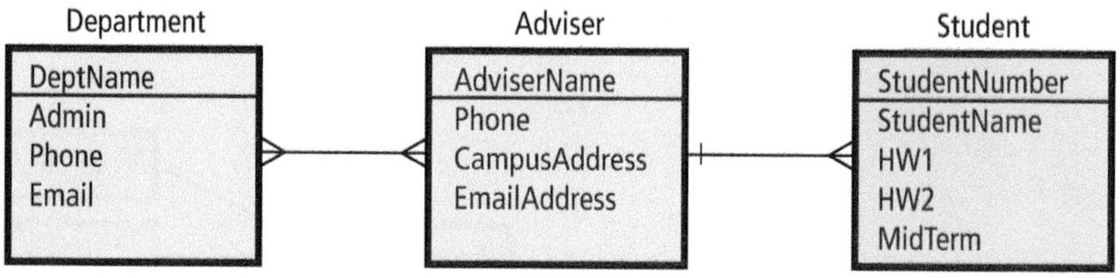

Department
DeptName
Admin
Phone
Email
Adviser
AdviserName
Phone
CampusAddress
EmailAddress
Student
StudentNumber
StudentName
HW1
HW2
MidTerm

FIGURE 21
Sample Relationships Version 2

Which, if either, of these versions is correct? Only the users know. These alternatives illustrate the kinds of questions you will need to answer when a database designer asks you to check a data model for correctness.

Figures 20 and 21 are typical examples of an entity-relationship diagram. Unfortunately, there are several different styles of entity-relationship diagrams. This one is called, not surprisingly, a **crow's-foot diagram** version. You may learn other versions if you take a database management class.

The crow's-foot notation shows the maximum number of entities that can be involved in a relationship. Accordingly, they are called the relationship's **maximum cardinality**. Common examples of maximum cardinality are 1:N, N:M, and 1:1 (not shown).

Another important question is "What is the minimum number of entities required in the relationship?" Must an adviser have a student to advise, and must a student have an adviser? Constraints on minimum requirements are called **minimum cardinalities**.

Figure 22 presents a third version of this E-R diagram that shows both maximum and minimum cardinalities. The second vertical bar on the lines means that at least one entity of that type is required. The small oval means that the entity is optional; the relationship *need not* have an entity of that type. Using this notation, if there are two vertical bars, both the minimum and maximum cardinality are one. If there is a vertical bar with a crow's foot, then the minimum cardinality is one and the maximum is many.

Thus, in Figure 22 a department is not required to have a relationship to any adviser, but an adviser is required to belong to a department. Similarly, an adviser is not required to have a relationship to a student, but a student is required to have a relationship to an adviser. Note, also, that the maximum cardinalities in Figure 22 have been changed so that both are 1:N.

Is the model in Figure 22 a good one? It depends on the policy of the university. Again, only the users know for sure.

Q6 How Is a Data Model Transformed into a Database Design?

Database design is the process of converting a data model into tables, relationships, and data constraints. The database design team transforms entities into tables and expresses relationships by defining foreign keys. Database design is a complicated subject; as with data modeling, it occupies weeks in a database management class. In this section, however, we will introduce two important database design concepts: normalization and the representation of two kinds of relationships.

Department
DeptName
Admin
Phone
Email
Adviser
AdviserName
Phone
CampusAddress
EmailAddress
Student
StudentNumber
StudentName
HW1
HW2
MidTerm

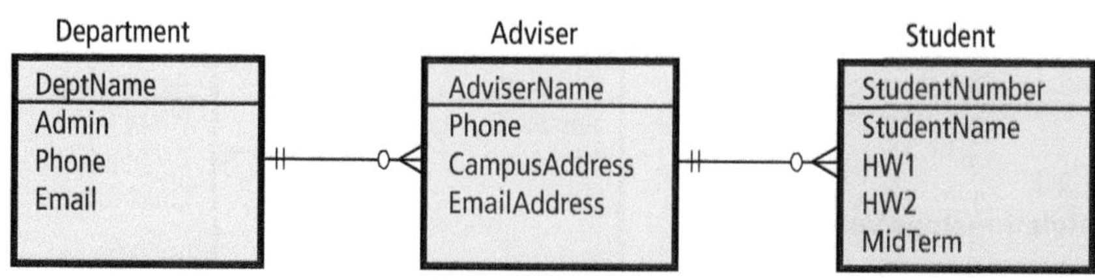

FIGURE 22
Sample Relationships Showing Both Maximum and Minimum Cardinalities

The first concept is a foundation of database design, and the second will help you understand important design considerations.

Normalization

Normalization is the process of converting a poorly structured table into two or more well-structured tables. A table is such a simple construct that you may wonder how one could possibly be poorly structured. In truth, there are many ways that tables can be malformed—so many, in fact, that researchers have published hundreds of papers on this topic alone.

Consider the *Employee* table in Figure 23a. It lists employee names, hire dates, email addresses, and the name and number of the department in which the employee works. This table seems innocent enough. But consider what happens when the Accounting department changes its name to Accounting and Finance. Because department names are duplicated in this table, every row that has a value of "Accounting" must be changed to "Accounting and Finance."

Data Integrity Problems

Suppose the Accounting name change is correctly made in two rows, but not in the third. The result is shown in Figure 23b. This table has what is called a **data integrity problem:** Some rows indicate that the name of Department 100 is "Accounting and Finance," and another row indicates that the name of Department 100 is "Accounting."

This problem is easy to spot in this small table. But consider a table like the *Customer* table in the Amazon.com database or the eBay database. Those databases have millions of rows. Once a table that large develops serious data integrity problems, months of labor will be required to remove them.

Data integrity problems are serious. A table that has data integrity problems will produce incorrect and inconsistent results. Users will lose confidence in the data, and the system will develop a poor reputation. Information systems with poor reputations become serious burdens to the organizations that use them.

Normalizing for Data Integrity

The data integrity problem can occur only if data are duplicated. Because of this, one easy way to eliminate the problem is to eliminate the duplicated data. We can do this by transforming the table

Employee

Name	HireDate	Email	DeptNo	DeptName
Jones	Feb 1, 2015	Jones@ourcompany.com	100	Accounting
Smith	Dec 3, 2017	Smith@ourcompany.com	200	Marketing
Chau	March 7, 2017	Chau@ourcompany.com	100	Accounting
Greene	July 17, 2016	Greene@ourcompany.com	100	Accounting

(a) Table Before Update

Employee

Name	HireDate	Email	DeptNo	DeptName
Jones	Feb 1, 2015	Jones@ourcompany.com	100	Accounting and Finance
Smith	Dec 3, 2017	Smith@ourcompany.com	200	Marketing
Chau	March 7, 2017	Chau@ourcompany.com	100	Accounting and Finance
Greene	July 17, 2016	Greene@ourcompany.com	100	Accounting

(b) Table with Incomplete Update

FIGURE 23
A Poorly Designed Employee Table

Employee

Name	HireDate	Email	DeptNo
Jones	Feb 1, 2015	Jones@ourcompany.com	100
Smith	Dec 3, 2017	Smith@ourcompany.com	200
Chau	March 7, 2017	Chau@ourcompany.com	100
Greene	July 17, 2016	Greene@ourcompany.com	100

Department

DeptNo	DeptName
100	Accounting
200	Marketing
300	Information Systems

FIGURE 24
Two Normalized Tables

design in Figure 23a into two tables, as shown in Figure 24. Here the name of the department is stored just once; therefore, no data inconsistencies can occur.

Of course, to produce an employee report that includes the department name, the two tables in Figure 24 will need to be joined back together. Because such joining of tables is common, DBMS products have been programmed to perform it efficiently, but it still requires work. From this example, you can see a trade-off in database design: Normalized tables eliminate data duplication, but they can be slower to process. Dealing with such trade-offs is an important consideration in database design.

The general goal of normalization is to construct tables such that every table has a *single* topic or theme. In good writing, every paragraph should have a single theme. This is true of databases as well; every table should have a single theme. The problem with the table design in Figure 23 is that it has two independent themes: employees and departments. The way to correct the problem is to split the table into two tables, each with its own theme. In this case, we create an *Employee* table and a *Department* table, as shown in Figure 24.

As mentioned, there are dozens of ways that tables can be poorly formed. Database practitioners classify tables into various **normal forms** according to the kinds of problems they have. Transforming a table into a normal form to remove duplicated data and other problems is called *normalizing* the table.[9] Thus, when you hear a database designer say, "Those tables are not normalized," she does not mean that the tables have irregular, not-normal data. Instead, she means that the tables have a format that could cause data integrity problems.

Summary of Normalization

As a future user of databases, you do not need to know the details of normalization. Instead, understand the general principle that every normalized (well-formed) table has one and only one theme. Further, tables that are not normalized are subject to data integrity problems.

Be aware, too, that normalization is just one criterion for evaluating database designs. Because normalized designs can be slower to process, database designers sometimes choose to accept non-normalized tables. The best design depends on the users' processing requirements.

Representing Relationships

Figure 25 shows the steps involved in transforming a data model into a relational database design. First, the database designer creates a table for each entity. The identifier of the entity becomes the key of the table. Each attribute of the entity becomes a column of the table. Next, the resulting

- Represent each entity with a table
  - Entity identifier becomes table key
  - Entity attributes become table columns
- Normalize tables as necessary
- Represent relationships
  - Use foreign keys
  - Add additional tables for N:M relationships

FIGURE 25
Transforming a Data Model into a Database Design

tables are normalized so that each table has a single theme. Once that has been done, the next step is to represent the relationships among those tables.

For example, consider the E-R diagram in Figure 26a. The *Adviser* entity has a 1:N relationship to the *Student* entity. To create the database design, we construct a table for *Adviser* and a second table for *Student*, as shown in Figure 26b. The key of the *Adviser* table is *AdviserName*, and the key of the *Student* table is *StudentNumber*.

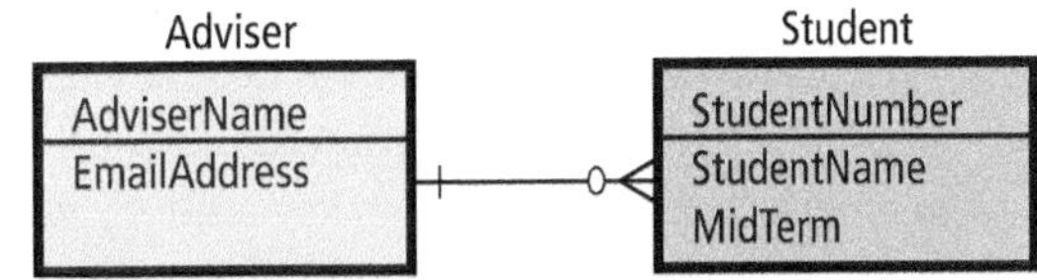

(a) 1:N Relationship Between Adviser and Student Entities

Adviser Table—Key Is AdviserName

AdviserName	EmailAddress
Jones	Jones@myuniv.edu
Choi	Choi@myuniv.edu
Jackson	Jackson@myuniv.edu

Student Table—Key Is StudentNumber

StudentNumber	StudentName	MidTerm
100	Lisa	90
200	Jennie	85
300	Jason	82
400	Terry	95

(b) Creating a Table for Each Entity

Adviser Table—Key Is AdviserName

AdviserName	EmailAddress
Jones	Jones@myuniv.edu
Choi	Choi@myuniv.edu
Jackson	Jackson@myuniv.edu

Student—Key Is StudentNumber

Foreign key column represents relationship

StudentNumber	StudentName	MidTerm	AdviserName
100	Lisa	90	Jackson
200	Jennie	85	Jackson
300	Jason	82	Choi
400	Terry	95	Jackson

(c) Using the *AdviserName* Foreign Key to Represent the 1:N Relationship

FIGURE 26
Representing a 1:N Relationship

Further, the *EmailAddress* attribute of the *Adviser* entity becomes the *EmailAddress* column of the *Adviser* table, and the *StudentName* and *MidTerm* attributes of the *Student* entity become the *StudentName* and *MidTerm* columns of the *Student* table.

The next task is to represent the relationship. Because we are using the relational model, we know that we must add a foreign key to one of the two tables. The possibilities are: (1) place the foreign key *StudentNumber* in the *Adviser* table or (2) place the foreign key *AdviserName* in the *Student* table.

The correct choice is to place *AdviserName* in the *Student* table, as shown in Figure 26c. To determine a student's adviser, we just look into the *AdviserName* column of that student's row. To determine the adviser's students, we search the *AdviserName* column in the *Student* table to determine which rows have that adviser's name. If a student changes advisers, we simply change the value in the *AdviserName* column. Changing *Jackson* to *Jones* in the first row, for example, will assign student 100 to Professor Jones.

For this data model, placing *StudentNumber* in *Adviser* would be incorrect. If we were to do that, we could assign only one student to an adviser. There is no place to assign a second adviser.

This strategy for placing foreign keys will not work for N:M relationships, however. Consider the data model in Figure 27a; here advisers and students have a many-to-many relationship. An adviser may have many students, and a student may have multiple advisers (for multiple majors).

To see why the foreign key strategy we used for 1:N relationships will not work for N:M relationships, examine Figure 27b. If student 100 has more than one adviser, there is no place to record second or subsequent advisers.

To represent an N:M relationship, we need to create a third table, as shown in Figure 27c. The third table has two columns, *AdviserName* and *StudentNumber*. Each row of the table means that the given adviser advises the student with the given number.

As you can imagine, there is a great deal more to database design than we have presented here. Still, this section should give you an idea of the tasks that need to be accomplished to create a database. You should also realize that the database design is a direct consequence of decisions made in the data model. If the data model is wrong, the database design will be wrong as well.

Users' Role in the Development of Databases

As stated, a database is a model of how the users view their business world. This means that the users are the final judges as to what data the database should contain and how the records in that database should be related to one another.

The easiest time to change the database structure is during the data modeling stage. Changing a relationship from one-to-many to many-to-many in a data model is simply a matter of changing the 1:N notation to N:M. However, once the database has been constructed and loaded with data and forms, reports, queries, and application programs have been created, changing a one-to-many relationship to many-to-many means weeks of work.

You can glean some idea of why this might be true by contrasting Figure 26c with Figure 27c. Suppose that instead of having just a few rows, each table has thousands of rows; in that case, transforming the database from one format to the other involves considerable work. Even worse, however, is that someone must change application components as well. For example, if students have at most one adviser, then a single text box can be used to enter *AdviserName*. If students can have multiple advisers, then a multiple-row table will need to be used to enter *AdviserName* and a program will need to be written to store the values of *AdviserName* into the *Adviser_Student_Intersection* table. There are dozens of other consequences, consequences that will translate into wasted labor and wasted expense.

Thus, *user review of the data model is crucial.* When a database is developed for your use, you must carefully review the data model. If you do not understand any aspect of it, you should ask for clarification until you do. *Entities must contain all of the data you and your employees need to do your*

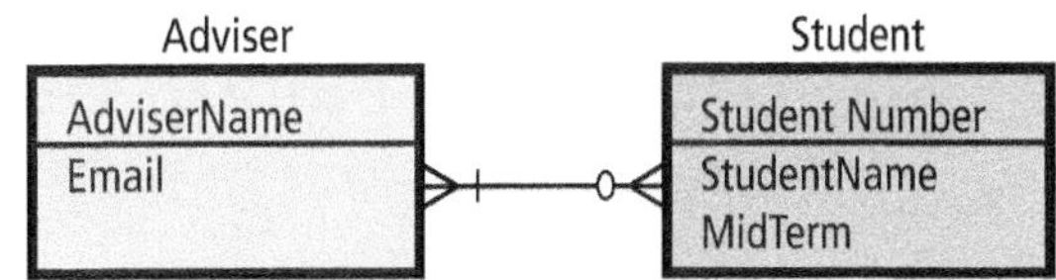

(a) N:M Relationship Between Adviser and Student

Adviser—Key Is AdviserName

AdviserName	Email
Jones	Jones@myuniv.edu
Choi	Choi@myuniv.edu
Jackson	Jackson@myuniv.edu

Student—Key Is StudentNumber

StudentNumber	StudentName	MidTerm	AdviserName
100	Lisa	90	Jackson
200	Jennie	85	Jackson
300	Jason	82	Choi
400	Terry	95	Jackson

No room to place second or third AdviserName

(b) Incorrect Representation of N:M Relationship

Adviser—Key Is AdviserName

AdviserName	Email
Jones	Jones@myuniv.edu
Choi	Choi@myuniv.edu
Jackson	Jackson@myuniv.edu

Student—Key Is StudentNumber

StudentNumber	StudentName	MidTerm
100	Lisa	90
200	Jennie	85
300	Jason	82
400	Terry	95

Adviser_Student_Intersection

AdviserName	StudentNumber
Jackson	100
Jackson	200
Choi	300
Jackson	400
Choi	100
Jones	100

Student 100 has three advisers

(c) Adviser_Student_Intersection Table Represents the N:M Relationship

FIGURE 27
Representing an N:M Relationship

jobs, and relationships must accurately reflect your view of the business. If the data model is wrong, the database will be designed incorrectly, and the applications will be difficult to use, if not worthless. Do not proceed unless the data model is accurate.

As a corollary, when asked to review a data model, take that review seriously. Devote the time necessary to perform a thorough review. Any mistakes you miss will come back to haunt you, and by then the cost of correction may be very high with regard to both time and expense. This brief introduction to data modeling shows why databases can be more difficult to develop than spreadsheets.

Q7 How Can Falcon Security Benefit from a Database System?

Falcon Security wants to be able to find videos by querying their characteristics. For example, it wants responses to questions like "Which videos do we have of the Beresford Building in October 2017, shot from 3,000 feet or less?" And, from time to time, Falcon employees analyze some of the videos, and they want to record comments about their analyses for potential later use.

Falcon can choose one of two database architectures. For one, it can store the video footage on a file server and keep metadata about each video in a relational database that it can query. That metadata will include the address of the video footage on the file server. Alternatively, Falcon can utilize one of the new NoSQL DBMS products like **MongoDB**—an open source document-oriented DBMS—to store the video footage in the same database as the metadata. (See Q8.)

Toshio Sato investigates these two alternatives and discusses his findings with Cam Forset. They are both intrigued by the possible use of MongoDB, but they know that their interest is, in part, a desire to learn something new. They don't really know how well that product works, nor do they know how robust the MongoDB query facility will be.

On the other hand, they can readily build a simple Access database to store the metadata. In the metadata, they can store the URL of the file server location that has the video (for example, *https://abc.Falcon.com/Video1*). In this way, they can use Access to store the data and then query it using the Access graphical query facility. Because Access can also process native SQL, they can use it for the most sophisticated query operations if needed.

Toshio and Cam discuss these alternatives and decide to use Access to store the metadata. They know this approach is less risky because it uses known technology. Also, both of them are skilled at using Access, and they can develop the database and application quickly with less risk. Toshio and Cam create a short presentation of this recommendation and present it to Mateo, who approves it.

After the approval, Toshio creates the E-R diagram shown in Figure 28 and discusses it with Cam. She thinks that they might want to add an Employee entity rather than just the employee's name in the Analysis entity. They decide, however, that they don't yet have that many employees and that adding the extra entity might make the application too hard to use, at least at present. So with that decision, they proceed to create the database and related applications. You'll have an opportunity to do the same with a team of your colleagues in Collaboration Exercise.

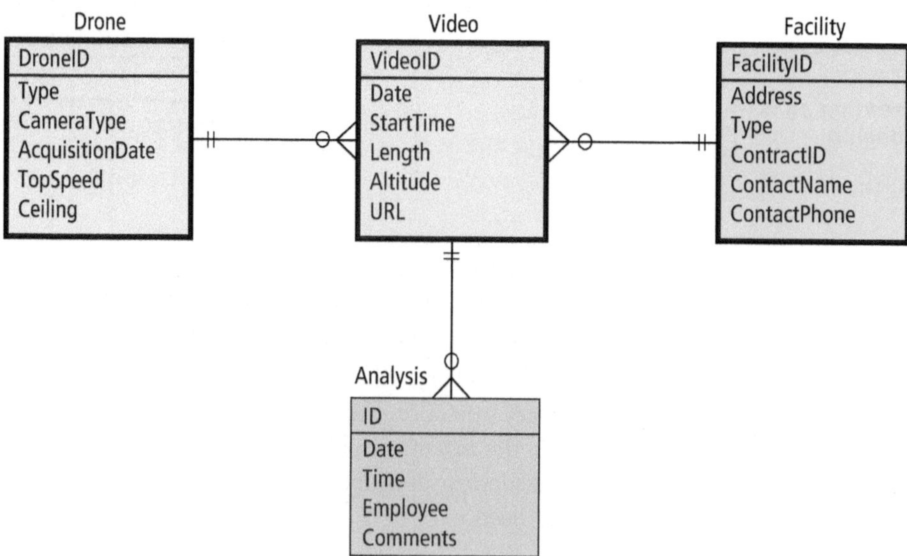

FIGURE 28
E-R Diagram for Falcon Security's Database

Q8 2027? 

With ever-cheaper data storage and data communications, we can be sure that the volume of database data will continue to grow, probably exponentially, through 2027. All that data contains patterns that can be used to conceive information to help businesses and organizations achieve their strategies. That will make business intelligence even more important. Furthermore, as databases become bigger and bigger, they're more attractive as targets for theft or mischief, as we saw in the 2016 attacks at MySpace (360 million accounts), LinkedIn (164 million accounts), and Tumblr (65 million accounts). Those risks will make database security even more important.

Additionally, the DBMS landscape is changing. While for years relational DBMS products were the only game in town, the Internet changed that by posing new processing requirements. As compared to traditional database applications, some Internet applications process many, many more transactions against much simpler data. A tweet has a much simpler data structure than the configuration of a Kenworth truck, but there are so many more tweets than truck configurations!

Also, traditional relational DBMS products devote considerable code and processing power to support what are termed **ACID** (atomic, consistent, isolated, durable) transactions. In essence, this acronym means that either all of a transaction is processed or none of it is (atomic), that transactions are processed in the same manner (consistent) whether processed alone or in the presence of millions of other transactions (isolated), and that once a transaction is stored it never goes away—even in the presence of failure (durable).

ACID transactions are critical to traditional commercial applications. Even in the presence of machine failure, Vanguard must process both the sell and the buy sides of a transaction; it cannot process part of a transaction. Also, what it stores today must be stored tomorrow. But many new Internet applications don't need ACID. Who cares if, one time out of 1 million, only half of your tweet is stored? Or if it's stored today and disappears tomorrow?

These new requirements have led to three new categories of DBMS:

1. **NoSQL DBMS**. This acronym is misleading. It really should be non-relational DBMS. It refers to new DBMS products that support very high transaction rates processing relatively simple data structures, replicated on many servers in the cloud, without ACID transaction support. MongoDB, Cassandra, Bigtable, and Dynamo are NoSQL products
2. **NewSQL DBMS**. These DBMS products process very high levels of transactions, like the NoSQL DBMS, but provide ACID support. They may or may not support the relational model. Such products are a hotbed of development with new vendors popping up nearly every day. Leading products are yet unknown.
3. **In-memory DBMS**. This category consists of DBMS products that process databases in main memory. This technique has become possible because today's computer memories can be enormous and can hold an entire database at one time, or at least very large chunks of it. Usually these products support or extend the relational model. SAP HANA is a computer with an in-memory DBMS that provides high volume ACID transaction support simultaneously with complex relational query processing. Tableau Software's reporting products are supported by a proprietary in-memory DBMS using an extension to SQL.

Does the emergence of these new products mean the death knell for relational databases? It seems unlikely because organizations have created thousands of traditional relational databases with millions of lines of application code that process SQL statements against relational data structures. No organization wants to endure the expense and effort of converting those databases and code to something else. There is also a strong social trend among older technologists to hang onto the relational model. However, these new products are loosening the stronghold that relational technology has enjoyed for decades, and it is likely that by 2027 many NoSQL, NewSQL, and in-memory databases will exist in commerce.

SECURITY GUIDE

BIG DATA...LOSSES

Do you enjoy trivia games? If so, you have probably flipped through the channels on a weeknight and stopped on the trivia game show *Jeopardy!* Successful contestants can quickly answer questions across a range of categories. Winners often repeat their success over several episodes. Long winning streaks are fairly uncommon, however, because they require mastery of an extensive set of topics. Viewers at home often resort to using their phones or computers to look up answers. If you have ever resorted to such tactics, you may have wondered how a computer would fare on *Jeopardy!*

Researchers at IBM had the same question in 2011. They had developed Watson, a supercomputer with advanced functionality that includes natural language processing and data mining. The data accessed by Watson when it competed on *Jeopardy!* included 500 gigabytes worth of dictionaries, encyclopedias, and other reference materials.[10] Since Watson's stunning defeat of two former *Jeopardy!* champions, IBM has been working to leverage Watson for a number of Big Data applications, including health care and marketing analytics.

Other companies witnessed the impressive performance of Watson on *Jeopardy!* and scrambled to develop their own Big Data analytics tools. However, some companies are still trying to figure out how Big Data applications can be used effectively. Furthermore, when focusing on perfecting powerful Big Data tools, some companies consider securing the data collected as an afterthought, if they consider it at all.

Security Loses, Again

Neglecting security for the sake of functionality and convenience is a common thread that runs through decades of technological advancement. For example, many car manufacturers now boast Internet connectivity in their advertisements but have done little to ensure the security and privacy of vehicles connected to the Internet. Technology-focused trade shows focus on the Internet of Things and feature home automation gadgets like Internet-connected lights, thermostats, door locks, and toasters. Unfortunately, the security features in these devices are often lacking or nonexistent.

The Big Data movement is another victim of the march toward technological advancement without thought of security ramifications. Many companies lack the ability to effectively use Big Data tools. As a result, their ability to secure these tools and the data that accompanies them is a grave concern.[11] Based on a recent scan of Big Data apps, a security audit conducted by a Swiss security company confirmed this suspicion. The company's analysis revealed that data on more than 39,000 NoSQL databases are exposed and 1.1 petabytes of this data were also available online.[12] But what

Source: © Dpa picture alliance/Alamy Stock Photo

leads to poor security protocols for these Big Data applications?

Rich in Data, Poor in Security

It turns out that security shortcomings in Big Data practices are not isolated. In fact, it is likely that poor database management practices translate into larger and more specialized Big Data "transfers." A recent survey conducted by *InformationWeek* reveals some troubling findings concerning the security issues plaguing Big Data. The survey identified poor database security practices in roughly 20 percent of survey respondents. They found that (1) databases containing sensitive information are not secured, (2) data breaches have occurred or it cannot be confirmed breaches have not occurred, and (3) security evaluations are not regularly conducted on respondents' databases.[13] These factors are driven by the larger problem of Big Data tools prioritizing security below other objectives like functionality, flexible access, and convenience.

In light of these security deficiencies, a number of best practices have been recommended to improve the state of Big Data security. These include logging and auditing all activity to permit the identification of unauthorized access, implementing strict access management protocols, and using better encryption to safeguard sensitive data.[14] Ultimately, securing the data generated and used by data-driven applications is as important as the accuracy and reporting capabilities of the applications themselves!

DISCUSSION QUESTIONS

1. Think about how the trend of capturing and storing data has affected you. What types of data have been generated about you, and where are these data located? What data have you generated yourself? Can you do anything to manage access to or the security of these data?
2. Search the Web to identify a new data-driven application being used by IBM's Watson. Describe how this new application might provide a competitive advantage for the adopting organization.
3. The feature mentions the continuing technological tension between security and convenience. How has this tension affected your own interactions with computers? Do you err on the side of security or convenience when creating and managing your own security "policies"?
4. Have you or anyone you know purchased home-automation devices? Based on a lack of security found in many of these devices, are you willing to accept the risk that comes with these devices in exchange for the convenience they provide?

Furthermore, existing DBMS vendors like Oracle, Microsoft, and IBM will not sit still. With substantial cash and highly skilled developers, they will likely incorporate features of these new categories of DBMS into their existing or new products. Acquisitions of some of the NewSQL startups, in particular, are likely.

What does that mean to you as a business professional? First, such knowledge is useful; stay abreast of developments in this area. When you are given a problem, like the need to query videos at Falcon, you might choose to utilize one of these new types of database. Unless you are an IT professional, however, you won't work with them directly. It will be to your advantage to know about them, however, and to suggest their use to the IS personnel who support your requirements.

Also, watch these developments from an investor's perspective. Not all such products will be open source; even if they are, there will be companies that integrate them into their product or service offerings, and those companies may well be good investment opportunities.

If you're interested in IS as a discipline or as a second major, pay attention to these products. You still need to learn the relational model and the processing of relational databases; they will be the bread-and-butter of the industry, even in 2027. But exciting new opportunities and career paths will also develop around these new DBMS products. Learn about them as well, and use that knowledge to separate yourself from the competition when it comes to job interviews.

Source: © Jacob Case

CAREER GUIDE

Name: Jacob Case
Company: Overstock.com
Job Title: Database Engineer
Education: University of Utah

1 How did you get this type of job?

After I got some hands-on experience analyzing data in the academic setting, I started networking with people about opportunities in the area I was living. After a while, I was offered a position at a startup company developing reports for the executive team. I've changed jobs a few times since then, and I think it's important to keep an eye out for opportunities to improve your career when the time is right.

2 What attracted you to this field?

I still remember my first database class. I just had a feeling that it was important because I knew businesses derive information and critical insights from data, and these insights are used to make critical business decisions. I knew that if I became proficient with managing and analyzing data I would always have a job. I also visualized how satisfying it could be to contribute to the process of extracting insights from data and helping assist in the process of developing business strategies.

3 What does a typical workday look like for you (duties, decisions, problems)?

It's a mix of technical work and requirements gathering. I would say that about 60 percent of my time is spent doing database development and the other 40 percent is spent interacting with people to either determine their needs or ensure that what we are developing meets their needs.

4 What do you like most about your job?

It's really interesting to observe how information is utilized by businesses and to see the nuts and bolts of how it works. Perhaps the most satisfying part is learning about the business processes that you are supporting. Some tasks are quite simple, and others can be very challenging, so you never get bored with the complexity of the work. I also really enjoy the people I've worked with in IS because most of them are very smart and professional.

5 What skills would someone need to do well at your job?

Over time, you develop a rich set of technical skills. But, early in your career, it's at least as important to have a great attitude, be a team player, and commit yourself to learning new things. Many of the skills you acquire and leverage in the field of IS are a function of continuing to learn. You don't have to be a genius, you just have to be patient and willing to learn and build upon what you have learned. Communication is also important. Bridging the gap between technical-speak and business-speak will help your career tremendously.

6 Are education or certifications important in your field? Why?

Both are important. A degree from a university gives you a higher-level perspective with a wider scope than a certification will, and it helps you to think about how the technologies you work with relate to each other. It also helps you to understand paradigms that are important to Information Systems. A certification gives you specific hands-on experience with a certain technology or process, which is invaluable when you jump into the job market.

7 What advice would you give to someone who is considering working in your field?

Don't be intimidated by the idea of working in the field of information systems. Your first job will probably be a junior-level position, but if you are commited to learning, are teachable, are a great team player, and have a good attitude, you will learn a tremendous amount. And, after a few years, you will be a really valuable employee with a lot of marketable skills. I have been on both sides of the hiring process, and I can tell you that hiring managers are just as concerned about your soft skills as they are about your technical skills.

8 What do you think will be hot tech jobs in 10 years?

I expect BigData technologies like NoSQL and distributed computing to continue flourishing because the amount of data businesses have is growing exponentially. Security is increasingly important, too, because the threat of sensitive information being stolen is so common these days. I'm really excited about the Internet of Things (IoT). I expect IoT to be highly disruptive. A background in information systems is just the place you need to be if you want to ride the wave that IoT will create. Cloud computing will be a critical part of how information systems are architected in the future. Companies will certainly be looking for cloud computing experts.

ACTIVE REVIEW

Use this Active Review to verify that you understand the ideas and concepts that answer the chapter's study questions.

Q1 What is the purpose of a database?

State the purpose of a database. Explain the circumstances in which a database is preferred to a spreadsheet. Describe the key difference between Figures 1 and 2.

Q2 What is a database?

Define the term *database*. Explain the hierarchy of data and name three elements of a database. Define *metadata*. Using the example of *Student* and *Office_Visit* tables, show how relationships among rows are represented in a database. Define the terms *primary key, foreign key,* and *relational database.*

Q3 What is a database management system (DBMS)?

Explain the acronym DBMS and name its functions. List five popular DBMS products. Explain the difference between a DBMS and a database. Summarize the functions of a DBMS. Define *SQL*. Describe the major functions of database administration.

Q4 How do database applications make databases more useful?

Explain why database tables, by themselves, are not very useful to buiness users. Name the four elements of a database application and describe the purpose of each. Explain the difference between a database application and a database application program. Describe the nature of traditional database applications. Explain why browser-based applications are better than traditional ones. Name the primary technologies used to support browser-based applications.

Q5 How are data models used for database development?

Explain why user involvement is critical during database development. Describe the function of a data model. Sketch the database development process. Define *E-R model, entity, relationship, attribute,* and *identifier*. Give an example, other than one in this text, of an E-R diagram. Define *maximum cardinality* and *minimum cardinality*. Give an example of three maximum cardinalities and two minimum cardinalities. Explain the notation in Figures 21 and 22.

Q6 How is a data model transformed into a database design?

Name the three components of a database design. Define *normalization* and explain why it is important. Define *data integrity problem* and describe its consequences. Give an example of a table with data integrity problems and show how it can be normalized into two or more tables that do not have such problems. Describe two steps in transforming a data model into a database design. Using an example not in this chapter, show how 1:N and N:M relationships are represented in a relational database. Describe the users' role in the database development. Explain why it is easier and cheaper to change a data model than to change an existing database. Use the examples of Figures 26c and 27c in your answer.

Q7 How can Falcon Security benefit from a database system?

Summarize the two database architectures that Falcon could use for its video database. Describe the architecture it used and explain the rationale for that choice.

Q8 2027?

Explain how an increase in database data in the next decade will affect business intelligence and security. Summarize two major requirements that some Internet database applications created. Explain the characteristics of the ACID processing of a transaction. Briefly describe the characteristics of NoSQL, NewSQL, and in-memory DBMS products. Summarize how you should respond to these developments.

Using Your Knowledge with Falcon Security

You can readily understand why the knowledge of this chapter would be useful to you if you have a job like Toshio or Cam. But what if you are Mateo (the CEO) or Joni (the CFO)? The knowledge in this chapter will prepare you to make better decisions like the one that Mateo made in Q7. It will also help Joni understand the level of budget required to fund this project. Even if you never create a single query during your career, you will make many decisions that involve the use, creation, and maintenance of databases.

KEY TERMS AND CONCEPTS

Access
ACID
Attributes
Byte
Columns
Crow's feet
Crow's-foot diagram
Data integrity problem
Data model
Database
Database administration
Database application
Database management system (DBMS)
DB2
Entity
Entity-relationship (E-R) data model
Entity-relationship (E-R) diagrams
Fields
File
Foreign keys
Graphical queries
Identifier
In-memory DBMS
Key
Lost-update problem
Many-to-many (N:M) relationships
Maximum cardinality
Metadata
Minimum cardinality
MongoDB
Multi-user processing
MySQL
NewSQL DBMS
Normal forms
Normalization
NoSQL DBMS
One-to-many (1:N) relationships
Oracle Database
Primary key
Records
Relation
Relational databases
Relationships
Rows
SQL server
Structured Query Language (SQL)
Table
Unified Modeling Language (UML)

MyMISLab™

To complete the problems with the MyMISLab, go to EOC Discussion Questions in the MyLab.

USING YOUR KNOWLEDGE

MyMISLab **1.** Draw an entity-relationship diagram that shows the relationships among a database, database applications, and users.

MyMISLab **2.** Consider the relationship between *Adviser* and *Student* in Figure 21. Explain what it means if the maximum cardinality of this relationship is:

a. N:1
b. 1:1
c. 5:1
d. 1:5

MyMISLab **3.** Identify two entities in the data entry form in Figure 29. What attributes are shown for each? What do you think are the identifiers?

4. Visit *www.acxiom.com*. Navigate the site to answer the following questions.

a. According to the Web site, what is Acxiom's privacy policy? Are you reassured by its policy? Why or why not?
b. Make a list of 10 different products that Acxiom provides.
c. Describe Acxiom's top customers.
d. Examine your answers in parts b and c and describe, in general terms, the kinds of data that Acxiom must be collecting to be able to provide those products to those customers.
e. What is the function of InfoBase?
f. What is the function of PersonicX?
g. In what ways might companies like Acxiom need to limit their marketing so as to avoid a privacy outcry from the public?
h. Should there be laws that govern companies like Acxiom? Why or why not?
i. Should there be laws that govern the types of data services that governmental agencies can buy from companies like Acxiom? Why or why not?

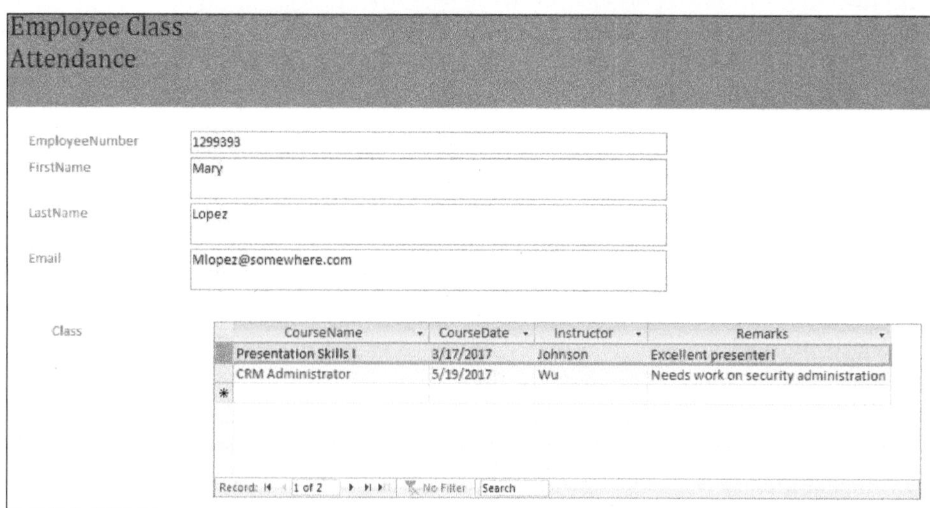

FIGURE 29
Sample Data Entry Form

COLLABORATION EXERCISE

Using the collaboration IS you built, collaborate with a group of students to answer the following questions.

The Falcon Security problem is an excellent example of the use of small databases in business. It is also within reach for you to develop as a practice exercise. To do so, work with your team to answer the following questions:

5. Study Figure 28 to understand the entities and their relationships. Justify each of the cardinalities in this model.
6. Working with your team, develop a list of seven queries that together use all of the entities in Figure 28.
7. Modify the E-R model in Figure 28 to include a *Contact* entity that is related to the Facility entity. Create the relationship, and specify and justify the relationship's cardinalities.
8. Discuss the advantages and disadvantages of the model you created in your answer to question 7 and the model in Figure 28.
9. Transform the data model in Figure 28 into a relational database design. *Hint:* Create a table for each entity and relate those tables as shown in 6.
10. Create an Access database for your design in question 9.
11. Fill your database with sample data. Because you do not have files on a server, leave the URL column blank.
12. Using the Access query facility, process each of the seven queries that you created in your answer to question 6.

CASE STUDY

Searching for Pianos ...

Dean Petrich is a certified piano tuner and technician who has been repairing and restoring pianos since 1973. He also has a career as Deano the Clown, a clown entertainer who performs children's parties in the Seattle, WA, metro area. (See Figure 30, *http://deanotheclown.com*). The schedule of his two businesses balance each other: He's busy as a clown in the late spring, summer, and fall, and during the rest of year, he repairs and restores pianos.

Over the past 20 years, the demand for pianos has dramatically declined. When Grandma dies, or the kids move out, or some other life change occurs, families have no further use for their piano, and when they find there is no market for it, they call Dean, who picks up that piano for a modest fee. For a number of years, Dean restored those pianos and either resold or rented them. Since the turn of the century, however, the decreasing demand for pianos has affected him as well, and over time, he's accumulated far too many pianos. Even discarding the worst of them, he has, today, nearly 100.

As you can imagine, 100 pianos consume considerable storage. At first, Dean stored them in his workshop. When he ran out

FIGURE 30
Deano the Clown
Source: Dean Petrich

of room in his workshop, he built and stored them in a large metal shed (Figure 31). When the shed overflowed with pianos, he moved them to plastic tents in a meadow on his property (Figure 32). Unfortunately, the plastic tents are prone to rips and tears, and because Dean lives in the Pacific Northwest, many pianos have been ruined by rain, even when he covers them with plastic tarps inside the plastic tents.

Two years ago, sinking in his steadily increasing piano inventory, Dean began to offer pianos for free. Not the very best pianos—those he hopes to sell—but he offers many quality pianos for free. However, Dean has two problems. First, he doesn't know which pianos are best and where they are located in the shop, shed, or tents. Second, few people are willing to crawl over the tops of the pianos in the large shed and tents (through refuse of squirrels, rats, and mice) looking for their perfect piano.

To resolve this issue, Dean created a Microsoft Access database with only one table: Piano. To fill the database with data, Dean had to first take an inventory of all the pianos and record the data shown in the columns of Figure 33.

As you know, a one-table database could just as easily have been stored in Excel, but Dean used Access because he wants to query his data in a variety of ways. He wants to know, for example, all of the pianos located in a tent that have a sound quality of 4 or higher. And he wants to know which pianos have a sound quality of 1 or less so he can dispose of them. Further, customers have particular needs. One might, for example, want a Baldwin spinet (a type of piano); without a database he has no idea whether he has one or where. Or, when he needs a replacement key top, he might want to know the location of all the pianos in the workshop that have ivory keys and a sound quality of 2 or less, and so on.

Because of the dynamic nature of his needs, Dean uses the Access query facility. Figure 34 shows an example query that returns all of the pianos of a sound quality higher than 4 that are located in a tent and Figure 35 shows the result of that query. Dean also suspects that the quality deteriorates faster in the tents than in the shed or the shop. To determine if this is the case, he created the report shown in Figure 36.

FIGURE 31
Pianos in Storage
Source: David Kroenke

FIGURE 32
Pianos in Tent
Source: David Kroenke

QUESTIONS

13. Explain why a one-table database could be stored just as readily in Excel as in Access.

14. Justify the decision to use Access to store the piano database.

15. Examine the columns in Figure 33. Name three characteristics of pianos that are not represented in this table.

  a. If you were a consultant advising Dean, what criteria should you and he use in deciding whether to include that additional data?

  b. Is this database a model of an inventory of pianos, or is it a model of Dean's model of an inventory of pianos? Explain the difference.

16 Suppose, in addition to the data about pianos, Dean wants to store data about the manufacturer such as its address (or last known address), its years of operation, and general comments about that manufacturer.

  a. Design a Manufacturer table.

  b. Alter the design of the Piano table (Figure 33) to represent the relationship between Piano and Manufacturer. State and justify any assumptions.

17. Using the data in Figure 36, draw conclusions about the effect of location on piano sound quality. Justify your statements using this data.

18. Explain the statement "A database is an abstraction of some aspect of a business." Using this example, explain the ways that processing an abstraction is more effective than examining pianos. Explain the ways that processing an abstraction is more efficient that examining pianos. Generalize your observation to databases for business in general.

19. This database will soon become useless if it is not kept up to date. List procedures that Dean needs to create and follow to keep his database current.

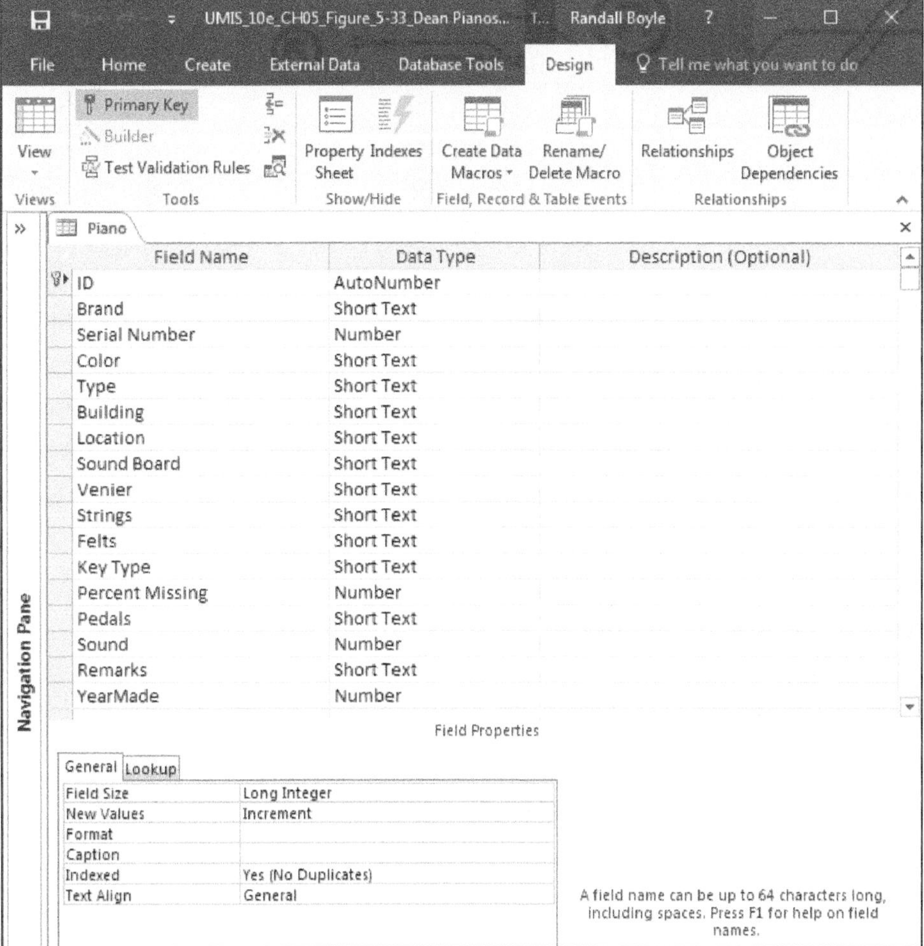

FIGURE 33
Columns in the Piano Table
Source: Windows 10, Microsoft Corporation.

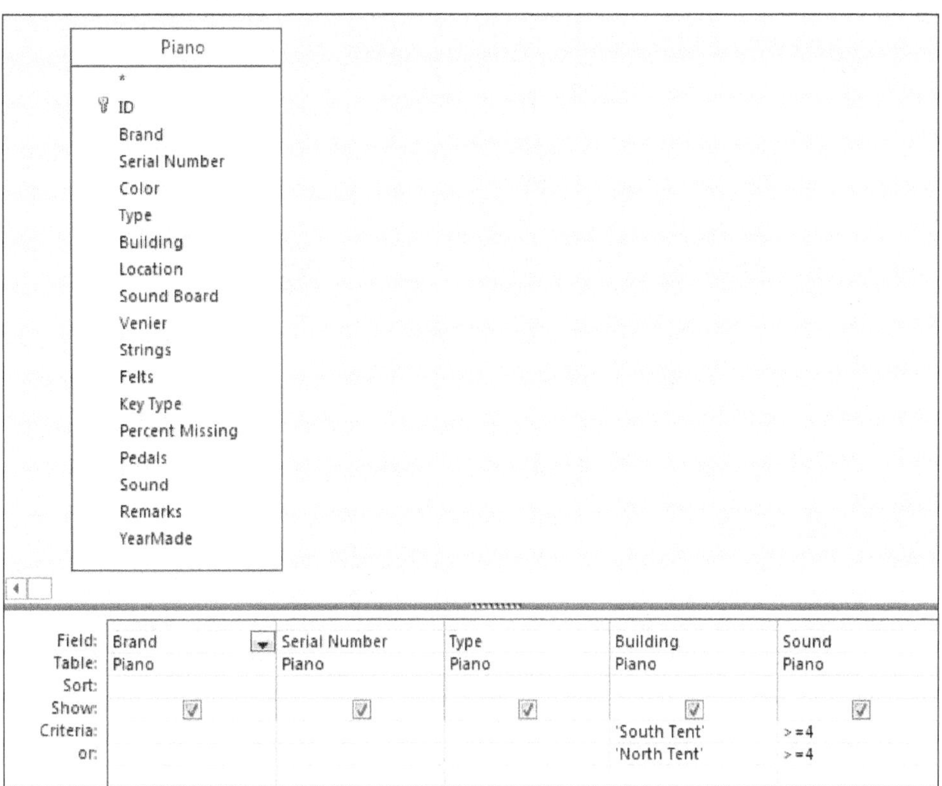

FIGURE 34
Example Query
Source: Windows 10, Microsoft Corporation.

Brand	Serial Number	Type	Building	Sound
Baldwin	70452	Spinet	South Tent	4
Esteu	20158	Upright	North Tent	4
H.G. Johnson	10749	Upright	North Tent	4
Winter ???	326493	Spinet	North Tent	4
Baldwin	637957	Spinet	North Tent	4
Briggs	80360	Upright	North Tent	4
Hobart Cable	77182	Upright	North Tent	4
Mehlin	28733	Upright	North Tent	4
Aeolian	182562	Spinet	North Tent	4
Farrand	27631	Upright	South Tent	4
Kurtzman	21398	Upright	South Tent	5
Mathushek	12963	Upright	South Tent	4

FIGURE 35
Results from Query in Figure 34
Source: Windows 10, Microsoft Corporation.

Piano Sound Quality by Building

Building	Sound Quality	Number Pianos
North Tent	1	1
North Tent	3	3
North Tent	4	8
Shed	0	10
Shed	1	1
Shed	2	7
Shed	3	13
Shed	4	12
Shop	0	2
Shop	1	2
Shop	3	5
Shop	4	2
South Tent	0	6
South Tent	2	3
South Tent	3	2
South Tent	4	3
South Tent	5	1

FIGURE 36
Piano Sound Quality by Building
Source: Windows 10, Microsoft Corporation.

MyMISLab™

Go to the Assignments section of your MyLab to complete these writing exercises.

20. Go to *http://aws.amazon.com* and search for AWS database offerings. Explain the differences among Amazon's RDS, DynamoDB, ElastiCache, and Redshift services. Which of these would you recommend for storing Falcon Security's data? (By the way, whenever you query the Internet for any AWS product, be sure to include the keyword "AWS" in your search. Otherwise, your search will result in Amazon's lists of books about the item you're searching for.)

21. Suppose you are the accounts manager at a wholesale auto parts distributor. You use spreadsheets to keep track of just about everything. So do your employees. You have hundreds of different spreadsheets to update, back up, and share. Some of them are getting extremely large and unwieldy. You're worried about losing track of them or, worse, having a malicious employee permanently destroy them. A new hire fresh out of college says building a database would solve most of your problems. How would you determine if a database would really solve your problems? If you chose to develop a centralized database, how would you choose the employees to create the database? What criteria would you use to select those employees? How would you justify allocating people and money to developing this database?

ENDNOTES

1. MySQL was supported by the MySQL company. In 2008, that company was acquired by Sun Microsystems, which was, in turn, acquired by Oracle later that year. However, because MySQL is open source, Oracle does not own the source code.
2. Clint Boulton, "Oil Company Hopes to Strike Efficiency with Cloud Analytics," *CIO.com*, November 10, 2015, accessed March 27, 2016, *www.cio.com/article/3003498/cloud-computing/oil-company-hopes-to-strike-efficiency-with-cloud-analytics.html.*
3. Ibid.
4. James Kobielus, "The All-Consuming Future of Cloud Analytics," *InfoWorld.com*, March 20, 2015, accessed March 27, 2016, *www.infoworld.com/article/2899662/big-data/the-all-consuming-future-of-cloud-analytics.html.*
5. Ibid.
6. Ibid.
7. Fahmida Y. Rashid, "The Dirty Dozen: 12 Cloud Security Threats," *InfoWorld.com*, March 11, 2016, accessed March 27, 2016, *www.infoworld.com/article/3041078/security/the-dirty-dozen-12-cloud-security-threats.html.*
8. Watch out for confusion between a *database application* and a *database application program*. A database application includes forms, reports, queries, and database application programs.
9. See David Kroenke and David Auer, *Database Concepts*, 7th ed., pp. 81–86 (Upper Saddle River, NJ: Pearson Education, 2015) for more information.
10. Elizabeth Dwoskin, "IBM to Sell Watson as a Big-Data Tool," *Digits: Tech Tools & Analysis From the WSJ*, March 6, 2016, *http://blogs.wsj.com/digits/2014/09/16/ibms-watson-computer-now-has-analytics.*
11. John Jordan, "The Risks of Big Data for Companies," *Wall Street Journal*, March 6, 2016, *www.wsj.com/articles/SB10001424052702304526204579102941708296708.*
12. John Leyden, "Misconfigured Big Data Apps Are Leaking Data Like Sieves," *The Register*, March 6, 2016, *www.theregister.co.uk/2015/08/13/big_data_apps_expose_data.*
13. Lorna Garey, "Big Data Brings Big Security Problems," *InformationWeek*, March 6, 2016, http://www.informationweek.com/big-data/big-data-analytics/big-data-brings-big-security-problems/d/d-id/1252747.
14. Ibid.

APPLICATION EXERCISES

All exercise files can be found on the following Web site: *www.pearsonhighered.com/kroenke*.

AE1. In some cases, users want to use Access and Excel together. They process relational data with Access, import some of the data into Excel, and use Excel's tools for creating professional-looking charts and graphs. You will do exactly that in this exercise.

Download the Access file **Ch05Ex01_U10e.accdb**. Open the database and select *DATABASE TOOLS/Relationships*. As you can see, there are three tables: *Product, Vendor-ProductInventory*, and *Vendor.* Open each table individually to familiarize yourself with the data.

For this problem, we will define *InventoryCost* as the product of *Industry-Standard-Cost* and *QuantityOnHand*. The query *InventoryCost* computes these values for every item in inventory for every vendor. Open that query and view the data to be certain you understand this computation. Open the other queries as well so that you understand the data they produce.

a. Sum this data by vendor and display it in a pie chart like that shown in Figure AE (your totals will be different from those shown). Proceed as follows:

(1) Open Excel and create a new spreadsheet.

(2) Click *DATA* on the ribbon and select *From Access* in the *Get External Data* ribbon category.

(3) Navigate to the location in which you have stored the Access file **Ch05Ex01_U10e.accdb**.

(4) Select the query that contains the data you need for this pie chart.

(5) Import the data into a worksheet.

(6) Format the appropriate data as currency.

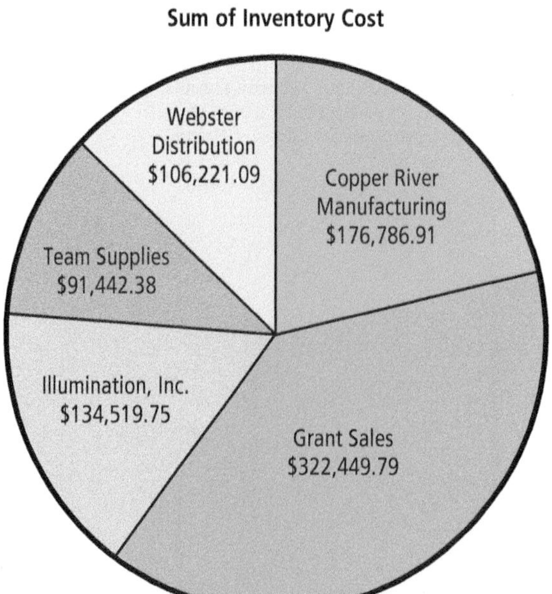

FIGURE AE
Data Displayed in Pie-Chart Format
Source: Microsoft Corporation

Inventory Cost by Category

Cost

$450,000
$400,000
$350,000
$300,000
$250,000
$200,000
$150,000
$100,000
$50,000
$0

Accessories Clothing Furniture Linens

FIGURE AE

Data Displayed in Bar-Chart Format

Source: Microsoft Corporation

(7) Select the range that contains the data, press the Function key, and proceed from there to create the pie chart. Name the data and pie chart worksheets appropriately.

h. Follow a similar procedure to create the bar chart shown in Figure AE. Again, your data will be different. Place the data and the chart in separate worksheets and name them appropriately.

AE2. Read Case Study 5. A copy of Dean's database is stored in the Access file **Ch05Ex02_U10e.accdb.** Download a copy of this file and create queries to provide the following data:

a. Sort the pianos from high quality to low.

b. Sort the pianos from high quality to low and, within each quality, sort by Building and then by Location within that building.

c. List the pianos in the shed and sort the results by manufacturer.

d. List all of the pianos with a Type of 'Spinet.'

e. Count the pianos for each value of quality (ranging from 1 to 5).

f. Write a query to produce the report in Figure 36.

AE3. 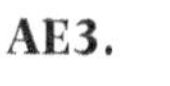  In this exercise, you will create a two-table database, define relationships, create a form and a report, and use them to enter data and view results.

a. Download the Excel file **Ch05Ex03_U10e.xlsx**. Open the spreadsheet and review the data in the *Employee* and *Computer* worksheets.

b. Create a new Access database with the name *Ch05Ex03_Solution*. Close the table that Access automatically creates and delete it.

c. Import the data from the Excel spreadsheet into your database. Import the *Employee* worksheet into a table named *Employee*. Be sure to check *First Row Contains Column Headings*. Select *Choose my own primary key* and use the ID field as that key.

d. Import the *Computer* worksheet into a table named *Computer*. Check *First Row Contains Column Headings*, but let Access create the primary key.

e. Open the relationships window and add both *Employee* and *Computer* to the design space. Drag ID from *Employee* and drop it on *EmployeeID* in *Computer*. Check *Enforce Referential Integrity* and the two checkmarks below. Ensure you know what these actions mean.

f. Open the Form Wizard dialog box (under *Create, More Forms*) and add all of the columns for each of your tables to your form. Select *View your data by Employee*. Title your form *Employee* and your subform *Computer*.

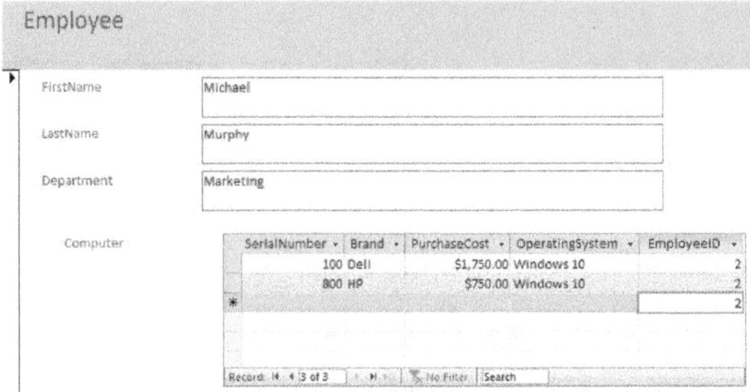

FIGURE AE
Employee Computer Assignment Form
Source: Microsoft Corporation

g. Open the *Computer* subform and delete *EmployeeID* and *ComputerID*. These values are maintained by Access, and it is just a distraction to keep them. Your form should appear like the one shown in Figure AE (Your data will be different.).

h. Use your form to add two new computers to *Michael Murphy*. Both computers are Dells, both use Windows 10, one costs $750, and the other costs $1,400.

i. Delete the Lenovo computer for Stan Larsen

j. Use the Report Wizard (under *Create*) to create a report having all data from both the *Employee* and *Computer* tables. Adjust the report design until you find a design you like. Correct the label alignment if you need to.

GLOSSARY

Access A popular personal and small workgroup DBMS product licensed by Microsoft. Included with some versions of Microsoft Office.

ACID An acronym standing for atomic, consistent, isolated, and durable. Used to describe the processing of transactions such that all of the transaction is processed or none of it is (atomic), transactions are processed in the same manner (consistent) whether processed alone or in the presence of millions of other transactions (isolated), and that once a transaction is stored it never goes away—even in the presence of failure (durable).

Attributes Characteristics of an entity. Example attributes of Order are *OrderNumber, OrderDate, SubTotal, Tax, Total,* and so forth. Example attributes of Salesperson are *SalespersonName, Email, Phone,* and so forth.

Columns Also called fields, or groups of bytes. A database table has multiple columns that are used to represent the attributes of an entity. Examples are PartNumber, EmployeeName, and SalesDate.

Crow's-foot diagram A type of entity-relationship diagram that uses a crow's foot symbol to designate a 1:N relationship.

Crow's feet Lines on an entity-relationship diagram that indicate a 1:N relationship between two entities.

Database administration A person or department that develops procedures and practices to ensure efficient and orderly multiuser processing of the database, to control changes to database structure, and to protect the database.

Database application A collection of forms, reports, queries, and application programs that facilitates users' processing of a database. A database can be processed by many different database applications.

Database A self-describing collection of integrated records.

Database management system (DBMS) A program for creating, processing, and administering a database. A DBMS is a large and complex program that is licensed like an operating system. Microsoft Access and Oracle Database are example DBMS products.

Data integrity problem In a database, the situation that exists when data item values disagree with one another. An example is two different names for the same customer.

Data model A logical representation of the data in a database that describes the data and relationships that will be stored in the database. Akin to a blueprint.

DB2 A popular, enterprise-class DBMS product licensed by IBM.

Entity-relationship (E-R) data model A tool for constructing data models that defines the entities stored in a database and the relationships among those entities.

Entity-relationship (E-R) diagrams A type of diagram used by database designers to document entities and their relationships to each other.

Entity In the E-R data model, a representation of some thing that users want to track. Some entities represent a physical object; others represent a logical construct or transaction.

Fields Also called columns; groups of bytes in a database table. A database table has multiple columns that represent the attributes of an entity. Examples are PartNumber, EmployeeName, and SaleDate.

File A group of similar rows or records. In a database, sometimes called a table.

Foreign keys A column or group of columns used to represent relationships. Values of the foreign key match values of the primary key in a different (foreign) table.

Graphical queries Queries in which criteria are created when the user clicks on a graphic.

Identifier An attribute (or group of attributes) whose value is associated with one and only one entity instance.

In-memory DBMS DBMS products that process databases stored in (very large) memories. Usually such DBMS utilize or extend the relational model. ACID support is common.

Key (1) A column or group of columns that identifies a unique row in a table. Also referred to as a primary key. (2) A string of bits used to encrypt data. The encryption algorithm applies the key to the original message to produce the coded message. Decoding (decrypting) a message is similar; a key is applied to the coded message to recover the original text.

Lost-update problem A problem that exists in database applications in which two users update the same data item, but only one of those changes is recorded in the data. Can be resolved using locking.

Many-to-many (N:M) relationships Relationships involving two entity types in which an instance of one type can relate to many instances of the second type, and an instance of the second type can relate to many instances of the first. For example, the relationship between Student and Class is N:M. One student may enroll in many classes, and one class may have many students. Contrast with one-to-many relationships.

Maximum cardinality The maximum number of entities that can be involved in a relationship. Common examples of maximum cardinality are 1:N, N:M, and 1:1.

Metadata Data that describes data.

Minimum cardinality The minimum number of entities that must be involved on one side of a relationship, typically zero or one.

MongoDB An open source, document-oriented, nonrelational DBMS.

Multi-user processing The situation in which multiple users process the database at the same time.

MySQL A popular open source DBMS product that is license-free for most applications.

NewSQL DBMS Relational DBMS with ACID support that provide processing speeds equivalent to those of NoSQL DBMS products.

Normal forms Definitions of table characteristics that identify various problems to which a table is subject.

Normalization The process of converting poorly structured tables into two or more better-structured tables.

One-to-many (1:N) relationships Relationships involving two entity types in which an instance of one type can relate to many instances of the second type, but an instance of the second type can relate to at most one instance of the first. For example, in most businesses, the relationship between Department and Employee is 1:N. A department may relate to many employees, but an employee relates to at most one department.

Oracle Database A popular, enterprise-class DBMS product from Oracle Corporation.

Primary key One or more columns in a relation whose values identify a unique row of that relation. Also known as a key.

Records Also called rows, groups of columns in a database table.

Relation A formal name for a database table.

Relational databases Databases that store data in the form of relations (tables with certain restrictions) and that represents record relationships using foreign keys.

Relationships Associations among entities or entity instances in an E-R model or an association among rows of a table in a relational database.

Rows Also called records, groups of columns in a database table.

SQL Server A popular enterprise-class DBMS product licensed by Microsoft.

Structured Query Language (SQL) An international standard language for processing database data. Can also be used to create and modify database structure.

Table Also called files, groups of similar rows or records in a database.

Unified Modeling Language (UML) A series of diagramming techniques that facilitates OOP development. UML has dozens of different diagrams for all phases of system development. UML does not require or promote any particular development process. Generally less popular that the E-R model.

NoSQL DBMS Nonrelational DBMS that support very high transaction rates processing relatively simple data structures, replicated on many servers in the cloud. No ACID support.

The Cloud

"What's your plan, Toshio?" Mateo Thomas, CEO of Falcon Security, is meeting with Toshio Sato, IT director, and Joni Campbell, CFO, to discuss Falcon Security's data storage costs.

"Right now, Mateo, we're fine. We just got our new NAS online, and we've increased our storage capacity by almost 30 percent, but ..." Toshio trails off.

Joni can't stand this. "Well, we're fine until you look at the bills we're running up. The money we've spent on storage has increased 350 percent *in 1 year*."

"Yes, Joni, it has, but our volume's gone up 400 percent," Toshio replies.

"True enough, but ..."

Mateo has had enough and interrupts. "We've been over this before. No need to rehash it. We all agree that our storage costs are too high. Toshio, I'd asked you to look into alternatives. What have you got?"

"The cloud."

"The *what?*" Joni hopes he's not losing it.

"The cloud," Toshio repeats. "We move all of our video to the cloud."

Mateo is curious. "OK, Toshio, I'll bite. What's the cloud?"

"It's a movement—I'd call it a fad, except I think it's here to stay."

"So how does it help us?" Mateo asks.

"We lease storage capacity from a third party."

Joni's confused. "You mean we'd lease hard drives rather than buy them?"

"Well, not exactly," Mateo explains. "We wouldn't be installing any more hard drives in our data center. We can lease online storage on very, very flexible, pay-as-you-go terms. If we get a large new client, we can acquire more storage and scale it to meet our needs."

"You mean each day? We can change the terms of our lease on a daily basis?" Joni thinks that's not possible. "OK, so how much does it cost? This can't be cheap."

"How about $10 per terabyte?"

Mateo's puzzled at that. "What do you mean, $10 per terabyte?"

"I mean we can get 1 terabyte of online storage for about $10 per month." Toshio grins as he says this.

"*What?*" Joni's dumbfounded.

"Yeah, that's it. We can get as much storage as we want, and our systems automatically upload all incoming data from our drones. The net difference would be that our average monthly storage costs would be at least 50 percent less than they are now. And that's not counting the power savings, the time saved doing backups, or the fact that we wouldn't have to configure any more new hardware." Toshio isn't quite sure, but he thinks the actual storage costs could be less.

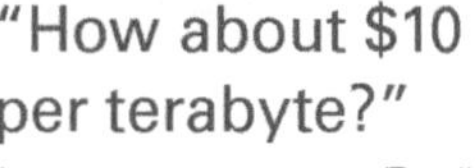

"How about $10 per terabyte?"

Image source: rommma/Fotolia

"Toshio, you've got to be kidding. We can save tens of thousands of dollars in storage costs. This is *huge*." As Joni says this, in the back of her mind she's thinking, "If it's true."

"Well, it's good; I don't know about huge. We'd have additional development costs to set up our systems, and that will take some time."

"Toshio, give me a plan. I want a plan." Mateo's thinking what these savings could mean to their next two quarters ... and beyond.

"I'll give you something next week," Toshio says.

"I want it by Friday, Toshio."

Study QUESTIONS

Q1 Why are organizations moving to the cloud?

Q2 How do organizations use the cloud?

Q3 What network technology supports the cloud?

Q4 How does the Internet work?

Q5 How do web servers support the cloud?

Q6 How can Falcon Security use the cloud?

Q7 How can organizations use cloud services securely?

Q8 2027?

Chapter PREVIEW

If you go into business for yourself, there's an excellent chance you'll have a problem just like Falcon Security's. What is the best way to support your Web site or other information systems? Should you use the cloud? Most likely, the answer will be yes. So, then, which of your applications should use it and how? You need the knowledge of this chapter to participate in the conversations you'll have. Of course, you could just rely on outside experts, but that doesn't work in the 21st century. Many of your competitors will be able to ask and understand those questions—and use the money their knowledge saves them for other purposes.

Or what if you work for a large company that has embraced the Internet of Things (IoT)? Will you make products that send and receive data across the Internet? How will your products connect to the cloud? Will a cloud offering make sense for you and your customers? How will you know without some knowledge of the cloud?

We begin this chapter with an overview of where the cloud came from, why organizations are moving toward it, and how they use it. Then, in Q3 and Q4, we will discuss local area networks and the fundamentals of the Internet. We then look at how Web servers function, basic steps for setting up a cloud presence, and cloud security. We'll wrap up with the cloud in 2027.

Q1 Why Are Organizations Moving to the Cloud?

We define the **cloud** as the *elastic* leasing of *pooled* computer resources *over the Internet*. The term *cloud* is used because most early diagrams of three-tier and other Internet-based systems used a cloud symbol to represent the Internet, and organizations came to view their infrastructure as being "somewhere in the cloud." To understand its importance, you need to first know where the term *the cloud* came from.

From about the early 1960s to the late 1980s, organizations primarily used **mainframes**, or large-scale high-speed centralized computers, for their internal data processing needs (see Figure 1). A **mainframe architecture** supported connections between a central mainframe and numerous **thin clients** (sometimes called **computer terminals**) which were essentially a screen, a keyboard, and a network connection. All applications, data, and processing power were located on the mainframe. There was no cloud as we currently understand it because the Internet had not yet arrived.

By the early 1990's, Internet usage had started taking off. Users were connecting their personal computers (stand-alone clients) to the Internet and organizations were buying servers to host their web sites and data (in-house hosting). A **client-server architecture** allows clients (users) to send requests across the Internet to severs. Servers respond to requests by sending data back to clients. For example, a user sitting at home can click on a link that sends a web request to a web server. The web server then sends a copy of the web page back to the user. As shown in Figure 2, applications and data storage can reside on clients, servers, or both. Processing load can also be shared between clients and servers.

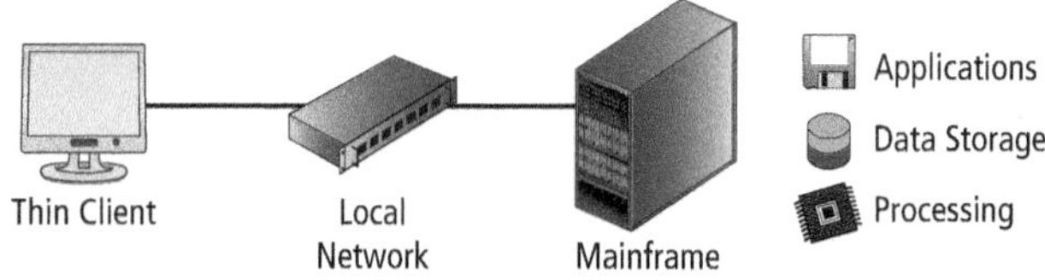

FIGURE 1
The Mainframe Era (1960s–1980s)

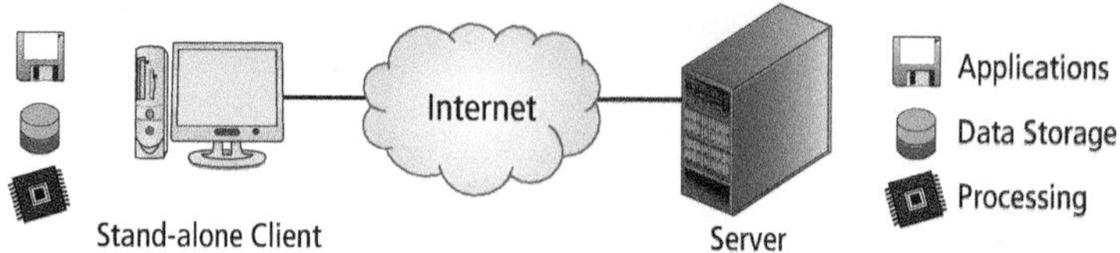

FIGURE 2
The Client-Server Era (1990s–2000s)

The client-server architecture was more appealing to organizations than mainframes because servers were much less expensive. Mainframes cost millions of dollars, but servers only cost thousands of dollars. Servers were also more **scalable**—or easily able to respond to incremental growth in demand—than mainframes because their incremental cost was lower. The client-server architecture also allowed users access systems from anywhere in the world as long as they had an Internet connection. What we now know as the cloud had arrived, but modern cloud computing was still a few years away. Mainframes didn't entirely go away with the advent of the client-server architecture. In fact, there are still some large organizations (e.g., large banks) that use mainframes to process daily transactions.

Cloud Computing

Until about 2008 or so, most organizations constructed and maintained their own computing infrastructure. Organizations purchased or leased hardware; installed it on their premises; and used it to support organizational email, Web sites, e-commerce sites, and in-house applications such as accounting and operations systems. After 2008, however, organizations began to move their computing infrastructure to the cloud.

Cloud computing architecture allows employees and customers to access organizational data and applications located in the cloud. As shown in Figure 3, applications, data, and processing power can be used remotely with a variety of devices including PCs, thin clients, mobile devices, and IoT devices. Organizations no longer need to purchase, configure, and maintain expensive computing infrastructure. Organizations are shifting to the cloud for some of the same reasons they shifted to a client-server architecture—reduced costs and improved scalability.

But there are additional benefits to using the cloud. At the beginning of this chapter we defined the cloud as the *elastic* leasing of *pooled* computer resources *over the Internet*. Consider each of the italicized terms in the definition to explore these benefits.

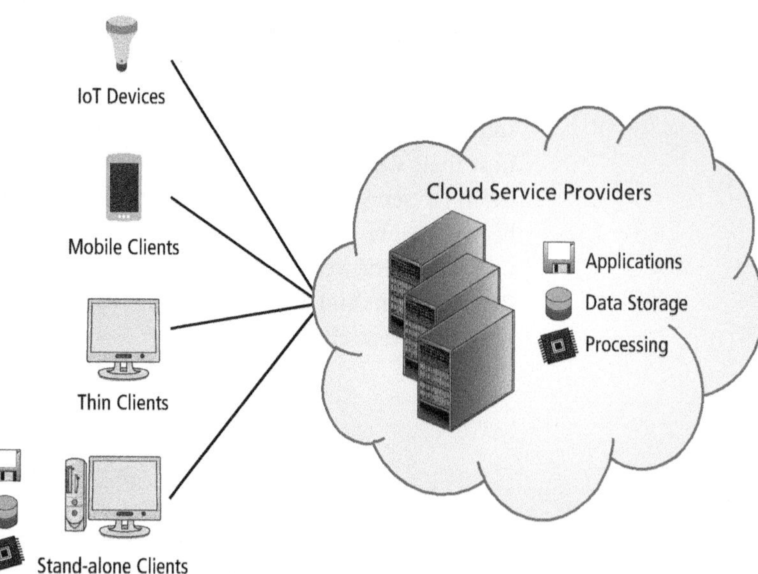

FIGURE 3
The Cloud Computing Era (2008–Current)

Elastic

The term **elastic**, which was first used this way by Amazon.com, means that leased computing resources can be increased or decreased dynamically, programmatically, in a short span of time and that organizations pay for only the resources they use.

Elasticity is not the same thing as scalability, which is the ability to respond to slow incremental growth in demand. A system's ability to add 1,000 new clients per year for the next 10 years (an increase) is an example of scalability. A small local news channel's ability to handle Web page requests from everyone on the planet about a one-time news story (massive increase *and decrease*) is an example of elasticity.

Cloud-based hosting offers considerable elasticity that traditional client-server environments don't offer. An organization could purchase enough server capacity to respond to any increase in demand, but it would be extremely expensive. The same organization could lease the capacity from a cloud vendor on an as-needed basis for a fraction of the price.

Pooled

The second key in the definition of the cloud is *pooled*. Cloud resources are **pooled** because many different organizations use the same physical hardware; they share that hardware through virtualization. Virtualization technology enables the rapid creation of new virtual machines. The customer provides (or creates in the cloud) a disk image of the data and programs of the machine it wants to provision. Virtualization software takes it from there.

Virtualization increases the scalability of an organization's systems because it can quickly respond to incremental growth in demand. New virtual machines can be created in a few minutes. But ordering, shipping, installing, and configuring a physical server can take days. Virtualization also reduces costs. Hundreds of virtual machines (virtual servers) can reside on a single physical server. Thus, the cost of the physical server is spread across each of the individual virtual machines.

Over the Internet

Finally, with the cloud, the resources are accessed **over the Internet**. "Big deal," you're saying. "I use the Internet all the time." Well, think about that for a minute. Accessing resources over the Internet means they aren't stored locally. From an organization's point of view, it doesn't have to have any servers on its premises anymore. It doesn't have to pay for power to run its servers, buy backup generators in case the power goes out, lease the additional commercial space to store the servers, heat and cool the server room, or install specialized fire suppression systems in case a fire breaks out. It also doesn't have to pay for someone to physically care for its servers by replacing broken parts or upgrading components. Physically managing your own computing infrastructure is costly. For many companies it has become too costly.

Why Do Organizations Prefer the Cloud?

It is likely that in the future all or nearly all computing infrastructure will be leased from the cloud, but we're not there yet. Not all organizations have fully embraced cloud computing. There are still racks of servers filling up in-house data centers. But the list of companies that have embraced cloud computing is growing rapidly. Well-known organizations like Netflix, Adobe Systems, the National Aeronautics and Space Administration (NASA), Juniper Networks, and Intuit Inc. have all shifted to the cloud.[1]

In fact, most people don't realize how quickly organizations have shifted to the cloud. Amazon launched Amazon Web Services (AWS) in 2006 largely as an experiment. Most industry analysts saw it as a cost center that probably wouldn't generate revenue for many years, if ever. As shown in Figure 4, by the first quarter of 2016 revenue from AWS was \$2.57B,[2] and annual revenue was expected to be \$12.5B.[3] That's tremendous growth in a short period of time. AWS also generated more than half of the operating income for Amazon as a whole and was growing twice as fast as

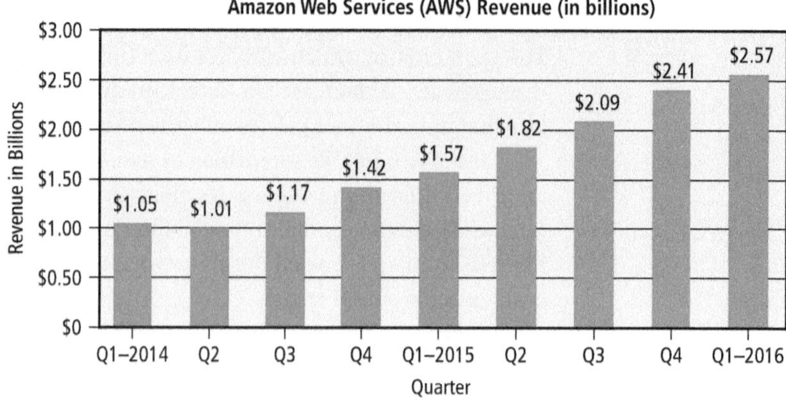

FIGURE 4
AWS Revenue Growth

its e-commerce counterpart. What is even more amazing is that Amazon boasts 31 percent market share of the cloud computing market with more than a million active customers![4] A million customers may not sound like a lot, but these aren't individual consumers buying items on Amazon.com; they are large companies like Adobe Systems ($48B market cap), Netflix Inc. ($37B market cap), and Pfizer Inc. ($205B market cap). One million of this type of customer is a lot.

Several factors have pushed organizations toward cloud-based hosting, including lower costs, ubiquitous access, improved scalability, and elasticity. But there are other reasons to shift to the cloud. Figure 5 compares and contrasts cloud-based and in-house (client-server) hosting. As you can see, the positives are heavily tilted toward cloud-based hosting. The cloud vendor Rackspace will lease you one medium server for less than a penny per hour. You can obtain and access that server today, actually within a few minutes. Tomorrow, if you need thousands of servers, you can readily scale up to obtain them. Furthermore, you know the cost structure; although you might have a surprise in terms of how many customers want to access your Web site, you won't have any surprises about how much it will cost.

Another positive is that as long as you're dealing with large, reputable organizations, you'll be receiving best-of-breed security and disaster recovery. In addition, you need not worry that you're investing in technology that will soon be obsolete; the cloud vendor is taking that risk. All of this is possible because the cloud vendor is gaining economies of scale by selling to an entire industry, not just to you. Finally, cloud computing allows you to focus on your business, not spend time maintaining infrastructure. You can outsource functions that are not your core competency and focus on those that give you a competitive advantage.

The negatives of cloud computing involve loss of control. You're dependent on a vendor; changes in the vendor's management, policy, and prices are beyond your control. Further, you don't know where your data—which may be a large part of your organization's value—is located. Nor do you know how many copies of your data there are or even if they're located in the same country as you are. Finally, you have no visibility into the security and disaster preparedness that is actually in place. Your competition could be stealing your data and you won't know it.

Companies can save a lot of money by using the cloud, and these savings translate into profit. This profit does not come without ethical concerns, however. The Ethics Guide given later in the chapter examines these concerns.

The positives and negatives of in-house hosting are shown in the second column of Figure 5. For the most part, they are the opposite of those for cloud-based hosting; note, however, the need for personnel and management. With in-house hosting, not only will you have to construct your own data center, you'll also need to acquire and train the personnel to run it and then manage those personnel and your facility.

When Does the Cloud Not Make Sense?

Storing valuable information online can be risky. The Security Guide given later in the chapter looks at why your information may not be as safe as you think.

Cloud-based hosting makes sense for most organizations. The only organizations for which it may not make sense are those required by law or by industry standard practice to have physical control over their data. Such organizations might be forced to create and maintain their own

Cloud	In-house
Positive:	
Small capital requirements	Control of data location
Speedy development	In-depth visibility of security and disaster preparedness
Superior scalability to growing or fluctuating demand	
Known cost structure	
Possibly best-of-breed security/disaster preparedness	
No obsolescence	
Industry-wide economies of scale, hence cheaper	
Focus on core business, not infrastructure	
Negative:	
Dependency on vendor	Significant capital required
Loss of control over data location	Significant development effort
Little visibility into true security and disaster preparedness capabilities	Difficult (impossible?) to accommodate fluctuating demand
	Ongoing support costs
	Staff and train personnel
	Increased management requirements
	Annual maintenance costs
	Cost uncertainties
	Obsolescence

FIGURE 5
Comparison of Cloud and In-House Alternatives

hosting infrastructure. A financial institution, for example, might be legally required to maintain physical control over its data. Even in this circumstance, however, it is possible to gain many of the benefits of cloud computing using private clouds and virtual private clouds, possibilities we consider in Q7.

Q2 How Do Organizations Use the Cloud?

Now that you know *what* the cloud is, we will look at specific examples of *how* organizations use the cloud. We'll look at how a car manufacturer can benefit from the cloud's resource elasticity, pooling, and unique Internet connectivity.

Resource Elasticity

Suppose a car manufacturer creates an ad to run during the Academy Awards. It believes it has a fantastic ad that will result in millions of hits on its Web site. However, it doesn't know ahead of time if there will be a thousand, a million, 10 million, or even more site visits. Further, the ad may appeal more to one nationality than to another. Will 70 percent of those visits arise in the United States and the rest in Europe? Or will there be millions from Japan? Or Australia? Given this uncertainty, how does the car manufacturer prepare its computing infrastructure? The car manufacturer knows that if it cannot provide very short response time (say, a fraction of a second), it will lose the benefit of an incredibly expensive ad. On the other hand, if the ad is a flop, preprovisioning of thousands of servers will add to the accumulation of wasted money.

Figure 6 shows an example of this situation, based on a real case supported by Amazon.com's CloudFront. Suppose Figure 6 shows the processing on the car manufacturer's Web site during the Academy Awards. Throughout the day, the car manufacturer is delivering less than 10 Gbps of its content to users. However, as soon as its ad runs (2 PM in the Hawaii-Aleutian time zone where the data was collected), demand increases sevenfold and stays high for half an hour. After the announcement of Best Picture, when the ad runs again, demand again increases to 30 and 40 Gbps for an hour and then returns to its base level.

Without an increase in servers, response time will be 3 or 5 seconds or more, which is far too long to maintain the attention of an Academy Awards viewer. However, the car manufacturer has contracted with its cloud vendor to add servers, wherever needed worldwide, to keep response time to less than 0.5 seconds. Using cloud technology, the cloud vendor will programmatically increase its servers to keep response time below the 0.5-second threshold. As demand falls after the ad runs a second time, it will release the excess servers and reallocate them at the end of the awards.

In this way, the car manufacturer need not build or contract for infrastructure that supports maximum demand. Had it done so, the vast majority of its servers would have been idle for most of the evening. And, as you'll learn, the cloud vendor can provision servers worldwide using the cloud; if a good portion of the excess demand is in Singapore, for example, it can provision extra servers in Asia and reduce wait time due to global transmission delays.

Pooling Resources

The servers that the car manufacturer needed for these few hours were much less costly because it only needed them for a short time. The servers that it used for the Academy Awards can be reallocated to CPA firms that need them later that same day, to textbook publishers who need them for online student activity on Monday, or to the hotel industry that needs them later the next week.

An easy way to understand the essence of this development is to consider electrical power. In the very earliest days of electric power generation, organizations operated their own generators to create power for their company's needs. Over time, as the power grid expanded, it became possible to centralize power generation so that organizations could purchase just the electricity they needed from an electric utility.

Both cloud vendors and electrical utilities benefit from *economies of scale*. According to this principle, the average cost of production decreases as the size of the operation increases. Major cloud vendors operate enormous Web farms. Figure 7 shows the building that contains the

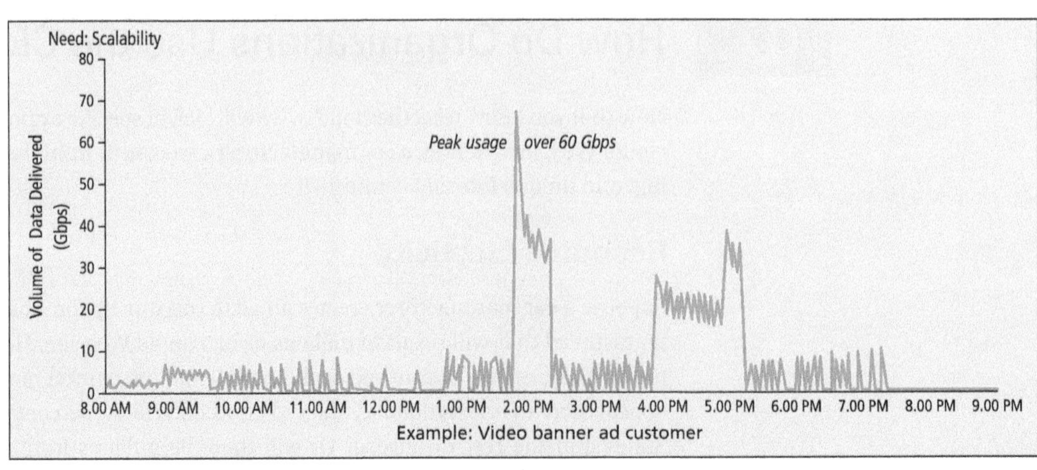

FIGURE 6
Example Video Banner Ad Customer

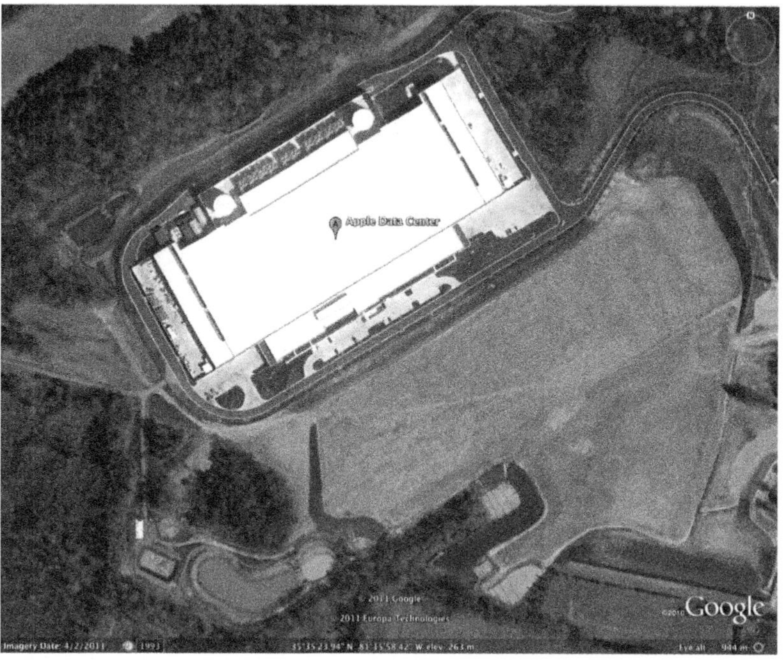

FIGURE 7
Apple Data Center in Maiden, NC
Source: Google Earth

computers in the Web farm that Apple constructed in 2011 to support its iCloud offering. This billion-dollar facility contains 505,000 square feet.[5] Amazon.com, IBM, Google, Microsoft, Oracle, and other large companies each operate several similar farms worldwide.

Over the Internet

The car manufacturer in the previous example has contracted with the cloud vendor for a maximum response time; the cloud vendor adds servers as needed to meet that requirement. As stated, the cloud vendor may be provisioning, nearly instantaneously, servers all over the world. How does it do that? And not for just one customer, like the car manufacturer, but for thousands?

In the old days, for such interorganizational processing to occur, developers from the car manufacturer had to meet with developers from the cloud vendor and design an interface. "Our programs will do this, providing this data, and we want your programs to do that, in response, sending us this other data back." Such meetings took days and were expensive and error-prone. Given the design, the developers then returned home to write code to meet the agreed-on interface design, which may not have been understood in the same way by all parties.

It was a long, slow, expensive, and prone-to-failure process. If organizations had to do that today, cloud provisioning would be unaffordable and infeasible.

Instead, the computer industry settled on a set of standard ways of requesting and receiving services over the Internet. You will learn about some of these standards in Q5. For now, just realize those standards enable computers that have never "met" before to organize a dizzying, worldwide dance to deliver and process content to users on PCs, iPads, Google phones, Xboxes, and even exercise equipment in a tenth of second or less. It is absolutely fascinating and gorgeous technology! Unfortunately, you will have the opportunity to learn only a few basic terms in Q3 and Q4.

Cloud Services from Cloud Vendors

Organizations can use the cloud in several different ways. The first and most popular way is obtaining cloud services from cloud service vendors. But not all organizations use cloud services to the same *extent*. You can use more of the cloud or less. It's up to you. As a business professional, you'll need to understand the differences in cloud service levels.

To help you understand these differences, we'll use a metaphor related to transportation and then relate it to cloud service offerings.

Transportation as a Service

Suppose you need to get to and from work each day. You have four options for satisfying your transportation needs. You can build a car, buy a car, rent a car, or take a taxi. Each has its own advantages and disadvantages. As shown in Figure 8, at one end of the spectrum, you manage your own transportation completely (building a car). At the other end of the spectrum, your transportation is managed by someone else (a taxi service).

For example, if you decide to buy a car rather than build one, you are essentially outsourcing some of your transportation to a car manufacturer. You don't have to buy the car parts, assemble the car, or test it to make sure it works properly. It might initially seem cheaper to build your own car. But realistically, you may not have the time, knowledge, skill, or patience to actually build a reliable car. It may end up cheaper to buy a car rather than build one.

Similarly, if you decide to rent a car, you're essentially outsourcing more of your transportation to someone else. By renting a car you don't have to pay for vehicle registration and taxes. You also don't have to make any repairs or clean the car. You're doing less work but potentially paying more. The same is true of the difference between renting a car and taking a taxi. If you take a taxi, you don't have to buy car insurance, drive the car, or buy gas. In fact, you don't even need a driver's license. Again, you're accomplishing the same thing—getting to and from work. You're just managing less of your transportation.

Types of Cloud Service Offerings

The "transportation as a service" metaphor helps explain how organizations use cloud services to move away from a traditional on-premises model in which they must provide all services internally. Depending on their choice of cloud services, organizations manage less of their infrastructure, platform, and software functions. In general, one type of service isn't necessarily better than another. What is best for an individual organization depends upon the way in which its managers want to use the cloud. Cloud-based service offerings can be organized into the three categories shown in Figure 9.

As shown in Figure 10, the most basic cloud offering is **infrastructure as a service (IaaS)**, which is the cloud hosting of a bare server computer, data storage, network, and virtualization. Rackspace Inc. provides hardware for customers to load whatever operating system they want, and Amazon.com licenses S3 (Simple Storage Service), which provides unlimited, reliable data storage in the cloud. The cost savings of IaaS over traditional on-premises hosting can be substantial.

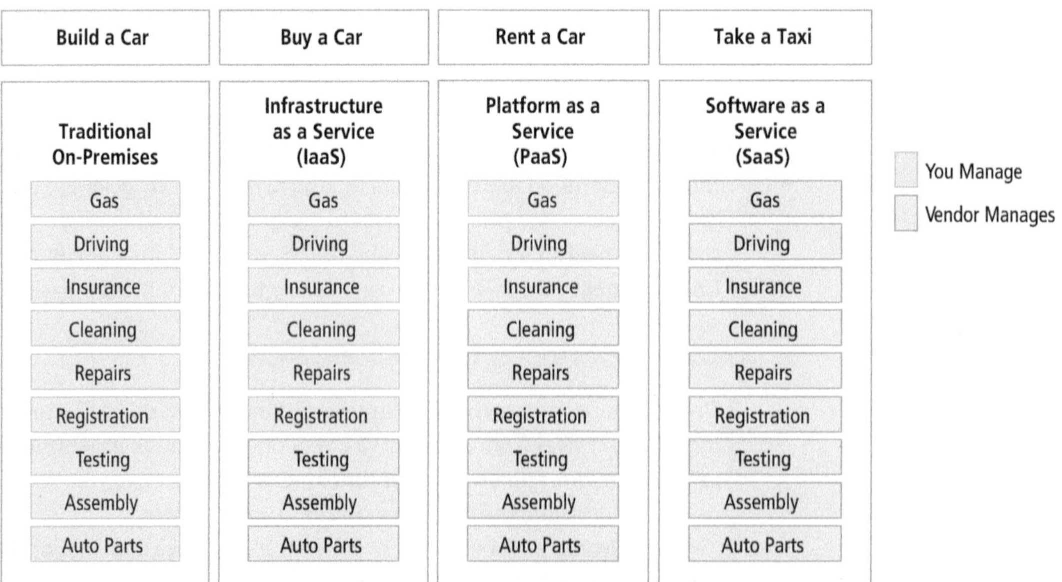

FIGURE 8
Transportation as a Service

FIGURE 9
Three Fundamental Cloud Types

Cloud Service	Users	Examples
SaaS	Employees Customers	Salesforce.com iCloud Office 365
PaaS	Application developers Application testers	Google App Engine Microsoft Azure AWS Elastic Beanstalk
IaaS	Network architects Systems administrators	Amazon EC2 (Elastic Compute Cloud) Amazon S3 (Simple Storage Service)

The second category of cloud hosting is **platform as a service (PaaS)**, whereby vendors provide hosted computers with an operating system, runtime environment, and middleware like a Web server or a DBMS. Microsoft Windows Azure, for example, provides servers installed with Windows Server. Customers of Windows Azure then add their own applications on top of the hosted platform. Microsoft SQL Azure provides a host with Windows Server and SQL Server. Oracle On Demand provides a hosted server with Oracle Database. Again, for PaaS, organizations add their own applications to the host. Amazon EC2 provides servers with Windows Server or Linux installed.

An organization that provides **software as a service (SaaS)** provides not only hardware infrastructure and an operating system but application programs and databases as well. For example, Salesforce.com provides hardware and programs for customer and sales tracking as a service. Similarly, Google provides Google Drive and Microsoft provides OneDrive as a service. With Office 365, Exchange, Skype for Business, and SharePoint applications are provided as a service "in the cloud."

For each of these applications, you just sign up for them and learn how to use them. You don't have to worry about buying hardware, loading an operating system, setting up a database, or installing software. All of that is managed by the cloud service provider. Much like using a taxi—you just jump in and go.

As a business professional you'll need to know the advantages and disadvantages of on-premises hosing, IaaS, PaaS, and SaaS. Your choice of cloud service will be driven by your competitive environment, business strategy, and technical resources. Much like the "transportation as a service" metaphor mentioned earlier, not everyone should build, own, or even rent a car.

If you're a working professional living in a big city, maybe taking a taxi is your best transportation option (SaaS). If you're always on the road traveling for business, renting a car in each city might be the right choice (PaaS). If you own a large package delivery company, you might want to

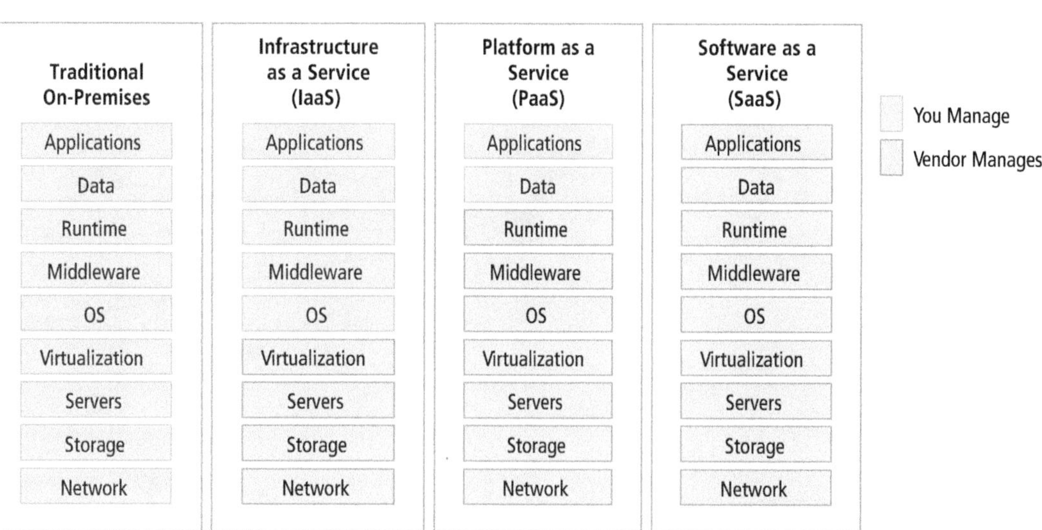

FIGURE 10
Cloud Service Offerings

buy a fleet of trucks (IaaS). If you're a high-performance racecar driver, you may need to build your own specialized racing vehicle (on-premises). Making the right choice between cloud services is really more about finding the right fit with your organization's needs.

Content Delivery Networks

Another major use of the cloud is to deliver content from servers placed around the world. A **content delivery network (CDN)** is a system of hardware and software that stores user data in many different geographical locations and makes those data available on demand. A CDN provides a specialized type of PaaS but is usually considered in its own category, as it is here. To understand how a CDN delivers content, let's compare it to how traditional servers deliver content.

Figure 11 shows a server located in California delivering content to users around the United States. Suppose this hypothetical California-based media company streams HD movies to millions of homes around the country. The bandwidth usage from this company would be tremendous. To give you an idea of how much this might be, reports indicate that Netflix traffic consumes 37 percent of all Internet traffic in North America during peak evening hours.[6] This level of bandwidth consumption would be costly to deliver and would slow content delivery from other companies.

Figure 12 shows how this online media company could use a CDN to store copies of its movies. The CDN vendor replicates movies on servers, possibly worldwide, in order to speed up response time. When a user at home requests a movie, the request is transmitted to a routing server that determines which CDN server will deliver the movie to the user the fastest. Because traffic changes rapidly, such determinations are made in real time. A request for content at one moment in time could be served by a computer in, say, San Diego, and a few moments later, that same request from that same user might be served by a computer in Seattle.

In addition to movies, CDNs are often used to store and deliver content that seldom changes. For example, the company banner on an organization's Web page might be stored on many CDN servers. Various pieces of the Web page could be obtained from different servers on the CDN; all such decisions are made in real time to provide the fastest content delivery possible.

Figure 13 summarizes CDN benefits. The first two are self-explanatory. Reliability is increased because data are stored on many servers. If one server fails, any of a potentially large number of other servers can deliver the content. For now, just understand that such security threats send so much data to a given server that the server's performance for legitimate traffic becomes unacceptable. By having multiple servers, CDNs help to protect against such attacks.

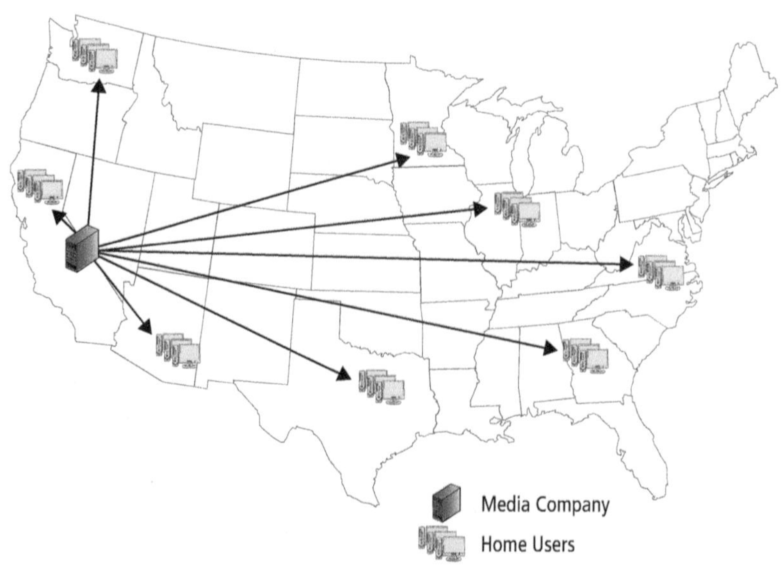

FIGURE 11
Traditional Server Content Distribution

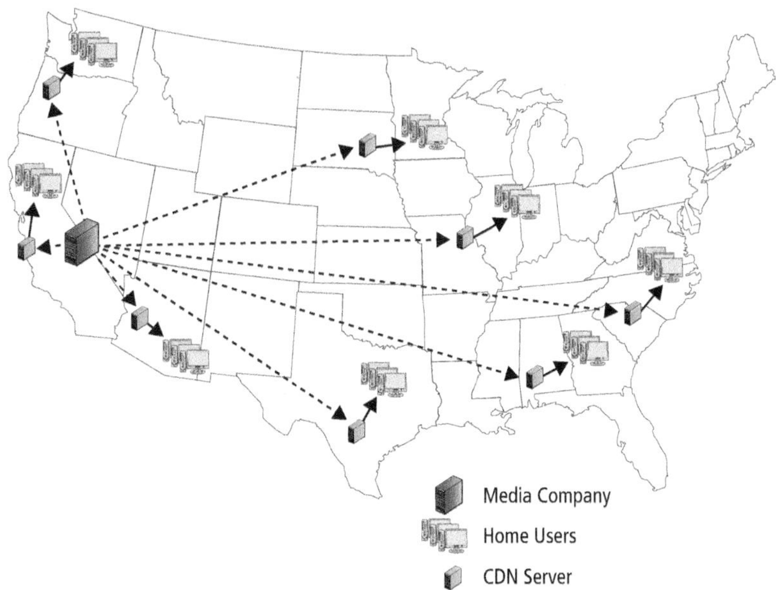

FIGURE 12
Distributed CDN Servers

In some cases, CDNs reduce access costs for mobile users (those who have a limited data account). By delivering the data faster, site connection charges can be reduced. Finally, many (but not all) CDN services are offered on a flexible, pay-as-you-go basis. Customers need not contract for fixed services and payments; they pay only for what they use, when they use it. Some of the leading CDN vendors include Amazon CloudFront, Akamai, CloudFlare CDN, and MaxCDN.

Using Web Services Internally

The final way that organizations can use cloud technology is to build internal information systems using Web services. Strictly speaking, this is not using the cloud because it does not provide elasticity or the advantages of pooled resources. It does advantageously use cloud standards, however, so we include it here.

Figure 14 shows a Web services inventory application at a hypothetical online bicycle part retailer named Best Bikes. In this example, Best Bikes is running its own servers on its own infrastructure. To do so, Best Bikes sets up a private internet within the company, an internet that is generally not reachable from outside the company. Best Bikes writes the applications for processing inventory using Web services standards, applications publish a WSDL, the Web services are accessed by other applications within the company using SOAP, and data are delivered using JSON. Application users access the inventory Web services using JavaScript that is sent down to the users' browsers. All of these will be discussed later in this chapter in Q5.

Users of the inventory Web services include Sales, Shipping, Customer Service, Accounting, and other departments. Internal applications can use the inventory Web services like building blocks. They can use the services that they need—and no more. Because the Web services are

FIGURE 13
Benefits of Content Delivery Networks

Benefits of Content Delivery Networks

- Decreased, even guaranteed, loadtime
- Reduced load on origin server
- Increased reliability
- Protection from DoS attacks
- Reduced delivery costs for mobile users
- Pay-as-you-go

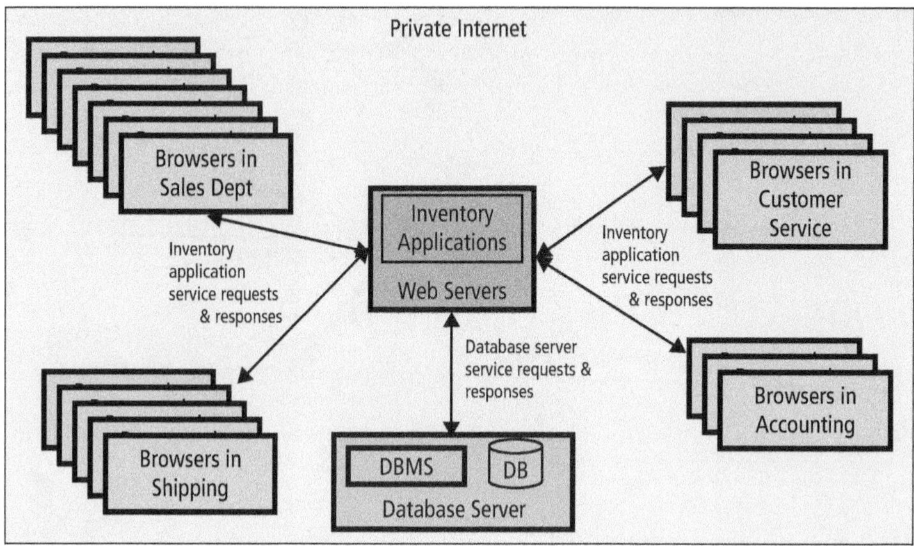

FIGURE 14
Web Services Principles Applied to Inventory Applications

encapsulated, the inventory system can be altered without affecting other applications. In this way, systems development is more flexible, and it will be faster and hence less costly.

As stated, however, this is not a cloud. In this example, Best Bikes has a fixed number of servers; no attempt is made to make them elastic. Also, the servers are dedicated to inventory. During idle periods, they are not dynamically reused for other purposes. Some organizations remove this limit by creating a private cloud, as discussed in Q7.

Q3 What Network Technology Supports the Cloud?

A computer **network** is a collection of computers that communicate with one another over transmission lines or wirelessly. As shown in Figure 15, the four basic types of networks are personal area networks, local area networks, wide area networks, and internets.

A **personal area network (PAN)** connects devices located around a *single person*. Most PAN devices connect wirelessly to other devices located within 10 meters. A **local area network (LAN)** connects computers that reside in a single geographic location on the premises of the company that operates the LAN. The number of connected computers can range from two to several hundred. The distinguishing characteristic of a LAN is *a single location.* A **wide area network (WAN)** connects computers at different geographic locations. The computers in two separated company sites must be connected using a WAN. To illustrate, a smartwatch or fitness tracker will create a PAN by connecting to a student's smartphone. The computers for a college of business located on a single campus can be connected via a LAN. The computers for a college of business located on multiple campuses must be connected via a WAN.

Type	Characteristic
Personal area network (PAN)	Devices connected around a single person
Local area network (LAN)	Computers connected at a single physical site
Wide area network (WAN)	Computers connected between two or more separated sites
The Internet and internets	Networks of networks

FIGURE 15
Basic Network Types

The single-versus multiple-site distinction between LANs and WANs is important. With a LAN, an organization can place communications lines wherever it wants because all lines reside on its premises. The same is not true for a WAN. A company with offices in Chicago and Atlanta cannot run a wire down the freeway to connect computers in the two cities. Instead, the company contracts with a communications vendor licensed by the government and that already has lines or has the authority to run new lines between the two cities.

An **internet** is a network of networks. Internets connect LANs, WANs, and other internets. The most famous internet is "**the Internet**" (with an uppercase letter *I*), the collection of networks you use when you send email or access a Web site. In addition to the Internet, private networks of networks, called *internets*, also exist. A private internet used exclusively within an organization is sometimes called an **intranet**.

The networks that make up an internet use a large variety of communication methods and conventions, and data must flow seamlessly across them. To provide seamless flow, an elaborate scheme called a *layered protocol* is used. The details of protocols are beyond the scope of this text. Just understand that a **protocol** is a set of rules and data structures for organizing communication. Computers need to use protocols so they can exchange data. People use similar protocols to communicate. People, for example, follow a conversational protocol that says when one person talks, the other person listens. They switch back and forth until they are done communicating. Without a protocol for conversations, people would continually talk over each other and nothing would be communicated.

There are many different protocols; some are used for PANs, some are used for LANs, some are used for WANs, some are used for internets and the Internet, and some are used for all of these. We will identify several common protocols in this chapter.

What Are the Components of a LAN?

See what a typical workday would look like for someone who manages networks in the Career Guide given later in the chapter.

As stated, a LAN is a group of computers connected together on a single site. Usually the computers are located within a half-mile or so of each other. The key distinction, however, is that all of the computers are located on property controlled by the organization that operates the LAN. This means that the organization can run cables wherever needed to connect the computers.

Figure 16 shows a LAN typical of those in a **small office or home office (SOHO)**. Typically, such LANs have fewer than a dozen or so computers and printers. Many businesses, of course, operate LANs much larger than this one. The principles are the same for a larger LAN, but the additional complexity is beyond the scope of this text.

The computers and printers in Figure 16 communicate via a mixture of wired and wireless connections. Some devices use wired connections, and others use wireless connections. The devices and protocols used differ for wired and wireless connectivity.

The Institute for Electrical and Electronics Engineers (IEEE, pronounced "I triple E") sponsors committees that create and publish protocol and other standards. The committee that addresses LAN standards is called the *IEEE 802 Committee*. Thus, IEEE LAN protocols always start with the numbers 802.

The **IEEE 802.3 protocol** is used for wired LAN connections. This protocol standard, also called **Ethernet**, specifies hardware characteristics, such as which wire carries which signals. It also describes how messages are to be packaged and processed for wired transmission over the LAN.

Most personal computers today support what is called **10/100/1000 Ethernet**. These products conform to the 802.3 specification and allow for transmission at a rate of 10, 100, or 1,000 Mbps (megabits per second). Switches detect the speed a given device can handle and communicate with it at that speed. If you check computer listings at Dell, Lenovo, and other manufacturers, you will see PCs advertised as having 10/100/1000 Ethernet. Today, speeds of up to 1 Gbps are possible on wired LANs.

By the way, the abbreviations used for communications speeds differ from those used for computer memory. For communications equipment, *K* stands for 1,000, not 1,024 as it does for

ETHICS GUIDE

CLOUDY PROFIT?

Alliance Partners (a fictitious name) is a data broker. Such companies acquire and buy consumer and other data from retailers, other data brokers, governmental agencies, and public sources and aggregate it into data profiles of individuals. Alliance specializes in acquiring and analyzing market, buyer, and seller data for real estate agents. Alliance sells an individual profile to qualified real estate agents for $100 to $1,500, depending on the amount of data and type of analysis requested.

Alliance is owned by three partners who started the business in 1999. They endured tough times during the dot-com collapse at the turn of the century but crawled out of that hole and were doing well until they encountered severe revenue shortfalls in the 2008 real estate collapse. In late 2008, in order to reduce operational costs to survive the downturn, Alliance transitioned its data storage and processing from its own Web farm to the cloud. The elastic flexibility of the cloud enables Alliance to improve the speed and quality of its data services at a fraction of prior costs. Furthermore, using the cloud enabled it to reduce the in-house hardware support staff by 65 percent.

The partners meet twice a year to review their financial performance, evaluate strategy, and plan for both the next six months and the longer term. In 2008, in the midst of their revenue shortfalls, they met in a small suite in the local Hamilton Inn, ate stale doughnuts, and drank watery orange juice. This year, they've rented a facility in the British Virgin Islands in the Caribbean. The following conversation occurred between two of the partners at the onset of this year's meeting:

"Bart, what are we doing here?" Shelly, the partner in charge of sales and marketing, is challenging Bart Johnson, Alliance's managing partner.

Source: Eunikas/Fotolia

"What do you mean, Shelly? Don't you like it here?"

"I *love* it here. So does my husband. But I also know we're paying $15,000 a night to rent this island!" Shelly rubs sunscreen on her hands as she talks.

"Well, we don't have the entire island." Bart sounds defensive.

"No, I guess not," she says. "They have to let some of the staff stay here. We're the only paying customers ... the only nonlocals.

"But," Shelly continues, "that's not my point. My point is, how can we afford this level of expense? We'll pay nearly $200,000 for this meeting alone. Where are we meeting next? Some five-star resort on the moon?"

"Look, Shelly, as you're about to hear, our gross margin last year was 74 percent. We're a money machine! We're swimming in profit! We can't spend money fast enough. One of the items on our agenda is whether we want to issue a $1 million, a $3 million, or a $5 million partners' distribution."

"No!" Shelly sounds stunned.

"Yup. Using the cloud, we've reduced our operational expense from 62 percent of our revenue to 9 percent. I'm plowing money back into R&D as fast as I can, but there's only so much that Jacob and his crew can absorb. Meanwhile, order the lobster and wait until you taste tonight's wines."

"That's disgusting."

"OK," Bart says. "Don't drink the wine. You want your distribution?"

"No; I mean yes, but this is crazy. It can't last."

"Probably not. But it's what we've got right now."

DISCUSSION QUESTIONS

When answering the following questions, assume that Alliance has done nothing illegal, including paying all federal, state, and local taxes on a timely basis.

1. From the perspective of Kant's categorical imperative, are Alliance's partners' meeting expenses and intended partner distribution unethical?
2. From the utilitarian perspective, are Alliance's partners' meeting expenses and intended partner distribution unethical?
3. Milton Friedman, world-renowned economist at the University of Chicago, stated that corporate executives have a responsibility to make as much money as possible as long as they don't violate rules embodied in law and in ethical custom.[7]
   - **a.** Do you agree with his statement? Why or why not?
   - **b.** Friedman defined *ethical custom* narrowly to mean no *fraud* or *deception*. Using his definition, has Alliance acted ethically?
   - **c.** Define, using your own words, *ethical custom*.
   - **d.** Using your definition of *ethical custom*, has Alliance acted ethically?
4. Do you find any of the following excessive? Explain your answers:
   - **a.** Spending nearly $200,000 on a five-day partners' meeting for three partners and their spouses?
   - **b.** Earning a 74 percent gross profit?
   - **c.** Paying a semiannual distribution of $1M, $3M, or $5M? If so, which level is excessive to you?
5. Describe the primary driver in Alliance's current profitability.
6. From the data presented, what else might Alliance have done with its excess profits?
7. Do you think profitable companies, especially very profitable companies, have an ethical obligation to:
   - **a.** Contribute to charity?
   - **b.** Lower prices when it is possible to do so and continue to earn a reasonable profit?
   - **c.** Contribute to environmental causes?
   - **d.** When possible, pay large bonuses to all employees, not just senior management?
8. To most students, someone who earns $500,000 a year in income is rich. To someone who makes $500,000 a year, partners who pay themselves $1M to $5M every 6 months are rich. To someone making $2M to $10M a year, billionaires are rich. What do you think classifies someone as rich?
9. Do you think rich people have an ethical obligation to:
   - **a.** Contribute to charity?
   - **b.** Contribute to environmental causes?
   - **c.** Forego governmental benefits to which they are entitled, for example, not take Social Security that they don't need?

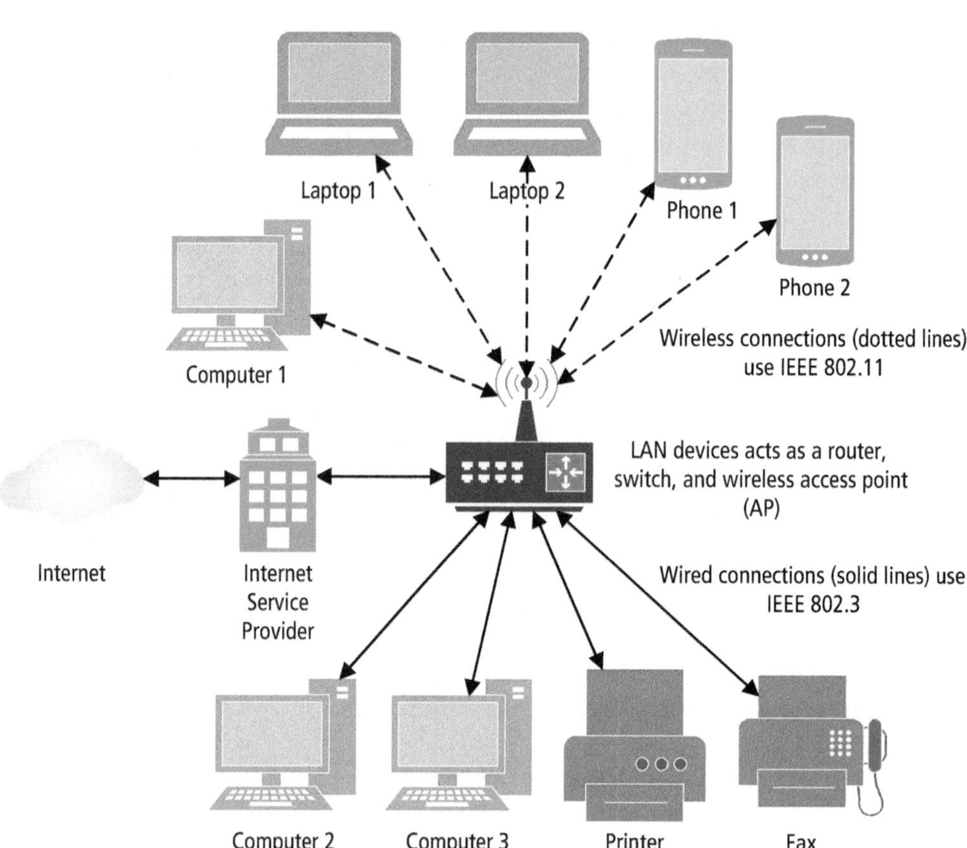

FIGURE 16
Typical Small Office/Home Office (SOHO) LAN

memory. Similarly, *M* stands for 1,000,000, not 1,024 * 1,024; *G* stands for 1,000,000,000, not 1,024 * 1,024 * 1,024. Thus, 100 Mbps is 100,000,000 bits per second. Also, communications speeds are expressed in *bits*, whereas memory sizes are expressed in *bytes*. These are different units of measurement. One byte consists of eight bits. This means a 1 MB file would consist of 8,388,608 bits. If you sent a 1 MB file over a 1 Mbps connection, it would take more than 8 seconds to send because your connection speed is measured in bits per second, not bytes per second.

Wireless LAN connections use the **IEEE 802.11 protocol**. Several versions of 802.11 exist, and as of 2016, the most current one is IEEE 802.11ac. The differences among these versions are beyond the scope of this discussion. Just note that the current standard, 802.11ac, allows speeds of up to 1.3 Gbps, though few users have an Internet connection fast enough to take full advantage of that speed.

Bluetooth is another common wireless protocol used to make PAN connections. It is designed for transmitting data over short distances, replacing cables. Devices, such as wireless mice, keyboards, printers, and headphones, use Bluetooth to connect to desktop computers. Other devices like smartwatches and fitness trackers can use Bluetooth to connect to smartphones and send data over the Internet. More and more devices like clothing, automobiles, and sports equipment are becoming Bluetooth enabled.

Connecting Your LAN to the Internet

Although you may not have realized it, when you connect your SOHO LAN, phone, iPad, or Kindle to the Internet, you are connecting to a WAN. You must do so because you are connecting to computers that are not physically located on your premises. You cannot start running wires down the street to plug in somewhere.

When you connect to the Internet, you are actually connecting to an **Internet service provider (ISP)**. An ISP has three important functions. First, it provides you with a legitimate Internet address. Second, it serves as your gateway to the Internet. The ISP receives the communications from your computer and passes them on to the Internet, and it receives communications from the Internet and passes them on to you. Finally, ISPs pay for the Internet. They collect money from their customers and pay access fees and other charges on your behalf.

Figure 17 shows the three common alternatives for connecting to the Internet. Notice that we are discussing how your computer connects to the Internet via a WAN; we are not discussing the structure of the WAN itself. WAN architectures and their protocols are beyond the scope of this text. Search the Web for "leased lines" or "PSDN" if you want to learn more about WAN architectures.

SOHO LANs (such as that in Figure 16) and individual home and office computers are commonly connected to an ISP in one of three ways: a special telephone line called a DSL line, a cable TV line, or a wireless-phone-like connection.

Digital Subscriber Line (DSL)

A **digital subscriber line (DSL)** operates on the same lines as voice telephones, but it operates so it does not interfere with voice telephone service. Because DSL signals do not interfere with telephone signals, DSL data transmission and telephone conversations can occur simultaneously. A device at the telephone company separates the phone signals from the computer signals and sends the latter signal to the ISP. Digital subscriber lines use their own protocols for data transmission.

Cable Line

A cable line is the second type of WAN connection. **Cable lines** provide high-speed data transmission using cable television lines. The cable company installs a fast, high-capacity optical fiber cable to a distribution center in each neighborhood it serves. At the distribution center, the optical fiber cable connects to regular cable-television cables that run to subscribers' homes or businesses. Cable signals do not interfere with TV signals.

FIGURE 17
Summary of LAN Networks

Type	Topology	Transmission Line	Transmission Speed	Equipment Used	Protocol Commonly Used	Remarks
Local area network	Local area network	UTP or optical fiber	Common: 10/100/1000 Mbps Possible: 1 Gbps	Switch NIC UTP or optical	IEEE 802.3 (Ethernet)	Switches connect devices, multiple switches on all but small LANs.
	Local area network with wireless	UTP or optical for nonwireless connections	Up to 600 Mbps	Wireless access point Wireless NIC	IEEE 802.11n, (802.11ac not yet common)	Access point transforms wired LAN (802.3) to wireless LAN (802.11).
Connections to the Internet	DSL modem to ISP	DSL telephone	Personal: Upstream to 1 Mbps, downstream to 40 Mbps (max 10 likely in most areas)	DSL modem DSL-capable telephone line	DSL	Can have computer and phone use simultaneously. Always connected.
	Cable modem to ISP	Cable TV lines to optical cable	Upstream to 1 Mbps Downstream 300 Kbps to 10 Mbps	Cable modem Cable TV cable	Cable	Capacity is shared with other sites; performance varies depending on others' use.
	WAN wireless	Wireless connection to WAN	500 Kbps to 1.7 Mbps	Wireless WAN modem	One of several wireless standards	Sophisticated protocols enables several devices to use the same wireless frequency.

Because as many as 500 user sites can share these facilities, performance varies depending on how many other users are sending and receiving data. At the maximum, users can download data up to 50 Mbps and can upload data at 512 Kbps. Typically, performance is much lower than this. In most cases, the download speed of cable lines and DSL lines is about the same. Cable lines use their own protocols.

WAN Wireless Connection

A third way you can connect your computer, mobile device, or other communicating device is via a **WAN wireless** connection. Amazon.com's Kindle, for example, uses a Sprint wireless network to provide wireless data connections. The iPhone uses a LAN-based wireless network if one is available and a WAN wireless network if not. The LAN-based network is preferred because performance is considerably higher. As of 2015, WAN wireless provides average performance of 1.0 Mbps with peaks of up to 3.0 Mbps, as opposed to the typical 50 Mbps for LAN wireless.

Q4 How Does the Internet Work?

This section will give you the basic understanding of how the Internet works and enable you to be an effective consumer of cloud services. The cloud resides in the Internet. So, in order to learn how the cloud works, you need a basic understanding of how the Internet works. With that background, you will learn how it is possible for a cloud vendor to provide dramatic elasticity to support the workload shown in Figure 6.

The Internet and the U.S. Postal System

The technology that underlies the Internet and the additional technology that enables the cloud to work are complicated. To explain how the Internet works, we'll use a simplified example, shown in Figure 18, comparing the movement of packages in the U.S. postal system to the movement of packets through the Internet. This is a highly simplified, but useful, example for explaining the basics of how the Internet works. We will stay at a high level and help you learn overarching concepts and basic definitions.

The Internet works much like the U.S. postal system in that both systems transport things from one location to another. The Internet transports email, while the U.S. postal system sends paper mail. Comparing the Internet to the U.S. postal system allows you to relate new Internet terms to a system with which you're already familiar (the U.S. postal system).

FIGURE 18
Comparison of the Postal System and the Internet

Steps to Send Package	Postal System	Internet Equivalent
1. Assemble package	Package	Packet
2. Put name on package	Person's name (e.g., BigBank Inc. or Jane Smith)	Domain name (e.g., www.BigBank.com)
3. Look up address	Phone book	DNS
4. Put address on package	Mailing address (e.g., 123 Park Ave, New York, NY, 10172)	IP address (e.g., 10.84.8.154)
5. Put registered mail sticker on package	Registered Mail	TCP
6. Ship package	Airlines (e.g., Delta Air Lines, Inc.) Airports (e.g., Seattle-Tacoma International Airport)	Carriers (e.g., Sprint Corp.) Routers

Step 1: Assemble Package (Packets)

Suppose you are sitting in your apartment in Seattle and you want to send a box of cookies to your friend, Jane Smith, working at BigBank Inc. in New York City. The Internet equivalent of this is sending a **packet**, or a formatted message that passes through networks, to BigBank's Web server requesting a copy of its main Web page. Packets wind their way through the Internet much the same way packages wind their way through the U.S. postal system. The cookies are created and boxed up by you, a person. The contents of the packet, on the other hand, are created by applications like Google Chrome, Firefox, Safari, Skype, or FileZilla.

Step 2: Put Name on Package (Domain Names)

The next step in sending a package through the U.S. postal system is to put a name on the package. On your package of cookies you might write "BigBank Inc." or "Jane Smith." On the packet you put a **domain name**, or a worldwide-unique name affiliated with a public IP address (discussed in Step 3). Examples of domain names include www.bigbank.com, www.microsoft.com, or www.university.edu.

It is not necessary for packets to contain a domain name. In fact, many don't. Just like with the U.S. postal system, the address is more important than the recipient name.

Step 3: Look Up Address (IP Address)

Before you can send your box of cookies to your friend you need to put a shipping address on the package (e.g., 123 Park Ave, New York, NY, 10172). Just like regular postal mail, every location on the Internet needs a unique address. For reasons beyond this discussion, an Internet address is called an **IP address**, which is a number that identifies a particular device. **Public IP addresses** identify a particular device on the public Internet. In order to get on the Internet, every device must have access to a public IP address.

IP Addresses

IP addresses have two formats. The most common form, called **IPv4**, has a four-decimal dotted notation such as 137.190.8.10. Unfortunately, there are only 4 billion IPv4 addresses that can be used by all 7 billion people on the earth. As a result, a second format of IP addresses called **IPv6** is being adopted—slowly. It has a longer format (e.g., 0:0:0:0:0:ffff:89be:80a), which accommodates 340 undecillion addresses. That's plenty of IP addresses—for now. In your browser, if you enter an IPv4 address like *http://137.190.8.10* or an IPv6 address like 0:0:0:0:0:ffff:89be:80a, your browser will connect with the device on the public Internet that has been assigned to this address.

DNS

Most people don't remember addresses. It's easier to remember a name like Jane Smith or BigBank Inc. and look up the mailing address in a phone book (or an Internet-based phone book). The Internet works the same way. Nobody wants to type IP addresses like *http://165.193.140.14* to find a particular site. It is easier to enter names like *www.pandora.com* or *www.woot.com* or *www.pearsonhighered.com*.

Because public IP addresses must be unique worldwide, their assignment is controlled by a public agency known as **ICANN (Internet Corporation for Assigned Names and Numbers)**. ICANN administers a directory naming system, like a phone book, called **Domain Name System (DNS)** that assigns domain names to IP addresses. When an organization or individual wants to register a domain name, it goes to a company that applies to an ICANN-approved agency to do so. GoDaddy (*www.godaddy.com*) is an example of such a company (Figure 19).

GoDaddy, or a similar agency, will first determine if the desired name is unique worldwide. If so, then it will apply to register that name to the applicant. Once the registration is completed, the

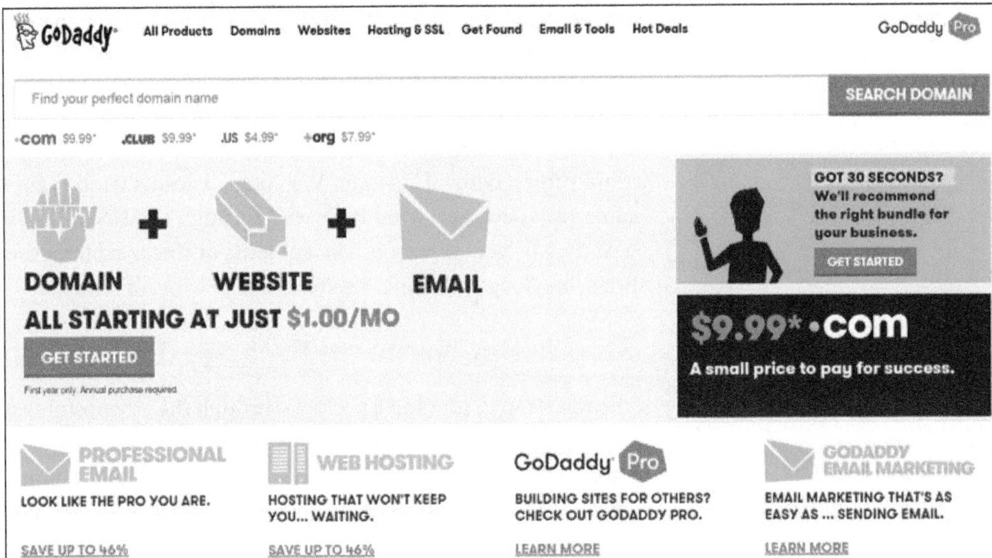

FIGURE 19
GoDaddy Screenshot
Source: © 2015 GoDaddy Operating Company, LLC. All rights reserved.

applicant can affiliate a public IP address with the domain name, much like your name is associated with a single postal address. From that point onward, traffic for the new domain name will be routed to the affiliated IP address.

In 2014, the U.S. Department of Commerce announced it was giving up oversight over ICANN. Critics worry that less-free countries will now try to force ICANN to disallow domain names for dissident groups, thereby kicking them off the Internet. At this point, it's still unclear how ICANN will be governed.

Step 4: Put Address on Package (IP Address on Packet)

Every time you enter a domain name (e.g., *www.washington.edu*) into your Web browser, your computer sends a lookup (resolution) request to a DNS server asking it for the IP address that corresponds with that domain name. The DNS server responds with the IP address that your operating system then puts on packets to be sent to that site.

Note two important points: First, several (or many) domain names can point to the same IP address. This is the real-world equivalent of multiple people (i.e., a family) sharing the same postal mailing address. Second, the affiliation of domain names with IP addresses is dynamic. The owner of the domain name can change the affiliated IP addresses at its discretion, much like you can change your affiliation with a specific mailing address if you decide to move.

Before we leave addressing, you need to know one more term. A **URL (Uniform Resource Locator)** is an address on the Internet. Commonly, it consists of a protocol (such as *http://* or *ftp://*) followed by a domain name or public IP address. A URL is actually quite a bit more complicated than this description, but that detailed knowledge is beyond the scope of this text, so we'll hurry along. The preferred pronunciation of *URL* is to say the letters *U, R, L*.

Step 5: Put Registered Mail Sticker on Package (TCP)

After your package is addressed, you need to guarantee that it gets delivered using registered mail. Registered mail guarantees delivery by requiring the recipient to sign a receipt that is then sent back to the sender. The same is true of packets. The **Transmission Control Protocol (TCP)** is a core Internet protocol that guarantees the reliable delivery of packets. TCP is the equivalent of registered mail in the postal system. TCP information is added to packets just like registered mail stickers are added to postal packages. They guarantee delivery by requiring the receiver to send back an acknowledgement that the packet was received. If no acknowledgement is received, it will keep trying to sending the packet a certain number of times before it gives up.

Step 6: Ship Package (Packets Transported by Carriers)

Figure 20 illustrates a simplified path that your packet may take through the Internet. To begin, note that this example is an internet because it is a network of networks. It consists of two LANs (yours and the bank's) and four networks. (In truth, the real Internet consists of tens of thousands of networks, but to conserve paper, we don't show all of them.) A **hop** is the movement from one network to another. This term is frequently used by cloud vendors when they discuss provisioning servers to minimize the number of hops. As drawn, in Figure 20, the shortest path from you to the bank's LAN consists of four hops. Your box of cookies will take a similar number of hops between postal facilities as it moves across the country.

At this point, we should mention that most hosts connected to a LAN share a single public IP address, much like a family living in a house shares a single postal address. Each internal host receives a **private IP address** that identifies a particular device on a private network. Private IP addresses are used for traffic going to other devices on the LAN. But all traffic leaving the LAN uses the single shared public IP address to cross the Internet. All private IP addresses are managed by a LAN device like the one shown in Figure 16.

Carriers

In the U.S. postal system, your package weaves its way toward its destination through multiple airports. It does so aboard airplanes owned by airlines like Delta Air Lines, Southwest Airlines, and United Airlines. Similarly, as your packet moves across the Internet, it passes through **routers** (airports), which are devices that connect different networks together. Routers, and many of the networks they're connected to, are owned by large telecommunication providers (airlines) known as **carriers**. Some of these large carriers include Sprint, AT&T, Verizon Business, and XO Communications. These large carriers exchange Internet traffic freely at physical locations called **Internet exchange points (IXP)**. Large carriers exchange traffic without charging each other access fees via **peering** agreements. Carriers make revenue by collecting subscription fees from end users but not from peers.

The problem with peering is that some people use more bandwidth than others. Netflix, for example, accounts for more than 30 percent of all Internet traffic in North America between 9 PM and 12 AM.[8] Carriers argue that they should be able to charge varying rates based on content, application, or the user requesting the data.

FIGURE 20
Using the Internet to Request a Web Page

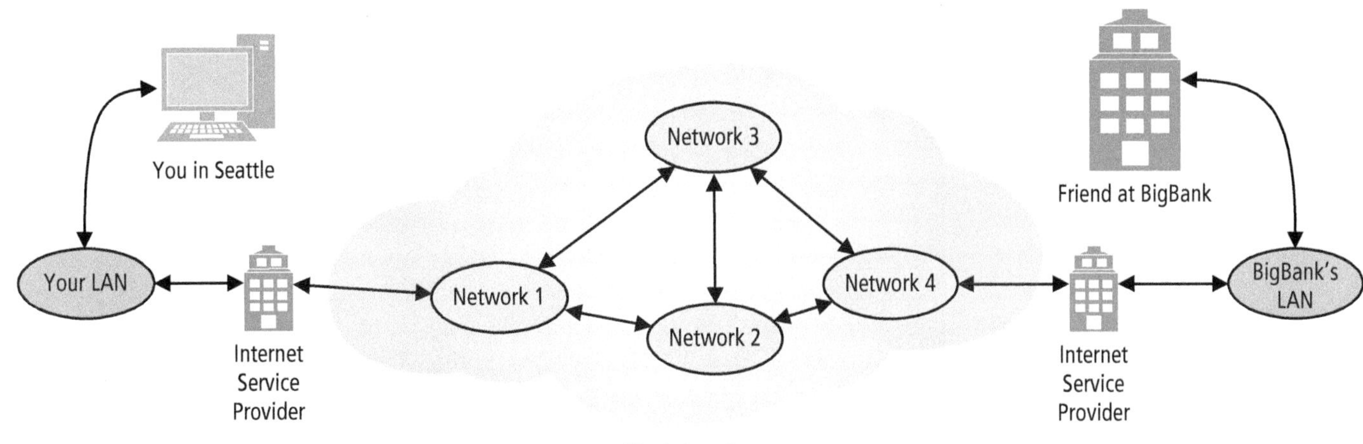

Net Neutrality

Netflix, eBay, Yahoo!, and Amazon.com say that allowing carriers to charge these varying rates could hurt consumers and innovation. They believe in the **net neutrality** principle, where all data is treated equally. They argue that carriers should not be allowed to decide which sites load quickly, which apps are allowed on a network, and which content is acceptable.

In 2015, the Federal Communications Commission (FCC) approved new net neutrality regulations that ensure ISPs cannot discriminate between different types of Internet traffic. This means all consumers have access to content on an equal basis. This ruling in many ways renders the Internet a utility like water or electricity that would be governed by comparable regulations. Several large carriers have begun fighting these new regulations in court.

Q5 How Do Web Servers Support the Cloud?

At this point, you know basic networking terms and have a high-level view of how the Internet works. To understand the value of the cloud as well as how it works and how your organization can use it, you need to know a bit about the processing that occurs on a Web server. For this discussion, we will use the example of a Web storefront, which is a server on the Web from which you can buy products.

Suppose you want to buy an item from zulily, a private buyer's site that sells clothing. To do so, you go to *www.zulily.com* and navigate to the product(s) you want to buy (see Figure 21). When you find something you want, you add it to your shopping cart and keep shopping. At some point, you check out by supplying credit card data. But what happens when your order data arrives at the server?

FIGURE 21

Sample of Commerce Server Pages; Product Offer Pages

Source: Courtesy of Zulily Inc. Used by permission.

When you enter *www.zulily.com* in your browser, the browser sends a request that travels over the Internet to a computer in the server tier at the zulily site. In response to your request, a server-tier computer sends back a **Web page**, which is a document coded in, usually, html probably includes CSS, JavaScript, and other data).

Three-Tier Architecture

Almost all Web applications use the **three-tier architecture**, which is a design of user computers and servers that consists of three categories, or tiers, as shown in Figure 22. The **user tier** consists of computers, phones, and other mobile devices that have browsers that request and process Web pages. The **server tier** consists of computers that run Web servers and process application programs. The **database tier** consists of computers that run a DBMS that processes requests to retrieve and store data. Figure 22 shows only one computer at the database tier. Some sites have multicomputer database tiers as well.

Web servers are programs that run on a server-tier computer and manage traffic by sending and receiving Web pages to and from clients. A **commerce server** is an application program that runs on a server-tier computer. Typical commerce server functions are to obtain product data from a database, manage the items in a shopping cart, and coordinate the checkout process. When a request comes to the server, the Web server examines it and sends it to the proper program for processing. Thus, the Web server passes e-commerce traffic to the commerce server. It passes requests for other applications to those applications. In Figure 22, the server-tier computers are running a Web server program, a commerce server application, and other applications having an unspecified purpose.

Watch the Three Tiers in Action!

Suppose the user of the Web page in Figure 21 clicks on shoes and then selects a particular shoe, say, the Darkish Gray Dorine Mary Jane shoe. When the user clicks on that shoe, the commerce server requests that shoe's data from the DBMS, which reads it from the database and then returns the data (including pictures) to the commerce server. That server then formats the Web page with the data and sends the html version of that page to the user's computer. The result is the page shown in Figure 23.

FIGURE 22
Three-Tier Architecture

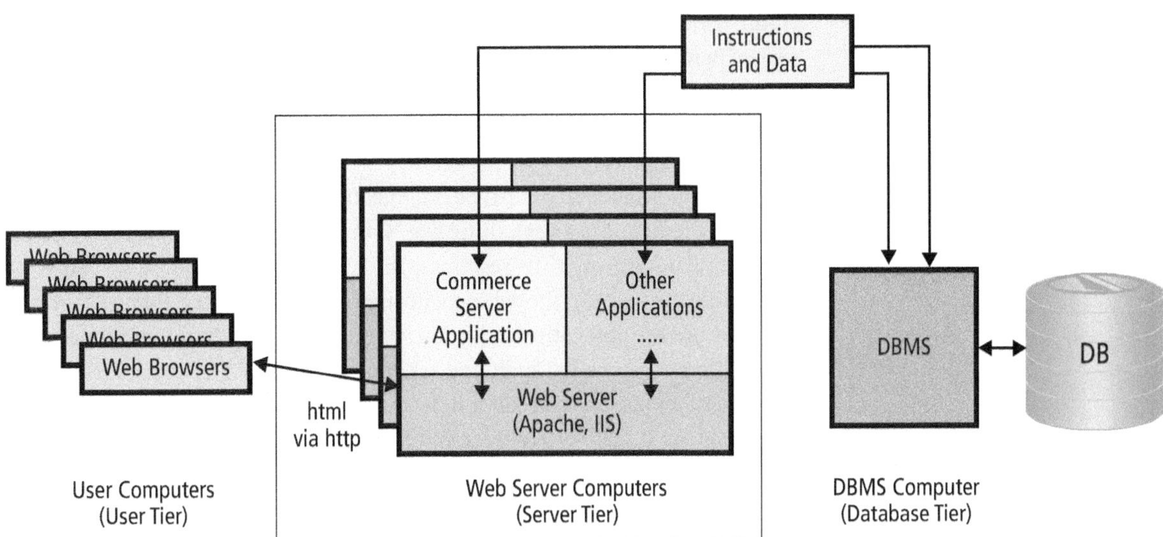

FIGURE 23
Product Page
Source: Courtesy of Zulily Inc. Used by permission

Service-Oriented Architecture (SOA)

The cloud would be impossible without a design philosophy called the **service-oriented architecture (SOA)**. According to this philosophy, all interactions among computing devices are defined as services in a formal, standardized way. This philosophy enables all the pieces of the cloud to fit together, as you will see. However, understanding SOA (pronounced SO-ah) in depth requires you to learn more computer science than you need as a business professional. So, the best way for you to understand SOA is via a business analogy.

A SOA Analogy

Figure 24 shows an arrangement of departments at a hypothetical online bicycle part retailer named Best Bikes. The Sales Department receives order requests and follows a process to have them approved for shipping. On request, the Credit Department verifies customer credit as needed to approve orders, and the Inventory Department verifies the availability of the inventory needed to fulfill an order.

In an informal, non-SOA-type organization, one salesperson would contact someone he or she knows in Credit and ask something like "Can you approve an allocation of $10,000 of credit to the ABC Bicycle Company?" In response, the credit person might say, "Sure," and the salesperson might note the name of the person who approved the amount. Some days, he or she might remember to record the date; other days, not so. Another salesperson might do something else, say, contact a different person in Credit and ask something like, "I need $5,000 in credit for Order 12345," and that other person in Credit might say, "I don't know, send the order over, and if I can, I'll write 'Approved' on it." Other irregular, but similar, interactions could occur between the Sales and the Inventory departments.

Such operations are definitely *not* service-oriented. People are asking for credit verification in different ways and receiving responses in different ways. The process for approving an order varies

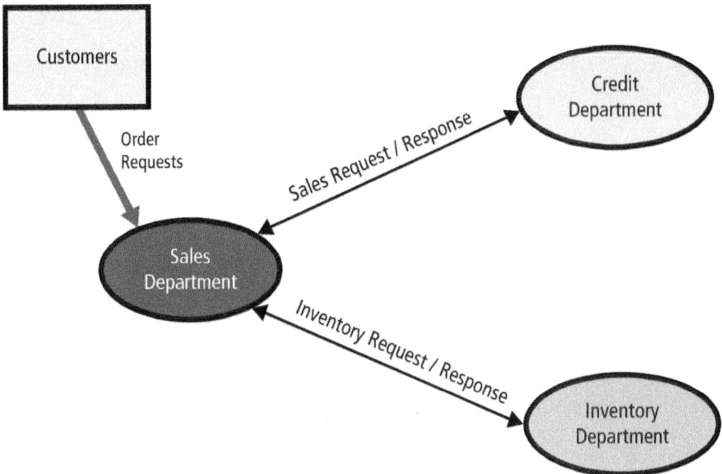

FIGURE 24
Approval Request Interactions Among Three Departments

from salesperson to salesperson, and possibly from day to day with the same salesperson. The records of approvals are inconsistent. Such an organization will have varying levels of process quality and inconsistent results, and should the company decide to open a facility in another city, these operations cannot be readily duplicated, nor should they be.

Using SOA principles, each department would formally define the services it provides. Examples are:

For the Credit Department:

- CheckCustomerCredit
- ApproveCustomerCredit

For the Inventory Department:

- VerifyInventoryAmount
- AllocateInventory
- ReleaseAllocatedInventory

Further, for each service, each department would formally state the data it expects to receive with the request and the data it promises to return in response. Every interaction is done exactly the same way. There is no personal contact between certain people in the departments; no salesperson need know who works in Credit or Inventory. Instead, requests are emailed to a generic email address in Credit or Inventory, and those departments decide who will process the request and how it will be processed. No department has or need have any knowledge of who works in another department nor how the department accomplishes its work. Each department is free to change personnel task assignments and to change the way it performs its services, and no other department needs to know that a change occurred. In SOA terms, we would say the work of the department is **encapsulated** in the department.

With this organization, if Best Bikes wants to add another Inventory Department in another city, it can do so and no salesperson need change the way he or she sets up, submits, or receives responses to requests. Sales continues to send a VerifyInventoryAmount service request, formatted in the standard way, to the same email address.

With multiple sites, the Inventory function would change the way it implements service requests to first identify which of the several Inventory Departments should process the request. Sales would not know, nor need to know, this happened. Best Bikes could dynamically create 1,000 Inventory Departments and the Sales Department need not change anything it does. Later, it could reduce those 1,000 Inventory Departments to three, and, again, sales need not make any change.

SOA for Three-Tier Architecture

From this discussion, you can see how SOA is used to enable cloud processing. The description and advantages and disadvantages of this analogy for SOA are the same for the cloud. Consider Figure 25, which shows the three-tier architecture with SOA drawn in. In this case, the commerce server application formally defines services that browsers can request, the data they must provide with the request, and the data that each will receive in response to the request. Sample services are:

- ObtainPartData
- ObtainPartImages
- ObtainPartQuantityOnHand
- OrderPart

And so forth. Again, each service also documents the data it expects and the data it will return.

Now, JavaScript (or another code language) is written to invoke these services correctly. That JavaScript is included as part of the Web pages the server sends to the browsers, and when users employ the browsers to purchase, the JavaScript behind the Web page invokes the services in the correct way.

The server tier can consist of three servers at 3 AM, 3,000 servers at 11 AM, 6,000 servers at 6 PM, and 100 servers at 10 PM. Furthermore, those servers can move around the world; at one time of day, they can be all located in the United States, and at another time of day, they can all be located in Europe, and so on. Nothing, absolutely nothing, in the browsers need change as these servers are adjusted.

To take advantage of the multiple Web servers, a load-balancing program receives requests and sends them to an available server. The load-balancing program keeps data about the speed and health of all its assigned Web servers and allocates work to maximize throughput.

In addition, on the back end, SOA services are defined between the Web server and the database server. Accordingly, the database server need do nothing as the number and location of Web servers is adjusted. And that's a two-way street. Nothing in the Web servers need be changed if the number and location of database servers is adjusted. However, load balancing for database servers is considerably more complicated.

Do not infer from this discussion that SOA services and the cloud are only used for three-tier processing. Such services and the cloud are used for multitudes of applications across the Internet. This three-tier application is just an example.

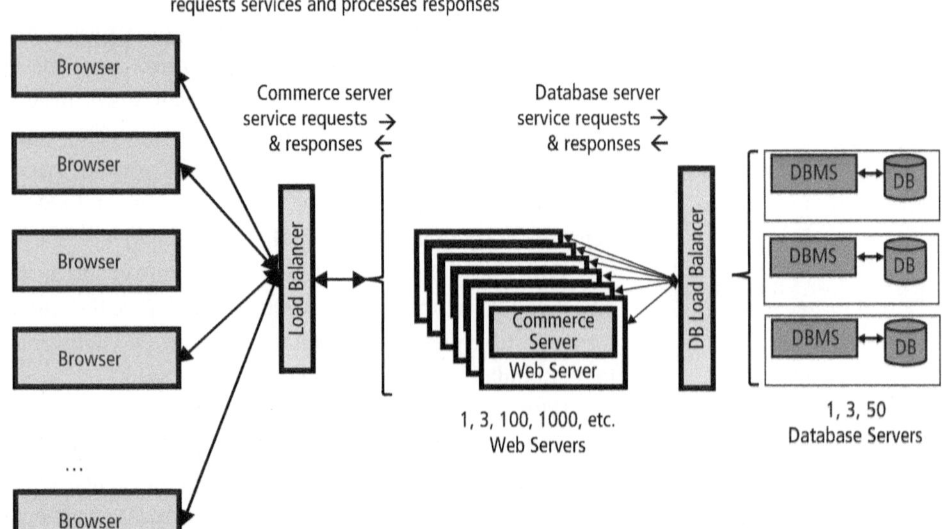

FIGURE 25
SOA Principles Applied to Three-Tier Architecture

From this discussion, you can understand how cloud elasticity is possible. However, for many organizations to use the cloud and to be able to mix and match Web services, they need to agree on standard ways of formatting and processing service requests and data. That leads us to cloud standards and protocols. Again, we discuss these at a very high level.

Internet Protocols

A protocol is a set of rules and data structures for organizing communication. Because the cloud's Web services use the Internet, the protocols that run the Internet also support cloud processing. We will start with them.

TCP/IP Protocol Architecture

The basic plumbing of the Internet is governed by protocols that are defined according to an arrangement called the **TCP/IP protocol architecture**. This architecture has five layers; one or more protocols are defined at each layer. Data communications and software vendors write computer programs that implement the rules of a particular protocol. (For protocols at the bottom layer, the physical layer, they build hardware devices that implement the protocol.)

Internet Protocols: http, https, smtp, and ftp

The only Internet protocols that you as a business professional are likely to encounter are those at the top, or the application layer of the TCP/IP architecture, shown in Figure 26. **Hypertext Transfer Protocol (http)** is the protocol used between browsers and Web servers. When you use a browser such as Chrome, Safari, or Firefox, you are using a program that implements the http protocol. At the other end there is a server that also processes http. Even though your browser and the server have never "met" before, they can communicate with one another because they both follow the rules of http. Similarly, in Figure 25, the browsers send and receive service requests to and from the commerce server using http.

There is a secure version of http called **https**. Whenever you see *https* in your browser's address bar, you have a secure transmission and you can safely send sensitive data like credit card numbers. When you are on the Internet, if you do not see *https*, then you should assume that all of your communication is open and could be published on the front page of your campus newspaper tomorrow morning. Hence, when you are using http, email, text messaging, chat, videoconferencing, or anything other than https, know that whatever you are typing or saying could be known by anyone else.

Two additional TCP/IP application-layer protocols are common. **smtp**, or **Simple Mail Transfer Protocol**, is used for email transmissions (along with other protocols). **ftp**, or **File Transfer Protocol**, is used to move files over the Internet. Google Drive and Microsoft OneDrive use ftp behind the scenes to transmit files to and from their cloud servers to your computer.

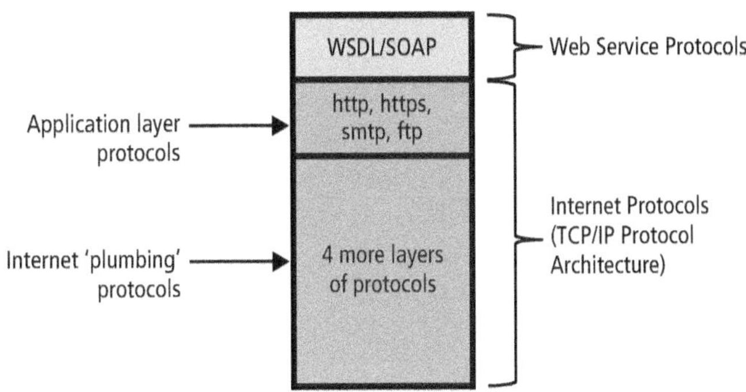

FIGURE 26
Protocols That Support Web Services

WSDL, SOAP, XML, and JSON

To wrap up the discussion, we will briefly consider four standards used extensively for Web services and the cloud. Those standards and their purpose are as follows:

WSDL (Web Services Description Language)	A standard for describing the services, inputs and outputs, and other data supported by a Web service. Documents coded according to this standard are machine readable and can be used by developer tools for creating programs to access the service.
SOAP (no longer an acronym)	A protocol for requesting Web services and for sending responses to Web service requests.
XML (eXtensible Markup Language)	A markup language used for transmitting documents. Contains much metadata that can be used to validate the format and completeness of the document, but includes considerable overhead (see Figure 27a).
JSON (JavaScript Object Notation)	A markup language used for transmitting documents. Contains little metadata and is preferred for transmitting volumes of data between servers and browsers. While the notation is the format of JavaScript objects, JSON documents can be processed by any language (see Figure 27b).

Service authors (computer programmers) create WSDL documents to describe the services they provide and the inputs and outputs required. These WSDL documents are seldom read by humans. Instead, developer tools like Microsoft Visual Studio read the WSDL to configure the programming environment for programmers who write code to access that service.

As shown in Figure 26, SOAP, which is not an acronym though it looks like one, is a protocol that sits on top of http and the lower-level Internet protocols. *Sits on top of* means that it uses http to send and receive SOAP messages. (SOAP can also use smtp.) Programs that use Web services issue SOAP messages to request services; the Web service uses SOAP messages to return responses to service requests.

Finally, XML and JSON are ways of marking up documents so that both the service requestor and the service provider know what data they're processing. Figure 27 shows a simple example of both. As you can see, XML documents contain as much metadata as they do application data. These metadata are used to ensure that the document is complete and properly formatted. XML is

```
<person>
    <firstName>Kelly</firstName>
    <lastName>Summers</lastName>
    <dob>12/28/1985</dob>
    <address>
        <streetAddress>309 Elm Avenue</streetAddress>
        <city>San Diego</city>
        <state>CA</state>
        <postalCode>98225</postalCode>
    </address>
    <phoneNumbers>
        <phoneNumber type="home">685 555-1234</phoneNumber>
        <phoneNumber type="cell">685 555-5678</phoneNumber>
    </phoneNumbers>
</person>
```

FIGURE 27a
Example XML Document

```
{
  "firstName": "Kelly",
  "lastName": "Summers",
  "dob": "12/28/1985",
  "address": {
    "streetAddress": "309 Elm Avenue",
    "city": "San Diego",
    "state": "CA",
    "postalCode": "98225"
  },
  "phoneNumber": [
    {
      "type": "home",
      "number": "685 555-1234"
    },
    {
      "type": "cell",
      "number": "685 555-5678"
    }
  ]
}
```


FIGURE 27b
Example JSON Document

used when relatively few messages are being transmitted and when ensuring a complete and correct document is crucial. Both WSDLs and SOAP messages are coded in XML.

As its name indicates, JSON uses the notation for JavaScript objects to format data. It has much less metadata and is preferred for the transmission of voluminous application data. Web servers use JSON as their primary way of sending application data to browsers.

With this technical background, you should no longer be skeptical that the benefits of the cloud are real. They are. However, this fact does not mean that every organization uses the cloud well. In the remainder of this chapter, we will describe generic ways that organizations can use the cloud, discuss how Falcon Security in particular can use the cloud, and, finally, discuss an exceedingly important topic: cloud security.

Q6 How Can Falcon Security Use the Cloud?

Falcon Security is an innovative startup company with a small IT department. As such, it is unlikely to have the resources necessary to develop a large server infrastructure. Instead, it is far more likely to take advantage of cloud services provided by cloud vendors.

SaaS Services at Falcon Security

Software as a service requires little investment in the hardware and software system components. The SaaS vendor administers and manages the cloud servers and makes the software available, usually as a thin client. Falcon will, however, need to transfer existing data, create new data, develop procedures, and train users.

Some of the SaaS products that Falcon could use are:

- Google Mail
- Google Drive
- Office 365
- Salesforce.com
- Microsoft CRM OnLine
- And many others

You already know what the first three SaaS offerings are. Salesforce.com and Microsoft's CRM OnLine are customer relationship management systems.

PaaS Services at Falcon Security

With PaaS, Falcon leases hardware and operating systems in the cloud from the cloud vendor. For example, it can lease EC2 (Elastic Cloud 2, a PaaS product offered by Amazon.com), and Amazon.com will preinstall either Linux or Windows Server on the cloud hardware. Given that basic capability, Falcon would then install its own software. For example, it could install its own, in-house developed applications, or it could install other applications licensed from a software vendor. It could also license a DBMS, say, SQL Server from Microsoft, and place it on an EC2 Windows Server instance. In the case of software licensed from others, Falcon must purchase licenses that permit replication because Amazon.com will replicate it when it increases servers.

Some cloud vendors include DBMS products in their PaaS services. Thus, Falcon could obtain Windows Servers with SQL Server already installed from the Microsoft Azure cloud offerings. That option is likely what Toshio was considering when he mentioned the $10 per TB per month.

DBMS are also included in other vendors' cloud offerings. As of May 2016, Amazon.com offers the following DBMS products with EC2:

Amazon Relational Database Service (RDS)	A relational database service supporting MySQL, Oracle, SQL Server, or PostgreSQL
Amazon DynamoDB	A fast and scalable NoSQL database service
Amazon ElastiCache	A very fast in-memory cache database service
Amazon Redshift	A petabyte-scale data warehouse

Finally, Falcon might use a CDN to distribute its content worldwide and to respond to leads generated from advertising as described in Q2.

IaaS Services at Falcon Security

As stated, IaaS provides basic hardware in the cloud. Some companies acquire servers this way and then load operating systems onto them. Doing so requires considerable technical expertise and management, and hence a company like Falcon is unlikely to do so.

Falcon might, however, obtain data storage services in the cloud. Amazon.com, for example, offers data storage with its S3 product. Using it, organizations can place data in the cloud and even have that data be made elastically available. Again, however, an organization like Falcon would more likely use SaaS and PaaS because of the added value they provide.

Q7 How Can Organizations Use Cloud Services Securely?

The Internet and cloud services based on Internet infrastructure provide powerful processing and storage services at a fraction of the cost of private data centers. However, the Internet is a jungle of threats to data and computing infrastructure. Some of the biggest threats to cloud services include insecure interfaces, data loss, and data leakage. How can organizations realize the benefits of cloud technology without succumbing to those threats?

The answer involves a combination of technologies that we will address, at a very high level, in this question. As you read, realize that no security story is ever over; attackers constantly strive to find ways around security safeguards, and occasionally they succeed. Thus, you can expect that cloud security will evolve beyond that described here throughout your career. We begin with a discussion of VPNs, a technology used to provide secure communication over the Internet.

Virtual Private Networks (VPNs)

A **virtual private network (VPN)** uses the Internet to create the appearance of private, secure connections. In the IT world, the term *virtual* means something that appears to exist but in fact does not. Here, a VPN uses the public Internet to create the appearance of a private connection on a secure network.

A Typical VPN

Figure 28 shows one way to create a VPN to connect a remote computer, perhaps used by an employee working at a hotel in Miami, to a LAN at a Chicago site. The remote user is the VPN client. That client first establishes a public connection to the Internet. The connection can be obtained by accessing a local ISP, as shown in Figure 28, or, in some cases, the hotel itself provides a direct Internet connection.

In either case, once the Internet connection is made, VPN software on the remote user's computer establishes a connection with the VPN server in Chicago. The VPN client and VPN server then have a secure connection. That connection, called a **tunnel**, is a virtual, private pathway over a public or shared network from the VPN client to the VPN server. Figure 29 illustrates the connection as it appears to the remote user.

To secure VPN communications over the public Internet, the VPN client software *encrypts*, or codes, messages so their contents are protected from snooping. Then the VPN client appends the Internet address of the VPN server to the message and sends that packet over the Internet to the VPN server. When the VPN server receives the message, it strips its address off the front of the message, *decrypts* the coded message, and sends the plain text message to the original address inside the LAN. In this way, secure private messages are delivered over the public Internet.

Using a Private Cloud

A **private cloud** is a cloud owned and operated by an organization for its own benefit. To create a *private* cloud, the organization creates a private internet and designs applications using Web services standards as shown in Figure 14. The organization then creates a farm of servers and manages those servers with elastic load balancing just as the cloud service vendors do. Because of the

FIGURE 28
Remote Access Using VPN; Actual Connections

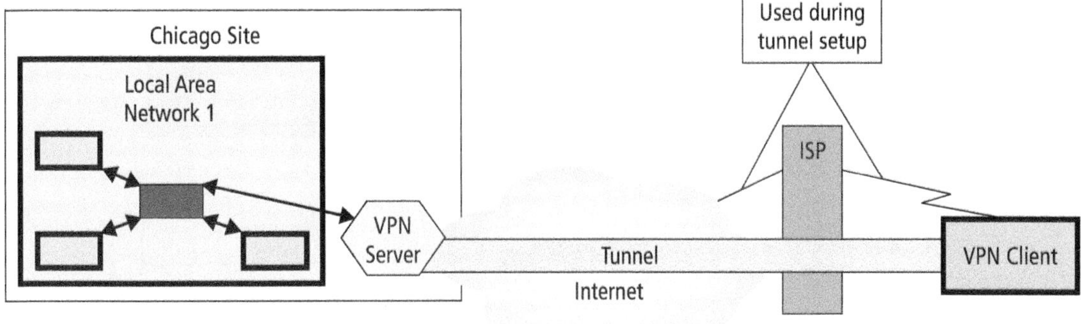

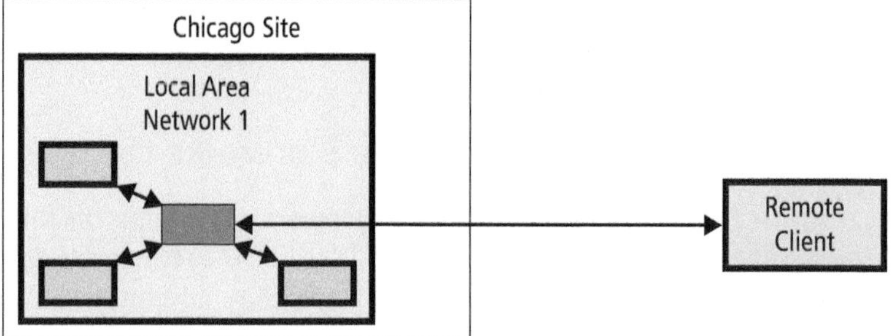

FIGURE 29
Remote Access Using VPN; Apparent Connection

complexity of managing multiple database servers, most organizations choose not to replicate database servers. Figure 30 illustrates this possibility.

Private clouds provide security *within* the organizational infrastructure but do not provide secure access from outside that infrastructure. To provide such access, organizations set up a VPN and users employ it to securely access the private cloud as shown in Figure 31.

Private clouds provide the advantages of elasticity, but to questionable benefit. What can organizations do with their idle servers? They could realize some cost savings by shutting down the idle servers. But unlike the cloud vendors, they cannot repurpose them for use by other companies. Possibly a large conglomerate or major international company could balance processing loads across subsidiary business units and across different geographical regions. 3M, for example, might balance processing for its different product groups and on different continents, but it is difficult to imagine that, in doing so, it would save money or time. A company like Falcon Security is very unlikely to develop a private cloud.

Amazon, Microsoft, IBM, Google, and other major cloud service vendors employ thousands of highly trained, very highly skilled personnel to create, manage, administer, and improve their cloud services. It is unimaginable that any non-cloud company, even large ones like 3M, could build and operate a cloud service facility that competes. The only situation in which this might make sense is if the organization is required by law or business custom to maintain physical control over its stored data. Even in that case, however, the organization is unlikely to be required to maintain physical control over all data, so it might keep critically sensitive data on-premises and place the rest of the data and related applications into the facilities of a public cloud vendor. It might also use a virtual private cloud, which we consider next.

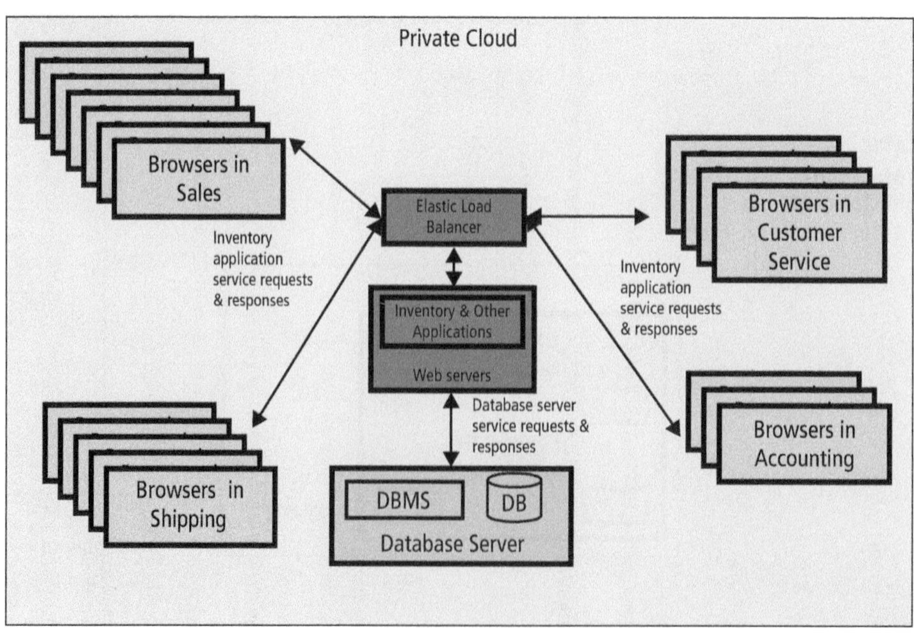

FIGURE 30
Private Cloud for Inventory and Other Applications

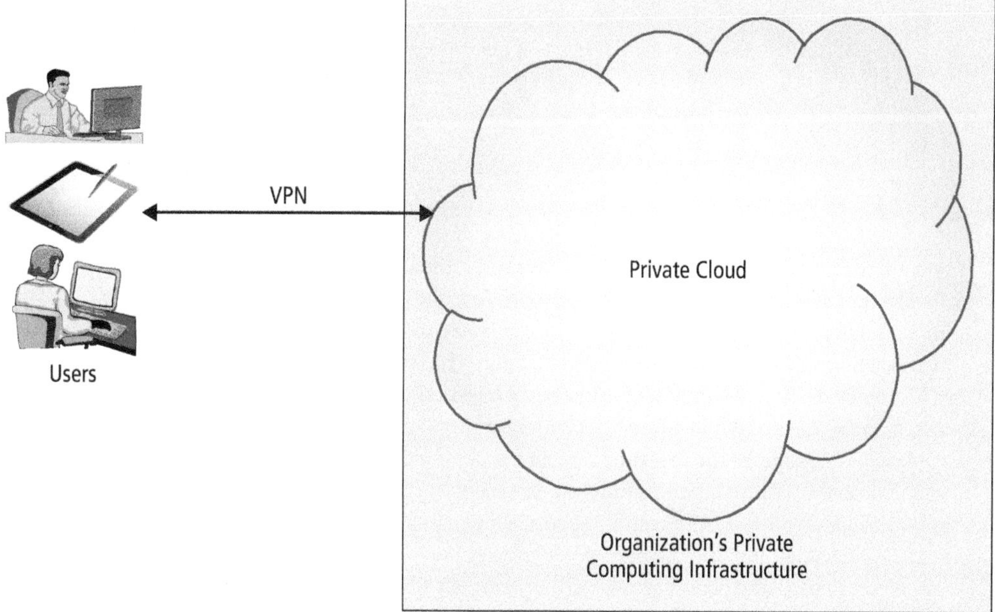

FIGURE 31
Accessing Private Cloud over a Virtual Private Network

Using a Virtual Private Cloud

A **virtual private cloud (VPC)** is a subset of a public cloud that has highly restricted, secure access. An organization can build its own VPC on top of public cloud infrastructure like AWS or that provided by other cloud vendors. The means by which this is done are beyond the scope of this text, but think of it as VPN tunneling on steroids.

Using a VPC, an organization can store its most sensitive data on its own infrastructure and store the less sensitive data on the VPC. In this way, organizations that are required to have physical control over some of their data can place that data on their own servers and locate the rest of their data on the VPC as shown in Figure 32. By doing so, the organization gains the advantages of cloud storage and possibly cloud processing for that portion of its data that it need not physically control.

In some cases, organizations have obtained permission from regulating bodies to store even their very sensitive data on a VPC. For example, Case Study discusses FinQloud, a VPC set up and managed by NASDAQ OMX, the owner of the NASDAQ and other financial exchanges.

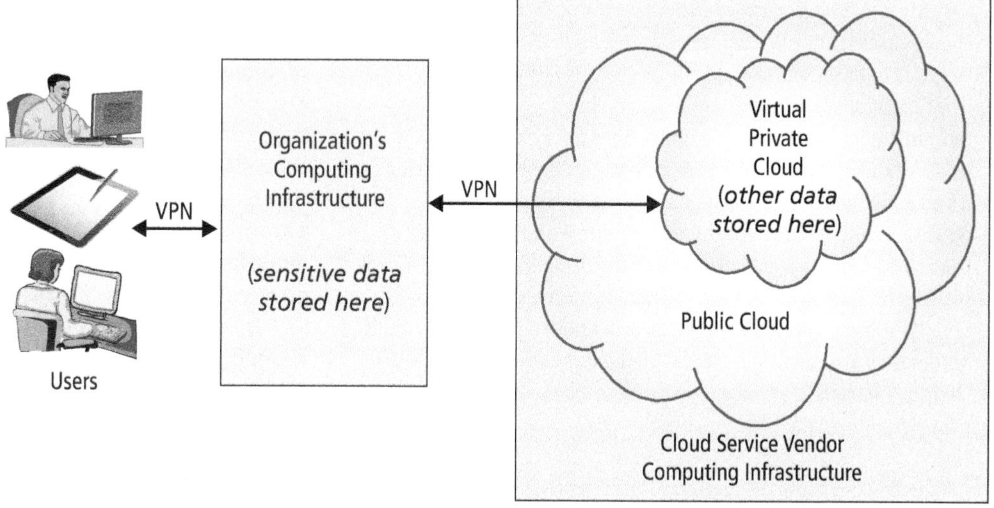

FIGURE 32
Using a Virtual Private Cloud (VPC)

SO WHAT?

QUANTUM LEARNING

If you are reading this text as part of a college course, then you probably already recognize the value of learning. Learning has been a fundamental part of your life for as long as you can remember. Some of the knowledge you have acquired has been "book" knowledge learned in school, while some has been "street smarts" learned while interacting with new people in new places. For example, the first time someone broke a promise to you, it probably affected the way you perceive the trustworthiness of others. As a result, the next time someone promised you something, a small part of you might have questioned whether that person would actually keep his word.

This ability of humans to interpret complex situations and social interactions, and remember and learn from past experiences, enables us to survive and thrive in dynamic and rapidly changing environments. What you may not realize is that computers are becoming better at learning in this dynamic way, too.

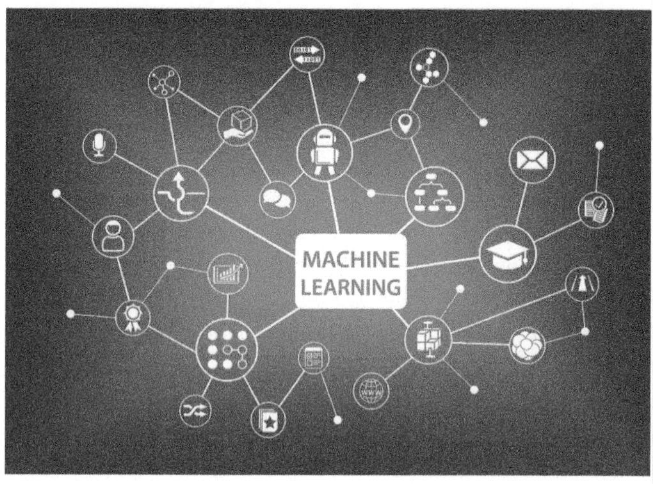

Source: © Iconimage/Fotolia

Learning to Learn

Many people perceive computers to be systems with very rigid operations; they can only carry out finite sets of tasks based on seemingly endless lines of computer code that tell them what to do. However, the walls of rigid computer code are breaking down as machine learning becomes more widely used in a number of industries. *Machine learning*, in a basic sense, is the ability of computers to learn dynamically rather than being explicitly told what to do via restrictive sets of coded instructions. Machine learning is based on the iterative generation of models; the computer has the ability to adapt to these models and interpret them differently over time. This capability is important because it allows the computer to identify patterns and other insights without being directed to the features it should analyze or being told where to find those features in large sets of data.[9]

The ability of computers to learn iteratively and dynamically has important implications for many real-world applications. Machine learning techniques have been used for fraud detection, credit score analysis, network intrusion detection, and image recognition.[10] Future applications of machine learning will likely include the development of artificial intelligence personal assistants and autonomous cars.[11]

As a more specific example, think about the ways in which companies are turning to social media for insight about how their products and services are perceived by customers. Companies use machine learning tools to analyze customer tweets. Then they identify trends in how customers feel about different advertising campaigns. Based on the results, companies can curtail campaigns that are not having the desired effect and roll out more effective campaigns on a larger scale.[12]

Computer scientists and executives are looking to the future of machine learning to see how advancements may change their industries. Many have an eye on the world of quantum computing as the next big advancement for machine learning due to its ability to increase the speed at which computers can process data.

One Quantum Step for Computers, One Giant Step for Learning

Quantum computing has been a topic of interest for scientists and innovators for many years. The fundamental difference between a quantum computer and a regular computer is the way in which computers manage information—bits. A standard computer uses 1s and 0s as the basis for all of its operations. For example, when you enter an *A* on the keyboard, the computer interprets this as "01000001." In contrast, a quantum computer can encode information in what are called *qubits*, which can be represented as a 1, a 0, or *both at the same time*. The capacity for this third state allows tasks to be carried out much more quickly and has the potential to yield exponential growth in the processing capability of computers.

Quantum computing also enhances computers' ability to learn. Right now there is still a huge gap between how computers adapt through machine learning and how humans learn. Quantum computing has the potential to narrow this gap as computers become increasingly able to learn how to interpret and adapt more complex datasets with little to no direction.[13]

The implications of quantum computing for machine learning and the creation of a more powerful artificial intelligence are profound. However, even if quantum computers have the capacity to process mammoth data sets, standardization of schemas and metadata will still be needed to ensure that the correct types of data are being considered for analysis.[14] Once infrastructure and data management hurdles are overcome, quantum computing stands to revolutionize almost everything that we do with 1s, 0s, or both!

Questions

1. Think about the last time you learned how to do something new. How long did it take for you to master it? What types of learning mechanisms did you use, and how varied were your approaches to learning? Think about the inherent limitations of computers in learning new operations. What would a computer have to do to master this same skill?
2. The feature provides the example of a company using social media analysis to evaluate customer sentiment and customize advertising based on consumers' tweets. Why would this type of analysis require a machine learning approach?
3. Conduct an Internet search to find the binary codes for ASCII keyboard characters. A common first task that programmers use to test their code is to have the system print "Hello World" on the screen. Use the binary codes for these characters to write "Hello World" as a computer would see it.
4. The article mentions that quantum computers will have tremendous processing power and revolutionize a number of computer applications. Conduct an Internet search to identify specific examples of how quantum computers may be used in the future.

Q8 2027? 

So where does the cloud go in the next 10 years? Absent some unknown factor such as a federal tax on Internet traffic, cloud services will become faster, more secure, easier to use, and cheaper. Fewer and fewer organizations will set up their own computing infrastructure; instead, they will benefit from the pooling of servers across organizations and from the economies of scale produced by cloud vendors.

But, looking a bit deeper, the cloud brings both good and bad news. The good news is that organizations can readily obtain elastic resources at very low cost. This trend will benefit everyone from individuals on the iCloud or Google Drive, to small groups using Office 365, to companies like Falcon Security using PaaS, to huge organizations like NASDAQ OMX (Case Study) using IaaS.

The overall size of the cloud is getting bigger too. For example, Google's Project Loon looks to seed the atmosphere with high-altitude balloons capable of providing Internet access to previously unreachable parts of the planet. And Google isn't stopping there. It's also making the cloud faster. Google Fiber aims to offer users 1 Gbps connections to the Internet. That's 100 times faster than the average broadband connection. Comcast responded to Google's plans by announcing its own gigabit-per-second service.

So what's the bad news? Remember that 500,000-square-foot Apple Web farm in Figure 7? Note the size of the parking lot. That tiny lot accommodates the entire operations staff. According to *Computerworld*, that building employs an operations staff of 50 people, which, spread over three shifts, 24/7, means that not many more than eight people will be running that center at any one time. Seems impossible, but is it? Again, look at the size of the parking lot.

And it's not just large companies like Apple. In 2016, every city of almost any size still supports small companies that install and maintain in-house email Exchange and other servers. If SaaS products like Google Drive or Office 365 replace those servers, what happens to those local jobs? They're gone! See Collaboration Exercise, for more on this topic.

But, with computing infrastructure so much cheaper, there have to be new jobs somewhere. By 2027, where will they be? For one, there will be more startups. Cheap and elastic cloud services enable small startups like the football player evaluation company Hudl (*www.hudl.com*) to access

SECURITY GUIDE

FROM ANTHEM TO ANATHEMA

Have you ever lost your smartphone, even just for an hour or two? If so, you probably recall the wave of panic that set in when you thought it might be gone forever. Losing any digital device can be extremely troubling for a number of reasons. First, mobile devices and laptops are not cheap. The thought of spending hundreds of dollars, or even a couple thousand dollars in the case of a laptop, to replace the lost device is distressing. However, what often creates the most panic is the thought of the person now possessing your device finding a way to access all of your data.

If you were to lose a digital device, what data would you be most concerned about—banking data, email archives, social media accounts, your collection of photos, or something else? There is no right or wrong answer to this question, and responses vary from person to person. However, what is certain is the likelihood that in the future someone will access your personal data. The frustrating part is that in most cases, the culprits will not even need physical access to your smartphone or laptop. Your data can be stolen just as easily from a company storing it in the cloud. Don't believe it? Just ask anyone covered by Anthem health care in February 2015.

Cloudy with a Chance of Theft

More and more data are being stored in the cloud. Why? Because data storage costs have plummeted and Internet access has become faster and cheaper. In 1990, 1 million transistors cost $527, a gigabyte of storage cost $569, and a gigabit per second of bandwidth cost $1,245.[19] But today 1 million transistors cost $0.05, a gigabyte of storage costs $0.02, and a gigabit per second of bandwidth costs $15.

Internet users want easy access to more and more data. Unfortunately, the downside to greater accessibility is that it becomes more accessible to hackers too.

In early 2015, Anthem Insurance Companies, Inc. reported a security breach resulting in the loss of roughly 80 million customer accounts.[20] Hackers stole sensitive account data like names, addresses, Social Security numbers, and salaries. While any nationally publicized security breach will cause concern, especially in light of the recent trend in breaches with the Target and Home Depot incidents, Anthem customers became more and more irate as details about the nature of the breach were reported. Anthem eventually disclosed that the account data stolen had been stored in plain text—not encrypted. This meant that hackers could immediately begin selling the data on the black market or using it for other nefarious purposes.

Security experts criticized Anthem for not encrypting sensitive customer account data. Numerous clients considered

Source: BillionPhotos.com/Fotolia

Anthem's failure to encrypt account records negligent, and they subsequently filed lawsuits.

Bad for Business or Business as Usual?

How would you feel if your account data had been part of the Anthem breach? Would this incident make you want to switch to a different healthcare provider, or would you recognize that large corporate data breaches are just a fact of life in a digital world and that your new healthcare provider could be equally vulnerable? The reality is that data breaches are so pervasive that it is not a matter of if but when a company holding data about you will be hacked. In fact, about a month after the Anthem data breach, Premera Blue Cross announced the loss of 11 million customer records. The lost customer records were even more sensitive because they included bank-account and medical data.[21]

Despite these threats, it is highly unlikely that companies will begin pulling data from the cloud. Consumers clearly want the ease of use that Web-based services provide. However, it is possible that corporations' security practices could evolve from being a necessary evil to becoming a competitive advantage. In fact, there could come a time when a company's reputation for information security could be more valuable than the very products or services it sells!

DISCUSSION QUESTIONS

1. Think about all of the cloud services you use. How vulnerable are you right now to having your data stolen?
2. What are some of the ways you can lower the chances of your personal data being stolen?
3. The feature explains how Anthem failed to encrypt sensitive account data. Why would encrypting account data make it more secure?
4. Have prior data breaches, like those at Home Depot or Target, affected your behavior as a consumer? How?
5. How can a greater awareness of security best practices help you in your current job?

CDN and other cloud services for next to nothing, a capability that would have taken years and thousands of dollars in the past. Go to its site to check its response time; it's fast!

There may be additional new cloud services beyond IaaS, PaaS, and SaaS. Cloud service providers may provide Analytics as a Service (AaaS) to help companies analyze the mountains of big data they're collecting. They may go even further and provide Business Process as a Service (BPaaS). Companies could then outsource common business processes like shipping and procurement. In fact, the cloud may evolve into Everything as a Service (EaaS) where all aspects of your business can be outsourced to a service provider—except the one aspect where you add value.

But what else? The cloud will foster new categories of work. By 2027, everything will be connected to everything else. Consider **remote action systems**, IS that provide computer-based activity or action at a distance. By enabling action at a distance, remote action systems save time and travel expense and make the skills and abilities of an expert available in places where he or she is not physically located. They also enable experts to scale their expertise. Let's look at a few examples.

Telediagnosis is a remote action system that healthcare professionals use to diagnose illness for patients in rural or remote areas. In 2016, more than a dozen online hospitals opened in China offering telediagnosis and treatment. Doctors videoconference with patients at local drugstores, where they can transmit diagnostic readings like blood pressure and temperature.[15] In Canada, Dr. Mehran Anvari regularly performs **telesurgery,** in which telecommunications link the surgeon to robotic equipment at distant locations, on patients more than 400 kilometers away.[16] Such examples, which are still somewhat rare, have problems that must be overcome, but they will become more common by 2027. In fact, the largest healthcare provider in the United States, UnitedHealthcare, recently announced that all video-based doctor visits will be covered just like regular doctor visits.[17]

Other uses for remote systems include **telelaw enforcement**, such as the RedFlex system that uses cameras and motion-sensing equipment to issue tickets for red-light and speeding violations. The RedFlex Group, headquartered in South Melbourne, Victoria, Australia, earns 87 percent of its revenue from traffic violations in the United States. It offers a turnkey traffic citation information system that includes all five components.

Many remote systems are designed to provide services in dangerous locations, such as robots that clean nuclear reactors or biologically contaminated sites. Drones and other unoccupied military equipment are examples of remote systems used in war zones. Private security and law enforcement will increasingly take advantage of remotely controlled flying drones and robots. You may see an upgraded form of Knightscope's 300-pound robot, named K5, patrolling your neighborhood in 2027.

But, even with these new opportunities, the news isn't all good. New York's Metropolitan Opera is arguably the finest opera company in the world. To see a live performance, you can drive to Manhattan, park your car, taxi to Lincoln Center, and pay $300 per seat. Or you can watch the same opera, remotely broadcast via Met Live, at a local movie theater, park your car for free, pay $12, and take a seat in the fourth row, where via the magic of digital broadcasting you can see details like the stitching on the singers' costumes. Details you just can't see from the $300 seats at the Met. And the sound quality is better. Wonderful, but now, who will go to a local opera performance?

Access to remote action systems reduces the value of local mediocrity. The claim "Well, I'm not the best, but at least I'm here" loses value in an interconnected world. In 1990, when former Secretary of Labor Robert Reich wrote *The Work of Nations*,[18] he could sensibly claim that those who provide routine face-to-face services are exempt from the dangers of offshoring. That claim loses validity in an interconnected world.

By 2027, the value of the top-notch performers increases, possibly exponentially. Four million people watch the average Met Live broadcast; agents for the artists who perform at that venue will negotiate a sizable part of that $120 million gate. A famous surgeon or skating coach can reach a bigger market, faster and better, and be much better paid. So, if you can be the world's best at something, do it!

But what about the rest of us? If you're not the world's expert at something, then find a way to be indispensable to someone who is. Own the theaters that broadcast Met Live. Own the skating rink for the remote figure skating coach. Be the vendor of the food at some teleaction event.

Or become essential to the development, use, and management of information systems that support these new opportunities. A business background with IS expertise will serve you very well between now and 2027.

Source: © Rebecca Cengiz Robbs

CAREER GUIDE

Name: Rebecca Cengiz-Robbs
Company: Carbonite
Job Title: Senior Network Manager
Education: University of Utah

1 How did you get this type of job?

I think it's a combination of skill, attitude, and networking. I was working as a network engineer when I was promoted to manager. I had been an engineer for four and a half years and hoped to stay in a technical position for a few more years. However, with my strong organizational skills and my willingness to volunteer for projects, it evolved into a management position. I also have a manager who is motivated to help his employees improve and advance.

2 What attracted you to this field?

I worked in the tourism industry before making a career change. I was attracted to IT by the wide variety of disciplines and the abundant opportunities, especially for women. After working as a network administrator and being able to get exposure to storage, backups, computing, security, and networking, I realized I liked networking the best.

3 What does a typical workday look like for you (duties, decisions, problems)?

I have remote engineers, so I host a daily team call so we all stay connected and aware of short- and long-term projects. I am responsible for negotiating and maintaining support contracts for network equipment; purchasing equipment for new projects and upgrades; coordinating with other teams on projects that impact infrastructure; monitoring and managing bandwidth capacity, network assets, and inventory; and managing the work and advancement of network engineers.

4 What do you like most about your job?

I like how there is always something to learn from day-to-day tasks, new projects, and my colleagues. At first I was intimidated by how much I didn't know. Now I'm glad I don't know everything and that I am surrounded by smart engineers who are willing to learn, teach, and help each other.

5 What skills would someone need to do well at your job?

When I am interviewing potential candidates I look for someone who is smart and happy. I've hired less experienced people because they were educated, intelligent, and organized and had a good attitude. Technical skills are easy to teach; attitude and intelligence are not.

6 Are education or certifications important in your field? Why?

This question is frequently debated by my colleagues. Most of the engineers at my company do not have a college degree. Some have certifications. I often hear that the only thing that matters is what you can do on the job, not a piece of paper. I believe education and certifications are both important in addition to technical skills. My degree gave me an advantage when I was looking for my first job. I had very little experience, but my manager was impressed with my academic accomplishments and took a chance on me. Based on my experience as a manager, I see that engineers with education have more motivation, focus, and ability to juggle multiple projects. They often communicate (verbally and in writing) better than engineers without degrees.

7 What advice would you give to someone who is considering working in your field?

In addition to technical skills and a good work ethic, I'd develop emotional intelligence and build a personal network. Often in IT, it's who you know and how you get along with people that will help you stand out and advance.

8 What do you think will be hot tech jobs in 10 years?

Anything to do with cloud computing: software engineering, network infrastructure and engineering, storage, computing, and automation.

ACTIVE REVIEW

Use this Active Review to verify that you understand the ideas and concepts that answer the chapter's study questions.

Q1 Why are organizations moving to the cloud?

Define *cloud* and explain the three key terms in your definition. Describe the differences between mainframe, client-server, and cloud architectures. Explain the difference between scalability and elasticity. Using Figure 5 as a guide, compare and contrast cloud-based and in-house hosting. What factors encourage organizations to move to the cloud? When does it not make sense to use a cloud-based infrastructure?

Q2 How do organizations use the cloud?

Describe how an organization can benefit from the cloud's resource elasticity, pooling, and unique Internet connectivity. Define *SaaS, PaaS,* and *IaaS*. Provide an example of each. For each, describe the business situation in which it would be the most appropriate option. Define *CDN* and explain the purpose and advantages of a CDN. Explain how Web services can be used internally.

Q3 What network technology supports the cloud?

Define *computer network.* Explain the differences among PANs, LANs, WANs, intranets, internets, and the Internet. Describe protocol and explain the purpose of protocols. Explain the key distinction of a LAN. Describe the purpose of each component in Figure 16. Define *IEEE 802.3* and *802.11* and explain how they differ. List three ways of connecting a LAN or computer to the Internet. Explain the nature of each.

Q4 How does the Internet work?

Describe how the Internet and the U.S. postal system are similar. Define *IP address* and explain why public IP addresses are necessary to deliver packets. Describe the purpose of a domain name and explain how such names are associated with public IP addresses. Explain the purpose of TCP. Explain the role for agencies like GoDaddy. Define *URL*. Define peering agreements and explain why carriers make them. Would a company like Netflix be for or against net neutrality? Explain why.

Q5 How do Web servers support the cloud?

Define *three-tier architecture* and name and describe the role of each tier. Explain the role of each tier in Figure 22 as well as how the pages in Figures 21 and 23 are processed. Using the department analogy, define *SOA* and explain why departments are encapsulated. Summarize the advantages of using SOA in the three-tier architecture. Define *TCP/IP protocol architecture* and explain, in general terms, the purpose of http, https, smtp, and ftp. Define the purpose and role of WSDL, SOAP, XML, and JSON. State a key difference between XML and JSON.

Q6 How can Falcon Security use the cloud?

First, state why Falcon is likely to use the cloud. Name and describe SaaS products that Falcon could use. Explain several ways that Falcon could use PaaS offerings. Summarize why it is unlikely that Falcon would use IaaS.

Q7 How can organizations use cloud services securely?

Explain the purpose of a VPN and describe, in broad terms, how a VPN works. Define the term *virtual* and explain how it relates to VPN. Define *private cloud.* Summarize why the benefits of a private cloud are questionable. What kind of organization might benefit from such a cloud? Explain why it is unlikely that even very large organizations can create private clouds that compete with public cloud utilities. Under what circumstance might a private cloud make sense for an organization? Define *VPC* and explain how and why an organization might use one.

Q8 2027?

What is the likely future for the cloud? Summarize the good and bad news the cloud brings. Explain why the photo in Figure 7 is disturbing. Describe three categories of remote action systems. Explain how remote systems will increase the value of super-experts but diminish local mediocrity. What can other-than-super-experts do? Summarize how this 2027 discussion pertains to your career hopes.

Using Your Knowledge with Falcon Security

Name the principal advantage of the cloud to Falcon Security. For hosting its data, which cloud offering—SaaS, PaaS, or IaaS—makes the most sense, given the size and nature of Falcon's business? Explain how Falcon could use that offering. If Falcon were larger and employed a more sophisticated IT staff, name another alternative that would make sense. Explain why.

KEY TERMS AND CONCEPTS

10/100/1000 Ethernet
Bluetooth
Cable line
Carrier
Client-server architecture
Cloud
Cloud computing architecture
Commerce server
Computer terminal
Content delivery network (CDN)
Database tier
Digital subscriber line (DSL)
Domain name
Domain Name System (DNS)
Elastic
Encapsulated
Ethernet
File Transfer Protocol (ftp)
Hop
https
Hypertext Transfer Protocol (http)
ICANN (Internet Corporation for Assigned Names and Numbers)
IEEE 802.3 protocol
IEEE 802.11 protocol
Infrastructure as a service (IaaS)
Internet
Internet exchange points (IXP)
Internet service provider (ISP)
Intranet
IP address
IPv4
IPv6
Local area network (LAN)
Mainframe architecture
Mainframes
Net neutrality
Network
Over the Internet
Packet
Peering
Personal area network (PAN)
Platform as a service (PaaS)
Pooled
Private cloud
Private IP address
Protocol
Public IP address
Remote action system
Routers
Scalable
Server tier
Service-oriented architecture (SOA)
Simple Mail Transfer Protocol (smtp)
Small office/home office (SOHO)
Software as a service (SaaS)
TCP/IP protocol architecture
Telediagnosis
Telelaw enforcement
Telesurgery
The Internet
Thin client
Three-tier architecture
Transmission Control Protocol (TCP)
Tunnel
URL (Uniform Resource Locator)
User tier
Virtual private cloud (VPC)
Virtual private network (VPN)
WAN wireless
Web page
Web servers
Wide area network (WAN)

To complete the problems with the MyMISLab, go to EOC Discussion Questions in the MyLab.

USING YOUR KNOWLEDGE

1. MyMISLab Define *cloud* and explain the three key terms in your definition. Compare and contrast cloud-based and in-house hosting using the comparison presented in Q1 as a guide. In your opinion, explain the three most important factors that make cloud-based hosting preferable to in-house hosting.

2. MyMISLab Apple invested more than $1B in the North Carolina data center mentioned in Q2. For Apple to spend such a sum, it must perceive the iCloud as being a key component of its future. Explain all the ways you believe the iCloud will give Apple a competitive advantage over other mobile device vendors.

3. MyMISLab Suppose you manage a group of seven employees in a small business. Each of your employees wants to be connected to the Internet. Consider two alternatives:

   Alternative A: Each employee has his or her own device and connects individually to the Internet.

   Alternative B: The employees' computers are connected using a LAN, and the network uses a single device to connect to the Internet.

   a. Sketch the equipment and lines required for each alternative.
   b. Explain the actions you need to take to create each alternative.
   c. Which of these two alternatives would you recommend?

4. Go to *http://aws.amazon.com.* and search for AWS database offerings. Explain the differences among Amazon's RDS, DynamoDB, ElastiCache, and Redshift services. Which of these would you recommend for storing Falcon Security's data? (By the way, whenever you query the Internet for any AWS product, be sure to include the keyword *AWS* in your search. Otherwise, your search will result in Amazon's lists of books about the item you're searching for.)

5. Suppose Toshio wants Falcon Security to set up a private internet, and he justifies this request on the basis of better security. Explain why that is not a good decision and rebut his claim about security by suggesting that Falcon use a VPC. Justify your suggestion.

6. In five sentences or fewer, explain how the cloud will affect job prospects for you between now and 2027.

COLLABORATION EXERCISE

Using the collaboration IS you built, collaborate with a group of students to answer the following questions.

The cloud is causing monumental changes in the information systems services industry. In every city, you will still see the trucks of local independent software vendors (ISVs) driving to their clients to set up and maintain local area networks, servers, and software. You'll know the trucks by the Microsoft, Oracle, and Cisco logos on their sides. For years, those small, local companies have survived, some very profitably, on their ability to set up and maintain LANs, connect user computers to the Internet, set up servers, sell Microsoft Exchange licenses, and install other software on both servers and user computers.

Once everything is installed, these companies continued to earn revenue by providing maintenance for problems that inevitably developed and support for new versions of software, connecting new user computers, and so forth. Their customers vary, but generally are smaller companies of, say, 3 to 50 employees—companies that are large enough to need email, Internet connections, and possibly some entry-level software applications such as QuickBooks.

7. Using the knowledge of this chapter and the intuition of the members of your team, summarize threats that cloud services present to such ISVs.

8. Suppose your team owns and manages one of these ISVs. You learn that more and more of your clients are choosing SaaS cloud services like Google for email, rather than setting up local email servers.
    - **a.** What, if anything, can you do to prevent the encroachment of SaaS on your business?
    - **b.** Given your answer to question 8a, identify three alternative ways you can respond.
    - **c.** Which of the three responses identified in your answer to question 8b would you choose? Justify your choice.

9. Even if SaaS eliminates the need for email and other local servers, there will still remain viable services that you can provide. Name and describe those services.

10. Suppose instead of attempting to adapt an existing ISV to the threat of cloud services, you and your teammates decide to set up an entirely new business, one that will succeed in the presence of SaaS and other cloud services. Looking at businesses in and around your campus, identify and describe the IS needs those businesses will have in the cloud services world.

11. Describe the IS services that your new business could provide for the business needs you identified in your answer to question 10.

12. Given your answers to questions 7 through 11, would you rather be an existing ISV attempting to adapt to this new world or an entirely new company? Compare and contrast the advantages and disadvantages of each alternative.

13. Changing technology has, for centuries, eliminated the need for certain products and services and created the need for new products and services. What is new, today, however, is the rapid pace at which new technology is created and adapted. Using cloud services as an example, create a statement of the posture that business professionals should take with regard to technology in order to thrive in this fast-changing environment. Notice the verb in this assignment is *thrive* and not just *survive.*

CASE STUDY

FinQloud Forever ... Well, at Least for the Required Interval ...

In 1937, the Securities and Exchange Commission (SEC) set out rules that stipulated records retention requirements for securities brokers and dealers. The SEC's concern was (and is) that records of financial transactions not be altered after the fact, that they be retained for a stipulated period of time, and that indexes be created so that the records can be readily searched.

In 1937, the rules assumed that such records were recorded on paper media. With the rise of information systems storage, in 1997 the SEC updated the rules by stating that such records can be kept electronically, provided that the storage devices are write once, read many times (WORM) devices. This rule was readily accepted by the financial services industry because the first CDs and DVDs were WORM devices.

However, as technology developed, broker-dealers and other financial institutions wanted to store records using regular disk storage and petitioned the SEC for guidance on how they might do that. In May 2003, the SEC interpreted the rule to enable the storage of such records on read-write media, provided that the storage mechanism included software that would prohibit data alteration:

> A broker-dealer would not violate the requirement in paragraph (f)(2)(ii)(A) of the rule if it used an electronic storage system that prevents the overwriting, erasing or otherwise altering of a record during its required retention period through the use of integrated hardware and software control codes. Rule 17a-4 requires broker-dealers to retain records for specified lengths of time. Therefore, it follows that the non-erasable and non-rewriteable aspect of their storage need not continue beyond that period.
>
> The Commission's interpretation does not include storage systems that only mitigate the risk a record will be overwritten or erased. Such systems—which may use software applications to protect electronic records, such as authentication and approval policies, passwords or other extrinsic security controls—do not maintain the records in a manner that is non-rewriteable and non-erasable. The external measures used by these other systems do not prevent a record from being changed or deleted. For example, they might limit access to records through the use of passwords. Additionally, they might create a "finger print" of the record based on its content. If the record is changed, the fingerprint will indicate that it was altered (but the original record would not be preserved). The ability to overwrite or erase records stored on these systems makes them non-compliant with Rule 17a-4(f).[22]

Notice the SEC specifically excludes extrinsic controls such as authentication, passwords, and manual procedures because it believes it would be possible for such systems to be readily misused to overwrite records. The SEC is striking a fine line in this ruling; if, for example, someone were to tamper with the storage systems' software, it would be possible to overwrite data. Apparently, the SEC assumes such tampering would be illegal and so rare as to not be a concern.

Given this ruling, organizations began to develop systems in compliance. The NASDAQ OMX Group, a multinational corporation that owns and operates the NASDAQ stock market as well as eight European exchanges, began to develop FinQloud, a cloud-based storage system that was developed to be compliant with the SEC's (and other regulating organizations') rulings. NASDAQ OMX operates in 70 different markets in 50 countries worldwide and claims that it processes one out of 10 stock transactions worldwide.[23]

Figure 33 shows the fundamental structure of the FinQloud system. On the back end, it uses Amazon's S3 product to provide scalable, elastic storage. When financial institutions submit records to FinQloud for storage, FinQloud processes the data in such a way that it cannot be updated, encrypts the data, and transmits the processed, encrypted data to AWS, where it is encrypted yet again and stored on S3 devices. Data is indexed on S3 and can be readily read by authorized users. After building the system,

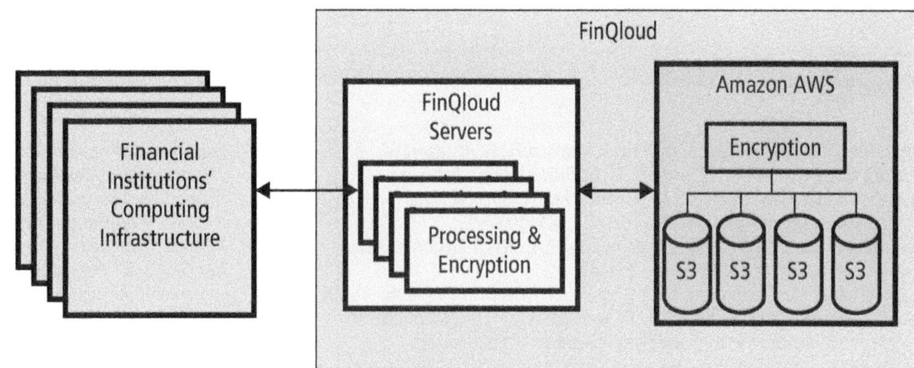

FIGURE 33
Components of the FinQloud System

NASDAQ OMX claimed that FinQloud's processing and encryption is done is such a way that it meets the SEC requirement.

Of course, NASDAQ OMX knew this statement would be perceived as self-serving, so it hired two independent companies to verify that claim: Jordan & Jordan, a securities industry consulting company, and Cohasset Associates, a document-processing consulting company. According to *The Wall Street Journal*, both organizations concluded that when properly configured, FinQloud meets the requirements of the SEC's rule (Rule 17a-3) as well as a similar rule set out by the Commodities Futures Trading Commission.[24]

Consequently, NASDAQ OMX customers can use FinQloud, and as long as they can demonstrate that they have properly configured it, their auditors will find this system to be in compliance with the SEC rulings.

QUESTIONS

14. In your own words, summarize the dealer-broker record retention requirements.

15. Reread the SEC's 2003 interpretation. In your own words, explain the difference between "integrated hardware and software control codes" and software applications that use "authentication and approval policies, passwords, or other extrinsic controls." Give an example of each.

16. Clearly, in the view of the SEC, the likelihood of compromise of an integrated system of hardware and software is considerably less than the likelihood of compromise of a system of authentication, passwords, and procedures. Justify this view.

17. Do you agree with the view in question 16? Why or why not?

18. Investigate Jordan & Jordan (*www.jandj.com*) and Cohasset Associates (*www.cohasset.com*). If you were a consultant to a financial institution, to what extent would you rely on the statements of these organizations?

19. If you were a consultant to a financial institution, what else might you do to verify that FinQloud complies with the SEC ruling and its 2003 interpretation?

20. Explain how the knowledge you have gained so far in this course helps you to understand the SEC's 2003 interpretation. Summarize how your knowledge would help you if you worked for a financial institution. Cast your answers to this question in a way that you could use in a job interview.

MyMISLab™

Go to the Assignments section of your MyLab to complete these writing exercises.

21. Suppose that you work at Falcon Security and Joni tells you that she doesn't believe that cheap, elastic provisioning of data storage is possible. "There has to be a catch somewhere," she says. Write a one-page memo to her explaining how the cloud works. In your memo, include the role of standards for cloud processing.

22. Suppose you manage a sales department that uses the SaaS product Salesforce.com. One of your key salespeople refuses to put his data into that system. "I just don't believe that the competition can't steal my data, and I'm not taking that risk." How do you respond to him?

ENDNOTES

1. Julie Bort, "Netflix, Juniper, and Intuit Explain How Amazon Is Eating the $3.5 Trillion IT Industry," *Business Insider*, January 13, 2016, accessed May 14, 2016, *www.businessinsider.com/netflix-intuit-juniper-go-all-in-on-amazon-cloud-2016-1*.
2. Yahoo! Finance, *SEC Filings*, accessed May 15, 2016, *http://finance.yahoo.com/q/sec?s=AMZN+SEC+Filings*.
3. John Divine, "Amazon.com, Inc.: Why AWS Growth Is VITAL to AMZN Stock," *InvestorPlace*, May 2, 2016, accessed May 15, 2016, *http://investorplace.com/2016/05/aws-growth-amazon-amzn-stock*.
4. Brandon Butler, "Amazon's Cloud Conference—By the Numbers," *NetworkWorld*, October 7, 2015, accessed May 15, 2016, *www.networkworld.com/article/2990421/cloud-computing/amazons-cloud-conference-by-the-numbers.html*.
5. Patrick Thibodeau, "Apple, Google, Facebook Turn N.C. into Data Center Hub," *Computerworld*, June 3, 2011, accessed June 3, 2016, *www.computerworld.com/article/2508851/data-center/apple-google-facebook-turn-n-c-into-data-center-hub.html*.

6. Victor Luckerson, "Netflix Accounts for More Than a Third of All Internet Traffic," *Time.com*, May 29, 2015, accessed May 17, 2016, *http://time.com/3901378/netflix-internet-traffic*.
7. Milton Friedman, "The Social Responsibility of Business Is to Increase Its Profits," *New York Times Magazine*, September 13, 1970.
8. Luckerson, "Netflix Accounts for More Than a Third of All Internet Traffic."
9. SAS, "Machine Learning: What It Is & Why It Matters," *SAS.com*, accessed March 27, 2016, *www.sas.com/it_it/insights/analytics/machine-learning.html*.
10. Ibid.
11. Lukas Biewald, "How Real Businesses Are Using Machine Learning," *TechCrunch.com*, March 19, 2016, accessed March 27, 2016, *http://techcrunch.com/2016/03/19/how-real-businesses-are-using-machine-learning*.
12. Ibid.
13. Tom Simonite, "Google's Quantum Dream Machine," *TechnologyReview.com*, December 18, 2015, accessed March 27, 2016, *www.technologyreview.com/s/544421/googles-quantum-dream-machine*.
14. Jennifer Ouellette, "How Quantum Computers and Machine Learning Will Revolutionize Big Data," *Wired*, October 14, 2013, accessed March 23, 2016, *www.wired.com/2013/10/computers-big-data*.
15. Ma Si and Wang Yanfei, "Net-Based Healthcare Services Set to Flourish in China," *ChinaDaily.com*, April 25, 2016, accessed June 11, 2016, *www.chinadaily.com.cn/business/2016-04/25/content_24808502.htm*.
16. Rose Eveleth, "The Surgeon Who Operates from 400km Away," *BBC.com*, May 16, 2014, accessed June 11, 2016, *www.bbc.com/future/story/20140516-i-operate-on-people-400km-away*.
17. Issie Lapowsky, "Video Is About to Become the Way We All Visit the Doctor," *Wired*, April 30,2015, accessed May 4, 2015, *www.wired.com/2015/04/united-healthcare-telemedicine*.
18. Robert Reich, *Work of Nations: Preparing Ourselves for Twenty-first Century Capitalism* (New York: Vintage Books, 1992), p. 176.
19. Gene Marks, "Why the Anthem Breach Just Doesn't Matter Anymore," *Forbes*, February 9, 2015, accessed June 2, 2016, *www.forbes.com/sites/quickerbettertech/2015/02/09/why-the-anthem-breach-just-doesnt-matter-anymore/#6954f59648de*.
20. Tom Huddleston, "Anthem's Big Data Breach Is Already Sparking Lawsuits," *Fortune*, February 6, 2015, accessed June 2, 2016, *http://fortune.com/2015/02/06/anthems-big-data-breach-is-already-sparking-lawsuits/*.
21. Coral Garnick, "Premera Negligent in Data Breach, 5 Lawsuits Claim," *Seattle Times*, March 27, 2015, accessed June 2, 2016, *www.seattletimes.com/seattle-news/premera-negligent-in-data-breach-5-lawsuits-claim/*.
22. U.S. Securities and Exchange Commission, "SEC Interpretation: Electronic Storage of Broker-Dealer Records," last modified May 5, 2003, accessed June 3, 2016, *www.sec.gov/rules/interp/34-47806.htm*.
23. NASDAQ OMX, "NASDAQ OMX Launches FinQloud Powered by Amazon Web Services (AWS)," accessed June 3, 2016, *http://ir.nasdaqomx.com/releasedetail.cfm?ReleaseID=709164*.
24. Greg MacSweeney, "Nasdaq OMX FinQloud R3 Meets SEC/CFTC Regulatory Requirements say Consultants," April 15, 2013, accessed June 3, 2016, *www.wallstreetandtech.com/data-management/nasdaq-omx-finqloud-r3-meets-sec-cftc-regulatory-requirements-say-consultants/d/d-id/1268024?*.

APPLICATION EXERCISES

All exercise files can be found on the following Web site: *www.pearsonhighered.com/kroenke.*

AE1. Numerous Web sites are available that will test your Internet data communications speed. You can find one good example at *www.speedtest.net.* (If that site is no longer active, Google or Bing "What is my Internet speed?" to find another speed-testing site. Use it.)

a. While connected to your university's network, go to Speedtest.net and test your speed against servers in Seattle, New York City, and Atlanta. Compute your average upload and download speeds.

b. Go home, or to a public wireless site, and run the Speedtest.net test again. Compute your average upload and download speeds. If you are performing this test at home, are you getting the performance you are paying for?

c. Contact a friend or relative in another state. Ask him or her to run the Speedtest.net test against those same three cities.

d. Compare the results in parts a–c. What conclusion, if any, can you draw from these tests?

AE2. Assume you have been asked to create an Office application to estimate cloud computing costs. You decide to create a spreadsheet into which your customers can provide their cloud computing needs and which you can then import into an Access database and use queries to compute cloud computing costs.

Figure AE shows the structure of the spreadsheet into which your customers will input their requirements. You can download this spreadsheet in the Excel file **Ch06Ex02_U10e.xlsx**. Figure AE shows an Access table that has costs corresponding to the requirements in Figure AE. You can download this database in the Access file **Ch06Ex02_U10e.accdb**.

a. Import the spreadsheet data into the Access database.

b. Write queries to compute the cost of each resource.

	A	B	C	D	E	F	G
1		Jan-18	Feb-18	Mar-18	Apr-18	May-18	Jun-18
2	**Compute requirements (hours):**						
3							
4	Extra Small Instance	1200	1200	1200	1200	1200	1200
5	Small Instance	2000	2000	2400	2400	0	3000
6	Medium Instance	900	1800	2700	3600	3600	3600
7	Large Instance	0	500	1000	1500	2000	2000
8	Extra Large Instance	0	0	0	1000	1500	2000
9							
10	Storage requirements:						
11	Storage Required (GB)	30	35	40	45	50	55
12	Storage Transactions (1000s)	30	30	35	35	40	50
13							
14	Database requirements (number of instances)						
15	10GB Database	2	2	2	2	1	1
16	20GB Database	0	3	3	3	3	3
17	30GB Database		4	5	6	6	7
18	40GB Database	0	0	0	3	3	4
19	50GB Database	0	0	2	2	3	0

FIGURE AE
Worksheet for Inputting Cloud Computing Requirements
Source: Microsoft Corporation

CloudCosts

ID	Resource Name	Units	Cost
1	Extra Small Instance	Hours	$0.03
2	Small Instance	Hours	$0.09
3	Medium Instance	Hours	$0.12
4	Large Instance	Hours	$0.37
5	Extra Large Instance	Hours	$0.55
6	StorageRequired	GB / month	$0.15
7	StorageTransactions	10,000	$0.01
8	10GB Database	Each	$9.99
9	20GB Database	Each	$149.98
10	30GB Database	Each	$199.97
11	40GB Database	Each	$299.96
12	50GB Database	Each	$399.95

FIGURE AE
Cloud Computing Costs
Source: Microsoft Corporation

c. Create a report that shows the cost for each type of resource for each month. Show the total costs for the 6-month period for each resource as well. Include a grand total of all the

d. Create a pie chart that breaks out the total costs by resource. *Hint:* You can import the query data back into Excel.

e. Create a pie chart that breaks out the total costs by month. *Hint:* You can import the query data back into Excel.

f. Assume that processing costs increase by 10 percent across the board. Repeat parts c, d, and e for the changed costs.

AE3. There are a few problems with cloud-based storage. First, it seems like there's never enough of it. This is especially true if it's free. Second, you always wonder if it's really secure. Yes, your storage provider says your data is secure. But is it really? Is there some way to be sure?

In this project, you will learn how to use 7-Zip to solve both of these problems. You'll learn how to compress and encrypt important files and directories. If you are storing confidential data in the cloud, it's important to make sure it's encrypted—by you. Using a third-party encryption tool like 7-Zip means only *you* can access your data. Trusting your cloud providers isn't necessary. 7-Zip is also a very efficient file archiver that will save you a lot of space.

a. Browse to *www.7-zip.org.*

b. Click on Download and install the latest version of 7-Zip for your operating system. (There are 7-Zip versions for Windows, Mac OS X, Linux, BSD, and UNIX.)

c. Go to your Downloads folder. (You can go to any folder that contains large files.)

d. Right-click on a large file.

e. Click 7-Zip and Add to archive.

f. Rename the file YourName.7z. (Replace "YourName" with your first and last names. If your name was John Doe, the file would be named JohnDoe.7z.)

g. In the Encryption section, enter a password—twice. (Choose a simple password you can remember.)

h. Take a screenshot and paste it into your document. (You can take a screenshot by pressing Alt + Print Screen.)

i. Click OK. (Notice that your original file remains unchanged.)

j. After your new YourName.7z file is compressed, right-click it and select 7-Zip and Extract to "YourName\".

k. Enter the password you set, and click OK. (Your file should start extracting.)
l. Explain why third-party encryption is important for highly confidential files.
m. Explain why compressing large files is important when using cloud-based storage.

GLOSSARY

10/100/1000 Ethernet A type of Ethernet that conforms to the IEEE 802.3 protocol and allows for transmission at a rate of 10, 100, or 1,000 Mbps (megabits per second).

Bluetooth A common wireless protocol designed for transmitting data over short distances, replacing cables.

Cable line Cable television lines that provide high-speed data transmission.

Carrier A telecommunications company that provides voice and data transportation services.

Client-server architecture Computing architecture that allows clients (users) to send requests across the Internet to servers, which respond and send data back.

Cloud A term that refers to elastic leasing of pooled computer resources over the Internet.

Cloud computing architecture Computing architecture that allows employees and customers to access organizational data and applications located in the cloud.

Commerce server An application program that runs on a server tier computer. A typical commerce server obtains product data from a database, manages items in users' shopping carts, and coordinates the checkout process.

Computer terminal A computing device consisting of a screen, keyboard, and network connection. Also called a *thin client*.

Content delivery network (CDN) An information system that serves content to Web pages over the Internet. To reduce wait time, data is typically stored and served from many geographic locations.

Database tier In the three-tier architecture, the tier that runs the DBMS and receives and processes requests to retrieve and store data.

Digital subscriber line (DSL) A communications line that operates on the same lines as voice telephones but does so in such a manner that its signals to not interfere with voice telephone service.

Domain name A worldwide unique name registered in the domain name system (DNS) and affiliated with a public IP address.

Domain Name System (DNS) A directory naming system that assigns domain names to IP addresses.

Elastic In cloud computing, the situation that exists when the amount of resource leased can be dynamically increased or decreased, programmatically, in a short span of time, and organizations pay for just the resources that they use. This term was first used in this way by Amazon.com.

Encapsulated A characteristic of systems design in which the details of a process are hidden from users of that process. A formal interface is defined for the process that specifies how the process is to be accessed, what data it requires, and the data that it will produce. The means by which that process creates those results are never exposed, nor do they need to be.

Ethernet Another name for the IEEE 802.3 protocol, Ethernet is a communications standard that specifies how messages are to be packaged, processed, and transmitted for wired transmission over a LAN.

File Transfer Protocol (ftp) An applications-layer protocol used to transfer files over the Internet.

Hop In an internet, the movement from one network to another.

https An indication that a Web browser is using the SSL/TLS protocol to provide secure communication.

Hypertext Transfer Protocol (http) An application-layer protocol used between browsers and Web servers.

ICANN (Internet Corporation for Assigned Names and Numbers) The organization responsible for managing the assignment of public IP addresses and domain names for use on the Internet. Each public IP address is unique across all computers on the Internet.

IEEE 802.11 protocol A standard for packaging and managing traffic on wireless local area networks.

IEEE 802.3 protocol A standard for packaging and managing traffic on wired local area networks.

Infrastructure as a service (IaaS) Hosting of a bare server computer, data storage, network, and virtualization by a vendor.

Internet exchange points (IXP) Physical locations where large carriers exchange traffic.

Internet service provider (ISP) An ISP provides users with Internet access. An ISP provides a user with a legitimate Internet address; it serves as the user's gateway to the Internet; and it passes communications back and forth between the user and the Internet. ISPs also pay for the Internet. They collect money from their customers and pay access fees and other charges on the users' behalf.

Internet When spelled with a small i, as in *internet*, a private network of networks. When spelled with a capital I, as in *Internet*, the public internet known as the Internet.

Intranet A private internet (note small i) used within a corporation or other organization.

IP address A series of dotted decimals in a format like 192.168.2.28 that identifies a unique device on a network or internet.

IPv4 The most commonly used Internet layer protocol; has a four-decimal dotted notation, such as 165.193.123.253.

IPv6 An Internet layer protocol that uses 128-bit addresses and is gradually replacing IPv4.

Local area network (LAN) A network that connects computers that reside in a single geographic location on the premises of the company that operates the LAN. The number of connected computers can range from two to several hundred.

Mainframe architecture Computing architecture that supports connections between a central mainframe and numerous thin clients.

Mainframes Large-scale high-speed centralized computers used for internal data processing needs.

Net neutrality The idea that all data should be treated equally as it passes between networks regardless of its type, source, or quantity.

Network A collection of computers that communicate with one another over transmission lines.

Over the Internet When applied to cloud computing, the provisioning of worldwide servers over the Internet.

Packet A formatted message that passes through networks.

Peering Exchanging information between telecommunication providers without charging an access fee.

Personal area network (PAN) A network connecting devices located around a single person.

Platform as a service (PaaS) Hosting of an operating system, runtime environment, and middleware by a vendor.

Pooled The situation in which many different organizations use the same physical hardware.

Private cloud In-house hosting, delivered via Web service standards, which can be dynamically configured.

Private IP address A type of IP address used within private networks and internets. Private IP addresses are assigned and managed by the company that operates the private network or internet.

Protocol A set of rules and data structures for organizing communication.

Public IP address An IP address used to identify a particular device on the Internet. Such IP addresses are assigned to major institutions in blocks by the Internet Corporation for Assigned Names and Numbers (ICANN). Each IP address is unique across all computers on the Internet.

Remote action system An information system that provides action at a distance, such as telesurgery or telelaw enforcement.

Routers Devices that connect different networks together.

Scalable Easily able to respond to incremental growth in demand.

Server tier In the three-tier architecture, the tier that consists of computers that run Web servers for generating Web pages and responding to requests from browsers. Web servers also process application programs.

Service-oriented architecture (SOA) A design philosophy that dictates that all interactions among computing devices are defined as services in a formal, standardized way. SOA makes the cloud possible.

Simple Mail Transfer Protocol (smtp) The protocol used for email transmission.

Small office/home office (SOHO) A business office with usually fewer than 10 employees often located in the business professional's home.

Software as a service (SaaS) Hosting of hardware infrastructure and operating system as well as application programs and databases by a vendor.

TCP/IP protocol architecture A protocol architecture having five layers and one or more protocols defined at each layer. Programs are written to implement the rules of a particular protocol.

Telediagnosis A remote access system used by healthcare professionals to provide expertise in rural or remote areas.

Telelaw enforcement A remote access system that provides law enforcement capability.

Telesurgery A remote access system that links surgeons to robotic equipment and patients at a distance.

The Internet The public collection of networks used for transmitting data, worldwide.

Thin client A computing device that consist of a screen, keyboard, and network connection. Also called a computer terminal.

Three-tier architecture Architecture used by most e-commerce server applications. The tiers refer to three different classes of computers. The user tier consists of users' computers that have browsers that request and process Web pages. The server tier consists of computers that run Web servers and in the process generate Web pages and other data in response to requests from browsers. Web servers also process application programs. The third tier is the database tier, which runs the DBMS that processes the database.

Transmission Control Protocol (TCP) A core Internet protocol that guarantees the reliable delivery of packets.

Tunnel A virtual, private pathway over a public or shared network from the VPN client to the VPN server.

URL (Uniform Resource Locator) An address on the Internet. Consists of a protocol followed by a domain name or public IP address.

User tier In the three-tier architecture, the tier that consists of computers, phones, and other mobile devices that have browsers and request or process Web pages and other services.

Virtual private cloud (VPC) A subset of a public cloud that has highly restricted, secure access.

Virtual private network (VPN) A WAN connection alternative that uses the Internet or a private internet to create the appearance of private point-to-point connections. In the IT world, the term virtual means something that appears to exist that does not exist in fact. Here a VPN uses the public Internet to create the appearance of a private connection.

WAN wireless A communications system that provides wireless connectivity to a wide area network.

Web page Document encoded in html that is created, transmitted, and consumed using the World Wide Web.

Web servers Programs that run on a server-tier computer and that manage http traffic by sending and receiving Web pages to and from clients and by processing client requests.

Wide area network (WAN) A network that connects computers at different geographic locations.

Processes, Organizations, and Information Systems

Zev Friedman, the owner of ARES; Ashley Turnwood, general manager; Cassie Castellon, marketing professional; Henri Kivi, IS professional; and Raj Agarwal, augmented reality guru; are having an introductory meeting at Friedman's luxurious house on a Saturday morning.

After polite conversation, Zev gets down to business.

"So ... where did Flores go wrong?" Zev asks. His eyes quickly move around the group looking for a response. Zev rarely asks questions to which he already knows the answer, but he asked this question for a reason. He needs to know if he's found a dedicated team with a strong leader.

Cassie unabashedly jumps in. "I think Flores is a good doctor who sincerely cares about helping people. But, quite frankly, he doesn't know how to run a business. He didn't have any sales beyond his own practice, but he kept paying developers for more and more features."

Ashley can tell that Zev is looking for something more substantial. Zev glances over at his newly hired general manager for a response. "That's true, but Flores probably wasn't going to sell the system to many doctors anyway. Doctors make money from expensive tests and procedures—not hardware, software, and advertising. The data from Flores's system may be interesting to healthcare professionals, but it won't pay their mortgages. He needed to market his system to people who would actually buy it. Medicine cures physical problems, but sales cure business problems."

"OK, so to whom are we going to sell this?" Zev asks.

"Well, right now, probably no one," Ashley replies dryly. "Flores was able to collect and integrate data from exercise equipment, mobile devices, and fitness trackers using a cloud-based system. He even made some good-looking reporting tools that can share data with other systems. That's nice, but now upgraded fitness trackers and smartwatches can collect and report exercise data too."

"We could also sell virtual spinning classes..."

Image source: andrew_rybalko/Fotolia

Cassie looks nervously at Ashley, and Zev leans back with a slight smile on his face.

Ashley continues, "But considering the people you've hired, that's not what you're going for anyway."

"What do you mean?" Zev replies.

"Well ... Raj is an expert in augmented reality from Stanford, and the rest of us love cycling. OK, maybe that's overstating it a bit. Henri and I *love* cycling; everyone else enjoys cycling. If you add Flores's software to the mix, you've got a hybrid entertainment-fitness company."

Zev nods slightly and says, "Good, so how are we going to make money?"

Henri chimes in, "We'll definitely make money selling the app for the AR headsets. An augmented reality app for stationary bikes would be cool. Both the headset and bike manufacturers would love this app because it will help them sell more units. The integration with Flores's system is going to be tricky, though."

Raj sees his opening. "We could also sell virtual spinning classes led by expert instructors. Imagine a group of 20 riders biking through Arches National Park in the early morning. That would be really cool." He pauses, clearly deep in thought, and then continues, "But I'm not sure if we have the bandwidth or backend resources to handle that."

"Cassie, what do you think?" Zev asks.

"Well," Cassie says, "I think we should consider placing ads into the AR interface. Google, Facebook, and Twitter all make most of their money from ads. There's a real opportunity there. Certain companies would *love* to put ads in front of cyclists. We also might be able make money from celebrity rides, charity events, and promotional contests. I'm not sure how we might make money using social media. Would users want to post their stats to Facebook? I'm not sure."

Ashley listens intently and then says, "You know, I think we could get referral fees from personal trainers if we could send them some of our users. They might even teach our virtual classes for free if they think it would attract clients. Large businesses might also be interested in using ARES for their wellness-at-work programs."

"Sounds good," Zev says approvingly. "Cassie, check into the ad revenue potential for ARES. Raj, see if it would be possible for our system to handle a virtual spinning class of 30 people. Henri, look at the costs of developing the apps and integrating the data on the backend system. Ashley, you look into the trainers and employers. Any questions?"

Everyone looks around the table; no one says a word.

"OK, see you next week."

Study QUESTIONS

Q1 What are the basic types of processes?

Q2 How can information systems improve process quality?

Q3 How do information systems eliminate the problems of information silos?

Q4 How do CRM, ERP, and EAI support enterprise processes?

Q5 What are the elements of an ERP system?

Q6 What are the challenges of implementing and upgrading enterprise information systems?

Q7 How do inter-enterprise IS solve the problems of enterprise silos?

Q8 2027?

Chapter PREVIEW

This chapter explores processes and their supporting information systems within levels of an organization. We will investigate three types of processes and the scope of information systems they use. We will also investigate the concept of process quality and explain how information systems can be used to increase it. Then we will discuss how the use of information systems at one level of organization leads to information silos, explain the problems of such silos, and then show how those problems can be solved by information systems at the next level of organization. In particular, we'll discuss how enterprise systems such as CRM, ERP, and EAI (you'll learn the meaning of those terms) solve problems caused by workgroup information silos. ERP systems play a particularly important role, and we'll discuss their purpose and components and the major ERP vendors. Then we'll survey the major challenges that occur when implementing enterprise systems. We'll wrap up the chapter by showing how inter-enterprise IS can solve the problems of enterprise-level silos and finally, in 2027, discuss the implications of mobility and the cloud on future enterprise and inter-enterprise IS.

Q1 What Are the Basic Types of Processes?

A business process is a network of activities that generate value by transforming inputs into outputs. Activities are subparts of processes that receive inputs and produce outputs. Activities can be performed by humans only, by humans augmented by computer systems, and by computer systems only.

Figure 1 shows a simplified view of a three-activity process for approving customer orders. Each of these activities is, itself, a subprocess of this overall process. You can see that each

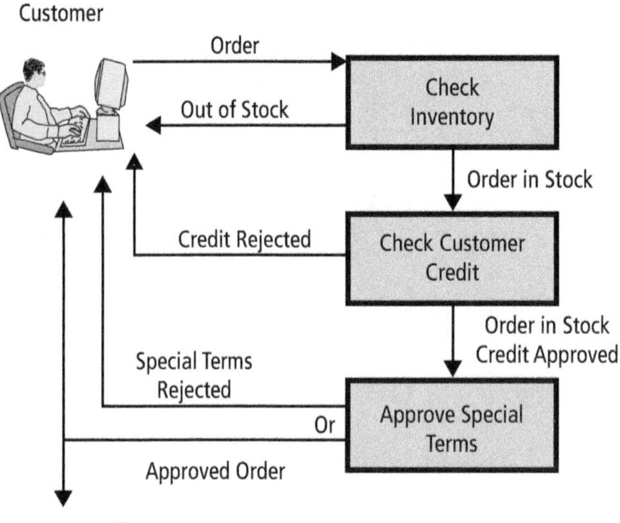

FIGURE 1
Business Process with Three Activities

step—check inventory, check customer credit, and approve special terms—receives inputs and transforms them into outputs. View Figure 1 as showing the gist of a typical business process.

How Do Structured Processes Differ from Dynamic Processes?

Businesses have dozens, hundreds, even thousands of different processes. Some processes are stable, almost fixed sequences of activities and data flows. For example, the process of a salesclerk accepting a return at Nordstrom, or other quality retail stores, is fixed. If the customer has a receipt, take these steps ... if the customer has no receipt, take these other steps. That process needs to be standardized so that customers are treated consistently and correctly, so that returned goods are accounted for appropriately, and so that sales commissions are reduced in a way that is fair to the sales staff.

Other processes are less structured, less rigid, and often creative. For example, how does Nordstrom's management decide what women's clothes to carry next spring? Managers can look at past sales, consider current economic conditions, and make assessments about women's acceptance of new styles at recent fashion shows, but the process for combining all those factors into orders of specific garments in specific quantities and colors is not nearly as structured as that for accepting returns.

In this text, we divide processes into two broad categories. **Structured processes** are formally defined, standardized processes that involve day-to-day operations: accepting a return, placing an order, purchasing raw materials, and so forth. They have the characteristics summarized in the left-hand column of Figure 2.

Dynamic processes are flexible, informal, and adaptive processes that normally involve strategic and less structured managerial decisions and activities. Deciding whether to open a new store location and how best to solve the problem of excessive product returns are examples, as is using Twitter to generate buzz about next season's product line. Dynamic processes usually require human judgment. The right-hand column of Figure 2 shows characteristics of dynamic processes.

We will discuss structured processes and information systems that support them in this chapter.

For the balance of this chapter, we will use the term *process* to mean *structured process.*

Structured	Dynamic
Support operational and structured managerial decisions and activities	Support strategic and less structured managerial decision and activities
Standardized	Less specific, fluid
Usually formally defined and documented	Usually informal
Exceptions rare and not (well) tolerated	Exceptions frequent and expected
Process structure changes slowly and with organizational agony	Adaptive processes that change structure rapidly and readily
Example: Customer returns, order entry, purchasing, payroll, etc.	**Example:** Collaboration; social networking; ill-defined, ambiguous situations

FIGURE 2
Structured Versus Dynamic Processes

How Do Processes Vary by Organizational Scope?

Processes are used at three levels of organizational scope: workgroup, enterprise, and inter-enterprise. In general, the wider the scope of the process, the more challenging the process is to manage. For example, processes that support a single workgroup function, say, accounts payable, are simpler and easier to manage than those that support a network of independent organizations, such as a supply chain. Consider processes at each of these three organizational scopes.

Workgroup Processes

A **workgroup process** exists to enable workgroups to fulfill the charter, purpose, and goals of a particular group or department. A physicians' partnership is a workgroup that follows processes to manage patient records, issue and update prescriptions, provide standardized postsurgery care, and so forth.

Figure 3 lists common workgroup processes. Notice that each of these processes is largely contained within a given department. These processes may receive inputs from other departments, and they may produce outputs used by other departments, but all, or at least the bulk of, the processes' activities lay within a single department.

A **workgroup information system** exists to support one or more processes within the workgroup. For example, an Operations department could implement an IS to support all three of the operations processes shown in Figure 3. Or an Accounting department might implement two or three different IS to support the accounting processes shown. Sometimes, workgroup information systems are called **functional information systems**. Thus, an operations management system is a functional information system, as are a general ledger system and a cost accounting system. The program component of a functional information system is called a **functional application**.

General characteristics of workgroup information systems are summarized in the top row of Figure 4. Typical workgroup information systems support 10 to 100 users. Because the procedures for using them must be understood by all members of the group, those procedures are often formalized in documentation. Users generally receive formal training in the use of those procedures as well.

When problems occur, they almost always can be solved within the group. If accounts payable duplicates the record for a particular supplier, the accounts payable group can make the fix. If the Web storefront has the wrong number of items in the inventory database, that count can be fixed within the storefront group.

(Notice, by the way, that the consequences of a problem are not isolated to the group. Because the workgroup information system exists to provide a service to the rest of the organization, its

Workgroup	Workgroup Example Processes
Sales and marketing	• Lead generation • Lead tracking • Customer management • Sales forecasting • Product and brand management
Operations	• Order entry • Order management • Finished goods inventory management
Manufacturing	• Inventory (raw materials, goods-in-process) • Planning • Scheduling • Operations
Customer service	• Order tracking • Account tracking • Customer support
Human resources	• Recruiting • Compensation • Assessment • HR planning
Accounting	• General ledger • Financial reporting • Cost accounting • Accounts receivable • Accounts payable • Cash management • Budgeting • Treasury management

FIGURE 3
Common Workgroup Processes

problems have consequences throughout the organization. The fix to the problem can usually be obtained within the group, however.)

Two or more departments within an organization can duplicate data, and such duplication can be very problematic to the organization, as we discuss in Q3. Finally, because workgroup information systems involve multiple users, changing them can be problematic. But, again, when problems do occur, they can be resolved within the workgroup.

Scope	Example	Characteristics
Workgroup	Doctor's office/ medical practice	Support one or more workgroup processes. 10–100 users; procedures often formalized; problem solutions within group; workgroups can duplicate data; somewhat difficult to change
Enterprise	Hospital	Support one or more enterprise processes. 100–1,000+ users; procedures formalized; problem solutions affect enterprise; eliminate workgroup data duplication; difficult to change
Inter-enterprise	Healthcare exchange	Support one or more inter-enterprise processes. 1,000+ users; systems procedures formalized; problem solutions affect multiple organizations; can resolve problems of duplicated enterprise data; very difficult to change

FIGURE 4
Characteristics of Information Systems

Enterprise Processes

The Ethics Guide demonstrates how one person's actions can affect an entire company

Enterprise processes span an organization and support activities in multiple departments. At a hospital, the process for discharging a patient supports activities in housekeeping, the pharmacy, the kitchen, nurses' stations, and other hospital departments.

Enterprise information systems support one or more enterprise processes. As shown in the second row of Figure 4, they typically have hundreds to thousands of users. Procedures are formalized and extensively documented; users always undergo formal procedure training. Sometimes enterprise systems include categories of procedures, and users are defined according to levels of expertise with the system as well as by level of authority.

The solutions to problems in an enterprise system involve more than one workgroup or department. As you will learn in this chapter, a major advantage of enterprise systems is that data duplication within the enterprise is either eliminated altogether or, if it is allowed to exist, changes to duplicated data are carefully managed to maintain consistency.

Because enterprise systems span many departments and involve potentially thousands of users, they are difficult to change. Changes must be carefully planned and cautiously implemented and users given considerable training. Sometimes users are given cash incentives and other inducements to motivate them to change.

CRM, ERP, and EAI are three enterprise information systems that we will define and discuss in Q4.

Inter-enterprise Processes

Inter-enterprise processes span two or more independent organizations. For example, the process of buying a healthcare insurance policy via a healthcare exchange (see Case Study) involves many insurance companies and governmental agencies. Each of these organizations has activities to fulfill, all of which are affected by laws, governmental policy, and competitive concerns of the insurance companies.

Inter-enterprise information systems support one or more inter-enterprise processes. Such systems typically involve thousands of users, and solutions to problems require cooperation among different, usually independently owned, organizations. Problems are resolved by meeting, by contract, and sometimes by litigation.

Data are often duplicated among organizations; such duplication is either eliminated or carefully managed. Because of their wide span, complexity, and use by multiple companies, such systems can be exceedingly difficult to change. Supply chain management is the classic example of an inter-enterprise information system.

Q2 How Can Information Systems Improve Process Quality?

Processes are the fabric of organizations; they are the means by which people organize their activities to achieve the organization's goals. As such, process quality is an important, possibly the most important, determinant of organizational success.[1]

The two dimensions of process quality are efficiency and effectiveness. **Process efficiency** is a measure of the ratio of process outputs to inputs. If an alternative to the process in Figure 1 can produce the same order approvals/rejections (output) for less cost or produce more approvals/rejections for the same cost, it is more efficient.

Process effectiveness is a measure of how well a process achieves organizational strategy. If an organization differentiates itself on quality customer service and if the process in Figure 1 requires 5 days to respond to an order request, then that process is ineffective. Companies that provide customized manufacturing might make their processes more effective by using 3D printing.

How Can Processes Be Improved?

Organizations can improve the quality (efficiency and/or effectiveness) of a process in one of three ways:

- Change the process structure.
- Change the process resources.
- Change both process structure and resources.

Change the Process Structure

In some cases, process quality can be changed just by reorganizing the process. The order approval process in Figure 1 might be made more efficient if customer credit was done first and inventory was checked second. This change might be more efficient because it would save the cost of checking inventory for customers whose credit will be denied. However, that change would also mean that the organization would pay for a credit check on customers for which it did not have appropriate inventory. Note that process structure has a strong bearing on process efficiency.

Changing process structure can also increase process effectiveness. If an organization chooses a cost-leader strategy, then that strategy might mean that no special terms should ever be approved. If the process in Figure 1 results in the authorization of orders with special terms, then eliminating the third activity will make it more effective (most likely it will save on operational costs as well).

Change Process Resources

Business process activities are accomplished by humans and information systems. One way to improve process quality is to change the allocation of those resources. For example, if the process in Figure 1 is not effective because it takes too long, one way to make it more effective is to identify the source of delays and then to add more resources. If delays are caused by the check customer credit activity, one way to increase process effectiveness is to add more people to that activity. Adding people should decrease delays, but it will also add cost, so the organization needs to find the appropriate balance between effectiveness and efficiency.

Another way to shorten the credit check process would be to use an information system to perform the customer credit checks. Depending on the development and operational costs of the new system, that change might also be less costly and therefore more efficient.

Change Both Process Structure and Process Resources

Of course, it is possible to improve process quality by changing both the process's structure and resources. In fact, unless a structure change is only a simple reordering of tasks, changing the structure of a process almost always involves a change in resources as well.

How Can Information Systems Improve Process Quality?

Information systems can be used to improve process quality by:

- Performing an activity.
- Augmenting a human who is performing an activity.
- Controlling data quality and process flow.

Performing an Activity

Information systems can perform the entirety of a process activity. In Figure 1, for example, the check credit activity could be entirely automated. When you purchase from Amazon or another major online retailer, information systems check your credit while your transaction is being processed. Reserving a seat on an airline is done automatically; all of the reservation activity is done by an information system. (Except, of course, the passenger's activities: When making a reservation, you must choose the seat from available locations, but your time is free to the airline.)

Augmenting a Human Performing an Activity

A second way that information systems can improve process quality is by augmenting the actions of a human who is performing that activity. Consider the process of managing patient appointments. To schedule an appointment, patients call the doctor's office and talk with a receptionist who uses an appointment information system. That information system augments the appointment creation activity.

Controlling Data Quality Process Flow

A third way that information systems can improve process quality is by controlling data quality and process flow.

One of the major benefits of information systems is to control data quality. The IS can not only ensure that correct data values are being input, it can also ensure that data are complete before continuing process activities. The cheapest way to correct for data errors is at the source, and it avoids the problems that develop when process activities are begun with incomplete data.

Information systems also have a role in controlling process flow. Consider the order approval process in Figure 1. If this process is controlled manually, then someone, say, a salesperson, will obtain the order data from the customer and take whatever actions are needed to push that order through the three steps in the order process. If the salesperson gets busy or is distracted or away from work for a few days, or if there are unexpected delays in one of the activities, it is possible for an order to be lost or the approval unnecessarily delayed.

If, however, an information system is controlling the order approval process, then it can ensure that steps are performed in accordance with an established schedule. The information system can also be relied upon to make correct process-routing decisions for processes that are more complicated than that in Figure 1.

Q3 How Do Information Systems Eliminate the Problems of Information Silos?

An **information silo** is the condition that exists when data are isolated in separated information systems. For example, consider the six workgroups and their information systems in Figure 3. Reflect on these information systems for a moment, and you'll realize that each one processes customer, sales, product, and other data, but each uses that data for its own purposes and will likely store slightly different data. Sales, for example, will store contact data for customers' purchasing agents, while Accounting will store contact data for customers' accounts payable personnel.

It's completely natural for workgroups to develop information systems solely for their own needs, but, over time, the existence of these separate systems will result in information silos that cause numerous problems.

What Are the Problems of Information Silos?

Figure 5 lists the major problems caused by information silos at the workgroup level, in this case, between the Sales and Marketing department and the Accounting department. First, data are duplicated. Sales and Marketing and Accounting applications maintain separate databases that store some of the same customer data. As you know, data storage is cheap, so the problem with duplication is not wasted disk storage. Rather, the problem is data inconsistency. Changes to customer data made in the Sales and Marketing application may take days or weeks to be made to the Accounting application's database. During that period, shipments will reach the customer without delay, but invoices will be sent to the wrong address. When an organization has inconsistent duplicated data, it is said to have a **data integrity** problem.

Additionally, when applications are isolated, business processes are disjointed. Suppose a business has a rule that credit orders over $15,000 must be preapproved by the Accounts Receivable department. If the supporting applications are separated, it will be difficult for the two activities to reconcile their data, and the approval will be slow to grant and possibly erroneous.

In the second row of Figure 5, Sales and Marketing wants to approve a $20,000 order with Ajax. According to the Sales and Marketing database, Ajax has a current balance of $17,800, so Sales and Marketing requests a total credit amount of $37,800. The Accounting database, however, shows Ajax with a balance of only $12,300 because the accounts receivable application has credited Ajax for a return of $5,500. According to Accounting's records, a total credit authorization of only $32,300 is needed in order to approve the $20,000 order, so that is all the department grants.

FIGURE 5
Problems Created by Information Silos

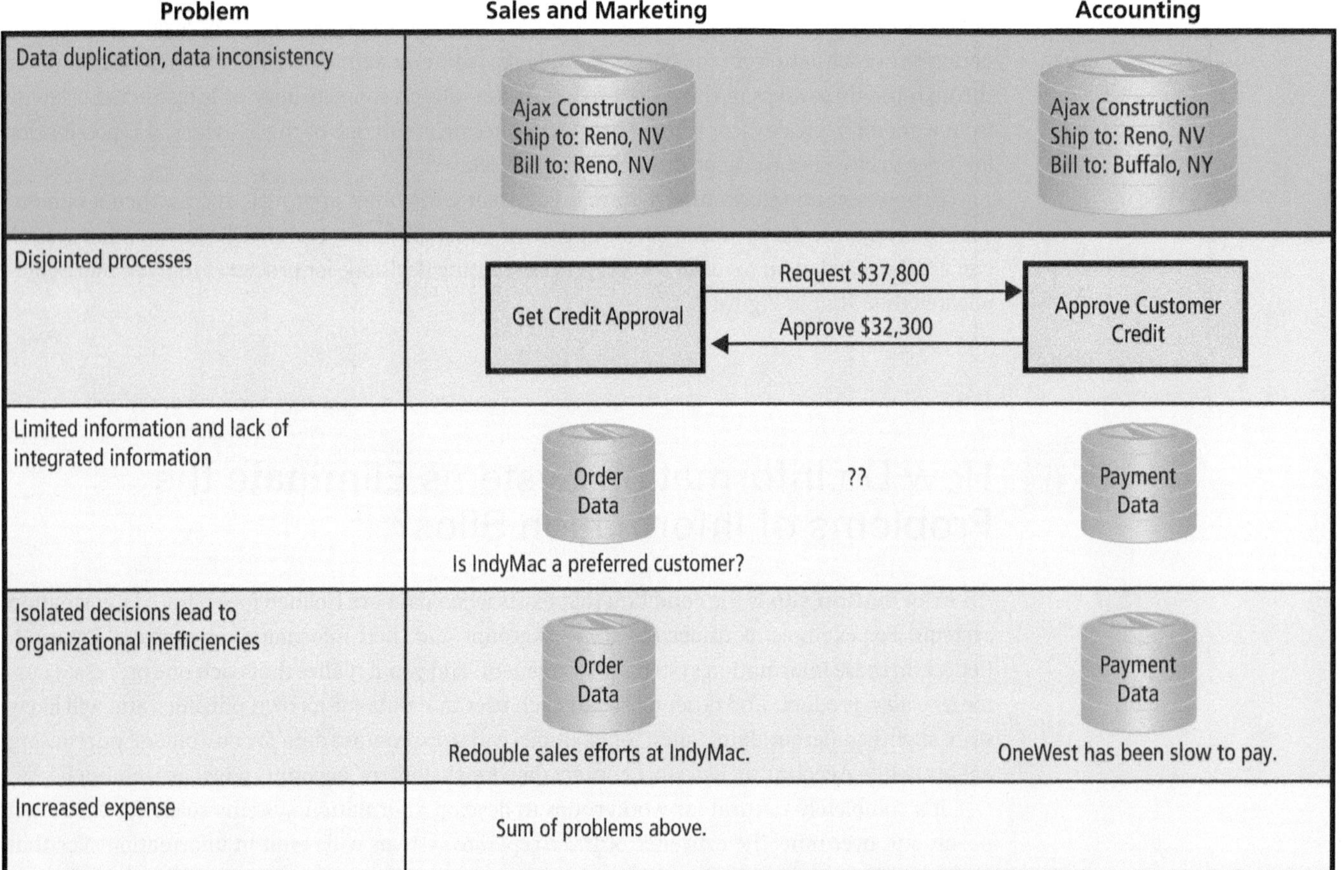

Sales and Marketing doesn't understand what to do with a credit approval of $32,300. According to its database, Ajax already owes $17,800, so if the total credit authorization is only $32,300, did Accounting approve only $14,500 of the new order? And why that amount? Both departments want to approve the order. It will take numerous emails and phone calls, however, to sort this out. These interacting business processes are disjointed.

A consequence of such disjointed activities is the lack of integrated enterprise information. For example, suppose Sales and Marketing wants to know if IndyMac is still a preferred customer. Assume that determining whether this is so requires a comparison of order history and payment history data. With information silos, that data will reside in two different databases and, in one of them, IndyMac is known by the name of the company that acquired it, OneWest Bank. Data integration will be difficult. Making the determination will require manual processes and days, when it should be readily answered in seconds.

This leads to the fourth consequence: inefficiency. When using isolated functional applications, decisions are made in isolation. As shown in the fourth row of Figure 5, Sales and Marketing decided to redouble its sales effort with IndyMac. However, Accounting knows that IndyMac was foreclosed by the FDIC and sold to OneWest and has been slow to pay. There are far better prospects for increased sales attention. Without integration, the left hand of the organization doesn't know what the right hand of the organization is doing.

Finally, information silos can result in increased cost for the organization. Duplicated data, disjointed systems, limited information, and inefficiencies all mean higher costs.

How Do Organizations Solve the Problems of Information Silos?

As defined, an information silo occurs when data is stored in isolated systems. The obvious way to fix such a silo is to integrate the data into a single database and revise applications (and business processes) to use that database. If that is not possible or practical, another remedy is to allow the isolation, but to manage it to avoid problems.

The arrows in Figure 6 show this resolution at two levels of organization. First, isolated data created by workgroup information systems are integrated using enterprise-wide applications.

Scope	Example	Example Information Silo	Enabling Technology
Workgroup	Doctor's office/ medical practice	Physicians and hospitals store separated data about patients. Unnecessarily duplicate tests and procedures.	Functional applications.
		⇩	Enterprise applications (CRM, ERP, EAI) on enterprise networks.
Enterprise	Hospital	Hospital and local drug store pharmacy have different prescription data for the same patient.	
		⇩	Distributed systems using Web service technologies in the cloud.
Inter-enterprise	Inter-agency prescription application	No silo: Doctors, hospitals, pharmacies share patients' prescription and other data.	

FIGURE 6
Information Silos as Drivers

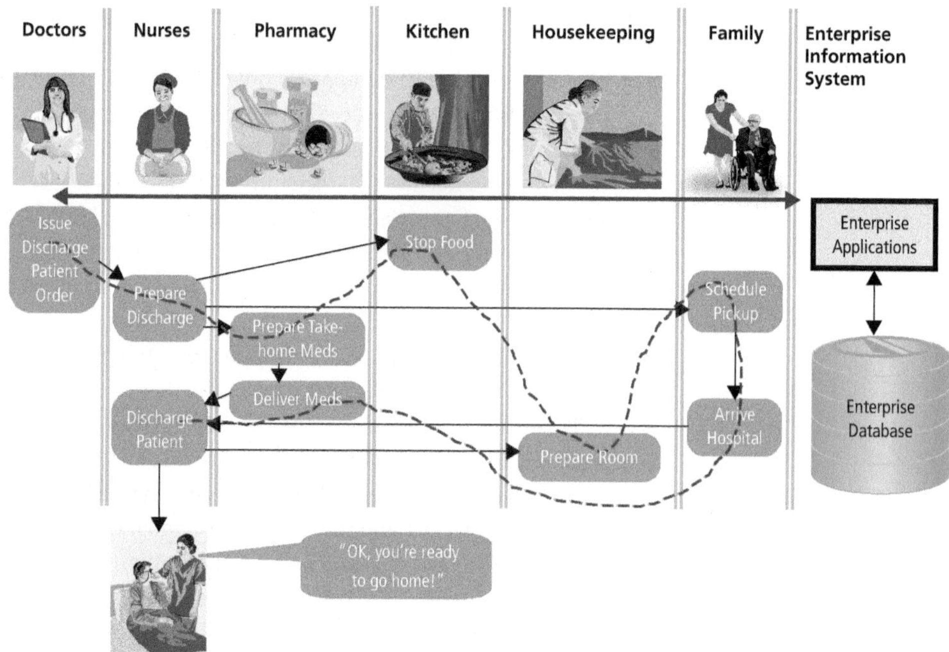

FIGURE 7
Example Enterprise Process and Information System

Second, today, isolated data created by information systems at the enterprise level are being integrated into inter-enterprise systems using distributed applications (such as ARES). These applications process data in a single cloud database or connect disparate, independent databases so that those databases appear to be one database. We will discuss inter-enterprise systems further in Q7.

For now, to better understand how isolated data problems can be resolved, consider an enterprise system at a hospital.

An Enterprise System for Patient Discharge

Figure 7 shows some of the hospital departments and a portion of the patient discharge process. A doctor initiates the process by issuing a discharge patient order. That order is delivered to the appropriate nursing staff, who initiates activities at the pharmacy, the patient's family, and the kitchen. Some of those activities initiate activities back at the nursing staff. In Figure 7, the enterprise process (supported by the IS) is represented by a dotted blue line.

Prior to the enterprise system, the hospital had developed procedures for using a paper-based system and informal messaging via the telephone. Each department kept its own records. When the new enterprise information system was implemented, not only was the data integrated into a database, but new computer-based forms and reports were created. The staff needed to transition from the paper-based system to the computer-based system. They also needed to stop making phone calls and let the new information system make notifications across departments. These measures involved substantial change, and most organizations experience considerable anguish when undergoing such transitions.

Q4 How Do CRM, ERP, and EAI Support Enterprise Processes?

Enterprise systems like the one in Figure 7 were not feasible until network, data communication, and database technologies reached a sufficient level of capability and maturity in the late 1980s and early 1990s. At that point, many organizations began to develop enterprise systems.

The Need for Business Process Engineering

As they did so, organizations realized that their existing business processes needed to change. In part, they needed to change to use the shared databases and to use new computer-based forms and reports. However, an even more important reason for changing business processes was that integrated data and enterprise systems offered the potential of substantial improvements in process quality. It became possible to do things that had been impossible before. Using Porter's language enterprise systems enabled the creation of stronger, faster, more effective *linkages* among value chains.

For example, when the hospital used a paper-based system, the kitchen would prepare meals for everyone who was a patient at the hospital as of midnight the night before. It was not possible to obtain data about discharges until the next midnight. Consequently, considerable food was wasted at substantial cost.

With the enterprise system, the kitchen can be notified about patient discharges as they occur throughout the day, resulting in substantial reductions in wasted food. But when should the kitchen be notified? Immediately? And what if the discharge is cancelled before completion? Notify the kitchen of the cancelled discharge? Many possibilities and alternatives exist. So, to design its new enterprise system, the hospital needed to determine how best to change its processes to take advantage of the new capability. Such projects came to be known as **business process reengineering**, which is the activity of altering existing and designing new business processes to take advantage of new information systems.

Unfortunately, business process reengineering is difficult, slow, and exceedingly expensive. Business analysts need to interview key personnel throughout the organization to determine how best to use the new technology. Because of the complexity involved, such projects require high-level, expensive skills and considerable time. Many early projects stalled when the enormity of the project became apparent. This left some organizations with partially implemented systems, which had disastrous consequences. Personnel didn't know if they were using the new system, the old system, or some hacked-up version of both.

The stage was set for the emergence of enterprise application solutions, which we discuss next.

Emergence of Enterprise Application Solutions

When the process quality benefits of enterprise-wide systems became apparent, most organizations were still developing their applications in-house. At the time, organizations perceived their needs as being "too unique" to be satisfied by off-the-shelf or altered applications. However, as applications became more and more complex, in-house development costs became infeasible. Systems built in-house are expensive not only because of their high initial development costs, but also because of the continuing need to adapt those systems to changing requirements.

In the early 1990s, as the costs of business process reengineering were coupled to the costs of in-house development, organizations began to look more favorably on the idea of licensing preexisting applications. "Maybe we're not so unique, after all."

Some of the vendors who took advantage of this change in attitude were PeopleSoft, which licensed payroll and limited-capability human resources systems; Siebel, which licensed a sales lead tracking and management system; and SAP, which licensed something new, a system called *enterprise resource management*.

These three companies, and ultimately dozens of others like them, offered not just software and database designs. They also offered standardized business processes. These **inherent processes**, which are predesigned procedures for using the software products, saved organizations from the expense, delays, and risks of business process reengineering. Instead, organizations could license the software and obtain, as part of the deal, prebuilt processes that the vendors assured them were based on "industry best practices."

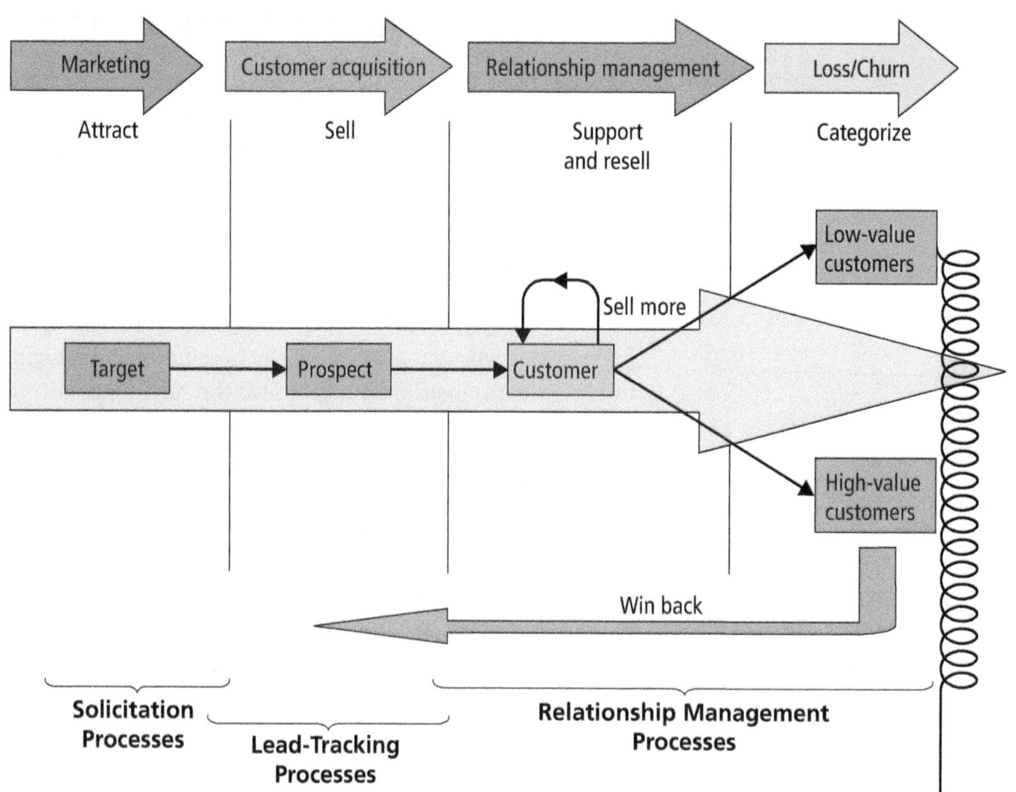

FIGURE 8
The Customer Life Cycle
Source: The Customer Life Cycle. Used with permission from Professor Douglas MacLachlan, Foster School of Business, University of Washington.

The Career Guide given later in the chapter to learn more about careers in managing the development of enterprise applications.

Some parts of that deal were too good to be true because, as you'll learn in Q5, inherent processes are almost never a perfect fit. But the offer was too much for many organizations to resist. Over time, three categories of enterprise applications emerged: customer relationship management, enterprise resource planning, and enterprise application integration. Consider each.

Customer Relationship Management (CRM)

A **customer relationship management (CRM) system** is a suite of applications, a database, and a set of inherent processes for managing all the interactions with the customer, from lead generation to customer service. Every contact and transaction with the customer is recorded in the CRM database. Vendors of CRM systems claim that using their products makes the organization *customer-centric.* Though that term reeks of sales hyperbole, it does indicate the nature and intent of CRM packages.

Figure 8 shows four phases of the **customer life cycle**: marketing, customer acquisition, relationship management, and loss/churn. Marketing sends messages to the target market to attract customer prospects. When prospects order, they become customers who need to be supported. Additionally, relationship management processes increase the value of existing customers by selling them more product. Inevitably, over time the organization loses customers. When this occurs, win-back processes categorize customers according to value and attempt to win back high-value customers.

Figure 9 illustrates the major components of a CRM application. Notice that components exist for each stage of the customer life cycle. As shown, all applications process a common customer database. This design eliminates duplicated customer data and removes the possibility of inconsistent data. It also means that each department knows what has been happening with the customer at other departments. Customer support, for example, will know not to provide $1,000 worth of support labor to a customer that has generated $300 worth of business over time. However, it will know to bend over backward for customers that have generated hundreds of thousands of dollars

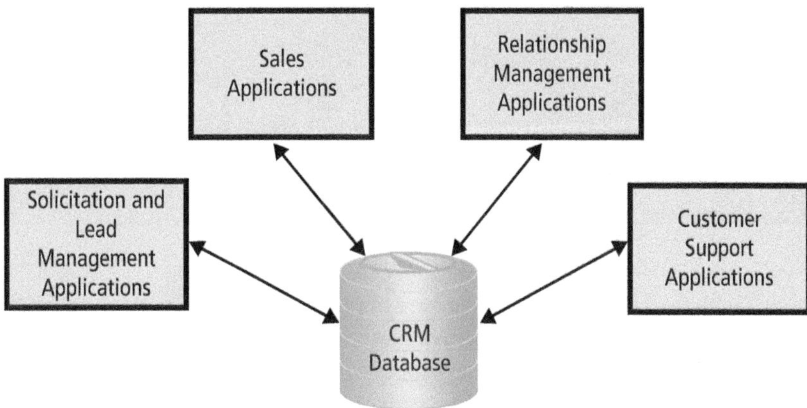

FIGURE 9
CRM Applications

of business. The result to the customers is that they feel like they are dealing with one entity, not many.

CRM systems vary in the degree of functionality they provide. One of the primary tasks when selecting a CRM package is to determine the features you need and to find a package that meets that set of needs. You might be involved in just such a project during your career.

Enterprise Resource Planning (ERP)

Large centralized databases can be attractive targets for disgruntled employees. For more information, see the Security Guide given later in the chapter.

Enterprise resource planning (ERP) is a suite of applications called **modules**, a database, and a set of inherent processes for consolidating business operations into a single, consistent, computing platform. An **ERP system** is an information system based on ERP technology. As shown in Figure 10, ERP systems include the functions of CRM systems but also incorporate accounting, manufacturing, inventory, and human resources applications.

The primary purpose of an ERP system is integration; an ERP system allows the left hand of the organization to know what the right hand is doing. This integration allows real-time updates globally, whenever and wherever a transaction takes place. Critical business decisions can then be made on a timely basis using the latest data.

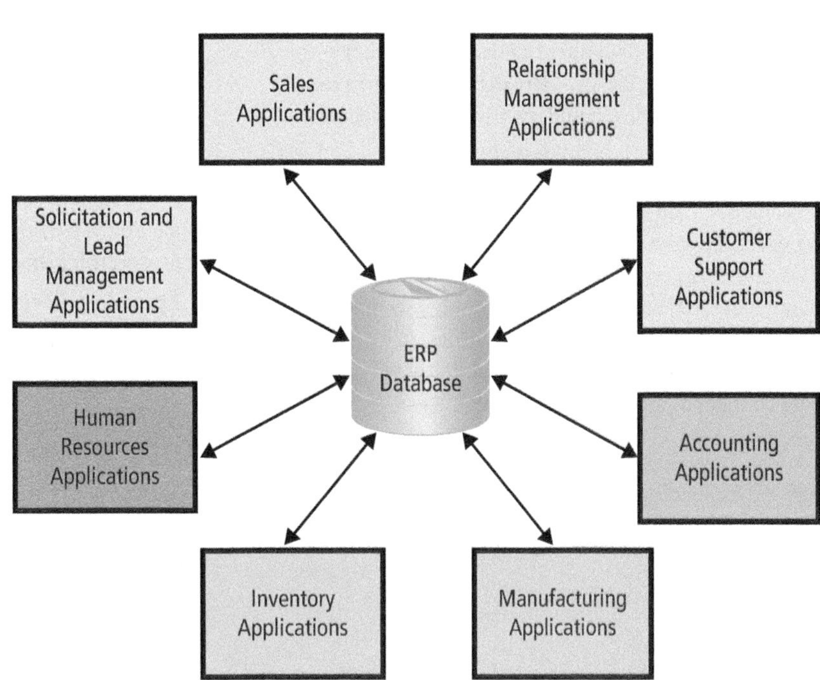

FIGURE 10
ERP Applications

SO WHAT?

WORKFLOW PROBLEMS

According to John Halamka, CIO of the Harvard Medical School and Group Health System, "Most IT problems are workflow problems, not software problems."[2] Using the knowledge of this chapter, you know that workflow problems concern either efficiency (ratio of costs to value delivered is too high) or effectiveness (not contributing to the competitive strategy). So what?

Who fixes a workflow problem? A computer programmer? A network engineer? A database administrator? No, no, and no. So who? Someone with knowledge of the business and, if the workflow involves an information system, someone who is knowledgeable and comfortable working with technical people.

Consider an example close to home. Suppose your university has a limited number of classrooms with sophisticated audiovisual display, and those classrooms are frequently assigned to professors who specialize in old-fashioned lecture and don't use audiovisual display. Meanwhile, professors who want to use, say, Learning Catalytics in their classrooms are making do with poor-quality, hard-to-view computer-based display.

How would you fix that problem? Change the software that allocates classrooms? But how? Who decides what changes need to be made? And does it need to be done in software? Could it be done by fixing a workflow? Is there a convenient point in the professor–class assignment process in which professors (or department chairs) can indicate which professors should teach in which classrooms? Or are classrooms allocated on a university-wide basis? Or maybe the audiovisual system is already generating metadata about its use, and without requiring anyone to provide any extra data, someone in the Assign-Classroom workflow could use this data to allocate the classrooms?

Who develops these alternatives? Who evaluates them? Who implements them with the workflow workers? You! Or it could be you. A *business analyst* is someone who knows business, who understands an organization's competitive strategy and ways to implement it, and who knows enough information systems technology to be able to model and design workflow changes and to work with technical personnel, when needed, to effectuate changes to information systems.

Source: Franz Pfluegl/Fotolia

To do this well, you need to know IS_and_something: IS_and_marketing, IS_and_ operations, IS_and_finance.

Questions

1. Using your own words, explain the meaning of the statement "Most IT problems are workflow problems, not software problems."
2. Consider the classroom assignment problem. Briefly describe three ways of solving that problem. Which of those three is the most promising? Why?
3. In your opinion, is the demand for professionals who know IS_and_something going to decrease? Increase? Stay about the same? Justify your response; search the Internet for data to support your claim.
4. If you were to become an expert in IS_and_something, what would the *something* be? Search the Internet for employment prospects for that career choice.
5. Examine your current plan of courses before you graduate. What courses do you need to add to your plan to learn IS_and_something? Will you add these courses? Why or why not?

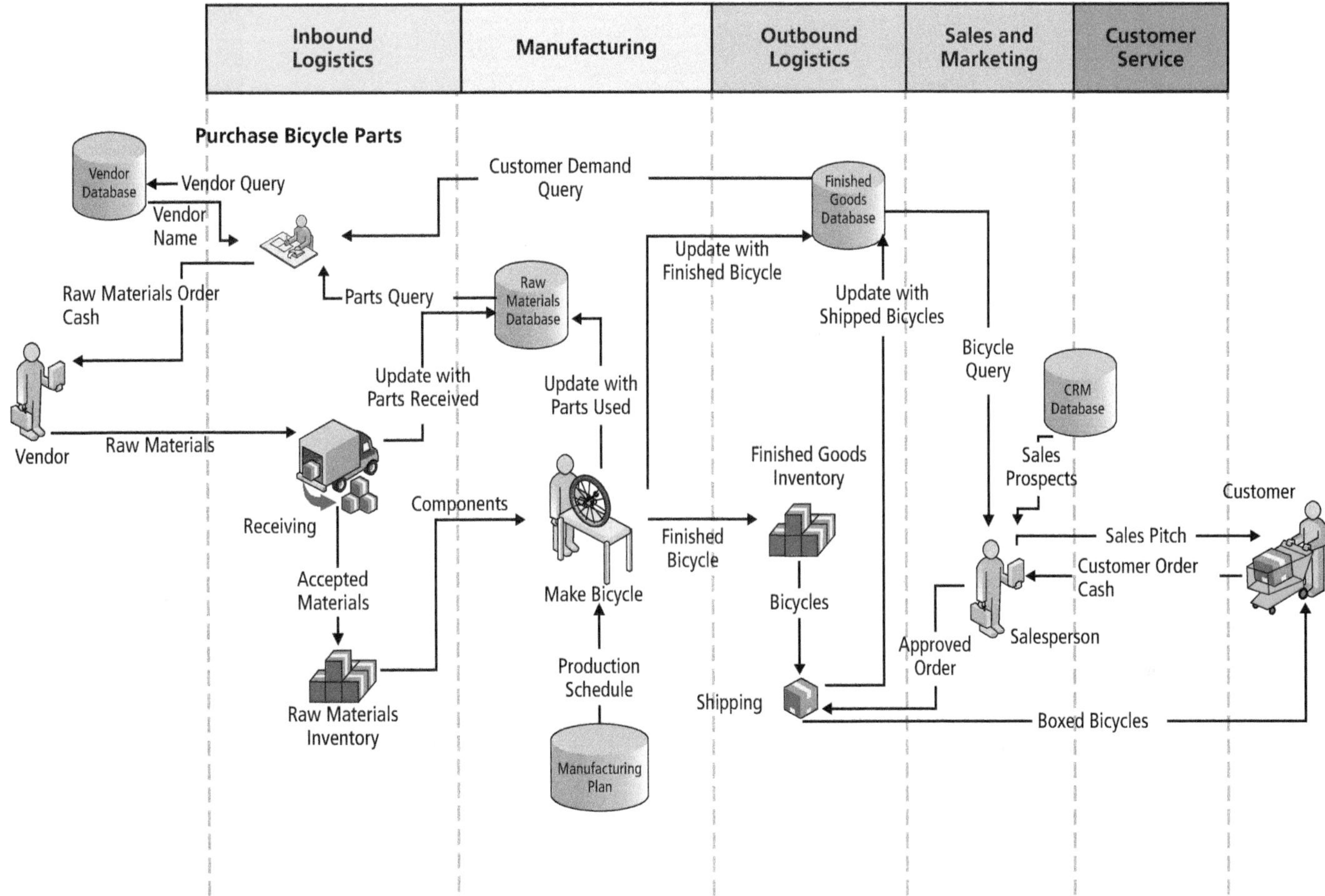

FIGURE 11
Pre-ERP Information Systems

To understand the utility of this integration, consider the pre-ERP systems shown in Figure 11. This diagram represents the processes used by a bicycle manufacturer. It includes five different databases, one each for vendors, raw materials, finished goods, manufacturing plan, and CRM. Consider the problems that appear with such separated data when the Sales department closes a large order, say, for 1,000 bicycles.

First, should the company take the order? Can it meet the schedule requirements for such a large order? Suppose one of the primary parts vendors recently lost capacity due to an earthquake, and the manufacturer cannot obtain parts for the order in time. If so, the order schedule ought not to be approved. However, with such separated systems this situation is unknown.

Even if parts can be obtained, until the order is entered into the finished goods database, purchasing is unaware of the need to buy new parts. The same comment applies to manufacturing. Until the new order is entered into the manufacturing plan, the Production department doesn't know that it needs to increase manufacturing. And, as with parts, does the company have sufficient machine and floor capacity to fill the order on a timely basis? Does it have sufficient personnel with the correct skill sets? Should it be hiring? Can production meet the order schedule? No one knows before the order is approved.

Figure 11 does not show accounting. We can assume, however, that the company has a separate accounting system that is similarly isolated. Eventually, records of business activity find their way to the Accounting department and will be posted into the general ledger. With such a pre-ERP system, financial statements are always outdated, available several weeks after the close of the quarter or other accounting period.

ETHICS GUIDE

PAID DELETION

Robin wound her way up to the third floor of the parking garage. As she began backing up into her assigned spot, she noticed that the car she expected to see in her side mirror was not there. Rather, a shiny new luxury car was parked in that spot. The space occupied by the car belonged to Eric Pittman, a colleague on their employer's search engine optimization team. Robin and Eric had both worked for the company—a leading Web search provider—for about 5 years. Based on conversations they'd had while out for drinks after work, they had comparable salaries, too. Robin wondered how Eric could afford such a nice car considering they were both struggling to afford basic living expenses in such an expensive city.

Robin's thoughts turned to the meetings she had lined up all morning—she probably wouldn't be able to check her email until after lunch. With a grimace, she descended to the first floor in the elevator. She counted the number of days until the weekend and let out a groan.

Eraser for Hire

Eric and Robin burst out of the conference room as quickly as they could. It was almost 6 o'clock and they had just left their last meeting of the day. "Do you want to grab a bite to eat at that Greek place?" Eric asked. "Sure," Robin replied. "I am happy to go anywhere that's at least a mile from this office!" They jumped into their cars and met up at the restaurant. They gossiped about some of their colleagues and poked fun at their bosses while they waited for the food to arrive. Once it arrived and Eric picked up his gyro to take a bite, Robin noticed his brand-new luxury watch.

"Time out!" Robin exclaimed. "You need to tell me what is going on! I parked my car next to your brand-new set of wheels this morning. I didn't want to say anything, but I just noticed that you have a brand-new watch, too. Did you get some sort of bonus that I don't know about?" she asked, half-kidding and half-worried. She wondered why *she* wouldn't

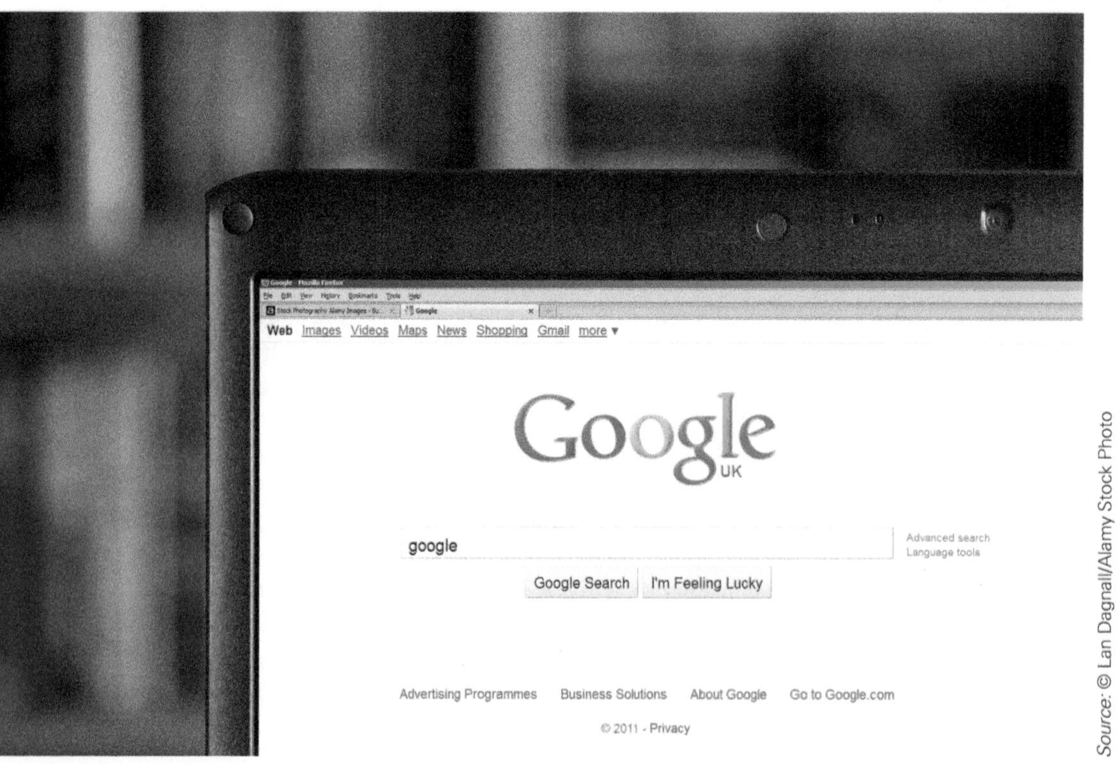

Source: © Lan Dagnall/Alamy Stock Photo

have received a bonus, too. Eric immediately had a concerned look on his face. "Can you keep a secret?" he asked.

Eric described an unraveling chain of events in which a number of companies operating in the area had approached him about the possibility of providing "reputation management" services. Each company had recently had some form of negative press, though each form was different. One large manufacturing company was dealing with environmental protection violations. A large retailer had to explain why it provided inadequate health benefits to its employees. A popular chain of restaurants had recently had a long list of health-code violations. The companies had come to Eric because his dad was a well-known consultant to many large companies in the area.

Each company had offered Eric a substantial financial incentive to tweak the results of Web searches using key terms relevant to these negative incidents. Eric had used his access to the search algorithms to make sure any negative press about these incidents showed up several pages deep in the search results, thus minimizing the likelihood that anyone would see them. In some cases, Eric even had the content completely removed from the search index.

Thanks to Eric, the negative stories had very little impact on the companies. His work limited the availability of information about these events via search engine. "With what they paid me, I paid off my student loans, prepaid the lease on my apartment for a whole year, and still had some left over to treat myself a bit," he said with pride. "Are you interested in being a part of this?"

Robin was astounded. She couldn't imagine what would happen to Eric if someone found out what he had done. She also couldn't bring herself to think about what would happen to their employer if someone found out its search results had been manipulated. Not only could Eric be in trouble, but the company could be severely damaged. She could lose her job, too.

But now that she knew about Eric's actions, she worried that she might be considered an accessory to search engine manipulation if she didn't report his behavior. Robin took another bite of her gyro; it didn't taste nearly as good as it had about 20 minutes before.

DISCUSSION QUESTIONS

1. According to the definitions of the ethical principles:
   a. Do you think that removing content on the Internet and manipulating search engine results for money is ethical according to the categorical imperative?
   b. Do you think that removing content on the Internet and manipulating search engine results for money is ethical according to the utilitarian perspective?
2. How might have Eric rationalized his fraudulent behavior?
3. How could an employer prevent this type of manipulation? What types of policies or procedures could be implemented to prevent this type of fraud?
4. Even if Eric were caught, would he be guilty of a crime? Which laws govern search engine management?
5. Would his employer be motivated to report this fraudulent behavior? Why or why not?

Contrast this situation with the ERP system in Figure 12. Here, all activity is processed by ERP application programs (called *modules*), and consolidated data are stored in a centralized ERP database. When Sales is confronted with the opportunity to sell 1,000 bicycles, the information it needs to confirm that the order, schedule, and terms are possible can be obtained from the ERP system immediately. Once the order is accepted, all departments, including purchasing, manufacturing, human resources, and accounting, are notified. Further, transactions are posted to the ERP database as they occur; the result is that financial statements are available quickly. In most cases, correct financial statements can be produced in real time. With such integration, ERP systems can display the current status of critical business factors to managers and executives, as shown in the sales dashboard in Figure 13.

Of course, the devil is in the details. It's one thing to draw a rectangle on a chart, label it "ERP Applications," and assume that data integration takes all the problems away. It is far more

FIGURE 12
ERP Information Systems

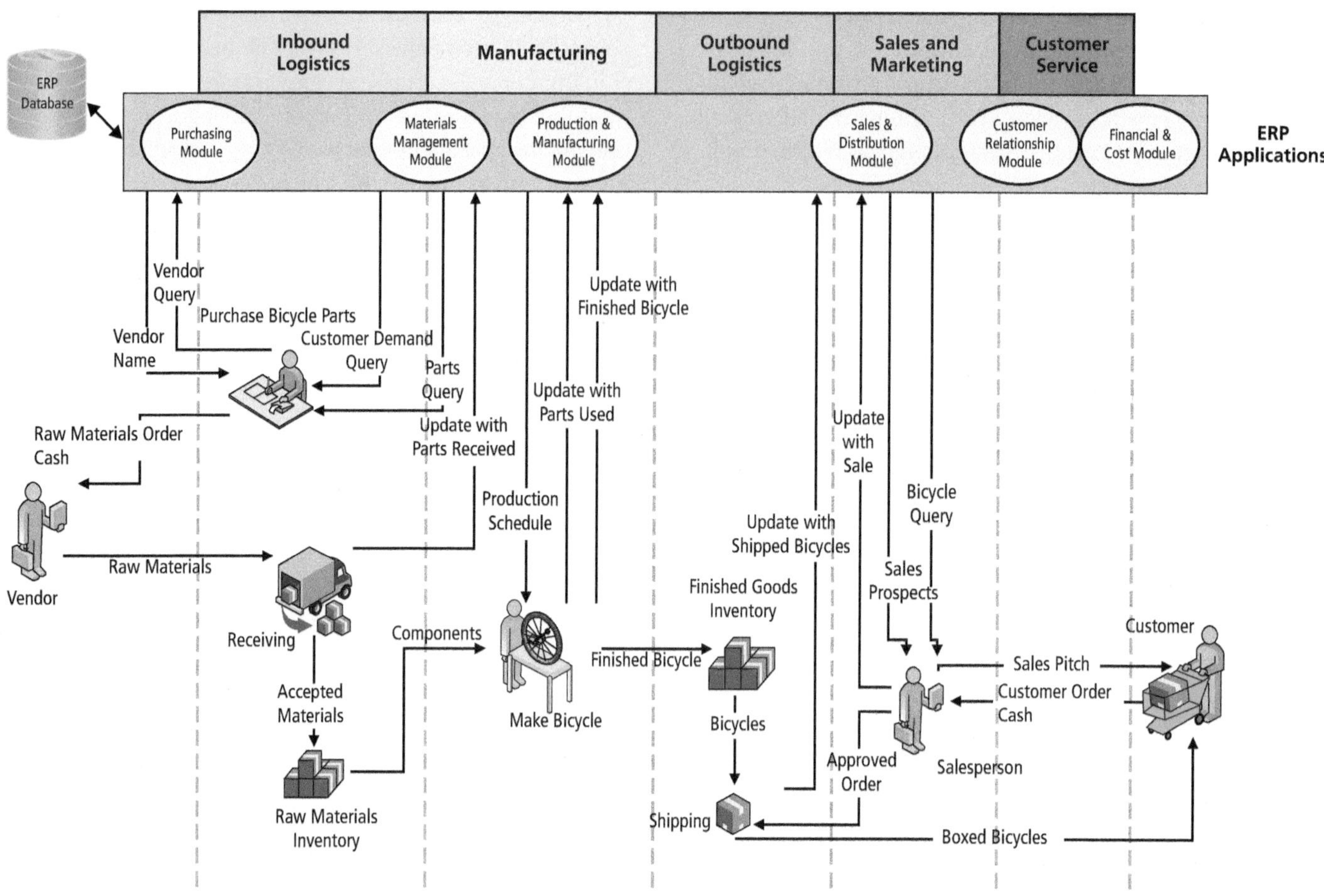

difficult to write those application programs and to design the database to store that integrated data. Even more problematic, what procedures should employees and others use to process those application programs? Specifically, for example, what actions should salespeople take before they approve a large order? Here are some of the questions that need to be answered or resolved:

- How does the Sales department determine that an order is considered large? By dollars? By volume?
- Who approves customer credit (and how)?
- Who approves production capacity (and how)?
- Who approves schedule and terms (and how)?
- What actions need to be taken if the customer modifies the order?
- How does management obtain oversight on sales activity?

As you can imagine, many other questions must be answered as well. Because of its importance to organizations today, we will discuss ERP in further detail in Q5. Before we do so, however, consider the third type of enterprise system: EAI.

Enterprise Application Integration (EAI)

ERP systems are not for every organization. For example, some nonmanufacturing companies find the manufacturing orientation of ERP inappropriate. Even for manufacturing companies, some find the process of converting from their current system to an ERP system too daunting. Others are quite satisfied with their manufacturing application systems and do not wish to change them.

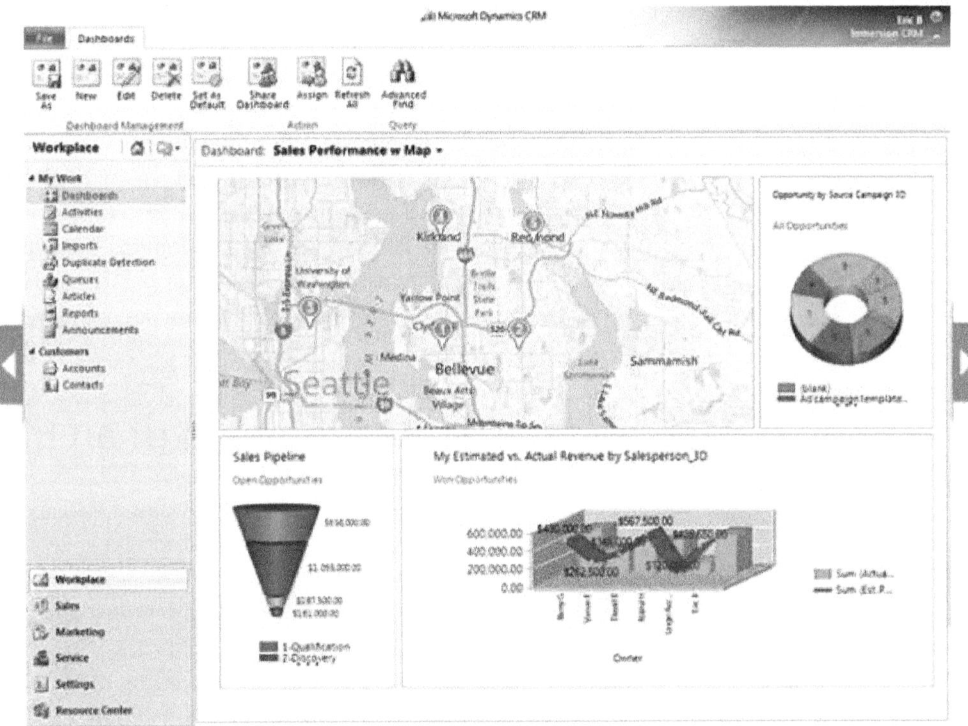

SOURCE: Courtesy of Microsoft

FIGURE 13
Sales Dashboard
Source: Windows 10, Microsoft Corporation.

Companies for which ERP is inappropriate still have the problems associated with information silos, however, and some choose to use **enterprise application integration (EAI)** to solve those problems. EAI is a suite of software applications that integrates existing systems by providing layers of software that connect applications together. EAI does the following:

- It connects system "islands" via a new layer of software/system.
- It enables existing applications to communicate and share data.
- It provides integrated information.
- It leverages existing systems—leaving functional applications as is but providing an integration layer over the top.
- It enables a gradual move to ERP.

The layers of EAI software shown in Figure 14 enable existing applications to communicate with each other and to share data. For example, EAI software can be configured to automatically carry out the data conversion required to make data compatible among different systems. When the CRM applications send data to the manufacturing application system, for example, the CRM system sends its data to an EAI software program. That EAI program makes the conversion and then sends the converted data to the ERP system. The reverse action is taken to send data back from the ERP to the CRM.

FIGURE 14
Design and Implementation for the Five Components

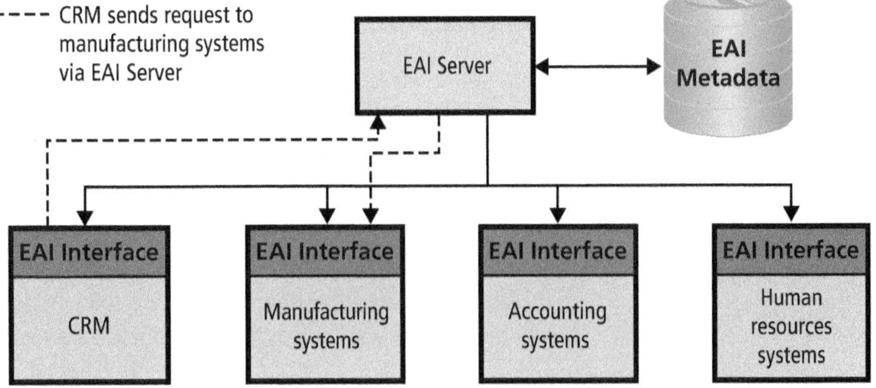

Although there is no centralized EAI database, the EAI software keeps files of metadata that describe data formats and locations. Users can access the EAI system to find the data they need. In some cases, the EAI system provides services that provide a "virtual integrated database" for the user to process.

The major benefit of EAI is that it enables organizations to use existing applications while eliminating many of the serious problems of isolated systems. Converting to an EAI system is not nearly as disruptive as converting to an ERP system, and it provides many of the benefits of ERP. Some organizations develop EAI applications as a stepping stone to complete ERP systems. Today, many EAI systems use Web services standards to define the interactions among EAI components. Some or all of the processing for those components can be moved to the cloud as well.

Q5 What Are the Elements of an ERP System?

Because of its importance to organizations today, we will consider ERP in more depth than CRM or EAI. To begin, the term *ERP* has been applied to a wide array of application solutions, in some cases erroneously. Some vendors attempted to catch the buzz for ERP by misapplying the term to applications that provided only one or two integrated functional applications.

The organization ERPsoftware360 publishes a wealth of information about ERP vendors, products, solutions, and applications. According to its Web site (*www.erpsoftware360.com/erp-101.htm*), for a product to be considered a true ERP product, it must include applications that integrate:

- Supply chain (procurement, sales order processing, inventory management, supplier management, and related activities)
- Manufacturing (scheduling, capacity planning, quality control, bill of materials, and related activities)
- CRM (sales prospecting, customer management, marketing, customer support, call center support)
- Human resources (payroll, time and attendance, HR management, commission calculations, benefits administration, and related activities)
- Accounting (general ledger, accounts receivable, accounts payable, cash management, fixed asset accounting)

An ERP solution is an information system and, as such, has all five components. We consider each in turn.

Hardware

Traditionally, organizations hosted ERP solutions on their own in-house, networked server computers. Such hosting is still the case for many large ERP applications, as well as for those ERP applications that were installed years ago and for which the hardware infrastructure is stable and well managed.

Increasingly, however, organizations are turning to cloud-based hosting in one of two modes:

- PaaS: Replace an organization's existing hardware infrastructure with hardware in the cloud. Install ERP software and databases on that cloud hardware. The using organization then manages the ERP software on the cloud hardware.
- SaaS: Acquire a cloud-based ERP solution. SAP, Oracle, Microsoft, and the other major ERP vendors offer their ERP software as a service. The vendor manages the ERP software and offers it to customers as a service.

During your career, existing in-house ERP solutions are likely to migrate to one of these two modes. Larger installations will likely move to PaaS; smaller and new ERP systems are likely to use SaaS.

ERP Application Programs

ERP vendors design application programs to be configurable so that development teams can alter them to meet an organization's requirements without changing program code. Accordingly, during the ERP development process, the development team sets configuration parameters that specify how ERP application programs will operate. For example, an hourly payroll application is configured to specify the number of hours in the standard workweek, hourly wages for different job categories, wage adjustments for overtime and holiday work, and so forth. Deciding on the initial configuration values and adapting them to new requirements is a challenging collaboration activity. It is also one that you might be involved in as a business professional.

Of course, there are limits to how much configuration can be done. If a new ERP customer has requirements that cannot be met via program configuration, then it needs to either adapt its business to what the software can do or write (or pay another vendor to write) application code to meet its requirements. Such custom programming is expensive, both initially and in long-term maintenance costs. Thus, choosing an ERP solution with applications that function close to the organization's requirements is critical to its successful implementation.

ERP Databases

An ERP solution includes a database design as well as initial configuration data. It does not, of course, contain the company's operational data. During development, the team must enter the initial values for that data as part of the development effort.

If your only experience with databases is creating a few tables in Microsoft Access, then you probably underestimate the value and importance of ERP database designs. SAP, the leading vendor of ERP solutions, provides ERP databases that contain more than 15,000 tables. The design includes the metadata for those tables, as well as their relationships to each other, and rules and constraints about how the data in some tables must relate to data in other tables. The ERP solution also contains tables filled with initial configuration data.

Reflect on the difficulty of creating and validating data models, and you will have some idea of the amount of intellectual capital invested in a database design of 15,000 tables. Also, consider the magnitude of the task of filling such a database with users' data!

Large organizational databases contain two types of program code. The first, called a **trigger**, is a computer program stored within the database that runs to keep the database consistent when certain conditions arise. The second, called a **stored procedure**, is a computer program stored in the database that is used to enforce business rules. An example of such a rule would be never to sell certain items at a discount. Triggers and stored procedures are also part of the ERP solution. Developers and business users need to configure the operation of such code during the ERP implementation as well.

Business Process Procedures

Another component of an ERP solution is a set of inherent procedures that implement standard business processes. ERP vendors develop hundreds, or even thousands, of procedures that enable the ERP customer organization to accomplish its work using the applications provided by the vendor. Figure 15 shows a part of the SAP ordering business process; this process implements a portion of the inbound logistics activities. Some ERP vendors call the inherent processes that are defined in the ERP solution **process blueprints**.

Without delving into the details, you should be able to understand the flow of work outlined in this process. Every function (rounded rectangles in Figure 15) consists of a set of procedures for accomplishing that function. Typically, these procedures require an ERP user to use application menus, screens, and reports to accomplish the activity.

As with application programs, ERP users must either adapt to the predefined, inherent processes and procedures or design new ones. In the latter case, the design of new procedures may

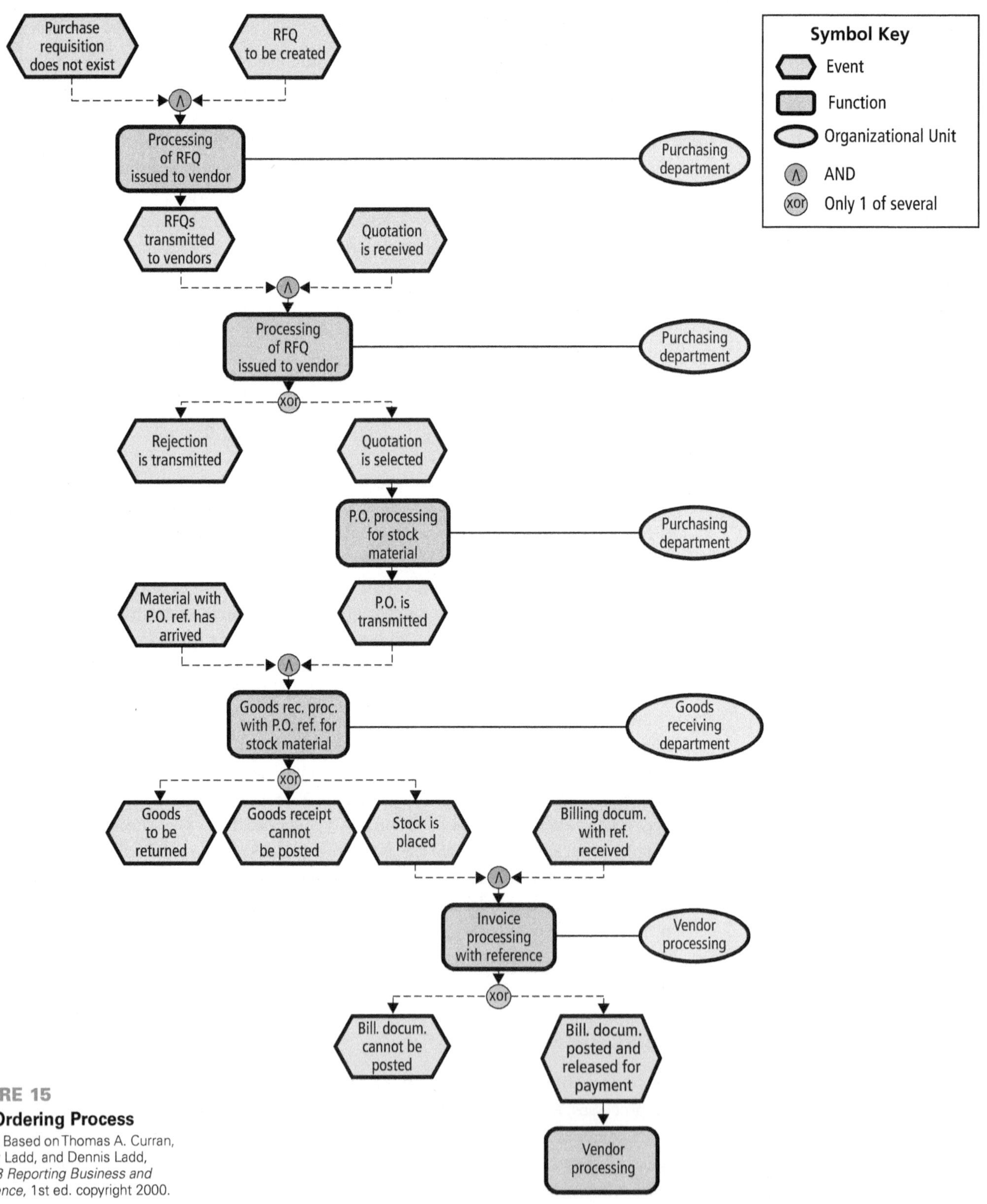

FIGURE 15
SAP Ordering Process
Source: Based on Thomas A. Curran, Andrew Ladd, and Dennis Ladd, *SAP/R/3 Reporting Business and Intelligence*, 1st ed. copyright 2000.

necessitate changes to application programs and to database structures as well. Perhaps you can begin to understand why organizations attempt to conform to vendor standards.

Training and Consulting

Because of the complexity and difficulty of implementing and using ERP solutions, ERP vendors have developed training curricula and numerous classes. SAP operates universities, in which customers and potential customers receive training both before and after the ERP implementation. In addition, ERP vendors typically conduct classes on site. To reduce expenses, the vendors sometimes train the organization's employees, called Super Users, to become in-house trainers in training sessions called **train the trainer**.

ERP training falls into two broad categories. The first category is training about how to implement the ERP solution. This training includes topics such as obtaining top-level management support, preparing the organization for change, and dealing with the inevitable resistance that develops when people are asked to perform work in new ways. The second category is training on how to use the ERP application software; this training includes specific steps for using the ERP applications to accomplish the activities in processes such as those in Figure 15.

ERP vendors also provide on-site consulting for implementing and using the ERP system. Additionally, an industry of third-party ERP consultants has developed to support new ERP customers and implementations. These consultants provide knowledge gained through numerous ERP implementations. Such knowledge is valued because most organizations go through an ERP conversion only once. Ironically, having done so, they now know how to do it. Consequently, some employees, seasoned by an ERP conversion with their employer, leave that company to become ERP consultants.

Industry-Specific Solutions

As you can tell, considerable work needs to be done to customize an ERP application to a particular customer. To reduce that work, ERP vendors provide starter kits for specific industries called **industry-specific solutions**. These solutions contain program and database configuration files as well as process blueprints that apply to ERP implementations in specific industries. Over time, SAP, which first provided such solutions, and other ERP vendors created dozens of such starter kits for manufacturing, sales and distribution, healthcare, and other major industries.

Company	ERP Market Rank	Remarks	Future
SAP	1	Led ERP success with client-server hardware. Largest vendor, most comprehensive solution. Largest customers. Expensive.	Technology older, but SAP is adapting to mobility and cloud trends. Expensive and seriously challenged by less expensive alternatives. Huge customer base. Future depends on effectively migrating traditional customers to the cloud. Claims number 1 in CRM.
Oracle	2	Combination of in-house and acquired (PeopleSoft, Siebel) products. Expensive.	Intensely competitive company with strong technology base. Large customer base. Flexible SOA architecture. Will leverage strong technology base into innovative and effective cloud-based solutions. Strong challenge to SAP market leadership. Claims number 1 in CRM.
Infor ERP	3	Privately held corporation that acquired an ERP product named Baan, along with more than 20 others.	Many solutions, not integrated, particularly specialized for manufacturing and supply chain management. Evolving with revolution in 3D printing practices.
Microsoft Dynamics	4	Four products acquired: AX, Nav, GP, and SL. AX and Nav more comprehensive. SL on the way out? Large VAR channel.	Products not well integrated with Office. Not integrated at all with Microsoft development languages. Solutions not integrated and product direction uncertain. Microsoft Azure hosts Oracle and SAP products. Conflict with Azure hosting of Microsoft ERP products.
Sage	5	Offers ERP, CRM, and financial-oriented functional system solutions.	Sage adapted many of its legacy applications and solutions for the cloud and for mobile computing. Offers inexpensive, cloud-based solutions for startups and small businesses. Broad product suite.

FIGURE 16

Characteristics of Top ERP Vendors

Source: Panorama Consulting Solutions, "Clash of the Titans 2016," *Panorama-consulting.com*, November 2015, *http://go.panorama-consulting.com/rs/603-UJX-107/images/Clash-of-the-Titans-2016.pdf;* Gartner, "ERP Software, Worldwide, 2015," *Gartner.com*, April 29, 2016, www.gartner.com/doc/3300322/market-share-analysis-erp-software.

Which Companies Are the Major ERP Vendors?

Although more than 100 different companies advertise ERP products, not all of those products meet the minimal ERP criteria. Even of those that do, the bulk of the market is held by the five vendors shown in Figure 16.[3] This figure shows market rank rather than market share because it is difficult to obtain comparable revenue numbers. Infor is owned by private equity investors and does not publish financial data. Its ranking is based on what little sales data is publicly available. Microsoft's ERP revenue is combined with its CRM revenue, and its true ERP revenue is unknown. Similarly, Oracle and SAP combine ERP revenue with revenue from other products. Sage revenue is an amalgam of ERP, CRM, and financial-oriented functional solutions.

Q6 What Are the Challenges of Implementing and Upgrading Enterprise Information Systems?

Implementing new enterprise systems, whether CRM, ERP, or EAI, is challenging, difficult, expensive, and risky. It is not unusual for enterprise system projects to be well over budget and a year or more late. In addition to new ERP implementations, numerous organizations implemented ERP 15 or 20 years ago and now need to upgrade their ERP installation to meet new requirements. If you work in an organization that is already using enterprise systems, you may find yourself engaged in a significant upgrade effort. Whether from a new implementation or an upgrade, expense and risks arise from five primary factors (see Figure 17).

Collaborative Management

Unlike departmental systems in which a single department manager is in charge, enterprise systems have no clear boss. Examine the discharge process in Figure 7; there is no manager of discharge. The discharge process is a collaborative effort among many departments (and customers).

With no single manager, who resolves the disputes that inevitably arise? All of these departments ultimately report to the CEO, so there is a single boss over all of them, but employees can't go to the CEO with a problem about, say, coordinating discharge activities between nursing and housekeeping. The CEO would throw them out of his or her office. Instead, the organization needs to develop some sort of collaborative management for resolving process issues.

Usually this means that the enterprise develops committees and steering groups for providing enterprise process management. Although this can be an effective solution, and in fact may be the *only* solution, the work of such groups is both slow and expensive.

Requirements Gaps

As stated in Q4, few organizations today create their own enterprise systems from scratch. Instead, they license an enterprise product that provides specific functions and features and that includes inherent procedures. But such licensed products are never a perfect fit. Almost always there are gaps between the organization's requirements and the application's capabilities.

- Collaborative management
- Requirements gaps
- Transition problems
- Employee resistance
- New technology

FIGURE 17
Five Primary Factors

The first challenge is identifying the gaps. To specify a gap, an organization must know both what it needs and what the new product does. However, it can be very difficult for an organization to determine what it needs; that difficulty is one reason organizations choose to license rather than to build. Further, the features and functions of complex products like CRM or ERP are not easy to identify. Thus, gap identification is a major task when implementing enterprise systems.

The second challenge is deciding what to do with gaps, once they are identified. Either the organization needs to change the way it does things to adapt to the new application, or the application must be altered to match what the organization does. Either choice is problematic. Employees will resist change, but paying for alterations is expensive, and the organization is committing to maintaining those alterations as the application is changed over time. Here, organizations fill gaps by choosing their lesser regret.

Transition Problems

Transitioning to a new enterprise system is also difficult. The organization must somehow change from using isolated departmental systems to using the new enterprise system, while continuing to run the business. It's like having heart surgery while running a 100-yard dash.

Such transitions require careful planning and substantial training. Inevitably, problems will develop. Knowing this will occur, senior management needs to communicate the need for the change to the employees and then stand behind the new system as the kinks are worked out. It is an incredibly stressful time for all involved.

Employee Resistance

People resist change. Change requires effort and engenders fear. Considerable research and literature exist about the reasons for change resistance and how organizations can deal with it. Here we will summarize the major principles.

First, senior-level management needs to communicate the need for the change to the organization and reiterate this, as necessary, throughout the transition process. Second, employees fear change because it threatens **self-efficacy**, which is a person's belief that he or she can be successful at his or her job. To enhance confidence, employees need to be trained and coached on the successful use of the new system. Word-of-mouth is a very powerful factor, and in some cases key users are trained ahead of time to create positive buzz about the new system. Video demonstrations of employees successfully using the new system are also effective.

Third, in many ways, the primary benefits of a new ERP system are felt by the accounting and finance departments and the senior management. Many of the employees who are asked to change their activities to implement ERP will not receive any direct benefit from it. Therefore, employees may need to be given extra inducement to change to the new system. As one experienced change consultant said, "Nothing succeeds like praise or cash, especially cash." Straight-out pay for change is bribery, but contests with cash prizes among employees or groups can be very effective at inducing change.

Implementing new enterprise systems can solve many problems and bring great efficiency and cost savings to an organization, but it is not for the faint of heart.

New Technology

Emerging, new technology affects all information systems, but it affects enterprise systems particularly because of their importance and their value. Consider, for example, the cloud. Because of the cost savings of cloud-based computing, organizations would like to move their enterprise systems to the cloud. But legal, risk, and business policy factors may make such a move infeasible. The organization may be required to keep physical control over its data. When moving it to the cloud, the cloud vendor controls the physical location of the data, and that location might not even be in the same country as the organization. So, some sort of hybrid model may need to be devised (see Q8).

Similar comments pertain to mobile technology. Employees want to use mobile devices to access and even modify enterprise system data. But mobile devices are just that—mobile. The enterprise system may be exposed to considerable risk while outside the control of the organization. And ERP data is a juicy target for crime. These factors don't mean organizations cannot use new technology with enterprise systems, but they do add challenges.

Q7 How Do Inter-enterprise IS Solve the Problems of Enterprise Silos?

The discussion in Q4 illustrates the primary ways in which enterprise systems solve the problems of workgroup information silos. In this question, we will use the ARES example to show you how inter-enterprise systems can accomplish the same for enterprise silos. (The transition is shown by the lower arrow leading to the bottom row in Figure 6.)

Figure 18 shows the information silos that exist among employers, health clubs, and principal ARES home users. Employers may maintain records of exercise programs, diet, weight, lab test results (e.g., cholesterol, blood sugar, etc.), and biometric readings from wearables (e.g., steps taken, heart rate, sleep patterns, etc.). Health clubs store membership, class, personal trainer, and exercise performance data in a club database. Data is gathered automatically from virtual cycling classes or from on-premises exercise equipment and member heart monitors. At home, individuals generate exercise data on heart monitors and equipment; that data is recorded on mobile devices via wearable exercise devices.

The isolation of this exercise data causes problems. For example, employers would like to have reports on exercise data stored in user devices and in health clubs. Users would like to have data like lab test results from their employer, as well as exercise data from their time at health clubs. Health clubs would like to have lab results and home workout data to integrate with the data they have. All three entities would like to produce reports from the integrated data.

Figure 19 shows the structure of an inter-enterprise system that meets the goals of the three types of participants. In this figure, the labeled rectangles inside the cloud represent mobile applications that could be native, thin-client, or both. Some of the application processing might be done on cloud servers as well as on the mobile devices. Those design decisions are not shown. As illustrated, this system assumes that all users receive reports on mobile devices, but because of the large amount of keying involved, employers submit and manage lab results using a personal computer.

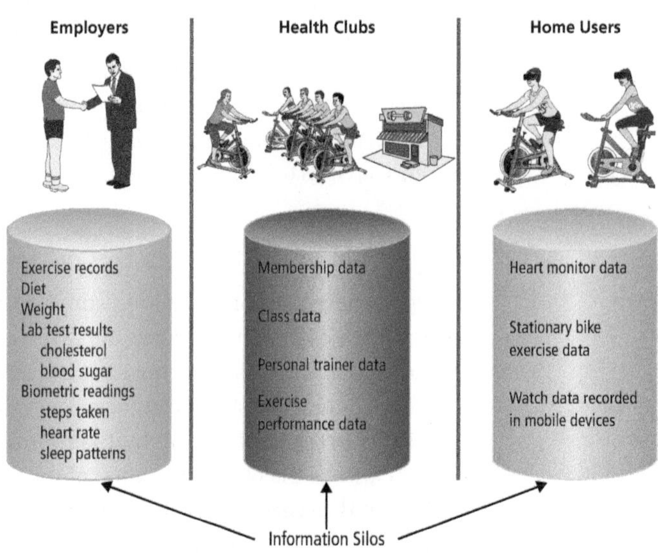

FIGURE 18
Information Silos Without ARES

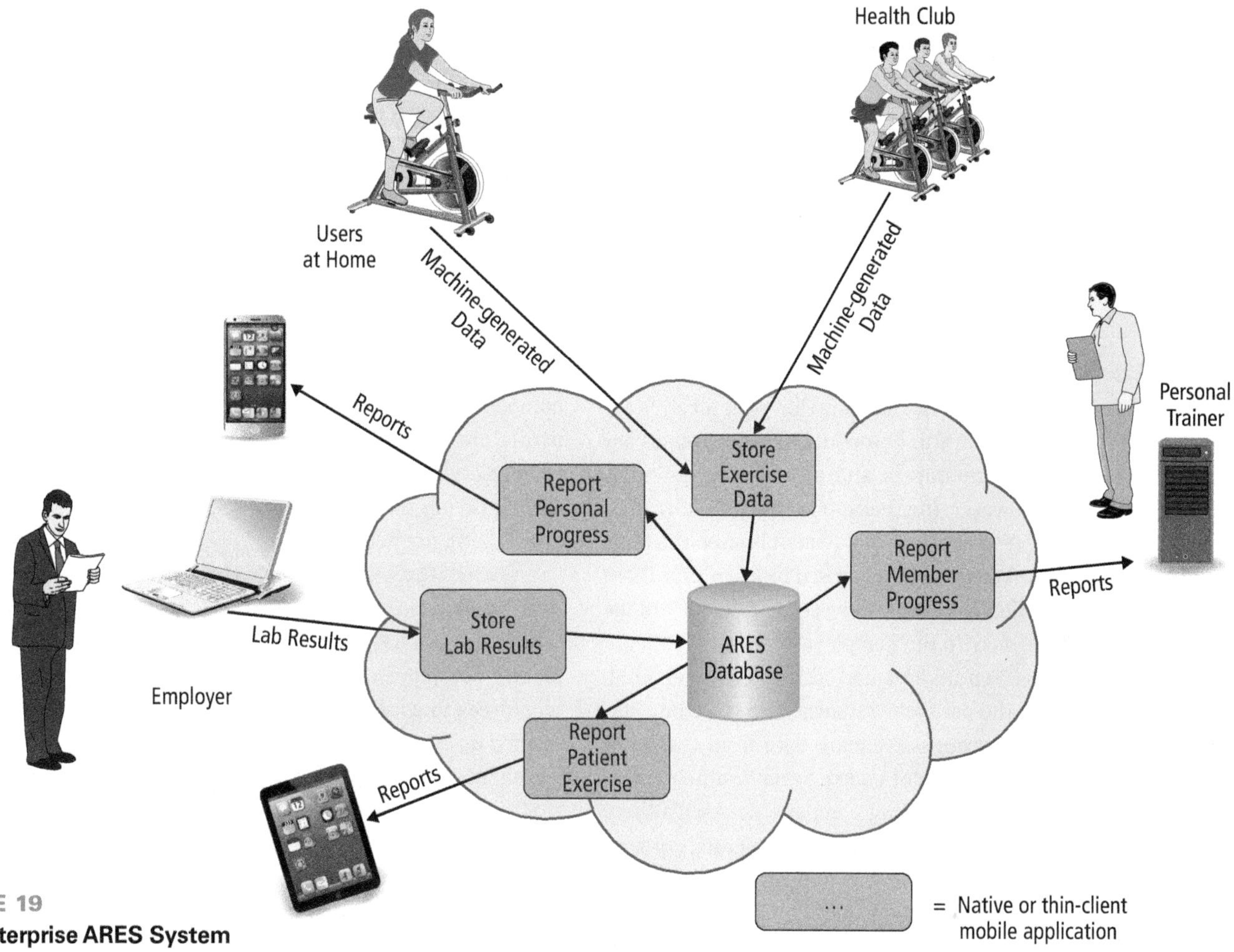

FIGURE 19
Inter-enterprise ARES System

As you can see, lab results and exercise data are integrated in the ARES database; that integrated data is processed by a reporting application to create and distribute the reports as shown.

Systems like that shown in Figure 19 are referred to as **distributed systems** because applications processing is distributed across multiple computing devices. Standards such as http, https, html5, css3, JavaScript, and SOA using Web services enable programs to receive data from and display data to a variety of mobile and desktop devices.

ARES data is requested and delivered using JSON.

Q8 2027? 

Within the next 10 years, ERP vendors and customers will have sorted out the problems of cloud-based ERP. In what is coming to be known as the **hybrid model**, ERP customers will store most of their data on cloud servers managed by cloud vendors and store sensitive data on servers that they manage themselves. Governmental agencies, financial analysts, and accountants will have defined standards against which organizations can be monitored for appropriate compliance. By the way, if you graduate as an accountant or financial analyst, this is interesting work in which you could be involved early in your career.

Mobility, however, will still present problems in 2027. Workers in the warehouse, loading dock, and shipping department will all carry mobile devices that enable them to process ERP and

SECURITY GUIDE

IT'S NOT ME ... IT'S YOU

If you have ever been asked to leave a job, then you understand how difficult it is. Learning that your services are no longer needed is stressful. Compounding the stresses are tense moments with managers and awkward interactions with coworkers. However, the realization that you now need to secure some other means of employment is often the most discouraging part. You may be surprised to learn that these factors commonly lead exiting employees to take advantage of their last moments with their employers.

A survey of 945 adults who had been laid off, been fired, or changed jobs in the past year revealed some startling statistics. Sixty percent reported stealing data from their employer before their employment ended. Seventy-nine percent admitted to knowing that taking company data with them was not permitted. They reported taking email lists, customers contact lists, employee records, and financial information.[4] It has been estimated that the financial damages inflicted by these types of incidents range from $5,000 to $3 million per incident.[5]

White Collar ... Dark Deeds

You may be wondering what factors contribute to the widespread theft of company data. To get "inside the minds" of data-stealing employees, we must look at the "fraud triangle." The fraud triangle contends that *pressure, opportunity,* and *rationalization* are the three key factors that govern an individual's propensity to commit white-collar crime.[6] In this context, employees in the process of leaving a company are pressured to find a job. They often think that they can increase the chances of finding a new position if they bring data assets with them. This is especially true if they are targeting a position at their employer's key competitor. What many employees fail to realize is that confidential customer lists and intellectual property are considered proprietary and are often governed by nondisclosure agreements. Giving this information to a new employer will likely harm them, not help them.

Factor two—opportunity—has continually increased over the past decade as interactions among employees, systems, and data have drastically changed. The rise of *telecommuting*—employees working from home—and the ability of employees to access their employer's data in the cloud have opened up countless opportunities for theft of data and intellectual assets. Shockingly, the employee survey also revealed that almost a quarter of employees said they still had the ability to connect to their employer's network after their employment had ended.[7] That's an opportunity!

Finally, rationalization is an element of data theft because employees have often created the data that they are attempting to take with them. They feel a sense of justification for taking the data because they created it.

Source: Putilov_Denis/Fotolia

I'm Not Disgruntled ... Are You?

In light of the ample opportunities for employees to take data from their companies and the feelings of pressure and rationalization for doing so, organizations are working to develop predictive tools that will help identify employees who may be preparing to steal data. A data loss prevention expert commented on the inadequacy of existing theft-prevention solutions by saying that most organizations fail to have the technological infrastructure in place to identify accidental employee dissemination of sensitive information. Identification of intentional, malicious incidents is even more difficult.[8]

The tools that are being developed to identify potential data theft search, monitor, analyze, and visualize the data originating from Web sites, applications, servers, networks, sensors, and mobile devices.[9] Encryption and continual monitoring of stored data are other tactics that can be used to thwart data theft. This includes encrypting and monitoring data stored within the organization and with third parties like the cloud vendors.

Most importantly, companies need to ensure that HR departments and technology groups are collaborating in real time to ensure that employee access to internal systems is revoked when an employee's time with the company has come to an end.

DISCUSSION QUESTIONS

1. Have you ever witnessed someone stealing something at work? If so, it was probably apparent to both you and the perpetrator that he or she was doing something wrong. Why do you think employees are so willing to steal data but might be hesitant to steal tangible items like cash, laptops, or other expensive organizational assets?
2. Take a moment to search the Internet for cases of white-collar crime. Find a specific example and see if you can identify the three elements of the white-collar triangle as being factors that contributed to that crime being committed.
3. How do you feel about the fact that many companies are investing in tools to monitor employee behavior? Would you want to work for a company that regularly audits your emails and analyzes your activity on the company's network?
4. The article mentions that encryption can be a tactic used to thwart employees from taking data with them. Explain how encryption can be used effectively in this context.

other enterprise applications from wherever they happen to be. Managers, decision makers, and other knowledge workers will have similar applications on their own phones or other mobile devices, devices that they can access from work, other offices, the street, or home.

However—and it's an enormous however—mobile devices are subject to severe security threats. Putting data online does make it easier to access. That's true for the good guys, but it's also true for the bad guys. In 2015 Anthem Inc., the largest for-profit health care company in the United States, lost healthcare records for 80 million people. Consider the enormity of that single data breach. There are only 320 million people in the United States. That means a single company lost records for one out of every four people you know.

Consider what would happen if some criminal, perhaps a malicious insider, were to infiltrate an ERP system. It would be possible to wreak havoc in, say, supply chain orders and inventories or in the operation of machinery on the factory floor. The hacked organization would have to shut down its ERP system, and thus its company, to sort out the mess. But allowing users mobile access to the ERP system will enable organizations to make significant improvements in process quality. So, in the next 10 years, organizations must engage in a delicate balancing act between risk of loss and improvement to processes.

Source: Andrew Yenchik

CAREER GUIDE

Name: Andrew Yenchik
Company: USAA
Job Title: IT Technical Manager
Education: Carnegie Mellon University

1 How did you get this type of job?

During my undergraduate studies, I worked as an unpaid intern—then later as a paid employee—for a software development and Web design company. While there, I learned networking, systems administration, and data center operations. I then completed a graduate degree and joined USAA. I worked in strategic planning and project management before moving into my current role as a technical manager. At USAA, I've focused on building my internal network, acquiring technical skills, and taking on leadership challenges. I've sought out difficult assignments and projects that force me to grow and learn.

2 What attracted you to this field?

I wanted to find a field that mixed business and technical skills and that requires a problem-solving mind-set. I didn't want to only have technical abilities and not understand the whys and hows of business functions. The field of information systems blends technical skills and business acumen. I spent time with professors and professionals in fields that interested me. This included job shadowing, lunch meetings, phone calls, and private meetings. These mentors provided valuable advice that led me to choose the information systems field.

3 What does a typical workday look like for you (duties, decisions, problems)?

I work daily with a team of software developers, analysts, scrum masters, and project managers. My team and I are globally dispersed. On occasion, I travel to spend time with my team members at their locales. As a technical manager, I provide technical leadership and am responsible for the execution and delivery of all project work. My current team develops and supports APIs and services for banking and financial systems. I also work closely with executive management regarding strategic, financial, technical, and human resource–related activities.

4 What do you like most about your job?

I enjoy the challenge of continual learning. I rarely have all the information or skills I need to make a decision or to execute a project. I enjoy the need to quickly learn and grow in order to be successful.

5 What skills would someone need to do well at your job?

Problem solving is a critical skill. I'm confronted with complex problems—such as fixing a technical outage or hiring the right person to join the team—on a daily basis. No matter the job, the ability to assess a problem, gather the right information and tools, and resolve the problem are key. Teamwork and leadership are other crucial skills. No single person knows all the answers. The abilities to work with, assist, teach, and motivate others in a collaborative manner are important.

6 Are education or certifications important in your field? Why?

Yes, education and certifications are important and provide career capital—the more you acquire, the more valuable you become. They provide a foundation of skills and competencies needed to be a successful IT professional. They illustrate your ability to study, learn, and gain knowledge. A degree from a reputable institution validates your acumen and skills.

7 **What advice would you give to someone who is considering working in your field?**

Stretch yourself to gain a broad range of skills and experiences while in school and in the early years of your career. Take a difficult class in an area outside your comfort zone—a class that is not an easy A—that will require a commitment of learning, work, and sacrifice on your part to pass the class. Ask questions and be inquisitive. Digging past the "what" and into the "why" will help you gain knowledge and abilities that will help you make good decisions and be a leader.

8 **What do you think will be hot tech jobs in 10 years?**

Network engineering—with an ever-increasing number of connected devices and the IoT revolution, network engineering skill sets will be in high demand. Information security—this rapid increase in the type and number of connected devices, coupled with the prevelance of technology in businesses and personal lives, make security a hot job.

Consider also the effect of the Internet of Things. Future users of ERP systems will be not just people but also devices and machines. ERP vendors are adapting their software to the particular requirements of 3D printing. In the future, when a salesperson enters an order, he or she may be starting a machine to make that part on demand. In addition, factory automation will also add to process quality improvements. Inventory-picking robots are one example, but self-driving cars and trucks are likely to have an even larger effect. And within the next 10 years, machines will be able to employ the ERP system to schedule their own maintenance. For example, on the factory floor a milling machine will be able to order a replacement for a dull cutter, one possibly made by a 3D printer. Machines will schedule both routine and emergency maintenance for themselves, thus carrying factory automation to a new level.

As we have stated many times so far, the future belongs not to those who specialize in existing methods, technology, and processes but rather to those who can find and implement innovative applications of emerging trends. Technology's effect on enterprise systems will be widespread because enterprise systems are widespread. Many opportunities will occur in the early years of your career.

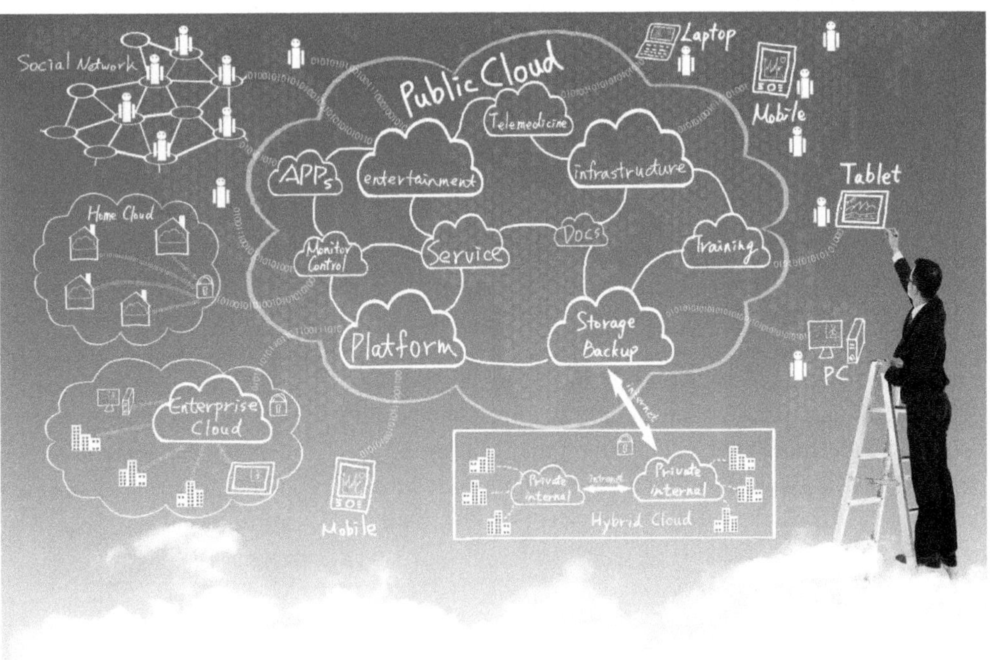

FIGURE 20
Designing a Future ERP System
Source: Tom Wang/Fotolia

ACTIVE REVIEW

Use this Active Review to verify that you understand the ideas and concepts that answer the chapter's study questions.

Q1 What are the basic types of processes?

Define *structured* and *dynamic processes* and compare and contrast them. Define *workgroup processes, enterprise processes,* and *inter-enterprise processes* and explain their differences and challenges. Define those same levels of information systems. Define *functional systems* and *functional applications.*

Q2 How can information systems improve process quality?

Name, define, and give an example of two dimensions of process quality. Name and describe three ways that organizations can improve process quality. Name and describe three ways that information systems can be used to improve process quality.

Q3 How do information systems eliminate the problems of information silos?

Define *information silo* and explain how such silos come into existence. When do such silos become a problem? Describe the two types of silos in Figure 6 and explain the meaning implied by the two arrows.

Q4 How do CRM, ERP, and EAI support enterprise processes?

Define *business process reengineering* and explain why it is difficult and expensive. Explain two major reasons why developing enterprise information systems in-house is expensive. Explain the advantages of inherent processes. Define and differentiate among *CRM, ERP,* and *EAI.* Explain how the nature of CRM and ERP is more similar to each other than that of EAI.

Q5 What are the elements of an ERP system?

Describe the minimum capability of a true ERP product. Explain the nature of each of the following ERP solution components: programs, data, procedures, and training and consulting. For each, summarize the work that customers must perform. List the top five ERP vendors in decreasing order of market share.

Q6 What are the challenges of implementing and upgrading enterprise information systems?

Name and describe five sources of challenges when implementing enterprise systems. Describe why enterprise systems management must be collaborative. Explain two major tasks required to identify requirements gaps. Summarize the challenges of transitioning to an enterprise system. Explain why employees resist change and describe three ways of responding to that resistance. Discuss the challenges that new technology poses for enterprise systems.

Q7 How do inter-enterprise IS solve the problems of enterprise silos?

Describe information silos that exist among employers health clubs, and individuals with regard to exercise data. Describe problems that those silos create. Explain how the system shown in Figure 19 will solve the problems caused by those silos. Define *distributed systems* and explain the benefits of SOA using Web services when implementing such systems.

Q8 2027?

Describe how the cloud, mobility, and the Internet of Things will affect enterprise systems in the next 10 years. Explain how these factors will create opportunities for business professionals. Explain how they will create opportunities for you!

Using Your Knowledge with ARES

Knowledge of this chapter will help you understand the fundamental value offered by solutions like ARES namely, the elimination of the problems of enterprise-level information silos. As you now know, silos caused by workgroup processes can be eliminated (or managed, in the case of EAI) with enterprise systems. Similarly, silos caused by enterprise processes can be eliminated with inter-enterprise systems like ARES Also, the knowledge of this chapter prepares you to understand the difficulty of adapting and of managing inter-enterprise systems. Finally, Figure 19 helps you understand how mobile devices and a cloud database can be used to implement an inter-enterprise system.

KEY TERMS AND CONCEPTS

Business process reengineering
Customer life cycle
Customer relationship management (CRM) system
Data integrity
Distributed systems
Dynamic processes
Enterprise application integration (EAI)
Enterprise information system
Enterprise processes
Enterprise resource planning (ERP)
ERP system
Functional application
Functional information systems
Hybrid model
Industry-specific solutions
Information silo
Inherent processes
Inter-enterprise information systems
Inter-enterprise processes
Modules
Process blueprints
Process effectiveness
Process efficiency
Self-efficacy
Stored procedure
Structured processes
Train the trainer
Trigger
Workgroup information system
Workgroup process

MyMISLab™

To complete the problems with the MyMISLab, go to EOC Discussion Questions in the MyLab.

USING YOUR KNOWLEDGE

1. MyMISLab Using the example of your university, give examples of information systems for each of the three levels of scope (workgroup, enterprise, and inter-enterprise) discussed in Q1. Describe three departmental information systems likely to duplicate data. Explain how the characteristics of these systems relate to your examples.

2. MyMISLab In your answer to question 1, explain how the three workgroup information systems create information silos. Describe the kinds of problems these silos are likely to cause. Refer to the discussion in Q3 as a guide.

3. MyMISLab Using your answer to question 2, describe an enterprise information system that will eliminate the silos. Would the implementation of your system require business process reengineering? Explain why or why not.

4. Google or Bing each of the top five ERP vendors discussed in Q5. In what ways have their product offerings changed since this text was written? Do these vendors have new products? Have they made important acquisitions? Have they been acquired? Have any new companies made important inroads into their market share?

5. How do you think mobile systems and the cloud will affect ERP solutions? Explain how mobile ERP might benefit the types of personnel discussed in the bicycle manufacturing example from Q4.

COLLABORATION EXERCISE

Using the collaboration IS you built, collaborate with a group of students to answer the following questions.

The county planning office issues building permits, septic system permits, and county road access permits for all building projects in a county in an eastern state. The planning office issues permits to homeowners and builders for the construction of new homes and buildings and for any remodeling projects that involve electrical, gas, plumbing, and other utilities, as well as the conversion of unoccupied spaces, such as garages, into living or working space. The office also issues permits for new or upgraded septic systems and permits to provide driveway entrances to county roads.

Figure 21 shows the permit process that the county used for many years. Contractors and homeowners found this process

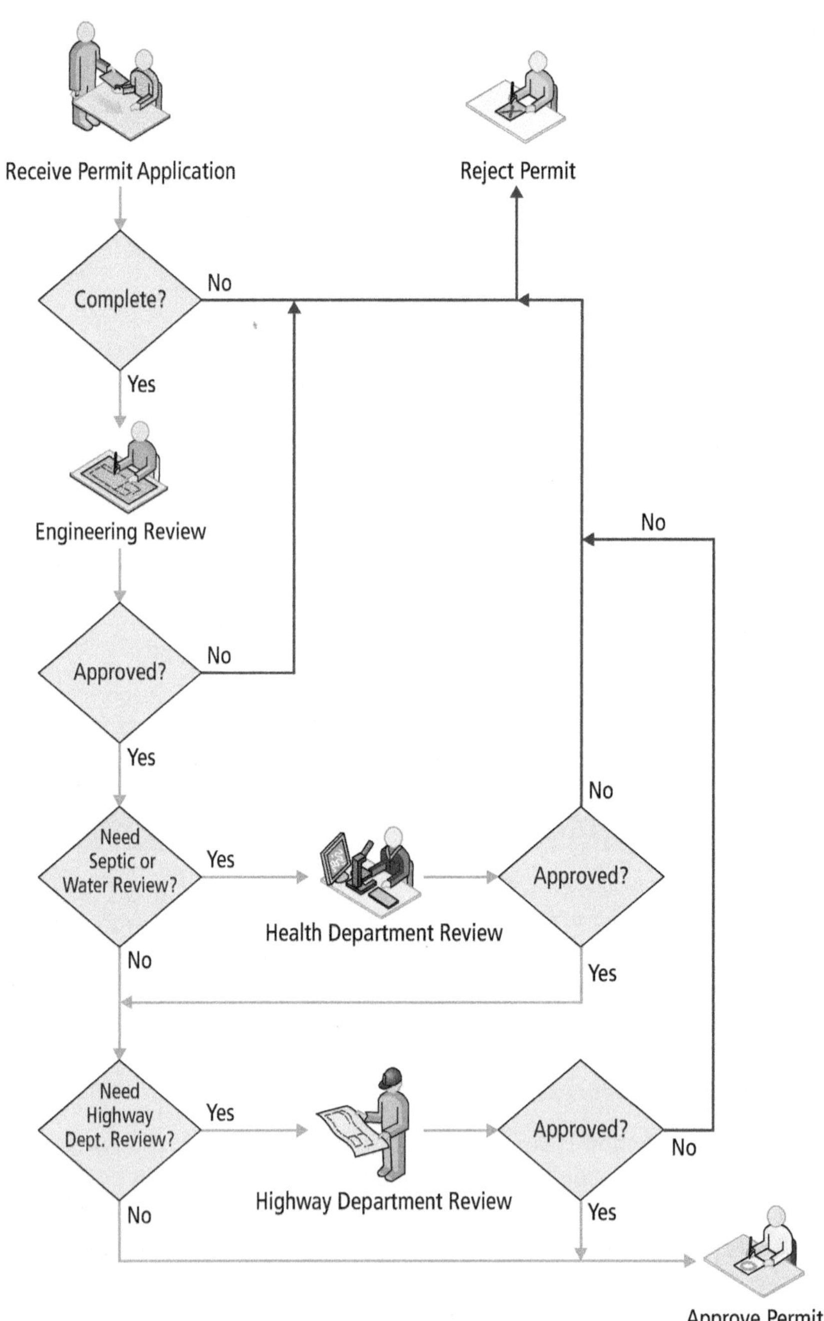

FIGURE 21
Building Permit Process, Old Version

slow and very frustrating. For one, they did not like its sequential nature. Only after a permit had been approved or rejected by the engineering review process would they find out that a health or highway review was also needed. Because each of these reviews could take 3 or 4 weeks, applicants requesting permits wanted the review processes to be concurrent rather than serial. Also, both the permit applicants and county personnel were frustrated because they never knew where a particular application was in the permit process. A contractor would call to ask how much longer, and it might take an hour or longer just to find which desk the permits were on.

Accordingly, the county changed the permit process to that shown in Figure 22. In this second process, the permit office made three copies of the permit and distributed one to each department. The departments reviewed the permits in parallel; a clerk would analyze the results and, if there were no rejections, approve the permit.

Unfortunately, this process had a number of problems, too. For one, some of the permit applications were lengthy; some included as many as 40 to 50 pages of large architectural drawings. The labor and copy expense to the county was considerable.

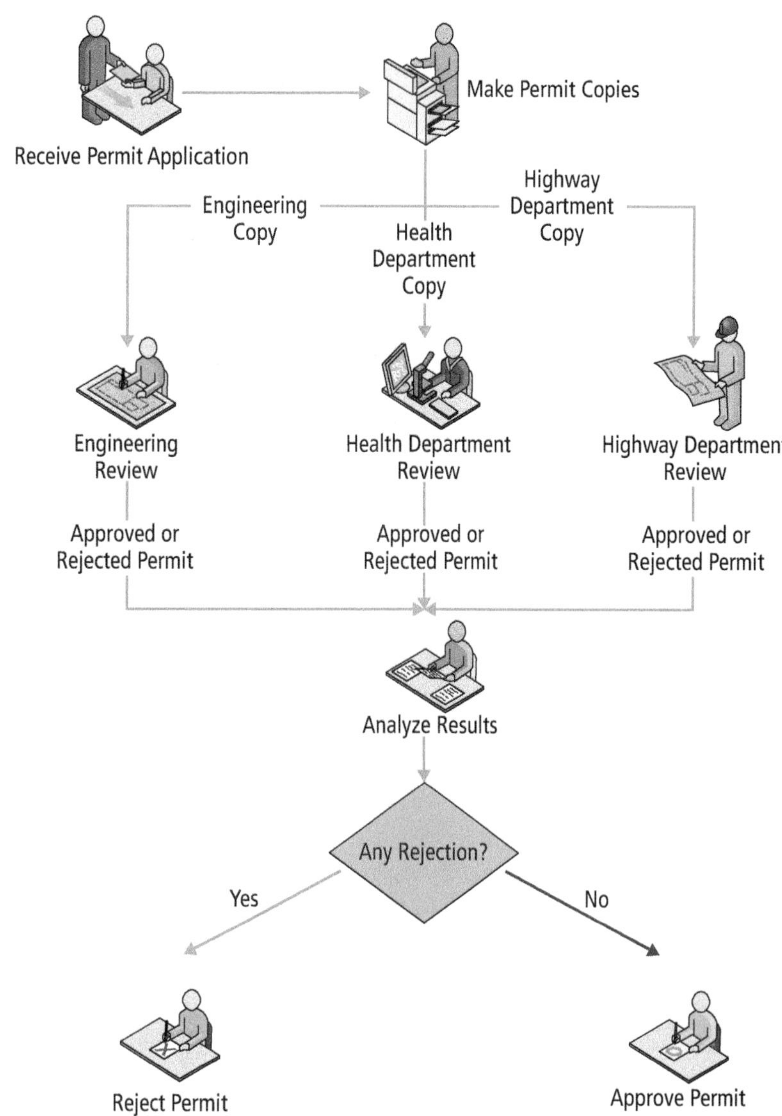

FIGURE 22
Building Permit Process, Revised Version

Second, in some cases departments reviewed documents unnecessarily. If, for example, the highway department rejected an application, then neither the engineering nor health departments needed to continue their reviews. At first, the county responded to this problem by having the clerk who analyzed results cancel the reviews of other departments when a rejection was received. However, that policy was exceedingly unpopular with the permit applicants, because once the problem in a rejected application was corrected, the permit had to go back through the other departments. The permit would go to the end of the line and work its way back into the departments from which it had been pulled. Sometimes this resulted in a delay of 5 or 6 weeks.

Cancelling reviews was unpopular with the departments as well, because permit-review work had to be repeated. An application might have been nearly completed when it was cancelled due to a rejection in another department. When the application came through again, the partial work results from the earlier review were lost.

6. Explain why the processes in Figures 21 and 22 are classified as enterprise processes rather than departmental processes. Why are these processes not interorganizational processes?
7. Using Figure 8 as an example, redraw Figure 21 using an enterprise information system that processes a shared database. Explain the advantages of this system over the paper-based system in Figure 21.
8. Using Figure 10 as an example, redraw Figure 22 using an enterprise information system that processes a shared database. Explain the advantages of this system over the paper-based system in Figure 22.

9. Assuming that the county has just changed from the system in Figure 21 to the one in Figure 22, which of your answers in questions 7 and 8 do you think is better? Justify your answer.

10. Assume your team is in charge of the implementation of the system you recommend in your answer to question 9. Describe how each of the five challenges discussed in Q6 pertain to this implementation. Explain how your team will deal with those challenges.

CASE STUDY

A Tale of Two Interorganizational IS

The Affordable Care Act (also known as Obamacare) requires the creation of healthcare exchanges that necessitate the development of interorganizational information systems. States were encouraged to set up exchanges for their own residents, but if they elected not to do so, the states' residents could use an exchange developed by the federal government. About half of the states decided to use the federal exchange. The remainder developed their own exchanges (and supporting information systems). These many parallel development projects give us a unique opportunity to learn from the experience of similar projects that had, in some cases, very different outcomes.

Consider, for example, Connecticut and Oregon. The state of Connecticut created an exchange named *Access CT*. It was delivered on time and on budget and has been such a success that the state of Maryland stopped developing its own system and licensed the Access CT solution instead.[11] Other states are considering licensing Access CT as well. On the other hand, the state of Oregon created an exchange named *Cover Oregon* that was a complete and utter failure. Cover Oregon was never operable despite costing more than $248 million in U.S. and Oregon tax dollars. In May 2014, the U.S. attorney's office in Portland opened a grand jury investigation into the project.[12]

Why were there such different outcomes? The two states started their projects about the same time, they had the same scope and goals, they began with about the same funding (Cover Oregon eventually spent nearly twice as much as Access CT), and they had the same required finish date. There is no substantial difference in the population of the two states; Connecticut has about 3.5 million people and Oregon about 3.9 million. What caused the different outcomes?

What Is a Healthcare Exchange?

To begin, a healthcare exchange is an online store that offers health insurance products to individuals and small businesses. Choosing medical insurance is a complex process with many different levels of coverage and costs, and selecting the right policy is difficult and confusing for most people. Exchanges are thus created not only to offer medical insurance policies, but also to simplify and partially automate the selection process. Exchanges also promote fair competition among health insurers.

Besides simplifying the selection of health insurance, another goal for exchanges is to help consumers navigate the complex array of governmental assistance options and possibilities. Depending on income, family size, and other circumstances, some consumers are entitled to Medicare and a variety of other governmental programs. Thus, when using an exchange, a consumer provides personal data about income and family situation, and the exchange uses automation to contact various governmental agencies to determine that consumer's eligibility. Given this determination, the exchange then offers insurance products appropriate to that particular consumer's situation. Exchanges are supposed to pay for themselves by charging a modest fee to insurers.

Figure 23 shows some of the organizations involved in a healthcare exchange. Clearly, an interorganizational information system is needed. As you know from this chapter, such projects are difficult to develop and manage, and it is not surprising that some states failed.

Access CT

Access CT is a quasi-public corporation. The chairman of the board is Connecticut's Lieutenant Governor, Nancy Wyman, who set out in the summer of 2012 to find an appropriate CEO. A nationwide searched identified 74 candidates, and in July 2012, the Connecticut governor hired Kevin Counihan.

Counihan had more than 30 years of experience working in the insurance industry and had been a key player in the development of the Massachusetts healthcare system (widely regarded as the model for Obamacare). Most recently, he had been the president of a private health exchange in California.[13]

Counihan holds a master's degree in marketing, and it shows. As soon as he was hired, he began a series of press conferences to explain the nature and goals of the project to the public. Within a few months, Counihan hired senior staff with deep experience in insurance, including Jim Wadleigh, Chief Information Officer. Wadleigh had been director of application development

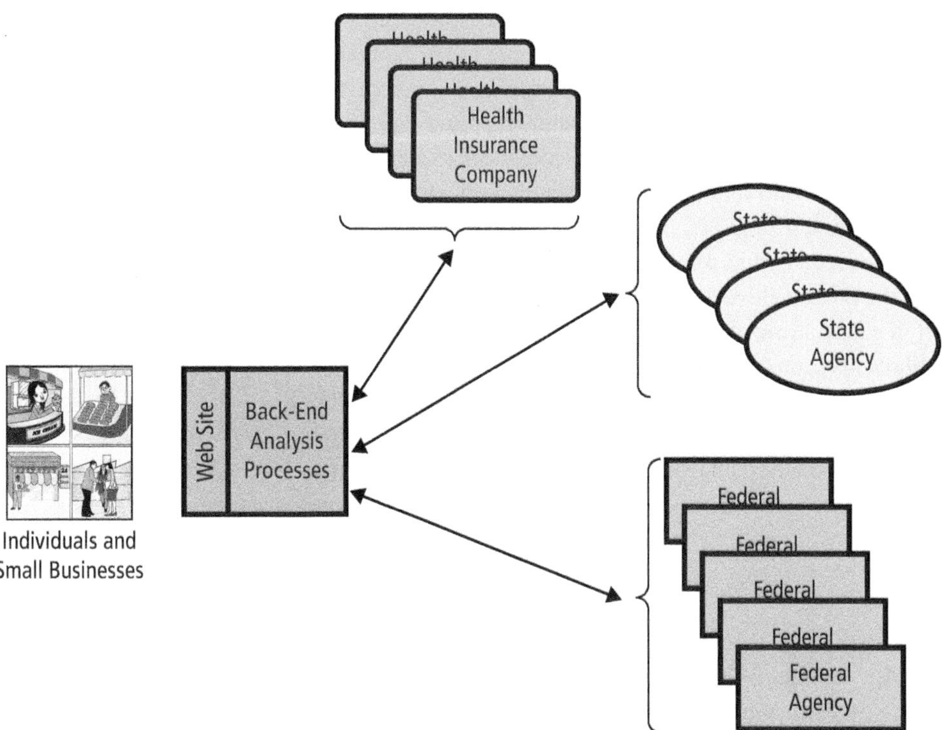

FIGURE 23
Healthcare Exchange Interorganizational IS

for CIGNA, a health services organization.[14] Wadleigh's primary assignment was to hire and manage an outside contractor to develop the exchange Web site and supporting backend code and to manage the implementation of the exchange information system.

By June 2012, Access CT had created a project plan and begun a search for the contractor to develop the site. By September 2012, it selected Deloitte Consulting LLP. At the time, Wadleigh stated, "With only 12 months until the Exchange goes live, we look forward to beginning our work with them immediately."[15]

That summer, in an interview on July 13, a local press reporter asked CEO Counihan, "Can you get it done on time?" His response: "This state's going to get it done in time."[16]

And it did. By the end of the federally mandated deadline, Access CT had enrolled 208,301 Connecticut residents,[17] and Connecticut had become a model for state-run exchanges.

Cover Oregon

The outcome was not so positive in Oregon. After spending nearly $250 million, the exchange was clearly inoperable, and the exchange's board of directors decided to stop development and utilize the federal exchange instead.[18] After this decision, the Oregon legislature hired an independent company, First Data Corporation, to investigate the causes of this debacle.[19]

Unlike in Connecticut, neither Oregon's governor nor any other elected official was directly involved in the project. In fact, in January 2014, the governor stated that he'd only become aware of the failure in "late October."[20] The site was to have gone operational on October 1, and it strains credulity to believe that it took 3 weeks for the news of the failure to reach him. In any case, it is safe to assume the governor was not a "hands-on manager" of the project, nor did he delegate any senior elected official to take that role.

According to First Data,[21] from the onset, the project suffered from divided direction. Cover Oregon is a quasi-independent corporation as is Access CT, but the exchange information system was to be developed by a different governmental agency, Oregon Health Authority (OHA). Personnel in the two agencies engaged in turf battles and held deep differences about project requirements. These differences resulted in always-changing, inconsistent direction to software developers.[22]

Further, unlike Access CT, OHA did not hire a supervising contractor for the project, but instead decided itself to take an active role in the software's development. Unfortunately, the agency suffered high employee turnover and had difficulty hiring and keeping qualified personnel. OHA did hire the services of a professional software development company to create major software components. However, of the three finalists for this work, two dropped out at the last minute, and the winner by default, Oracle Corporation, became in essence a sole source vendor. Consequently, Oracle was able to negotiate time and materials contracts rather than contracts for specific deliverables at specific prices. Later, when problems developed, Oracle was paid tens of millions of additional money for change orders on that same time and materials basis. OHA also attempted to do much of its own programming, but the team had no experience with Oracle and lacked both developers and managers.[23]

Ironically, because of prior problems with technology projects, the Oregon legislature required the state to hire a quality assurance contractor, Maximus Corporation, to oversee the project. From the project's start, Maximus reported significant problems involving divided control, lack of clear requirements, inappropriate contracting methodology, lack of project planning, and lack of progress. It is unclear to whom those reports were delivered or what was done with them. In January 2013, when the head of the OHA project received another negative report in a long string of such negative reports, she threatened to withhold Maximus' payment.[24]

Alas, when, in January 2013, *The Oregonian* asked Rocky King, the director of Cover Oregon, whether the system would work, he responded, "I haven't the foggiest idea."[25] Sadly, when the fog cleared, the exchange failed. In March 2015, Cover Oregon was shuttered.

Questions

11. Summarize the purpose and intended benefits of a healthcare exchange.

12. Explain why a healthcare exchange requires an interorganizational information system.

13. Using knowledge from this chapter, summarize the difficulties and challenges of developing interorganizational information systems.

14. Healthcare exchanges must utilize personal and confidential data about their users. Write a one-paragraph policy that stipulates responsible processing and storage of this data.

15. Explain what you believe are the reasons for the Access CT success.

16. Read the Executive Summary of the First Data report located at *www.oregon.gov/DAS/docs/co_assessment.pdf*. Summarize the report's findings.

17. Using the facts described in this case and your answer to question 16, list five key learnings you can take from the Access CT and Cover Oregon projects.

MyMISLab™

Go to the Assignments section of your MyLab to complete these writing exercises.

18. Using the patient discharge process in Q3, explain how the hospital benefits from an ERP solution. Describe why integration of patient records has advantages over separated databases. Explain the value of an industry-specific ERP solution to the hospital.

19. Go to *www.microsoft.com* and search for *Microsoft Dynamics*. Ignore Dynamics CRM. Have any important changes occurred in Microsoft's ERP product offerings since this edition was written? Has Microsoft brought a cloud-based ERP solution to market? Have any of the four ERP systems described in the chapter been better integrated with Office or the Microsoft Developer's platform? Using your knowledge guided by experience, what do you think are Microsoft's intentions with regard to ERP?

ENDNOTES

1 The subject of this chapter is structured processes, and we will discuss process quality in terms of them. Note, however, that all of the concepts in this question pertain equally well to dynamic processes.

2 D. Peak, "An Interview with John Halamka, MD, Chief Information Officer, Harvard Medical School and CareGroup Health System, USA," *Journal of IT Case and Application Research*, 10, no. 1 (2008): 70.

3 Panorama Consulting Solutions, "Clash of the Titans 2016," *Panorama-consulting.com*, November 2015, *http://go.panorama-consulting.com/rs/603-UJX-107/images/Clash-of-the-Titans-2016.pdf*.

4 Brian Krebs, "Data Theft Common by Departing Employees," *Washington Post*, March 7, 2016, *www.washingtonpost.com/wp-dyn/content/article/2009/02/26/AR2009022601821.html*.

5 Devlin Barrett, "FBI Warns of Rise in Disgruntled Employees Stealing Data," *Wall Street Journal*, March 7, 2016, *www.wsj.com/articles/fbi-warns-of-rise-in-disgruntled-employees-stealing-data-1411516389*.

6 Bill Barrett, "Inside the Mind of the White-Collar Criminal," *Accounting Web*, March 7, 2016, *www.accountingweb.com/technology/trends/inside-the-mind-of-the-white-collar-criminal*.

7 Krebs, "Data Theft Common by Departing Employees."

8 Ibid.

9 Stacy Collett, "5 Signs an Employee Plans to Leave with Your Company's Data," *CIO*, March 7, 2016, *www.cio.com/article/2975774/data-protection/5-signs-an-employee-plans-to-leave-with-your-companys-data.html*.

11 Andrea Walker, Meredith Cohn, and Erin Cox, "Md. Votes to Adopt Health Exchange Software Used in Connecticut," *Baltimore Sun*, April 2, 2014, accessed May 25, 2016, *http://articles.baltimoresun.com/2014-04-02/health/bs-hs-exchange-board-vote-20140401_1_isabel-fitzgerald-new-website-federal-exchange*.

12 Maeve Reston, "U.S. Prosecutors Investigate Oregon's Failed Health Insurance Exchange," *Los Angeles Times*, May 21, 2014, accessed May 25, 2016, *www.latimes.com/nation/nationnow/la-na-us-attorneys-office-probes-oregons-health-insurance-exchange-20140521-story.html.*

13 Matthew Sturdevant, "CT Health Exchange Has A New Chief Executive," *Hartford Courant*, June 21, 2012, accessed May 25, 2016, *http://articles.courant.com/2012-06-21/health/hc-health-exchange-ceo-20120621_1_health-insurance-exchange-health-care-victoria-veltri*

14 Healthcare IT Connect, "Jim Wadleigh," accessed May 25, 2016, *www.healthcareitconnect.com/jim-wadleigh/*.

15 accessed May 25, 2016, *http://ct.gov/hix/lib/hix/HIX-DELOITTE-RELEASE.pdf.*

16 Matthew Sturdevant, "Health Exchange Chief Explains How It Will Work," *Hartford Courant*, July 13, 2012, accessed May 25, 2016, *www.courant.com/health/connecticut/hc-health-exchange-20120712,0,4877364.story.*

17 Arielle Levin Becker, "Obamacare Exchange's Final Tally: 208,301 People Signed Up," *The CT Mirror*, April 17, 2014, accessed May 25, 2016, http://ctmirror.org/2014/04/17/obamacare-exchanges-final-tally-208301-people-signed-up/.

18 Jeff Manning, "Cover Oregon: State Moves to Federal Exchange, but Oracle Technology Lives On," *The Oregonian*, May 6, 2014, accessed May 25, 2016, www.oregonlive.com/health/index.ssf/2014/05/cover_oregon_state_moves_to_fe.html

19 "Cover Oregon Website Implementation Assessment," April 23, 2014, accessed May 25, 2016, http://portlandtribune.com/documents/artdocs/00003481205618.pdf

20 Dusty Lane, "'We Look Like Fools:' A History of Cover Oregon's Failure," *Katu.com*, January 10, 2014, accessed May 25, 2016, www.althycommunitiesoregon.com/lanecounty/2014/01/we-look-like-fools-a-history-of-cover-oregons-failure/.

21 "Cover Oregon Website Implementation Assessment."

22 Nick Budnick, "Cover Oregon: Health Exchange Failure Predicted, but Tech Watchdogs' Warnings Fell on Deaf Ears," *The Oregonian*, January 18, 2014, accessed May 25, 2016, *www.oregonlive.com/health/index.ssf/2014/01/cover_oregon_health_exchange_f.html.*

23 Nick Budnick, "Oregon Health Exchange Technology Troubles Run Deep due to Mismanagement, Early Decisions," *The Oregonian*, December 14, 2013, accessed May 25, 2016, *www.oregonlive.com/health/index.ssf/2013/12/oregon_health_exchange_technol.html.*

24 Budnick, "Cover Oregon: Health Exchange Failure Predicted."

25 Ibid.

APPLICATION EXERCISES

All exercise files can be found on the following Web site: *www.pearsonhighered.com/kroenke.*

AE1. Suppose your manager asks you to create a spreadsheet to compute a production schedule. Your schedule should stipulate a production quantity for seven products that is based on sales projections made by three regional managers at your company's three sales regions.

a. Create a separate worksheet for each sales region. Use the data in the Word file **Ch07Ex01_U10e.docx**. This file contains each manager's monthly sales projections for the past year, actual sales results for those same months, and projections for sales for each month in the coming quarter.

b. Create a separate worksheet for each manager's data. Import the data from Word into Excel.

c. On each of the worksheets, use the data from the prior four quarters to compute the discrepancy between the actual sales and the sale projections. This discrepancy can be computed in several ways: You could calculate an overall average, or you could calculate an average per quarter or per month. You could also weight recent discrepancies more heavily than earlier ones. Choose a method that you think is most appropriate. Explain why you chose the method you did.

d. Modify your worksheets to use the discrepancy factors to compute an adjusted forecast for the coming quarter. Thus, each of your spreadsheets will show the raw forecast and the adjusted forecast for each month in the coming quarter.

e. Create a fourth worksheet that totals sales projections for all of the regions. Show both the unadjusted forecast and the adjusted forecast for each region and for the company overall. Show month and quarter totals.

f. Create a bar graph showing total monthly production. Display the unadjusted and adjusted forecasts using different colored bars.

AE2. Figure AE is a sample bill of materials (BOM), a form that shows the components and parts used to construct a product. In this example, the product is a child's wagon. Such bills of materials are an essential part of manufacturing functional applications as well as ERP applications.

This particular example is a form produced using Microsoft Access. Creating such a form is a bit tricky, so this exercise will guide you through the steps required. You can then apply what you learn to produce a similar report. You can also use Access to experiment on extensions of this form.

a. Create a table named *PART* with columns *PartNumber, Level, Description, QuantityRequired,* and *PartOf. Description* and *Level* should be text, *PartNumber* should be AutoNumber, and *QuantityRequired* and *PartOf* should be numeric, long integer. Add the *PART* data shown in Figure AE to your table.

b. Create a query that has all columns of *PART*. Restrict the view to rows having a value of 1 for *Level*. Name your query *Level1*.

c. Create two more queries that are restricted to rows having values of 2 or 3 for *Level*. Name your queries *Level2* and *Level3*, respectively.

d. Create a form that contains *PartNumber, Level,* and *Description* from *Level1*. You can use a wizard for this if you want. Name the form *Bill of Materials*.

Ajax Toy Manufacturing
Bill of Materials

PartNumber	Level	Description
1	1	Deluxe Wagon III

Parts Contained

PartNumber	Level	Description	QuantityRequired	PartOf
2	2	Handle Bar	1	1

PartNumber	Level	Descrption	QuantityRequir	PartOf
3	3	Bar Grip	2	2
4	3	Bar Tang	1	2
14	3	Bar Stock	1	2
(New)			0	2

PartNumber	Level	Description	QuantityRequired	PartOf
5	2	Wagon Body, Metal	1	1

PartNumber	Level	Descrption	QuantityRequir	PartOf
(New)			0	5

PartNumber	Level	Description	QuantityRequired	PartOf
6	2	Front Wheel Assembly	1	1

PartNumber	Level	Descrption	QuantityRequir	PartOf
7	3	Front Wheels	2	6
8	3	Axle	1	6
9	3	Wheel retainer	2	6
(New)			0	6

PartNumber	Level	Description	QuantityRequired	PartOf
10	2	Rear Wheel Assembly	1	1

PartNumber	Level	Descrption	QuantityRequir	PartOf
11	3	Rear Wheels	2	10
12	3	Axle	1	10
13	3	Wheel retainer	2	10
(New)			0	10

PartNumber	Level	Description	QuantityRequired	PartOf
(New)			0	1

Record: 1 of 4 No Filter Search

FIGURE AE
Bill of Materials Example
Source: Microsoft Corporation

e. Select the Subform/Subreport tool in the Controls section of the DESIGN ribbon and create a subform in your form in part d. Set the data on this form to be all of the columns of *Level2*. After you have created the subform, ensure that the Link Child Fields property is set to *PartOf* and that the Link Master Fields property is set to *PartNumber*. Close the *Bill of Materials* form.

f. Open the subform created in part e and create a subform on it using the Subform/Subreport control. Set the data on this subform to be all of the columns of *Level3*. After you have created the subform, ensure that the Link Child Fields property is set to *PartOf* and that the Link Master Fields property is set to *PartNumber*. Close the *Bill of Materials* form.

g. Open the *Bill of Materials* form. It should appear as in Figure AE. Open and close the form and add new data. Using this form, add sample BOM data for a product of your own choosing.

h. Following the process similar to that just described, create a *Bill of Materials Report* that lists the data for all of your products.

i. **(Optional, challenging extension)** Each part in the BOM in Figure AE can be used in at most one assembly (there is space to show just one *PartOf* value). You can change your design to allow a part to be used in more than one assembly as follows: First, remove *PartOf* from PART. Next, create a second table that has two columns: *AssemblyPartNumber* and *ComponentPartNumber*. The first contains a part number of an assembly, and the second contains a part number of a component. Every component of a part will have a row in this table. Extend the views described above to use this second table and to produce a display similar to Figure AE.

GLOSSARY

Business process reengineering The activity of altering existing and designing new business processes to take advantage of the capabilities of new information systems technology.

Customer life cycle Taken as a whole, the processes of marketing, customer acquisition, relationship management, and loss/churn that must be managed by CRM systems.

Customer relationship management (CRM) system A suite of applications, a database, and a set of inherent processes for managing all the interactions with the customer, from lead generation to customer service.

Data integrity In a database or a collection of databases, the condition that exists when data values are consistent and in agreement with one another.

Distributed systems Systems in which application processing is distributed across multiple computing devices.

Dynamic processes Flexible, informal, and adaptive processes that normally involve strategic and less specific managerial decisions and activities.

Enterprise application integration (EAI) A suite of software applications that integrates existing systems by providing layers of software that connect applications together.

Enterprise information system Information systems that support cross-functional processes and activities in multiple departments.

Enterprise processes Processes that span an organization and support activities in multiple departments.

Enterprise resource planning (ERP) A suite of applications called modules, a database, and a set of inherent processes for consolidating business operations into a single, consistent, computing platform.

ERP system An information system based upon ERP technology.

Functional application Software that provides features and functions necessary to support a particular business activity or department (function).

Functional information systems Workgroup information systems that support a particular business function.

Hybrid model An enterprise system in which some of the data is stored in the cloud and managed by cloud vendors and other data is stored in the premises of the using organization and managed by it.

Industry-specific solutions An ERP template designed to serve the needs of companies or organizations in specific industries. Such solutions save time and lower risk. The development of industry-specific solutions spurred ERP growth.

Information silo A condition that exists when data are isolated in separated information systems.

Inherent processes The procedures that must be followed to effectively use licensed software. For example, the processes inherent in ERP systems assume that certain users will take specified actions in a particular order. In most cases, the organization must conform to the processes inherent in the software.

Inter-enterprise information systems Information systems that support one or more inter-enterprise processes.

Inter-enterprise processes Processes that support activities in multiple, independent companies or other organizations.

Modules A suite of applications in an ERP system.

Process blueprints In an ERP application, comprehensive sets of inherent processes for all organizational activities, each of which is documented with diagrams that use a set of standardized symbols.

Process effectiveness A measure of how well a process achieves organizational strategy.

Process efficiency A measure of the ratio of process outputs to inputs.

Self-efficacy A person's belief that he or she can successfully perform the tasks required in his or her job.

Stored procedure A computer program stored in the database that is used to enforce business rules.

Structured processes Formally defined, standardized processes that involve day-to-day operations; accepting a return, placing an order, and purchasing raw materials are common examples.

Train the trainer Training sessions in which vendors train the organization's employees, called Super Users, to become in-house trainers in order to improve training quality and reduce training expenses.

Trigger A computer program stored within the database that runs to keep the database consistent when certain conditions arise.

Workgroup information system An information system that supports a particular department or workgroup.

Workgroup process A process that exists to enable workgroups to fulfill the charter, purpose, and goals of a particular group or department.

Business Intelligence Systems

"So how's it going with the employer wellness programs? Are they interested in a system like ARES?" Henri, the technology manager at ARES, asks as he sets down his protein shake.

"Pretty good," Ashley, the general manager, responds, nodding slightly as she unwraps her sandwich. "I looked up the largest 50 employers in the state with employee wellness programs and started making calls."

"And?"

"And they were all interested. They liked the idea that they could get actual exercise data."

Henri looks surprised. "They don't already collect it?"

"No. Most of them do require employees to successfully complete an annual fitness exam and blood test, but the exercise requirements are all self-reported. They just don't have a way to collect the data."

"So they just take the employees' word for it?"

"Yep."

"Wow. Seems like something that could be manipulated pretty easily."

"I showed them our existing ARES reporting tools, and they were impressed that we were able to pull in data from existing exercise equipment and fitness bands. They also liked the fact that they could promote the entertainment angle of ARES to get employees exercising together."

"Sounds like a win-win. The companies get the data they need to ensure that their employees are staying healthy and not gaming the system. And the employees get a fun AR cycling experience."

"Maybe." Ashley frowns slightly. "But I did have one HR representative who was concerned about privacy. She was worried that employees might think the data could be analyzed and used against them somehow. You know, Big Brother plus Big Data equals big trouble."

"Hmm. What about the personal trainer angle? Do you think we could get referral fees from trainers if we send them users?"

"Yes, but I need your help," Ashley says with a smile.

"Anything for the boss."

"I need to know where our users live so I can refer them to a trainer at a local gym. I can't refer users in Texas to a trainer in California. Do we have geographic location data?"

Henri grabs a marker and starts drawing on the white board. "Well, the system currently collects data related to distance, speed, time, beats per minute, calories burned, resistance, sweat, and watts. But we could use their IP address to determine their location."

"Data analysis, where you don't know the second question to ask until you see the answer to the first one."

Image source: andrew_rybalko/Fotolia

"How does that work?"

"Well, every device that accesses the Internet must have an IP address. Computers, phones, AR headsets, and networked exercise bikes need an IP address. A given range of IP addresses are usually used within the same city. Would city-level location be accurate enough?"

"I'm not quite sure what I want."

"That's typical for BI."

"What's BI?"

"Business intelligence. Data analysis where you don't know the second question to ask until you see the answer to the first one."

Study QUESTIONS

Q1 How do organizations use business intelligence (BI) systems?

Q2 What are the three primary activities in the BI process?

Q3 How do organizations use data warehouses and data marts to acquire data?

Q4 How do organizations use reporting applications?

Q5 How do organizations use data mining applications?

Q6 How do organizations use Big Data applications?

Q7 What is the role of knowledge management systems?

Q8 What are the alternatives for publishing BI?

Q9 2027?

"Yeah. That's it exactly! That's where I am right now."

"OK, let me gather some IP address data from the existing system and put it in a spreadsheet for you. Then I'll show you how to look up the area for that IP address range. Then you'll know where our current users are generally located."

"That might work," Ashley says, sitting back in her chair.

"Yes, well, if it does work and you want to build something for users, do some serious data mining, or set up a data mart, then you'll need to come up with some money for my budget."

Ashley laughs. "If I can turn your data into dollars, that won't be a problem."

Henri smiles as he picks up his protein shake. "That's always the tricky part."

Chapter PREVIEW

This chapter considers business intelligence (BI) systems: information systems that can produce patterns, relationships, and other information from organizational structured and unstructured social data as well as from external, purchased data. In addition to this data, another rich source of knowledge is employees themselves. Employees come to the organization with expertise, and as they gain experience in the organization they add to that expertise. Vast amounts of collective knowledge exist in every organization's employees. How can that knowledge be shared?

As a future business professional, business intelligence is a critical skill. According to a recent survey by PricewaterhouseCoopers, 50 percent of U.S. CEOs see *very high value* of digital technology in data analytics (business intelligence). Eighty percent reported that data mining and analytics were strategically important to their organizations.[1] In 2016, Gartner found that one of the top priorities for CEOs is managing the digital transformation of their businesses (e.g., Internet of Things, self-driving cars, etc). More than half of CEOs believe that their industries will undergo such tremendous digital transformations in the next 5 years that they will be nearly unrecognizable. As you will learn, business intelligence is a key technology supporting such digital transformation.[2]

This chapter begins by summarizing the ways organizations use business intelligence. It then describes the three basic activities in the BI process and illustrates those activities using a parts selection problem. We then discuss the role of data warehouses and data marts followed by survey reporting, data mining, artificial intelligence, machine learning, Big Data, and knowledge management BI applications. After that, you'll learn alternatives for publishing the results of BI applications. We will wrap up the chapter with a 2027 observation that many people find frightening.

Q1 How Do Organizations Use Business Intelligence (BI) Systems?

Business intelligence (BI) systems are information systems that process operational, social, and other data to identify patterns, relationships, and trends for use by business professionals and other knowledge workers. These patterns, relationships, trends, and predictions are referred to as **business intelligence**. As information systems, BI systems have the five standard components: hardware, software, data, procedures, and people. The software component of a BI system is called a **BI application**.

In the context of their day-to-day operations, organizations generate enormous amounts of data. AT&T, for example, processes 1.9 trillion call records in its database and Google stores a database with more than 33 trillion entries.[3] Business intelligence is buried in that data, and the function of a BI system is to extract it and make it available to those who need it.

The boundaries of BI systems are blurry. In this text, we will take the broad view shown in Figure 1. Source data for a BI system can be the organization's own operational data, social media data, data that the organization purchases from data vendors, or employee knowledge. The BI application processes the data with reporting applications, data mining applications, Big Data applications, and knowledge management applications to produce business intelligence for knowledge workers. Today such workers include not only analysts in the home office but also operations and field personnel who use BI to approve loans, order goods, and decide when to prescribe, to take a few examples.

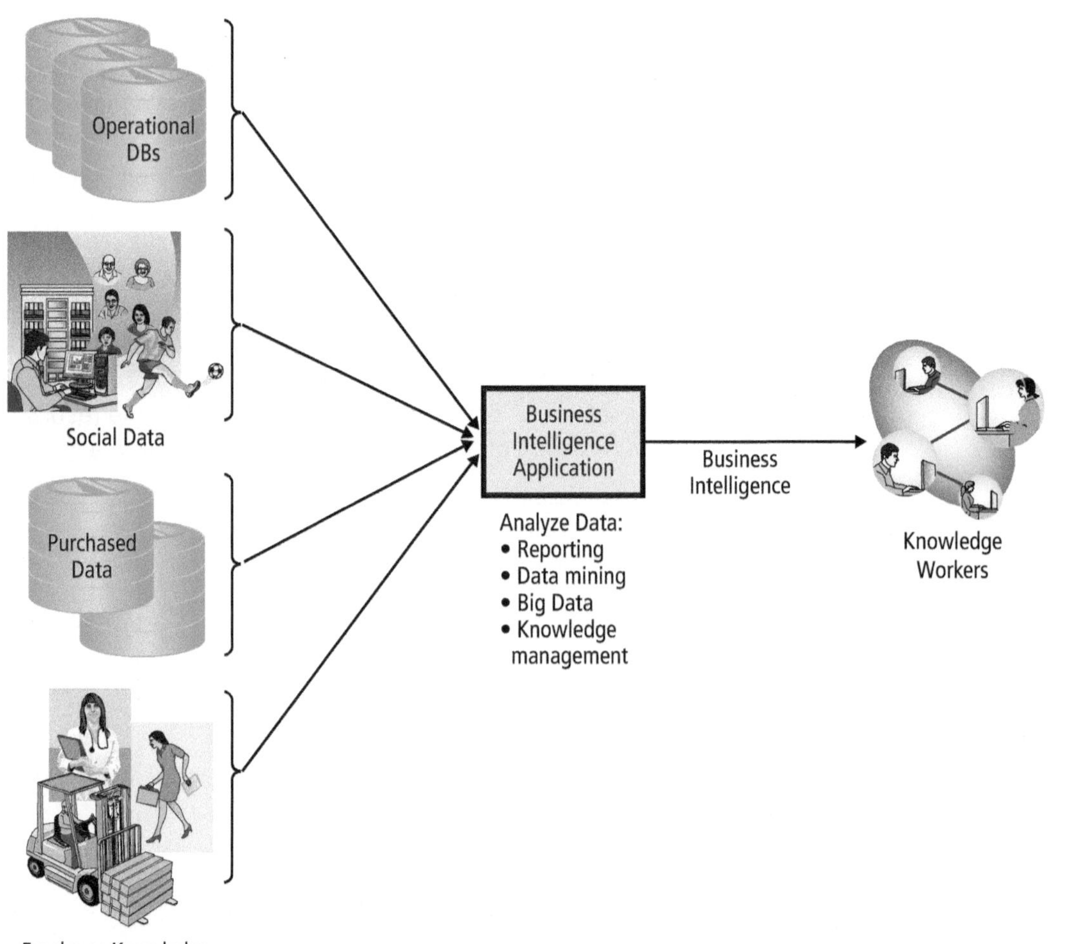

FIGURE 1
Components of a Business Intelligence System

How Do Organizations Use BI?

As shown in Figure 2, organizations use BI for all four of the collaborative tasks. Starting with the last row of Figure 2, business intelligence can be used just for informing. Personal trainers can use ARES to learn how clients are using the new system. At the time of the analysis, the trainers may not have any particular purpose in mind, but are just browsing the BI results for some future, unspecified purpose. At Falcon Security, Mateo may just want to know how Falcon's current sales compare to the forecast. He may have no particular purpose in mind; he just wants to know "how we're doing."

Moving up a row in Figure 2, some managers use BI systems for decision making. ARES could use BI on its user data to determine the location of the closest health club to each user. It could then generate referral fees by recommending users contact personal trainers working at those health clubs. Falcon Security could use a BI analysis of flight failures to decide when it is time to service drones and related camera equipment.

(By the way, some authors define BI systems as supporting decision making only, in which case they use the older term **decision support systems** as a synonym for decision-making BI systems. We take the broader view here to include all four of the tasks in Figure 2 and will avoid the term *decision support systems*.)

Problem solving is the next category of business intelligence use. Again, a problem is a perceived difference between what is and what ought to be. Business intelligence can be used for both sides of that definition: determining *what is* as well as *what should be*. If revenue is below expectations, ARES can use BI to learn what factors to change to obtain more user activity and more health club referral fees. Falcon Security could use BI to determine whether it could save costs by rerouting its drone flights.

Finally, business intelligence can be used during project management. ARES can be used to support a project to create targeted partnerships with local health clubs. When Falcon Security wants to expand to new geographic locations, it can use business intelligence to determine which locations will be the most advantageous.

As you study Figure 2, recall the hierarchical nature of these tasks. Deciding requires informing; problem solving requires deciding (and informing); and project management requires problem solving (and deciding [and informing]).

What Are Typical BI Applications?

See what a typical workday would look like for someone who manages data and analytics in the Career Guide given later in the chapter.

This section summarizes three BI applications that will give you a flavor of what is possible. Because *business intelligence* and the related term *Big Data* are hot topics today, a Web search will produce dozens of similar examples. After you read this chapter, search for more applications that appeal to your particular interests.

Task	ARES Example	Faclon Security Example
Project Management	Create partnership programs between ARES users and local health clubs.	Expand geographically.
Problem Solving	How can we increase revenue from health clubs?	How can we save money by rerouting drone flights?
Deciding	Which health club is closest to each user? Refer users to local trainers.	Which drones and related equipment are in need of maintenance?
Informing	In what ways are clients using the new system?	How do sales compare to our sales forecast?

FIGURE 2
Example Uses of Business Intelligence

Identifying *Changes* in Purchasing Patterns

Most students are aware that business intelligence is used to predict purchasing patterns. Amazon made the phrase "Customers who bought ... also bought" famous; when we buy something today, we expect the e-commerce application to suggest what else we might want. Later in this chapter, you'll learn some of the techniques that are used to produce such recommendations.

More interesting, however, is identifying *changes* in purchasing patterns. Retailers know that important life events cause customers to change what they buy and, for a short interval, to form new loyalties to new brands. Thus, when people start their first professional job, get married, have a baby, or retire, retailers want to know. Before BI, stores would watch the local newspapers for graduation, marriage, and baby announcements and send ads in response. That is a slow, labor-intensive, and expensive process.

Target wanted to get ahead of the newspapers and in 2002 began a project to use purchasing patterns to determine that someone was pregnant. By applying business intelligence techniques to its sales data, Target was able to identify a purchasing pattern of lotions, vitamins, and other products that reliably predicts pregnancy. When Target observed that purchasing pattern, it sent ads for diapers and other baby-related products to those customers.

Its program worked—too well for one teenager who had told no one she was pregnant. When she began receiving ads for baby items, her father complained to the manager of the local Target store, who apologized. It was the father's turn to apologize when he learned that his daughter was, indeed, pregnant.[4]

BI for Entertainment

Amazon, Netflix, Pandora, Spotify, and other media-delivery organizations generate billions of bytes of data on consumer media preferences. Using that data, Amazon has begun to produce its own video and TV, basing plots and characters and selecting actors on the results of its BI analysis.[5]

Netflix decided to buy *House of Cards*, starring Kevin Spacey, based on its analysis of customers' viewing patterns. Similarly, Spotify processes data on customers' listening habits to determine locations where particular bands' songs are heard most often. Using that data, it then recommends the best cities for popular bands and other musical groups to perform.[6]

A popular adage among marketing professionals is that "buyers are liars," meaning they'll say they want one thing but purchase something else. That characteristic reduces the efficacy of marketing focus groups. BI produced from data on watching, listening, and rental habits, however, determines what people actually want, not what they say. Will this enable data miners like Amazon to become the new Hollywood? We will see.

Just-in-Time Medical Reporting

Practice Fusion Inc., a medical record startup, provides injection notification services to doctors during exams. As the doctor enters data, the software analyzes patient's records, and if injections are needed, it recommends that the doctor prescribe them as the exam progresses. It seems to work, too. During a 4-month study period, patients whose doctors were using the recommendation service prescribed 73 percent more vaccinations than those in a control group who did not use the service.[7]

The service is free to doctors. Practice Fusion is paid by Merck, a pharmaceutical company. While Practice Fusions software recommends many products that are not sold by Merck, it also recommends many that are. Hence, the service stands on the blurry edge of medical ethics. Should a drug company provide software that recommends its products to doctors "for free"? If the injections are truly needed, who could object? On the other hand, how unbiased is the Practice Fusion software?

Setting the ethical issues aside, Practice Fusion provides an excellent example of data mining and reporting in real time. During your career, there likely will be many examples of middle-of-the-sales-call sales assistance.

Given these examples, we next consider the process used to create business intelligence.

Q2 What Are the Three Primary Activities in the BI Process?

Figure 3 shows the three primary activities in the BI process: acquire data, perform analysis, and publish results. These activities directly correspond to the BI elements in Figure 1. **Data acquisition** is the process of obtaining, cleaning, organizing, relating, and cataloging source data. We will illustrate a simple data acquisition example later in this question and discuss data acquisition in greater detail in Q3.

BI analysis is the process of creating business intelligence. The four fundamental categories of BI analysis are reporting, data mining, Big Data, and knowledge management. We will illustrate a simple example of a reporting system later in this question and describe each of the categories of BI analysis in greater detail in Q4 through Q7, respectively.

Publish results is the process of delivering business intelligence to the knowledge workers who need it. **Push publishing** delivers business intelligence to users without any request from the users; the BI results are delivered according to a schedule or as a result of an event or particular data condition. **Pull publishing** requires the user to request BI results. Publishing media include print as well as online content delivered via Web servers, specialized Web servers known as *report servers*, and BI results that are sent via automation to other programs. We will discuss these publishing options further in Q8. For now, consider a simple example of the use of business intelligence.

Using Business Intelligence to Find Candidate Parts

3D printing offers the possibility for customers to print parts they need rather than order them from a retailer or distributor. One large distributor of bicycle parts wanted to stay on top of this potential change in demand and decided to investigate the possibility of selling 3D printing files for the parts rather than the parts themselves. Accordingly, it created a team to examine past sales data to determine which part designs it might sell. To do so, the company needed to identify qualifying parts and compute how much revenue potential those parts represent.

To address this problem, the team obtained an extract of sales data from its IS department and stored it in Microsoft Access. It then created five criteria for parts that might quality for this new program. Specifically, it looked for parts that were:

1. Provided by certain vendors (starting with just a few vendors that had already agreed to make part design files available for sale)
2. Purchased by larger customers (individuals and small companies would be unlikely to have 3D printers or the needed expertise to use them)

FIGURE 3
Three Primary Activities in the BI Process

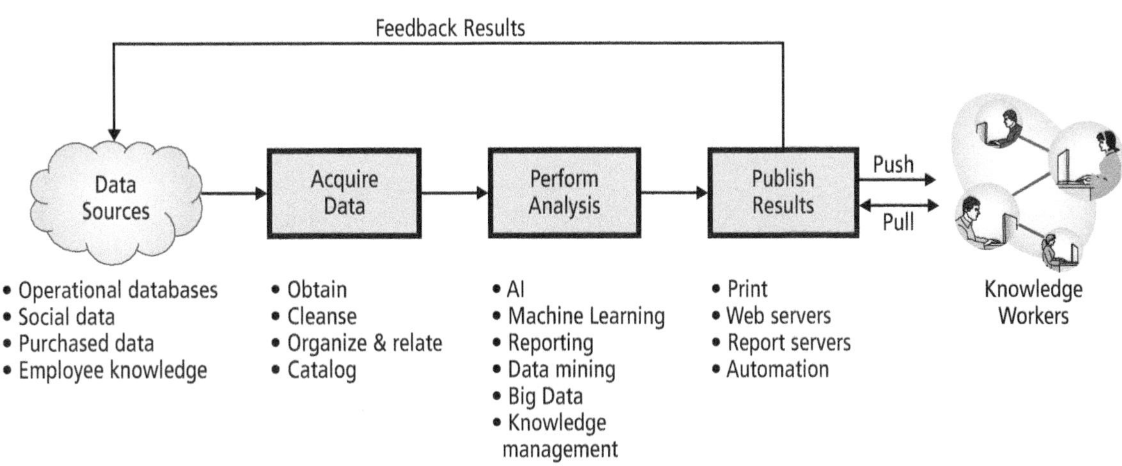

3. Frequently ordered (popular products)
4. Ordered in small quantities (3D printing is not suited for mass production)
5. Simple in design (easier to 3D print)

The team knew that the fifth criterion would be difficult to evaluate because the company doesn't store data on part complexity per se. After some discussion, the team decided to use part weight and price as surrogates for simplicity, operating under the assumption that "If it doesn't weigh very much or cost very much, it probably isn't complex." At least, the team decided to start that way and find out. Accordingly, the team asked the IS department to include part weight in the extract.

Acquire Data

As shown in Figure 3, acquiring data is the first step in the BI process. In response to the team's request for data, the IS department extracted operational data to produce the following two tables:

Sales (CustomerName, Contact, Title, Bill Year, Number Orders, Units, Revenue, Source, PartNumber)

Part (PartNumber, Shipping Weight, Vendor)

Sample data for these two tables is shown in Figure 4. As team members examined this data, they concluded they had what they needed and actually wouldn't need all of the data columns in the Sales table. They were surprised that the data was divided into different billing years, but because they planned to sum item sales over those years, that division wouldn't affect their analysis.

Analyze Data

The team's first step was to combine the data in the two tables into a single table that contained both the sales and part data. Also, because team members had already selected certain vendors to work with (those they knew would agree to release 3D part design files), they set filtering criteria for those vendor names, as shown in Figure 5. In this Access query, the line between PartNumber in Order Extract and PartNumber in Part Data means that rows of the two tables are to be combined if they have matching values of PartNumber.

The result of this query is shown in Figure 6. Notice there are some missing and questionable values. Numerous rows have missing values of Contact and Title, and some of the rows have a

Island Biking	John Steel	Marketing Manager	2017	10	39	$195.22	AWS
Island Biking	John Steel	Marketing Manager	2016	14	59	$438.81	Internet
Island Biking	John Steel	Marketing Manager	2016	21	55	$255.96	AWS
Island Biking	John Steel	Marketing Manager	2017	4	11	$85.55	Internet
Kona Riders	Renate Messne	Sales Representative	2014	43	54	$349.27	Internet
Kona Riders	Renate Messne	Sales Representative	2015	30	53	$362.45	Internet
Kona Riders	Renate Messne	Sales Representative	2016	1	2	$14.34	Internet
Lone Pine Crafters	Jaime Yorres	Owner	2017	4	14	$108.89	Internet
Lone Pine Crafters	Jaime Yorres	Owner	2017	2	2	$15.56	Internet
Lone Pine Crafters	Jaime Yorres	Owner	2018	2	2	$15.56	Internet
Moab Mauraders	Carlos Gonzále	Accounting Manager	2017	2	4	$4,106.69	Internet
Moab Mauraders	Carlos Gonzále	Accounting Manager	2017	3	7	$7,404.18	Internet
Moab Mauraders	Carlos Gonzále	Accounting Manager	2017	2	6	$6,346.44	Internet
Sedona Mountain Trails	Felipe Izquierd	Owner	2017	6	7	$73.46	Internet
Sedona Mountain Trails	Felipe Izquierd	Owner	2017	3	7	$39.14	Phone
Sedona Mountain Trails	Felipe Izquierd	Owner	2017	3	9	$74.59	Phone
Sedona Mountain Trails	Felipe Izquierd	Owner	2016	5	20	$153.00	Phone
Sedona Mountain Trails	Felipe Izquierd	Owner	2014	3	8	$37.14	Phone
Sedona Mountain Trails	Felipe Izquierd	Owner	2015	1	0	$89.30	Internet
Sedona Mountain Trails	Felipe Izquierd	Owner	2015	6	20	$73.13	Phone
Sedona Mountain Trails	Felipe Izquierd	Owner	2014	4	8	$67.41	Internet
Flat Iron Riders	Maria Anders	Sales Representative	2015	7	22	$11,734.25	Internet
Flat Iron Riders	Maria Anders	Sales Representative	2017	2	1	$595.00	Internet
Flat Iron Riders	Maria Anders	Sales Representative	2016	10	29	$16,392.25	Internet
Flat Iron Riders	Maria Anders	Sales Representative	2017	20	32	$12,688.80	AWS

FIGURE 4a
Sample Extracted Data: Order Extract Table
Source: Windows 10, Microsoft Corporation.

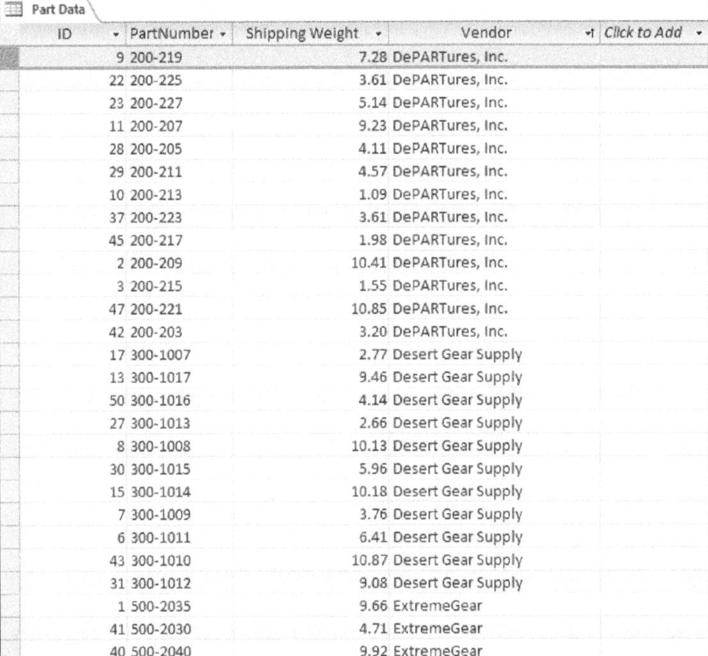

Part Data

ID	PartNumber	Shipping Weight	Vendor	Click to Add
9	200-219	7.28	DePARTures, Inc.	
22	200-225	3.61	DePARTures, Inc.	
23	200-227	5.14	DePARTures, Inc.	
11	200-207	9.23	DePARTures, Inc.	
28	200-205	4.11	DePARTures, Inc.	
29	200-211	4.57	DePARTures, Inc.	
10	200-213	1.09	DePARTures, Inc.	
37	200-223	3.61	DePARTures, Inc.	
45	200-217	1.98	DePARTures, Inc.	
2	200-209	10.41	DePARTures, Inc.	
3	200-215	1.55	DePARTures, Inc.	
47	200-221	10.85	DePARTures, Inc.	
42	200-203	3.20	DePARTures, Inc.	
17	300-1007	2.77	Desert Gear Supply	
13	300-1017	9.46	Desert Gear Supply	
50	300-1016	4.14	Desert Gear Supply	
27	300-1013	2.66	Desert Gear Supply	
8	300-1008	10.13	Desert Gear Supply	
30	300-1015	5.96	Desert Gear Supply	
15	300-1014	10.18	Desert Gear Supply	
7	300-1009	3.76	Desert Gear Supply	
6	300-1011	6.41	Desert Gear Supply	
43	300-1010	10.87	Desert Gear Supply	
31	300-1012	9.08	Desert Gear Supply	
1	500-2035	9.66	ExtremeGear	
41	500-2030	4.71	ExtremeGear	
40	500-2040	9.92	ExtremeGear	

FIGURE 4b
Sample Extracted Data: Part Data Table
Source: Windows 10, Microsoft Corporation.

value of zero for Units. The missing contact data and title data wasn't a problem. But the values of zero units might be problematic. At some point, the team might need to investigate what these values mean and possibly correct the data or remove those rows from the analysis. In the immediate term, however, the team decided to proceed even with these incorrect values. You will learn in Q3 that, for a number of reasons, such problematic data is common in data extracts.

The data in Figure 6 has been filtered for their first criterion, to consider parts only from particular vendors. For their next criterion, team members needed to decide how to identify large customers. To do so, they created the query in Figure 7, which sums the revenue, units, and average price for each customer. Looking at the query results in Figure 8, team members decided to consider only customers having more than $200,000 in total revenue; they created a query having just those customers and named that query Big Customers.

Next, team members discussed what they meant by frequent purchase and decided to include items ordered an average of once a week or roughly 50 times per year. You can see that they set

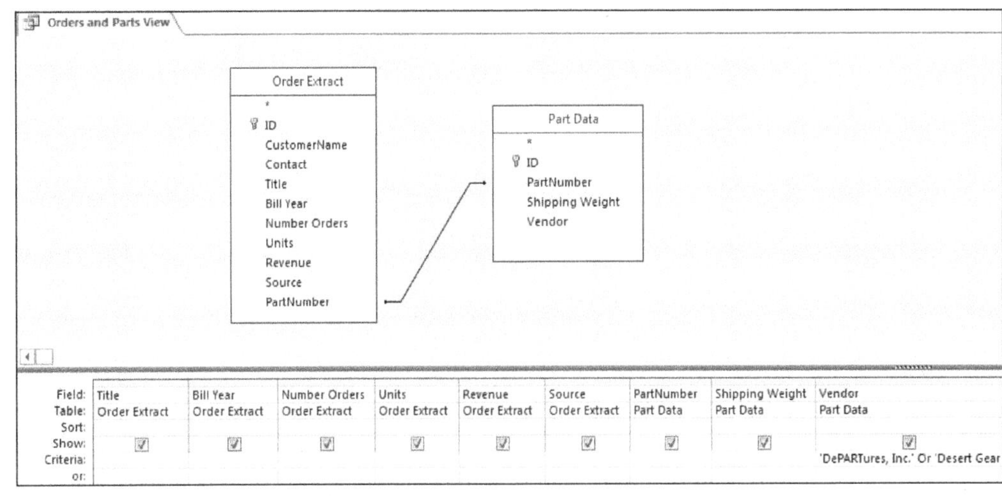

FIGURE 5
Joining *Orders Extract* and Filtered *Parts* Tables
Source: Windows 10, Microsoft Corporation.

Orders and Parts View

CustomerName	Contact	Title	Bill Year	Number Orders	Units	Revenue	Source	PartNumber	Shipping Weight	Vendor
Gordos Dirt Bikes	Sergio Gutiérrez	Sales Repres	2016	43	107	$26,234.12	Internet	100-108	3.32	Riley Manufacturing
Island Biking			2017	59	135	$25,890.62	Phone	500-2035	9.66	ExtremeGear
Big Bikes			2015	29	77	$25,896.00	AWS	700-1680	6.06	HyperTech Manufacturing
Lazy B Bikes			2014	19	30	$25,576.50	Internet	700-2280	2.70	HyperTech Manufacturing
Lone Pine Crafters	Carlos Hernández	Sales Repres	2017	1	0	$25,171.56	Internet	500-2030	4.71	ExtremeGear
Seven Lakes Riding	Peter Franken	Marketing M	2014	15	50	$25,075.00	Internet	500-2020	10.07	ExtremeGear
Big Bikes			2017	10	40	$24,888.00	Internet	500-2025	10.49	ExtremeGear
B' Bikes	Georg Pipps	Sales Manage	2017	14	23	$24,328.02	Internet	700-1680	6.06	HyperTech Manufacturing
Eastern Connection	Isabel de Castro	Sales Repres	2017	48	173	$24,296.17	AWS	100-105	10.73	Riley Manufacturing
Big Bikes	Carine Schmitt	Marketing M	2014	22	71	$23,877.48	AWS	500-2035	9.66	ExtremeGear
Island Biking	Manuel Pereira	Owner	2016	26	45	$23,588.86	Internet	500-2045	3.22	ExtremeGear
Mississippi Delta Riding	Rene Phillips	Sales Repres	2017	9	33	$23,550.25	Internet	700-2180	4.45	HyperTech Manufacturing
Uncle's Upgrades			2017	9	21	$22,212.54	Internet	700-1680	6.06	HyperTech Manufacturing
Big Bikes			2015	73	80	$22,063.92	Phone	700-1680	6.06	HyperTech Manufacturing
Island Biking			2017	18	59	$22,025.88	Internet	100-108	3.32	Riley Manufacturing
Uncle's Upgrades			2016	16	38	$21,802.50	Internet	500-2035	9.66	ExtremeGear
Hard Rock Machines			2017	42	57	$21,279.24	Internet	100-108	3.32	Riley Manufacturing
Kona Riders			2017	11	20	$21,154.80	Internet	700-1880	2.28	HyperTech Manufacturing
Moab Mauraders			2017	6	20	$21,154.80	Internet	700-2180	4.45	HyperTech Manufacturing
Lone Pine Crafters			2017	35	58	$21,016.59	Internet	100-106	6.23	Riley Manufacturing
Big Bikes	Carine Schmitt	Marketing M	2015	9	36	$20,655.00	Internet	500-2035	9.66	ExtremeGear
East/West Enterprises			2016	14	60	$20,349.00	Internet	100-104	5.80	Riley Manufacturing
Jeeps 'n More	Yvonne Moncada	Sales Agent	2017	47	50	$20,230.00	AWS	500-2030	4.71	ExtremeGear
East/West Enterprises			2014	14	60	$20,178.15	AWS	500-2035	9.66	ExtremeGear
Lone Pine Crafters			2017	20	54	$20,159.28	Internet	100-106	6.23	Riley Manufacturing
Lone Pine Crafters	Carlos Hernández	Sales Repres	2017	1	0	$20,137.27	Internet	500-2030	4.71	ExtremeGear
Lazy B Bikes			2017	21	29	$19,946.78	AWS	700-1580	7.50	HyperTech Manufacturing
Eastern Connection	Isabel de Castro	Sales Repres	2017	42	173	$19,907.06	Phone	100-105	10.73	Riley Manufacturing
Lazy B Bikes			2017	8	30	$19,724.25	AWS	700-1580	7.50	HyperTech Manufacturing
Sedona Mountain Trails			2015	12	22	$19,677.29	Internet	700-2080	8.63	HyperTech Manufacturing
Mississippi Delta Riding	Maria Larsson	Owner	2015	17	20	$19,507.50	Internet	700-1880	2.28	HyperTech Manufacturing
Seven Lakes Riding	Peter Franken	Marketing M	2016	39	53	$19,400.40	AWS	500-2020	10.07	ExtremeGear
Lazy B Bikes			2016	6	20	$19,218.50	Internet	700-1580	7.50	HyperTech Manufacturing

FIGURE 6

Sample *Orders* and *Parts View* Data

Source: Windows 10, Microsoft Corporation.

that criterion for Number Orders in the query in Figure 9. To select only parts that are ordered in small quantities, they first created a column that computes average order size (Units / [Number Orders]) and then set a criterion on that expression that the average must be less than 2.5. Their last two criteria were that the part be relatively inexpensive and that it be lightweight. They decided to select parts with a unit price (computed as Revenue / Units) less than 100 and a shipping weight less than 5 pounds.

The results of this query are shown in Figure 10. Of all the parts that the company sells, these 12 fit the criteria that the team created.

The next question was how much revenue potential these parts represent. Accordingly, the team created a query that connected the selected parts with their past sales data. The results are shown in Figure 11.

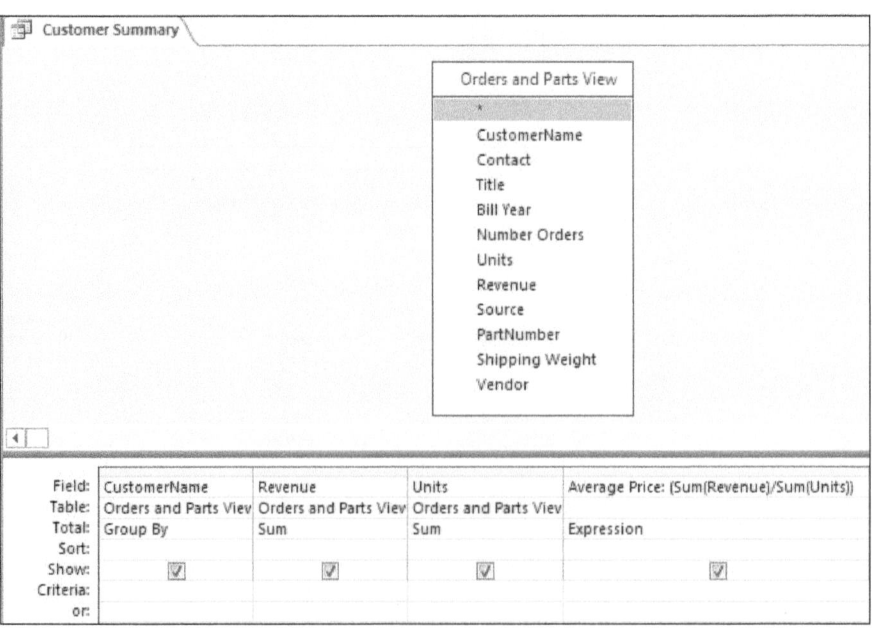

FIGURE 7

Creating the Customer Summary Query

Source: Windows 10, Microsoft Corporation.

Customer Summary

CustomerName	SumOfRevenue	SumOfUnits	Average Price
Great Lakes Machines	$1,760.47	142	12.3976535211268
Seven Lakes Riding	$288,570.71	5848	49.3451963919289
Around the Horn	$16,669.48	273	61.0603611721612
Dewey Riding	$36,467.90	424	86.0092018867925
Moab Mauraders	$143,409.27	1344	106.7033234375
Gordos Dirt Bikes	$113,526.88	653	173.854335068913
Mountain Traders	$687,710.99	3332	206.395855432173
Hungry Rider Off-road	$108,602.32	492	220.736416056911
Eastern Connection	$275,092.28	1241	221.669848186946
Mississippi Delta Riding	$469,932.11	1898	247.593315542676
Island Biking	$612,072.64	2341	261.457770098249
Big Bikes	$1,385,867.98	4876	284.222310233798
Hard Rock Machines	$74,853.22	241	310.594267219917
Lone Pine Crafters	$732,990.33	1816	403.629038215859
Sedona Mountain Trails	$481,073.82	1104	435.755269474638
Flat Iron Riders	$85,469.20	183	467.044808743169
Bottom-Dollar Bikes	$72,460.85	154	470.5250201298
Uncle's Upgrades	$947,477.61	1999	473.975794047023
Ernst Handel Mechanics	$740,951.15	1427	519.236962438683
Kona Riders	$511,108.05	982	520.476624439919
Lazy B Bikes	$860,950.72	1594	540.119648619824
Jeeps 'n More	$404,540.62	678	596.667583185841
French Riding Masters	$1,037,386.76	1657	626.063224984912
B' Bikes	$113,427.06	159	713.377735849057
East/West Enterprises	$2,023,402.09	2457	823.525474074074
Bon App Riding	$65,848.90	60	1097.48160833333

FIGURE 8
Customer Summary
Source: Windows 10, Microsoft Corporation.

Publish Results

Publish results is the last activity in the BI process shown in Figure 3. In some cases, this means placing BI results on servers for publication to knowledge workers over the Internet or other networks. In other cases, it means making the results available via a Web service for use by other applications. In still other cases, it means creating PDFs or PowerPoint presentations for communicating to colleagues or management.

In this case, the team reported these results to management in a team meeting. Judging just by the results in Figure 11, there seems to be little revenue potential in selling designs for these parts. The company would earn minimal revenue from the parts themselves; the designs would have to be priced considerably lower, and that would mean almost no revenue.

In spite of the low revenue potential, the company might still decide to offer 3D designs to customers. It might decide to give the designs away as a gesture of goodwill to its customers; this analysis indicates it will be sacrificing little revenue to do so. Or it might do it as a PR move intended to

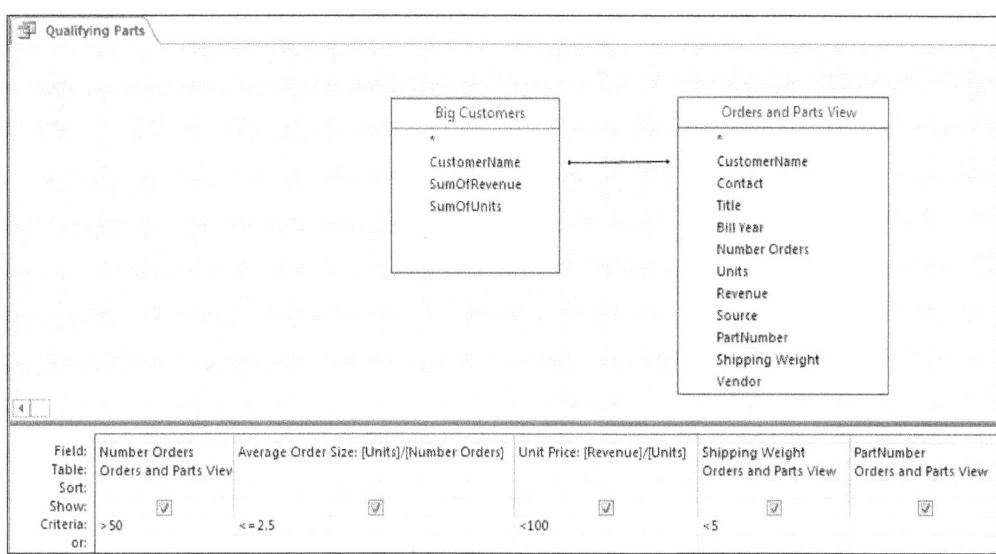

FIGURE 9
Qualifying Parts Query Design
Source: Windows 10, Microsoft Corporation.

Qualifying Parts

Number Orders	Average Order Size	Unit Price	Shipping Weight	PartNumber
275	1	9.14173854545455	4.14	300-1016
258	1.87596899224806	7.41284524793388	4.14	300-1016
110	1.18181818181818	6.46796923076923	4.11	200-205
176	1.66477272727273	12.5887211604096	4.14	300-1016
139	1.0431654676259	6.28248965517241	1.98	200-217
56	1.83928571428571	6.71141553398058	1.98	200-217
99	1.02020202020202	7.7775	3.20	200-203
76	2.17105263157895	12.0252206060606	2.66	300-1013
56	1.07142857142857	5.0575	4.57	200-211
73	1.15068493150685	5.0575	4.57	200-211
107	2.02803738317757	6.01096405529954	2.77	300-1007
111	2.07207207207207	6.01096434782609	2.77	300-1007

FIGURE 10
Qualifying Parts Query Results
Source: Windows 10, Microsoft Corporation.

Revenue Potential

Total Orders	Total Revenue	PartNumber
3987	$84,672.73	300-1016
2158	$30,912.19	200-211
1074	$23,773.53	200-217
548	$7,271.31	300-1007
375	$5,051.62	200-203
111	$3,160.86	300-1013
139	$1,204.50	200-205

FIGURE 11
Sales History for Selected Parts
Source: Windows 10, Microsoft Corporation.

show that it's on top of the latest manufacturing technology. Or it might decide to postpone consideration of 3D printing because it doesn't see that many customers ordering the qualifying parts.

Of course, there is the possibility that the team members chose the wrong criteria. If they have time, it might be worthwhile to change their criteria and repeat the analysis. Such a course is a slippery slope, however. They might find themselves changing criteria until they obtain a result they want, which yields a very biased study.

This possibility points again to the importance of the human component of an IS. The hardware, software, data, and query-generation procedures are of little value if the decisions that the team made when setting and possibly revising criteria are poor. Business intelligence is only as intelligent as the people creating it!

With this example in mind, we will now consider each of the activities in Figure 3 in greater detail.

Q3 How Do Organizations Use Data Warehouses and Data Marts to Acquire Data?

Although it is possible to create basic reports and perform simple analyses from operational data, this course is not usually recommended. For reasons of security and control, IS professionals do not want data analysts processing operational data. If an analyst makes an error, that error could cause a serious disruption in the company's operations. Also, operational data is structured for fast and reliable transaction processing. It is seldom structured in a way that readily supports BI analysis. Finally, BI analyses can require considerable processing; placing BI applications on operational servers can dramatically reduce system performance.

For these reasons, most organizations extract operational data for BI processing. For small organizations, the extraction may be as simple as an Access database. Larger organizations, however, typically create and staff a group of people who manage and run a **data warehouse**, which is a facility for managing an organization's BI data. The functions of a data warehouse are to:

- Obtain data
- Cleanse data
- Organize and relate data
- Catalog data

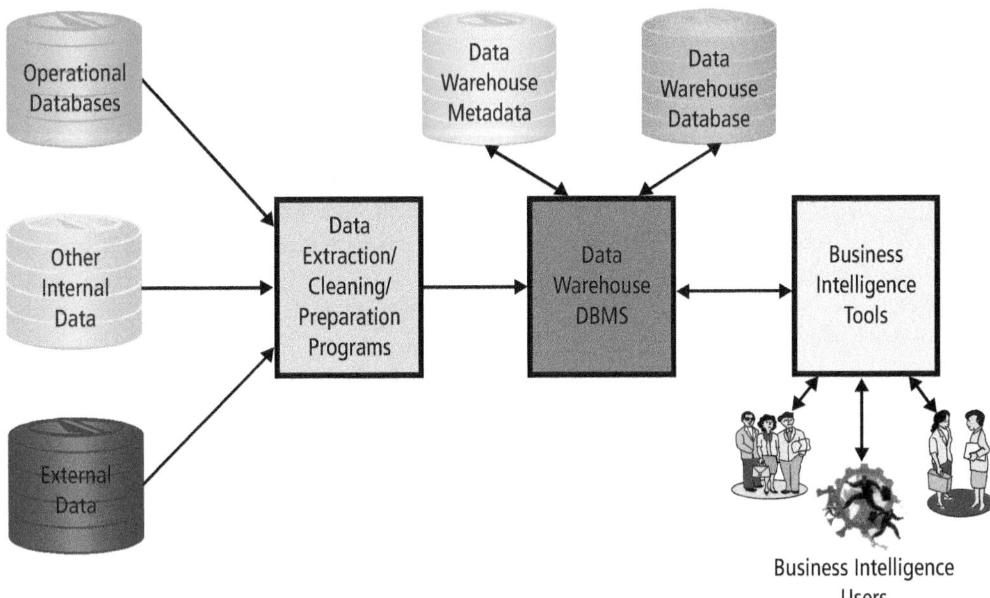

FIGURE 12
Components of a Data Warehouse

Figure 12 shows the components of a data warehouse. Programs read operational and other data and extract, clean, and prepare that data for BI processing. The prepared data is stored in a data warehouse database using a data warehouse DBMS, which can be different from the organization's operational DBMS. For example, an organization might use Oracle for its operational processing, but use SQL Server for its data warehouse. Other organizations use SQL Server for operational processing, but use DBMSs from statistical package vendors such as SAS or SPSS in the data warehouse.

Data warehouses include data that is purchased from outside sources. The purchase of data about organizations is not unusual or particularly concerning from a privacy standpoint. However, some companies choose to buy personal consumer data (e.g., marital status) from data vendors such as Acxiom Corporation. Figure 13 lists some of the consumer data that can be readily purchased. An amazing (and, from a privacy standpoint, frightening) amount of data is available.

Metadata concerning the data—its source, its format, its assumptions and constraints, and other facts about the data—is kept in a data warehouse metadata database. The data warehouse DBMS extracts and provides data to BI applications.

The term *business intelligence users* is different from *knowledge workers* in Figure 1. BI users are generally specialists in data analysis, whereas knowledge workers are often nonspecialist users of BI results. A loan approval officer at a bank is a knowledge worker, but not a BI user.

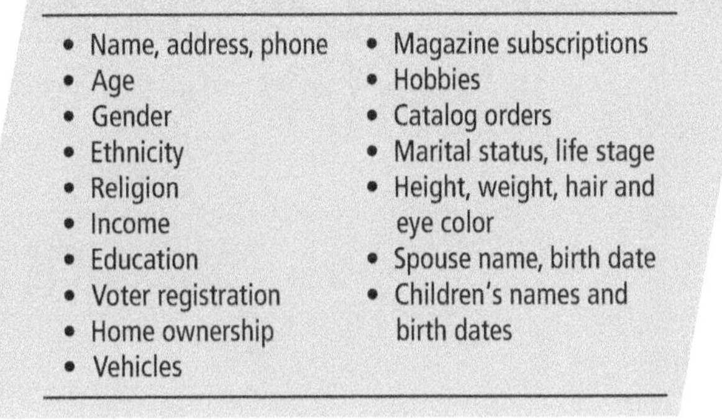

FIGURE 13
Examples of Consumer Data That Can Be Purchased

Problems with Operational Data

Most operational and purchased data has problems that inhibit its usefulness for business intelligence. Figure 14 lists the major problem categories. First, although data that is critical for successful operations must be complete and accurate, marginally necessary data need not be. For example, some systems gather demographic data in the ordering process. But, because such data is not needed to fill, ship, and bill orders, its quality suffers.

Security concerns about access to data are problematic. See the Security Guide given later in the chapter for more information.

Problematic data is termed dirty data. Examples are a value of B for customer gender and of 213 for customer age. Other examples are a value of 999-999-9999 for a U.S. phone number, a part color of "gren," and an email address of WhyMe@GuessWhoIAM.org. The value of zero for Units in Figure 6 is dirty data. All of these values can be problematic for BI purposes.

Purchased data often contains missing elements. The contact data in Figure 6 is a typical example; orders can be shipped without contact data, so its quality is spotty and has many missing values. Most data vendors state the percentage of missing values for each attribute in the data they sell. An organization buys such data because for some uses, some data is better than no data at all. This is especially true for data items whose values are difficult to obtain, such as Number of Adults in Household, Household Income, Dwelling Type, and Education of Primary Income Earner. However, care is required here because for some BI applications a few missing or erroneous data points can seriously bias the analysis.

Inconsistent data, the third problem in Figure 14, is particularly common for data that has been gathered over time. When an area code changes, for example, the phone number for a given customer before the change will not match the customer's number afterward. Likewise, part codes can change, as can sales territories. Before such data can be used, it must be recoded for consistency over the period of the study.

Some data inconsistencies occur from the nature of the business activity. Consider a Web-based order-entry system used by customers worldwide. When the Web server records the time of order, which time zone does it use? The server's system clock time is irrelevant to an analysis of customer behavior. Coordinated Universal Time (formerly called Greenwich Mean Time) is also meaningless. Somehow, Web server time must be adjusted to the time zone of the customer.

Another problem is nonintegrated data. A particular BI analysis might require data from an ERP system, an e-commerce system, and a social networking application. Analysts may wish to integrate that organizational data with purchased consumer data. Such a data collection will likely have relationships that are not represented in primary key/foreign key relationships. It is the function of personnel in the data warehouse to integrate such data somehow.

Data can also have the wrong **granularity**, a term that refers to the level of detail represented by the data. Granularity can be too fine or too coarse. For the former, suppose we want to analyze the placement of graphics and controls on an order-entry Web page. It is possible to capture the customers' clicking behavior in what is termed *clickstream data*. Those data, however, include everything the customer does at the Web site. In the middle of the order stream are data for clicks on the news, email, instant chat, and a weather check. Although all of that data may be useful for a study of consumer browsing behavior, it will be overwhelming if all we want to know is how customers respond to an ad located differently on the screen. To proceed, the data analysts must throw away millions and millions of clicks.

- Dirty data
- Missing values
- Inconsistent data
- Data not integrated
- Wrong granularity
  - Too fine
  - Not fine enough
- Too much data
  - Too many attributes
  - Too many data points

FIGURE 14
Possible Problems with Source Data

Data can also be too coarse. For example, a file of regional sales totals cannot be used to investigate the sales in a particular store in a region, and total sales for a store cannot be used to determine the sales of particular items within a store. Instead, we need to obtain data that is fine enough for the lowest-level report we want to produce.

In general, it is better to have too fine a granularity than too coarse. If the granularity is too fine, the data can be made coarser by summing and combining. This is what team members did with the sales data in Figure 6. Sales by Bill Year were too fine for their needs, so they summed sales data over those years. If the granularity is too coarse, however, there is no way to separate the data into constituent parts.

The final problem listed in Figure 14 is to have too much data. As shown in the figure, we can have either too many attributes or too many data points. We can have too many columns or too many rows.

Consider the first problem: too many attributes. Suppose we want to know the factors that influence how customers respond to a promotion. If we combine internal customer data with purchased customer data, we will have more than a hundred different attributes to consider. How do we select among them? In some cases, analysts can ignore the columns they don't need. But in more sophisticated data mining analyses, too many attributes can be problematic. Because of a phenomenon called the *curse of dimensionality*, the more attributes there are, the easier it is to build a model that fits the sample data but that is worthless as a predictor. There are other good reasons for reducing the number of attributes, and one of the major activities in data mining concerns efficient and effective ways of selecting attributes.

The second way to have an excess of data is to have too many data points—too many rows of data. Suppose we want to analyze clickstream data on CNN.com. How many clicks does that site receive per month? Millions upon millions! In order to meaningfully analyze such data we need to reduce the amount of data. One good solution to this problem is statistical sampling. Organizations should not be reluctant to sample data in such situations.

Data Warehouses Versus Data Marts

To understand the difference between data warehouses and data marts, think of a data warehouse as a distributor in a supply chain. The data warehouse takes data from the data manufacturers (operational systems and other sources), cleans and processes the data, and locates the data on the shelves, so to speak, of the data warehouse. The data analysts who work with a data warehouse are experts at data management, data cleaning, data transformation, data relationships, and the like. However, they are not usually experts in a given business function.

A **data mart** is a data collection, smaller than the data warehouse, that addresses the needs of a particular department or functional area of the business. If the data warehouse is the distributor in a supply chain, then a data mart is like a retail store in a supply chain. Users in the data mart obtain data that pertain to a particular business function from the data warehouse. Such users do not have the data management expertise that data warehouse employees have, but they are knowledgeable analysts for a given business function.

Figure 15 illustrates these relationships. In this example, the data warehouse takes data from the data producers and distributes the data to three data marts. One data mart is used to analyze clickstream data for the purpose of designing Web pages. A second analyzes store sales data and determines which products tend to be purchased together. This information is used to train salespeople on the best way to up-sell to customers. The third data mart is used to analyze customer order data for the purpose of reducing labor for item picking from the warehouse. A company like Amazon, for example, goes to great lengths to organize its warehouses to reduce picking expenses.

As you can imagine, it is expensive to create, staff, and operate data warehouses and data marts. Only large organizations with deep pockets can afford to operate a system like that shown in Figure 12. Smaller organizations operate subsets of this system, but they must find ways to solve the basic problems that data warehouses solve, even if those ways are informal.

ETHICS GUIDE

MIS-DIAGNOSIS

Fred Bolton stared at his computer screen until his eyes glazed over. He had been working 15-hour days for the past week trying to solve a serious problem that could have a devastating impact on the future of his employer. Fred had worked at A+Meds for almost a decade, and he was proud to be affiliated with a world-leading pharmaceutical company. He started out at the bottom of the IT department but had moved up quickly. He was a fast learner with a never-give-up attitude. But today he was on the verge of giving up.

Fred was astounded at how much the pharmaceutical industry had changed over the previous 10 years. When he first started at A+Meds, the company could drive up sales using direct marketing techniques. Doctors met with company representatives who convinced them that A+Meds were the best on the market. Now, technology had started to permeate every aspect of the healthcare industry. Doctors were relying more and more on artificial intelligence (AI)-driven expert systems to select the most appropriate medications and treatments. These systems made recommendations based on drug profiles submitted to the system by pharmaceutical companies. The companies could update the drug profiles if any aspect of the drug changed, but this didn't happen very often if the changes were minor.

Recently, the sales of a new drug had been underperforming. A+Meds had invested tens of millions of dollars in developing it. Company executives and new product developers were convinced that the product was superior to competing drugs. The problem, they believed, was that the expert systems used by doctors were not recommending the product. Sales were suffering, profitability was down, and employee compensation was in jeopardy.

Fred had been tasked with doing a rigorous investigation of the AI recommendation system. He was supposed to identify the problem and see if there was something the company could do to improve the system's "perception" of the product. During his testing, Fred found that minor modifications to the drug's profile made a big difference. But some of the numbers he used to modify the profile were not accurate. Even if they were, the changes he made would warrant a regulatory review, which could take an extensive amount of time. The financial damage to the company would be done long before the review was complete. Fred was not looking forward to reporting his findings.

Information Manipulation

Fred kept looking at the clock on his computer monitor. It was time for his meeting, but he was trying to find an excuse to linger at his desk. He came up empty handed and headed over to the boardroom. He took a seat at the end of a long conference table and joined Patricia Tanner, a high-level A+Meds sales executive. "So, Fred, what did you find out?" Patricia asked. "Good news, I hope!" Fred explained that, in spite of his extensive analysis of the recommendation system, he was unable to identify a solution that would cause the system to select their product over competing products—unless they tweaked the profile.

"But our drug is superior and safer!" she exclaimed. "I was a sales executive at our competitor when they were putting a similar drug through trials, and I know for a fact that our drug is the better choice."

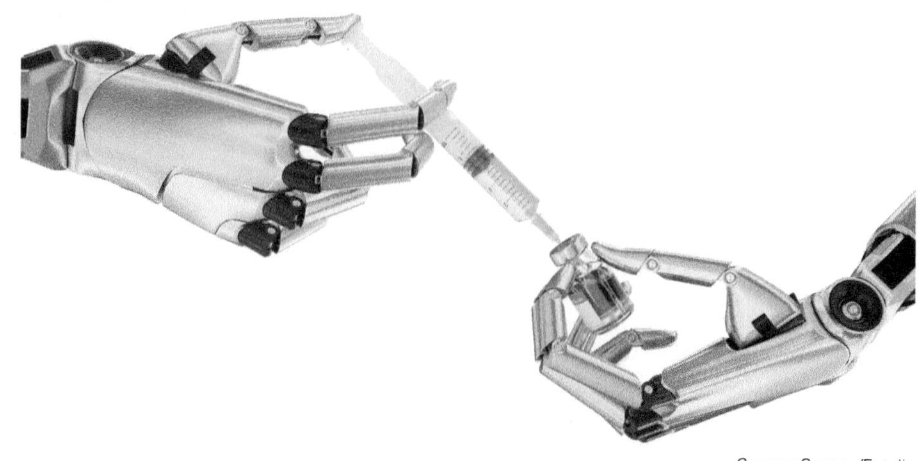

Source: Sergey/Fotolia

"That may be," Fred replied cautiously, "but our profile is based on our current approval guidelines. The drug's current profile is causing us to lose out to competing drugs."

They both sat for a minute before Patricia slowly replied, "What if we submit a new profile that the system perceives as more favorable, even though some of the data was a bit of a stretch?"

Fred couldn't believe she'd just asked that question. He wasn't sure how to respond without putting his job in jeopardy. "Wouldn't the addition of inaccurate information to the system be considered a violation? Wouldn't we be liable if something happened to a patient who took our drug based on *altered* information?" Fred asked. Patricia replied that drug companies did stuff like this all of the time. Investigations were extremely rare and only occurred if there were numerous patient-related incidents of a serious nature.

Patricia looked over at him with a funny look on her face and said, "Do you think it is right to have people using what we *know* to be an inferior drug simply based on how this system interprets drug profiles? What if people get sick or if something more serious happens to them because they should have taken our drug but didn't because of the system? Wouldn't you feel bad about that?" Fred hadn't thought about it like that. Maybe Patricia was right. Fred did believe their drug was the better choice. But he wasn't a doctor. Adhering to federal regulations seemed like the right choice, but not at the risk of keeping people from the medication they *should* be getting. He let out a sigh and leaned back in his chair. He wasn't sure what to say.

DISCUSSION QUESTIONS

1. According to the definitions of the ethics principles:
   a. Do you think that manipulating the recommendation of an AI system even though the new recommendation may be for the better drug is ethical according to the categorical imperative?
   b. Do you think that manipulating the recommendation of an AI system even though the new recommendation may be for the better drug is ethical according to the utilitarian perspective?
2. How would you respond if you were placed in Fred's shoes? Do you think it is appropriate to submit inaccurate information because the drug may be better and safer than the competition?
3. How should Fred handle the fact that Patricia made the suggestion to manipulate the drug's profile? Is her willingness to use this type of tactic cause for concern in its own right?
4. How do you feel about the growing use of AI and other technological solutions in helping people make decisions? Would you want a doctor treating you based on recommendations from an automated system? Consider other arenas as well. For example, would you trust the recommendation of an automated financial investment system over the advice of a human financial advisor?

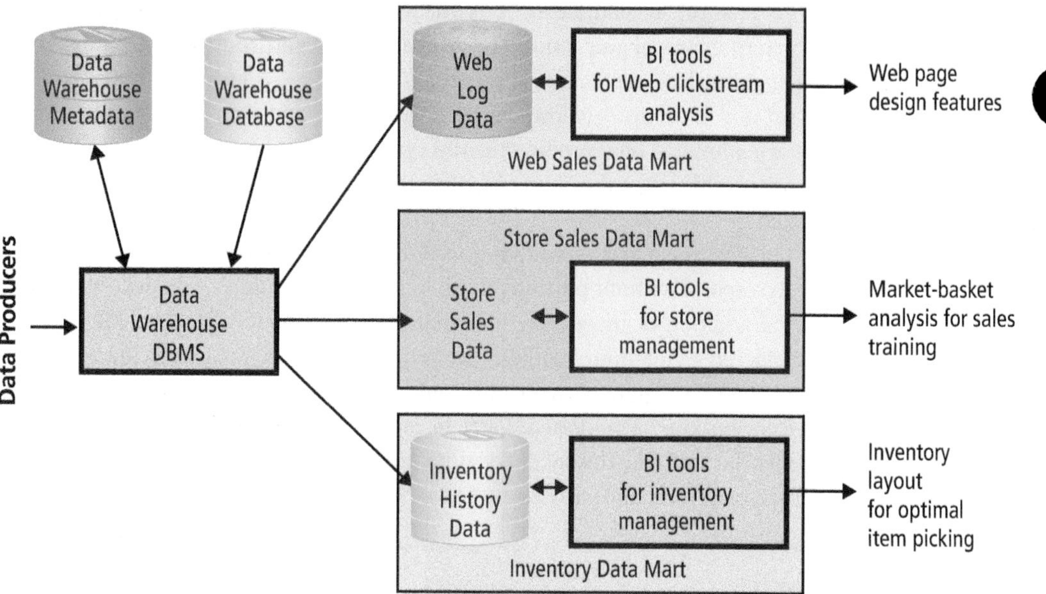

FIGURE 15
Data Mart Examples

How Do Organizations Use Reporting Applications?

A **reporting application** is a BI application that inputs data from one or more sources and applies reporting operations to that data to produce business intelligence. We will first summarize reporting operations and then illustrate two important reporting applications: RFM analysis and OLAP.

Basic Reporting Operations

Reporting applications produce business intelligence using five basic operations:

- Sorting
- Filtering
- Grouping
- Calculating
- Formatting

None of these operations is particularly sophisticated; they can all be accomplished using SQL and basic HTML or a simple report writing tool.

The team that analyzed parts in Q3 used Access to apply all five of these operations. Examine, for example, Figure 11. The results are *sorted* by Total Revenue, *filtered* for particular parts, sales are *grouped by* PartNumber, Total Orders and Total Revenue are *calculated*, and the calculations for Total Revenue are *formatted* correctly as dollar currency.

These simple operations can be used to produce complex and highly useful reports. Consider RFM analysis and Online Analytical Processing as two prime examples.

RFM Analysis

RFM analysis, a technique readily implemented with basic reporting operations, is used to analyze and rank customers according to their purchasing patterns.[8] RFM considers how *recently* (R) a customer has ordered, how *frequently* (F) a customer ordered, and how much *money* (M) the customer has spent.

To produce an RFM score, the RFM reporting tool first sorts customer purchase records by the date of their most recent (R) purchase. In a common form of this analysis, the tool then divides the customers into five groups and gives customers in each group a score of 5 to 1. The 20 percent of the customers having the most recent orders are given an R score of 5, the 20 percent of the customers having the next most recent orders are given an R score of 4, and so forth, down to the last 20 percent, who are given an R score of 1.

The tool then re-sorts the customers on the basis of how frequently they order. The 20 percent of the customers who order most frequently are given an F score of 5, the next 20 percent of most frequently ordering customers are given a score of 4, and so forth, down to the least frequently ordering customers, who are given an F score of 1.

Finally, the tool sorts the customers again according to the amount spent on their orders. The 20 percent who have ordered the most expensive items are given an M score of 5, the next 20 percent are given an M score of 4, and so forth, down to the 20 percent who spend the least, who are given an M score of 1.

Figure 16 shows sample RFM results. The first customer, Big 7 Sports, has ordered recently and orders frequently. Big 7 Sports' M score of 3 indicates, however, that it does not order the most expensive goods. From these scores, the sales team can conclude that Big 7 Sports is a good, regular customer and that it should attempt to up-sell more expensive goods to Big 7 Sports.

The second customer in Figure 16 could represent a problem. St. Louis Soccer Club has not ordered in some time, but when it did order in the past, it ordered frequently, and its orders were of the highest monetary value. This data suggests that St. Louis Soccer Club might have taken its business to another vendor. Someone from the sales team should contact this customer immediately.

No one on the sales team should even think about the third customer, Miami Municipal. This company has not ordered for some time; it did not order frequently; and, when it did order, it bought the least expensive items and not many of them. Let Miami Municipal go to the competition; the loss will be minimal.

The last customer, Central Colorado State, is right in the middle. Central Colorado State is an OK customer, but probably no one in sales should spend much time with it. Perhaps sales can set up an automated contact system or use the Central Colorado State account as a training exercise for an eager departmental assistant or intern.

Online Analytical Processing (OLAP)

Online analytical processing (OLAP), a second type of reporting application, is more generic than RFM. OLAP provides the ability to sum, count, average, and perform other simple arithmetic operations on groups of data. The defining characteristic of OLAP reports is that they are dynamic. The viewer of the report can change the report's format, hence the term *online*.

An OLAP report has measures and dimensions. A **measure** is the data item of interest. It is the item that is to be summed or averaged or otherwise processed in the OLAP report. Total sales, average sales, and average cost are examples of measures. A **dimension** is a characteristic of a measure. Purchase date, customer type, customer location, and sales region are all examples of dimensions.

Customer	RFM Score
Big 7 Sports	5 5 3
St. Louis Soccer Club	1 5 5
Miami Municipal	1 2 1
Central Colorado State	3 3 3

FIGURE 16
Example RFM Scores

FIGURE 17
Example Grocery Sales OLAP Report
Source: Windows 10, Microsoft Corporation.

	A	B	C	D	E	F	G
1							
2							
3	Store Sales Net	Store Type					
4	Product Family	Deluxe Supermarket	Gourmet Supermarket	Mid-Size Grocery	Small Grocery	Supermarket	Grand Total
5	Drink	$8,119.05	$2,392.83	$1,409.50	$685.89	$16,751.71	$29,358.98
6	Food	$70,276.11	$20,026.18	$10,392.19	$6,109.72	$138,960.67	$245,764.87
7	Non-Consumable	$18,884.24	$5,064.79	$2,813.73	$1,534.90	$36,189.40	$64,487.05
8	Grand Total	$97,279.40	$27,483.80	$14,615.42	$8,330.51	$191,901.77	$339,610.90

Figure 17 shows a typical OLAP report. Here, the measure is *Store Sales Net*, and the dimensions are *Product Family* and *Store Type*. This report shows how net store sales vary by product family and store type. Stores of type *Supermarket* sold a net of $36,189 worth of nonconsumable goods, for example.

A presentation like that in Figure 17 is often called an **OLAP cube** or sometimes simply a *cube*. The reason for this term is that some software products show these displays using three axes, like a cube in geometry. The origin of the term is unimportant here, however. Just know that an *OLAP cube* and an *OLAP report* are the same thing.

The OLAP report in Figure 17 was generated by Microsoft SQL Server Analysis Services and is displayed in an Excel pivot table. The data was taken from a sample instructional database, called Food Mart, that is provided with SQL Server.

It is possible to display OLAP cubes in many ways besides with Excel. Some third-party vendors provide more extensive graphical displays. For more information about such products, check for OLAP vendors and products at the Data Warehousing Review at *http://dwreview.com/OLAP/index.html*. For an example of a superb, easy-to-use OLAP tool, visit *www.TableauSoftware.com*. Tableau has a liberal student-use policy as well.

As stated earlier, the distinguishing characteristic of an OLAP report is that the user can alter the format of the report. Figure 18 shows such an alteration. Here, the user added another dimension, *Store Country* and *Store State*, to the horizontal display. Product-family sales are now broken out by store location. Observe that the sample data only includes stores in the United States, and only in the western states of California, Oregon, and Washington.

With an OLAP report, it is possible to **drill down** into the data. This term means to further divide the data into more detail. In Figure 19, for example, the user has drilled down into the stores located in California; the OLAP report now shows sales data for the four cities in California that have stores.

Notice another difference between Figures 18 and 19. The user has not only drilled down, she has also changed the order of the dimensions. Figure 18 shows *Product Family* and then store location within *Product Family*. Figure 19 shows store location and then *Product Family* within store location.

FIGURE 18
Example of Expanded Grocery Sales OLAP Report
Source: Windows 10, Microsoft Corporation.

	A	B	C	D	E	F	G	H	I
1									
2									
3	Sum of store_sales			Column Labels					
4	Row Labels	Store Country	Store State	Deluxe Superma	Gourmet Supermar	Mid-Size Groce	Small Grocery	Supermarket	Grand Total
5	Drink	USA	CA		$3,940.54		$373.72	$9,888.98	$14,203.24
6			OR	$7,394.25				$4,743.04	$12,137.29
7			WA	$6,092.91		$2,348.79	$768.89	$13,285.09	$22,495.68
8		USA Total		$13,487.16	$3,940.54	$2,348.79	$1,142.61	$27,917.11	$48,836.21
9	Drink Total			$8,119.05	$2,392.83	$1,409.50	$685.89	$16,751.71	$29,358.98
10	Food	USA	CA		$33,424.17		$3,275.80	$78,493.20	$1,15,193.17
11			OR	$62,945.01				$39,619.66	$1,02,564.67
12			WA	$54,143.86		$17,314.24	$6,899.50	$1,12,920.15	$1,91,277.75
13		USA Total		$1,17,088.87	$33,424.17	$17,314.24	$10,175.30	$2,31,033.01	$4,09,035.59
14	Food Total			$70,276.11	$20,026.18	$10,392.19	$6,109.72	$138,960.67	$245,764.87
15	Non-Consumable	USA	CA		$8,385.53		$791.66	$20,594.24	$29,771.43
16			OR	$16,879.02				$10,696.09	$27,575.11
17			WA	$14,607.19		$4,666.20	$1,776.81	$28,969.59	$50,019.79
18		USA Total		$31,486.21	$8,385.53	$4,666.20	$2,568.47	$60,259.92	$1,07,366.33
19	Non-Consumable Total			$18,884.24	$5,064.79	$2,813.73	$1,534.90	$36,189.40	$64,487.05
20	Grand Total			$1,62,062.24	$45,750.24	$24,329.23	$13,886.38	$3,19,210.04	$5,65,238.13

	A	B	C	D	E	F	G
1	Sum of store_sales	Column Labels					
2	Row Labels	Deluxe Supermarket	Gourmet Supermarket	Mid-Size Grocery	Small Grocery	Supermarket	Grand Total
3	USA	$162,062.24	$45,750.24	$24,329.23	$13,886.38	$319,210.04	$565,238.13
4	CA		$45,750.24		$4,441.18	$108,976.42	$159,167.84
5	Beverly Hills		$45,750.24				$45,750.24
6	Drink		$3,940.54				$3,940.54
7	Food		$33,424.17				$33,424.17
8	Non-Consumable		$8,385.53				$8,385.53
9	Los Angeles					$54,545.28	$54,545.28
10	Drink					$4,823.88	$4,823.88
11	Food					$39,187.46	$39,187.46
12	Non-Consumable					$10,533.94	$10,533.94
13	San Diego					$54,431.14	$54,431.14
14	Drink					$5,065.10	$5,065.10
15	Food					$39,305.74	$39,305.74
16	Non-Consumable					$10,060.30	$10,060.30
17	San Francisco				$4,441.18		$4,441.18
18	Drink				$373.72		$373.72
19	Food				$3,275.80		$3,275.80
20	Non-Consumable				$791.66		$791.66
21	OR	$87,218.28				$55,058.79	$142,277.07
22	Portland					$55,058.79	$55,058.79
23	Salem	$87,218.28					$87,218.28
24	WA	$74,843.96		$24,329.23	$9,445.20	$155,174.83	$263,793.22
25	Bellingham				$4,739.23		$4,739.23
26	Bremerton					$52,896.30	$52,896.30
27	Seattle					$52,644.07	$52,644.07
28	Spokane					$49,634.46	$49,634.46
29	Tacoma	$74,843.96					$74,843.96
30	Walla Walla				$4,705.97		$4,705.97
31	Yakima			$24,329.23			$24,329.23
32	Grand Total	$162,062.24	$45,750.24	$24,329.23	$13,886.38	$319,210.04	$565,238.13

FIGURE 19

Example of Drilling Down into Expanded Grocery Sales OLAP Report

Source: Windows 10, Microsoft Corporation.

Both displays are valid and useful, depending on the user's perspective. A product manager might like to see product families first and then store location data. A sales manager might like to see store locations first and then product data. OLAP reports provide both perspectives, and the user can switch between them while viewing the report.

Unfortunately, all of this flexibility comes at a cost. If the database is large, doing the necessary calculating, grouping, and sorting for such dynamic displays will require substantial computing power. Although standard commercial DBMS products do have the features and functions required to create OLAP reports, they are not designed for such work. They are designed, instead, to provide rapid response to transaction-processing applications, such as order entry or manufacturing planning. Consequently, some organizations tune DBMS products on dedicated servers for this purpose. Today, many OLAP servers are being moved to the cloud.

Q5 How Do Organizations Use Data Mining Applications?

Data mining is the application of statistical techniques to find patterns and relationships among data for classification and prediction. As shown in Figure 20, data mining resulted from a convergence of disciplines, including artificial intelligence and machine learning. The recent surge in the popularity of artificial intelligence, machine learning, and data mining has been driven by

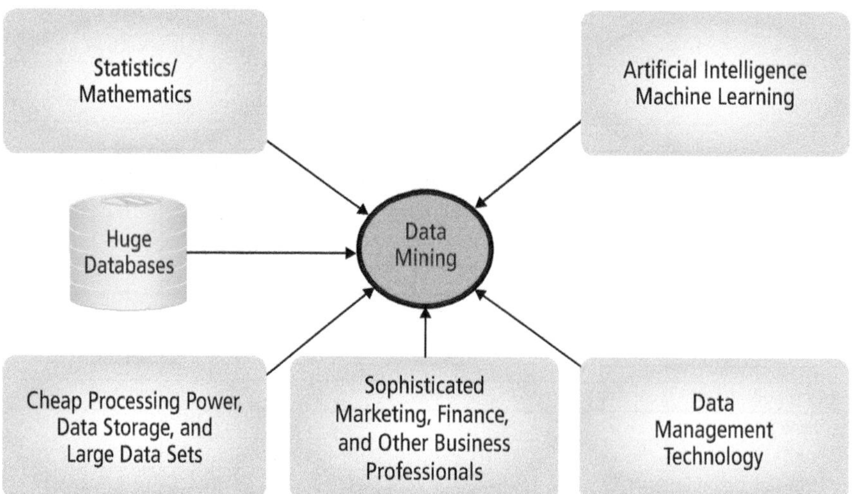

FIGURE 20
Source Disciplines of Data Mining

exponential increases in processing power and inexpensive data storage and by the creation of large data sets.

Intelligent Machines

Artificial intelligence (AI) is the ability of a machine to simulate human abilities such as vision, communication, recognition, learning, and decision making. Organizations hope to use AI to automate mundane tasks typically done by humans. For example, a professor at Georgia Tech trained IBM's AI, named Watson, to be a teaching assistant in his class. It was responsible for answering a portion of nearly 10,000 student questions. None of the students realized "Jill Watson" was a machine until the end of the semester when the professor identified their cybernetic classmate.[9]

A subset of AI is **machine learning**, or the extraction of knowledge from data based on algorithms created from training data. Machine learning is a close cousin to data mining but differs in its approach. Machine learning is focused on predicting outcomes based on previously known training data. Conversely, data mining is focused on discovering *new* patterns among data without prior training.

For example, machine learning can be used to teach a system to recognize and classify dog breeds. A machine learns to recognize each breed of dog by analyzing millions of dog images. In fact, Microsoft has made an app named Fetch! that does just that. You can even submit your own photo and see what dog breed you most closely resemble (*www.what-dog.net*). The applications of machine learning go far beyond dog breed classification. Entire courses are taught on machine learning. However, for our purposes we'll focus on data mining techniques.

Data mining techniques emerged from artificial intelligence and machine-learning fields in computer science and from statistics and mathematics. As a result, data mining terminology is an odd blend of terms from these different disciplines. Sometimes people use the term knowledge discovery in databases (KDD) as a synonym for data mining.

Most data mining techniques are sophisticated, and many are difficult to use well. Such techniques are valuable to organizations, however, and some business professionals, especially those in finance and marketing, have become experts in their use. In fact, today there are many interesting and rewarding careers for business professionals who are knowledgeable about data mining techniques.

Data mining techniques fall into two broad categories: unsupervised and supervised. We explain both types in the following sections.

Unsupervised Data Mining

With **unsupervised data mining**, analysts do not create a model or hypothesis before running the analysis. Instead, they apply a data mining application to the data and observe the results. With this method, analysts create hypotheses *after the analysis*, in order to explain the patterns found.

One common unsupervised technique is **cluster analysis**. With it, statistical techniques identify groups of entities that have similar characteristics. A common use for cluster analysis is to find groups of similar customers from customer order and demographic data.

Artifical intelligence (AI) applications are being used to help users process large amounts of data and make decisions. What happens when these decisions include recommendations for competing products? The Ethics Guide given later in the chapter considers these questions.

For example, suppose a cluster analysis finds two very different customer groups: One group has an average age of 33, owns four Android phones and three iPads, has an expensive home entertainment system, drives a Lexus SUV, and tends to buy expensive children's play equipment. The second group has an average age of 64, owns Arizona vacation property, plays golf, and buys expensive wines. Suppose the analysis also finds that both groups buy designer children's clothing.

These findings are obtained solely by data analysis. There is no prior model about the patterns and relationships that exist. It is up to the analyst to form hypotheses, after the fact, to explain why two such different groups are both buying designer children's clothes.

Supervised Data Mining

With **supervised data mining**, data miners develop a model *prior to the analysis* and apply statistical techniques to data to estimate parameters of the model. For example, suppose marketing experts in a communications company believe that cell phone usage on weekends is determined by the age of the customer and the number of months the customer has had the cell phone account. A data mining analyst would then run an analysis that estimates the effect of customer and account age.

One such analysis, which measures the effect of a set of variables on another variable, is called a **regression analysis**. A sample result for the cell phone example is:

$$\text{CellphoneWeekendMinutes} = 12 + (17.5 \times \text{Customer Age}) + (23.7 \times \text{NumberMonthsOfAccount})$$

Using this equation, analysts can predict the number of minutes of weekend cell phone use by summing 12, plus 17.5 times the customer's age, plus 23.7 times the number of months of the account.

As you will learn in your statistics classes, considerable skill is required to interpret the quality of such a model. The regression tool will create an equation, such as the one shown. Whether that equation is a good predictor of future cell phone usage depends on statistical factors, such as t values, confidence intervals, and related statistical techniques.

Neural networks are another popular supervised data mining application used to predict values and make classifications such as "good prospect" or "poor prospect" customers. The term *neural networks* is deceiving because it connotes a biological process similar to that in animal brains. In fact, although the original *idea* of neural nets may have come from the anatomy and physiology of neurons, a neural network is nothing more than a complicated set of possibly nonlinear equations. Explaining the techniques used for neural networks is beyond the scope of this text. If you want to learn more, search *http://kdnuggets.com* for the term *neural network*.

In the next sections, we will describe and illustrate two typical data mining tools—market-basket analysis and decision trees—and show applications of those techniques. From this discussion, you can gain a sense of the nature of data mining. These examples should give you, a future manager, a sense of the possibilities of data mining techniques. You will need additional coursework in statistics, data management, marketing, and finance, however, before you will be able to perform such analyses yourself.

Market-Basket Analysis

Suppose you run a dive shop, and one day you realize that one of your salespeople is much better at up-selling to your customers. Any of your sales associates can fill a customer's order, but this one salesperson is especially good at selling customers items *in addition* to those for which they ask. One day, you ask him how he does it.

"It's simple," he says. "I just ask myself what is the next product they would want to buy. If someone buys a dive computer, I don't try to sell her fins. If she's buying a dive computer, she's already a diver and she already has fins. But these dive computer displays are hard to read. A better mask makes it easier to read the display and get the full benefit from the dive computer."

A **market-basket analysis** is an unsupervised data mining technique for determining sales patterns. A market-basket analysis shows the products that customers tend to buy together. In marketing transactions, the fact that customers who buy product X also buy product Y creates a **cross-selling** opportunity; that is, "If they're buying X, sell them Y" or "If they're buying Y, sell them X."

Figure 21 shows hypothetical sales data from 400 sales transactions at a dive shop. The number on the diagonal (shaded) in the first set of rows is the total number of times an item was sold. For example, the 270 on the diagonal cell for Masks means that 270 of the 400 transactions

	Mask	Tank	Fins	Weights	Dive Computer
Mask	270	10	250	10	90
Tank	10	200	40	130	30
Fins	250	40	280	20	20
Weights	10	130	20	130	10
Dive Computer	90	30	20	10	120
	Support				
Num Trans	400				
Mask	0.675	0.025	0.625	0.025	0.225
Tank	0.025	0.5	0.1	0.325	0.075
Fins	0.625	0.1	0.7	0.05	0.05
Weights	0.025	0.325	0.05	0.325	0.025
Dive Computer	0.225	0.075	0.05	0.025	0.3
	Confidence				
Mask	1	0.05	0.892857143	0.076923077	0.75
Tank	0.037037037	1	0.142857143	1	0.25
Fins	0.925925926	0.2	1	0.153846154	0.166666667
Weights	0.037037037	0.65	0.071428571	1	0.083333333
Dive Computer	0.333333333	0.15	0.071428571	0.076923077	1
	Lift (Improvement)				
Mask		0.074074074	1.322751323	0.113960114	1.111111111
Tank	0.074074074		0.285714286	2	0.5
Fins	1.322751323	0.285714286		0.21978022	0.238095238
Weights	0.113960114	2	0.21978022		0.256410256
Dive Computer	1.111111111	0.5	0.238095238	0.256410256	

FIGURE 21
Market-Basket Analysis at a Dive Shop
Source: Windows 10, Microsoft Corporation.[2]

included masks. The 120 in the diagonal cell for Dive Computer means that 120 of the 400 transactions included dive computers.

We can use the number of times an item sold to estimate the probability that a customer will purchase an item. Because 270 of the 400 transactions were masks, we can estimate the probability that a customer will buy a mask to be 270/400, or .675. The probabilty of selling a dive computer is .3.

In market-basket terminology, **support** is the probability that two items will be purchased together. To estimate that probability, we examine sales transactions and count the number of times that two items occurred in the same transaction. For the data in Figure 21, fins and masks appeared together 250 times, and thus the support for fins and a mask is 250/400, or .625. Similarly, the support for fins and weights is 20/400, or .05.

These data are interesting by themselves, but we can refine the analysis by taking another step and considering additional probabilities. For example, what proportion of the customers who bought a mask also bought fins? Masks were purchased 270 times, and of those individuals who bought masks, 250 also bought fins. Thus, given that a customer bought a mask, we can estimate the probability that he or she will buy fins to be 250/270, or .926. In market-basket terminology, such a conditional probability estimate is called the **confidence**.

Reflect on the meaning of this confidence value. The likelihood of someone walking in the door and buying fins is 250/400, or .625. But the likelihood of someone buying fins, given that he or she bought a mask, is .926. Thus, if someone buys a mask, the likelihood that he or she will also buy fins increases substantially, from .625 to .926. Thus, all sales personnel should be trained to try to sell fins to anyone buying a mask.

Now consider dive computers and fins. Of the 400 transactions, fins were sold 280 times, so the probability that someone walks into the store and buys fins is .7. But of the 120 purchases of dive computers, only 20 appeared with fins. So the likelihood of someone buying fins, given he or she bought a dive computer, is 20/120, or .1666. Thus, when someone buys a dive computer, the likelihood that he or she will also buy fins falls from .625 to .1666.

The ratio of confidence to the base probability of buying an item is called **lift**. Lift shows how much the base probability increases or decreases when other products are purchased. The lift of fins and a mask is the confidence of fins given a mask, divided by the base probability of fins. In Figure 21, the lift of fins and a mask is .926/.7, or 1.32. Thus, the likelihood that people buy fins when they buy a mask increases by 32 percent. Surprisingly, it turns out that the lift of fins and a mask is the same as the lift of a mask and fins. Both are 1.32.

We need to be careful here, though, because this analysis shows only shopping carts with two items. We cannot say from this data what the likelihood is that customers, given that they bought a mask, will buy both weights and fins. To assess that probability, we need to analyze shopping carts with three items. This statement illustrates, once again, that we need to know what problem we're solving before we start to build the information system to mine the data. The problem definition will help us decide if we need to analyze three-item, four-item, or some other sized shopping cart.

Many organizations are benefiting from market-basket analysis today. You can expect that this technique will become a standard CRM analysis during your career.

Decision Trees

A **decision tree** is a hierarchical arrangement of criteria that predict a classification or a value. Here we will consider decision trees that predict classifications. Decision tree analyses are an unsupervised data mining technique: The analyst sets up the computer program and provides the data to analyze, and the decision tree program produces the tree.

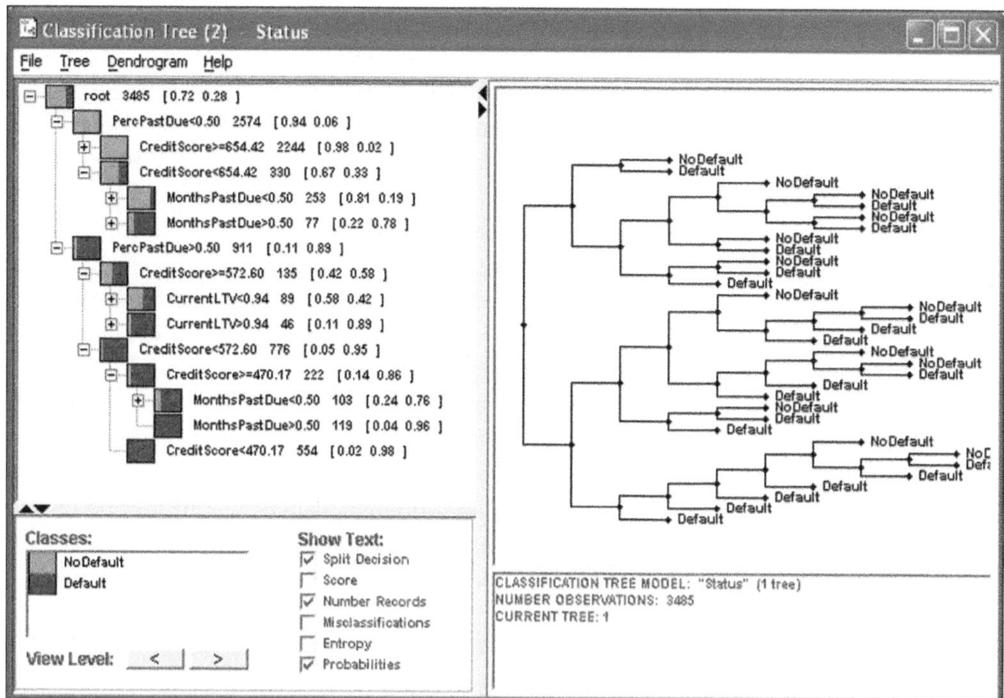

FIGURE 22
Credit Score Decision Tree
Source: Used with permission of TIBCO Software Inc. Copyright © 1999-2005 TIBCO Software Inc. All rights reserved.

A common business application of decision trees is to classify loans by likelihood of default. Organizations analyze data from past loans to produce a decision tree that can be converted to loan-decision rules. A financial institution could use such a tree to assess the default risk on a new loan. Sometimes, too, financial institutions sell a group of loans (called a *loan portfolio*) to one another. An institution considering the purchase of a loan portfolio can use the results of a decision tree program to evaluate the risk of a given portfolio.

Figure 22 shows an example provided by Insightful Corporation, a vendor of BI tools. This example was generated using its Insightful Miner product. This tool examined data from 3,485 loans. Of those loans, 72 percent had no default and 28 percent did default. To perform the analysis, the decision tree tool examined six different loan characteristics.

In this example, the decision tree program determined that the percentage of the loan that is past due (*PercPastDue*) is the best first criterion. Reading Figure 22, you can see that of the 2,574 loans with a *PercPastDue* value of 0.5 or less (amount past due is less than half the loan amount), 94 percent were not in default. Reading down several lines in this tree, 911 loans had a value of *PercPastDue* greater than 0.5; of those loans, 89 percent were in default.

These two major categories are then further subdivided into three classifications: *CreditScore* is a creditworthiness score obtained from a credit agency; *MonthsPastDue* is the number of months since a payment; and *CurrentLTV* is the current ratio of outstanding balance of the loan to the value of the loan's collateral.

With a decision tree like this, the financial institution can develop decision rules for accepting or rejecting the offer to purchase loans from another financial institution. For example:

- If percent past due is less than 50 percent, then accept the loan.
- If percent past due is greater than 50 percent *and*
- If *CreditScore* is greater than 572.6 *and*
- If *CurrentLTV* is less than .94, then accept the loan.
- Otherwise, reject the loan.

Of course, the financial institution will need to combine this risk data with an economic analysis of the value of each loan to determine which loans to take.

Decision trees are easy to understand and, even better, easy to implement using decision rules. They also can work with many types of variables, and they deal well with partial data. Organizations can use decision trees by themselves or combine them with other techniques. In some cases, organizations use decision trees to select variables that are then used by other types of data mining tools. For example, decision trees can be used to identify good predictor variables for neural networks.

Q6 How Do Organizations Use Big Data Applications?

Big Data (also spelled BigData) is a term used to describe data collections that are characterized by huge *volume*, rapid *velocity*, and great *variety*. In general, the following statements are true of Big Data:

- Big Data data sets are at least a petabyte in size, and usually larger.
- Big Data is generated rapidly.
- Big Data has structured data, free-form text, log files, possibly graphics, audio, and video.

MapReduce

Because Big Data is huge, fast, and varied, it cannot be processed using traditional techniques. **MapReduce** is a technique for harnessing the power of thousands of computers working in parallel. The basic idea is that the Big Data collection is broken into pieces, and hundreds or thousands of independent processors search these pieces for something of interest. That process is referred to as the *Map* phase. In Figure 23, for example, a data set having the logs of Google searches is broken into pieces, and each independent processor is instructed to search for and count search keywords. Figure 23, of course, shows just a small portion of the data; here you can see a portion of the keywords that begin with *H*.

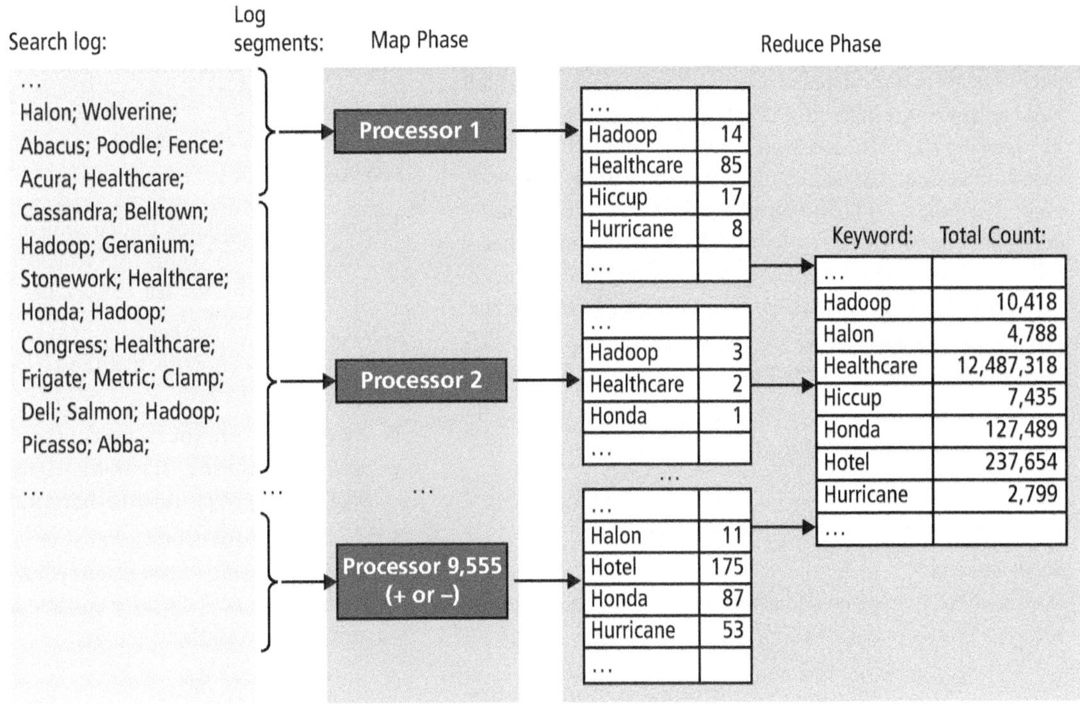

FIGURE 23
MapReduce Processing Summary

SO WHAT? BI FOR SECURITIES TRADING?

Since the 1970s there have been rumors of large computers buried in nondescript offices near Wall Street, cranking out analyses for smart stock trading. Do they work? Who knows? If you found a correlation between, say, a decrease in the dollar-to-euro exchange rate that influenced the price of 3M stock, would you publish it? No, you'd trade on it and hope that no one else noticed that correlation. Or if your hedge fund developed a model that failed miserably, would you publish that failure? No. So, due to a lack of data, no controlled study of the success and failure of model-based trading has been done (nor is likely to be done).

Still, it is known that traders such as Alexander Migdal, a former Soviet physicist, made millions of dollars in a high-frequency trading firm[10] that he started. The firm and others like it earn small gains on hundreds of thousands of automated transactions.[11] Unfortunately, such high-frequency trading places severe stresses on the market and was responsible for the near melt-downs in 2007 and 2008.[12] Still such trading continues, if with a bit more control.

Critics say there is far too much noise in the market for any reliable-over-time predictive analysis to work. Consider, for example, the factors that influence the price of 3M stock: global exchange rates, oil prices, the overall stock market, recent patent filings, patents that are about to expire, employee and customer tweets, product failures—the list goes on and on. No model can account for such complexity.

Or can it?

Today a new class of quantitative applications is using Big Data and business intelligence to analyze immense amounts of data over a broad spectrum of sources. These applications both build and evaluate investment strategies. Two Sigma (*www.twosigma.com*) is in the forefront of this new style of quantitative analysis. According to the firm, it analyzes vast amounts of data, including corporate financial statements, developing news, Twitter activity, weather reports, and other data sources. From those analyses, it develops and tests investment strategies.[13] They could, in theory, model all of the factors that influence stocks like 3M.

Two Sigma uses a five-step process:

1. Acquire data
2. Create models
3. Evaluate models
4. Analyze risks
5. Place trades[14]

Does it work? Two Sigma and other firms claim it does. We will see.

Source: Freshidea/Fotolia

We can, however, make one important observation: It has never been easy, some would say even possible, for regular investors to *time the market* by buying just before an upturn or selling just before a downturn. But today, if you try that, you're not only trying to beat the market, you're competing with Two Sigma, with its hundreds of PhDs and massive computing power, and with a slew of similar companies. For most of us, John Bogle, founder of Vanguard, had it right. Buy an index fund, take your 6 percent, and be happy. And, over 30 years, that 6 percent will net a near sixfold increase.

Questions

1. Consider two publicly traded companies: Apple and Alaska Airlines. List 10 factors that you believe influence the price of those two stocks. The factors may be different.
2. Pick one of the two companies in your answer to question 1. Briefly explain how each of the 10 factors influences the price of the stock.
3. For the factors in your answer to question 2, list sources of data for measuring each of the 10 factors. What role would Big Data play in processing that data?
4. If you had the data in your answer to question 3, how would you go about determining how much each of the factors influences the price of the stock? What kinds of BI techniques would you employ?

5. Assuming you had used BI to answer question 4 and now had a model of how your 10 factors influence the price of that stock, how would you determine how good your model is? How would you know that the 10 factors you choose were the right 10 factors?
6. Suppose it is possible to obtain the data needed and to build a model to predict with 51 percent accuracy the price of a stock. Is that a usable model? What do you need to make such a model effective?
7. Suppose you've misjudged your model and it predicts with only 49 percent accuracy. What is likely to happen?
8. Summarize what you have learned from this exercise.

As the processors finish, their results are combined in what is referred to as the *Reduce* phase. The result is a list of all the terms searched for on a given day and the count of each. The process is considerably more complex than described here, but this is the gist of the idea.

By the way, you can visit Google Trends to see an application of MapReduce. There you can obtain a trend line of the number of searches for a particular term or terms. Figure 24 compares the search trends for the terms *Web 2.0* and *Hadoop*. Go to *www.google.com/trends* and enter the terms *Big Data, BigData*, and *data analytics* to see why learning about them is a good use of your time.

Hadoop

Hadoop is an open source program supported by the Apache Foundation[15] that implements MapReduce on potentially thousands of computers. Hadoop could drive the process of finding and counting the Google search terms, but Google uses its own proprietary version of MapReduce to do so instead.

Hadoop began as part of Cassandra, but the Apache Foundation split it off to become its own product. Hadoop is written in Java and originally ran on Linux. Some companies implement Hadoop on server farms they manage themselves, and others run Hadoop in the cloud. Amazon.com supports Hadoop as part of its EC3 cloud offering. Microsoft offers Hadoop on its Azure platform as a service named HDInsight. Hadoop includes a query language titled **Pig**.

At present, deep technical skills are needed to run and use Hadoop. Judging by the development of other technologies over the years, it is likely that higher-level, easier-to-use query products will be implemented on top of Hadoop. For now, understand that experts are required to use it; you may be involved, however, in planning a Big Data study or in interpreting results.

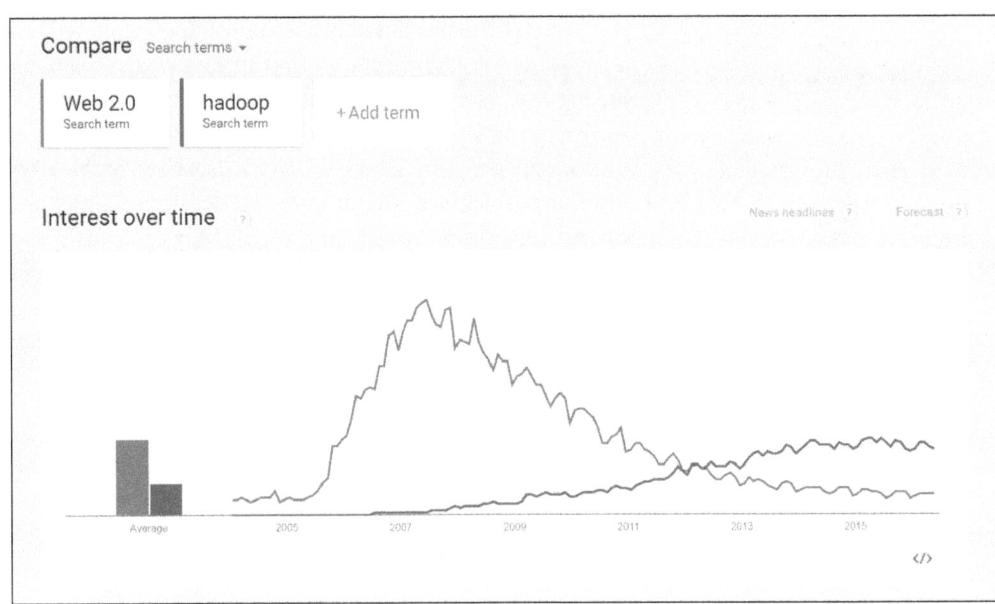

FIGURE 24
Google Trends on the Terms *Web 2.0* and *Hadoop*
Source: Google and the Google logo are registered trademarks of Google Inc., Used with permission.

Big Data analysis can involve both reporting and data mining techniques. The chief difference is, however, that Big Data has volume, velocity, and variation characteristics that far exceed those of traditional reporting and data mining.

Q7 What Is the Role of Knowledge Management Systems?

Nothing is more frustrating for a manager to contemplate than the situation in which one employee struggles with a problem that another employee knows how to solve easily. Or to learn of a customer who returns a large order because the customer could not perform a basic operation with the product that many employees (and other customers) can readily perform. Even worse, someone in the customer's organization may know how to use the product, but the people who bought it didn't know that.

Knowledge management (KM) is the process of creating value from intellectual capital and sharing that knowledge with employees, managers, suppliers, customers, and others who need that capital. The goal of knowledge management is to prevent the kinds of problems just described.

Knowledge management was done before social media, and we discuss two such KM systems. However, notice in the first sentence of this paragraph that the scope of KM (employees, managers, suppliers, customer, and others...) is the same scope as that of the use of SM in hyper-social organizations. In fact, modern knowledge management ascribes to hyper-social organization theory, as we will discuss.

Before we turn to those specific technologies, however, consider the overall goals and benefits of KM. KM benefits organizations in two fundamental ways:

- Improve process quality
- Increase team strength

As you know, process quality is measured by effectiveness and efficiency, and knowledge management can improve both. KM enables employees to share knowledge with each other and with customers and other partners. By doing so, it enables the employees in the organization to better achieve the organization's strategy. At the same time, sharing knowledge enables employees to solve problems more quickly and to otherwise accomplish work with less time and other resources, hence improving process efficiency.[16]

Successful teams not only accomplish their assigned tasks, they also grow in capability, both as a team and as individuals. By sharing knowledge, team members learn from one another, avoid making repetitive mistakes, and grow as business professionals.

For example, consider the help desk at any organization, say, one that provides support for electronic components like iPhones. When a user has a problem with an iPhone, he or she might contact Apple support for help. The customer service department has, collectively, seen just about any problem that can ever occur with an iPhone. The organization, as a whole, knows how to solve the user's problem. However, that is no guarantee that a particular support representative knows how to solve that problem. The goal of KM is to enable employees to be able to use knowledge possessed collectively by people in the organization. By doing so, both process quality and team capability improve.

What Are Expert Systems?

The earliest KM systems, called expert systems, attempted to directly capture employee expertise. They existed long before social media and in fact were in use long before the Internet.

Expert systems are rule-based systems that encode human knowledge in the form of **If/Then rules**. Such rules are statements that specify if a particular condition exists, then to take some action.

```
Other rules here...

IF CardiacRiskFactor = 'Null' THEN Set CardiacRiskFactor = 0
IF PatientSex = 'Male' THEN Add 3 to CardiacRiskFactor
IF PatientAge >55 THEN Add 2 to CardiacRiskFactor
IF FamilyHeartHistory = 'True' THEN Add 5 to CardiacRiskFactor
IF CholesterolScore = 'Problematic' THEN Add 4 to CardiacRiskFactor
IF BloodPressure = 'Problematic' THEN Add 3 to CardiacRiskFactor
IF CardiacRiskFactor >15 THEN Set EchoCardiagramTest = 'Schedule'
...
Other rules here...
```

FIGURE 25
Example of If/Then Rules

Figure 25 shows an example of a few rules that could be part of a medical expert system for diagnosing heart disease. In this set of rules, the system examines various factors for heart disease and computes a *CardiacRiskFactor.* Depending on the value of that risk factor, other variables are given values.

The set of rules shown here may need to be processed many times because it is possible that *CardiacRiskFactor* is used on the If side of a rule occurring before these rules. Unlike this example, an operational expert system may consist of hundreds, if not thousands, of rules.

The programs that process a set of rules are called **expert systems shells**. Typically, the shell processes rules until no value changes. At that point, the values of all the variables are reported as results.

To create the system of rules, the expert system development team interviews human experts in the domain of interest. The rules in Figure 25 would have been obtained by interviewing cardiologists who are known to be particularly adept at diagnosing cardiac disease. Such a system encodes the knowledge of those highly skilled experts and makes it available to less-skilled or less-knowledgeable professionals.

Many expert systems were created in the late 1980s and early 1990s, but only a few have enjoyed success. They suffer from three major disadvantages. First, they are difficult and expensive to develop. They require many labor hours from both experts in the domain under study and designers of expert systems. This expense is compounded by the high opportunity cost of tying up domain experts. Such experts are normally some of the most sought-after employees in an organization.

Second, expert systems are difficult to maintain. Because of the nature of rule-based systems, the introduction of a new rule in the middle of hundreds of others can have unexpected consequences. A small change can cause very different outcomes. Unfortunately, such side effects cannot be predicted or eliminated. They are the nature of complex rule-based systems.

Finally, expert systems were unable to live up to the high expectations set by their name. Initially, proponents of expert systems hoped to be able to duplicate the performance of highly trained experts, like doctors. It turned out, however, that no expert system has the same diagnostic ability as knowledgeable, skilled, and experienced doctors. Even when expert systems were developed that came close in ability, changes in medical technology required constant changing of the expert system, and the problems caused by unexpected consequences made such changes very expensive.

The few expert systems that have been successful have addressed more restricted problems than duplicating a doctor's diagnostic ability. They address problems such as checking for harmful prescription drug interactions and configuring products to meet customer specifications. These systems require many fewer rules and are therefore more manageable to maintain.

However, unless expert systems technology gets a boost from massively parallel computing (think MapReduce and Hadoop), their problems will cause them to fade from use.

What Are Content Management Systems?

Another form of knowledge management concerns knowledge that is encoded in documents. **Content management systems (CMS)** are information systems that support the management and delivery of documents including reports, Web pages, and other expressions of employee knowledge.

Typical users of content management systems are companies that sell complicated products and want to share their knowledge of those products with employees and customers. Someone at Toyota, for example, knows how to change the timing belt on the four-cylinder 2017 Toyota Camry. Toyota wants to share that knowledge with car owners, mechanics, and Toyota employees.

What Are the Challenges of Content Management?

Content management systems face serious challenges. First, most content databases are huge; some have thousands of individual documents, pages, and graphics. Second, CMS content is dynamic. Imagine the frequency of Web page changes at Apple or Google or Amazon.com that must occur each day!

Another complication for content management systems is that documents do not exist in isolation from each other. Documents refer to one another, and when one changes, others must change as well. To manage these connections, content management systems must maintain linkages among documents so that content dependencies are known and used to maintain document consistency.

A fourth complication is that document contents are perishable. Documents become obsolete and need to be altered, removed, or replaced. Consider, for example, what happens when a new product is announced. Figure 26 shows the main page for Microsoft.com less than 2 hours after its announcement of Surface. We can only wonder how many other pages on Microsoft.com needed to be changed within those 2 hours.

Finally, content is provided in many languages. 3M has tens of thousands of products, some of which are harmful when used improperly. 3M must publish product safety data for all such products in all the languages shown. Every document, in whatever language it was authored, must be translated into all languages before it can be published on 3M's site. And when one of them changes, all of the translated versions must change as well.

FIGURE 26
Microsoft.com Main Page Less Than 2 Hours After Surface Announcement
Source: Windows 10, Microsoft Corporation.

What Are Content Management Application Alternatives?

Three common alternatives for content management applications are:

- In-house custom
- Off-the-shelf
- Public search engine

In the past, organizations developed their own *in-house content management applications*. A customer support department, for example, might develop in-house database applications to track customer problems and their resolution. Operations might develop an in-house system to track machine maintenance procedures. Like all custom applications, however, custom content management applications are expensive to develop and maintain. Unless the domain of the content management is crucial to the organization's strategy and no off-the-shelf solution is available, most organizations today choose not to support a custom CMS application.

Because of the expense of custom applications, many organizations today use *off-the-shelf* software. Horizontal market products like Microsoft SharePoint provide generalized facilities to manage documents and other content types. Some organizations choose vertical market off-the-shelf applications. An accounting firm, for example, may license a vertical market application to manage document flow for the processing of tax returns or the management of audit documents.

Such off-the-shelf products have considerably more functionality than most in-house systems, and they are far less expensive to maintain. Keep in mind, however, that organizations need to develop data structures and procedures for managing their content; they also need to train users.

Some organizations just rely on *Internet search engines*, such as Google or Bing, to manage their content. Because these engines search through all public sites of all organizations, they are usually the fastest and easiest way to find public documents, even within the organization. It may be easier, for example, for a General Motors employee to find a General Motors document using Google than using an in-house search engine.

This is content management on the cheap. Just put documents on a public server and let Google or Bing do the rest! However, documents that reside behind a corporate firewall are not publicly accessible and will not be reachable by Google or other search engines. Organizations must index their own proprietary documents and provide their own search capability for them.

How Do Hyper-Social Organizations Manage Knowledge?

In recent years, social media has changed the orientation of knowledge management. In the past, the focus was on structured systems such as expert systems and content management systems. These KM techniques relied on planned and prestructured content management and delivery methods. Social media fosters emergence. In the KM context, employees and others express their knowledge in a variety of modes and media, and the mechanisms for managing and delivering that knowledge emerge from usage.

Hyper-social knowledge management is the application of social media and related applications for the management and delivery of organizational knowledge resources. Progressive organizations encourage their employees to Tweet, post on Facebook or other social media sites, write blogs, and post videos on YouTube and any of the other sites. Of course, such organizations need to develop and publish an employee social media policy as well.

Hyper-organization theory provides a framework for understanding this new direction in KM. In this frame, the focus moves from the knowledge and content per se to the fostering of authentic relationships among the creators and the users of that knowledge.

Blogs provide an obvious example. An employee in customer support who writes a daily blog on current, common customer problems is expressing authentic opinions on the company's products, positive and possibly negative. If perceived as authentic, customers will comment upon blog entries and, in the process, teach others how they solved those problems themselves.

The open airing of product use issues may make traditional marketing personnel uncomfortable, but this KM technique does insert the company in the middle of customer conversations about possible product problems, and, while it does lose control, the organization is at least a party to those conversations.

Hyper-Social KM Alternative Media

Figure 27 lists common hyper-social KM alternative media, whether each medium is used for public, private, or either, and the best group type. Except for rich directories, you know what each of these is already, and we need not discuss them further.

A **rich directory** is an employee directory that includes not only the standard name, email, phone, and address but also organizational structure and expertise. With a rich directory, it is possible to determine where in the organization someone works, who is the first common manager between two people, and what past projects and expertise an individual has. For international organizations, such directories also include languages spoken. Microsoft's product Active Directory is the most popular rich directory.

Rich directories are particularly useful in large organizations where people with particular expertise are unknown. For example, who at 3M knows which 3M product is the best to use to glue teak wood to fiberglass? Probably dozens, but who are they and who is the closest to a factory in Brazil? If no one is near Brazil, is there anyone who speaks Portuguese?

Resistance to Knowledge Sharing

Two human factors inhibit knowledge sharing in organizations. The first is that employees can be reluctant to exhibit their ignorance. Out of fear of appearing incompetent, employees may not submit entries to blogs or discussion groups. Such reluctance can sometimes be reduced by the attitude and posture of managers. One strategy for employees in this situation is to provide private media that can be accessed only by a smaller group of people who have an interest in a specific problem. Members of that smaller group can then discuss the issue in a less-inhibiting forum.

The other inhibiting human factor is employee competition. "Look," says the top salesperson. "I earn a substantial bonus from being the top salesperson. Why would I want to share my sales techniques with others? I'd just be strengthening my competition." This understandable perspective may not be changeable. A hyper-social KM application may be ill-suited to a competitive group. Or the company may be able to restructure rewards and incentives to foster sharing of ideas among employees (e.g., giving a bonus to the group that develops the best idea).

Media	Public or Private	Best for:
Blogs	Either	Defender of belief
Discussion groups (including FAQ)	Either	Problem solving
Wikis	Either	Either
Surveys	Either	Problem solving
Rich directories, (e.g., Active Directory)	Private	Problem solving
Standard SM (Facebook, Twitter, etc.)	Public	Defender of belief
YouTube	Public	Either

FIGURE 27
Hyper-Social KM Media

If these two factors are limiting knowledge sharing, strong management endorsement can be effective, especially if that endorsement is followed by strong positive feedback. Concerning employee resistance, "Nothing wrong with praise or cash ... especially cash."

Q8 What Are the Alternatives for Publishing BI?

The previous discussions have illustrated the power and utility of reporting, data mining, and knowledge management BI applications. But, for BI to be actionable, it must be published to the right user at the right time. In this question, we will discuss the primary publishing alternatives and the functionality of BI servers, a special type of Web server.

Characteristics of BI Publishing Alternatives

Figure 28 lists four server alternatives for BI publishing. **Static reports** are BI documents that are fixed at the time of creation and do not change. A printed sales analysis is an example of a static report. In the BI context, most static reports are published as PDF documents.

Dynamic reports are BI documents that are updated at the time they are requested. A sales report that is current at the time the user accessed it on a Web server is a dynamic report. In almost all cases, publishing a dynamic report requires the BI application to access a database or other data source at the time the report is delivered to the user.

Pull options for each of the servers in Figure 28 are the same. The user goes to the site, clicks a link (or opens an email), and obtains the report. Because they're the same for all four server types, they are not shown in Figure 28.

Push options vary by server type. For email or collaboration tools, push is manual; someone, say, a manager, an expert, or an administrator, creates an email with the report as an attachment (or URL to the collaboration tool) and sends it to the users known to be interested in that report. For Web servers and SharePoint, users can create alerts and RSS feeds to have the server push content to them when the content is created or changed, with the expiration of a given amount of time, or at particular intervals. SharePoint workflows can also push content.

A BI server extends alert/RSS functionality to support user **subscriptions**, which are user requests for particular BI results on a particular schedule or in response to particular events. For example, a user can subscribe to a daily sales report, requesting that it be delivered each morning. Or the user might request that RFM analyses be delivered whenever a new result is posted on the server, or a sales manager might subscribe to receive a sales report whenever sales in his region exceed $1M during the week. We explain the two major functions of a BI server in the next section.

FIGURE 28
BI Publishing Alternatives

Server	Report Type	Push Options	Skill Level Needed
Email or collaboration tool	Static	Manual	Low
Web server	Static/Dynamic	Alert/RSS	Low for static High for dynamic
SharePoint	Static/Dynamic	Alert/RSS Workflow	Low for static High for dynamic
BI server	Dynamic	Alert/RSS Subscription	High

The skills needed to create a publishing application are either low or high. For static content, little skill is needed. The BI author creates the content, and the publisher (usually the same person) attaches it to an email or puts it on the Web or a SharePoint site, and that's it. Publishing dynamic BI is more difficult; it requires the publisher to set up database access when documents are consumed. In the case of a Web server, the publisher will need to develop or have a programmer write code for this purpose. In the case of SharePoint and BI servers, program code is not necessarily needed, but dynamic data connections need to be created, and this task is not for the technically faint of heart. You'll need knowledge beyond the scope of this class to develop dynamic BI solutions. You should be able to do this, however, if you take a few more IS courses or major in IS.

What Are the Two Functions of a BI Server?

A **BI server** is a Web server application that is purpose-built for the publishing of business intelligence. The Microsoft SQL Server Report manager (part of Microsoft SQL Server Reporting Services) is the most popular such product today, but there are other products as well.

BI servers provide two major functions: management and delivery. The management function maintains metadata about the authorized allocation of BI results to users. The BI server tracks what results are available, what users are authorized to view those results, and the schedule upon which the results are provided to the authorized users. It adjusts allocations as available results change and users come and go.

As shown in Figure 29, all management data needed by any of the BI servers is stored in metadata. The amount and complexity of such data depends, of course, on the functionality of the BI server.

BI servers use metadata to determine what results to send to which users and, possibly, on which schedule. Today, the expectation is that BI results can be delivered to "any" device. In practice, *any* is interpreted to mean computers, smartphones, tablets, applications such as Microsoft Office, and SOA Web services.

FIGURE 29
Elements of a BI System

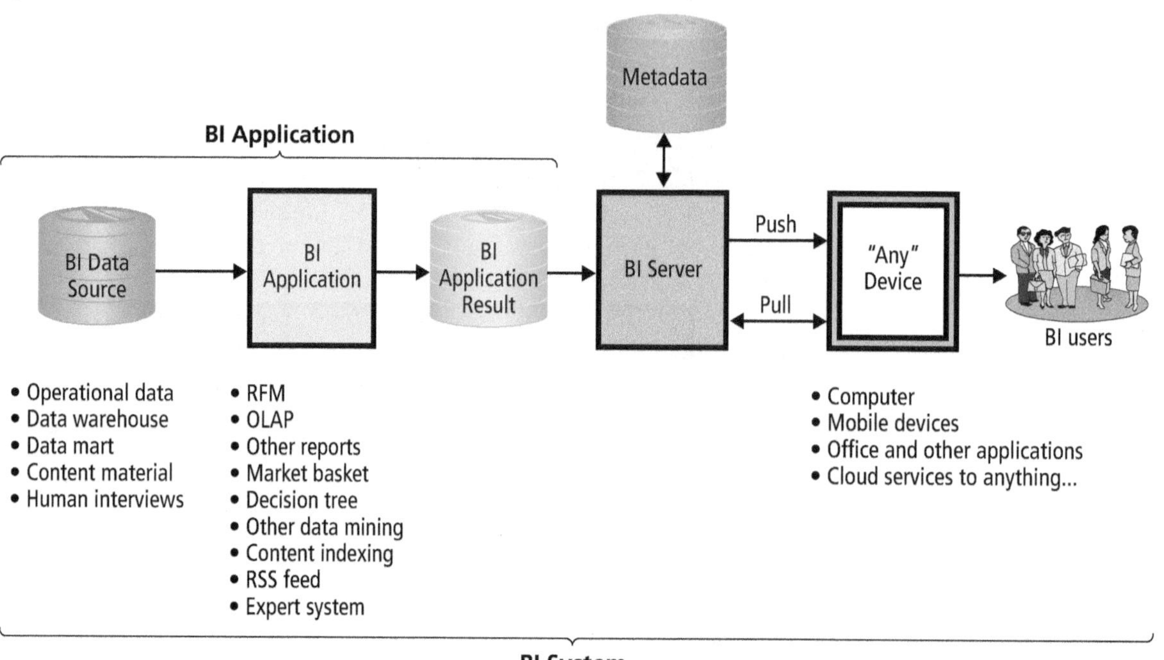

Q9 2027? 

BI systems truly add value. Not every system is a success, but simple ones like RFM and OLAP often are, and even complicated and expensive data mining applications can generate tremendous return if they are applied to appropriate problems and are well designed and implemented.

For example, suppose you never buy expensive jewelry on your credit card. If you travel to South America and attempt to buy a $5,000 diamond bracelet using that credit card, watch what happens! Especially if you make the attempt on a credit card other than the one for which you paid for the travel. A data mining application integrated into the credit card agency's purchase-approval process will detect the unusual pattern, on the spot, and require you to personally verify the purchase on the telephone or in some other way before it will accept the charge. Such applications are exceedingly accurate because they are well designed and implemented by some of the world's best data miners.

How will this change by 2027? We know that data storage is free, that CPU processors are becoming nearly so, that the world is generating and storing exponentially more information about customers, and that data mining techniques are only going to get better. It is likely that by 2027 some companies will know more about your purchasing psyche than you, your mother, or your analyst.

In fact, it may be important to ask the question: How unsupervised do we want unsupervised data mining to be? Today, a data miner extracts a data set and inputs it into an unsupervised data mining application for analysis. The application finds patterns, trends, and other business intelligence and reports the results to the human analyst. The BI analyst examines the results and possibly iterates by finding more data and running more analyses.

But what happens when BI applications become sophisticated enough to replace the BI analyst? What happens when the unsupervised data mining application has features and functions to find its own data sets and to evaluate those data sets based on the results of a prior BI analysis? And then decides which BI analysis to perform next?

Machines work faster than humans, and they work 24/7. At some point, will machines know so much about us that we are incapable of understanding the results? What happens when, because of complexity, such BI machines can only communicate with other BI machines?

Ray Kurzweil developed a concept he calls **the Singularity**, which is the point at which computer systems become sophisticated enough that they can adapt and create their own software and hence adapt their behavior without human assistance. Apply this idea to unsupervised data mining.[17] What happens when machines can direct their own data mining activities? There will be an accelerating positive feedback loop among the BI machines. Then what will they know about us? Is it important that at that date we will lack the capacity to know what the machines will know?

This line of thinking exposes a future flaw that runs through this text. We've defined information as something possessed only by humans. If it's on a piece of paper or on a screen, it's data. If it's in the mind of a human, it is (or can be) information. When we're talking about simple reporting operations such as grouping and filtering, and so on, that's legitimate. But, in the day when unsupervised data mining truly is unsupervised, machines will possess and create information for themselves.

Do you know what your data mining application is doing tonight?

SECURITY GUIDE

SEMANTIC SECURITY

Security is a very difficult problem—and risks grow larger every year. Not only do we have cheaper, faster computers (remember Moore's Law), we also have more data, more systems for reporting and querying that data, and easier, faster, and broader communication. We have organizational data in the cloud that is not physically under our control. All of these combine to increase the chances that private or proprietary information is inappropriately divulged.

Access security is hard enough: How do we know that the person (or program) who signs on as Megan Cho really is Megan Cho? We use passwords, but files of passwords can be stolen. Setting that issue aside, we need to know that Megan Cho's permissions are set appropriately. Suppose Megan works in the HR department, so she has access to personal and private data of other employees. We need to design the reporting system so that Megan can access all of the data she needs to do her job, and no more.

Also, the delivery system must be secure. A BI server is an obvious and juicy target for any would-be intruder. Someone can break in and change access permissions. Or a hacker could pose as someone else to obtain reports. Application servers help the authorized user, resulting in faster access to more information. But without proper security reporting, servers also ease the intrusion task for unauthorized users.

All of these issues relate to access security. Another dimension to security is equally serious and far more problematic: **semantic security**. Semantic security concerns the unintended release of protected information through the release of a combination of reports or documents that are independently not protected. The term **data triangulation** is also used for this same phenomenon.

Take an example from class. Suppose I assign a group project, and I post a list of groups and the names of students assigned to each group. Later, after the assignments have

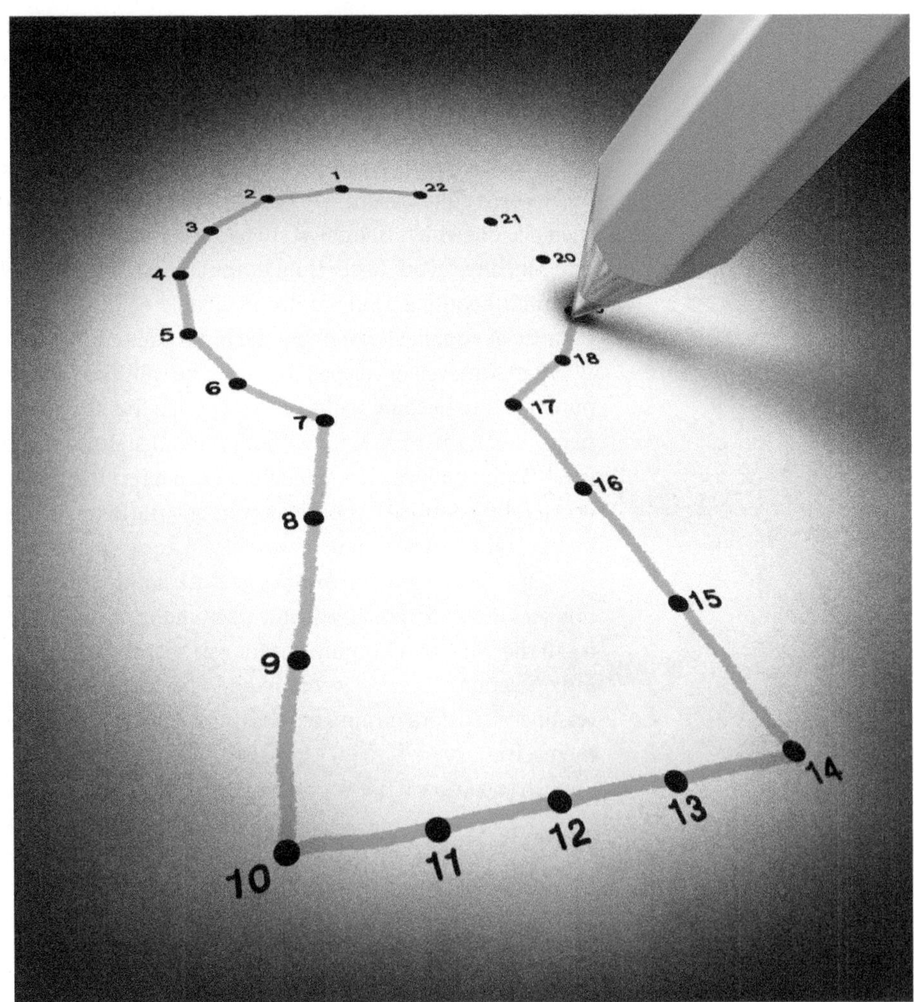

Source: Freshidea/Fotolia

been completed and graded, I post a list of grades on the Web site. Because of university privacy policy, I cannot post the grades by student name or identifier, so instead I post the grades for each group. If you want to get the grades for each student, all you have to do is combine the list from Lecture 5 with the list from Lecture 10. You might say that the release of grades in this example does no real harm—after all, it is a list of grades from one assignment.

But go back to Megan Cho in HR. Suppose Megan evaluates the employee compensation program. The COO believes salary offers have been inconsistent over time and that they vary too widely by department. Accordingly, the COO authorizes Megan to receive a report that lists *SalaryOfferAmount* and *OfferDate* and a second report that lists *Department* and *AverageSalary*.

Those reports are relevant to her task and seem innocuous enough. But Megan realizes that she could use the information they contain to determine individual salaries—information she does not have and is not authorized to receive. She proceeds as follows.

Like all employees, Megan has access to the employee directory on the Web portal. Using the directory, she can obtain a list of employees in each department, and using the facilities of her ever-so-helpful report-authoring system she combines that list with the department and average-salary report. Now she has a list of the names of employees in a group and the average salary for that group.

Megan's employer likes to welcome new employees to the company. Accordingly, each week the company publishes an article about new employees who have been hired. The article makes pleasant comments about each person and encourages employees to meet and greet them.

Megan, however, has other ideas. Because the report is published on SharePoint, she can obtain an electronic copy of it. It's an Acrobat report, and using Acrobat's handy Search feature, she soon has a list of employees and the week they were hired.

She now examines the report she received for her study, the one that has *SalaryOfferAmount* and the offer date, and she does some interpretation. During the week of July 21, three offers were extended: one for $35,000, one for $53,000, and one for $110,000. She also notices from the "New Employees" report that a director of marketing programs, a product test engineer, and a receptionist were hired that same week. It's unlikely that they paid the receptionist $110,000; that sounds more like the director of marketing programs. So, she now "knows" (infers) that person's salary.

Next, going back to the department report and using the employee directory, she sees that the marketing director is in the marketing programs department. There are just three people in that department, and their average salary is $105,000. Doing the arithmetic, she now knows that the average salary for the other two people is $102,500. If she can find the hire week for one of those other two people, she can find out both the second and third person's salaries.

You get the idea. Megan was given just two reports to do her job. Yet she combined the information in those reports with publicly available information and was able to deduce salaries, for at least some employees. These salaries are much more than she is supposed to know. This is a semantic security problem.

DISCUSSION QUESTIONS

1. In your own words, explain the difference between access security and semantic security.
2. Why do reporting systems increase the risk of semantic security problems?
3. What can an organization do to protect itself against accidental losses due to semantic security problems?
4. What legal responsibility does an organization have to protect against semantic security problems?
5. Suppose semantic security problems are inevitable. Do you see an opportunity for new products from insurance companies? If so, describe such an insurance product. If not, explain why.

CAREER GUIDE

Source: Lindsey Tsuya

Name: Lindsey Tsuya
Company: American Express Company
Job Title: Manager, Data and Analytics
Education: University of Utah

1 How did you get this type of job?

I was referred by a friend who was already working at American Express. Luckily, I have been referred for every position I have held since graduation. In addition, upon graduation I entered into a technology rotation program that enabled me to explore different areas of technology. This allowed me to determine the type of technology that best suited me. The program enabled me to understand what I was passionate about in technology. I strongly recommend that anyone who has a similar opportunity take it.

2 What attracted you to this field?

As a college student, I worked in the service industry. When I was selecting my degree, I knew I wanted two things. First, I wanted a degree that made money. Second, I wanted a job that did not involve direct provision of service to the public. By choosing information systems, I knew I would be doing more of a behind-the-scenes job.

3 What does a typical workday look like for you (duties, decisions, problems)?

I am responsible for the majority of the reporting needs for my department. We have multiple weekly reports that must be sent out. We have monthly and quarterly reports as well. I also handle the majority of ad hoc requests from the department. We are a global team located in Singapore, London, Sydney, New York, and Salt Lake City. These reports may be ad hoc data analyses or data mining that looks for certain things in the data.

4 What do you like most about your job?

I love my job because I am passionate about what I do. I love data. I love analyzing data and determining what story the data is telling me. Because I am in a financial services company, I have to look at many drivers to determine the story. What I like most about my job is that it is always different. No two ad hoc requests are the same. Every day is different, and I like that.

5 What skills would someone need to do well at your job?

Good analytical skills and the ability to analyze large amounts of data are essential. Critical thinking skills and the ability to think outside the box are also important. Soft skills that differentiate people are passion and a can-do attitude. Those two things coupled together will take anyone far in life.

6 Are education or certifications important in your field? Why?

I would say in any field, education and certifications assist with career development and credibility.

7 What advice would you give to someone who is considering working in your field?

No matter what field you choose, make sure it is something you are passionate about because if you are not passionate about it, work will feel like... work. If you are passionate about what you do, then work feels like play. You will spend so many hours of your life working, and you should not waste it doing something you don't love.

ACTIVE REVIEW

Use this Active Review to verify that you understand the ideas and concepts that answer the chapter's study questions.

Q1 How do organizations use business intelligence (BI) systems?

Define *business intelligence* and *BI system*. Explain the components in Figure 1. Give an example, other than one in this text, of one way that an organization could use business intelligence for each of the four collaborative tasks in Figure 2. Describe one use of BI in retailing, entertainment, and medicine.

Q2 What are the three primary activities in the BI process?

Name and describe the three primary activities in the BI process. Using Figure 3 as a guide, describe the major tasks for each activity. Summarize how the team at the parts distribution company used these activities to produce BI results. Explain the role of Figures 4 through 11.

Q3 How do organizations use data warehouses and data marts to acquire data?

Describe the need and functions of data warehouses and data marts. Name and describe the role of data warehouse components. List and explain the problems that can exist in data used for data mining and sophisticated reporting. Use the example of a supply chain to describe the differences between a data warehouse and data mart.

Q4 How do organizations use reporting applications?

Name and describe five basic reporting operations. Define *RFM analysis* and explain the actions that should be taken with customers who have the following scores: [5, 5, 5,], [1, 5, 5,], [5, 5, 3], and [5, 2, 5]. Explain OLAP and describe its unique characteristics. Explain the roles for measure and dimension in an OLAP cube. Illustrate an OLAP cube with a single measure and five dimensions, two dimensions on one axis and three on another. Show how drill down applies to your example.

Q5 How do organizations use data mining applications?

Define *data mining* and explain how its use typically differs from reporting applications. Define artificial intelligence and describe its potential benefits. Describe the difference between machine learning and data mining. Explain why data mining tools are difficult to use well. Describe the differences between unsupervised and supervised data mining. Use an example to illustrate cluster analysis and regression analysis. Define *neural networks* and explain why the term is a misnomer. Define *support, confidence,* and *lift* and describe these terms using the data in Figure 21. Describe a good application for market-basket analysis results. Describe the purpose of decision trees and explain how the data in Figure 22 is used to evaluate loans for possible purchase.

Q6 How do organizations use Big Data applications?

Name and explain the three *v's* of Big Data. Describe the general goal of MapReduce and explain, at a conceptual level, how it works and how it could generate the data for Figure 24. Explain the purpose of Hadoop and describe its origins. Describe the ways organizations can deploy Hadoop. Define *Pig.*

Q7 What is the role of knowledge management systems?

Define *knowledge management.* Explain five key benefits of KM. Briefly describe three types of KM systems. Define *expert systems, If/Then rules,* and *expert system shell.* Explain how expert system rules are created. Differentiate expert system If/Then rules from decision tree If/Then rules. Summarize the three major disadvantages of expert systems and assess their future. Define *content management system (CMS).* Describe five challenges organizations face for managing content. Name three CMS application alternatives and explain the use of each.

Explain how social media has changed the orientation of knowledge management. Define *hyper-social knowledge management.* Explain the hyper-social KM use of each medium in Figure 28. Explain the entries in the second and third columns of this figure. Define *rich directory* and explain three uses for it. Summarize possible employee resistance to hyper-social knowledge sharing and name two management techniques for reducing it.

Q8 What are the alternatives for publishing BI?

Name four alternative types of server used for publishing business intelligence. Explain the difference between static and dynamic reports; explain the term *subscription.* Describe why dynamic reports are difficult to create.

Q9 2027?

Summarize the function of the credit card approval application. Explain how you think that application uses data. Summarize the way that unsupervised data mining could spiral out of the control of humans. In your opinion, is this a problem? Why or why not? Describe how Kurzweil's singularity pertains to data mining applications. Explain the potential flaw in the use of the term *information* that runs throughout this text.

Using Your Knowledge with ARES

From this chapter, you know the three phases of BI analysis, and you have learned common techniques for acquiring, processing, and publishing business intelligence. This knowledge will enable you to imagine innovative uses for data that your employer generates and also to know some of the constraints of such use. At ARES, the knowledge of this chapter will help you understand possible uses for employer and exercise data to increase ad revenue, the critical driver for the success of ARES Systems.

KEY TERMS AND CONCEPTS

Artificial intelligence (AI)
BI analysis
BI application
BI server
Big Data
Business intelligence (BI)
Business intelligence (BI) systems
Cluster analysis
Confidence
Content management systems (CMS)
Cookie
Cross-selling
Data acquisition
Data mart
Data mining
Data triangulation
Data warehouse
Decision support systems
Decision tree
Dimension
Drill down
Dynamic reports
Expert systems
Expert systems shells
Granularity
Hadoop
Hyper-social knowledge management
If/Then rules
Knowledge management (KM)
Lift
Machine learning
MapReduce
Market-basket analysis
Measure
Neural networks
OLAP cube
Online analytical processing (OLAP)
Pig
Publish results
Pull publishing
Push publishing
Regression analysis
Reporting application
RFM analysis
Rich directory
Semantic security
Static reports
Subscriptions
Supervised data mining
Support
The Singularity
Third-party cookie
Unsupervised data mining

MyMISLab™

To complete the problems with the MyMISLab, go to EOC Discussion Questions in the MyLab.

USING YOUR KNOWLEDGE

MyMISLab

1. In Q1, the Practice Fusion software that advises doctors is paid for by Merck, a pharmaceutical company. According to the categorical imperative, is this ethical? Is it ethical according to utilitarianism? Do you believe it is ethical?

MyMISLab

2. Explain in your own words how the sales analysis team in Q2 implemented each of the five criteria it developed. Use the data and tables shown in Q2 in your answer.

MyMISLab

3. In Q2, the sales analysis team created a query that connected the selected parts with their past sales data (Sales History for Selected Parts). Explain why the query results do not show promise for the selling of these part designs. In light of these results, should the team look at changing its criteria? If so, how? If not, why not?

4. Given the results from the Sales History for Selected Parts query, list three actions that the company can take. Recommend one of these actions and justify your recommendation.

5. Suppose you work at Costco or another major, national big-box store; you do a market-basket analysis and identify the 25 pairs of items in the store that have the highest lift and the 25 pairs that have the lowest lift. What would you do with this knowledge? Costco (or your big-box store) doesn't have salespeople, so up-selling is not an option. What else might you do with information about these items' lift? Consider advertising, pricing, item location in stores, and any other factor that you might adjust. Do you think the lift calculations are valid for all stores in the United States (or other country)? Why or why not? Are the 50 pairs of products with the highest and lowest lift the best place to focus your attention? What other 50 pairs of products might you want to consider? Explain.

6. Describe a use for RFM analysis for Costco. Explain what you would do for customers who have the following scores: [5, 5, 5], [3, 5, 5], [5, 2, 5], [3, 3, 5], [5, 5, 3]. Is this analysis useful to Costco? Explain your answer.

7. Describe an application for market-basket analysis for your local bookstore. Explain how you would use the knowledge that two items have a lift of 7. Explain how you would use the knowledge that two items have a lift of .003. If they have a lift of 1.03? If they have a lift of 2.1?

8. Define the characteristics of Big Data. Identify and describe three student-related applications at your university that meet Big Data characteristics. Describe patterns and relationships that might be found within that data.

COLLABORATION EXERCISE

Using the collaboration IS you built, collaborate with a group of students to answer the following questions.

Read Case Study if you have not already done so. Undeniably, third-party cookies offer advantages to online sellers. They also increase the likelihood that consumers will receive online ads that are close to their interests; thus, third-party cookies can provide a consumer service as well. But at what cost to personal privacy? And what should be done about them? Working with your team, answer the following questions:

9. Summarize the ways that third-party cookies are created and processed. Even though cookies are not supposed to contain personally identifying data, explain how such data can readily be obtained.

10. Numerous browser features, add-ins, and other tools exist for blocking third-party cookies. Search the Web for *block third-party cookies for xxx,* and fill in the *xxx* with the name and version of your browser. Read the instructions, and summarize the procedures that you need to take to view the cookies issued from a given site.

11. In large measure, ads pay for the free use of Web content and even Web sites themselves. If, because of a fear of privacy, many people block third-party cookies, substantial ad revenue will be lost. Discuss with your group how such a movement would affect the valuation of Facebook and other ad-revenue-dependent companies. Discuss how it would affect the delivery of free online content such as that supplied by *Forbes* or other providers.

12. Many companies have a conflict of interest with regard to third-party cookies. On the one hand, such cookies help generate revenue and pay for Internet content. On the other hand, trespassing on users' privacy could turn out to be a PR disaster. As you learned in your answer to question 10, browsers include options to block third-party cookies. However, in most cases, those options are turned off in the default browser installation. Discuss why that might be so. If sites were required to obtain your permission before installing third-party cookies, how would you determine whether to grant it? List criteria that your team thinks you would actually use (as opposed to what the team thinks you *should* do). Assess the effectiveness of such a policy.

13. The processing of third-party cookies is hidden; we don't know what is being done behind the scenes with the data about our own behavior. Because there is so much of it and so many parties involved, the possibilities are difficult to comprehend, even if the descriptions were available. And if your privacy is compromised by the interaction of seven different companies working independently, which is to be held accountable? Summarize consequences of these facts on consumers.

14. Summarize the benefits of third-party cookies to consumers.

15. Given all you have learned about third-party cookies, what does your team think should be done about them? Possible answers are: a) nothing; b) require Web sites to ask users before installing third-party cookies; c) require browsers to block third-party cookies; d) require browsers to block third-party cookies by default, but enable them at the users' option; e) something else. Discuss these alternatives among your team and recommend one. Justify your recommendation.

CASE STUDY

Hadoop the Cookie Cutter

A **cookie** is data that a Web site stores on your computer to record something about its interaction with you. The cookie might contain data such as the date you last visited, whether you are currently signed in, or something else about your interaction with that site. Cookies can also contain a key value to one or more tables in a database that the server company maintains about your past interactions. In that case, when you access a site, the server uses the value of the cookie to look up your history. Such data could include your past purchases, portions of incomplete transactions, or the data and appearance you want for your Web page. Most of the time cookies ease your interaction with Web sites.

Cookie data includes the URL of the Web site of the cookie's owner. Thus, for example, when you go to Amazon, it asks your browser to place a cookie on your computer that includes its name, *www.amazon.com*. Your browser will do so unless you have turned cookies off.

A **third-party cookie** is a cookie created by a site other than the one you visited. Such cookies are generated in several ways, but the most common occurs when a Web page includes content from multiple sources. For example, Amazon designs its pages so that one or more sections contain ads provided by the ad-servicing company, DoubleClick. When the browser constructs your Amazon page, it contacts DoubleClick to obtain the content for such sections (in this case, ads). When it responds with the content, DoubleClick instructs your browser to store a DoubleClick cookie. That cookie is a third-party cookie. In general, third-party cookies do not contain the name or any value that identifies a particular user. Instead, they include the IP address to which the content was delivered.

On its own servers, when it creates the cookie, DoubleClick records that data in a log, and if you click on the ad, it will add that fact of that click to the log. This logging is repeated every time DoubleClick shows an ad. Cookies have an expiration date, but that date is set by the cookie creator, and they can last many years. So, over time, DoubleClick and any other third-party cookie owner will have a history of what they've shown, what ads have been clicked, and the intervals between interactions.

But the opportunity is even greater. DoubleClick has agreements not only with Amazon, but also with many others, such as Facebook. If Facebook includes any DoubleClick content on its site, DoubleClick will place another cookie on your computer. This cookie is different from the one that it placed via Amazon, but both cookies have your IP address and other data sufficient to associate the second cookie as originating from the same source as the first. So, DoubleClick now has a record of your ad response data on two sites. Over time, the cookie log will contain data to show not only how you respond to ads, but also your pattern of visiting various Web sites on all those sites in which it places ads.

You might be surprised to learn how many third-party cookies you have. The browser Firefox has an optional feature called *Lightbeam* that tracks and graphs all the cookies on your computer. Figure 30 shows the cookies that were placed on my computer as I visited various Web sites. As you can see, in Figure 30a, when I started my computer and browser, there were no cookies. The cookies on my computer after I visited *www.msn.com* are shown in Figure 30b. At this point, there are already eight third-party cookies tracking. After I visited five sites I had 27 third-party cookies, and after I visited seven sites I had 69, as shown in Figures 30c and d.

Who are these companies that are gathering my browser behavior data? If you hold your mouse over one of the cookies, Lightbeam will highlight it in the data column on the right. As you can see in Figure 30d, after visiting seven sites, DoubleClick was connected to a total of 16 other sites, only seven of which can be sites I visited. So, DoubleClick is connecting to sites I don't even know about and on my computer. Examine the connection column on the right. I visited MSN, Amazon, MyNorthwest, and WSJ, but who are Bluekai and Rubiconproject? I never heard of them until I saw this display. They, apparently, have heard of me, however!

Third-party cookies generate incredible volumes of log data. For example, suppose a company, such as DoubleClick, shows 100 ads to a given computer in a day. If it is showing ads to 10 million computers (possible), that is a total of 1 billion log entries per day, or 365 billion a year. Truly this is Big Data.

Storage is essentially free, but how can they possibly process all that data? How do they parse the log to find entries just for your computer? How do they integrate data from different cookies on the same IP address? How do they analyze those entries to determine which ads you clicked on? How do they then characterize differences in ads to determine which characteristics matter most to you? The answer, as you learned in Q6, is to use parallel processing. Using a MapReduce algorithm, they distribute the work to thousands of processors that work in parallel. They then aggregate the results of these independent processors and then, possibly, move to a second phase of analysis where they do it again. Hadoop, the open-source program that you learned about in Q6, is a favorite for this process.

(See the collaboration exercise for a continuation of the discussion: third-party cookies—problem? Or opportunity?)

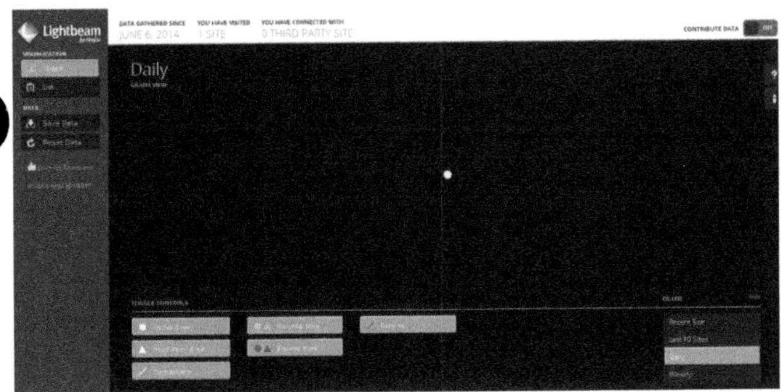

a. Display on Startup

b. After MSN.com and Gmail

c. Five Sites Visited Yield 27 Third Parties

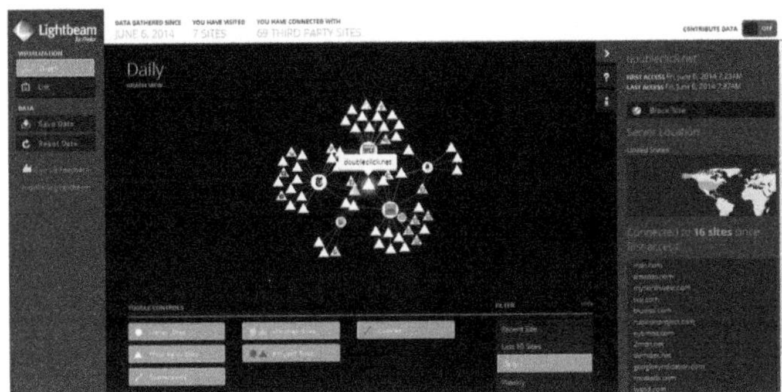

d. Sites Connected to DoubleClick

FIGURE 30
Third-Party Cookie Growth
Source: © Mozilla Corporation

QUESTIONS

16. Using your own words, explain how third-party cookies are created.

17. Suppose you are an ad-serving company, and you maintain a log of cookie data for ads you serve to Web pages for a particular vendor (say, Amazon).

- **a.** How can you use this data to determine which are the best ads?
- **b.** How can you use this data to determine which are the best ad formats?
- **c.** How could you use records of past ads and ad clicks to determine which ads to send to a given IP address?
- **d.** How could you use this data to determine how well the technique you used in your answer to question c was working?
- **e.** How could you use this data to determine that a given IP address is used by more than one person?
- **f.** How does having this data give you a competitive advantage vis-à-vis other ad-serving companies?

18. Suppose you are an ad-serving company, and you have a log of cookie data for ads served to Web pages of all your customers (Amazon, Facebook, etc.).

- **a.** Describe, in general terms, how you can process the cookie data to associate log entries for a particular IP address.
- **b.** Explain how your answers to question 10 change, given that you have this additional data.
- **c.** Describe how you can use this log data to determine users who consistently seek the lowest price.
- **d.** Describe how you can use this log data to determine users who consistently seek the latest fashion.
- **e.** Explain why users like those in parts c and d above are only possible with MapReduce or a similar technique.

19. As stated, third-party cookies usually do not contain, in themselves, data that identifies you as a particular person. However, Amazon, Facebook, and other first-party cookie vendors know who you are because you signed in. Only one of them needs to reveal your identity to the ad-server, and your identity can then be correlated with your IP address. At that point, the ad-server and potentially all of its clients know who you are. Are you concerned about the invasion of your privacy that third-party cookies enable? Explain your answer.

MyMISLab™

Go to the Assignments section of your MyLab to complete these writing exercises.

20. Reflect on the differences among reporting systems, data mining systems, and Big Data systems. What are their similarities and differences? How do their costs differ? What benefits does each offer? How would an organization choose among them?

21. Install Firefox, if you do not already have it, and then install the Lightbeam add-on. Visit the sites you normally visit first thing in your day.

a. How many third-party sites are you connected to?

b. Find DoubleClick in the Lightbeam display. List the companies that DoubleClick is connected to that you did not visit.

c. Choose one of the companies in your answer to question 21b. Google it and describe what it does.

22. Suppose you work for an online sporting goods retailer. You've been hired as a business analyst with the task of increasing sales. Describe how you could use RFM and market-basket analysis to increase the sales of sporting goods. If used effectively, how could RFM and market-basket analysis affect customer satisfaction?

ENDNOTES

1. PricewaterhouseCoopers. *2015 U.S. CEO Survey*, accessed May 29, 2016, *www.pwc.com/us/en/ceo-survey/index.html*.
2. Clint Boulton, "Why CEOs Must Go Big in Digital (or Go Home)," *CIO.com*, May 2, 2016, accessed May 29, 2016, *www.cio.com/article/3064592/cio-role/why-ceos-must-go-big-in-digital-or-go-home.html*.
3. Nipun Gupta, "Top 10 Databases in the World," May 4, 2014, accessed May 29, 2016, *http://csnipuntech.blogspot.com/2014/05/top-10-largest-databases-in-world.html*.
4. Charles Duhigg, "How Companies Learn Your Secrets," *New York Times*, last modified February 16, 2012, *www.nytimes.com/2012/02/19/magazine/shopping-habits.html*.
5. Alistair Barr, "Crowdsourcing Goes to Hollywood as Amazon Makes Movies," *Reuters*, last modified October 10, 2012, *www.reuters.com/article/2012/10/10/us-amazon-hollywood-crowd-idUSBRE8990JH20121010*.
6. Martin U. Müller, Marcel Rosenbach, and Thomas Schulz, "Living by the Numbers: Big Data Knows What Your Future Holds,"*Der Spiegel*, accessed May 29, 2016, *www.spiegel.de/international/business/big-data-enables-companies-and-researchers-to-look-into-thefuture-a-899964.html*.
7. Elizabeth Dwoskin, "The Next Marketing Frontier: Your Medical Records," *Wall Street Journal*, March 3, 2015, accessed May 29, 2016, *http://www.wsj.com/articles/the-next-marketing-frontier-your-medical-records-1425408631*.
8. Arthur Middleton Hughes, "Quick Profits with RFM Analysis," *Database Marketing Institute*, May 31, 2016, *www.dbmarketing.com/articles/Art149.htm*.
9. Paul Miller, "Professor Pranksman Fools His Students with a TA Powered by IBM's Watson," *The Verge*, May 6, 2016, accessed June 1, 2016, *www.theverge.com/2016/5/6/11612520/ta-powered-by-ibm-watson*.
10. Bradley Hope, "5 Things to Know About High Frequency Trading," *Wall Street Journal*, April 2, 2014, accessed May 29, 2016, *http://blogs.wsj.com/briefly/2014/04/02/5-things-to-know-about-high-frequency-trading/*.
11. Bradley Hope, "How Computers Troll a Sea of Data for Stock Picks, *Wall Street Journal*, April 2, 2015, accessed May 29, 2016, *www.wsj.com/articles/how-computers-trawl-a-sea-of-data-for-stock-picks-1427941801*.
12. Scott Patterson, *The Quants: How a New Breed of Math Whizzes Conquered Wall Street and Nearly Destroyed It* (1st ed.). New York: Crown Business, 2010.
13. Two Sigma, accessed May 29, 2016, *www.twosigma.com/about.html*.
14. Hope, "How Computers Troll a Sea of Data for Stock Picks."
15. A nonprofit corporation that supports open source software projects, originally those for the Apache Web server but today for a large number of additional major software projects.
16. Meridith Levinson, "Knowledge Management Definition and Solutions," *CIO Magazine*, accessed May 29, 2016, *www.cio.com/article/2439279/enterprise-software/knowledge-management-definition-and-solutions.html*.
17. "The Singularity Is Near," accessed May 29, 2016, *www.singularity.com*.

APPLICATION EXERCISES

All exercise files can be found on the following Web site: *www.pearsonhighered.com/kroenke*.

AE1. OLAP cubes are very similar to Microsoft Excel pivot tables. For this exercise, assume that your organization's purchasing agents rate vendors similar to the situation described in AE8-2.

a. Open the Excel file **Ch09Ex01_U10e.xlsx**. The spreadsheet has the following column names: *VendorName, EmployeeName, Date, Year,* and *Rating*.

b. Under the *INSERT* ribbon in Excel, click *Pivot Table*.

c. When asked to provide a data range, drag your mouse over the column names and data values so as to select all of the data. Excel will fill in the range values in the open dialog box. Place your pivot table in a new worksheet. Click OK.

d. Excel will create a field list on the right-hand side of your spreadsheet. Underneath it, a grid labeled Drag fields between areas below: should appear. Drag and drop the field named *VendorName* into the area named ROWS. Observe what happens in the pivot table to the left (in column A). Now drag and drop *EmployeeName* on to COLUMNS and *Rating* on to VALUES. Again observe the effect of these actions in the pivot table to the left. Voilà! You have a pivot table.

e. To see how the pivot table works, drag and drop more fields onto the grid in the bottom right hand side of your screen. For example, drop *Year* just underneath *EmployeeName*. Then move *Year* above *Employee*. Now move *Year* below *Vendor*. All of this action is just like an OLAP cube, and, in fact, OLAP cubes are readily displayed in Excel pivot tables. The major difference is that OLAP cubes are usually based on thousands or more rows of data.

AE2. It is surprisingly easy to create a market-basket report using table data in Access. To do so, however, you will need to enter SQL expressions into the Access query builder. Here, you can just copy SQL statements or type them in. If you take a database class, you will learn how to code SQL statements like those you will use here.

a. Create an Access database with a table named *Order_Data* having columns *OrderNumber, ItemName,* and *Quantity*, with data types Number (*LongInteger*), Short Text (50), and Number (*LongInteger*), respectively. Define the key as the composite (*OrderNumber, ItemName*). (You can do this in the table designer by highlighting both columns and clicking the Primary Key icon.)

b. Import the data from the Excel file **Ch09Ex02_U10e.xlsx** into the *Order_Data* table.

c. Now, to perform the market-basket analysis, you will need to enter several SQL statements into Access. To do so, click *CREATE/Query Design*. Click Close when the Show Table dialog box appears. Right-click in the gray section above the grid in the window. Select SQL View. Enter the following expression exactly as it appears here:

```
SELECT    T1.ItemName as FirstItem,
          T2.ItemName as SecondItem
FROM      Order_Data T1, Order_Data T2
WHERE     T1.OrderNumber =
          T2.OrderNumber
AND       T1.ItemName <> T2.ItemName;
```

Click the red exclamation point in the toolbar to run the query. Correct any typing mistakes and, once it works, save the query using the name TwoItem Basket.

d. Now enter a second SQL statement. Again, click *CREATE/Query Design*. Click Close when the Show Table dialog box appears. Right-click in the gray section above the grid in the window. Select SQL View. Enter the following expression exactly as it appears here:

```
SELECT      TwoItemBasket.FirstItem,
            TwoItemBasket.SecondItem,
            Count(*) AS SupportCount
FROM        TwoItemBasket
GROUP BY    TwoItemBasket.FirstItem,
            TwoItemBasket.SecondItem;
```

Correct any typing mistakes and, once it works, save the query using the name SupportCount.

e. Examine the results of the second query and verify that the two query statements have correctly calculated the number of times that two items have appeared together. Explain further calculations you need to make to compute support.

f. Explain the calculations you need to make to compute lift. Although you can make those calculations using SQL, you need more SQL knowledge to do it, and we will skip that here.

g. Explain, in your own words, what the query in part c seems to be doing. What does the query in part d seem to be doing? Again, you will need to take a database class to learn how to code such expressions, but this exercise should give you a sense of the kinds of calculations that are possible with SQL.

AE3. Suppose you work for the bicycle parts distributor mentioned in Q-2 of this chapter. The team was investigating the possibility of selling 3D printable plans for bike parts rather than the parts themselves. The team needed to identify qualifying parts and compute how much revenue potential those parts represent. Download the Access file **Ch09Ex03_U10e.accdb**, which contains the data extract the team used.

a. Suppose Desert Gear Supply decides not to release its 3D design files at any price. Remove parts provided by it from consideration and repeat the data analysis in this chapter.

b. The team decides, in light of the absence of Desert Gear Supply's part designs, to repeat its analysis with different criteria as follows:

- Large customers are those who have ordered more than 900 parts.
- Frequent purchases occur at least 25 times per year.
- Small quantities have an average order size of 3 or less.
- Inexpensive parts cost less than $75.
- Shipping weight is less than 4 pounds.

Repeat the data analysis in this chapter.

c. How does the second set of criteria change the results?

d. What recommendations would you make in light of your analysis?

GLOSSARY

Artificial intelligence (AI) The ability of a machine to simulate human abilities such as vision, communication, recognition, learning, and decision making.

BI analysis The process of creating business intelligence. The four fundamental categories of BI analysis are reporting, data mining, Big Data, and knowledge management.

BI application The software component of a BI system.

Big Data A term used to describe data collections that are characterized by huge volume, rapid velocity, and great variety.

BI server A Web server application that is purpose-built for the publishing of business intelligence.

Business intelligence (BI) systems Information systems that produce business intelligence.

Business intelligence (BI) The processing of operational data, social data, purchased data, and employee knowledge to expose solutions, patterns, relationships, and trends of importance to the organization.

Cluster analysis Unsupervised data mining using statistical techniques to identify groups of entities that have similar characteristics. A common use for cluster analysis is to find groups of similar customers in data about customer orders and customer demographics.

Confidence In market-basket terminology, the probability estimate that two items will be purchased together.

Content management systems (CMS) Information systems that support the management and delivery of documentation including reports, Web pages, and other expressions of employee knowledge.

Cookie A small file that is stored on the user's computer by a browser. Cookies can be used for authentication, for storing shopping cart contents and user preferences, and for other legitimate purposes. Cookies can also be used to implement spyware.

Cross-selling The sale of related products to customers based on salesperson knowledge, market-basket analysis, or both.

Data acquisition In business intelligence systems, the process of obtaining, cleaning, organizing, relating, and cataloging source data.

Data mart A data collection, smaller than a data warehouse, that addresses the needs of a particular department or functional area of a business.

Data mining The application of statistical techniques to find patterns and relationships among data for classification and prediction.

Data triangulation See *semantic security*.

Data warehouse A facility for managing an organization's BI data.

Decision support systems Some authors define business intelligence (BI) systems as supporting decision making only, in which case they use this older term as a synonym for decision-making BI systems.

Decision tree A hierarchical arrangement of criteria that predict a classification or a value.

Dimension A characteristic of an OLAP measure. Purchase date, customer type, customer location, and sales region are examples of dimensions.

Drill down With an OLAP report, to further divide the data into more detail.

Dynamic reports Business intelligence documents that are updated at the time they are requested.

Expert systems Rule-based systems that encode human knowledge in the form of If/Then rules.

Expert systems shells A program in an expert system that processes a set of rules, typically many times, until the values of the variables no longer change, at which point the system reports the results.

Granularity The level of detail in data. Customer name and account balance is large granularity data. Customer name, balance, and details of all contacts with that customer, orders, and payments is smaller granularity.

Hadoop An open source program supported by the Apache Foundation that manages thousands of computers and that implements MapReduce.

Hyper-social knowledge management The application of social media and related applications for the management and delivery of organizational knowledge resources.

If/Then rules Statements that specify that if a particular condition exists, then a particular action should be taken. Used in different ways, by both expert systems and decision tree data mining.

Knowledge management (KM) The process of creating value from intellectual capital and sharing that knowledge with employees, managers, suppliers, customers, and others who need it.

Lift In market-basket terminology, the ratio of confidence to the base probability of buying an item. Lift shows how much the base probability changes when other products are purchased. If the lift is greater than 1, the change is positive; if it is less than 1, the change is negative.

Machine learning The extraction of knowledge from data based on algorithms created from training data.

MapReduce A two-phase technique for harnessing the power of thousands of computers working in parallel. During the first phase, the Map phase, computers work on a task in parallel; during the second phase, the Reduce phase, the work of separate computers is combined, eventually obtaining a single result.

Market-basket analysis A data mining technique for determining sales patterns. A market-basket analysis shows the products that customers tend to buy together.

Measure The data item of interest on an OLAP report. It is the item that is to be summed, averaged, or otherwise processed in the OLAP cube. Total sales, average sales, and average cost are examples of measures.

Neural networks A popular supervised data mining technique used to predict values and make classifications, such as "good prospect" or "poor prospect."

OLAP cube A presentation of an OLAP measure with associated dimensions. The reason for this term is that some products show these displays using three axes, like a cube in geometry. Same as OLAP report.

Online analytical processing (OLAP) A dynamic type of reporting system that provides the ability to sum, count, average, and perform other simple arithmetic operations on groups of data. Such reports are dynamic because users can change the format of the reports while viewing them.

Pig Query language used with Hadoop.

Publish results The process of delivering business intelligence to the knowledge workers who need it.

Pull publishing In business intelligence (BI) systems, the mode whereby users must request BI results

Push publishing In business intelligence (BI) systems, the mode whereby the BI system delivers business intelligence to users without any request from the users, according to a schedule, or as a result of an event or particular data condition.

Regression analysis A type of supervised data mining that estimates the values of parameters in a linear equation. Used to determine the relative influence of variables on an outcome and also to predict future values of that outcome.

Reporting application A business intelligence application that inputs data from one or more sources and applies reporting operations to that data to produce business intelligence.

RFM analysis A technique readily implemented with basic reporting operations to analyze and rank customers according to their purchasing patterns.

Rich directory An employee directory that includes not only the standard name, email, phone, and address but also expertise, organizational relationships, and other employee data.

Semantic security Also called data triangulation; concerns the unintended release of protected data through the release of a combination of reports or documents that are not protected independently.

Static reports Business intelligence documents that are fixed at the time of creation and do not change.

Subscriptions User requests for particular business intelligence results on a stated schedule or in response to particular events.

Supervised data mining A form of data mining in which data miners develop a model prior to the analysis and apply statistical techniques to determine the validity of that model and to estimate values of the parameters of the model.

Support In market-basket terminology, the probability that two items will be purchased together.

The Singularity According to Ray Kurzweil, the point at which computer systems become sophisticated enough that they can create and adapt their own software and hence adapt their behavior without human assistance.

Third-party cookie A cookie created by a site other than the one visited.

Unsupervised data mining A form of data mining whereby the analysts do not create a model or hypothesis before running the analysis. Instead, they apply the data mining technique to the data and observe the results. With this method, analysts create hypotheses after the analysis to explain the patterns found.

Index

D

E

F

G

H

Q

R

S

T

U

V

W

X

Y